*New Beacon Bible Commentary

HEBREWS
A Commentary in the Wesleyan Tradition

Kevin L. Anderson

BEACON HILL PRESS
OF KANSAS CITY

Copyright 2013
by Beacon Hill Press of Kansas City

ISBN 978-0-8341-2946-7

Cover Design: J.R. Caines
Interior Design: Sharon Page

Unless otherwise indicated all Scripture quotations are from the *Holy Bible, New International Version*® (NIV®). Copyright © 1973, 1978, 1984 by Biblica, Inc.™ Used by permission of Zondervan. All rights reserved worldwide. www.zondervan.com.

King James Version (KJV).

Tyndale New Testament (1534 edition) (TYNDALE)

The following copyrighted versions of the Bible are used by permission:

The *Common English Bible* (CEB), copyright 2011. All rights reserved.

The *Contemporary English Version* (CEV). Copyright © by the American Bible Society, 1991, 1992.

The Holy Bible, English Standard Version (ESV), copyright © 2001 by Crossway Bibles, a division of Good News Publishers. All rights reserved.

Good News Translation® (*Today's English Version*, Second Edition) (GNT). Copyright © 1992 American Bible Society. All rights reserved.

GOD'S WORD® (GW). Copyright © 1995 by God's Word to the Nations. Used by permission of Baker Publishing Group. All rights reserved.

Holman Christian Standard Bible® (HCSB), copyright © 1999, 2000, 2002, 2003, 2009 by Holman Bible Publishers. Used by permission. Holman Christian Standard Bible®, Holman CSB®, and HCSB® are federally registered trademarks of Holman Bible Publishers.

The *Lexham English Bible* (LEB), Fourth Edition. Copyright 2010, 2012 Logos Bible Software, 1313 Commercial St., Bellingham, WA 98225. http://www.logos.com.

The *New American Bible* (NAB). Copyright © 1970 by the Confraternity of Christian Doctrine, 3211 4th St. N.E., Washington, DC 20017-1194. All rights reserved.

The *New American Standard Bible*® (NASB®), © copyright The Lockman Foundation 1960, 1962, 1963, 1968, 1971, 1972, 1973, 1975, 1977, 1995.

The *New Century Version* (NCV). Copyright © 1987, 1988, 1991 by Thomas Nelson, Inc. All rights reserved.

The *New English Bible* (NEB), © the Delegates of the Oxford University Press and the Syndics of the Cambridge University Press 1961, 1970.

The *NET Bible*® (NET), copyright © 1996-2006 by Biblical Studies Press, L.L.C., http://bible.org. Quoted by permission. All rights reserved.

The *Holy Bible, New International Version*® (NIV¹¹®). Copyright © 1973, 1978, 1984, 2011 by Biblica, Inc.™ Used by permission. All rights reserved worldwide.

The *New Jerusalem Bible* (NJB), copyright © 1985 by Darton, Longman & Todd, Ltd., and Doubleday, a division of Bantam Doubleday Dell Publishing Group, Inc. Reprinted by permission.

The *New King James Version* (NKJV). Copyright © 1979, 1980, 1982 Thomas Nelson, Inc.

The *Holy Bible, New Living Translation* (NLT), copyright 1996, 2004. Used by permission of Tyndale House Publishers, Inc., Carol Stream, IL 60188. All rights reserved.

The *New Revised Standard Version* (NRSV) of the Bible, copyright 1989 by the Division of Christian Education of the National Council of the Churches of Christ in the USA. All rights reserved.

The New Testament in Modern English (PHILLIPS). Revised Student Edition, by J. B. Phillips, translator. Reprinted with permission of the Macmillan Publishing Company. Copyright 1958, 1960, 1972 by J. B. Phillips.

The *Revised English Bible* (REB). Copyright © 1989 by Oxford University Press and Cambridge University Press.

The *Revised Standard Version* (RSV) of the Bible, copyright 1946, 1952, 1971 by the Division of Christian Education of the National Council of the Churches of Christ in the USA. All rights reserved.

Holy Bible, Today's New International Version® (TNIV®). Copyright © 2001, 2005 by Biblica. All rights reserved worldwide.

Library of Congress Cataloging-in-Publication Data

Anderson, Kevin L. (Kevin Lee), 1966-
  Hebrews / Kevin Anderson.
    pages cm. — (New Beacon Bible commentary)
  Includes bibliographical references.
  ISBN 978-0-8341-2946-7 (pbk.)
  1. Bible. N.T. Hebrews—Commentaries. I. Title.
  BS2775.53A53 2013
  227'.8707—dc23

2013002483

DEDICATION

For Mom. Your love for God's Word and
passion for ministry have had an indelible effect on me.

COMMENTARY EDITORS

General Editors

Alex Varughese
 Ph.D., Drew University
 Professor of Biblical Literature
 Mount Vernon Nazarene University
 Mount Vernon, Ohio

Roger Hahn
 Ph.D., Duke University
 Dean of the Faculty
 Professor of New Testament
 Nazarene Theological Seminary
 Kansas City, Missouri

George Lyons
 Ph.D., Emory University
 Professor of New Testament
 Northwest Nazarene University
 Nampa, Idaho

Section Editors

Joseph Coleson
 Ph.D., Brandeis University
 Professor of Old Testament
 Nazarene Theological Seminary
 Kansas City, Missouri

Robert Branson
 Ph.D., Boston University
 Professor of Biblical Literature
  Emeritus
 Olivet Nazarene University
 Bourbonnais, Illinois

Alex Varughese
 Ph.D., Drew University
 Professor of Biblical Literature
 Mount Vernon Nazarene University
 Mount Vernon, Ohio

Jim Edlin
 Ph.D., Southern Baptist Theological
  Seminary
 Professor of Biblical Literature and
  Languages
 Chair, Division of Religion and
  Philosophy
 MidAmerica Nazarene University
 Olathe, Kansas

Kent Brower
 Ph.D., The University of Manchester
 Vice Principal
 Senior Lecturer in Biblical Studies
 Nazarene Theological College
 Manchester, England

George Lyons
 Ph.D., Emory University
 Professor of New Testament
 Northwest Nazarene University
 Nampa, Idaho

CONTENTS

General Editors' Preface	7
Author's Preface	9
Abbreviations	11
Bibliography	19
Table of Sidebars	27
INTRODUCTION	29
A. Mystery and Revelatory Power	29
B. Author	31
C. Destination	38
D. Date and Situation of the Audience	42
E. Genre	44
F. Purpose	46
G. Theology	48
COMMENTARY	57
I. Hearing the Apostle and High Priest of Our Confession: Hebrews 1:1—4:13	57
A. Hearing God's Son in These Last Days: Jesus the Merciful and Faithful High Priest (1:1—2:18)	58
1. We Must Heed God's Definitive Revelation in the Son (1:1—2:4)	58
a. God's Definitive Action in the Son (1:1-4)	61
b. Scriptural Arguments for the Son's Majesty over Angels (1:5-14)	70
c. Heed What Was Spoken in the Son (2:1-4)	76
2. Jesus Perfected as a Merciful and Faithful High Priest (2:5-18)	82
a. The Humiliation and Exaltation of Jesus (2:5-9)	85
b. Jesus' Identification with Humanity (2:10-18)	92
B. Hearing God's Word Today: Jesus the Apostle and High Priest of Our Confession (3:1—4:13)	104
1. Commitment as Christ's Partners, God's House (3:1-6)	106
2. Entering God's Rest: Warning and Promise (3:7—4:13)	118
a. The Peril of Defying God's Voice (3:7-19)	118
b. Warning Not to Fall Short of the Promised Rest (4:1-13)	128
II. Jesus' Superior High Priesthood: Hebrews 4:14—10:18	153
A. The Qualifications of the Great High Priest (4:14—5:10)	153
1. The Great High Priest (4:14-16)	157
2. Qualifications of Ordinary High Priests (5:1-4)	162
3. Qualifications of the High Priest like Melchizedek (5:5-10)	164

- B. Preparing for Advanced Teaching on Christ's High Priesthood (5:11—6:20) — 175
  1. Reproof Concerning Arrested Spiritual Development (5:11-14) — 177
  2. Exhortation to Go on to Maturity (6:1-3) — 183
  3. Warning About Irreversible Apostasy (6:4-8) — 187
  4. Words of Reassurance (6:9-12) — 193
  5. Powerful Encouragement Based on God's Trustworthiness (6:13-20) — 196
- C. The High Priest like Melchizedek: The Son Perfected Forever (7:1-28) — 210
  1. The Greatness of Melchizedek's Priesthood (7:1-10) — 212
  2. The Imperfection of the Levitical Priesthood (7:11-19) — 219
  3. The Son's Permanent and Perfect Priesthood (7:20-28) — 224
- D. The Superior Ministry of the Son's High Priesthood (8:1—10:18) — 233
  1. Introduction to Christ's Superior Ministry (8:1-13) — 235
  2. The Better and More Perfect Tabernacle (9:1-14) — 240
  3. Christ's Sacrificial Death Inaugurated the New Covenant (9:15-28) — 250
  4. Christ's One Obedient Offering Perfects Worshipers Forever (10:1-18) — 257

III. Call to Persevering Faith and Acceptable Worship: Hebrews 10:19—13:25 — 269
- A. Exhortations to Persevere in Faith (10:19—12:13) — 271
  1. Confidence and Perseverance in Faith (10:19-39) — 271
     a. Invocation to Worship and Faithful Living (10:19-25) — 272
     b. Fearful Expectation of Judgment for Apostates (10:26-31) — 280
     c. Praise for Past Endurance (10:32-34) — 284
     d. Exhortation to Endure in Faith (10:35-39) — 288
  2. Worthy Examples of Faith (11:1-40) — 291
     a. From Creation to Flood (11:1-7) — 293
     b. From Abraham to Joseph (11:8-22) — 299
     c. From Moses to Rahab (11:23-31) — 306
     d. Many More Faithful: From Triumph to Suffering (11:32-40) — 310
  3. Training for Enduring Faith (12:1-13) — 314
- B. Exhortations to Offer Acceptable Worship (12:14—13:25) — 328
  1. Receive the Unshakable Kingdom with Gratitude and Worship (12:14-29) — 329
     a. Pursue Peace and Holiness (12:14-17) — 331
     b. Mountain of Terror and Mountain of Celebration (12:18-24) — 335
     c. Listen to the Heavenly Voice (12:25-29) — 340
  2. Instructions for Worship as a Way of Life (13:1-25) — 344
     a. Exhortations to Love, Purity, and Trust (13:1-6) — 345
     b. Final Call to Commitment and Worship (13:7-19) — 350
     c. Benediction and Postscript (13:20-25) — 360

GENERAL EDITORS' PREFACE

The purpose of the New Beacon Bible Commentary is to make available to pastors and students in the twenty-first century a biblical commentary that reflects the best scholarship in the Wesleyan theological tradition. The commentary project aims to make this scholarship accessible to a wider audience to assist them in their understanding and proclamation of Scripture as God's Word.

Writers of the volumes in this series not only are scholars within the Wesleyan theological tradition and experts in their field but also have special interest in the books assigned to them. Their task is to communicate clearly the critical consensus and the full range of other credible voices who have commented on the Scriptures. Though scholarship and scholarly contribution to the understanding of the Scriptures are key concerns of this series, it is not intended as an academic dialogue within the scholarly community. Commentators of this series constantly aim to demonstrate in their work the significance of the Bible as the church's book and the contemporary relevance and application of the biblical message. The project's overall goal is to make available to the church and for her service the fruits of the labors of scholars who are committed to their Christian faith.

The *New International Version* (NIV) is the reference version of the Bible used in this series; however, the focus of exegetical study and comments is the biblical text in its original language. When the commentary uses the NIV, it is printed in bold. The text printed in bold italics is the translation of the author. Commentators also refer to other translations where the text may be difficult or ambiguous.

The structure and organization of the commentaries in this series seeks to facilitate the study of the biblical text in a systematic and methodical way. Study of each biblical book begins with an **Introduction** section that gives an overview of authorship, date, provenance, audience, occasion, purpose, sociological/cultural issues, textual history, literary features, hermeneutical issues, and theological themes necessary to understand the book. This section also includes a brief outline of the book and a list of general works and standard commentaries.

The commentary section for each biblical book follows the outline of the book presented in the introduction. In some volumes, readers will find section ***overviews*** of large portions of scripture with general comments on their overall literary structure and other literary features. A consistent feature of the commentary is the paragraph-by-paragraph study of biblical texts. This section has three parts: **Behind the Text, In the Text,** and **From the Text.**

The goal of the ***Behind the Text*** section is to provide the reader with all the relevant information necessary to understand the text. This includes specific historical situations reflected in the text, the literary context of the text, sociological and cultural issues, and literary features of the text.

In the Text explores what the text says, following its verse-by-verse structure. This section includes a discussion of grammatical details, word studies, and the connectedness of the text to other biblical books/passages or other parts of the book being studied (the canonical relationship). This section provides transliterations of key words in Hebrew and Greek and their literal meanings. The goal here is to explain what the author would have meant and/or what the audience would have understood as the meaning of the text. This is the largest section of the commentary.

The ***From the Text*** section examines the text in relation to the following areas: theological significance, intertextuality, the history of interpretation, use of the Old Testament scriptures in the New Testament, interpretation in later church history, actualization, and application.

The commentary provides ***sidebars*** on topics of interest that are important but not necessarily part of an explanation of the biblical text. These topics are informational items and may cover archaeological, historical, literary, cultural, and theological matters that have relevance to the biblical text. Occasionally, longer detailed discussions of special topics are included as ***excurses***.

We offer this series with our hope and prayer that readers will find it a valuable resource for their understanding of God's Word and an indispensable tool for their critical engagement with the biblical texts.

Roger Hahn, Centennial Initiative General Editor
Alex Varughese, General Editor (Old Testament)
George Lyons, General Editor (New Testament)

AUTHOR'S PREFACE

The Letter to the Hebrews is one of the most challenging books in the Bible. The challenge is on two levels. The first, and more important, is its relentless summons to steadfast commitment to Christ. The second is the sophisticated way it develops its message: with profound interpretations of OT passages and masterful rhetorical argumentation. Much of what we read in Hebrews is foreign to contemporary readers. The text presents a multitude of challenges for the commentator.

Hence, my trepidation when invited to write a commentary on Hebrews for the New Beacon Bible Commentary series. Upon completion of the commentary, I am still humbled at the opportunity to offer my own small contribution to the understanding of this book. I have felt like a runner, often wearied by the race set before me, but cheered on by a great cloud of witnesses (commentators and scholars) who have gone before me. The scholarship on Hebrews is enormous, impossible for anyone to master. Regrettably, Gareth Cockerill's 2012 commentary came into my hands too late for me to interact with it here.

My own journey with Hebrews has had three important influences. My first formal introduction to Hebrews was in a college course on the epistle taught by Sam Brelo at Trinity Bible College. Sam's approach to studying and teaching Hebrews was infectious. He modeled for me the fusion of tremendous passion with technical, scholarly precision. My second major influence came from William Lane's study, *Call to Commitment* (1985), the forerunner to his major commentary on Hebrews (1991). Lane opened up the world of Hebrews as a sermon addressed to a faith community in crisis. His recognition of Hebrews as a sermon meant to be *heard* was revolutionary to me at the time—and still is. My third influence was a course in Hebrews with Morris Weigelt (now professor emeritus of New Testament) at Nazarene Theological Seminary. Morris taught me that Hebrews (and the Bible as a whole) is not a book we master but a book we live with. Even after writing a commentary on Hebrews, I feel as if I've only begun to live with this majestic book.

In writing this commentary I have benefited from the support of many people. I would like to thank the Faculty Development Committee and administration of Asbury University, which granted me a sabbatical during the fall of 2009. The work never could have been completed without this important release time. I would also like to thank my colleagues in the Christian Studies and Philosophy Department who have followed this project with interest and encouragement. I am grateful for the tireless work of George Lyons in editing the manuscript. The end result is so much better due to his efforts, though any deficiencies that remain are mine. Last, but not least, my wife, Sandi, has been an indispensable source of love and support.

My prayer is that this commentary will help in some small way to extend the challenging message of Hebrews. As Scripture, Hebrews summons each new generation to pay heed to God's voice in his Son, and our Great High Priest, Jesus Christ.

Kevin Anderson
May 16, 2012

ABBREVIATIONS

With a few exceptions, these abbreviations follow those in *The SBL Handbook of Style* (Alexander 1999).

General

→	see the comment on
‖	parallel(s)
A.D.	anno Domini
B.C.	before Christ
BDAG	W. Bauer, F. W. Danker, W. F. Arndt, and F. W. Gingrich, *Greek-English Lexicon of the New Testament and Other Early Christian Literature*. 3d ed. Chicago and London: University of Chicago Press, 2000.
ca.	circa
d.	died
EDNT	*Exegetical Dictionary of the New Testament*. Edited by H. Balz and G. Schneider. Grand Rapids: Eerdmans, 1990-93.
esp.	especially
fl.	flourished (Latin: *flōruit*)
Gk.	Greek
Heb.	Hebrew
ktl.	*kai ta loipa* ("and the remaining") = etc. (for Greek)
Lat.	Latin
lit.	literally
L&N	*Greek-English Lexicon of the New Testament: Based on Semantic Domains*. Edited by J. P. Louw and E. A. Nida. 2d ed. New York: United Bible Societies, 1989.
LCL	Loeb Classical Library
LSJ	H. G. Liddell, R. Scott, and H. S. Jones, *A Greek-English Lexicon*. 9th ed. with revised supplement. Oxford and New York: Oxford University Press, 1996.
LXX	Septuagint
mg	marginal reading (e.g., NIV^{mg})
MM	J. H. Moulton and G. Milligan, *Vocabulary of the Greek New Testament*. London: Hodder & Stoughton, 1930. Repr. Peabody, Mass.: Hendrickson, 1997.
MS/MSS	manuscript/manuscripts
MT	Masoretic Text
n.	note
n.p.	no page, no place
NIDB	*New Interpreter's Dictionary of the Bible*. Edited by Katharine Doob Sakenfeld. 5 vols. Nashville: Abingdon, 2006-9.
NIDNTT	*New International Dictionary of New Testament Theology*. Edited by C. Brown. 4 vols. Grand Rapids: Zondervan, 1975-85.
NT	New Testament
OT	Old Testament
𝔓	papyrus manuscript
PGL	*Patristic Greek Lexicon*. Edited by G. W. H. Lampe. Oxford: Oxford University Press, 1968.
pl.	plural
rev.	revised
sg.	singular
Str-B	H. L. Strack and P. Billerbeck, *Kommentar zum Neuen Testament aus Talmud und Midrasch*. 6 vols. Munich: C. H. Beck, 1922-61.
supp.	supplement
TDNT	*Theological Dictionary of the New Testament*. Edited by G. Kittel and G. Friedrich. Translated by G. W. Bromiley. 10 vols. Grand Rapids: Eerdmans, 1964-76.
TLNT	C. Spicq, *Theological Lexicon of the New Testament*. Translated and edited by J. D. Ernest. 3 vols. Peabody, Mass.: Hendrickson, 1994.

English Versions

CEB	Common English Bible
CEV	Contemporary English Version

ESV	English Standard Version
GNT	Good News Translation (= Today's English Version)
GW	GOD'S WORD Translation
HCSB	Holman Christian Standard Bible
KJV	King James Version
LEB	Lexham English Bible
NAB	New American Bible
NASB	New American Standard Bible (1977 and 1995)
NASB95	New American Standard Bible (1995 update)
NCV	New Century Version
NEB	New English Bible
NET	New English Translation
NIV	New International Version (1984)
NIV11	New International Version (2011)
NIVmg	New International Version, marginal reading
NJB	New Jerusalem Bible
NKJV	New King James Version
NLT	New Living Translation
NRSV	New Revised Standard Version
PHILLIPS	New Testament in Modern English
REB	Revised English Bible
RSV	Revised Standard Version
TNIV	Today's New International Version
TYNDALE	Tyndale's New Testament (1534 ed.)

Print Conventions for Translations

Bold font	NIV (bold without quotation marks in the text under study; elsewhere in the regular font, with quotation marks and no further identification)
Bold italic font	Author's translation (without quotation marks)

Behind the Text: Literary or historical background information average readers might not know from reading the biblical text alone
In the Text: Comments on the biblical text, words, phrases, grammar, and so forth
From the Text: The use of the text by later interpreters, contemporary relevance, theological and ethical implications of the text, with particular emphasis on Wesleyan concerns

Old Testament

Gen	Genesis	Dan	Daniel	**New Testament**	
Exod	Exodus	Hos	Hosea	Matt	Matthew
Lev	Leviticus	Joel	Joel	Mark	Mark
Num	Numbers	Amos	Amos	Luke	Luke
Deut	Deuteronomy	Obad	Obadiah	John	John
Josh	Joshua	Jonah	Jonah	Acts	Acts
Judg	Judges	Mic	Micah	Rom	Romans
Ruth	Ruth	Nah	Nahum	1—2 Cor	1—2 Corinthians
1—2 Sam	1—2 Samuel	Hab	Habakkuk		
1—2 Kgs	1—2 Kings	Zeph	Zephaniah	Gal	Galatians
1—2 Chr	1—2 Chronicles	Hag	Haggai	Eph	Ephesians
Ezra	Ezra	Zech	Zechariah	Phil	Philippians
Neh	Nehemiah	Mal	Malachi	Col	Colossians
Esth	Esther	(Note: Chapter and verse numbering in the MT and LXX often differ compared to those in English Bibles. To avoid confusion, all biblical references follow the chapter and verse numbering in English translations, even when the text in the MT and LXX is under discussion.)		1—2 Thess	1—2 Thessalonians
Job	Job			1—2 Tim	1—2 Timothy
Ps/Pss	Psalm/Psalms			Titus	Titus
Prov	Proverbs			Phlm	Philemon
Eccl	Ecclesiastes			Heb	Hebrews
Song	Song of Songs/ Song of Solomon			Jas	James
				1—2 Pet	1—2 Peter
Isa	Isaiah			1—2—3 John	1—2—3 John
Jer	Jeremiah			Jude	Jude
Lam	Lamentations			Rev	Revelation
Ezek	Ezekiel				

Apocrypha
Ep Jer	Epistle of Jeremiah
1—4 Macc	1—4 Maccabees
Pr Azar	Prayer of Azariah
Sir	Sirach/Ecclesiasticus
Sus	Susanna
Tob	Tobit
Wis	Wisdom of Solomon

Old Testament Pseudepigrapha
Apoc. Ab.	Apocalypse of Abraham
Apoc. El.	Apocalypse of Elijah
Apoc. Zeph.	Apocalypse of Zephaniah
Ascen. Isa.	Martyrdom and Ascension of Isaiah 6—11
2 Bar.	2 Baruch (Syriac Apocalypse)
3 Bar.	3 Baruch (Greek Apocalypse)
1 En.	1 Enoch (Ethiopic Apocalypse)
2 En.	2 Enoch (Slavonic Apocalypse)
3 En.	3 Enoch (Hebrew Apocalypse)
Eup.	Eupolemus
4 Ezra	4 Ezra
Jub.	Jubilees
L.A.B.	Liber antiquitatum biblicarum (Pseudo-Philo)
L.A.E.	Life of Adam and Eve
Let. Aris.	Letter of Aristeas
Odes Sol.	Odes of Solomon
Ps.-Phoc.	Pseudo-Phocylides
Pss. Sol.	Psalms of Solomon
Ques. Ezra	Questions of Ezra
Sib. Or.	Sibylline Oracles
T. 12 Patr.	Testaments of the Twelve Patriarchs
T. Benj.	Testament of Benjamin
T. Dan	Testament of Dan
T. Jud.	Testament of Judah
T. Levi	Testament of Levi
T. Naph.	Testament of Naphtali
T. Reub.	Testament of Reuben
T. Sim.	Testament of Simeon
T. 3 Patr.	Testments of the Three Patriarchs
T. Ab.	Testament of Abraham
T. Isaac	Testament of Isaac
T. Jac.	Testament of Jacob
T. Job	Testament of Job

Jewish Writings
Dead Sea Scrolls
1QH^a	Hodayot^a or Thanksgiving Hymns^a
1QS	Rule of the Community
1QSb	Rule of the Blessings (Appendix b to Rule of the Community [1QS])
4Q212	Letter of Enoch
4QFlor	Florilegium
11QMelch	Melchizedek
CD	Cairo Genizah copy of the Damascus Document

Josephus
Ag. Ap.	Against Apion
Ant.	Jewish Antiquities
C. Ap.	Contra Apionem
J.W.	Jewish War

Philo
Abraham	On the Life of Abraham
Agriculture	On Agriculture
Alleg. Interp.	Allegorical Interpretation
Cherubim	On the Cherubim

Confusion	On the Confusion of Tongues
Congr.	De congressu eruditionis gratia
Creation	On the Creation of the World
Decalogue	On the Decalogue
Dreams	On Dreams
Drunkenness	On Drunkenness
Embassy	On the Embassy to Gaius
Flight	On Flight and Finding
Giants	On Giants
God	On God
Good Person	That Every Good Person Is Free
Heir	Who Is the Heir?
Migration	On the Migration of Abraham
Moses 1, 2	On the Life of Moses 1, 2
Names	On the Change of Names
Planting	On Planting
Posterity	On the Posterity of Cain
Prelim. Studies	On the Preliminary Studies
QG	Questions and Answers on Genesis
Rewards	On Rewards and Punishments
Sacrifices	On the Sacrifices of Cain and Abel
Sobriety	On Sobriety
Spec. Laws	On the Special Laws
Unchangeable	That God Is Unchangeable
Virtues	On the Virtues
Worse	That the Worse Attacks the Better

Rabbinic Works (preceding b. = Babylonian Talmud; y. = Jerusalem Talmud; t. = tractates of the Tosefta; e.g., b. Sanh.)

Ḥag.	Ḥagigah
Midr.	Midrash
Ned.	Nedarim
Pesaḥ.	Pesaḥim
Pesiq. Rab.	Pesiqta Rabbati
Pirqe R. El.	Pirqe Rabbi Eliezer
Rab.	Rabbah (+ biblical book; e.g., Gen. Rab.)
Rosh. Hash.	Rosh HaShanah
Sanh.	Sanhedrin
Šhabb.	Šhabbat
Tanḥ.	Tanḥuma
Tg. Neof.	Targum Neofiti
Tg. Ps.-J.	Targum Pseudo-Jonathan
Yoma	Yoma (= Kippurim)

Early Christian Writings

Apos. Con.	Apostolic Constitutions and Canons
Barn.	Barnabas
1—2 Clem.	1—2 Clement
Diogn.	Diognetus
Herm. Mand.	Shepherd of Hermas, Mandate
Herm. Sim.	Shepherd of Hermas, Similitude
Herm. Vis.	Shepherd of Hermas, Vision
Ign. Eph.	Ignatius, To the Ephesians
Ign. Magn.	Ignatius, To the Magnesians
Ign. Rom.	Ignatius, To the Romans

Gnostic Texts

Gos. Thom.	Gospel of Thomas
NHC	Nag Hammadi Codices

Church Fathers

Ambrose

Paen.	De paenitentia

Clement of Alexandria
    Strom.   *Stromata*
Cyprian
    Ep.   *Epistles*
Epiphanius
    Pan.   *Panarion (Adversus haereses)* = Refutation of All Heresies
Eusebius
    Hist. eccl.   *Ecclesiastical History*
    Praep. ev.   *Preparation for the Gospel*
Hippolytus
    Trad. ap.   *The Apostolic Tradition*
Jerome
    Epist.   *Epistles*
Justin
    1 Apol.   *First Apology*
    Dial.   *Dialogue with Trypho*
Origen
    Cels.   *Against Celsus*
Pseudo-Justin
    Coh. ad Graec.   *Cohortatio ad Graecos*
Tertullian
    An.   *De anima (On the Soul)*
    Bapt.   *Baptism*
    Pud.   *De pudicitia (On Modesty)*

Other Ancient Writings

Aeschylus
    Ag.   *Agamemnon*
Aesop
    Fab.   *Fables*
Antoninus Liberalis
    Metam.   *Metamorphōseōn synagōgē (Collection of Transformations)*
Appian
    Hisp.   *Hispanica (Wars in Spain)*
Aristotle
    Eth. nic.   *Nichomachean Ethics*
    Pol.   *Politics*
    Rhet.   *Rhetoric*
Artemidorus Daldianus
    Onir.   *Onirocritica*
Cicero
    Inv.   *De inventione rhetorica*
    Leg.   *De legibus*
    Part. or.   *Parititiones oratoriae*
    Rab. Perd.   *Pro Rabirio Perduellionis Reo*
Diodorus Siculus
    Library   *Library of History*
Diogenes Laertius
    Diog. Laert.   *Lives of the Eminent Philosophers*
Epictetus
    Diatr.   *Diatribai (Dissertationes)*
    Frag.   *Fragments*
Euripides
    Alc.   *Alcestis*
    Orest.   *Orestes*
Heliodorus
    Aeth.   *Aethiopica*
Hermogenes
    Inv.   *On Invention*
    Prog.   *Progymnasmata*
Herodotus
    Hist.   *Histories*

Homer
    Od.   *Odyssey*
Horace
    Carm.   *Carmina (Odes)*
Isocrates
    Archid.   *Archidamus*
    Demon.   *To Demonicus*
    De pace   *On Peace*
    Nic.   *To Nicocles*
    Phil.   *To Philip*
Juvenal
    Sat.   *Satires*
Lucian
    History   *How to Write History*
    Icar.   *Icaromenippus*
    Peregr.   *The Passing of Peregrinus*
    Tox.   *Toxaris*
Lucretius
    Nat.   *On the Nature of Things*
Ovid
    Metam.   *Metamorphoses*
Pindar
    Ol.   *Olympian Odes*
Plato
    Leg.   *Leges (Laws)*
    Resp.   *Respublica (Republic)*
    Tim.   *Timaeus*
Plutarch
    Mor.   *Moralia*
    Quaest. conv. *Quaestionum convivialium libri IX*
    Sol.   *Solon*
    Suave viv.   *Non posse suaviter vivi secundum Epicurum*
Pollux
    Onom.   *Onomasticon*
Polybius
    Hist.   *Histories*
Quintilian
    Inst.   *Institutio oratoria*
    Rhet. Alex.   *Rhetorica ad Alexandrum*
    Rhet. Her.   *Rhetorica ad Herennium*
Seneca
    Ben.   *De beneficiis*
    Ep.   *Moral Epistles*
Sextus Empiricus
    Pyr.   *Outlines of Pyrrhonism*
Stobaeus
    Flor.   *Florilegium*
Suetonius
    Claud.   *Divus Claudius*
Tacitus
    Ann.   *Annales*
Theophrastus
    Char.   *Characters*
Xenophon
    Anab.   *Anabasis*
    Cyr.   *Cyropaedia*

Greek Transliteration

Greek	Letter	English
α	alpha	a
β	bēta	b
γ	gamma	g
γ	gamma nasal	n (before γ, κ, ξ, χ)
δ	delta	d
ε	epsilon	e
ζ	zēta	z
η	ēta	ē
θ	thēta	th
ι	iōta	i
κ	kappa	k
λ	lambda	l
μ	mu	m
ν	nu	n
ξ	xi	x
ο	omicron	o
π	pi	p
ρ	rhō	r
ρ	initial *rhō*	rh
σ/ς	sigma	s
τ	tau	t
υ	upsilon	y
υ	upsilon	u (in diphthongs: *au, eu, ēu, ou, ui*)
φ	phi	ph
χ	chi	ch
ψ	psi	ps
ω	ōmega	ō
ʽ	rough breathing	h (before initial vowels or diphthongs)

Hebrew Consonant Transliteration

Hebrew/Aramaic	Letter	English
א	alef	ʼ
ב	bet	b
ג	gimel	g
ד	dalet	d
ה	he	h
ו	vav	v or w
ז	zayin	z
ח	khet	ḥ
ט	tet	ṭ
י	yod	y
כ/ך	kaf	k
ל	lamed	l
מ/ם	mem	m
נ/ן	nun	n
ס	samek	s̱
ע	ayin	ʽ
פ/ף	pe	p; f (spirant)
צ/ץ	tsade	ṣ
ק	qof	q
ר	resh	r
שׂ	sin	ś
שׁ	shin	š
ת	tav	t; th (spirant)

BIBLIOGRAPHY

COMMENTARIES
Attridge, Harold W. 1989. *The Epistle to the Hebrews*. Hermeneia. Philadelphia: Fortress.
Barclay, William. 1976. *The Letter to the Hebrews*. Daily Study Bible Series. Rev. ed. Philadelphia: Westminster.
Bengel, John Albert. 1877. *Gnomon of the New Testament*. Revised and edited by A. R. Fausset. 5 vols. From the Latin 2d ed. of 1759. Translated by James Bryce. 7th ed. Edinburgh: T&T Clark.
Bruce, F. F. 1990. *The Epistle to the Hebrews*. New International Commentary on the New Testament. Rev. ed. Grand Rapids: Eerdmans.
Buchanan, G. W. 1972. *To the Hebrews*. Anchor Bible 36. Garden City, N.Y.: Doubleday.
Calvin, John. 1976. *The Epistle of Paul the Apostle to the Hebrews and the First and Second Epistles of St. Peter*. Translated by W. B. Johnston. Edinburgh: Oliver and Boyd, 1963. Repr. Grand Rapids: Eerdmans.
Carter, Charles W. 1966. Hebrews. Pages 1-194 in vol. 6 of *The Wesleyan Bible Commentary*. 6 vols. Edited by Charles W. Carter. Grand Rapids: Eerdmans.
Chrysostom. 1996. *Homilies on the Gospel of St. John and the Epistle to the Hebrews*. In vol. 14 of *The Nicene and Post-Nicene Fathers*. Series 1. Edited by Philip Schaff. 14 vols. Edinburgh: T&T Clark, 1886-89; Repr. Grand Rapids: Eerdmans.
Clarke, Adam. 1977. *The New Testament of Our Lord and Saviour Jesus Christ*. Vol. 3 of *Clarke's Commentary*. 3 vols. Repr. Nashville: Abingdon.
Cockerill, Gareth Lee. 2012. *The Epistle to the Hebrews*. New International Commentary on the New Testament. Grand Rapids: Eerdmans.
Delitzsch, Franz. 1871-72. *Commentary on the Epistle to the Hebrews*. Translated by T. L. Kingsbury. 2 vols. Edinburgh: T&T Clark.
deSilva, David A. 2000a. *Perseverance in Gratitude: A Socio-Rhetorical Commentary on the Epistle "to the Hebrews."* Grand Rapids: Eerdmans.
Dods, Marcus. 1960. The Epistle to the Hebrews. Pages 219-381 in vol. 4 of *The Expositor's Greek Testament*. Edited by W. Robertson Nicoll. 5 vols. New York: G. H. Doran, 1897. Repr. Grand Rapids: Eerdmans.
Dunning, H. Ray. 2001. *Superlative Christ: Devotional Studies in Hebrews*. Kansas City: Beacon Hill Press of Kansas City.
Ellingworth, Paul. 1993. *The Epistle to the Hebrews*. The New International Greek Testament Commentary. Grand Rapids: Eerdmans.
France, R. T. 2006. Hebrews. Pages 17-195 in vol. 13 of *The Expositor's Bible Commentary*. Edited by Tremper Longman III and David E. Garland. 2d ed. Grand Rapids: Zondervan.
Guthrie, Donald. 1983. *Hebrews*. Tyndale New Testament Commentaries 15. Grand Rapids: Eerdmans.
Guthrie, George H. 1998. *Hebrews*. NIV Application Commentary Series. Grand Rapids: Zondervan.
_____. 2002. Hebrews. Pages 2-85 in vol. 4 of *Zondervan Illustrated Bible Backgrounds Commentary*. Edited by Clinton E. Arnold. 4 vols. Grand Rapids: Zondervan.
Hagner, Donald A. 1990. *Hebrews*. New International Biblical Commentary 14. Peabody, Mass.: Hendrickson.
_____. 2002. *Encountering the Book of Hebrews*. Encountering Biblical Studies. Grand Rapids: Baker.
Heen, Erik M., and Philip D. W. Krey. 2005. *Hebrews*. Ancient Christian Commentary on Scripture: New Testament 10. Edited by Thomas C. Oden. Downers Grove, Ill.: InterVarsity.
Hughes, Philip Edgcumbe. 1977. *A Commentary on the Epistle to the Hebrews*. Grand Rapids: Eerdmans.
Isaacs, Marie E. 2002. *Reading Hebrews and James: A Literary and Theological Commentary*. Reading the New Testament. Macon, Ga.: Smyth & Helwys.
Jewett, Robert. 1981. *Letter to Pilgrims: A Commentary on the Epistle to the Hebrews*. New York: Pilgrim.

Johnson, Luke Timothy. 2006. *Hebrews*. The New Testament Library. Louisville, Ky.: Westminster John Knox.
Kistemaker, Simon J. 1984. *Exposition of the Epistle to the Hebrews*. New Testament Commentary. Grand Rapids: Baker.
Koester, Craig R. 2001. *Hebrews*. Anchor Bible 36. Garden City, N.Y.: Doubleday.
Lane, William L. 1985. *Call to Commitment: Responding to the Message of Hebrews*. Nashville: Thomas Nelson.
_____. 1991. *Hebrews*. Word Biblical Commentary 47A-B. Dallas: Word.
Lünemann, Göttlieb. 1890. Commentary on the Epistle to the Hebrews. Pages 327-748 in *Critical and Exegetical Hand-Book to the Epistles to Timothy and Titus and to the Epistle to the Hebrews*. Meyer's Commentary on the New Testament. Translated from the German 4th ed. by M. J. Evans. New York and London: Funk & Wagnalls.
Michaels, J. Ramsey. 2009. Hebrews. Pages 305-478 in vol. 17 of *Cornerstone Biblical Commentary*. Edited by Philip W. Comfort. 18 vols. Carol Stream, Ill.: Tyndale House.
Moffatt, James. 1924. *A Critical and Exegetical Commentary on the Epistle to the Hebrews*. International Critical Commentary. Edinburgh: T&T Clark.
Montefiore, Hugh. 1964. *A Commentary on the Epistle to the Hebrews*. New York: Harper; London: Black.
Morris, Leon. 1981. Hebrews. Pages 3-158 in vol. 12 of *The Expositor's Bible Commentary*. Edited by Frank E. Gæbelein. 12 vols. Grand Rapids: Zondervan, 1976-92.
Murray, Andrew. 1993. *The Holiest of All: An Exposition of the Epistle to the Hebrews*. Repr. Grand Rapids: Revell.
O'Brien, Paul T. 2010. *The Letter to the Hebrews*. Pillar New Testament Commentary. Grand Rapids: Eerdmans.
Owen, John. 1812. *An Exposition to the Epistle to the Hebrews with Preliminary Exercitations*. 7 vols. 2d ed. Edinburgh: J. Ritchie.
Pfitzner, Victor C. 1997. *Hebrews*. Abingdon New Testament Commentaries. Nashville: Abingdon.
Purkiser, W. T. 1974. *Hebrews, James, Peter*. Vol. 11 of *Beacon Bible Expositions*. Edited by W. M. Greathouse and W. H. Taylor. 12 vols. Kansas City: Beacon Hill Press of Kansas City.
Spicq, C. 1952-53. *L'Épître aux Hébreux*. 2 vols. *Études Bibliques*. Paris: Gabalda.
Stedman, Ray C. 1992. *Hebrews*. The IVP New Testament Commentary Series 15. Downers Grove, Ill.: InterVarsity.
Taylor, Richard S. 1967. Hebrews. Pages 18-183 in vol. 10 of the *Beacon Bible Commentary*. Edited by A. F. Harper et al. 10 vols. Kansas City: Beacon Hill Press of Kansas City, 1964-69.
Thompson, James W. 2008. *Hebrews*. Paideia Commentaries on the New Testament. Grand Rapids: Baker Academic.
Turner, George Allen. 1975. *The New and Living Way: A Fresh Exposition of the Epistle to the Hebrews*. Minneapolis: Bethany Fellowship.
Wesley, John. n.d. *Explanatory Notes upon the New Testament*. 16th ed. New York: Phillips & Hunt; Cincinnati: Cranston & Stowe.
Westcott, B. F. 1909. *The Epistle to the Hebrews: The Greek Text with Notes and Essays*. 3d ed. London: Macmillan.
Whedon, Daniel D. 1880. *Commentary on the New Testament*. 5 vols. New York: Phillips & Hunt; Cincinnati: Cranston & Stowe, 1860-80.
Wiley, H. Orton. 1984. *The Epistle to the Hebrews*. Revised by Morris A. Weigelt. Original ed., 1959. Kansas City: Beacon Hill Press of Kansas City.
Witherington, Ben, III. 2007. *Letters and Homilies for Jewish Christians: A Socio-Rhetorical Commentary on Hebrews, James, and Jude*. Downers Grove, Ill.: InterVarsity.
Wright, Tom. 2004. *Hebrews for Everyone*. 2d ed. London: SPCK; Louisville, Ky.: Westminster John Knox.

OTHER WORKS

Achtemeier, Paul J., Joel B. Green, and Marianne Meye Thompson. 2001. *Introducing the New Testament: Its Literature and Theology*. Grand Rapids: Eerdmans.
Agnew, Milton S. 1975. *The Better Covenant: Studies in the Epistle to the Hebrews*. Kansas City: Beacon Hill Press of Kansas City.
Aherne, Cornelius. 1912. Epistles to Timothy and Titus. *The Catholic Encyclopedia*. Vol. 14. Cited 31 October 2012. Online: http://www.newadvent.org/cathen/14727b.htm.

Aitken, Ellen Bradshaw. 2005. Portraying the Temple in Stone and Text: The Arch of Titus and the Epistle to the Hebrews. Pages 131-48 in *Hebrews: Contemporary Methods—New Insights.* Edited by Gabriella Gelardini. Biblical Interpretation Series 75. Atlanta: Society of Biblical Literature.

Alexander, P. 1983. 3 (Hebrew Apocalypse of) Enoch: A New Translation and Introduction. Pages 223-315 in vol. 1 of *The Old Testament Pseudepigrapha.* Edited by James H. Charlesworth. 2 vols. Garden City, N.Y.: Doubleday.

Alexander, Paul. H. et al. 1999. *The SBL Handbook of Style: For Ancient Near Eastern, Biblical, and Early Christian Studies.* Peabody, Mass.: Hendrickson.

Allen, David. 2010. *Lukan Authorship of Hebrews.* NAC Studies in Bible and Theology 8. Nashville: Broadman and Holman.

Anderson, Kevin L. 2006. *"But God Raised Him from the Dead": The Theology of Jesus' Resurrection in Luke-Acts.* Paternoster Biblical Monographs. Milton Keynes, England: Authentic Media.

———. 2011. "The Holy Spirit Says": Hearing and Preaching the Scriptures according to the Letter to the Hebrews. Pages 405-19 in *The Bible Tells Me So: Reading the Bible as Scripture.* Edited by Richard P. Thompson and Thomas Jay Oord. Nampa, Idaho: SacraSage.

Annas, Julia E. 1992. *Hellenistic Philosophy of Mind.* Hellenistic Culture and Society 8. Berkeley, Calif.: University of California Press.

Aristotle. 1926-79. Translated by Harold P. Cooke et al. 23 vols. LCL. Cambridge: Harvard University Press.

Arterbury, Andrew E. 2007. Hospitality. Page 901 in vol. 2 of *NIDB.*

Aulén, Gustaf. 2003. *Christus Victor: An Historical Study of the Three Main Types of the Idea of Atonement.* Translated by A. G. Herbert. London: SPCK, 1931. Repr. Eugene, Ore.: Wipf and Stock.

Backhaus, Knut. 1996. *Der Neue Bund und das Werden der Kirche: Die Diatheke-Deutung des Hebräerbriefs im Rahmen der frühchristlichen Theologiegeschichte.* Neutestamentliche Abhandlungen 29. Münster: Aschendorff.

Balz, Horst. 1991a. *"eulabeia, as, hē."* Pages 78-79 in vol. 2 of *EDNT.*

———. 1991b. *"leitourgia, as, hē."* Page 347 in vol. 2 of *EDNT.*

———. 1991c. *"hosios."* Page 536 in vol. 2 of *EDNT.*

———. 1993a. *"Siōn."* Page 246 in vol. 3 of *EDNT.*

———. 1993b. *"stenazō."* Page 272 in vol. 3 of *EDNT.*

Banks, Robert. 1994. *Paul's Idea of Community: The Early House Churches in Their Cultural Setting.* Rev. ed. Peabody, Mass.: Hendrickson.

Barrett, C. K. 1956. The Eschatology of the Epistle to the Hebrews. Pages 363-93 in *The Background of the New Testament and Its Eschatology.* Edited by W. D. Davies and D. Daube. Cambridge: Cambridge University Press.

Bateman, Herbert W., IV, ed. 2007a. *Four Views on the Warning Passages in Hebrews.* Grand Rapids: Kregel.

———. 2007b. Introducing the Warning Passages in Hebrews: A Contextual Orientation. Pages 23-85 in *Four Views on the Warning Passages in Hebrews.* Edited by Herbert W. Bateman IV. Grand Rapids: Kregel.

Beck, Frederick A. G., and Rosalind Thomas. 1996. Education, Greek. Pages 506-9 in *The Oxford Classical Dictionary.* Edited by Simon Hornblower and Antony Spawforth. 3d ed. Oxford and New York: Oxford University Press.

Behm, J. 1965. *"sklērokardia."* Pages 613-14 in vol. 3 of *TDNT.*

Bennett, Maxwell R. 2007. Development of the Concept of Mind. *Australian and New Zealand Journal of Psychiatry* 41:943-56.

Berman, Joshua. 2002. The "Sword of Mouths" (Jud. iii 16; Ps. cxlix 6; Prov. v 4): A Metaphor and Its Ancient Near Eastern Context. *Vetus Testamentum* 52:291-303.

Bettenson, Henry, ed. 1963. *Documents of the Christian Church.* 2d ed. London, Oxford, and New York: Oxford University Press.

Bloch, Renée. 1957. Midrash. Columns 1263-81 in vol. 5 of *Dictionnaire de la Bible: Supplément.* Edited by L. Pirot, A. Robert, and H. Cazelles. Paris: Librairie Letouzey et Ané, 1928—.

Böcher, O. 1990. *"haima, atos, to."* Page 37 in vol. 1 of *EDNT.*

Boyd, George Richard. 2012. Sonship: Central Theological Motif and Unifying Theme of Hebrews. Ph.D. diss., Brunel University.

Brown, Raymond. 1997. *An Introduction to the New Testament.* Anchor Bible Reference Library. New York: Doubleday.

Büchsel, Friedrich. 1965. *"hiketēria."* Pages 296-97 in vol. 3 of *TDNT.*

Buhl, Frants, Emil G. Hirsch, and Solomon Schechter. 1925. Esau. Pages 206-8 in vol. 5 of *The Jewish Encyclopedia*. Edited by I. Singer. 12 vols. New York: Funk and Wagnalls.

Burridge, Richard A. 2004. *What Are the Gospels? A Comparison with Graeco-Roman Biography*. 2d ed. Grand Rapids: Eerdmans.

CathNewsUSA. 2012. Keira Knightley Covets Catholic Perk. No pages. Cited 12 May 2012. Online: http://www.cathnewsusa.com/2012/05/keira-knightley-wishes-she-could-be-catholic/

Charlesworth, James H., ed. 1983. *The Old Testament Pseudepigrapha*. 2 vols. New York: Doubleday.

Cockerill, Gareth L. 2007. A Wesleyan Arminian View. Pages 257-92 in *Four Views on the Warning Passages in Hebrews*. Edited by Herbert W. Bateman IV. Grand Rapids: Kregel.

———. 2008. Melchizedek Without Speculation: Hebrews 7.1-25 and Genesis 14.17-24. Pages 128-44 in *A Cloud of Witnesses: The Theology of Hebrews in Its Ancient Contexts*. Edited by Richard Bauckham et al. Library of New Testament Studies 387. New York: T&T Clark.

Cole, Susan Guettel. 1988. Greek Cults. Pages 887-908 in vol. 2 of *Civilization of the Ancient Mediterranean: Greece and Rome*. Edited by Michael Grant and Rachel Kitzinger. 3 vols. New York: Charles Scribner's Sons.

Cosby, Michael R. 1988. *The Rhetorical Composition and Function of Hebrews 11 in Light of Example Lists in Antiquity*. Macon, Ga.: Mercer University Press.

Cross, F. L., and E. A. Livingstone. 1997a. Cardinal Virtues. Page 287 of *The Oxford Dictionary of the Christian Church*. Edited by F. L. Cross and E. A. Livingstone. 3d ed. New York: Oxford University Press.

———. 1997b. Theological Virtues. Page 1604 of *The Oxford Dictionary of the Christian Church*. Edited by F. L. Cross and E. A. Livingstone. 3d ed. New York: Oxford University Press.

Croy, N. Clayton. 1998. *Endurance in Suffering: Hebrews 12.1-13 in Its Rhetorical, Religious, and Philosophical Context*. Society for New Testament Studies Monograph Series 98. Cambridge and New York: Cambridge University Press.

D'Angelo, Mary R. 1979. *Moses in the Letter to the Hebrews*. Society of Bible Literature Dissertation Series 42. Missoula, Mont.: Scholars.

Decker, Rodney J. 2007. The Alexamenos Graffito. No pages. Cited 31 October 2012. Online: http://ntresources.com/alex_graffito.htm.

de Lacy, Phillip, ed. with trans. and commentary. 1984. *Galeni de Placitis Hippocratis et Platonis*. 3 vols. Berlin: Akademie.

Delling, Gerhard. 1964. "aisthanomai, aisthēsis, aistētērion." Pages 187-88 in vol. 1 of *TDNT*.

———. 1971. "stoicheion." Pages 670-87 in vol. 7 of *TDNT*.

deSilva, David A. 1997. Heaven, New Heavens. Pages 439-43 in *Dictionary of the Later New Testament and Its Developments*. Edited by Ralph P. Martin and Peter H. Davids. Downers Grove, Ill.: InterVarsity.

———. 2000b. *Honor, Patronage, Kinship & Purity: Unlocking New Testament Culture*. Downers Grove, Ill.: InterVarsity.

———. 2001. *New Testament Themes*. St. Louis: Chalice.

Dewald, Carolyn. 1988. Greek Education and Rhetoric. Pages 1077-1107 in vol. 2 of *Civilization of the Ancient Mediterranean: Greece and Rome*. Edited by Michael Grant and Rachel Kitzinger. 3 vols. New York: Charles Scribner's Sons.

Diogenes Laertius. 1972. *Lives of Eminent Philosophers*. Translated by R. D. Hicks. 2 vols. LCL. Cambridge: Harvard University Press.

Elliott, J. Keith. 1977. Is Post-Baptismal Sin Forgivable? *Bible Translator* 28:330-32.

Eusebius. 1926-32. Translated by Kirsopp Lake and J. E. L. Oulton. 2 vols. LCL. Cambridge: Harvard University Press.

Evans, Craig A. 2006. Jewish Exegesis. Pages 380-84 in *Dictionary for Theological Interpretation of the Bible*. Edited by Kevin J. Vanhoozer. London: SPCK; Grand Rapids: Baker Academic.

Fanning, Buist M. 2007. A Classical Reformed View. Pages 172-219 in *Four Views on the Warning Passages in Hebrews*. Edited by Herbert W. Bateman IV. Grand Rapids: Kregel.

Feine, Paul, Johannes Behm, and Werner Georg Kümmel. 1966. *Introduction to the New Testament*. 14th rev. ed. Nashville: Abingdon.

Filson, Floyd V. 1967. *"Yesterday": A Study of Hebrews in the Light of Chapter 13*. Studies in Biblical Theology (Second Series), 4. London: SCM.

Finney, Charles G. 1980. The Rest of Faith, No. 1 and The Rest of Faith, No. 2. Pages 201-10 and 210-16 in *The Promise of the Spirit*. Compiled and edited by Timothy L. Smith. Minneapolis: Bethany House.

———. 1984. Rest of the Saints. Pages 256-68 in *Principles of Holiness*. Compiled and edited by Louis G. Parkhurst Jr. Minneapolis: Bethany House.
Fitzgerald, John T. 1992. Virtue/Vice Lists. Pages 857-59 in vol. 6 of *The Anchor Bible Dictionary*. Edited by D. N. Freedman. 6 vols. New York: Doubleday.
Fitzmyer, Joseph A. 1991. *"monogenēs."* Page 439 in vol. 2 of *EDNT*.
Gelardini, Gabriella. 2005. Hebrews, an Ancient Synagogue Homily for *Tisha be-Av*: Its Function, Its Basis, Its Theological Interpretation. Pages 107-27 in *Hebrews: Contemporary Methods—New Insights*. Edited by Gabriella Gelardini. Biblical Interpretation Series 75. Atlanta: Society of Biblical Literature.
Gess, J. 1979. Image [*charaktēr*]. Pages 288-89 in vol. 2 of *NIDNTT*.
Gleason, Randall C. 2007a. Moderate Reformed Response (to Cockerill 2007). Pages 322-35 in *Four Views on the Warning Passages in Hebrews*. Edited by Herbert W. Bateman IV. Grand Rapids: Kregel.
———. 2007b. A Moderate Reformed View. Pages 336-77 in *Four Views on the Warning Passages in Hebrews*. Edited by Herbert W. Bateman IV. Grand Rapids: Kregel.
Godbey, W. B. 1893. *Holiness or Hell?* Louisville, Ky.: Pentecostal Publishing Company.
Gould, John. 2003. *Myth, Ritual, Memory, and Exchange: Essays in Greek Literature and Culture*. Oxford: Oxford University Press.
Gowan, Donald E. 2009. Repentance in the OT. Pages 764-65 in vol. 4 of *NIDB*.
Gray, Patrick. 2003. *Godly Fear: The Epistle to the Hebrews and Greco-Roman Critiques of Superstition*. Society of Biblical Literature Academia Biblica 16. Atlanta: Society of Biblical Literature.
Greenlee, J. Harold. 1990. Hebrews 11:11: Sarah's Faith or Abraham's? *Notes on Translation* 4, 37-42.
Gunter, W. Stephen, et al. 1997. *Wesley and the Quadrilateral: Renewing the Conversation*. Nashville: Abingdon.
Günther, W., and H. Krienke. 1979. Remnant, Leave. Pages 247-53 in vol. 3 of *NIDNTT*.
Guthrie, Donald. 1990. *New Testament Introduction*. 4th ed. Downers Grove, Ill.: InterVarsity.
Guthrie, George H. 2001. The Case for Apollos as the Author of Hebrews. *Faith and Mission* 18/2: 41-56.
Hahn, F. 1993. *"Christos, ou, ho."* Page 474 in vol. 3 of *EDNT*.
Harder, Günther. 1971. *"spoudazō, spoudē, spoudaios."* Pages 559-68 in vol. 7 of *TDNT*.
Harrison, R. K. 1996. Cherubim. Page 183 in *New Bible Dictionary*. Edited by D. R. W. Wood et al. 3d ed. Downers Grove, Ill.: InterVarsity.
Hauck, Friedrich. 1964. *"bebēlos, bebēloō."* Pages 604-6 in vol. 1 of *TDNT*.
———. 1965. *"katabolē."* Pages 620-21 in vol. 3 of *TDNT*.
Hewett, James Allen. 1986. *New Testament Greek: A Beginning and Intermediate Grammar*. Peabody, Mass.: Hendrickson.
Hildebrandt, Franz, and Oliver A. Beckerlegge, eds. 1989. *A Collection of Hymns for the Use of the People Called Methodists*. Vol. 7 in *The Works of John Wesley*. Nashville: Abingdon.
Hofius, Otfried. 1970. *Katapausis: Die Vorstellung vom endzeitlichen Ruheort im Hebräerbrief*. Wissenschaftliche Untersuchungen zum Neuen Testament 11. Tübingen: J. C. B. Mohr (Paul Siebeck).
Hollander, H. W. 1991. *"makrothymia, as, hē ktl."* Page 380 in vol. 2 of *EDNT*.
———. 1993. *"hypostasis, eōs, hē."* Page 406 in vol. 3 of *EDNT*.
Hoppin, Ruth. 2009. *Priscilla's Letter: Finding the Author of the Epistle to the Hebrews*. Fort Bragg, Calif.: Lost Coast Press.
Hurst, L. D. 1990. *The Epistle to the Hebrews: Its Background of Thought*. Society for New Testament Studies Monograph Series 65. Cambridge: Cambridge University Press.
Jameson, Michael H. 1988. Sacrifice and Ritual: Greece. Pages 959-79 in vol. 2 of *Civilization of the Ancient Mediterranean: Greece and Rome*. Edited by Michael Grant and Rachel Kitzinger. 3 vols. New York: Charles Scribner's Sons.
Josephus, Flavius. 1895. *The Works of Flavius Josephus (JOE)*. Translated by William Whiston. Auburn and Buffalo, N.Y.: John E. Beardsley. BibleWorks version 8.
Just, Felix. 2005. New Testament Statistics, n.p. Cited October 16, 2012. Online: http://catholic-resources.org/Bible/NT-Statistics-Greek.htm.
Justin Martyr. 1994. *First Apology*. In vol. 1 of *The Ante-Nicene Fathers*. Edited by Alexander Roberts and James Donaldson. 1885-87. Repr. Peabody, Mass.: Hendrickson.
Kennedy, George A., trans. 2005. *Invention and Method: Two Rhetorical Treatises of the Hermogenic Corpus*. Society of Biblical Literature: Writings from the Greco-Roman World 15. Atlanta: Society of Biblical Literature.

Kertelge, K. 1991. *"lytron, ou, to."* Page 364 in vol. 2 of *EDNT*.
Koenig, John. 1992. Hospitality. Pages 299-301 in vol. 3 of *The Anchor Bible Dictionary*. Edited by D. N. Freedman. 6 vols. New York: Doubleday.
Koester, Helmut. 1962. "Outside the Camp": Hebrews 13:9-14. *Harvard Theological Review* 55:299-315.
_____. 1972. *"hypostasis."* Pages 572-89 in vol. 8 of *TDNT*.
Kuhn, H.-W. 1990. *"anastauroō."* Page 92 in vol. 1 of *EDNT*.
Lane, William L. 1979. Want, Lack, Need. Pages 952-56 in vol. 3 of *NIDNTT*.
_____. 1998. Living a Life of Faith in the Face of Death: The Witness of Hebrews. Pages 247-69 in *Life in the Face of Death*. Edited by Richard N. Longenecker. Grand Rapids: Eerdmans.
Lausberg, Heinrich. 1998. *Handbook of Literary Rhetoric: A Foundation for Literary Study*. Translated by Matthew T. Bliss, Annemiek Jansen, and David E. Orton. Edited by David E. Orton and R. Dean Anderson. Leiden, Boston, and Köln: Brill.
Lewis, C. S. 1978. *Mere Christianity*. Repr. New York: Macmillan, 1952.
Liddell, H. G., and R. Scott. 1995. *An Intermediate Greek-English Lexicon Founded upon the Seventh Edition of Liddell and Scott's Greek-English Lexicon*. First ed., 1889. Repr. Oxford: Oxford University Press.
Lincoln, Andrew T. 1982. Sabbath, Rest, and Eschatology in the New Testament. Pages 197-220 in *From Sabbath to Lord's Day: A Biblical, Historical, and Theological Investigation*. Edited by D. A. Carson. Grand Rapids: Zondervan.
_____. 2006. *Hebrews: A Guide*. London and New York: T&T Clark.
Lindars, Barnabas. 1991. *The Theology of the Letter to the Hebrews*. New Testament Theology. Edited by James D. G. Dunn. Cambridge: Cambridge University Press.
Link, H.-G. 1979. Swear, Oath. Pages 737-43 in vol. 3 of *NIDNTT*.
Long, A. A. 1974. *Hellenistic Philosophy: Stoics, Epicureans, Sceptics*. London: Duckworth.
Longenecker, Bruce W. 2005. *Rhetoric at the Boundaries: The Art and Theology of New Testament Chain-Link Transitions*. Waco, Tex.: Baylor University Press.
Longenecker, Richard N. 1975. *Biblical Exegesis in the Apostolic Period*. Grand Rapids: Eerdmans.
Maddox, Randy. 1981. The Use of the Aorist Tense in Holiness Exegesis. *Wesleyan Theological Journal* 16, 2:106-18.
Manson, T. W. 1949. The Problem of the Epistle to the Hebrews. *Bulletin of the John Rylands Library* 32:1-17.
Marrou, H. I. 1964. *A History of Education in Antiquity*. New York and Toronto: Mentor. Reprint of *A History of Education in Antiquity*. Translated by George Lamb. New York: Sheed and Ward, 1956. Translation of *Histoire de l'Education dans l'Antiquité*. 3d ed. Paris: Editions du Seuil, 1948.
Marshall, I. Howard. 1966. James Denney. Pages 203-38 in *Creative Minds in Contemporary Theology*. Edited by Philip Edgcumbe Hughes. Grand Rapids: Eerdmans.
_____. 2004. *New Testament Theology: Many Witnesses, One Gospel*. Downers Grove, Ill.: InterVarsity.
Martin, Luther H. 1987. *Hellenistic Religions: An Introduction*. New York and Oxford: Oxford University Press.
McCown, Wayne. 1981. Holiness in Hebrews. *Wesleyan Theological Journal* 16, 2:58-78.
McKnight, Scot. 1992. The Warning Passages of Hebrews: A Formal Analysis and Theological Conclusions. *Trinity Journal* 13:21-59.
Metzger, Bruce M. 1994. *A Textual Commentary on the Greek New Testament*. 2d ed. Stuttgart: Deutsche Bibelgesellschaft.
Mundle, W. 1979. *"eulabeia."* Pages 90-91 in vol. 2 of *NIDNTT*.
Naiden, F. S. 2007. *Ancient Supplication*. Oxford: Oxford University Press.
Newman, Judith H. 2009. Prayer. Pages 579-89 in vol. 4 of *NIDB*.
Oden, Thomas C. 2001a. *The Word of Life*. Vol. 2 of *Systematic Theology*. 3 vols. New York: HarperCollins, 1992. Repr. Peabody, Mass.: Prince Press.
_____. 2001b. *Life in the Spirit*. Vol. 3 of *Systematic Theology*. 3 vols. New York: HarperCollins, 1992. Repr. Peabody, Mass.: Prince Press.
Olson, Roger. 2002. *The Mosaic of Christian Belief: Twenty Centuries of Unity and Diversity*. Downers Grove, Ill.: InterVarsity.
Osborne, Grant R. 2007a. A Classical Arminian View. Pages 86-128 in *Four Views on the Warning Passages in Hebrews*. Edited by Herbert W. Bateman IV. Grand Rapids: Kregel.

———. 2007b. Classical Arminian Response (to Fanning 2007). Pages 220-32 in *Four Views on the Warning Passages in Hebrews*. Edited by Herbert W. Bateman IV. Grand Rapids: Kregel.
———. 2007c. Classical Arminian Response (to Gleason 2007b). Pages 378-95 in *Four Views on the Warning Passages in Hebrews*. Edited by Herbert W. Bateman IV. Grand Rapids: Kregel.
Pfitzner, Victor C. 1967. *Paul and the Agon Motif: Traditional Athletic Imagery in the Pauline Literature*. Leiden: E. J. Brill.
Philo. 1929-62. Translated by F. H. Colson and G. H. Whitaker. 12 vols. LCL. Cambridge: Harvard University Press.
Plato. 1921-86. Translated by H. N. Fowler et al. 12 vols. LCL. Cambridge: Harvard University Press.
Plümacher, E. 1991. "*moicheuō ktl.*" Page 436 in vol. 2 of *EDNT*.
———. 1993a. "*stoicheion, ou, to.*" Page 277 in vol. 3 of *EDNT*.
———. 1993b. "*philadelphia, as, hē.*" Page 424 in vol. 3 of *EDNT*.
Plutarch. 1927-96. Translated by F. C. Babbitt et al. 16 vols. LCL. Cambridge: Harvard University Press.
Powell, Mark Allan. 2009. *Introducing the New Testament: A Historical, Literary, and Theological Survey*. Grand Rapids: Baker Academic.
Procksch, Otto. 1964. "*hagios ktl.*" Pages 89-115 in vol. 1 of *TDNT*.
Proulx, Pierre, and Luis Alonso Schökel. 1973. Heb 4,12-13: componentes y estructura. *Biblica* 54:331-39.
Quintilian. *Institutio oratoria*. 1920-22. Translated by H. E. Butler. 2 vols. LCL. Cambridge: Harvard University Press. Cited October 16, 2012. Online: http://penelope.uchicago.edu/Thayer/E/Roman/Texts/Quintilian/Institutio_Oratoria/home.html.
Rapske, Brian. 1994. *Paul in Roman Custody*. Vol. 3 of *The Book of Acts in Its First Century Setting*. Edited by Bruce W. Winter. Grand Rapids: Eerdmans.
Rickaby, John, S.J. 1908. Cardinal Virtues. *The Catholic Encyclopedia*. Vol. 3. Cited October 16, 2012. Online: http://www.newadvent.org/cathen/03343a.htm.
Robertson, A. T. 1934. *A Grammar of the Greek New Testament in the Light of Historical Research*. 4th ed. Nashville: Broadman.
Robinson, John A. T. 1976. *Redating the New Testament*. Philadelphia: Westminster.
Sand, A. 1993. "*peithō.*" Page 63 in vol. 3 of *EDNT*.
Sänger, D. 1991. "*mesitēs, ou, hē.*" Page 410 in vol. 2 of *EDNT*.
Schenck, Kenneth. 2007. *Cosmology and Eschatology in Hebrews: The Settings of the Sacrifice*. Society for New Testament Studies Monograph Series 143. Cambridge: Cambridge University Press.
Schneider, Johannes. 1967. "*orkos ktl.*" Pages 457-67 in vol. 5 of *TDNT*.
Scott, E. F. 1922. *The Epistle to the Hebrews: Its Doctrine and Significance*. Edinburgh: T&T Clark.
See, Isaac M. 1871. *The Rest of Faith*. New York: W. C. Palmer.
Seeseman, Heinrich. 1967. "*panēgyris.*" Page 722 in vol. 5 of *TDNT*.
Seneca. 1917-72. Translated by John W. Basore et al. 10 vols. LCL. Cambridge: Harvard University Press.
Smyth, Herbert Weir. 1984. *Greek Grammar*. Revised by Gordon M. Messing. Cambridge, Mass.: Harvard University Press.
Son, Kiwoong. 2005. *Zion Symbolism in Hebrews: Hebrews 12:18-24 as a Hermeneutical Key to the Epistle*. Paternoster Biblical Monographs. Milton Keynes, England: Authentic Media.
Spicq, Ceslas. 1994a. "*metechō, metochē, metochos.*" Pages 478-82 in vol. 2 of *TLNT*.
———. 1994b. "*spoudazō ktl.*" Pages 276-85 in vol. 3 of *TLNT*.
———. 1994c. "*hypostasis.*" Pages 421-23 in vol. 3 of *TLNT*.
———. 1994d. "*hystereō ktl.*" Pages 427-31 in vol. 3 of *TLNT*.
Spittler, R. P. 1983. Testament of Job: A New Translation and Introduction. Pages 829-68 in vol. 1 of *The Old Testament Pseudepigrapha*. Edited by James H. Charlesworth. 2 vols. Garden City, N.Y.: Doubleday.
Steele, Daniel. 1909. *Half-Hours with St. Paul*. N.p.: McDonald & Gill, 1894. Repr. Chicago and Boston: Christian Witness.
Suetonius. 1997-98. *Lives of the Twelve Caesars*. Translated by J. C. Rolfe. Cambridge: Harvard University Press.
Tertullian. *On the Soul*. 1950. In vol. 10 of *The Fathers of the Church*. Edited by Roy Joseph Defarrari. Washington, D.C.: Catholic University of America Press, 1947—.
Thiselton, Anthony C. 2009. Oath. Pages 309-12 in vol. 4 of *NIDB*.
Thompson, James W. 1982. *The Beginnings of Christian Philosophy: The Epistle to the Hebrews*. Catholic Biblical Quarterly Monograph Series 13. Washington, D.C.: Catholic Biblical Association.

Thorsen, Donald A. D. 2005. *Wesleyan Quadrilateral: Scripture, Tradition, Reason, and Experience as a Model of Evangelical Theology.* Lexington, Ky.: Emeth.

Traub, Helmut, and Gerhard von Rad. 1967. *"ouranos ktl."* Pages 497-543 in vol. 5 of *TDNT.*

Trotter, Andrew H., Jr. 1997. *Interpreting the Epistle to the Hebrews.* Guides to New Testament Exegesis. Grand Rapids: Baker.

Übelacker, Walter G. 1989. *Der Hebräerbrief als Appell. Untersuchungen zu exordium, narratio, und postscriptum (Hebr 1-2 und 13,22-25).* Coniectanea Biblica: New Testament Series 21. Lund: Wallin & Dalholm.

Vanhoye, Albert. 1959. De "apectu" obationis Christi secundum Epistulam ad Hebraeos. *Verbum Domini* 37:32-38.

———. 1996. La *"teleiôsis"* du Christ: Point capital de le christologie sacerdotale d'Hébreux. *New Testament Studies* 42:321-38.

Wallace, Daniel B. 1996. *Greek Grammar Beyond the Basics: An Exegetical Syntax of the New Testament.* Grand Rapids: Zondervan.

Wesley, John. 1986. A Call to Backsliders (1778). Sermon 86 in *Sermons III.* Edited by Albert C. Outler. Vol. 3 of *The Bicentennial Edition of the Works of John Wesley.* Nashville: Abingdon, 1976—.

Westfall, Cynthia Long. 2005. *A Discourse Analysis of the Letter to the Hebrews: The Relationship between Form and Meaning.* Library of New Testament Studies 297. London and New York: T&T Clark.

Whitehead, David, trans. 2011. *"hiketēria."* Suda Online. No pages. Cited February 2, 2013. Online: http://www.stoa.org/sol-entries/iota/265.

———. 2013a. *"hiketeia."* Suda Online. No pages. Cited February 2, 2013. Online: http://www.stoa.org/sol-entries/iota/264.

———. 2013b. *"hiketēs."* Suda Online. No pages. Cited February 2, 2013. Online: http://www.stoa.org/sol-entries/iota/266.

Wilckens, U. 1972. *"hysteros ktl."* Pages 592-601 in vol. 8 of *TDNT.*

Williamson, Ronald. 1974-75. Hebrews 4:15 and the Sinlessness of Jesus. *Expository Times* 86:4-8.

Witherington, Ben, III. 2005. *The Problem with Evangelical Theology: Testing the Exegetical Foundations of Calvinism, Dispensationalism, and Wesleyanism.* Waco, Tex.: Baylor University Press.

———. 2009. The Conquest of Faith and the Climax of History (Hebrews 12:1-4, 18-29). Pages 432-37 in *The Epistle to the Hebrews and Christian Theology.* Edited by Richard Bauckham et al. Grand Rapids: Eerdmans.

Wolter, M. 1993. *"pherō."* Page 418 in vol. 3 of *EDNT.*

Wooten, Cecil W. 1988. Roman Education and Rhetoric. Pages 1109-20 in vol. 2 of *Civilization of the Ancient Mediterranean: Greece and Rome.* Edited by Michael Grant and Rachel Kitzinger. 3 vols. New York: Charles Scribner's Sons.

Worley, David R. 1981. God's Faithfulness to Promise: The Hortatory Use of Commissive Language in Hebrews. Ph.D. diss., Yale University.

Wray, Judith Hoch. 1998. *Rest as a Theological Metaphor in the Epistle to the Hebrews and the Gospel of Truth: Early Christian Homiletics of Rest.* Society of Biblical Literature Dissertation Series 166. Atlanta, Ga.: Scholars Press.

Wright, N. T. 2003. *The Resurrection of the Son of God.* Minneapolis: Fortress.

Wuest, Kenneth S. 2004. *Word Studies from the Greek New Testament.* Repr., Grand Rapids: Eerdmans, 1973.

Zerwick, Maximilian. 1983. *Biblical Greek: Illustrated with Examples.* English edition (1963), adapted from the 4th Latin edition by Joseph Smith. Scripta Pontificii Instituti Biblici 114. Repr., Rome: Biblical Institute.

Zerwick, Max, and Mary Grosvenor. 1981. *A Grammatical Analysis of the Greek New Testament.* Rome: Biblical Institute.

TABLE OF SIDEBARS

Title	Location
Aliens and Strangers	11:13
Ancient Images of Educational Progress	5:13
Ancient Philosophy on the Fear of Death	2:15
Ancient Thinkers Dissect the Soul	4:12
"Better" Things in Hebrews	1:4
"Bookends" of 4:14-16 and 10:19-23, The	4:14—5:10 Behind the Text
"By the grace of God" or "apart from God" (2:9)?	2:9
Chain-Linking	4:6-7
Christology in Rhyme	1:3
Conscience, The	9:8-10
Cultural Imagery	5:11—6:20 Behind the Text
"The Day"	10:24-25
Different Foundations, Different Priesthoods	7:15-17
Education in the Hellenistic World	5:12
Enlightenment and Baptism	6:4a
Esau the Immoral in Jewish Tradition	12:15-16
Eschatology in Hebrews	2:5
Eternal Fate of the Exodus Generation, The	4:3b-5
Five Warnings Against Apostasy	Introduction, F. Purpose
"Four Hundred Years of Silence"	1:1
God's "House"	3:2
God's Revelation: Past and Present	1:1-4
Hardened Hearts	3:7b-8
"The Heavens" in Ancient Cosmology and in Hebrews	4:14
Holiness in Hebrews	3:1
Hortatory Subjunctives in Hebrews	4:1
Hospitality in the Ancient World	13:2
Interpreting Scripture with Scripture in Hebrews	6:18-20
Jesus the Champion	2:10
John Wesley on Restoration from Apostasy	5:11—6:20 From the Text
Legal Jargon in Hebrews	6:13-20
"Let us . . ."	4:1
Literary and Historical Background of Hebrews 5:7-10, The	5:7
Mediator	8:6
Midrash	3:7-19 Behind the Text
Moses: Handsome and High-Class from Birth	11:23
Mysterious Melchizedek	7:7-8

No Second Repentance or No Second Baptism?	6:6
Outward Sign, Inward Grace	10:22
Partners with Christ	3:14
Philo and Hebrews on God Swearing by Himself	6:13-15
Playing with Beginnings and Endings	5:9
Precise Contrasts	10:11-14
Priesthoods Old and New	7:23-25
Prison in the Ancient Roman World	10:34
Propitiation, Expiation, or Atonement?	2:17-18
Proposed Authors of Hebrews	Introduction, B. Author
Psalm 22: Jesus as Sufferer and Worship Leader	2:12
Psalm 110 in Hebrews	1:13
Quoting Scripture in Hebrews	1:5-14
Rending of the Temple Veil	10:20
Repeating the Proposition	4:15
Rest and Salvation in Hebrews	4:1-13 Behind the Text
Sabbath Rest and the World to Come	4:1-13 Behind the Text
Scandal of Christ's Suffering, The	2:5-18 Behind the Text
Seneca and Hebrews on Suffering and Divine Discipline	12:11
Sons vs. Slaves in Biblical Times	3:5-6*a*
Use of Comparison, The	3:1-6 Behind the Text
Use of the Name "Jesus" in Hebrews	2:9
Verbal Analogy	4:3*b*-5
Virtues	6:10
Whatever Happened to Timothy?	13:23
Why the Comparison of Jesus with Angels in Hebrews?	2:2
Wisdom Christology and Hymnody in 1:2*b*-3	1:2*b-c*
Zion and the Heavenly Jerusalem: Images of God's Temple	12:22*a*

INTRODUCTION

A. Mystery and Revelatory Power

The nineteenth-century Scottish theologian James Denney explained that in interpreting the documents of the NT, "the chief business of the commentator is to elucidate their significance as vehicles of revelation" (cited in Marshall 1966, 207). This task is all but thwarted on multiple fronts when it comes to the Epistle to the Hebrews. Definitive answers to fundamental questions of literary analysis simply elude us. What kind of work is it? Who wrote it? To whom was he writing? Where was the author? Where were his recipients? When did he write? What was the situation of the audience and the purpose of the author in writing to them? What is the discernible structure of the work?

Readers do not get far before realizing that Hebrews is a difficult text to understand. For example: Why the extensive comparison of Christ with angels? What does it mean to be "made perfect"? What is entering into God's rest? Is it really impossible to repent again after falling away? Who is the obscure figure, Melchizedek, and why would the author look to him to explain the priestly role of Jesus?

Even statements that at first seem straightforward and informative raise more questions than they answer. For example, the mention of Timothy in 13:23 assumes the audience's awareness of information we would like to know. Is this the Timothy who was the Apostle Paul's trusted coworker? Does his "release" indicate imprisonment? If so, where? Where will Timothy go to meet the author? What was the relationship of both the author and Timothy to the readers? Or in 13:24, does the expression "those from Italy" suggest that the author is writing *from* or *to* recipients in Italy?

In light of the many literary, sociohistorical, and theological questions arising from Hebrews, William Lane declared it "a delight for the person who enjoys puzzles" (1991, xlvii). In 1906 William Wrede called his study *The Literary Riddle of the Epistle to the Hebrews* (translation of the German; Brown 1997, 689-90). E. F. Scott's (1922, 1) description of the perplexity of Hebrews is particularly memorable: "Among early Christian writings it stands solitary and mysterious, 'without father, without mother, without genealogy,' like that Melchizedek on whom its argument turns."

Despite our difficulty in elucidating the significance of Hebrews, it still functions as a vehicle of divine revelation. Many passages in Hebrews contain such powerful language and imagery that they have the capacity to transcend their literary and rhetorical contexts to speak to us directly. "For the word of God is living and active. Sharper than any double-edged sword . . ." (4:12). "Jesus Christ is the same yesterday and today and forever" (13:8). "Because he himself suffered when he was tempted, he is able to help those who are being tempted" (2:18). "Let us then approach the throne of grace with confidence, so that we may receive mercy and find grace to help us in our time of need" (4:16). What Christian has not been inspired by the great "hall of faith" in Heb 11 or the benediction of 13:20-21?

Some of the great hymns of the church draw upon the Epistle to the Hebrews for inspiration. Charles Wesley's hymn "Love Divine, All Loves Excelling" echoes the theme of divine rest (4:1-11): "Let us all in Thee inherit, / Let us find that second rest." "How Firm a Foundation" utilizes the language of taking refuge (6:18) and the promise, "Never will I leave you; never will I forsake you" (13:5): "What more can He say than to you He hath said, / To you who for refuge to Jesus have fled?" and "That soul, though all hell should endeavor to shake, / I'll never, no never, no never forsake." The hymn "The Solid Rock" freely incorporates the imagery of Hebrews (6:17-19; 7:22; 13:20): "In every high and stormy gale, / My anchor holds within the veil" and "His oath, His covenant, His blood, / Support me in the whelming flood. / When all around my soul gives way, / He then is all my hope and stay" (Lincoln 2006, 7).

No Christian who reads Hebrews with interest can come away from it without being struck by two aspects of its message. First, it magnifies Christ as God's definitive revelation and means of salvation. Second, it urges radical commitment to Christ. These points are so unmistakable and important that they must not be lost in all the tangles of literary, historical, and theological questions surrounding Hebrews. The anonymous author would probably be surprised that his work has generated so many puzzles. Surely he would urge us not to concentrate too long on those matters that are in the end only tangential to the vital message he communicated.

B. Author

Curious students of Hebrews invariably ask: "Who do you think wrote it?" This question has occupied readers since ancient times. With the exception of the Pentateuch, no other book in the Bible has had so much energy and imagination devoted to the question of its authorship. We consider first a profile of the author discernible from the book itself. Then we look at the three most significant proposals for authorship.

What kind of man wrote Hebrews? The writer of Hebrews does not go out of his way to reveal personal details about himself. In comparison to the intensely personal and autobiographical statements we find in Paul's letters, the author of Hebrews is self-effacing (Ellingworth 1993, 11). Yet many facts about the author emerge in the course of his writing. A mundane but basic fact is revealed in his use of a masculine participle in 11:32, namely, that he is indeed a "he." Therefore, we are not dealing with a female author, such as Priscilla or the Blessed Virgin. Six major aspects of the author's profile emerge from the text of Hebrews (see Lane 1991, xlix-li; Trotter 1997, 42-47; G. Guthrie 2001, 50-52):

(1) In 2:3 the author ranks himself, not among the apostles, but as one of those who received from them the saving message of the gospel. He defers to past leaders of the community he addresses (13:7), perhaps familiar apostolic messengers. He classifies himself among the community's present leaders. He exhorts his audience to obey and pray for their leaders (13:17-18). His request for prayers for his speedy return to them (13:19) suggests that he was intimately involved with the community.

(2) Mention of Timothy (13:23) probably indicates the author's connection with the Pauline circle. Unfortunately, he offers insufficient details to determine whether he writes before or after Paul's death. And he says nothing specific about Timothy's imprisonment and recent release.

(3) The writer was highly educated. His facility with Greek may well be the finest in the NT. Even in English, Hebrews gives the sense that we are dealing with a towering intellect. His command of various fields of knowledge shines through the text. He easily recalls technical terms from many facets of culture, such as business, education, law, and medicine (→ 5:11—6:20 sidebar, "Cultural Imagery"; and 6:13-20 sidebar, "Legal Jargon in Hebrews"). Educational metaphors form a key part of his direct address to the audience's situation (→ 5:11—6:1; 12:4-11; and 5:13 sidebar, "Ancient Images of Educational Progress"). He is familiar with philosophical concepts from Platonism and Stoicism. Lane (1991, l) suggests that our author had an education comparable to Philo's.

The author seems to have attained the highest level of educational training: rhetoric (→ 5:12 sidebar, "Education in the Hellenistic World"). The rich vocabulary, arrangement, rhetorical devices, and methods of argumentation in Hebrews reflect someone with considerable rhetorical skill.

(4) The author's exceptional learning was applied to his interpretation of the Hebrew Scriptures. He had a vast knowledge of the Scriptures in Greek, though the Pentateuch and Psalms were the major sources for his quotations (Lane 1991, cxvi). He employed rabbinic hermeneutical techniques in use in Hellenistic synagogues of the first century.

Two interpretive principles are integral to the development of ideas in Hebrews: verbal analogy and the argument from lesser to greater (G. Guthrie 2001, 51). The author of Hebrews is capable of scriptural exposition marked by careful attention to the biblical text, creative insights, and powerful application for his audience.

(5) The author's religious sensibilities were shaped within distinctly Jewish and Christian settings. His thinking is saturated with the cultic language of the LXX. His central arguments in 7:1—10:18 are devoted to matters related to the Levitical priesthood, tabernacle, and covenant. His knowledge and interest in defilement, blood, and purgation are essential to his interpretation of Christ's death. He is also familiar with Jewish ceremonial washings and food regulations (6:2; 9:10; 13:9). This mental framework suggests he had serious and long exposure to worship and study in Hellenistic Jewish synagogues.

He was also an heir to the traditions and confessions of the primitive Christian churches. Central to the author's understanding of salvation is the confession of Christ's person and work. He repeatedly urges his listeners to commit themselves to Christ by way of this confession (3:1; 4:14; 10:23; 13:15). The concrete reality of the historical Jesus provides the hermeneutical key that unlocks the Scriptures. Jesus' suffering, which perfected him as high priest, and his exaltation to God's right hand, constitute the turning point in history (2:5-18; 5:7-10; 7:11, 14-16; 9:26). The writer shares with the earliest churches the belief that they are now living in the "last days" (1:2), are already participating in the realities of the age to come (2:5; 6:4-5; 10:1), and are awaiting the ultimate inheritance and salvation in accordance with God's promises (e.g., 1:14; 6:12; 9:15, 28; 13:14). These christological and eschatological commitments are foundational to authentic Christian faith.

(6) The author has a pastor's heart. He marshals his learning, interpretive skill, and oratorical ability to fashion a "word of exhortation" to address the fears and struggles of a specific community. He knows enough about them (10:25, 32-34; 13:7-24) to boldly confront them about their shortcomings (5:11-14), warn them about the consequences of failure (2:1-4; 3:7—4:13; 6:4-8; 10:26-39; 12:14-29), and encourage them to persevere in their commitment to Christ (10:19—12:13). As a gifted preacher and interpreter, the author deploys penetrating expositions of Scripture in the service of rhetorically powerful exhortations to his audience.

Who was the author? Scholars repeatedly propose three likely authors of Hebrews.

Paul. The King James Version preserves a title for Hebrews that occurs in the Greek manuscript tradition: "The Epistle of Paul the Apostle to the Hebrews." It was certainly not original, since the earlier, simpler superscription "To the Hebrews" was itself added by an early compiler. Nevertheless, in the eastern part of the Roman Empire, Christians attributed Hebrews to Paul fairly early on (but not unanimously). Western acceptance of Hebrews was slower and more difficult.

The earliest existing collection of Paul's letters (the Beatty Papyrus II, $\mathfrak{P}^{46}$), dating to about A.D. 200, places Hebrews between Romans and 1 Corinthians. Around the same time, some Christian scholars in Egypt included Hebrews among Paul's letters, with qualification. Clement of Alexandria claimed that his teacher, Pantaenus, taught that Paul wrote Hebrews. But two problems were immediately apparent.

First, Hebrews is anonymous. Many speculated that Paul withheld his name out of modesty. The apostle to the Gentiles did not want to give the impression that he was imposing himself upon the Jews as an apostle in place of the Lord himself (Eusebius, *Hist. eccl.* 6.14.3-4).

Second, the style of Hebrews differs markedly from Paul's. Some explain this by speculating that the work was originally written in Hebrew. Based upon stylistic similarities, Clement thought Luke translated it and published it for the Greeks (Eusebius, *Hist. eccl.* 6.14.2).

Clement's successor, Origen, affirmed Pauline authorship, with reservations. For Origen, variance in style was a major hurdle. Hebrews' diction is manifestly superior to Paul's, who by his own admission is "rude in speech" (2 Cor 11:6 KJV). Origen thought a student of Paul wrote Hebrews, yet deferred to the tradition of Pauline authorship (Eusebius, *Hist. eccl.* 6.25.11-14). He consistently referred to the fourteen epistles of Paul and introduced passages from Hebrews with "the Apostle says" or "Paul says" (Ellingworth 1993, 5).

Origen was aware of other proposals regarding authorship, namely, Clement of Rome and Luke. His uncertainty probably made him bold enough to press gently against strong tradition. Origen's final verdict is legendary: "But who wrote the epistle, in truth God knows" (Eusebius, *Hist. eccl.* 6.25.14).

In the West, Hebrews was not accepted initially as one of Paul's letters. It was not included in the Muratorian Canon (dated as early as A.D. 180), a list of authoritative NT books accepted in Rome. According to Photius (*Bibliotheca*, 232), both Irenaeus (second century) and Hippolytus (early third century) claimed that Hebrews was not written by Paul. Tertullian (early third century) attributed it to Barnabas. Eusebius (early fourth century) reported ongoing challenges to Pauline authorship in Rome (*Hist. eccl.* 3.3.5; 6.20.3).

Only in the late fourth century did the West include Hebrews among Paul's letters. This came at the prodding of the heavyweights, Jerome and Augustine, and for the sake of church unity between East and West. Because Hebrews was a valuable weapon in the fight against Arianism, both urged its acceptance, despite continuing doubts about Pauline authorship. Jerome wrote (*Epist.*, 129, cited in Lincoln 2006, 4), "It makes no difference whose it is, since it is from a churchman, and is celebrated in the daily readings of the Churches."

From this time forward the status of Hebrews as the fourteenth epistle of Paul seemed secure. However, during the Reformation (early fifteenth century), the judgment against Pauline authorship by the Catholic scholar Erasmus and the Protestant Reformers, Luther and Calvin, began a sea change. A century later, William Tyndale, in his prologue to Hebrews, expressed doubt concerning Pauline authorship. By the seventeenth century, the Puritan divine John Owen felt the need to mount a rigorous defense of Pauline authorship (1812, 1:62-90). Today, if scholars—both Catholic and Protestant—can come to consensus on anything concerning Hebrews, it is that Paul certainly did *not* write it. The evidence against Pauline authorship is overwhelming (see Achtemeier, Green, and Thompson 2001, 468):

(1) The work is anonymous, which is out of character for Paul. It is not credible that Paul would conceal his identity, as Pantaenus and Clement of Alexandria claimed. Paul always identifies himself at the beginning of letters, and (according to 2 Thess 3:17) "signs off" with a postscript in his own hand. Hebrews includes none of the autobiographical and personal references typical in Paul's letters.

(2) The vocabulary and literary style of Paul and Hebrews are worlds apart. Ellingworth presents an impressive list of differences in vocabulary (1993, 7-12). As a signal example, Paul frequently uses *dikaiosynē* and its cognates to describe forensic justification. But in Hebrews the word group is used primarily of ethical righteousness (i.e., obedience to God's will; see, e.g., 1:9; 12:11; Trotter 1997, 56).

Ancient Greek readers could not help but detect Hebrews' superior literary style. His rhetorical planning is executed with far more discipline than Paul's. Lane observes that the author of Hebrews possessed "an architectural mind" (1991, xlix). He states a thesis and then develops it by way of analysis. Even his digressions seem deliberate, unlike Paul who sometimes gets sidetracked and never returns to his original point.

(3) There are numerous differences in theological emphasis, not least in Hebrews' presentation of Jesus as high priest, entirely missing in Paul. Hebrews uses other distinctive titles for Christ, such as "author [*archēgos*]" (2:10; 12:2) or "apostle" (3:1), not in Paul. Paul's distinctive emphases on justification by faith and union with Christ are absent from Hebrews. Whereas Paul highlights the forensic and redemptive aspects of Christ's death, Hebrews accents its cultic aspects as a cleansing, sanctifying, and perfecting sacrifice. Hebrews' appropriation of a key Pauline text (Hab 2:4 in 10:37-39) is strikingly different from Paul's in Rom 1:17 and Gal 3:11 (see D. Guthrie 1990, 672-73; Trotter 1997, 56-57).

(4) The decisive evidence against Pauline authorship is the author's claim that the message of salvation, first proclaimed by the Lord, "was confirmed to us by those who heard him" (2:3). Paul would never have made such a clear line of separation between himself and the apostles. Instead, Paul forcefully asserts his apostleship and his reception of the gospel by direct revelation from Jesus (see 1 Cor 9:1; Gal 1:1, 12).

A college professor of mine, when a student expressed the opinion that Hebrews represents "a piece of Paul," replied curtly, "Paul? Baloney! You don't know Paul!"

Proposed Authors of Hebrews

Proposed Author	Rationale	Proponent(s)
Paul	Attested in the earliest collection of Paul's letters ($\mathfrak{P}^{46}$); mention of Timothy (13:23); supported by Eastern church fathers	Pantaenus; Clement of Alexandria (late second century); most Greek fathers thereafter; church consensus after the fourth century until modern times
Clement of Rome	Verbal and conceptual parallels with 1 Clement	Eusebius (*Hist. eccl.* 3.38); Erasmus; Calvin (as a possibility)
Barnabas	A Levite familiar with Jewish cultic rituals and sacrifice; called "Son of Encouragement" (Acts 4:36; compare Heb 13:22)	Tertullian (late second century); John A. T. Robinson; Philip Hughes
Apollos	Description of him in Acts 18:24-28 and Paul's letters admirably fits the profile of authorship for Hebrews.	Martin Luther; many modern NT scholars
Luke (as translator of Paul's work)	Stylistic similarities between Hebrews and Luke-Acts	Clement of Alexandria
Luke (as sole author)	Stylistic similarities between Hebrews and Luke-Acts; theological affinities; historical reconstruction regarding Luke's involvement with Paul in his final days and with the composition of the Pastoral Epistles	Calvin (as a possibility); Grotius; David Allen (2010)
Timothy (with a postscript by Paul)	Paul sent this sermon by Timothy (who was in prison), adding his own "cover letter" at the end.	J. D. Legg; J. Ramsey Michaels (2009, 310-11)

Silas/Silvanus	Member of the Pauline circle; literary resemblances with 1 Peter	Boehme; T. Hewitt
Priscilla (assisted by Aquila)	Feminine touches (e.g., women mentioned in ch 11); was an instructor of Apollos	Adolf von Harnack; Ruth Hoppin (2009)
Epaphras	Similar concerns about gnostic heresy (see Col 1:7; 4:12-13)	C. P. Anderson; Robert Jewett (1981, 7-9)
Philip	Writing from Caesarea, Philip commends Paul's gospel to Jewish Christians in Jerusalem.	Sir William Ramsay
Mary the mother of Jesus (with assistance from John and Luke)	Feminine touches	J. Massyngberde Ford

Barnabas. This is one of the few alternative proposals to Paul that originated in ancient times (other than Luke and Clement of Rome). Tertullian (ca. A.D. 200) named Barnabas as the author of Hebrews. He did so casually enough, that it may not have been his own idea. But, if he depended on tradition, it must have been confined to North Africa. Two centuries later, Jerome was aware of Tertullian's proposal (see Ellingworth 1993, 14). Some modern scholars have made a case for Barnabas' authorship (notably Robinson [1976, 217-20] and Hughes [1977, 24-25, 29]). Three lines of evidence support this view:

(1) Barnabas was a Levite and a native of Cyprus (Acts 4:36). His Levitical ancestry would account for his interest in the priesthood and sacrificial cult, such as we find in Hebrews. As a Diaspora Jew, he would have been most familiar with the LXX.

(2) The name Barnabas was a nickname (for Joseph), which Acts 4:36 interprets as "Son of Encouragement [*paraklēseōs*]." Did this originate with his gift as a troubleshooter and mediator in the early church (Acts 9:26-30; 11:22-30; 15:22-39; Robinson 1976, 218)? Perhaps Barnabas fulfilled this role in sending Hebrews as a "word of exhortation [*paraklēseōs*]" (Heb 13:22) to a troubled church in Rome (→ C. Destination).

(3) Barnabas was noted for his exemplary self-sacrifice and generosity (Acts 4:37). He sponsored, with Paul, a famine relief mission for the churches in Judea (Acts 11:29). An important concern in Hebrews is freedom from greed (13:5-6). It commends the joyful loss of possessions (10:34) and the demonstration of love and true sacrifice through sharing with others (6:10-11; 13:16).

The impressive correlations between Barnabas and Hebrews may be no more than coincidences. They can neither prove nor disprove his authorship. Other reasons argue *against* Barnabas as the author:

First, whether Rome is the origin or destination of the work (13:24), it is remarkable that the identity of Barnabas as its author was unknown there. There is no evidence that Barnabas had any dealings in Rome, except according to the historically unreliable *Clementine Recognitions* (1.7-13; see Robinson 1976, 217).

Second, some confusion may have existed between Hebrews and the spurious *Epistle of Barnabas*. Tertullian clearly cites Hebrews (6:4-8), yet calls the work he is quoting both "an epistle to the Hebrews" and "the epistle of Barnabas" (*Pud.* 20).

Third, the quality of Hebrews' style surpasses Paul's. Yet it was Paul, not Barnabas, who acted as "the chief speaker" during the first missionary journey (Acts 14:12). This does not prove Barnabas could not have had the oratorical skill to match the rhetorical display in Hebrews. However, Acts takes note of rhetorical prowess when it is present (e.g., Stephen [6:10] and Apollos [18:23-28]).

Apollos. This is the brilliant suggestion made by Martin Luther. Since the nineteenth century, many scholars have argued for Apollos as the author, including F. Bleek, F. W. Farrar, T. Zahn, T. W. Manson, H. Montefiore, R. C. H. Lenski, and C. Spicq. Many recent scholars tip their hat to this view as the most viable (e.g., Lane, Ellingworth, Hagner, Pfitzner, L. T. Johnson; see D. Guthrie 1990, 679-80; G. Guthrie 2001, 42-49).

Apollos, in accordance with the description in Acts 18:24-28 and additional details from Paul's letters, matches our profile of the author of Hebrews (→ *What kind of man wrote Hebrews?* above). He was not an apostle but could claim that the message he preached was confirmed by the apostles. He was in touch with the Pauline circle. He had dealings with Priscilla and Aquila, and Paul himself in Ephesus (Acts 18:26; 1 Cor 16:12). Some scholars speculate that "those from Italy" (Heb 13:24) is an oblique reference to Priscilla and Aquila. Acts calls Apollos a "learned man [*anēr logios*]" (Acts 18:24), an expression employed by Philo and others to signify both great learning and eloquence (Lane 1991, 1; BDAG, 598). His native city also bespeaks his high level of education, since Alexandria was the premier center of Hellenistic culture and higher learning in the first-century Roman world.

Apollos was "mighty [*dynatos*]" (KJV), that is, "an authority" on the Scriptures (Acts 18:24 NAB). He was capable of bold speech and vigorous argumentation with Jews in the synagogue (18:26, 28). He taught accurately concerning Jesus and proved from the Scriptures that Jesus is the Messiah (18:25, 28), as do the scriptural expositions in Hebrews. His past adherence to the teaching of John the Baptist provides a plausible background for Hebrews' references to "baptisms" (Heb 6:2; 9:10), as well as its undeveloped doctrine of the Holy Spirit (compare Acts 18:25 with 19:1-6).

Apollos is also described as nurturing the faith of new converts in Achaia (Acts 18:27; 1 Cor 3:6). He appears as a church leader, working in cooperation with the apostle Paul (1 Cor 16:12). The last time we see him, he has traveled to Crete on his way to another assignment (Titus 3:13). Thus, Apollos appears to have been in demand as a gifted and passionate preacher who was effective at confirming the faith of believers.

The strength of Apollonian authorship is that there are no hard facts against it (D. Guthrie, 1990). Nevertheless, there are three impediments to consider:

First, Apollos was not named as the author until the time of Luther. If Apollos had penned Hebrews, it is remarkable that no one in the early church remembered it. Neither do we have knowledge that he engaged in any literary activity. Although the lack of early positive testimony or literary remains falls short of proving that Apollos was the author, it does not disprove it.

Second, some scholars admit that Apollos fits the general profile for authorship but insist that there must have been others in the early church who were his equal in exegetical and rhetorical ability (Attridge 1989, 4). G. Guthrie counters this assumption by pointing to the especially strong language Luke uses to describe Apollos in Acts 18:24-28 (2001, 52). Apollos so impressed the church at Corinth with his learning and eloquence that some inappropriately elevated him above the apostles Peter and Paul (1 Cor 1:12; 3:4). By all accounts, Apollos was an exceptional figure. There was not someone like him standing at every corner in the early Christian movement.

Third, if Apollos were the author, it could weaken the case for a Roman destination of Hebrews (→ C. Destination, below). But this is an argument from silence. We do not know where Apollos traveled or resided prior to his arrival in Ephesus (Acts 18:24). Beyond his work in Corinth, Ephesus, and later in Crete, we know nothing certain about his movements.

Priscilla and Aquila returned to Rome (after Claudius' expulsion order lapsed [Acts 18:1; Rom 16:3-5]). And Paul ended up there as a prisoner (Acts 28:11-31). Apollos cooperated with all three of these early church leaders. Paul envisioned establishing a base in Rome for a projected mission to Spain (Rom 15:24, 28). So some involvement of Apollos with the churches at Rome by the late fifties is not improbable (G. Guthrie 2001, 53).

Alas, we cannot know with certainty who wrote Hebrews. Any proposal concerning authorship is inevitably speculative, based on the paltry information available to us. We are left with Origen's well-worn pronouncement: "But who wrote the epistle, in truth God knows."

C. Destination

Numerous possible destinations have been proposed for the Epistle to the Hebrews: Colosse, Ephesus, Galatia, Corinth, Syria (possibly Antioch), Cyprus, and even Berea (see D. Guthrie 1990, 700-701). Three proposals have garnered the most support: Jerusalem, Alexandria, and Rome.

Jerusalem. The title "To the Hebrews [*Pros Hebraious*]" is not original. Probably added in the second century when Hebrews was compiled into a collection of Paul's letters (like 𝔓⁴⁶), it was created to match other titles indicating addressees (e.g., "To the Romans [*Pros Rōmaious*]"). The earliest mention of the Epistle to the Hebrews by this title goes back to Irenaeus (noted in Eusebius, *Hist. eccl.* 5.26). This is the title we find later in Tertullian, Clement of Alexandria, and Origen. The title was likely an educated guess, based on the contents of the work. It signified a Jewish audience, more specifically Jewish Christians. Implied, as well, was a destination in the Holy Land. John Chrysostom (late fourth century) was the first to make this explicit, stating that the recipients were "in Jerusalem and Palestine" (1996, 364).

From around the fourth century until modern times the traditional view has been that Hebrews was written to a group of Jewish Christians in Jerusalem or its environs. A twentieth-century variation identified the recipients as converted priests in Palestine (see Acts 6:7). Among them were Essenes who were either associated with or former members of the community at Qumran (Spicq 1952, 1:226-31; Hughes 1977, 10-15). This theory emerged in the fervor over the discovery of the Dead Sea Scrolls but has not survived detailed scholarly investigation.

There are many incongruities concerning a destination of Jerusalem (see Brown 1997, 698-99; Trotter 1997, 37; Koester 2001, 48-49):

(1) It is odd that the author would have written in such polished Greek to an audience whose native tongue was Aramaic. Clement of Alexandria perceived this problem and made the impossible suggestion that Paul originally wrote the work in Hebrew (= Aramaic) and Luke translated it into Greek.

(2) The author wrote as though none of his readers had been firsthand witnesses to Jesus (2:3) or had risen to the role of teachers (5:11-14). Both claims ill-suit the primitive church in Jerusalem.

(3) The past persecutions described in 10:32-34, as well as the comment in 12:4, suggest that no one in the community had experienced martyrdom. But persecutions of early Christians in Jerusalem had resulted in the deaths of Stephen and James the brother of John (Acts 7:58—8:3; 12:1-2).

(4) The readers of Hebrews were exemplary in their generosity to others (6:10; 10:34; 13:16). But we know that the believers in Judea were notably poor and often in need of assistance themselves (Acts 24:17; Rom 15:26; Gal 2:10).

(5) It also seems strange that the author's lengthy discussion of the Levitical priesthood and cult makes repeated references to the ancient tabernacle and none to the temple in Jerusalem.

(6) The book of Acts attests to Jewish Christians—Paul included—taking part in worship activities in the Jerusalem temple (Acts 21:23-24, 26). If Hebrews were written before A.D. 70, what good would it do to direct them not to go back to rituals they never gave up? After A.D. 70, how could Jewish Christians return to a sacrificial cult that no longer existed?

(7) Is it plausible that any author, much less a second-generation Pauline Christian, would think he could persuade Jewish Christians in Jerusalem to renounce cultic activities in the temple? The Jewish piety modeled by the prominent leader of the Jerusalem church, James the brother of Jesus (d. A.D. 61), would not have given way easily to argument. This was especially true in the years leading up to the Jewish War and ultimate destruction of the temple, when Jewish nationalism was at a fever pitch.

Alexandria. A fashionable view in the last two centuries has advocated a target audience in Alexandria, based upon "Alexandrian colouring" or supposed similarities with Philo (D. Guthrie 1990, 700; see Bruce 1990, 12-13). But it is hardly credible, since the earliest scholars to propose (wrongly) that Paul composed Hebrews were in Alexandria. In any event, the "colouring" of the epistle may tell us more about the author than his audience. The decline of this theory seems to correspond with the increasing rejection of the once popular view that Hebrews was influenced profoundly by Philonic or Platonic thought (see Hurst 1990, 7-42).

Rome. Since the mid-1700s the view that Hebrews was addressed to a Christian community in Rome has gained increasing favor (see D. Guthrie 1983, 27; Bruce 1990, 13-14; Hagner 1990, 5; Lane 1991, lviii-lx; Ellingworth 1993, 29; Pfitzner 1997, 30-31; G. Guthrie 1998, 20-21; Koester 2001, 49; France 2006, 22-23; O'Brien 2010, 15). The only explicit marker in the text, "those from Italy," is ambiguous (→ 13:24). The more likely interpretation is that the author sends greetings from some of his Italian companions to their fellow Christians back home. A number of connections between external and internal evidence cohere with a Roman destination:

(1) The earliest uses of Hebrews were associated with Rome. Clement of Rome quoted extensively from Hebrews in his letter to the Corinthians (*1 Clement;* ca. A.D. 96). The *Shepherd of Hermas,* also written from Rome (late first century), was indebted to Hebrews (see point 2 below). Irenaeus was the first to mention Hebrews by its title ("To the Hebrews"). Before he became a bishop in Gaul, he resided in Rome. Both he and his disciple, Hippolytus of Rome, denied that Paul wrote Hebrews.

(2) In terms of content, there are several correlations between the earliest Roman sources (*1 Clement* and *Hermas*) and Hebrews:

First, the vocabulary used to describe Christian "leaders" appears to be distinctive to Rome. The terms are not used as titles for Christian leaders in any sources apart from those originating there (*hēgoumenoi*: Heb 13:7, 17, 24; *1 Clem.* 1.3; *proēgoumenoi*: *1 Clem.* 21.6; *Herm. Vis.* 2.2.6; 3.9.7).

Second, the *Shepherd of Hermas* is aware of the rigorist doctrine in Hebrews (that it is impossible to repent again after conversion and subsequent apostasy). A heavenly messenger modifies this teaching, making allowance for one additional opportunity for repentance after baptism (*Herm. Mand.* 4.3.1-7; see *Herm. Vis.* 2.2.4-5). This relaxation of Hebrews' position drew fire from Tertullian, who dubbed *Hermas* "that apocryphal Shepherd of adulterers" (*Pud.* 20).

A third, though less certain, correlation concerns the motive for apostasy. In *Hermas*, certain believers would not "cleave" to the saints (*Herm. Sim.* 8.8.1; 8.9.1), because they were wealthy or entangled in business affairs (9.20.1-2). Robinson (1976, 211-12) detects the same reason for some of Hebrews' readers holding back from "love and good deeds" and withdrawing from the Christian assembly (10:24-25). At least some of them were wealthy. In the past they had been generous (6:10) and willing to relinquish possessions rather than deny their commitment to Christ (10:34). But now they needed to be warned against greed (13:5) and reminded to share with others (13:16; see 6:10-11). Robinson also points out the preponderance of commercial images: God is a wage-payer (11:6); salvation is a "reward" (10:35; 11:26), possessions/property (10:34), or coming into an inheritance (1:2, 4, 14; 6:12, 17; 9:15; 11:8; 12:17); obedience is enjoined because their leaders must "give [an] account," and a bad reckoning would be "unprofitable" (13:17 KJV).

(3) The church's record of generosity is in keeping with celebrations of the generosity of the Roman Christians (Ign. *Rom.* Opening; Eusebius, *Hist. eccl.* 4.23.10; Pfitzner 1997, 31).

(4) At an early date there were Christians in Rome (Rom 1:7; 16:3-5, 14-15) and in its port city, Puteoli (Acts 28:13-15). There had long been Jewish communities in these two cities (Josephus, *J.W.* 2.104; Philo, *Embassy*, 155). The churches founded in these cities had many Gentile members (Rom 1:5-6, 13-15), although they included prominent Jewish Christians (e.g., Priscilla and Aquila [Rom 16:3]). Many Roman Christians remained heavily invested in their Jewish heritage (see Rom 9—11; *1 Clement*). Ambrosiaster commented in the preface to his exposition of Romans: "The Romans had embraced the faith of Christ, albeit according to the Jewish rite." Hippolytus of Rome (*Trad. ap.* 20.5) mentions Christians who prescribed purifying baths similar to Jewish rites (Lane 1991, lix). This Jewish identity among the Roman churches coheres with concerns treated in Hebrews.

In his letter to the Romans, Paul is aware of several house churches in Rome (16:3-16). Hebrews is likely written to one of these. The exhortations to remember, obey, and greet the leaders (Heb 13:7, 17, 24) hints at a loose organizational structure acknowledged by the various house churches. Did the pulling away from "meeting together" (10:25) involve individuals abandoning the house church? Or did the house church itself refrain from larger public gatherings with the other houses churches in Rome?

(5) Concern for Timothy's situation (13:23) fits a Roman destination, since the churches there were in touch with leaders in the orbit of Paul's ministry (Rom 16:3, 7). The Roman churches knew Timothy and others identified by Paul as Jewish Christians (Rom 16:21; see 16:7, 11).

D. Date and Situation of the Audience

We are no more certain about the date of Hebrews or the exact situation of its original readers than we are about its author. Hebrews indicates that some time had passed since the community first accepted the message of salvation (2:1-4; 3:14; 5:12; 6:10; 10:32-34; 13:7). Since both the author and his readers were familiar with the Pauline circle (13:23), Hebrews cannot be dated earlier than the late 50s. Its latest plausible date seems to be A.D. 96, when Hebrews is first quoted by Clement of Rome (e.g., *1 Clem.* 36.1-5).

The destruction of Jerusalem and its temple in A.D. 70 was for Jews in some ways similar to the leveling of the Twin Towers in New York City on 9/11/2001 for Americans. The Roman conquest of Judea was world news. It was celebrated and propagandized by the Romans in various ways: a triumphal procession in A.D. 71; the minting of Judea Capta coins for twenty-five years under the emperor Vespasian and his sons, Titus and Domitian; the housing of the spoils from the Jerusalem temple in the newly constructed Temple of Peace next to the Roman Forum, dedicated in A.D. 75; and in the Arch of Titus, erected around A.D. 81 after the death of Titus (Aitken 2005, 137-38, 145). If Hebrews was written after the sack of Jerusalem, it is extraordinary that it never mentions the destruction of the Jerusalem temple.

This argument from silence that Hebrews was written prior to A.D. 70 has not convinced many scholars. Not only does its author never mention the temple's destruction, but he makes no reference whatsoever to the temple in Jerusalem. Hebrews refers exclusively to the wilderness tabernacle and the Levitical priesthood and offerings as described in the Pentateuch. Of course, this demonstrates only the scriptural and exegetical focus of the author. It says nothing about the continuance of the temple cult in Jerusalem. Might the author have purposely ignored mentioning the temple so as not to legitimate it?

Hebrews regularly refers to priestly actions in the present tense (e.g., 7:27-28; 8:4-5; 9:6-7; 13:11). This might suggest that the temple cult was still in operation. Critics are quick to point out, however, that others writing after A.D. 70 refer to the temple or sacrificial offerings in the present tense (Josephus, *Ant.* 3.224-57; *C. Ap.* 2.77, 193-98; *1 Clem.* 41.2; *Diogn.* 3.5).

However, several statements in Hebrews could hardly have been expressed in the same way if the temple were already in ruins. The author speaks of "the present time" when "gifts and sacrifices [are] being offered" (9:9). He writes of "the same sacrifices repeated endlessly year after year" (10:1) and that "day after day every priest stands and performs his religious duties" (10:11). These sacrifices can never remove sins or perfect worshipers. If they could, "would they not have stopped being offered?" (10:2). If the temple were already destroyed, would not the statement in 8:13 be even more pointed than it is: "what is obsolete and aging will soon disappear"?

If the author wrote after the destruction of the temple, could he have resisted comment on the cessation of the temple cult, particularly in light of the work's argument? The *Epistle of Barnabas* is the only other early Christian work, which, like Hebrews, presents a sustained argument for the superiority of Christ and his sacrificial death to the sacrifices and ritual practices of Judaism. Clearly written after A.D. 70 (ca. 130), Pseudo-Barnabas does precisely what we would expect: he explicitly refers to the fall of Jerusalem and its temple to bolster his argument (*Barn.* 16.1-5). He is the first Christian writer to do so (Robinson 1976, 313).

Likewise, had the temple been razed prior to the writing of Hebrews, "it would have dotted the i's and crossed the t's of everything the author was labouring to prove" (Robinson 1976, 204). The author of Hebrews discerned the Holy Spirit's demonstration that a way into the most holy place would not be revealed "as long as the first tabernacle was still standing" (9:8). How much more, then, would he have traced the intent of the Holy Spirit in the actual destruction of the Jerusalem temple?

Thus, we may be reasonably confident that Hebrews was written prior to the destruction of Jerusalem. Analogously, in our own day, we would expect books written specifically about global terrorism not to refer to the destruction of the World Trade Center in New York City only if they had been written *before* September 11, 2001. Nevertheless, as with so many other matters regarding Hebrews, we cannot be dogmatic concerning its date.

Is it possible to zoom in even closer on the times and situation of the early Christian community to whom Hebrews was written? Sketching a coherent picture from the little data we have is an exercise in historical reconstruction. We must be mindful that it is provisional and subject to revision or rejection. The best proposal is William Lane's (1985, 22-25; 1991, lxiii-lxvi). It builds upon the argument that Hebrews was written to an early Jewish Christian community in Rome. Hebrews reveals to us two main periods in the community's life.

The first period was during "those earlier days" after they were originally enlightened by the gospel (10:32; see 3:14; 6:4) in response to the preaching of the word of God (2:3; 13:7). The community was undergoing a "great contest" of suffering on account of their confession of Christ (10:32). The persecution endured by the community fits the distress Jewish Christians experienced in A.D. 49 in Rome. The Roman biographer Suetonius reported riots in the Jewish quarter of Rome "at the instigation of Chrestus" (*Claud.* 25.4). Historians regard the slave name "Chrestus" a mistaken form of "Christus" (Christ).

Jewish Christians were evidently evangelizing in the Jewish quarter, proclaiming the crucified and risen Jesus as the promised Messiah (the Christ). Vitriolic responses to their preaching erupted in violence. The unrest and rioting prompted swift, decisive action by the emperor Claudius. He expelled many Jews from Rome (Suetonius, *Claud.* 25.4), including Jewish Christians such as Aquila and Priscilla (Acts 18:2). Other hardships noted in Heb 10:32-34 are consistent with such imperial action: public exposure to verbal and physical abuse, imprisonment, and seizure of property.

The second period was concurrent with the writing of Hebrews, approximately fifteen years later. About ten years earlier, a number of banished Jewish Christians, including Priscilla and Aquila, had resettled in Rome after the death of Claudius (A.D. 54; see Rom 16:3-5). Then, in A.D. 64 a great fire devastated over 70 percent of Rome. Christians, who were already the objects of public ridicule and suspicion, now became targets of official persecution. To deflect rumors that he had caused the fire, the emperor Nero shifted the blame to the Christians (Tacitus, *Ann.* 15.44). Prominent Christians were arrested and tortured. Many others were sentenced to death.

We cannot be certain this was the setting of Hebrews' original audience. But their experience was consistent with it. Hebrews addressed a community under so severe a threat that they were enslaved by the "fear of death" (2:14-15). This paralysis of fear was making them increasingly resistant to listening to God's word (2:1, 3; 3:7, 15; 4:7; 5:11; 12:25). Their spiritual growth was stunted (5:11-14); and they were suffering from a failure of nerve to forge ahead in their faith (6:1-3, 11-20). They were growing weary and losing heart (12:3, 12-13). They needed to be emboldened in their confession of Christ (3:6; 4:14; 10:23, 35).

The backdrop of the Neronian persecution also fits Hebrews' emphasis on the example of Jesus' perfection through suffering and death (2:9-10; 5:8-9). Repeated exhortations to persevere are backed up by examples of the past faithful who endured alienation (11:13), imprisonment, torture, exile, and execution (11:35-40). These worthy men and women are "a great cloud of witnesses" to the readers' present struggle (12:1). But Jesus' endurance of crucifixion is the supreme pattern for the readers' own perseverance in faith (12:2-3). They have not yet struggled to the point of bloodshed (12:4). But they had to be prepared to give their all in devotion to Christ. The climactic call to commitment is in 13:13: "Let us, then, go to him [Jesus] outside the camp, bearing the disgrace he bore."

Although far from certain, the setting of Hebrews plausibly fits into the troubled period for Christians in Rome between the great fire of A.D. 64 and Nero's suicide in 68. This early date squares with Hebrews' expectation of the imminent return of Christ (10:25, 37-39; see 9:28) and awareness of Timothy's active role in the early churches (13:23; Lane 1991, lxvi).

E. Genre

H. E. Dana said Hebrews "begins like a treatise, proceeds like a sermon, and closes like an epistle" (quoted in Brown 1997, 690). Debate surrounds the identification of Hebrews' genre. But recent scholars increasingly agree that it is written with deep pastoral concern to a real community in crisis (see Lane

1991, lxxiv; Lincoln 2006, 11). Despite its majestic opening and rich theology, Hebrews is not a theological treatise.

The author describes his own composition as a "word of exhortation" (→ 13:22). The same label in Acts 13:15 designates a synagogue sermon Paul delivers after the reading of the Law and the Prophets (on Hebrews as a synagogue homily, see Gelardini 2005). Several features in Hebrews confirm this identification:

(1) While Hebrews is obviously a written composition, it assumes primarily oral forms of expression. Prior to the postscript (13:22-25), the author deliberately avoids references to reading or writing. Rather, he consistently refers to speaking (2:4-5; 5:11; 6:9; 8:1; 9:5; 11:32; 13:6) and listening (2:1, 3; 3:7, 15-16; 4:2, 7; 5:11). God's speaking is of ultimate concern in Hebrews (e.g., 1:1-2a; 12:25-27).

(2) The author sustains a personal tone throughout. This can be seen in his frequent identification with his audience through the use of the first person plural ("we" and "us"; his use of the hortatory subjunctive is illustrative; → 4:1 sidebar, "Let us . . ."). He also skillfully interweaves direct addresses to his listeners in the second person ("you"; see 5:11—6:20; 10:19-39). For example, even in the midst of technical legal arguments in ch 7, the author interjects bits of pastoral encouragement (vv 19, 22, 25, 26).

(3) The author's approach to interpreting Scripture was common in ancient Jewish and Hellenistic synagogues and in later rabbinic Judaism. Midrash (→ 3:7-19 Behind the Text sidebar, "Midrash"), as it is called, incorporates various interpretive strategies such as verbal analogy, typology, argument from silence, and argument from lesser to greater (→ 4:3b-5 sidebar, "Verbal Analogy"; → 7:1-28 Behind the Text). The author's alternation between expositions of biblical texts and exhortations to his listeners is itself characteristic of ancient homilies (see Acts 13:16-41; Lincoln 2006, 10-11).

(4) Hebrews is the finest rhetorical display in the NT. The author utilizes many elegant rhetorical figures and patterns of argumentation. A short list includes *inclusio*, comparison (*synkrisis*), chiasm, alliteration, anaphora, antithesis, examples (*exempla*), wordplay, and the frequent lesser to greater argument (for convenient explanations, see Trotter 1997, 66-75, 164-80; Lincoln 2006, 19-21). Throughout the commentary, we give English readers insights into the rhetorical force of such techniques, the rhetorical structuring of the work, as well as Hebrews' stylistic command of Greek.

Because Hebrews is a sermon, I often refer to the author as "the preacher." Nevertheless, Hebrews is also an epistle; and its author, a letter writer. Chapter 13 contains many elements of the closing of ancient letters (→ 13:1-25 Behind the Text). The urgency of the audience's situation and the preacher's inability to deliver his "word of exhortation" in person necessitated an epistolary mode. He committed his sermon to writing and sent it to them by way of a letter (13:22b). Thus, we can justifiably refer to "The Epistle to the

Hebrews," although the controlling genre of the work is that of a homily or sermon.

F. Purpose

The purpose of Hebrews is directly responsive to the situation of the audience (→ D. Date and Situation of the Audience above). Hebrews presents "strong encouragement" (6:18 ESV, RSV, NASB; see 12:5; 13:22) to a group of Jewish Christians who are presently or will soon be subjected to a great trial of suffering. The society around them is branding them with dishonor and shame on account of their confession of Jesus Christ. Feelings of vulnerability, insecurity, isolation, and fear are shaking their confidence and certainty in the Christian faith.

Extreme discouragement has overtaken some members of the little house church. As a result, some are guilty of flagging commitment to Christ. This tendency has made them inattentive to advanced Christian teaching (5:11; 6:1-3). Their moral clarity and spiritual maturity are on the decline (5:12-14; 12:5-11). The preacher is concerned that their sluggishness (5:11; 6:12) and weakened resolve (12:12-13) will lead to disbelief and disobedience (3:12; 4:11). This may ultimately result in outright abandonment of their Christian commitment. Thus, Hebrews contains five frightening warnings about the danger of apostasy (2:1-4; 3:7—4:13; 5:11—6:12; 10:19-39; 12:14-29; see Bateman 2007a).

Five Warnings Against Apostasy

Hebrews	Warning
2:1-4	Inattentiveness to and drifting away from the message of salvation announced by the Lord is more perilous than lawbreaking under the old covenant.
3:7—4:13	Even as the hard-hearted Israelites were destroyed in the wilderness because of their unbelief and disobedience, so also will those who disbelieve and disobey the gospel be barred from entry into God's final rest.
5:11—6:12	It is impossible to be restored to repentance after sharing in the blessings of salvation and then decisively repudiating the Son of God.
10:19-39	Deliberate, persistent, and knowing desecration of the Son of God, his covenant sacrifice, and gracious Spirit leaves one with no effective sacrifice for sins or deliverance from the fearful expectation of divine judgment.

12:14-29	It is imperative to prefer the heavenly realities of God's unshakable kingdom over earthly concerns. Failure to do so risks forfeiture of God's promised inheritance (like Esau) and exposure to the consuming fire of God's judgment.

Hebrews exhorts the readers to avoid falling away or turning back from their allegiance to Christ. But the preacher does not explicitly state what they would shrink back to—except unbelief and destruction (3:12-19; 4:1, 11; 10:39). The traditional view is that they were tempted to slip back into the beliefs and practices of Judaism to which they were accustomed prior to their reception of the gospel. Devotion to Christ left them exposed to persecution. Judaism was a protected religion under the Roman state. So the logical and safe option would be simply to revert back to their pre-Christian Jewish identity and commitments.

The traditional perspective has been criticized in recent scholarship (→ 13:13-14). David deSilva, for example, rejects both the threat of violence and the attractive option of returning to Judaism as motivating factors for apostasy (2000a, 16-20; see Attridge 1989, 13). Continued alienation from the surrounding culture and the lack of esteem and wealth that could be available to them through a good standing in society were sufficient causes for turning away from the Christian confession. The expected rewards for commitment to Christ have not materialized. The community has become worn down by the external pressure and mistreatment from their neighbors and the internal desire for an honorable status and favorable reputation in society.

Analysis of the social dynamics of the readers' precarious position is a welcome contribution to our understanding of the audience's sociocultural setting. It does not, however, possess adequate explanatory scope and power to account for the theological and religious dimensions of Hebrews' purpose. Hebrews makes a sustained comparison and contrast between God's past revelation through the Prophets and the definitive, eschatological revelation in the Son (1:1-2*a*). God's revelation in the Son is superior to the message delivered through angels (1:4—2:4). Jesus holds a more exalted position as the Son over God's house, in comparison with Moses who was a faithful servant in God's house (3:1-6). Hebrews painstakingly argues that Christ's high priesthood, new covenant, heavenly sanctuary, and atoning sacrifice are superior to the cultic arrangements under the Mosaic law (7:1—10:18; → 7:23-25 sidebar, "Priesthoods Old and New," for an overview of contrasts). Rhetorical climaxes of the work include the contrast between the earthly Mount Sinai and heavenly Mount Zion (12:18-29) and the appeal to identify with Jesus' suffering outside the city gate/camp of Jerusalem (13:11-14). These must have had some relevance for the audience's religious attachments, not simply their social predicament.

"Such a massive interest in the relationship of the two dispensations" is likely to have had a bearing on the live options being considered by the readers (Lincoln 2006, 58). There are no credible indications that the audience had any inclinations toward paganism (e.g., "acts that lead to death" do not imply idolatry; → 6:1b). If they were pulling away from their devotion to Christ, backsliding into their "previous way of life in Judaism" (Gal 1:13) would be a natural alternative. This is strongly suggested in the readers' sluggish response to in-depth exposition of the Christian confession (5:10-11). It is also implicit in their apparent willingness to stand pat on basic theological beliefs that did not stipulate the centrality of Christ for which the preacher was contending (6:1-6). The traditional view, therefore, remains the most viable interpretation of Hebrews' purpose.

G. Theology

The author of Hebrews ranks among the Evangelists and Paul as one of the most creative theological minds in the NT. He is a consummate pastoral theologian. The theological truths he conveys are best grasped through exposure to the work itself. Only in this way can we experience the masterful biblical exposition, the subtle argumentation, and the appropriation of Christian claims for the situation of the audience. Separating the content from the form flattens out the depth and texture of Hebrews' theology and weakens its expressive and persuasive force. Nevertheless, it is advantageous to orient readers in the basic theological framework of Hebrews.

Eschatology: The Old and the New. In simplest terms, eschatology is "the study of last times" (*eschata*, "last things" + *logos*, "discourse, reason"). Applied to Hebrews, eschatology is the belief that God's revelation and saving action are culminating at the end of the ages through the Son. This eschatological perspective is immediately visible in Hebrews' majestic opening (1:1-4). Divine revelation (God "has spoken" [1:2a]) and salvation have been decisively introduced "in these last days" (1:2a) through the Son's provision of purification for sins and in his subsequent exaltation (1:3c).

Eschatology is at the heart of Hebrews' theological method. It underlies the author's interpretation of scriptural texts and his mode of argumentation. The author reads the Scriptures with an eye toward how they point to a future time of fulfillment. For example, Pss 110:1 (Heb 1:13) and 8:4-6 (Heb 2:6b-8a) are interpreted as prophecies concerning the subjection of "the world to come," not to angels, but to the Son (2:5; see 2:8b-c). Moses testified to "what would be said in the future" (3:5). The Mosaic law is only a shadow of "the good things that are coming" (10:1).

The preacher finds indications in the biblical texts that an old order of the past was flawed, weak, and temporary. It was in need of being replaced by a future "new order" that is perfect, steadfast, and eternal (9:10; see 4:8; 7:11, 17-19; 8:7-8, 13; 9:8-10; 10:9; 12:15-26). A fundamental text in this regard is the prophecy in Jer 31:31-34 (Heb 8:8-12; see 10:16-17) concerning God's establishment of a "new covenant." This "better covenant" is guaranteed by a new and superior high priesthood (7:22). It has been inaugurated in a "greater and more perfect tabernacle" (9:11) by Christ's definitive ("once for all") sacrifice offered "at the end of the ages" (9:26). This pervasive method of comparing the old to the new is borne out in the author's frequent references to the aspects of God's work in these final days as "better" or "superior" (→ 1:4 sidebar, "'Better' Things in Hebrews"; see Lane 1991, cxxix).

In line with this eschatological viewpoint is the important theme of perfection. The language of perfection (cognates of *telos*, "end, goal") indicates bringing something or someone to a desired end or purpose. Jesus himself was fitted or qualified ("perfected") for his role as high priest through suffering (2:10; 5:8-9). He became "the author and perfecter" of faith (12:2). His once-for-all sacrifice "at the end of the ages" accomplished what none of the provisions under the old covenant could do (9:26). Neither the Levitical priesthood nor any of the legal arrangements under the old covenant could bring about "perfection" (7:11, 19).

With regard to God's people, Hebrews describes perfection in terms of the cleansing of the conscience from sin, which animal sacrifices could never procure (9:9; 10:1). Christ's sacrifice has decisively removed (9:26, 28; 10:4, 11) and cleansed sins (9:14; 10:2, 22) so that believers are "made perfect forever" (10:14). That is, they are completely sanctified and suited for worship in the holy presence of God.

While the coming of Christ has inaugurated a time of fulfillment, Hebrews is keenly aware that God's purposes are not yet complete. All things are presently subjected under the exalted Son (2:8). But the full realization of this dominion will not occur until all his enemies are finally vanquished ("made his footstool" [10:13]). Believers now experience "the powers of the coming age" (6:5). But the final attainment of salvation is consistently expressed in terms of hope (3:6; 6:11, 18; 7:19; 10:23; 11:1). Only at the second coming of Christ will salvation become a reality for believers (9:28), and judgment will come upon those who have opposed God (9:27; 10:27, 30, 37-38). We will explore the future dimension of salvation more fully below (→ Salvation below; → 2:5 sidebar, "Eschatology in Hebrews," for additional treatment of the "already" and the "not yet" in Hebrews).

Christology: Son and High Priest. Hebrews makes one of the most recognizable declarations about Jesus: "Jesus Christ is the same yesterday and today and forever" (13:8). In Hebrews' "high Christology" Jesus is not merely a human being who lived and died. He is the Son of God who existed before the creation of the world and is now exalted at the right hand of God. The preacher has a full understanding of Christ's nature and work, corresponding to what we find elsewhere in the NT. But he supplements this with creative insights and emphases that have had a lasting impact on Christian faith and theological formulation. (For further reading on the Christology of Hebrews, see Marshall 2004, 621-25; Lincoln 2006, 85-89; Powell 2009, 435-39.)

Hebrews relates a complete picture of Christ's life: preexistence (1:2; 10:5), incarnation (2:14-18; 5:5-7), suffering and death (2:9-10, 18; 5:8; 9:15, 26; 12:2; 13:12), resurrection (13:20), exaltation (1:3, 13; 4:14; 7:26; 8:1; 9:24; 10:12; 12:2), heavenly intercession (7:25; see 2:18; 4:15-16; 8:1-2; 12:24), and second coming to bring salvation and judgment (9:27-28; 10:25, 37-39).

Hebrews employs the familiar titles "Christ" and "Lord." Their significance is not as pronounced as we find in other NT authors. The former occurs a dozen times, but chiefly as a proper name for Jesus. In a few instances it may function as a title pointing to Jesus as "Messiah" (6:1; 11:26; perhaps also "Jesus Christ" [10:10; 13:8, 21] = "Jesus the Christ"?). "Lord" is used unambiguously of Jesus only four times: twice in relation to his earthly career (2:3; 7:14), twice of his exalted status (1:10; 13:20), but never with the emphasis we find in Paul (e.g., 1 Cor 12:3; 2 Cor 4:5; Phil 2:11). Then there is the rare term "author [*archēgos*]" (Heb 2:10; 12:2). It is a primitive title, found elsewhere only on the lips of Peter and the early apostles in proclaiming Jesus as the crucified and risen Savior (Acts 3:15; 5:31; → 2:10 sidebar, "Jesus the Champion").

Two titles are integral to Hebrews' distinctive Christology: "Son" and "high priest." They are joined by a third, the simple name of "Jesus" (→ 2:9 sidebar, "Use of the Name 'Jesus' in Hebrews"). By presenting Christ under these terms, Hebrews proves to be a key NT source for the central Christian confession that he is both fully divine and fully human.

The sermon we call Hebrews opens with an impressive tribute to Christ's preeminence as the Son. The Son is the reflection of divine glory and the exact expression of God's nature (1:3*a*). He is the agent through whom God created and sustains the universe (1:2*c*, 3*b*, 10). His righteous rule is eternal (1:8-9) and his divine character is unchanging (1:7, 11-12). Indeed, the Son is directly addressed as "God" (1:8).

The eternal Son of God was also appointed "heir of all things" (1:2*b*). But God's "firstborn" was not given dominion over "the world to come" (1:6; 2:5) solely on account of his divine status. God saw it as both fitting and necessary (2:10, 17) for the Son to share in the humiliation of humanity's flesh-and-blood mortality. Only then could he vanquish the power of death that held its fearful sway over humanity, and bring many sons with him into the glory of the divine inheritance (2:5-18).

More explicitly than any other NT author, Hebrews makes a case for why the Son had to become human. He had to enter fully into the human condition—"yet . . . without sin" (4:15)—so that he could become a "merciful and faithful high priest" (2:17). As to his faithfulness, in order to become the author or source of eternal salvation (2:10; 5:9; see 7:28), Jesus had to be "made perfect" through suffering. Such perfection, paradoxically, involved the eternal Son learning obedience through suffering (5:8-9; → 4:14—5:10 From the Text for a discussion of this paradox). Jesus demonstrated his faithfulness as our high priest by doing the will of God (10:5-10; see 5:7). This meant offering himself (9:7, 14, 25, 26; or his body: 10:5, 10, 20) as an atonement for sins (2:17).

Passing through the ultimate trial—the suffering of death—also equipped Jesus to be a merciful high priest. He can completely identify with the human struggle against temptation and provide real help and compassionate intercession for those who are tempted (2:18; 4:15-16; 7:25). His triumph over sin and his perfection as high priest were signaled by his subsequent exaltation into heaven (4:14; 7:26-28; 8:1). Jesus' endurance of the suffering and shame of the cross makes him credible as the "author and perfecter" of faith for those who follow his example of faithful perseverance (12:1-4; see 13:13).

Sonship is a traditional christological identification (e.g., abundant in the Gospels and in Paul). It also remains central to Hebrews' Christology, notwithstanding the frequent and distinctive designation of Jesus as high priest. The apostle and high priest of our confession is, after all, "the Son" (3:1, 6). Our "great high priest who has gone through the heavens" is "Jesus the Son of God" (4:14; see 5:4-6; 7:3, 28; 10:21, 23, 29; Pfitzner 1997, 38). Jesus is not attested as high priest anywhere else in the early Christian tradition (but see the priestly description of the heavenly Christ in Rev 1:12-16). What could possibly suggest it, since—as Hebrews admits (7:13)—Jesus did not descend from the priestly tribe of the Levites? Hebrews was compelled to provide reasonable evidence and argumentation for this identification.

The warrant for Jesus' high priesthood is presented to us through a comparison of the Son with the mysterious figure Melchizedek, mentioned in only two OT texts (Gen 14:18-20; Ps 110:4). The preacher's ingenious midrash on these texts, as well as his carefully developed arguments, are best appreciated by reading the commentary on Heb 7. But two main points emerge in defense of the Son's high priesthood.

First, like Melchizedek (7:3, 6) and in accordance with the oracle from Ps 110:4 (Heb 7:11-19), Jesus was appointed as high priest expressly at God's command.

Second, like Melchizedek (7:3, 8) and in accordance with Ps 110:4 (Heb 7:20-25), God has declared on oath that the Son will enjoy a permanent priesthood: "You are a priest forever." Unlike the Levitical priests, Jesus was not appointed on the basis of the Mosaic law's stipulation regarding natural ancestry, but because he possesses "the power of an indestructible life" (7:16). Therefore, there is no longer any need for one generation after another of earthly priests. The Son is the ultimate high priest. Furthermore, Jesus' moral excellence and exaltation to heaven meant that he did not need to offer repeated animal sacrifices for his own sins, as ordinary priests did. Jesus offered himself as the "once for all" sacrifice for sins (7:26-28).

Salvation. Salvation in Hebrews is regularly spoken of in relation to Christ's work. It comes as a result of Christ's proclamation (2:3), sacrificial death (2:10; 5:8-9), high-priestly intercession (7:25), and second coming (9:28). Salvation is a thoroughly eschatological reality, for it is broadly conceived in terms of its future realization. It is a future inheritance (1:14; see 6:12, 17; 9:15) described as entrance into glory (2:10). Even its present blessings and privileges are a participation in the spiritual and heavenly vitality of "the coming age" (6:4-5; see 2:4).

The breadth of imagery for salvation that we find throughout the NT is represented in Hebrews (Lincoln 2006, 90). Forensic concepts of divine judgment and human accountability are clearly present (4:12-13; 6:2, 7-8; 9:27; 10:27, 30-31). However, the language of righteousness is not employed in the typical Pauline sense of justification by faith, but rather to denote faithfulness and ethical righteousness (see 10:37-39; 11:4, 7).

Imagery from both the battlefield (victory over powers hostile to God and humanity) and the slave market (redemption) describe salvation in 2:14-15. Indeed, here we find one of the clearest NT examples of the Christus Victor motif (see Aulén 2003). Christ destroyed the one who holds the power of death (the devil) and delivers his children from the enslaving fear of death. These ideas, however, are not developed further. The vocabulary of redemption appears in 9:15 concerning Christ's "ransom" of people from the slavery to sins that continued under the first covenant.

Paul's rich conception of salvation as reconciliation with God is not present in Hebrews. Nevertheless, in Hebrews the restoration of people's relationship to God is expressed through the domestic imagery of belonging to God's family or "house" (2:11-13, 17; 3:6; 10:21), the commercial language of partnership with Christ (3:14; see 3:1; 6:4), the OT promise of God's new covenant (8:6-13; see 7:22; 9:15-22; 10:15-18), and the cultic action of drawing near to God in worship (4:16; 7:19, 25; 10:22; 12:22).

Salvation in Hebrews is articulated predominantly through the cultic imagery of sacrifice and worship. The aim of Christ's saving work is to make people holy (2:11). He accomplishes this by cleansing them from the defilement of sin (9:14), making them fit to approach a holy God in worship. Three main elements of salvation are related to Christ's sacrificial death:

First, Christ's death provided atonement for sins (2:17). This involved expiation: the decisive removal of the sins that acted as a barrier between God and humankind (9:26, 28; 10:4, 11). Implicit, as well, is propitiation: turning aside God's fierce anger and judgment against sinners (see 3:10-11; 6:7-8; 9:27; 10:26-31; 12:25-27, 29).

Second, Christ's sacrifice provided the requisite sanctification to inaugurate a new, eternal covenant relationship between God and his people. Hebrews envisions Christ's sacrifice in terms of the Day of Atonement (9:6-14; 13:11-14), the sacrifice of the red heifer (9:13), and the covenant inauguration under Moses (9:18-22). Both the people and place of worship (see 9:23-24) were made ready through a sacrifice that provides purification/cleansing (1:3; 9:13-14, 22-23) or the forgiveness of sins (9:22). In this way, they are made holy or sanctified. That is, they are separated from everything that is unholy or defiled and devoted entirely to the service and worship of God in holiness. Christ's sacrifice decisively effected the sanctification of God's people (2:11; 9:13-14; 10:10, 15, 29; 13:12). Christ our mediator (8:6; 9:15; 12:24) has brought us into a new covenant relationship with God through the purifying effects of his covenant blood (9:20; 10:29; 12:24; 13:20).

Third, Christ's self-offering "made perfect forever" those who are sanctified (10:14). For Hebrews, preparation to approach God involves more than outward ceremonial purification (9:10, 13). The problem of human sin runs much deeper, requiring a profound moral transformation of the inner person. Christ's sacrifice is superior to the ineffective animal sacrifices under the old covenant. They were unable to remove the effects of sin on the human heart. Unlike the Levitical priests, Christ was sinless, and so he did not have to offer sacrifices for himself. The sacrifice of himself "at the end of the ages" was therefore a definitive sacrifice that needed to be offered only "once for all" (9:26; see 7:27; 9:12, 28; 10:10).

The decisive nature of the sacrifice means that it accomplished something that previous, ineffective sacrifices could not do: it makes worshipers "perfect" with respect to their conscience (9:9 NRSV; 10:1-2; see 9:14; 10:22). The conscience is so thoroughly cleansed from guilt that people can enter into the very presence of God with a sense of complete freedom and confidence (4:16; 10:19). Such conclusive purgation and inward moral renewal is the fulfillment of the promises of the new covenant (10:15-18). The salvation achieved through Christ's obedient offering of his own body is appropriately called "a new and living way" into the most holy place (10:19-20; see 9:8).

The notion of Jesus opening up a pathway through his sacrificial death connects with the future orientation of salvation. Jesus is the mighty champion over death who leads "many sons to glory" (2:10, 14-15). He is the forerunner who has anchored our hope "behind the curtain" in the presence of God (6:19-20). Thus, salvation is Christ's grand achievement on our behalf, initiated and bestowed by the grace of God. Yet it is also a summons—a "heavenly calling" (3:1)—for believers to embark on a journey, a pilgrimage toward the heavenly kingdom. This is expressed through four images that include the idea of motion or travel:

First, the cultic language used in the exhortations to "approach/draw near [*proserchōmetha*]" to God (4:16; 10:22) is consonant with the pattern of Christ's reentrance into God's presence (6:19-20; see 4:14; 8:1; 9:24; 12:2). In one sense, worshipers presently enjoy access into the most holy place as a result of Christ's work; already they "have come" (*proselēlythate*) to the heavenly Mount Zion (12:22). In another crucial sense, believers are still in the process of receiving the future, unshakable kingdom (12:28). Salvation will not be brought to them in its fullness until Christ's second coming (9:28).

Second, an image that precedes the call to draw near to God is found in the urgent, repeated exhortations "to enter" into God's eschatological rest (4:1-11; → 4:1-13 Behind the Text sidebar, "Sabbath Rest and the World to Come").

Third, believers are invited to identify with Abraham, the sojourner in Canaan. He was called "to go out [*exelthein*]" of his country of origin to a place he would receive as his inheritance (11:8 ESV, KJV; compare "had gone out [*exebēsan*]" in 11:15 ESV). The patriarchs lived as "aliens and strangers on earth" (11:13), for they welcomed from afar God's promises of a better, heavenly homeland and a future city built by God alone (11:10, 16). Like the ancients, who suffered for their faithfulness as they looked forward to their reward (11:26; see 11:13, 39), the readers, too, must risk the possibility of suffering and disgrace as they "go out" to Jesus (13:13). "For here we do not have an enduring city, but we are looking for the city that is to come" (13:14).

Finally, the preacher characterizes the Christian life as a footrace. "The race marked out for us" will demand resistance to sin (12:1, 4) through persevering faith and strength of character that come only through the divine program of discipline (12:5-13). Christ is the exemplar for those who are running the race, since his own faithful endurance was demonstrated in his suffering and exaltation (12:2). He has already gained the prize as our victorious "forerunner" (6:20 NIV[11]).

Faith and Perseverance. The future-oriented dimension of the Christian life permeates Hebrews' conception of what it means to commit oneself fully to Christ. The foundation of Christian teaching begins with repentance and faith in God (6:1). The preacher describes the first step on the Christian journey as receiving "the knowledge of the truth" (10:26) or being "enlightened" (6:4; 10:32). The latter may be associated with submitting to Christian baptism.

The initial and ongoing basis for the life of faith is a deep-seated "conviction" (3:14 NIV[11]) or commitment to partnership with Christ "till the end." This commitment is described as a fixed gaze on Jesus, "the apostle and high priest of our confession" (3:1 CEB, ESV, NASB, NKJV, NRSV; see 12:2). This entails a firm hold on our confession of Jesus (4:14) and on the hope afforded to us by that confession (10:23). Steadfast commitment is an indispensable safeguard for continued inclusion in God's family and eventual reception of the promised inheritance (3:6; 6:11, 18; 7:19; 11:1).

Hebrews' call to commitment is frequently expressed in terms of attentive and faithful response to God's voice (2:1-3; 3:7, 15-16; 4:2, 7; 12:25). Failure to heed the divine message of salvation is perilous, as Hebrews' many warnings against apostasy make clear (→ F. Purpose sidebar, "Five Warnings

Against Apostasy"). But commitment or steadfast faith is not a matter of sheer willpower. Hebrews grounds "the full assurance of hope" (6:11 ESV, KJV, LEB, NASB, NRSV) and "the full assurance of faith" (10:22 ESV, KJV, LEB, NASB, NIV, NRSV, TNIV) in the trustworthiness of God's character (6:16-18; 10:23; 11:11) and the faithfulness of Jesus (2:17; 3:2, 5-6; 6:19-20).

Faith itself is defined as a guarantee of "what we hope for" and the evidence or proof of "what we do not see" (→ 11:1). It is a way of seeing and taking possession of future, heavenly realities. Genuine faith, by its very nature, does not shrink back in the face of adversity (10:38-39). It is a forward-looking, promise-grasping virtue, taking its confidence and encouragement from the unchanging nature of God's purpose (6:17-18). Faith is the firm basis for the kind of perseverance exhibited by the saints of old (6:12, 15; 11:1-40) and by Jesus in his faithful death on the cross (12:2). These examples of persevering faith are for all who need to endure the hardships of this life, and finally receive the "better and lasting possessions" of our inheritance (10:34-36; 12:1, 3, 7; see 10:32).

COMMENTARY

I. HEARING THE APOSTLE AND HIGH PRIEST OF OUR CONFESSION: HEBREWS 1:1—4:13

The first part of Hebrews focuses on paying attention to and being accountable to the word of God. The book opens with the declaration that God has spoken definitively "by his Son" (1:1-2*a*). The first part ends by emphasizing the word of God as "living and active," a "double-edged sword" of judgment that penetrates to our innermost motivations; and God as the judge to whom "we must give account" (4:12-13).

The theme of heeding God's word threads its way through 1:1—4:13. In 2:1 the preacher makes his first call for readers to "pay more careful attention" to the message of salvation spoken through the Son. The wilderness generation serves as an object lesson of the negative consequences for refusing to listen to the voice of God (3:7—4:13). A repeated scriptural refrain from this tragic history addresses the readers: "Today, if you hear his voice, do not harden your hearts" (3:7-8, 15; 4:7). The theme will be picked up in the second part (4:14—10:18), particularly in the reference to the readers' slowness to listen (5:11, lit., "sluggish hearing"). The theme will come to its climax in the exhortation not to refuse the One who speaks from heaven and will shake heaven and earth (12:25-27).

The message we should heed concerns the confession of Jesus as "the apostle and high priest" (3:1). In 1:1—2:18 Jesus is presented as the One who is most suited to bring salvation to humanity. He is the exalted Son of God who shares the very nature of God (1:1-14), yet he provided purification for sins (1:3*c*). The author of salvation achieved his fitting and necessary perfection by identifying with humanity to the point of suffering death (2:5-18).

The sweep of Christ's movement from eternal Son, to humiliation and suffering in the incarnation, to his exaltation before God leads to the thesis or proposition of the entire sermon in 2:17-18. Jesus' solidarity with humanity makes him a "merciful and faithful high priest." His suffering and death provided atonement for sin. But his faithful death and subsequent exaltation as our high priest provide us respectively with a worthy example of endurance under the pressure of temptation, as well as timely help for those who are presently undergoing temptation (compare 4:14-16; 7:25).

Hebrews 3:1—4:13 paves the way for the rest of the sermon by focusing on the readers' need to commit themselves fully to Christ. The positive example of the superiority of Christ to Moses as the faithful Son over God's house (3:1-6) and the negative example of Israel's disobedience in the wilderness (3:7—4:13) serve this end. The audience is urged to "hold on" boldly to their confession of Christ (3:1, 6, 14) and to exercise due diligence to enter into final salvation (God's rest [4:11]; see 4:1, 6, 9). Christ's suffering, as the prime example of perseverance and faith and the definitive sacrifice for sins, forms the foundation for the Son's exaltation as high priest. It is also the basis for the calls to radical commitment to Christ repeated throughout the sermon (4:14-16; 10:19-25; 12:1-4; 13:13).

A. Hearing God's Son in These Last Days: Jesus the Merciful and Faithful High Priest (1:1—2:18)

The preacher to the Hebrews faithfully attends to two tasks throughout his sermon. On the one hand, he fixes his gaze on Jesus, the "merciful and faithful high priest" (2:17) and "author of [our] salvation" (2:10). On the other hand, he encourages his audience to share in his vision of the Son of God, so that they might respond appropriately to the gracious word and work of Christ and enter fully into worship and service before a holy God. This dual set of concerns is in evidence in this, the first section of part one.

This section consists of two units. In the first unit (1:1—2:4), the introduction to the entire discourse, the preacher pairs an exposition of the exalted Son with a powerful exhortation to heed the message of salvation. The second unit (2:5-18) plays a supportive role. It does so by demonstrating the necessity and appropriateness of the incarnation for perfecting the Son as Savior and high priest.

1. We Must Heed God's Definitive Revelation in the Son (1:1—2:4)

BEHIND THE TEXT

Hebrews 1:1—2:4: An Exordium. Hebrews 1:1—2:4 easily functions as a formal introduction to the sermon. In classical rhetoric the introduction to a speech was known in Latin as the *exordium*, in Greek as the prooemium. Many commentators have viewed only 1:1-4 as the *exordium* and have had difficulty describing its relationship to the following subunits (1:5-14 and 2:1-4). There are three reasons, however, for recognizing all of 1:1—2:4 as a carefully constructed introduction.

(1) *Length*. Hebrews 1:1-4 is too brief to serve as the *exordium* for a discourse of this size and complexity. The introduction to a speech was usually 200 to 300 words in length, or several minutes long in delivery time. Since Hebrews would take about forty-five to fifty minutes to deliver, an *exordium* occupying about three to four minutes' time (1:1—2:4 equaling about 320 words) would be well within appropriate limits (Koester 2001, 175; for general instructions on length of exordia, see Quintilian, *Inst.* 4.1.62).

(2) *Framing*. The unit 1:1—2:4 is admirably framed, beginning with a carefully balanced sentence in 1:1-4 and concluding with another in 2:2-4. The opening line of each framing subsection is designed for the ear in Greek, using alliteration with the *p* sound (→ In the Text on 1:1 and 2:1). Thematically, the two subunits (1:1-4; 2:1-4) frame the discussion within the context of the modes of divine speech (using forms of the Greek verb *laleō* ["speak," "utter"] in 1:1, 2; 2:2, 3, 5), and emphasize the definitive nature of God's revelation via the Son. It is no coincidence that the author also frames the introduction by making reference to the recipients of God's ultimate revelation, namely, himself and his audience ("we" [2:1, 3]; "us" [1:2; 2:3]).

(3) *Structure and Movement*. The *exordium* to Hebrews follows a careful structure. Its elegant opening in 1:1-4 sets up a comparison of God's revelation in the Son with that of previous divine messengers. This comparison is focalized in the following subunit through a contrast between the Son and angels. The conclusion to this comparison is stated up front in 1:4, and supported (note the "for [*gar*]" in 1:5) through a chain of seven scriptural quotations (1:5-14). Finally, the author draws the *exordium* to a close (2:1-4). He employs a prominent "therefore [*Dia touto*]" in 2:1, and brings the dignity and majesty of the ultimate agent of divine revelation to bear upon his listeners' response to the message of salvation.

The movement within the *exordium*, from christological exposition to powerful exhortation, is assisted by a vertical movement of the author's thinking regarding the Son. In 1:1-4 the preacher moves from the varied modes of revelation in the past to God's ultimate revelation in the Son who "sat down at the right hand of the Majesty in heaven" (1:3, echoing Ps 110:1) and received the supreme inheritance (1:4).

In 1:5-14 the movement is repeated. Scriptural citations demonstrate the preeminence of the Son over angels, building in intensity toward the key text from Ps 110:1: "Sit at my right hand until I make your enemies a footstool for your feet" (Heb 1:13). The listeners, too, are associated with the Son's dignity, since through him they are heirs of salvation and are served by the heavenly host (1:14).

This upward vision will be significant in the next section (see 2:9), but in the *exordium* it is used to press forward a principal persuasive aim: to impress upon listeners the absolute necessity of paying attention to God's saving message in the Son (2:1-4). Listeners will shrug off this revelation only at their own peril, and this urgency will be stressed repeatedly throughout the sermon (3:7, 15, 16; 4:7; 6:1-8; 10:19-39) and climactically in 12:25-29 (observe the dramatic reappearance of God as "him who speaks" [12:25; compare 1:1-2]).

The concluding exhortation, therefore, provides the *exordium* with its proper rhetorical "payoff." It is not enough to marvel at the glory of the Son; we must respond with due attention to "such a great salvation" (2:3). The gravity of the response is indicated also by the "crowded stage" that rounds out the introduction (Westfall 2005, 98). All of the important players populate the preacher's first exhortation in 2:1-4: author, recipients, angels, the Lord Jesus, apostolic witnesses, and God. This underscores the all-importance of our response to the divine revelation. Completing the rhetorical circuit from persuasive argument to necessary response in 1:1—2:4 is what gives this *exordium* its unmatched integrity and dynamism, and characterizes its function as a true rhetorical introduction.

The Purposes of an Exordium. The *exordium* in ancient speeches served at least two functions. First, it introduced the leading ideas developed within the speech. Aristotle advised that exordia "provide a sample of the subject, in order that hearers may know beforehand what it is about, and that the mind may not be kept in suspense, for that which is undefined leads astray; so then he who puts the beginning, so to say, into the hearer's hand enables him, if he holds fast to it, to follow the story" (*Rhet*. 3.14.6). The *exordium* to Hebrews masterfully anticipates the topic that will be amplified throughout the sermon, namely Jesus as Son and Great High Priest (see 1:3). It also employs persuasive strategies we shall see throughout the discourse, like comparison (*synkrisis*), considerations based upon logic and Scripture (1:5-14), exhortation (2:1), and the argument from lesser to greater (2:2-4).

Second, the *exordium* prepares listeners to attend to the remainder of the speech. The ancient rhetorical handbooks concur that exordia must be designed to render listeners "well-disposed, attentive, and receptive" (Cicero, *Inv*. 1.15.20; see Quintilian, *Rhet. Her*. 1.4.6-7; *Inst*. 4.1.5; *Rhet. Alex*. 1436a35). The writer to the Hebrews seems to have had no need to secure the goodwill of his audience. Nowhere in the sermon do we find a hint of ill will toward him that he would need to dispel. He seems to have had a warm, personal relationship with them (13:18-19, 23-24). The pressing issue is the response of the hearers to the word of God, and upon this the preacher lays considerable stress. The persuasive power of Hebrews' *exordium* may be found in the author's decision to privilege, not his own speech, but God's (see Koester 2001, 175-76). So, apart from his display of accomplished rhetorical skill, the preacher makes no effort to establish his own character or authority as a speaker. Rather, he includes himself among the "we" (or "us") who are accountable to God's mighty word (1:2; 2:1, 3).

One's approach to making listeners attentive depends upon the type of cause one is promoting, whether honorable, mean, doubtful, extraordinary, obscure, or even scandalous (Quintilian, *Inst.* 4.1.40). The cause in Hebrews is obscure (*dysparakoloutheton*, "hard to follow"), though the preacher will not reveal this uncomfortable fact until later. He will state that his exposition of Jesus as high priest in the order of Melchizedek is "hard to explain" (*dysermēneutos*) because his audience has grown "dull of hearing" (5:11 ESV, KJV, NASB, NKJV, RSV; see 6:12).

For now, in the introduction, the preacher seeks to win attention through the grandeur and seriousness of the subject matter itself, and through a direct appeal for his listeners to "pay attention [*prosechein*]" (2:1; compare the repeated use of this verb with respect to exordia in *Rhet. Alex.* 1436b5-15, 1438a1). "The receptive hearer is one who is willing to listen attentively" (*Rhet. Her.* 1.4.7), and the way to make hearers attentive is to relate to them matters "that are important, that concern their interests, that are astonishing, that are agreeable" (Aristotle, *Rhet.* 3.14.7). This is precisely what the preacher to the Hebrews does, not only in the introduction, but throughout his sermon.

IN THE TEXT

a. God's Definitive Action in the Son (1:1-4)

The opening line to Hebrews sounds forth a "euphonious introduction" (Wiley 1984, 24). The author appeals to the ear through rhythmic Greek, incorporating alliteration (with the repetition of the *p* sound at the beginning of words) and assonance (rhyming of words), which can be fairly appreciated in English transliteration:

<u>Polymerōs</u> kai polytropōs palai ho the<u>os</u> lalē<u>sas</u> tois patrasin en tois prophētais (1:1).

All of 1:1-4 is one periodic sentence in Greek. A period is a "close-packed and uninterrupted group of words embracing a complete thought" (*Rhet. Her.* 4.19.27). Usually it is comprised of carefully balanced clauses, used to express antitheses (Aristotle, *Rhet.* 3.9.5-8; *Rhet. Alex.* 1435b25-35). The opening to Hebrews presents two contrasts: the first in 1:1-2; the second in 1:3-4. In these the Son is compared with the prophets and angels respectively.

God's Revelation: Past and Present

Hebrews 1:1-2a contains a carefully constructed contrast between God's modes of revelation from past to present:

God spoke . . .				
	TIME	RECIPIENTS	AGENCY	MANNER
1	In the past	to our forefathers	through the prophets	at many times and in various ways
2a	in these last days	to us	by his Son	[by implication: definitively]

(1) God's Word from Past Days to Last Days (1:1-2)

These two verses contain the main clause of the preacher's opening statement. The author sets up a contrast that he will unpack later in the sermon (e.g., between the Levitical priesthood and Christ's [ch 7] or the old and new covenants [ch 8]). But here the discontinuity between divine modes of revelation, past and present, is drawn together in continuity through God's speaking. The same **God** (the subject of the main clause) who **spoke** to ancient Israel (1:1) **has** also **spoken** (the leading verb of the main clause) in Jesus Christ (1:2*a*).

The preacher never detracts from God's authoritative words in the Hebrew Scriptures but does insist that the revelation of God through the Son is *more* authoritative, and that the Scriptures themselves point to this (e.g., 3:5; 8:7-8, 13; 12:18-29). The preacher expresses contrasts among the instances of God's revelation with respect to their manner, time, recipients, and agency in 1:1-2*a*.

■ 1 The author begins with a consideration of the nature of God's past revelation. In the Greek text the *manner* of the revelation appears first: **at many times and in various ways** (*polymerōs kai polytropōs*). The first word (*polymerōs*) may be translated temporally, **at many times** (ESV; see NLT; "at sundry times" [KJV]), but it is more likely that **in many parts** is intended (compare "fragmentary" [NEB]; "partial" [NAB]; "in many portions" [NASB]). The author may well be tapping into a common ancient sentiment that the simple, whole, basic, or pure is to be preferred to the complex, composite, fragmented, or alloyed.

The second adverb, **various** (*polytropōs*), indicates the variety of modes through which the revelation took place. These would include vision and prophecy, poetry and proverb, parable and history. Earlier interpreters, such as Chrysostom, took the adverbial phrase *polymerōs kai polytropōs* as a hendiadys (two words joined together by a conjunction to express one point), meaning "all sorts of ways." However, later commentators are probably correct that the author expresses two ideas. This is elegantly captured by the NEB: "When in former times God spoke to our forefathers, he spoke in *fragmentary* and *varied fashion* through the prophets" (emphasis added). God's past revelation was diverse, scattered, and incomplete.

The *time* of God's earlier revelation was **in the past**. This is a reference to the distant past, as in the translation "long ago" (ESV, GW, LEB, NASB, NET, NLT, NRSV).

"Four Hundred Years of Silence"

For Jews the time of revelation had long since vanished with the last of the Hebrew prophets, Malachi. The chronicler of the Maccabeans recorded a time of great distress during that period of Israel's history, "such as had not been since the time that prophets ceased to appear among them" (1 Macc 9:27 NRSV; see also 14:41). Thus, the intertestamental period is often called "Four Hundred Years of Silence," because of the discontinuance of the prophetic voice. This perspective continued among Jews after the destruction of Jerusalem in A.D. 70. This is reflected in the apocalyptic author who wrote under the pseudonym of Baruch:

> Further, know that our fathers in former times and former generations had helpers, righteous prophets and holy men. . . . But now the righteous have been assembled, and the prophets are sleeping. Also we have left our land, and Zion has been taken away from us, and we have nothing now apart from the Mighty One and his Law. (2 Bar. 85:1, 3)

It is no wonder that when Jesus came on the scene, announcing the kingdom of God and performing all manner of miracles, one response was, "A great prophet has appeared among us" (Luke 7:16). The NT authors identify Jesus as "the prophet like Moses" foretold by the Lord through the ancient Lawgiver himself (Deut 18:15, 18; 34:10; see Luke 24:19; John 6:14; 7:40; Acts 3:22-23; 7:37). For the author of Hebrews, the Son is more than a prophet. He is the definitive revelation of God.

The *recipients* of the age-old revelations were **our forefathers** (lit., **the fathers**). Only twice more will the preacher mention **the fathers,** both in scriptural quotations. In these he refers to the wilderness generation whom the Lord brought out of Egypt (3:9; 8:9; "our fathers" in 12:9 is a general reference to male ancestors). He will also refer to "the ancients [*presbyteroi*]" (11:2).

The *agents* of God's past revelation were **the prophets.** Once more the preacher will speak of "the prophets," and then only in a rapid-fire listing of faithful worthies (11:32). Prophets were the primary means of divine communication with ancient Israel. But they were merely a shadow of the Lord's clear, face-to-face communication with Moses (Num 12:6-8). "I spoke to the prophets, gave them many visions and told parables through them," spoke the Lord through Hosea (12:10). "The LORD used a prophet to bring Israel up from Egypt, by a prophet he cared for him" (Hos 12:13). The Lord reliably spoke to Israel through "my servants the prophets" (2 Kgs 9:7; 17:13; Ezek 38:17; Zech 1:6), as God repeatedly reminded them in Jeremiah (26:5; 29:19; 35:15; 44:4). The preacher to the Hebrews has a profound awareness that the reading of prophetic texts makes God's voice audible (→ 1:5-14 sidebar, "Quoting Scripture in Hebrews").

■ **2a** The antithesis or counterpart to 1:1 is given in 1:2. Here the preacher sets forth the time, recipients, and agency of God's definitive revelation. In relating the *time* of God's ultimate disclosure, the author displays his eschatological perspective. The God who spoke through the prophets has now spoken **in the last days.** The preacher perhaps first encountered the phrase *at the end of the days* (*ep' eschatou tōn hēmerōn*) in his Bible, the LXX. The exact phrase occurs four times (Num 24:14; Jer 23:20; 49:39; Dan 10:14), and many more times in slightly different forms (Gen 49:1; Deut 4:30; 8:16; Josh 24:27; Isa 2:2; Jer 37:24; Ezek 38:16; Dan 2:28, 29, 45; Hos 3:5; Mic 4:1).

The expression, in keeping with its Hebrew original (*bē'ăḥărît hayyāmîm*, "in the last days"), refers to the final period in history when God will act decisively to bring judgment and salvation. Our author shares with other NT writers the conviction that the final epoch of salvation history has already arrived (see Acts 2:17; 2 Pet 3:3). He writes not simply of the last days, but "**these** last days" ("this the final age" [REB]).

Christ "has appeared once for all at the end of the ages" (Heb 9:26) and has inaugurated the messianic era of fulfillment, to which all the prophets pointed (1 Pet 1:10-11). As Paul explained, "But when the time had fully come, God sent his Son" (Gal 4:4), and so Christ's followers are those "on whom the fulfillment of the ages has come" (1 Cor 10:11).

The preacher includes himself among those to whom God addresses his final word: **to us.** These are the *recipients* of God's ultimate revelation. They realize their identity as an end-times community. This is not only because of the incarnation of the Son but also because God has made his saving presence known to them by the Holy Spirit in miraculous ways (2:4), through the community's taste of "the powers of the coming age" (6:5).

In Hebrews the supreme *agent* of God's self-revelation is the Son. Other NT witnesses showcase Jesus' position as Son—such as the Synoptic Gospels' narration of Jesus' baptism (Mark 1:9-11 par.), the Gospel of John's "only Son" (1:14, 18; 3:16, 18; 1 John 4:9), and Paul's many references to the Son (Rom 1:3, 4, 9; 8:3, 29, 32; Gal 1:15; 2:20; 4:4, etc.). Hebrews adds his unique voice to the chorus. The preacher will return repeatedly to the identity of Jesus as Son as a key point in his argument.

This identification is introduced in 1:2*a*: **in these last days** God **has spoken to us by his Son.** The author's simple two-word phrase in Greek (*en huiō*) is more compact and insightful than English can convey, though the NRSV comes close with "by a Son" (compare "through a son" [NAB]; "in a son" [NET]). One might expect the definite article (God spoke "by *the* Son"); but the lack of the article is deliberate. The preacher emphasizes the *qualitative* importance of God's eschatological revelation through "One who is Son" (Westcott 1909, 7).

The author of Hebrews will refer to our Lord (1:10; 2:3*b*) primarily as Son in the *exordium*, and not by his personal name, Jesus, until 2:9. According to the descriptions of the Son in ch 1, and throughout the whole discourse, the priority of God's revelation in the Son is to be found not only in what Jesus says but supremely in who he is and what he has accomplished *as Son.*

Before proceeding to the descriptions of the Son in 1:2b-4, it should be noted that there is no formal parallel in 1:2a to the *manner* of revelation found in 1:1 ("at many times and in various ways"). The implication of the omission is unmistakable: God's revelation through the Son is unique and decisive. Later the preacher will accent the "once for all" nature of Christ's work (*hapax*: 9:26, 28; *ephapax*: 7:27; 9:12; 10:10). Here the contrast between the old and new occurs in two ways.

First, the nature of the comparison in 1:1-2a is typical of the exordia in speeches and history writing. In them, for example, a multiplicity of past works may be weighed (usually unfavorably) against the author's present work (Luke 1:1-4 serves as a possible biblical example; see also Josephus, *J.W.* Preface 1, 3-4; *Ag. Ap.* Preface 1).

Second, the preacher will demonstrate at length the primacy and uniqueness of the Son's majesty over the created order in the remainder of this chapter.

■ **2b-c** Two subordinate clauses supply the first two descriptions of the Son in terms of God's further actions through him. Already we have learned that God "has spoken" by the Son. God is still the subject of the verbs in these clauses (**appointed** and **made**), though the topical focus is on the Son by way of the relative pronoun **whom**.

The first subordinate clause modifies "Son" by stating that he is the one **whom he** [i.e., God] **appointed heir.** Inheritance was a key element in God's covenant with ancient Israel, involving continued blessing from God and possession of the promised land (see 11:8; 12:17). In the NT there has been an expansion of the divine inheritance. It is now truly cosmic in scope, as evidenced by Jesus' modification of Ps 37:11 ("But the meek will inherit the land") to "Blessed are the meek, for they will inherit the earth" (Matt 5:5).

In the Son is fulfilled the coronation promise delivered to Israel's kings, "Ask me, and I will make the nations your possession" (Ps 2:8 CEB). Perhaps Ps 2:8 was in the preacher's mind, given his quotation of Ps 2:7 in Heb 1:5. The Son is **heir of all things.** As divine heir, the Son is "lord of all" (Gal 4:1 KJV), that is, master of the whole created order.

Importantly, the Son was **appointed,** not created, heir. The Son eternally shares the divine nature, attributes, and dominion. There was never a time when the Son was not the Son. There was never a time when he did not radiate the divine glory, or reflect the divine image. He has ever been the fount of existence for every created thing.

Then why did he need to be appointed heir of all things, if he already owned them? Theodoret of Cyr answered: "Christ the Lord is heir of all things, not as God, but as man" (Heen and Krey 2005, 8). The eternal Son was not appointed heir for his own sake, but for the sake of humanity. People were created to partake of the divine glory, but fall short of it through sin (Rom 3:23). The Son was appointed heir so that we might "inherit salvation" (Heb 1:14;

9:15). The Son restored the divine inheritance to humanity by entering into the human predicament of sin, suffering, and death, and prevailing over them through his atoning death and exaltation.

Hebrews also emphasizes the eschatological character of the inheritance. Other NT writers do the same when they mention inheriting eternal life (Matt 19:29; Titus 3:7) or the kingdom of God (Matt 25:34; 1 Cor 6:9, 10; 15:50; Gal 5:21; Eph 5:5; Jas 2:5). The Son appeared "at the end of the ages" to do away with sin through "the sacrifice of himself" (Heb 9:26), and his appointment as heir involves his installation as king over "the world to come" (2:5; compare 1:6).

The second description of the Son relates his role in creation: **and through whom [= the Son] he [= God] made the universe.** John, Paul, and Hebrews speak with one voice concerning the Son's intermediate agency in God's creation of the world (using the Greek preposition *dia*, "by," **through**; see John 1:3; 1 Cor 8:6; Col 1:16). In his creative role, the Son is understood as divine Wisdom. The Greek word *aiōnas*, **universe** or *ages*, denotes here "the whole created universe of time and space" (Bruce 1990, 47).

Lane (1991, 12) considers the order of the two descriptions—heir first, creation second—ironic. But it is perfectly fitting that the preacher would, in two parallel clauses (note the correspondence between "all things" and "universe"), announce both the glorious destiny and origin of creation in the Son.

Wisdom Christology and Hymnody in 1:2b-3

Jewish Wisdom literature was a veritable treasure-house for early Christian reflection on the preexistence and nature of Christ. Personified Wisdom as an agent of divine creation was viewed as directly applicable to the Son, not only in Hebrews, but also by other NT writers (John 1:3, 10; Rom 11:36; 1 Cor 8:6; Col 1:16). Several aspects of "Wisdom Christology" appear in Heb 1:2b-3:

Hebrews	Wisdom Literature
through whom he made the universe (1:2b)	"I [wisdom] was there when he set the heavens in place . . . marked out the horizon on the face of the deep . . . established the clouds . . . fixed securely the fountains of the deep . . . gave the sea its boundary . . . marked out the foundations of the earth. . . . I was the craftsman at his side" (Prov 8:27-30). "O God of my ancestors . . . who have made all things by your word, and by your wisdom have formed humankind. . . . [W]isdom . . . was present when you made the world" (Wis 9:1-2, 9 NRSV).
the radiance of God's glory (1:3a)	"She [wisdom] is . . . a pure emanation of the glory of the Almighty . . . a reflection of eternal light" (Wis 7:25-26 NRSV).

| and the exact representation of his being (1:3a) | "She [wisdom] is . . . a spotless mirror of the working of God, and an image of his goodness" (Wis 7:26 NRSV). |

Given that the form and content of 1:2b-3 resemble other hymn-like confessions of Christ (see Phil 2:6-11; Col 1:15-18; John 1:1-18; 1 Tim 3:16; 1 Pet 3:18-19, 22), many scholars have contended that the author has incorporated an early christological hymn at this point. However, there is no agreement on whether this is so and, if it is, whether the original hymn would have begun at 1:2b with the first relative pronoun "whom," or in 1:3a (see Attridge 1989, 41-42). Regardless of whether the preacher has chimed in with a Christ-hymn already familiar to his listeners, or has composed one of his own, he has opened his sermon with a sample of the sort of "confession" to which he will later urge his readers to hold fast (3:1; 4:14; 10:23).

(2) The Majesty of the Son Above the Angels (1:3-4)

■ 3 The Son (*hos*, "who") is the subject of another major, though secondary, clause in the author's opening statement. The main verbs in this clause are **sat down** (1:3d) and "inherited" (1:4). These form the climax to the description of the Son in comparison to the angels. Embedded in this grammatical skeleton are four clauses that flesh out the preacher's confession of the Son's majesty. The first clause (beginning with the Greek participle *ōn*, "being," **is**) introduces a pair of complementary statements that describe the Son's unique role as the *revealer* of God.

First, he is **the radiance of God's glory.** Interpreters have long wrestled with whether the Greek word *apaugasma* should be taken in an active or passive sense. Actively it means "radiance" (ESV, LEB, NASB, NET, REB, TNIV; "radiates" [NLT]), "brightness" (KJV), or "refulgence" (NAB). Passively it means "reflection" (NJB, NRSV). The difference is comparable to that between the sun and moon. Actively, a ray of light shines forth from the sun and possesses a brilliance continuous with the sun itself. Passively, moonlight is the reflection from a body other than the light's origin. The distinction was critical to the Trinitarian controversies of the fourth century, and the active reading was enshrined in the Nicene Creed: "Light of Light, very God of very God."

The second statement, **the exact representation of his being,** likewise figured largely in the christological controversies of the fourth and fifth centuries. The NRSV's "exact imprint of God's very being" can scarcely be improved upon. The Greek word *charaktēr* (**exact representation**) often referred to the embosser or stamp used to imprint coins, or to the imprinted coins themselves, and then to the characteristics of something or someone, such as writing style or an individual's unique, inborn personality (Gess 1979, 288). The word translated **being** (*hypostasis*) referred to what is basic or foundational, hence, the nature or essence of a person or thing. The Son perfectly reveals

God, so that if one has seen the Son, that person "has seen the Father" (John 14:9; see 1:14, 18; 14:7).

Calvin rightly cautions against needless speculation, making due allowance for the limits of creaturely analogy in describing the divine. The preacher's "intention was not to describe the likeness of the Father to the Son within the Godhead, but . . . to build up our faith fruitfully, so that we may learn that God is revealed to us in no other way than in Christ. . . . [W]hile God is incomprehensible to us in Himself, yet His form appears to us in the Son" (Calvin 1976, 8).

The second clause declares the Son's providential role as *governor* over the whole created order. The participle **sustaining** (*pherōn*) conveys the action of "bearing up" (TYNDALE) or "upholding" (ESV, KJV, RSV; see NASB). This is not an image of Jesus carrying the world on his shoulders, "for the Son is not an Atlas sustaining the dead weight of the world" (Westcott 1909, 13-14). Nor is it simply that "all things hold together" in him (Col 1:17). The idea is one not only of supporting but also of acting, moving, or guiding creation toward God's intended aims (see Erasmus's comments, cited in Hughes 1977, 45 n. 22).

This action is closely linked to the previous statement about the Son as divine revealer. The two are joined by the connecting word *te* in Greek. It can be translated "so" or "thus" (Smyth 1984, 666 §2968; Westcott 1909, 13). It is his divine prerogative to rule, "and *so* he bears **all things**." Christ's all-encompassing providential authority is executed merely **by his powerful word** (the Greek has a Semitic flavor, "by the word of his power" [KJV]).

Christology in Rhyme

The preacher's rhetorical skill is apparent in his use of *paromoiōsis*, which is selecting words with similar sounds at the beginning or end of clauses (Aristotle, *Rhet.* 3.9.9; *Rhet. Alex.* 1436a5-14). Hebrews masterfully uses this rhyming technique at both the beginning and end of the four clauses in 1:3 to enhance the acoustic impact of this confession of the Son's majesty:

Who being [*hos ōn*] **the radiance of his glory**
   and stamp of his being [*tēs hypostaseōs autou*],
bearing [*pherōn*] **all things**
   by the word of his power [*tēs dynameōs autou*],
purification [*katharismon*]
   of sins having made [*poiēsamenos*],
he sat [*ekathisen*] **at the right hand**
   of the Majesty on high [*en hypsēlois*].

The third embedded clause, **after he had provided purification for sins** (1:3c), introduces an important shift in the preacher's train of thought. This is expressed in two ways:

First, the participle that governs this clause (*poiēsamenos*, **having made, after he had provided**) is placed at the end of the Greek clause. In the previous two clauses, the participles appear instead at the beginning. Perhaps this participle was chosen for its capacity to extend the rhyme (*hypostaseōs . . . dynameōs . . . poiēsamenos;* → 1:3 sidebar, "Christology in Rhyme").

Second, the previous two participles—**being** and **sustaining**—are in the present tense. But this one is in the aorist tense (a Greek past tense). The Son's revealing the nature of God and sustaining the universe are ongoing activities. His sacrifice of atonement is a completed, historic act.

Many interpreters have noted the author's use of the Greek middle voice here. This may convey what an ancient addition to the text sought to clarify: that the Son provided purification "by himself" (KJV) or "in his awne [= own] person" (TYNDALE). But it is more likely that the middle voice is only a variation in style. Greek authors often employed the verb "to make [*poieō*]" in the middle voice with verbal nouns (such as *katharismos*, **purification**) to express the same action as the corresponding simple verb (*katharizō*, "to purify"; see Smyth 1984, 391 §1722).

The preacher touches only briefly on a topic to which he will devote considerable space later, namely, the Son as our Great *High Priest*. The atoning death of Christ was of paramount importance to the preacher. This is evidenced by its appearance both here in his opening statement and in the proposition for the entire sermon (2:17). Barnabas Lindars suggests that the first readers of Hebrews were terribly concerned about the defilement of their postbaptismal sins. This explains the author's reminder that the definitive work of cleansing for sins was accomplished on the cross (1991, 41).

The climax to the opening statement is that **he sat down at the right hand** (1:3*d*). This alludes to a key text for the author's Christology: Ps 110:1 (→ 1:13 sidebar, "Psalm 110 in Hebrews"). Having described the Son as revealer, governor, and priest, the preacher now speaks of the Son as *royal heir*. The circumlocution for "God," **the Majesty in heaven,** serves to heighten the dignity and honor the Son possesses. The title, which indirectly refers to God, indicates that the Son enjoys a status on par with God the Father. The word **Majesty** is rare in the NT (twice in Hebrews [1:3; 8:1], once in Jude [25]), and used only of God.

■ **4** A fourth and final embedded participial clause in Greek rounds out the opening statement with a comparison between the Son and angels. The heavenly enthronement of the Son demonstrates his superiority to angels: **So he became as much superior to the angels as the name he has inherited is superior to theirs.** To inherit a great name is to receive recognition and honor.

The name he inherited can be none other than "Son" (see 1:5; 5:5). Preexisting as God, he already possessed every divine attribute and prerogative. So it was as a human being who suffered, died, and was exalted that he restored the divine favor and sonship to humanity, which had been lost with Adam.

By mentioning the Son as heir toward the beginning (1:1-2a), and his inheritance of the superior name, "Son," at its end (1:4), the preacher encloses the opening statement. And by moving from a comparison with the prophets in the first half (1:1-2) to a comparison with angels in the second (1:3-4), he prepares his readers for the arguments to follow in 1:5-14.

"Better" Things in Hebrews

The word "better [*kreittōn, kreissōn*]" is a key word in Hebrews, used thirteen times. It is sometimes translated "greater" or "superior" in the NIV.

Reference to	"better..."	Hebrews
the Son	"superior" to the angels	1:4
audience	the preacher is confident of "better things" pertaining to their salvation	6:9
Melchizedek	"greater" than Abraham	7:7
hope	"better" than the Law	7:19
God's oath	Jesus, the guarantee of a "better covenant"	7:22
ministry of Jesus	mediator of a "better covenant," founded on "better promises"	8:6 (two times)
heavenly things	purified with "better sacrifices"	9:23
audience's past loss of freedom and possessions	endured in the expectation of "better and lasting possessions"	10:34
the patriarchs	longed for "a better country"	11:16
Maccabean martyrs	refused to escape torture to gain a "better resurrection"	11:35
all the saints before Christ	the "something better" God provided: that they would be perfected along with us	11:40
sprinkled blood of Christ	"speaks... better" than the blood of Abel	12:24

b. Scriptural Arguments for the Son's Majesty over Angels (1:5-14)

A catena, or chain, of scriptural passages in 1:5-14 buttresses the proposition made in 1:4 concerning the superiority of the Son to angels. But this is not simply a series of proof texts. Rather, the author marshals them into logical arguments, called enthymemes in ancient rhetoric.

An enthymeme is like a formal syllogism, except that any one (or two) of the components of the syllogism—major premise, minor premise, or conclusion—can be missing (i.e., implied). The preacher stacks one enthymeme upon another in 1:5-14. He employs a scriptural passage (or passages) at the heart of each logical argument. They build to a climax in 1:13, followed by a conclusion in 1:14.

The scriptural chain is carefully forged. Three OT texts—two at the beginning and one at its end—are introduced with a similar formula: **To which of the angels did God ever say . . . ?** (1:5, 13). All three (Ps 2:7; 2 Sam 7:14; Ps 110:1) were generally accepted as messianic texts. The chain proceeds in three definable steps: The first presents the Son's installation as royal heir (1:5-6); the second, the Son's constancy (1:7-12); the third, the Son's exaltation (1:13-14).

Quoting Scripture in Hebrews

The writer of Hebrews reads and quotes the Holy Scriptures (i.e., the OT) primarily to hear the voice of God. Almost without exception, he is uninterested in noting the human authors of biblical quotations (see 4:7; 9:19-20). Even in 4:7, in which David is identified as the author of Ps 95, this is done to establish a time frame important to the preacher's interpretation. In any case, it is God speaking "through David." The preacher vaguely introduces Ps 8:4-6 in Heb 2:6 with "there is a place where someone has testified" (see 4:4). But the preacher customarily introduces scriptural texts as divine speech.

Of Hebrews' thirty-five OT quotations, twenty are ascribed to God (1:5*a*, 5*b*, 6, 7, 8-9, 10-12, 13; 4:4; 5:5, 6; 6:14; 7:17, 21; 8:5, 8-12; 10:30*a*, 30*b*, 37-38; 12:26; 13:5), four to the Son (2:12, 13*a*, 13*b*; 10:5-9), and five to the Holy Spirit (3:7*b*-11 [see 3:15]; 10:15; and evidently 4:3, 5, 7; see also 9:8; Lane 1991, cxvii).

Importantly, the preacher never begins quotations with the formula "as it is written," common among other NT authors. Instead, he prefers to use verbs for speaking, and often in the present tense (e.g., *legō* [fourteen times]: 1:6, 7; 2:6, 12; 3:7, 15; 4:7; 5:6; 6:14; 7:21; 8:8; 10:5, 8; 12:26; *phēmi*: 8:5). Hebrews recognizes in Scripture the divine voice of warning (8:5), criticism (8:8), promise (6:13; 12:26), and solemn testimony (2:6; 7:17; 10:15). Scripture is not a dead letter from the historic past, but the "living and active" word of God in the present (4:12-13). His approach to Scripture serves as an example to us. For when reading the Holy Scriptures we, too, ought to listen for the voice of God speaking in and through them.

(1) The Son's Installation as Royal Heir (1:5-6)

■ **5** The opening rhetorical question, **For to which of the angels did God ever say** (1:5*a*), links the catena to the comparison between the Son and the angels begun in 1:4. The author introduces three scriptural texts. The second and third are linked with the first through similar introductory formulae: **or again** [*kai palin*] (1:5*c*); "And again [*de palin*]" (1:6*a*).

The first quotation comes from Ps 2:7: **You are my Son; today I have become your Father.** Psalm 2 is a royal psalm, already alluded to in the opening statement (Ps 2:8 in 1:2*b*). The psalm includes solemn words spoken at the coronation of a new Israelite king. Christian appropriation of the psalm associated Ps 2:7 with the declaration of Jesus as God's Son at his baptism (Mark 1:11||), transfiguration (Mark 9:7||), and resurrection (Acts 13:33).

The second quotation from 2 Sam 7:14 appears within the context of God's covenant promise of perpetual kingship to the house of David: **I will be his Father, and he will be my Son** (1:5*d*). This text is not quoted elsewhere in the NT. But a messianic interpretation of the promise to David's "seed" in 2 Sam 7:12 appears in several passages (John 7:42; Acts 13:23; Rom 1:3; see Luke 1:32-33). The connection of divine sonship and Israelite kingship is implicit in John 1:49. That Ps 2:7 and 2 Sam 7:12 were viewed in tandem as messianic prophecies is confirmed by a text from Qumran (4QFlor I, 10-11).

These two texts are used in the deployment of the preacher's first logical argument. The major premise, already set forth in Heb 1:4, is that the name Son is superior to any other name. The minor premise is that God is the One who called this person his Son, and this is given authoritative support by Ps 2:7 and 2 Sam 7:14. The conclusion has already been stated at the end of the opening statement: he has therefore inherited a better name than the angels (1:4).

■**6** The third scriptural citation in 1:6 is a bit more difficult to identify. **Let all God's angels worship him** resembles both Deut 32:43 and Ps 97:7 in the LXX. However, it corresponds exactly to a version of the "Song of Moses" in the *Odes of Solomon* (2:34), appended to the Psalms in a manuscript tradition of the LXX (Codex A, 55; see also Justin, *Dial.* 130). Apparently the preacher appeals to a liturgical adaptation of a biblical text. This is comparable to preachers today who point to a biblical truth expressed in one of the great hymns of the church.

The introductory formula, **when God brings his firstborn into the world**, also presents a difficulty. First, some interpreters think this refers to the second coming. But this incorrectly takes the adverb **again** with the verb **brings**. Actually, **again** is the last marker for this series of quotations ("did God ever say . . . ? Or again . . . **And again** . . ." [Heb 1:5-6]).

Second, others understand God's bringing the Son into the world as a reference to the incarnation. However, in Hebrews the incarnation of Jesus does not mark the Son's exaltation, but his humiliation, his being "made a little lower than the angels" (2:9, 7). Also, Hebrews uses the word *kosmos* ("world"), rather than *oikoumenē* (→ below), to refer to this created world (4:3; 9:26; 11:7, 38; see 9:1 [*kosmikon*, "earthly"] and 10:5 [Christ's entrance into the *kosmos* at his incarnation]).

A third interpretation is preferable. The **world** (*oikoumenē*) is further defined as the "world to come" in 2:5. Thus, the author is speaking about the ascension-glorification of Christ. Only at the conclusion of Christ's earthly life (5:7)—after he had endured suffering and death—was he "crowned with glory and honor" (2:9). It is at his enthronement that God commanded the angels to bow down before him.

The honorific title **firstborn** does not refer to Jesus' birth, either with regard to his eternal generation from the Father or his incarnation. Instead, it signifies his preeminence as the divine-human heir "over all creation" (Col 1:15) as the Risen One (Col 1:18; Rev 1:5) and forerunner of all "those who will inherit salvation" (Heb 1:14; see Rom 8:29).

This sets up another logical argument, with the major premise: One who is worshiped is greater than the worshiper. This is an unexpressed axiom on the order of Heb 7:7: "And without doubt the lesser person is blessed by the greater." The minor premise is once again supported by a scriptural quotation: the angels worship the Son (1:6). The unexpressed conclusion is pervasive to this entire chapter: the Son is superior to the angels.

(2) The Son's Constancy (1:7-12)

■ **7** A second subunit is comprised of three scriptural passages, stitched together as follows. The author signals the beginning of a contrast in the introduction to the first passage: **In speaking of the angels** *on the one hand* (*kai pros men tous angelous legei* [1:7]). The counterpart is expressed in 1:8a: "But [or *on the other hand*] about the Son he says [*pros de ton huion*]," followed by the second scripture (1:8b-9). A third passage continues the second half of the contrast in 1:10-12, introduced with, "He also says."

The major premise of this argument was a truism in the ancient world, especially for those influenced by Platonism. This philosophy held that things that do not change are superior to those that do.

The minor premise is that, whereas angels are changeable (1:7), the Son is unchangeable (1:8-12). The angels are clearly unstable, created beings. Psalm 104:4 (LXX) states that God **makes** (*poiōn*) them become fleeting, elemental forces of nature, such as wind or fire. **He makes his angels winds, his servants flames of fire** (Heb 1:7). It should be noted that the word for **winds** can also be translated "spirits" (CEB, KJV, NET, TNIV), as in 1:14. Thus, the angels are part of the changing created order.

■ **8** The Son, however, is constant and eternal. The preacher demonstrates this by quotations from Ps 45:6-7 (LXX) in Heb 1:8-9 and Ps 102:25-27 (LXX) in Heb 1:10-12. The Ps 45 quotation underlines the Son's constancy in sovereignty and righteous judgment.

The enthroned Son is addressed as God: **Your throne, O God, will last for ever and ever** (Heb 1:8b). Not only will the Son's sovereignty endure, but it will be executed in righteousness: **and righteousness will be the scepter of your kingdom** (1:8c). The **scepter** is used figuratively (by metonymy) to refer to all that was entailed in a monarch's exercise of sovereignty. This is much like our association of kings with crowns, judges with gavels, police officers with badges. The Son's authority is not only symbolized but realized in his establishment of righteousness.

■ **9 You have loved righteousness and hated wickedness** (v 9a). Israel's kings were expected to administer righteousness and justice (see 1 Kgs 3:28; 10:9; 2 Chr 9:8; Ps 71:1; Prov 16:12-13; 20:8, 28; 25:5; 29:4; Jer 22:15). They were subject to God's curse when they did not, for God was the Righteous King they were to emulate (Ps 99:4). The prophets foretold a coming king, the "righteous Branch" from the house of David (Jer 23:5). This is the Messiah, the Righteous One (Isa 53:11; Acts 3:14; 7:52; 1 John 2:1), whose kingdom is established in justice and righteousness forever (Isa 9:7).

The preacher's gaze moves, as it always does, to the exaltation (= anointing) of the Son as king: **therefore God, your God, has set you above your companions by anointing you with the oil of joy** (Heb 1:9b-c). Prophets, priests, and kings were anointed in the OT. Anointing with oil signified God's special appointment, consecration, and spiritual enablement of persons for his service. Also, it would not be lost on Greek readers that the word for "anoint [*chriō*]" is related to the word for "Christ [*Christos*, 'Anointed One']."

■ **10** The quotation from Ps 102:25-27 in Heb 1:10-12 emphasizes the contrast between the constancy of the Son as Creator and the contingency of the created order. **In the beginning, O Lord, you laid the foundations of the earth, and the heavens are the work of your hands** (v 10). The eternal Son existed before creation, and creation came into being at his command (see 1:2c; 3:3-4). The author does not hesitate to attribute to Christ what the OT author attributed to God.

■ **11-12** The Son is contrasted with a changing and deteriorating creation: **They will perish, but you remain; they will all wear out** [lit., *become old*] **like a garment** (1:11).

Not only is the universe perishable, but the Son—the eternal Creator (1:2c)—could withdraw his sustaining power (1:3c) and bring the present universe to an end as easily as one can remove and put away clothing: **You will roll them up like a robe; like a garment they will be changed** (1:12a-b).

The Son is unlike the ever-changing cosmos: **But you remain the same, and your years will never end** (1:12c). The preacher will later sum up this truth in the memorable statement, "Jesus Christ is the same yesterday and today and forever" (13:8). Given the major and minor premises of this argument, the conclusion is once again clear. The Son who is eternal and constant is superior to angels who, as part of the created order, are ever changing.

(3) The Son's Exaltation (1:13-14)

■ **13** A seventh and final scriptural quotation, Ps 110:1, completes the chain. This is one of the preacher's favorite passages. He has already alluded to it in Heb 1:3d and will again several more times (8:1; 10:12; 12:2).

The catena started (1:5a), and now ends, with a similar formula expressed as a rhetorical question, **To which of the angels did God ever say . . . ?** (1:13a). There is a subtle but important difference between the two formulae, which is difficult to represent in English translation. In 1:5*a* the author used the simple past tense (aorist, *eipon*), translated as an emphatic past tense in the NIV (**did . . . say**). Here in 1:13*a* he uses the Greek perfect tense, **has . . . said** (*eirēken*). The perfect tense describes an action as having been completed in the past but having lasting effects. The pronouncement from Ps 110:1, never spoken concerning any angel, has now been spoken resolutely of the Son: **Sit at my right hand until I make your enemies a footstool for your feet** (Ps 110:1 in Heb 1:13*b-c*). The climax of enthronement at God's right hand, which appeared toward the close of the opening statement (1:3*d*), is repeated here at the close of the catena (1:5-14).

Psalm 110 in Hebrews

It may be an exaggeration to claim, as G. W. Buchanan has (1972, xix-xxx), that Hebrews is a "homiletic midrash" on Ps 110. But this psalm, nevertheless, plays a pivotal role in supporting the main proposition of the sermon—that Jesus is our high priest (see 1:17-18).

The key text in 8:1 summarizes the message of the sermon in terms of Ps 110:1, 4: "The point of what we are saying is this: We do have such a high priest"—i.e., in the order of Melchizedek (as in Ps 110:4). The author made this point in the preceding discussion (Heb 5—7). He continues by saying that this priest "sat down at the right hand of the Majesty in heaven" (as in Ps 110:1; see 1:3).

The preacher alludes to Ps 110:1 at the beginning of Heb 1 (v 3) and explicitly quotes it toward the end of the same chapter (v 13). He also echoes this verse in many other passages (8:1; 10:12, 13; 12:2; perhaps also 4:14 and 7:26). He uses Ps 110:4 even more extensively. He cites it initially in Heb 5:6, picks up its language about Melchizedek's high priesthood and God's oath in chs 5—7 (5:10; 6:17, 20; 7:3, 11, 15, 20, 24, 28), and quotes it twice more in 7:17, 21 (see Lincoln 2006, 12-13).

Clearly, Psalm 110 serves as the backbone for christological reflection in Hebrews. It is the wellspring for the preacher's inspired exposition of Jesus as the "great high priest who has gone through the heavens" (4:14).

■ **14** This scripture (Ps 110:1), too, is part of a logical argument in Heb 1:14. The major premise, yet another truism, is that the one who rules is superior to those who serve him (see John 13:16; 15:20). The minor premise is that the Son is ruler (as demonstrated in the quotation from Ps 110:1 in Heb 1:13). By way of contrast, **all angels** are servants (1:14). The servitude of angels is underscored in two ways:

First, they are **ministering spirits** (*leitourgika pneumata*). This echoes the language of Ps 104:4 in Heb 1:7. The preacher may well be thinking of the ministry of worship angels carry out before the throne of God in heaven (1:6; 12:22).

Second, angels are **sent to serve** (lit., ***sent for service***). Angels are divinely commissioned to assist human beings on earth.

The particular beneficiaries of this angelic service are **those who will inherit salvation**. The Son is "the heir" par excellence (1:2b). Believers are drawn into the divine inheritance through their union with Christ. Thus, angels are dedicated not only to the service of God but also to his people. There is no doubt about the conclusion to this final argument: the Son is superior to the angels.

c. Heed What Was Spoken in the Son (2:1-4)

To say that either 1:1-4 or 1:1-14 comprises the *exordium* to Hebrews would be woefully inadequate. Clearly, 2:1-4 constitutes the interpretive point of everything that precedes it. The author does not switch from exposition and argument (1:1-14) to exhortation (2:1-4) in order merely to insert a homiletical digression. No, this warning is the destination toward which the introduction has been heading all along. This is indicated by the emphatic **therefore** (*Dia touto*) that heads this subunit.

This exhortation harks back to the starting point in 1:1-2a: ***the God who speaks.*** The verb "to utter, speak [*laleō*]" returns (**spoken** [2:2]; **announced** [2:3]; see 1:1, 2a), but now along with its important counterpart, hearing the message (2:1, 3b). Also, even as 1:2a referenced the recipients of the divine word (**to us**), so now **we** are the ones who must pay utmost attention (2:1), and **we** will not escape if we "neglect such a great salvation" (2:3a ESV, RSV), which was confirmed **to us** by the apostles (2:3b).

In 2:1-4 the preacher brings his comparison (*synkrisis*) of the Son and the angels to its proper conclusion (→ 2:5, 16). We can now determine the reason for this comparison. It lies in the lesser-to-greater comparison between the messages delivered by angels and by the Son. The conclusion is that we disregard God's word in the Son at our own peril.

This closing paragraph of the *exordium* consists of two sentences. The first sentence in 2:1 contains alliteration using the letter *p* (*perissoterōs prosechein . . . pararyōmen*) as in 1:1. The second is another periodic sentence (2:2-4), as in the opening statement (1:1-4). It constructs an a fortiori (lesser-to-greater) argument in the form of a rhetorical question containing a condition (**if . . .** [2:2]) and proposed outcome (**how shall we escape . . . ?** [2:3-4]). Although 2:2-4 is one complex sentence in Greek, 2:3b-4 details the foundation for the great salvation about which the author is speaking, and so may be explored under a separate heading.

(1) Exhortation to Pay Utmost Attention (2:1)

■ 1 The upshot of all the comparisons between the Son and angels presented in ch 1 is that **We must pay more careful attention, therefore, . . . to what we have heard.** The use of the verb **must** (*dei*) with the adverb ***more carefully*** (*perissoterōs*) is emphatic, and the sense is captured well in the rendering, "we are bound to pay all the more heed" (REB). The verb translated **pay ... attention** (*prosechein*) is used in nautical contexts of directing a ship toward a harbor to anchor there (LSJ, 1512). This would hardly seem relevant, if it were not for the following purpose clause, **so that we do not drift away**. The verb **drift away** (*pararyōmen*) can refer to drifting off course (LSJ supp., 240; see REB). The nautical imagery vividly communicates the insidious danger of neglecting the message of salvation.

(2) The Peril of Neglecting the Message (2:2-3a)

■ **2** Now the preacher leverages his comparison of the Son to angels for maximum persuasive effect. What follows provides a further basis for the exhortation in 2:1 (note the **For** [*gar*]). He begins with a condition: **if the message spoken by angels** (2:2). The **message** is the law of Moses. Hebrews is not alone in claiming that the Law was given to Moses through angelic intermediaries (see Acts 7:38; Gal 3:19). The legal aspect of the message is punctuated by judicial vocabulary. The message **was binding** (*bebaios*, "firm," "valid," "in force"), **and every violation and disobedience** [lit., *refusal to listen*] **received its just punishment**. The Mosaic law contained sanctions for disobedience, summed up well in Paul's quotation from Deut 27:26 in Gal 3:10: "Cursed is everyone who does not continue to do everything written in the Book of the Law."

Why the Comparison of Jesus with Angels in Hebrews?

The sustained comparison between Christ and the angels in Heb 1—2 has tantalized scholars. Is the author addressing a specific problem among his readers?

One suggestion is that, like the Colossians (see Col 2:18), there was a problem with the worship of angels (Manson 1949, 1-17; Jewett 1981, 5-7, 39). However, since there is no explicit polemic against such practice—especially in light of the already clear tradition of angelic refusal of worship (Tob 12:16-22; Rev 19:10; 22:9; *Apoc. Zeph.* 6:11-15; *Ascen. Isa.* 7:18-23; 8:5)—this view is not compelling.

Another suggestion is that the preacher is combating an angelic Christology. Various models of Jewish reflection about the eschatological, high-priestly, or sometimes messianic roles of angels may have played a part in speculation about the nature and function of Jesus the Christ (for a detailed survey, see Attridge 1989, 51-52). In Daniel, for example, the archangel Michael contends for the children of Israel (Dan 12:1). At Qumran, Melchizedek was viewed as an end-time messianic king and priest, who may also have been thought of as an angel (11QMelch; → Heb 7:7-8 sidebar, "Mysterious Melchizedek"). Philo often described the intermediary figure, the Logos, as an angel (*Embassy* 3.177.62; *God* 1.182; *Flight* 1.5; *Names* 1.87; *Dreams* 1.239).

We also know that such Jewish angelic models informed christological formulations among certain Christians into the second century (see Justin, *Dial.* 34.2; *Herm. Sim.* 8.3.3; 9.12.7-8; *Apos. Con.* 8.12.7, 23; *Gos. Thom.* 13 [34,34]). Perhaps Hebrews wanted to emphasize Jesus as not just one of the "sons of God," even if the most exalted one (i.e., angels; → In the Text on 2:7). Christ is the eternal and unique Son of God. Once again, in the absence of explicit rebuttals to an angelic Christology in Hebrews, this view can be little more than speculation.

More firmly grounded in the text of Hebrews is a background in which angels were considered mediators of the law of Moses (2:2) and governors over the present cosmic order (2:5). A widespread belief among Jews in the intertestamental period, as well as in the NT, was that the Law was not directly given to Moses by Yahweh, but through the intermediate agency of angels (*Jub.* 1:27, 29; 2:1; Josephus, *Ant.* 15.136; Acts 7:53; Gal 3:19; Heb 2:2). In connection with this capacity, angels were leaders of the heavenly liturgy and Israel's worship of God (Isa 6:3; *1 En.* 39:10-13; *Jub.* 2:2, 18; 15:27; 31:14; *T. Levi* 3:5; 1QSb 4:25-26; *Ascen. Isa.* 7:37; 8:17; 9:28-33; *3 En.* 1:12). According to *Jubilees*, angels observed the Sabbath, the Feast of Weeks, and were even created circumcised (*Jub.* 2:17-18; 6:18; 15:26-27).

Beyond this, angels were believed to be responsible for the governance of the entire universe, including nations (Deut 32:8 LXX; Dan 10:13, 20-22; 12:1), heavenly realms (*T. Levi* 3; *1 En.* 3-20), and the physical processes of the cosmos, such as heavenly bodies, weather phenomena, and the growth of plants and animals (*Jub.* 2:2; *1 En.* 60:16-22; 82:9-20; *1 En.* 19; 1QH^a 1:10-11). One may wonder whether Paul in Galatians was tapping into such traditions in his associating the Torah with both angels (Gal 3:19) and the *stoicheia* ("elemental spirits" [Gal 4:3, 9 NRSV; see Col 2:8, 20]).

Like other NT authors, Hebrews declares the supremacy of Christ over every cosmic power (Eph 1:20-21; Col 1:16; 1 Pet 3:22). While angels did and continue to serve God in this present age (Heb 1:6, 14; 12:22; 13:2), the Son of God plays a preeminent role "in these last days" (1:2a) or "the world to come" (2:5). The old order has given way to the new order of salvation, now focused on the atoning death of the Son (12:24) and his heavenly intercession for God's people (7:25). If angels once served as God's vice-regents and intermediaries, now the Son reigns as king and high priest, through whom alone we may gain access to God. Membership in God's household, therefore, requires honoring and worshiping God through the Son, not through the practices under the old covenant, which were under the guidance of angels.

■ **3a** The condition is followed by a proposed outcome. If the message, communicated through inferior messengers (angels), stipulated such severe consequences for noncompliance, **how shall we escape if we ignore such a great salvation?** (2:3a). This, of course, is a rhetorical question. The implied answer is, "We won't!" To **ignore** is not casual neglect, but an active, contemptuous disregard. It is not a loss of memory or an unintended oversight, but a culpable lack of concern (such as in our phrase "child neglect"; see 8:9). Because the disregard is for a salvation so great, it entails dishonoring the source of every benefit, God himself (deSilva 2000a, 106).

(3) The Pedigree of Such Great Salvation (2:3b-4)

■ **3b-c** The remainder of the *exordium* is a series of clauses that further modifies "salvation" in 2:3a. **It was first announced by the Lord** (2:3b). The preacher uses an expression in the style of the finest Classical Greek to suggest, not simply chronological priority, but that the message had its origin in the **Lord**'s (i.e., Jesus') preaching of the gospel ("announced originally" [NAB]; see Mark 1:1; 1 John 2:7, 24; 3:11; 2 John 5-6).

It was confirmed to us by those who heard him (2:3*c*). The verb **was confirmed** (*bebaiōthē*) is a cognate of the adjective "binding" (2:2*a*) and has the connotation of legal validation. Especially in Luke-Acts, we see Jesus' apostles appointed as qualified witnesses to what they had "seen and heard" (Acts 4:20; 22:15), particularly with regard to Jesus' resurrection (Luke 24:48; Acts 1:8, 21-22; 2:32; 3:15; 5:32; 10:39, 41; 13:31; see Anderson 2006, 34-37, 188-93).

■ **4** But if this were not enough, **God also testified to it.** The verb *synepimartyreō* is yet another legal term meaning "to bear witness at the same time," "bear witness along with," or ***corroborate.***

The elements of divine corroboration include **signs** and **wonders.** In the OT this is a stock expression for God's mighty works in connection with the exodus (Exod 7:3; Deut 4:34; 6:22; 7:19; 29:3; Ps 135:9; Jer 32:20-21). In the NT the expression refers to **various miracles** performed by Jesus (Acts 2:22) and at the hands of the apostles (Acts 2:43; 4:30; 5:12; 6:8; 14:3; 15:12; Rom 15:19; 2 Cor 12:12). The word **miracles** (*dynameis*) refers to miraculous powers.

Finally, though the preacher speaks of ***distributions*** or ***dividings*** (*merismoi*; **distributed**), surely he intends a partitioning not **of the Holy Spirit** but of the **gifts of the Holy Spirit.** Determining whether **according to his will** refers to the intention of the Holy Spirit or to God (as Codex Bezae specifies) is unnecessary. In a parallel passage in 1 Cor 12:11 it is clearly the Spirit who apportions gifts "just as he determines." Yet Paul teaches in 1 Cor 12:4-7 that every person of the triune God operates in the gifting of the body of Christ.

FROM THE TEXT

Hebrews begins where every theology must begin: divine revelation. "God spoke" (1:1). The author of Hebrews is a master theologian and preacher who brings before his audience the full-orbed revelation of God. His is a pattern for every other preacher of the gospel. Our goal should be to usher listeners into the presence of an awesome, holy, and gracious God.

The author of Hebrews' apprehension and appropriation of divine revelation has some similarities to the so-called Wesleyan quadrilateral. This is an approach to interpretation that seeks to apprehend divine revelation by way of Scripture, tradition, reason, and experience (see Gunter 1997; Olson 2002, ch 2; Thorsen 2005).

First, the author's main storehouse of revelation is the Scriptures. Of course, the Son is God's ultimate revelation to humankind. But the preacher diligently searches the Scriptures in order to hear the voice of the triune God. He makes abundant use of allusions and quotations in ch 1, including the wisdom traditions in Scripture. He exploits these to explain the nature and destiny of the Son. Scriptural exegesis will continue to be basic to the preacher's strategy for pastoral ministry to his readers.

Second, the preacher acknowledges his indebtedness—which he has in common with his listeners—to the witness of the apostles. The message of salvation was first spoken by the Lord Jesus, but it was mediated and confirmed to us by "those who heard him" (2:3c). For us today it is still true that the church is "built on the foundation of the apostles and prophets, with Christ Jesus himself as the chief cornerstone" (Eph 2:20). We must never forget the historical rootedness of our faith. We must not neglect two thousand years of church history. Throughout its history, the flame of truth has been passed along by faithful believers, preachers, and theologians.

From the time of the early church fathers until now, God has guided the church's understanding of the faith, sometimes called the Great Tradition. Many ambitious believers have struck out on their own, trying to restore Christianity to the pristine glory the church supposedly enjoyed at the time of Jesus and the apostles. However, these are almost always proud and unworkable attempts to figure out the faith within the small circle of one individual's human understanding.

The fact is that we cannot help but stand on the shoulders of spiritual giants in Christ's church. This begins with apostles—Peter, James, John, and others. Then it embraces those who passed on the apostolic baton throughout the history of the church. Names such as Justin Martyr, the Cappadocian fathers, Augustine, Aquinas, Luther, Calvin, Wesley, and Barth come readily to mind. The Westminster Abbey of Heb 11 has been considerably enlarged since the preacher first preached his sermon!

Third, the preacher presses reason into service for the cause of the gospel. He has already used comparisons, considerations (more technically called enthymemes), and logical arguments (such as a fortiori). In the first-century world, the highest attainment of education was rhetoric, and the preacher is quite accomplished in it. The book of Hebrews stands as a shining example of how an educated human being can be used by God for the proclamation of the gospel through winsome language, ordered and logical thinking, and persuasive argumentation.

Fourth, the preacher points out the breaking through of God's revelation into the experience of his listeners. God has spoken *to us* in the Son (1:2a). When the gospel is preached, God bears corroborating testimony to it through "signs, wonders . . . miracles, and gifts of the Holy Spirit" (2:4). The preacher was at one with the apostles in realizing that this miraculous divine testimony is an indicator of the change of times. The death, resurrection, and exaltation of Jesus marked a transition from the old age of sin and death to the coming age of righteousness and life.

Theological method should not overshadow the stunning christological claim made in Hebrews' *exordium* (1:1—2:4). Few passages in the NT are as lucid as this one in declaring the deity of Jesus Christ. Only the prologue to the Gospel of John (1:1-18) is as equally explicit and emphatic, especially in its opening line: "In the beginning was the Word, and the Word was with God, and the Word was God" (John 1:1).

Not surprisingly, the Gospel of John and Hebrews were primary weapons in the arsenal against the Arian heresy that began in the fourth century. Arius held that the Son is not of the same nature as God the Father. The Son did not exist eternally but was the first created being.

The powerful testimony to Jesus' divine nature and eternal existence in Heb 1 led some Arians to dispute the book's status as apostolic. Others twisted texts in Hebrews to suit Arian doctrine (Epiphanius, *Pan.* 69.37). They seized upon the statement in 1:4 that the Son "became" superior to the angels but more commonly pointed to the assertion that the Son was faithful to God who "made" him (→ 3:2).

Defensively, supporters of orthodox, Trinitarian belief could handily refute these interpretations (e.g., see Athanasius on 1:4 [Heen and Krey 2005, 19] and Epiphanius on 3:2 [*Pan.* 69.37-39]). Offensively, many elements of Heb 1 were interpreted to support the full deity and eternity of the Son:

- That the universe (lit., "the ages") was created through the Son (1:2c) means that he existed before all ages. Only God, according to Ps 55:19 LXX, has existed "before the ages" (Theodore of Mopsuestia; Heen and Krey 2005, 8).
- That the Son is "the radiance of God's glory" (Heb 1:3a) indicates that the Son has the same nature as God (Theodore of Mopsuestia; Heen and Krey 2005, 11). It is impossible to conceive of the Light of God existing eternally without eternally radiating the brightness of the Son. Likewise, 1:3b says that the Son was "the exact representation of [God's] being." Therefore, the Arians are wrong in saying "There was once when he was not" (Athanasius; Theodoret of Cyr; Heen and Krey 2005, 12, 14-15, 16).
- "Sustaining all things by his powerful word" (1:3c) evidences the Son's divine, creative power. He keeps the universe from falling apart into nonexistence (Chrysostom; Gregory of Nyssa; Heen and Krey 2005, 16).
- We are forbidden in Scripture to worship created things. That angels are commanded to worship the Son (1:6) implies that he is to be worshiped as God (Didymus the Blind; Heen and Krey 2005, 24).
- The Son is addressed as "God," and it is declared that his kingdom will be everlasting (1:8; Theodoret of Cyr; Heen and Krey 2005, 24).

We could go on. Hebrews 1 fits into the pattern of biblical revelation behind the truth confessed about Christ in the Nicene Creed (A.D. 325): "of the same essence of the Father, God of God, Light of Light, very God of very God, begotten, not made, being of one substance with the Father."

The revelation of Jesus Christ as more than an exalted figure, but the divine Son, who is superior even to the angels, is not simply for the purpose of making a doctrinal statement about the deity of Christ. In Hebrews, the aim of this high view of Christ is to impress upon the readers the magnitude of their accountability to the message of salvation spoken by the Son (2:1-4). The preacher does not want us simply to express belief in Jesus as the Son of God. He wants us to commit ourselves to him as our Savior, who makes us holy through his atoning death and leads us into the glory of his inheritance.

2. Jesus Perfected as a Merciful and Faithful High Priest (2:5-18)

BEHIND THE TEXT

Having solicited the full attention of his listeners in the *exordium* (1:1—2:4), the preacher now turns to a statement of facts (2:5-16) and proposition (2:17-18). Called the *narratio* (Lat.; Gk. *diēgēsis*) by ancient teachers of rhetoric, the statement of facts serves three important functions in a speech. First, it presents the relevant background story for the following arguments. Second, it gives the nature of the subject at hand. Third, it leads up to the proposition of the speech, which often immediately follows the statement of facts (Quintilian, *Inst.* 4.4.1). The proposition relates the central point(s) of the speech. As a conclusion to the statement of facts, it is a summing up of its contents and an introduction to the succeeding arguments (Übelacker 1989, 193).

One had considerable flexibility in composing a statement of facts (see *Rhet. Her.* 1.8.12-13). In deliberative speeches it could narrate past events, catalog a series of present facts, or forecast future events (*Rhet. Alex.* 1338a5). Since Hebrews is a brief sermon, the statement of facts is not a complete rundown of the arguments to follow. It is a staging platform upon which everything else in the sermon is built. It has in view the present and future state of affairs (namely, the current subjection of the world to come in 2:5) as a result of the grand drama of the incarnation. It tackles head-on the central challenge to the listeners' commitment to the lordship of Christ: the off-putting notion that the Son of God came to suffer and die. In rhetorical terms, this is "the head of the whole business [*kephalaion estin*]" (Quintilian, *Inst.* 3.10.27). Without dealing with this matter up-front, the preacher would not be able to persuade his listeners, not with any number of other arguments, of the high priesthood of Christ or the expediency of their holding allegiance to him. The *narratio* is the appropriate place to grapple with a matter so fundamental to the entire case being argued.

The Scandal of Christ's Suffering

A primary hurdle that Hebrews must overcome is the tremendous scandal of Christ's suffering. Gods appearing as humans was not a foreign idea to the Greeks (see Acts 14:11-12; Ovid, *Metam.* 8.611-725), and Jews were aware of angels appearing in human guise (Gen 18:1-15; Josh 5:13-15; Judg 13:1-7; Tob 12:19; see Heb 13:2). However, the notion of divine or angelic figures so participating in the human condition as to suffer and die—especially a criminal's death on a cross—was ridiculous, repulsive, and scandalous to Jews and Gentiles alike (1 Cor 1:23).

The crucifixion of Christ served as the basis for negative assessments of Christian faith. Tacitus could hardly find enough disparaging adjectives to describe the Christians persecuted under Nero. That Christ, their founder, "suffered the extreme penalty" (i.e., crucifixion) under Pontius Pilate sufficiently demonstrated their disreputable beginnings (*Ann.* 15.44). According to Justin Martyr, pagan critics of Christians believed it was "madness . . . that we give to a crucified man a place second to the unchangeable and eternal God, the Creator of all" (*1 Apol.* 13.4). Justin also reported the protest Trypho raised among Jews: "But this so-called Christ of yours was dishonourable and inglorious, so much so that the last curse contained in the law of God fell on him, for he was crucified" (*Dial.* 32.1).

Such criticism of the suffering Christ led the preacher to the Hebrews to insist that Christ suffered nobly and courageously on behalf of others to bring them the benefits of eternal salvation.

2:5-18

The statement of facts should be concise, clear, and credible (see *Rhet. Alex.* 1438a20-b10; *Rhet. Her.* 1.9.14-16; Quintilian, *Inst.* 4.2.31-60). The statement of facts in Hebrews is certainly clear and concise. It details God's action of placing all things under the authority of the Son, bringing salvation to humankind through the incarnation, and defeating death and the devil, all in relatively short compass.

The most important quality of the statement of facts is that it be credible (Quintilian, *Inst.* 4.2.32-34; other rhetoricians add plausible, probable, or convincing [see Quintilian, *Inst.* 4.2.31-32; *Rhet. Alex.* 1438a20]). This is achieved, "if in regard to facts that are improbable we bring forward reasons [*aitiai*] that will make the events that we allege seem likely to have taken place" (*Rhet. Alex.* 1438b1; see Quintilian, *Inst.* 4.2.52).

Both the rationale and purpose behind God's actions in Jesus are privileged in the *narratio* of Hebrews. Notice the frequency of inferential connectives such as "so [*di' hēn aitian*]" (2:11b), "since [*epei oun*]" (2:14a), "for surely [*gar dēpou*]" (2:16), and "for this reason [*hothen*]" (2:17a), and purpose clauses like "so that [*hopōs*]" (2:9b), "so that"/"in order that [*hina*]" (2:14b, 17b), and "that [*eis to*]" (2:17c). Moreover, there are references to God's or Christ's actions as gracious (2:9c), appropriate ("fitting" [2:10]), sacred (2:11a), honorable ("crowned with glory and honor" [2:9b]; "not ashamed" [2:11b]), and necessary ("he had to" [2:17]). Other telltale signs indicate that 2:5-18 constitutes the statement of facts and proposition of the sermon:

First, the preacher opens the statement by denying that the world to come has been subjected to angels (2:5). Ancient rhetoricians insisted (see Quintilian, *Inst.* 4.2.132) that the statement should end where the issue to be determined began. So we see the statement beginning and ending with a negation of the angels as beneficiaries of divine salvation (2:5, 16). The conversational tone of both 2:5 and 16 also lends to our identification of 2:5-16 as the statement of facts. The proposition immediately follows in 2:17-18.

Second, the preacher introduces Jesus by name for the first time, and emphatically so (→ 2:9 sidebar, "Use of the Name 'Jesus' in Hebrews"). Jesus is also given titles that have an archaic Jewish ("son of man" [2:6]) and Hellenistic ("author [*archēgos*]" [2:10]) flavor, and evoke images of a great champion for the people of God. Most notable, though, is the appearance of Jesus as a speaker. "What really carries weight in deliberative speeches," writes Quintilian (*Inst.* 3.8.12), "is the authority of the speaker." So it is significant that the preacher brings forward statements by the authoritative figure of Jesus himself in 2:12-13. Only in one other place will the author quote Jesus directly (10:5-7)—again, significantly, regarding Christ's incarnation.

Finally, the preacher appeals to his readers' emotions (see Quintilian, *Inst.* 4.2.111-15). What is potentially the most incredible aspect of his case, namely Jesus' humiliating suffering and death, the preacher sets forth as the chief strength of God's work for humanity in the incarnation. Jesus' suffering may not be regarded as senseless or contemptible, because his was a noble death. He died for others, for everyone (2:9), to exalt them to glory (2:10*a*), make them holy (2:11*a*), and claim them as members of God's family (2:11*b*-13). Indeed, it was appropriate for God to "perfect" Jesus as "the author of their salvation . . . through suffering" (2:10*c*). What's more, Jesus came to destroy the devil, who held the power of death, and free his siblings from the greatest fear of all, the fear of death (2:14-15). Thus, the preacher appeals to his listeners' feelings of admiration, gratitude, and courage in contrast to his eliciting their fear in the *exordium* (2:1-4).

The statement of facts is developed as follows. It begins with a consideration of the main question: Whether the future inheritance and kingdom of God truly belong to the Son, over against the domain that has existed under the administration of angels (2:5-9). The preacher uses Ps 8:4-6 as an authoritative guide to understanding the course of events in the incarnation. He introduces the issue of Jesus' suffering as the necessary prelude to his exaltation. Then, in Heb 2:10-15, the preacher looks at the appropriateness and necessity of the Son's complete identification with mortal humanity in order to bring salvation. In 2:16 he returns to where the discussion began, by stating that Jesus' powerful leadership concerns the children of Abraham, not angels.

The discussion of Jesus' fellowship in human suffering leads up to the proposition or thesis in 2:17-18 (note "For this reason" in 2:17). The proposition is twofold, corresponding to the expository and hortatory goals of the sermon:

On the expository side, Jesus' identification with humanity qualifies him as a high priest who is compassionate and faithful and who provides atonement for sins. The image of Jesus as the Great High Priest is, of course, key to the preacher's argument in Hebrews (compare 2:17 with 3:1; 4:14-15; 5:1, 5-6, 10; 6:20; 7:11, 15-17, 21, 26; 8:1; 9:11, 25; 10:12, 21; 13:11).

On the hortatory side, the preacher wishes to encourage his listeners to endure every temptation and suffering with the help of and in allegiance to this Great High Priest (compare 2:18 with 3:1, 6; 4:14-16; 6:18-20; 10:19-39; 12:1-28). We can see, then, how the statement of facts and proposition are critical to framing the rhetorical aims of the entire sermon.

IN THE TEXT

a. The Humiliation and Exaltation of Jesus (2:5-9)

■ **5** This passage is closely tied to the preceding *exordium* through the use of the conjunction *for* (*gar* [2:5]; untranslated in NIV). The preacher builds upon his previous arguments for the supremacy of the Son over angels: **For it is not to angels that he has subjected the world to come.**

Ancient Jews thought angels had jurisdiction over the nations of the earth, based on such texts as Deut 32:8 LXX: "When the Most High divided the nations, when he scattered the sons of Adam, he established boundaries for the nations according to the number of the angels of God." Thus, in the OT the prophet Daniel recognized angelic princes over Israel and Persia (Dan 10:13, 20-22; 12:1).

In the NT angels are classed among cosmic rulers and powers (Rom 8:38; 1 Pet 3:22; → Heb 2:2 sidebar, "Why the Comparison of Jesus with Angels in Hebrews?"). However, **he** (i.e., God) has not granted sovereignty to angels in the coming kingdom of God. That privilege belongs to Christ and his church (see 1 Cor 3:21-23; 6:2-3; Eph 1:20-23; 3:10; Col 1:13; 2 Tim 2:12; Heb 12:28; Jas 2:5; 2 Pet 1:11; Rev 1:5-6, 9; 5:10; 22:5).

The verb **subjected,** according to the Latin etymology behind our English word, as well as the Greek here in Heb 2:5 (*hypotassō*), means "to place under," that is, "to bring something under the firm control of someone" (L&N 37.31). The use of this verb anticipates its appearance in the last line of the psalm quotation in 2:6*b*-8*a*, as well as its recurrences in the preacher's interpretation of Ps 8:4-6 in Heb 2:8*b*-*c*.

The object of this subjection is **the world to come**. The **world** here is the same as that found in 1:6. There the angels were commanded to worship the Son when he was introduced "into the world." The **world** (*oikoumenē*) is that realm of authority and dignity into which Christ entered when he had made "purification for sins" and "sat down at the right hand of the Majesty" on high (1:3). Here in 2:5 the preacher more clearly refers to that realm as the world **to come** (*mellousan*) or "future world" (NLT). This is the world Jesus inherited through his death and exaltation. It is the present and sure reality of the coming kingdom of God (see 1:8; 12:26-28) **about which we are speaking** ("which is our theme" [REB]).

Eschatology in Hebrews

The preacher's eschatology (understanding of last things) mirrors the "already-but-not-yet" tension throughout the NT. On the one hand, the exaltation of Jesus has ushered in the realization of "the good things to come" (10:1 NRSV), which were but shadowed in the Law. Jesus "has appeared once for all at the end of the ages" to deal decisively with sin through his self-sacrifice (9:26). So even now believers taste of "the powers of the coming age" (6:5) and are in the process of entering into the promised end-time "rest" (4:3). Jesus has already entered into "the world to come" (2:5; see 1:6), so that the church presently participates with him in the realities of the heavenly city of Jerusalem (12:22-24).

On the other hand, "we are looking for the city that is to come" (13:14). Our entrance into divine rest lies in the future (→ 4:11), as does God's "eternal judgment" (6:2; see 9:27; 10:27, 30; 13:4). Since our inheritance of salvation is a future prospect (1:14), the preacher consistently speaks of it in terms of "hope" (3:6; 6:11, 18; 7:19; 10:23; 11:1). The Son is already invested with universal authority over the world to come; "yet at present we do not see everything subject to him" (2:8c), not until the unshakable kingdom of God is fully revealed (12:26-28; see 10:13).

The tension between the "already" and the "not yet" is due to our living between the two pivotal moments of God's saving action in Christ: "so Christ was sacrificed once to take away the sins of many people; and he will appear a second time, not to bear sin, but to bring salvation to those who are waiting for him" (9:28). From the perspective of time, then, we have the *hope* of salvation; from the perspective of eternity, we are receiving the *reality* of salvation. The link between the two is *faith* (see 11:1), by which we receive God's promises (4:1-3; 6:12; 10:22-23, 36; 11:6, 9, 13, 17, 33). For further discussion on Hebrews' eschatology, see C. K. Barrett (1956, 363-93) and Lincoln (2006, 92-100).

■ **6-7** In 2:6-8a the witness of Scripture contradicts (**But**, *de* [2:6a]) the notion that angels will rule the world to come (already negated in 2:5). The nondescript introduction—**there is a place where someone** (lit., ***somewhere someone***)—does not indicate ignorance regarding the location and authorship of the following quotation. Perhaps being vague gives the audience the pleasure of recognizing for themselves such a well-known quote. More likely, like the Alexandrian Jewish scholar Philo and later Jewish rabbis, the preacher is de-emphasizing the human medium of the scriptural text and focusing on the fact that it is ultimately *God* who **has testified** in the Scriptures (→ 1:5-14 sidebar, "Quoting Scripture in Hebrews").

The psalmist in Ps 8 revels in the majesty of God and the grandeur of God's creation. In Ps 8:4-6 (quoted in Heb 2:6b-8a) he reflects on the irony of humanity's insignificance by comparison to its divinely granted predominance in the world. Surely, the preacher to the Hebrews was well aware of the psalmist's commentary on human nature, and its indebtedness to Gen 1:26-28. But for Hebrews, as for Paul, the dignity and divine destiny of humanity is only realized through "the man from heaven" (1 Cor 15:47-49), Jesus Christ, the true image of God (Heb 1:3; 2 Cor 4:4; Col 1:15). The preacher's christological approach to Ps 8:4-6 is apparent in several ways.

First, as we have already seen, his reading of the text is concerned with the governance of "the world to come" (Heb 2:5), to which he has already alluded throughout ch 1. Two verbal links between 2:5 and the psalm quotation in 2:6b-8a make this clear: **angels** (2:5, 7a) and **subjected** (*hypotassō* [2:5, 8a—**put . . . under**]).

Second, it is no coincidence that the quotation from Ps 8:4-6 in Heb 2:6b-8a appears in proximity to Ps 110:1 in Heb 1:13. Early Christians interpreted these texts in tandem as prophecies regarding the exaltation of Jesus, using a rabbinic hermeneutical technique called *gezerah shawah* (→ 4:3b-5 sidebar, "Verbal Analogy"). This was a principle of analogy, whereby two texts were mutually interpreted based on catchwords or phrases appearing in both of them, as follows:

Ps 110:1   "until I make your enemies a footstool for *your feet*"
Ps 8:6   "put everything under *his feet*"

Paul draws together the same two texts as dual testimony to the fact that God has placed "all things" or "enemies" under the feet of the exalted Christ (1 Cor 15:25-27; Eph 1:20-22; see Phil 3:21; 1 Pet 3:22). Hebrews is probably an heir to this interpretive heritage.

Third, in the two parallel clauses of the Ps 8:4, **What is man that you are mindful of him, the son of man that you care for him?** (Heb 2:6b-c), a straightforward reading would equate **man** (i.e., humanity) with **son of man** ("mere human beings" [GNT]). Synonymous parallelism is common in Hebrew poetry and would tend to support such a reading. The preacher would also know from his extensive knowledge of the OT that the expression **son of man** can be employed simply as an equivalent for **man** (e.g., ninety-three times in Ezekiel).

However, it is difficult to escape what must have leapt off the page for early Christian readers. It is "the man Christ Jesus" (1 Tim 2:5; see Rom 5:15, 17) who in the NT is "the Son of Man" (Heb 2:6c GW). They identified him with the regal figure in Dan 7:13-14, who is granted universal dominion (as in Ps 110:1 and Ps 8:6). This is the Son of Man sitting (or standing in Acts 7:56) at the right hand of God (Matt 26:64; Mark 14:62; Luke 22:69; see Heb 1:3, 13).

The lack of the definite article **the** before **son of man** in the Greek text (Ps 8:5 LXX in Heb 2:6c) does not rule out interpreting the expression as a christological title, since identical wording elsewhere refers to Jesus as Son of Man (John 5:27; Rev 1:13; 14:14). It is significant to note, as well, that Heb 2:5-18 is enclosed by sections (1:1—2:4 and 3:1-6) in which Jesus is prominently identified as the divine "Son" (1:2, 5 [two times], 8; 3:6), as he is throughout Hebrews ("Son" [5:5, 8; 7:28]; "Son of God" [4:14; 6:6; 7:3; 10:29]). In Hebrews, Jesus is both the quintessential human being in his complete identification with suffering and mortal humanity, and Son of Man in his regal authority at God's right hand.

Fourth, in 2:7-8a the preacher reads this selection from Ps 8 in a way that highlights the proper sequence of major events related to the incarnation. The preacher's use of the Greek version of the OT (the LXX) facilitated his unique and inspired interpretation of the psalm. The Hebrew text of Ps 8:5 clearly expresses the idea of humanity's preeminence within the created order. In the Hebrew text humanity ranks only a little lower than "God" (HCSB, NASB, NIV^{mg}, NLT, NRSV; "a god" [NAB, NJB, REB]). The common Hebrew word for "God [*Ělōhîm*]" may also be translated "heavenly beings" (ESV, NIV) or "angels" (KJV, NCV), following the LXX. For the preacher, however, the psalmist is not making a statement about the exalted state of humanity, but the humiliation of the Son of Man.

An interpretive possibility in the LXX (quoted in Hebrews) lends itself to this reading. The NIV's **a little** (2:7a, 9a) preserves the ambiguity of the LXX's *brachy ti*. This expression may faithfully render the almost certain idea of space or degree in the Hebrew text of Ps 8:5a ("a little bit"). But both in the LXX and in Heb 2:7a, 9a it more likely conveys the idea of a brief period of time: **for a little while** (NIV^{mg}, ESV, NAB, NASB, NET, NIV^{11mg}, NRSV; "for a season" [TYNDALE]).

Thus, instead of the two clauses in Ps 8:5 being parallel and synonymous, they are viewed as antithetical. **You made him for a little while [NIV^{mg}] lower than the angels** refers to the Son's entrance "into the world" (10:5), commencing "the days of Jesus' life on earth" (5:7). This is the first phase of Christ's incarnation, when he participated fully in the frailty and mortality of human life (2:14) and provided for the purification of sins (1:3; 10:10). **You crowned him with glory and honor** is the second phase, the exaltation that followed the Son's temporary humiliation. It is his enthronement at God's right hand (1:3c, 13; 8:1; 10:12; 12:2). The third phase of the Son's fulfillment of the divine purpose is envisioned in 2:8a.

■ **8** Another pair of parallel clauses appears in Ps 8:6, but the quotation in Hebrews passes over the first of them ("You made him ruler over the works of your hands"). As a result, the preacher's reading of the psalm text does not expand upon the dominion of humanity over creation celebrated in Ps 8:5. Rather, it foretells the culmination, not only of the Son's life of obedience and suffering, but of world history under the Son's authority in the age to come: God **put everything under his feet** (see Heb 1:13; 10:13). The three-part movement of the incarnation (from suffering and death, to exaltation, to final supremacy over all creation) will be clarified in the interpretation of the psalm text that follows in 2:8b-9.

A brief interpretation of Ps 8:4-6 begins in Heb 2:8b-c by seizing upon the phrase **put everything under** from the last line of the quotation. The verb *subjected* (**put . . . under**; *hypotassō*) was introduced in 2:5 in anticipation of the Scripture quotation. It is now repeated twice (**putting . . . under** [2:8b]; **subject** [2:8c]) and joined by the related adjective **not subject** (*anypotakton* [2:8b]).

The first statement in 2:8b is a synonymy (or "interpretation") in which a speaker restates an idea to deepen its impact on the audience (*Rhet. Her.* 4.28.38):

> *For* **in putting everything under him,**
> **God left nothing that is not subject to him**.

Not as easily seen in English is the chiastic (x-shaped, ABB'A') pattern in Greek:

subjecting (*hypotaxai*)   all things (*panta*)

                              x

nothing (*ouden*)   unsubjected (*anypotakton*)

Thus, the preacher states categorically that the Son has dominion over everything. Many scholars think this verse is about humankind, as reflected in the translation "to them" (NIV[11], NRSV; see REB) instead of **to him** (*autō*). Others think the author is intentionally being ambiguous, so that **him** can refer either to humanity or to Jesus (deSilva 2000a, 109-10). These interpretations are not impossible, especially since the glorious destiny of the people of God intertwines with that of the Son in 2:10-18. However, the christological thrust of the quotation and interpretation of the psalm seems uppermost (→ 2:6-7).

Shockingly, the preacher presents an apparent challenge to the Son's universal authority: **Yet at present we do not see everything subject to him.** The author does not directly contradict the statement in 2:8b. He does not say that everything is *not* subject to him. Rather, he says we do not presently see (emphasis added) everything that already has been (as the Greek perfect tense suggests) and indeed is **subject** (*hypotetagmena*) to him. Other translations clarify an important detail in Greek: we do **not yet** (*oupō*) see everything subjected to him (ESV, HCSB, KJV, NASB, NCV, NET, NRSV, REB).

The preacher's concern is eschatological as well as perceptual. **Yet at present** contrasts with "the world to come" (2:5), which has already been subjected to the Son but has not been finally manifested in divine judgment and salvation. Psalm 8:6b (in Heb 2:8a), as we have already seen, may be correlated with Ps 110:1 (in Heb 1:13). The paradox, readily apparent in Paul's exposition of both texts in 1 Cor 15:24-28, is that indeed God has placed all things under Christ's feet (1 Cor 15:27-28; see Eph 1:20-22), yet "he must reign until he has put all his enemies under his feet" (1 Cor 15:25).

So also Heb 10:12-13 neatly distinguishes between the enthronement of the Son at God's right hand and the final subjugation of his enemies. Therefore, by faith we can see "the Day approaching" (10:25) when our salvation will be complete and the last enemy destroyed (see 1 Cor 15:26). But **at present we do not yet see** it with our eyes. There is a sustained interplay between what is seen by faith and what is seen or not yet seen with the eyes in Heb 11:1, 3, 7, 13, 26-27.

■ **9** Verse 8b-c focuses on the last line of the psalm (Ps 8:6b in Heb 2:8a). In 2:9 the two previous lines (Ps 8:5 in Heb 2:7) serve as the basis for an authoritative interpretation of the incarnation and its implications for humanity. The intricacy of the Greek composition is difficult to capture in English translation. Here is my own literal translation of 2:9, which attempts to do so:

> *But it is the one who for a little while was made lower than the angels whom we see, Jesus, because of the suffering of death crowned with glory and honor, so that by the grace of God he might taste death for everyone.*

Observe that what we do not now see in 2:8c stands in contrast to what we do see here in 2:9. The word translated **we see** (*blepomen*) is the principal verb of the entire sentence. **Jesus,** described with language from the psalm quotation, is the object of our seeing. Note how the name of the One borne witness to in the psalm is flung to the end of the first clause in Greek (see the ESV and NASB). This arrangement heightens the suspense, since this is the first occurrence of his proper name in Hebrews.

Use of the Name "Jesus" in Hebrews

Deferred placement of Jesus' name for emphasis is unique to Hebrews. Out of the nine occurrences of the name Jesus by itself (not, e.g., "Jesus Christ"), eight times it stands emphatically in Greek either at the end of a clause (2:9; 6:20; 12:2, 24; see 4:14) or sentence (3:1; 7:22; 10:19; 13:20). In this way the preacher draws attention to the humanity of the One who bears that incomparable name: Jesus.

The psalm quoted in 2:7a bears witness to the temporary abasement of Jesus. The word order of the psalm in Greek (**You made him for a little while** [NIVmg] **lower than the angels**) is altered here to *for a little while made lower than the angels.* The phrase **for a little while** is pushed toward the beginning of the sentence to prioritize the idea of brevity. (→ 2:6-8 on **for a little while** [NIVmg].) However, that Jesus' humiliation is temporary does not minimize its importance; indeed, his exaltation depends upon it.

The psalm also testifies to Jesus' high position, **now crowned with glory and honor.** The image of crowning is associated with the recognition of someone's athletic victory (1 Cor 9:25; 2 Tim 2:5) or reward for faithful endurance (Jas 1:12; 1 Pet 5:4; Rev 2:10). Jesus' crowning was the fitting sequel to his having been made low. More precisely, he was crowned **because *of the suffering of death*.** Both the grammatical construction and the understanding of Jesus' suffering throughout Hebrews (2:10, 18; 5:8; 9:26; 13:12) suggest that the preacher is talking about suffering that *is* death. Thus, the NIV helpfully translates, **because he suffered death.**

For the writer to the Hebrews, then, Ps 8:7 would be one of the very prophecies that "predicted the sufferings of Christ and the glories that would follow" (1 Pet 1:11). Jesus himself spoke of his messianic destiny foretold by the prophets, "Did not the Christ have to suffer these things and then enter his glory?" (Luke 24:26). This suffering-to-glory theme is also evident in Paul's famous Christ-hymn, in which (as in Hebrews) it is precisely **because** of Christ's humble, obedient, and disgraceful death (i.e., on a cross) that, "Therefore God exalted him to the highest place" (Phil 2:9).

Finally, the purpose of Jesus' incarnation, and more particularly his death, finds expression at the end of Heb 2:9 (**so that** . . .). The greatest scandal of the Christian faith is Christ crucified. Paul said it is "a stumbling block to Jews and foolishness to Gentiles" (1 Cor 1:23). In the next section the preacher will demonstrate the appropriateness and necessity of Jesus' complete identification with humanity through suffering. For now, though, he anticipates that discussion by stating three important things about the purpose of Jesus' death:

First, the death of Jesus was initiated **by the grace of God.** Grace is at the heart of the gospel, in that God "did not spare his own Son, but gave him up for us all" (Rom 8:32). Death had come through Adam, but "how much more did God's grace and the gift that came by the grace of the one man, Jesus Christ, overflow to the many!" (Rom 5:15). These are passages Chrysostom points out in his homily on our present text (1996, 383). He could have also pointed to Eph 1:6-7: "to the praise of his glorious grace, which he has freely given us in the One he loves. In him we have redemption through his blood, the forgiveness of sins, in accordance with the riches of God's grace." God's grace is mentioned explicitly only a half-dozen more times in Hebrews (see 4:16 [two times]; 10:29; 12:15; 13:9, 25), but stands no less as the foundation (along with holiness) of God's dealings with humanity, for his throne is "the throne of grace" (4:16).

"By the grace of God" or "apart from God" (2:9)?

The reading "by the grace of God [*chariti theou*]" has early and widespread support among Greek NT manuscripts, including the important and early 𝔓⁴⁶. However, the variant reading "apart from God [*chōris theou*]," meagerly attested in late Greek manuscripts and versions, was amply defended by many church fathers. Origen found it in some manuscripts as early as the third century.

Both readings figured into christological controversies. Orthodox writers, such as Athanasius and Ambrose, argued from the reading "apart from God" that the divine nature did not participate in Christ's suffering (the doctrine of divine impassibility). Other Orthodox fathers, such as Oecumenius and Theophylact, accused the Nestorians of introducing this reading into the text (see the hurling of accusations back and forth in the selections from Oecumenius and Theodore of Mopsuestia in Heen and Krey 2005, 38-39).

While "apart from God" is the more difficult reading, its appearance is easily explained: a scribe mistook the word "by grace [*chariti*]" for "apart from [*chōris*]." Or, a marginal note ("apart from God") for Heb 2:8, inspired by Paul's qualification of Ps 8:6 in I Cor 15:27, was mistaken as a correction for the reading "by the grace of God" in Heb 2:9. A later scribe then transferred this marginal note into the text of 2:9.

Given the overwhelming textual support for "by the grace of God," and the transcriptional probabilities for the rise of the variant reading "apart from God," the former is likely to have been the original reading. Besides, that Jesus tasted death "by the grace of God" makes much more sense in the context (for more detailed discussion of this textual issue, see Metzger 1994, 594; Hughes 1977, 94-97).

Second, the death of Jesus was real. The phrase **taste death** may give the impression of a mere sampling, as some would interpret it (e.g., Chrysostom and Luther). However, this is a biblical idiom that indicates the real and personal experience of death (see Matt 16:28; Mark 9:1; Luke 9:27; John 8:52). Jesus drank his fill of death; he drained the bitter cup to its dregs.

Third, the death of Jesus was vicarious, that is, it was experienced on behalf of others. The scope of Jesus' representation was universal. He tasted death **for everyone.** Jesus did not die for only a chosen few, but for the whole world (so, e.g., 1 John 2:2; 2 Cor 5:14-15; 1 Tim 2:4-6). He died even for those who might turn aside from him, and effectively crucify him all over again (Heb 6:6), trample him under foot, and desecrate his covenant blood that sanctified them (10:29).

b. Jesus' Identification with Humanity (2:10-18)

Having mentioned the suffering of Jesus' death in 2:9, the preacher now turns to an explanation of why it is that the Son became fully human—even to the point of death. The discussion is framed by statements about the appropriateness (2:10) and necessity (2:17*a*) of Jesus' suffering.

The first part of the discussion (2:10-13) demonstrates the divine intention for Jesus to be in full solidarity with the people of God, not least with scriptural declarations by Jesus himself to this effect (2:12-13). The second part (2:14-18) details the benefits of Jesus' sharing in our humanity, especially his deliverance of the people of God from the fear of death (2:14-16), and his preparation for high-priestly service on their behalf before God (2:17-18).

■ 10 The core assertion in 2:10 is stunning: it was appropriate for God to perfect the author of salvation through suffering. The verb **it was fitting** (*eprepen*) stands at the head of the sentence in Greek. It refers to something that is fitting, suitable, or appropriate to someone or to a set of circumstances. The verb occurs only six other times in the NT in contexts where something is fitting in the sense either of being appropriate to meeting a need (as in 7:26) or being morally proper (Matt 3:15; 1 Cor 11:13; Eph 5:3; 1 Tim 2:10; Titus 2:1). Only here is the word used in reference to **God.**

There seems to be something inappropriate in deliberating about what might or might not be fitting for God. It is a train of thought much more at home in Hellenistic philosophy than in Jewish theology. Yet even in Hellenistic Jewish thought it would have been an impropriety to identify God with suffering humanity. Here in Hebrews, as in the rest of the NT, the appropriateness of God's action in the death of Christ is not in its accommodation to human need but in the fulfillment of God's eternal purpose. God is the One **for whom and through whom everything exists** (see Rom 11:36; 1 Cor 8:4-6). That is, in God may be found the origin and destiny of all things. The human tragedy of sin and death did not derail God from "the unchanging nature of his purpose" (Heb 6:17). The death of Christ was in accordance with the express will of God (10:5-10).

So how is it that the Son's death was appropriate for God? It was appropriate to God, whose essential character is described throughout all the Scriptures as gracious (or loving) and holy. These very same essential divine attributes flank our present verse, with grace in 2:9 and holiness in 2:11. The identification of Jesus with humanity through suffering and death fulfills both aspects of God's nature, while at the same time accomplishing God's purpose for humanity. How this is so will unfold only as we learn more concerning Jesus' atoning death and high-priestly ministry in Hebrews.

The purpose of God in perfecting Christ is to be found **in bringing many sons to glory.** Scholars debate whether the participle **bringing** (*agagonta*) belongs with God or with Jesus (i.e., **the author of . . . salvation**). Choosing between the two options is of no real consequence, though the latter is more likely. On the one hand, God's purpose is to bring many sons to glory—in other words, **their salvation.** Glorification is God's desired end for those who are in Christ (see Rom 8:30). On the other hand, the participle most certainly belongs with the following word in the Greek text (**author** [*archēgon*]), since the two words are in grammatical agreement (see deSilva 2000a, 112 n. 56). So, in fulfillment of God's purpose, Jesus is the One who brings **many sons to glory.** He stooped down into our world of suffering and was consequently crowned with glory and honor (2:7, 9), so that as our "forerunner" (6:20 NIV[11]) he could lead us into the glorious presence of God.

In characteristic style, the preacher engages in a clever wordplay in this verse. The title for Jesus, **author** (*archēgos*), is difficult to render into English (→ 2:10 sidebar, "Jesus the Champion"). It is played off against two related words in this verse. The second part of *archēgos* is derived from the verb *agō* ("to lead, bring"), which is the root of the participle we have already encountered (*agagonta*, **bringing, leading**). Jesus, the "leader [*archēgos*]," "leads [*agagonta*]" **many sons to glory**.

The first part of the word *archēgos* is derived from the noun *archē*, "beginning." This produces a pun with the word for **make . . . perfect** (*teleiōsai*), which means to bring something to its proper end or goal (→ 5:9 sidebar, "Playing with Beginnings and Endings"). Aside from this wordplay, to **make . . . perfect** also carries the connotation of Jesus' being prepared or qualified for priestly ministry. The language of perfection (the verb *teleioō* and noun *teleiōsis*) occurs in connection with the consecration of priests in the law of Moses (Exod 29:9, 29, 33, 35; Lev 4:5; 7:27; 8:33; 16:32; 21:10; Num 3:3; see Lane 1991, 57-58).

Jesus the Champion

The title for Jesus in 2:10 (**author** [*archēgos*]) is difficult to translate, as evidenced by the many translations of the word: "author" (NASB, NIV); "leader" (NAB, NJB, NLT); "pioneer" (NIV[11], NRSV, REB); "founder" (ESV); "source" (GW, HCSB); "captain" (KJV); "lorde" (TYNDALE). While not a rare word, neither is it commonplace, occurring twenty-seven times in the LXX with many different meanings, and only four times in the NT (Acts 3:15; 5:31; Heb 2:10; 12:2), solely as a title for the risen, exalted Jesus.

The word had an archaic, literary flavor that conjured up images of ancient founders of cities, renowned patrons, or divine heroes. The context of 2:10-18 suggests that Jesus is being portrayed as a champion for the people of God, almost like the famous Greek hero Hercules who was the "champion [*archēgos*]" and "savior [*sōtēr*]" who triumphed over Death, "the dark-robed lord of the dead" (Euripides, *Alc.* 2.843-44; see Lane 1991, 56-57; Witherington 2007, 149). Jesus took on flesh and blood in order to triumph in mortal combat with the devil and deliver people from the fear of death. Thus, Jesus is the "the champion who initiates and perfects our faith" (12:2 NLT).

■ **11** That the perfection of God's champion through suffering meant his qualification as high priest is confirmed in 2:11. Here Jesus is designated as the **one who makes *people*** [NIV[11]] **holy**. To make **holy** (*hagiazō*), or to sanctify or consecrate, is the principal function of a priest. In a Jewish context, it involved cleansing people from their sins so as to prepare them for worship (1:3; 9:13-14, 22; 10:2, 22), marking them off as holy, that is, devoted to God. This is now accomplished through Jesus' sacrificial death (10:10, 14, 29; 13:12).

The perfection of Jesus through suffering was appropriate and necessary, because the only way for people to be identified with a holy God is through holiness (12:10, 14). **Both the one who makes *people* [NIV¹¹] holy [*ho' hagiazōn*] and those who are made holy** (*hoi hagiazomenoi*) are related to God through holiness.

Indeed, the source of all holiness is God. Both the sanctifier and the sanctified are "all of one" (as the KJV literally renders *ex henos pantes*). English versions generally translate the expression *ex henos* ("from one") as a reference to God ("one Father" [HCSB, NASB, NRSV]; "same Father" [GW, NLT]), a reference more generally to "origin" (ESV, NAB, NET, RSV), or to membership in the **same family** (CEV, NCV, NIV; "of the same stock" [NJB]; "of one stock" [REB]). The following train of thought, focused on Jesus' kinship with humanity, speaks in favor of the rendering **of the same family.** However, this translation too quickly puts the *result* of God's work in Christ (note the **So** in 2:11*b*) in place of its *source* (implied by the preposition *ek/ex*, "from"). Furthermore, the masculine gender of the word *henos* ("one"), as well as the preceding designation of God as the One "for whom and through whom everything exists" (2:10), seem to indicate that the association between sanctifier and sanctified stems from only one source, God.

So, or more precisely, "For this reason [*di' hēn aitian*]" (NRSV) introduces the result of God's holy work in perfecting Jesus and leading many sons to glory through his death and exaltation: **Jesus is not ashamed to call them brothers.** The preacher uses a figure of speech called litotes—understatement (e.g., when "not a little" means "a lot, many" in Acts 12:18; 14:28; 15:2; 17:4, 12; 19:23; 26:29; 27:20). When it says Jesus is **not ashamed,** it means that he is *honored* to call them siblings (see Rom 1:16). God spoke similarly about the faithful patriarchs (Heb 11:16).

The irony is that the path to such an honorable position for both Christ and his siblings was through the disgrace of his suffering and death (see 13:12-13). Endurance of present disgrace in view of future glory was the same path pursued by Moses (11:26), and has already been experienced in some measure by the audience (10:36); but it is Jesus' own example ("despising the shame" [12:2 ESV, KJV, NASB, NKJV, RSV]; "bearing the disgrace" [13:13]) that encourages the Hebrew Christians to persevere in their faith to continue on as members of God's family (3:6).

The words "brothers and sisters" (NIV¹¹) anticipate their appearance in the first Scripture quotation that follows in the next verse. A prominent facet of God's saving work in Christ Jesus is the adoption of believers as children of God (Rom 8:15, 23; Gal 4:5; Eph 1:5) or heirs of the kingdom (Rom 8:17; 1 Cor 6:9-10; 15:50; Gal 3:29; 4:7; 5:21; Eph 1:14, 18; 5:5; Col 3:24; Titus 3:7; Heb 1:14; 6:17; 9:15; 1 Pet 1:4; 3:9; Rev 21:7). "For those God foreknew," writes Paul, "he also predestined to be conformed to the likeness of his Son, that he might be the firstborn among many brothers" (Rom 8:29).

■ **12** The scriptural demonstration of Jesus' sibling relationship with those he has sanctified follows in 2:12-13. Three passages from the OT are quoted. Two things are significant about them.

First, they are cited as quotations from Jesus himself. The word translated **He says** at the head of 2:12 does not actually start a new sentence in Greek. Rather, it completes the thought in 2:11 that Jesus is not ashamed to call them brothers, **saying** . . . (*legōn*). To regard the scriptures as not only being about Christ, but spoken by him, is a unique aspect of Hebrews' use of Scripture.

Second, the author selects Scripture passages from contexts that were already well-known for their testimony to Christ, as we shall see.

The first quotation from Ps 22 was a scripture that deeply enriched the early church's understanding of Jesus' death. The preacher hears the voice of Jesus speaking in Ps 22:22: **I will declare your name to my brothers; in the presence of the congregation I will sing your praises.** Jesus acknowledges his "brothers and sisters" (NIV[11]) in the **congregation** (*ekklēsia*, **church;** see Heb 12:23). The One who is worshiped by angels (1:6) humbled himself below angels to become the leader of the worshiping community. In Hebrews, Jesus' high-priestly ministry prepares believers to draw near to God in worship (4:16; 7:19; 10:19-22; 12:22-29 [esp. vv 24 and 28]; 13:15).

Psalm 22: Jesus as Sufferer and Worship Leader

2:12-13

Psalm 22 is notably connected with the passion of Christ in the NT (Ps 22:7 [Matt 27:39 and Mark 15:29]; 22:7-8 [Matt 27:43 and Luke 23:35-36]; 22:15 [John 19:28]; 22:18 [Matt 27:35; Mark 15:24; Luke 23:34; John 19:24]). Indeed, its very first line (Ps 22:1*a*) served as Jesus' last words from the cross in Mark 15:34 and Matt 27:46: "My God, my God, why have you forsaken me?"

Hebrews likely quotes from this psalm because it was already recognized as a rich source for christological reflection. Uniquely, however, Hebrews quotes from the latter portion of the psalm, where the righteous sufferer praises God for his help (Ps 22:22). Here he actually hears the voice of Jesus himself, as the exalted high priest, leading the church into the presence of God to worship.

■ **13** The second and third passages in 2:13 come from the eighth chapter of Isaiah. Isaiah 8:14 was an important prophecy concerning the Christ as a stumbling block for Israel (Luke 2:34; Rom 9:33; 1 Pet 2:8). In the original context of Isaiah, Yahweh foretold both doom and salvation for Israel by way of the names of Isaiah's children (Isa 8:1, 3; 7:3). In a time of national turmoil and unfaithfulness, the prophet resolved to trust God (Isa 8:17) and hold on to the tokens of divine providence given to him in the names of his children (Isa 8:18).

Once again, Hebrews hears in these verses the contemporary voice of Jesus. Perhaps the proximity of the prophecies concerning Immanuel in Isa

7:14 and the Wonderful Counselor in Isa 9:6 contributed to his being attuned to hearing the Messiah's voice in Isa 8.

In the second of the three scriptures, a quotation from Isa 8:17, Jesus says, **I will put my trust in him** (Heb 2:13*a*). Jesus has entered into solidarity with humanity through his unqualified trust in God. The hallmark of his humanity in Hebrews is his faithful obedience to God, especially in the face of suffering (5:7-8). His faithfulness qualifies him as the honored Son who is given charge over God's family (or "house"), and he is thus the great example of faithfulness for anyone who is a member of that household (3:1-6). Jesus' faithful endurance makes him "the author and perfecter" of faith (12:2). Paul, too, spoke of the key significance of "the faithfulness of Jesus Christ" (Rom 3:22 CEB, NET; Gal 2:16 CEB, NET; 3:22 CEB, NET).

The third passage in Heb 2:13*b* is added (**and again he says**) to complete the thought that Jesus has been united with the people of God. **Here am I**, Jesus says in the words of Isa 8:18, **and the children God has given me.** Those who belong to the family of God are not part of a club instituted by human beings. They are people who have responded to the divine call (3:1; 9:15; see Rom 8:28). They are, as Jesus asserts repeatedly in the Gospel of John, those whom the Father has given him (John 6:39; 10:29; 17:2, 6, 7, 9, 24; 18:9).

■ **14** The Son participated fully in humanity so as to come to its rescue (Heb 2:14). The incarnation was a result (***Therefore*** [*oun*]; untranslated in the NIV) of the divine intention for humanity's salvation. Likewise, the Son's suffering allowed him to experience fully the predicament of humanity. This was only appropriate, given the character of God revealed in Scripture (→ 2:10).

Picking up on the language from the scripture just quoted in 2:13*b*, the author points to **the children** whom Christ came to save. It is **since the children have flesh and blood** that **he too shared in their humanity.** What humanity ***holds in common*** (*kekoinōnēken*, **have**) is **flesh and blood**. The idiom **flesh and blood** does not refer simply to bodily existence. That could equally be communicated by the expression "flesh and bones" (Luke 24:39; see Gen 2:23; Job 2:5). **Flesh and blood** emphasizes the inferiority of humanity to God (Matt 16:17; Gal 1:16), as well as frailty and mortality (1 Cor 15:50; see Sir 14:18). The latter connotation fits the following references to the power and fear of death (Heb 2:14*b*, 15). In Hebrews the word order is inverted to ***blood and flesh*** (as in Eph 6:11). By placing **blood** first, the author may subtly hint at Jesus' sacrificial death, a central theme in Hebrews (Isaacs 2002, 43).

Jesus' full participation in the human condition is expressed forcefully in the clause **he too shared in their humanity**. First, **he** is an emphatic personal pronoun in the Greek text, often translated "he himself" (ESV, KJV, NASB, NRSV). Second, Jesus' complete identification with humanity is doubly expressed. He ***in just the same way*** (*paraplēsiōs*, "similarly, likewise"; **too**) shared ***in the same things*** (*tōn autōn*, see ESV, NRSV; **their humanity**). Jesus' humanity was no shadow or phantom. Hebrews stresses the identity of Jesus as a human being "in every way" (2:17).

Yet there is a distinction between humanity's sharing in flesh and blood and Jesus' participation in the same. Humanity's participation is a long-standing state of affairs characteristic of its identity (perfect tense *kekoinōnēken*, "share, have a share," **have**). But for Christ, human nature was not native to him. The divine Son **partook** of or **shared** (aorist tense *meteschen*) in human nature as a historical act in obedience to God's will (10:5-10). Bengel notes that the verb for **shared** (*meteschen*) may express the likeness of one to the rest; **hold in common** (*kekoinōnēken*) to the likeness of many among one another (Bengel 1877, 4:364).

The incarnation has a twofold purpose: First, negatively, to destroy the one who held the power of death. Second, positively, to deliver those who were held captive by the fear of death.

The first prong of the purpose statement (*hina*, so that) is in 2:14*b*. Jesus came to **destroy him who holds the power of death—that is, the devil**. Nowhere else in the Bible is the **power of death** so expressly attributed to **the devil**. However, a Christian reading of the story of humanity's fall in Gen 3 reveals the devil's role in deceiving Adam and Eve to take the path toward death (see also Wis 2:23-24). According to John 8:44 the devil is the primal murderer and liar, and in 1 John 3:12 Cain's murder of his brother is the sin most intimately associated with one who belongs to the evil one.

The devil does not possess the power of death inherently, but only by way of trickery and intimidation (Acts 13:10; Eph 6:11; 1 Tim 3:6-7; 2 Tim 2:26; Rev 12:9; 20:10), and cannot inflict a mortal blow unless God allows it (Job 1:12; 2:6). Christ came to **destroy** the devil. Here is the same verb (*katargeō*, "render powerless or ineffective") used by Paul of the last enemy to be "destroyed"—death (1 Cor 15:26; see 2 Thess 2:8; 2 Tim 1:10; 1 John 3:8).

The means by which Jesus dealt a deathblow to the devil was **by his own death**. How can this be so? The preacher does not explain, but we may infer several things from what he says elsewhere in Hebrews about Jesus' death: His death was in obedience to the will of God (10:10; see 5:7). His death was undeserved, for when tested through suffering he never sinned (2:18; 4:15). He is "holy, blameless, pure, set apart from sinners" (7:26) who endured such hostility from sinners (12:3).

Therefore, since he did not die on account of any sin he had done, his was a death purely for others. He "taste[d] death for everyone" (2:9) to ransom them from their sins (9:15; see 1:3; 2:17; 7:27; 9:26, 28; 10:12). Because his death was not due to his own sins, but an act of holy obedience, "it was impossible for death to keep its hold on him" (Acts 2:24; see Heb 7:16). In this way Jesus the champion (*archēgos* [2:10]) wielded the devil's own instrument of terror and enslavement against him.

■ 15 The second, related purpose of Jesus' death is to **free** people from the **fear of death**. The dire condition of death's victims is described as persistent, enslaving fear. This death phobia is a chronic condition of human existence. It is "lifelong" (ESV; **all their lives**), so that it holds sway over all of our attitudes, decisions, and relationships. The enslavement is expressed redundantly as being **held in** [*enochoi*, "subject to" (ESV, KJV, NAB, NASB)] **slavery** (*douleias*).

Ancient Philosophy on the Fear of Death

Greco-Roman authors commonly compared the fear of death to slavery. Euripides wrote, "Are you a slave and afraid of death, which might set you free from suffering?" (*Orest.* 1522). Others commented on this famous line. Philo wrote "that nothing is so calculated to enslave the mind as fearing death through desire to live" (*Good Person* 22). Plutarch wrote, "Who can be a slave if he gives no heed to death" (*Mor.* 34b).

Ancient moral philosophers often spoke of the emotional well-being achieved by overcoming the fear of death. Epicureans sought to dissuade their students from fearing death by rationalizing that in the end it is really nothing at all. Death is merely the termination of one's existence, so one has no reason to fear eternal punishment (Lucretius, *Nat.* 1.102-26). The typical Epicurean epitaph was, "I wasn't, I was, I am not, I don't care." Stoics pointed to death as the ultimate escape from suffering or appealed to a sense of honor by encouraging people to face death nobly, as Socrates did. Seneca wrote that human reason "makes us joyful in the very sight of death, strong and brave no matter in what state the body may be" (*Ep.* 30.3).

In Hebrews, however, the preacher does not tackle the fear of death by diminishing its reality (9:27). Nor does he present Jesus' valiant battle with death merely as a noble example of how to endure suffering, though that it is. More than this, Jesus' own triumph over death means that he can "save completely" (7:25) from death's tyranny (2:14-15). Through his own suffering, the Son was perfected as "the source of eternal salvation for all who obey him" (5:9). Believers have the hope that they are on the path to glory that their champion, Jesus, trail-blazed for them.

■ 16 The preacher interjects in a conversational manner, **For surely it is not angels he helps, but Abraham's descendants**. First, he marks his words emphatically with the word **surely** or ***of course*** (*dēpou*). Second, he abruptly switches to the present tense (**helps**). But what may appear as an interruption helps to tie together the discussions in 2:5-9 and 2:10-18 through references to angels (2:5, 7, 9, 16). The sermon has thus far been punctuated with comparisons between Jesus and angels (see also 1:4, 5, 6, 7, 13; 2:2). (Only two more references to angels will occur toward the close of the discourse [12:22; 13:2].) The reference to angels in 2:16 signals a conclusion to the introductory parts of the sermon and leads into the statement of facts (→ 2:17-18 and Behind the Text on 2:5-18).

The meaning of the verb *epilambanetai* (**helps**) has been the subject of debate. The church fathers (both Greek and Latin) unanimously translated this verb as "takes hold of," and understood it to mean that the Son took upon himself human nature. This view was maintained by the Scholastics, as well as Reformers such as Calvin. Modern scholars have generally rejected this classical interpretation, opting instead for another attested meaning of the verb, "assist, help, be concerned about" (see esp. Sir 4:11). They have been followed by most English translations ("helps" [ESV, GNT, GW, HCSB, NAB, NASB, NCV, NIV, NLT, NRSV]; "concern" [NET]; "is concerned" [RSV]), with few exceptions ("took [or taketh] on" [KJV, TYNDALE]; "took [or takes] to himself" [NEB, NJB]; "become" [PHILLIPS]).

Neither of these interpretations does justice to the text of Hebrews. On the one hand, both **angels** and **Abraham's descendants** are classes of beings, not anything as abstract as human nature or as concrete as "flesh and blood" that one would "take on." In any case, despite the opinion of the church fathers (driven as it was by christological controversy), the verb *epilambanomai* is never employed in the sense "assume the nature of." Even Chrysostom, who promotes the patristic interpretation, acknowledges that the text of Hebrews reads "takes hold of" not "took on him" (1996, 388).

On the other hand, a translation such as **helps** or "be concerned with" is far too weak. The verb strongly conveys the action of grasping, seizing, or taking hold of. Looking forward to 2:18, the preacher will only then explicitly state that Jesus comes to our aid, using the common and expected verb for **help** (*boētheō*). But grasping the meaning of *epilambanomai* in 2:16 is achieved by looking backward to the string of vivid images in 2:14-15.

Jesus is described as "break[ing] the power" (NIV[11]) of the devil, who has death in his grip (*ton to kratos echonta*; lit., "who has the hold" [2:14]; note the cognate verb *krateō*, "hold fast" [4:14 ESV, KJV, LEB, NASB, NRSV; 6:18 ESV, LEB]). Consequently, Jesus can "free" or release (*apallaxē* [2:15]) people who have been "held" in slavery to the fear of death (*enochos*; "pert. to being held in or constrained" [BDAG, 338]). So Jesus *releases* people from the devil's *hold* on death. He **takes hold of** (*epilabanetai* [2:16]) those who were *held* in slavery to the fear of death. The verb *epilambanomai* occurs only once more in Hebrews, in the quotation from Jer 31:32 in Heb 8:9. There likewise the action of grasping is for the purpose of deliverance.

Why does Jesus take hold of **Abraham's descendants** (lit., "seed of Abraham") rather than humanity in general? This expression has particular theological significance in connection with the theme of divine inheritance. That theme has resonated in the first chapter concerning both the Son (1:1, 4) and those he saves (1:14) in contrast with angels. The Son brings to fulfillment the promise to Abraham of numerous descendants (see 11:12) in his "bringing many sons to glory" (2:10). The heirs of the promise to Abraham are those who hold on firmly to the hope of salvation in Jesus Christ (6:11-20).

True, this hope is available to all, since Jesus tasted death for everyone (2:9). However, it avails only for those who become true sons (2:10; 12:5, 7-8). It is for those who are sanctified (2:11a) and are therefore brothers (2:11b, 12, 17; see 3:1, 12; 10:19; 13:1, 22), partners with Christ (3:1, 14), members of the church (*ekklēsia* [2:12]; see 12:23), God's children (2:13-14), and God's "people [*laos*]" (2:17; see 4:9; 13:12).

■ **17-18** The comparison of Christ with angels ends in v 16. Thus, 2:17-18 serves as a conclusion, not only to the discussion in 2:10-18 concerning Jesus' solidarity with the people of God, but to everything spoken up to this point in the sermon. These two verses also comprise the proposition for the entire discourse. This announces the theme that will occupy the balance of the sermon.

The preacher announces for the first time that Jesus is the **high priest** (*archiereus* [2:17]). This is perhaps intended to play phonetically with the title *archēgos* ("author") in 2:10. One of Jesus' primary high-priestly actions is his making **atonement for . . . sins**. This forms a link with the beginning of the sermon, where the Son is said to have "provided purification for sins" (1:3c). The introduction of Jesus as high priest (2:17) is coupled with encouragement about his assistance in times of testing (2:18). We have in miniature, then, the preacher's procedure throughout the sermon: exposition about Christ as high priest and exhortation to persevere.

For this reason points forward to the purpose (**in order that**) for which Jesus' complete identification with humanity "was essential" (2:17 NJB). The suffering that was regarded as "fitting" (2:10) is a high-priestly obligation (2:17). The verb translated **he had to** (*ōpheilen*) is used in a similar context in 5:3 of a high priest's obligation to offer sacrifices.

Here the effectiveness of Jesus' high-priestly ministry depends upon his having **to be made like** humanity **in every way** (*kata panta*). Of course, **every way** encompasses his suffering and death. **To be made like** (*homoiōthēnai*) means that Jesus shared (*meteschen*) in the very same things that the children have in common (*kekoinōnēken* [2:14]). Specifically, he shared in the frailty and mortality of humanity. This made possible his perfection as high priest through suffering (2:10). Paul similarly says that God sent his Son "in the likeness [*en homoiōmati*] of sinful man to be a sin offering" (Rom 8:3).

Jesus' ministry extends to **his brothers**, already proudly named in 2:11, 12. This anticipates the preacher's direct address to the Hebrews as "holy brothers" in 3:1 and the succeeding discussion of the Son's leadership over God's household (3:1-6).

Thus, Jesus' complete identification with suffering humanity qualified him to **become a merciful and faithful high priest.** He is **merciful** (*eleēmōn*; "compassionate" [NJB]) in that he is able to "sympathize with our weaknesses" because he "has been tempted in every way, just as we are [*kata panta kath' homoiotēta*]—yet was without sin" (4:15; compare **he was tempted . . . those who are being tempted** [2:18]). Therefore, we can "approach the throne of grace with confidence" to "receive mercy [*eleos*] and find grace to help us in our time of need [*boētheia*]" (4:16; compare **help,** *boēthēsai* [2:18]). One can see how the complete likeness, mercy, and help in temptation in 4:15-16 mirror what we find in 2:17-18.

Jesus' high-priestly ministry is **in service to God** (*ta pros ton theon;* lit., "in things pertaining to God" [NASB]). This somewhat uncommon biblical expression is used in contexts in which a minister represents God (Exod 4:16; 18:19; Deut 31:27; Rom 15:17). Both occurrences of the expression in Hebrews (2:17; 5:1) relate to a high priest's representation of the people in matters pertaining to God, especially in connection with offering sacrifices: **that he might make atonement for the sins of the people.**

Propitiation, Expiation, or Atonement?

For the rendering **that he might make atonement** the NIV offers another translation in a footnote: "that he might turn aside God's wrath, taking away [the sins of the people]" (2:17 NIV^mg). This combines two competing views of how to translate the Greek verb *hilaskomai* (and the related words *hilastērion* [Rom 3:23] and *hilasmos* [1 John 2:2; 4:10]).

First, "That he might turn aside God's wrath" reflects the traditional translation "make propitiation" (HCSB, ESV, NASB, NKJV). Second, "taking away [sins]" reflects "make expiation" (REB, RSV; or "expiate" [NAB, NJB]). A more recent trend is to translate the verb as **make atonement** (NIV, NET) or "make a sacrifice of atonement" (NRSV). This avoids the theological debate, as well as the contested sacrificial terms with which most English readers are unfamiliar.

Many modern NT scholars deny the notion of appeasing or conciliating God in the biblical use of the verb *hilaskomai,* despite its widespread use in this sense in the ancient Greek world. It seems objectionable that God's wrath would need to be averted through Christ's sacrifice. Therefore, arguments have been made for interpreting this word group in connection with removing or wiping out sins (expiation) rather than placating God's anger toward sins (propitiation).

However, God's steady, holy hostility toward sin (i.e., his wrath and judgment; see Heb 2:3; 3:10-12, 17-18; 4:3; 6:7-8) is not incompatible with his equally strong love for sinners. Only through the cross could both aspects of the divine nature be adequately put into action: God's condemnation of sin (in which his wrath toward it is exhausted) and his love for sinful humanity.

In Hebrews, continued commitment to the sanctifying work of Christ's sacrifice is essential to being delivered from God's wrath. Missing out on the grace of God (12:15) and sinfully rejecting Christ's sacrifice (10:26, 29) can only expose one to "a fearful expectation of judgment and of raging fire that will consume the enemies of God" (10:27; see 12:29). "It is a dreadful thing to fall into the hands of the living God" (10:31). Therefore, God graciously sent Jesus to "taste death for everyone" (2:9), "to make propitiation for the sins of the people" (2:17 ESV).

In line with what has already been noted (see comments on "Abraham's descendants" [2:16]), Christ's high-priestly work is effected especially on behalf of the **people** of God whom he represents. This people is in historical continuity with the people of Israel, but not merely genetically. The most important links between the Hebrews addressed by the preacher and God's ancient people of Israel are viewed through examples of faithful (6:12-18; 11:1—12:2) or unfaithful responses to God's promises (3:7—4:13; 12:16-17). It is to this topic that the preacher will turn in chs 3—4.

Jesus' ability **to help** [*boēthēsai*] **those who are being tempted** (2:18) is a clear example of his qualification as a **merciful . . . high priest, . . . because he himself suffered when he was tempted.** That Jesus is **faithful** (*pistos*) is likewise associated with his faithful obedience to God in the face of suffering and death (→ 2:13*a* above). Jesus' faithfulness will be highlighted in the following passage (3:1-6).

FROM THE TEXT

Hebrews is one of the most important contributors to our understanding of Christology. The preacher could scarcely relate more fully both the deity and humanity of Christ. Chapter 1 clearly demonstrated the deity of the Son. Chapter 2 (particularly vv 10-16) could not more strongly articulate the full extent of Jesus' identification with humanity. The preacher is not concerned with the debates in philosophical theology pertaining to the two natures of Christ. This was not settled until A.D. 451 with the Definition of Chalcedon. Rather, he is concerned with the question so ably put by Anselm of Canterbury in the title of his influential work on the atonement, *Cur Deus Homo* ("Why God Became Man").

Hebrews captures the cosmic drama of the Son's descent "for a little while lower than the angels" to reach the lowest ebb of human existence—death. He is fully aware that Christ's death was degrading and base in the eyes of the culture around him (→ above Behind the Text sidebar, "The Scandal of Christ's Suffering"). But Jesus' death was actually honorable and courageous, since it was for a noble cause (see Aristotle's exposition of courage in *Eth. nic.* 1115a1-1115b12). Hebrews 2:14-15 may well be the earliest vivid portrayal of the so-called Christus Victor ("Christ the Victor") understanding of the atonement. Jesus is the *archēgos* or champion who successfully takes on the Herculean task of destroying the devil and rescuing humanity from death's tyrannical grip of fear. Yet Jesus' death is also viewed as a propitiatory sacrifice (2:17*c*).

The death of Christ was appropriate because it was grounded in the nature of God, who is gracious and holy (2:9*c*, 11). But it was also necessary because it was only through taking on mortality that he could defeat it. So Jesus, as Anselm explained, did what only God *could* do but what only human beings *ought* to do. It was in his obedient humanity, in fact, that Jesus revealed the love and holiness of God most clearly. Christ as "the man for others" (to borrow Dietrich Bonhoeffer's phrase) was the quintessential man for God.

What then should our response be to this mighty champion who in an epic struggle with the devil freed us from the paralyzing fear of death? For modern readers the conclusion in 2:17-18 might almost seem like an anticlimax, since we are not familiar with the figure of a high priest and we are not nearly as obsessed with the dangers of temptation as first-century Jews and Christians were. The great achievement on our behalf by Jesus, the Great High Priest, is that through his death and exaltation he brings us to God. But "bringing many sons to glory" requires them to be "made holy" (2:10-11). This is why being cleansed from sin and avoiding yielding to temptation are so important.

In Hebrews we can see the beginnings of the doctrine of *theosis* ("divinization") formulated by Greek fathers such as Irenaeus and Athanasius. In Jesus, God became human, so that we could become like God. In the language of Hebrews, Jesus shared (*meteschen* [2:14]) in our humanity so that we could also be sharers (*metochoi*) in his "heavenly calling" (3:1; see 3:14; 6:4; 12:8). This becomes possible because we share in the family likeness of Jesus' faithfulness, courage, hope, and, holiness (2:11*a*; see 12:14). This is why he came, to make us true children of God (2:11*b*, 13*b*; see 12:4-17).

B. Hearing God's Word Today: Jesus the Apostle and High Priest of Our Confession (3:1—4:13)

Normally the statement of facts would be followed by a series of proofs, that is, the main arguments of a speech. (→ Behind the Text for 2:5-18.) But this is not what we find in chs 3—4 of Hebrews. Rather, we find a kind of "second *exordium*," as Quintilian might call it, which "may form a very useful preparation for the examination of the main question," and can be offered "with a view to exciting or mollifying the judge or disposing him to lend a favouring ear to our proofs" (*Inst.* 4.3.9).

Such a digression (Gk. *parekbasis*; Lat. *egressus* or *eggressio*) is "the handling of some theme, which must however have some bearing on the case, in a passage that involves digression from the logical order of the speech" (Quintilian, *Inst.* 4.3.14). It could be used in virtually any part of a speech. It could involve amplifying or abridging a topic, making an emotional appeal, or introducing topics that add charm and elegance to oratory, such as "luxury, avarice, religion, duty." "But these would hardly seem to be digressions as they are so closely attached to arguments on similar subjects that they form part of the texture of the speech" (*Inst.* 4.3.15).

Hebrews 3—4 is a sort of repeat performance of the *exordium* in 1:1—2:4. It compares Jesus and Moses (3:1-6), albeit more succinctly than the comparison between the Son and angels in 1:1-14. In both instances Jesus proves to be superior, with a better name in 1:4 and "greater honor" in 3:3.

In 3:7—4:13 the preacher makes an even more pointed and expansive appeal to his audience than in 2:1-4. He uses Israel's disobedient wilderness experience as a negative example of warning and promise for entering God's Sabbath rest. In rhetorical practice, a speaker uses digression to "extol persons or places, describe regions, record historical examples or even legendary occurrences" (Quintilian, *Inst.* 4.3.12). The preacher does two of these things: he extols Jesus through the comparison with Moses in 3:1-6; he points to the historical precedent of Israel's disobedience (3:7—4:13) and its fearful consequences (3:16-19; 4:1, 5-6, 11).

The theme of hearing God's word returns. What was spoken (*laleō*) by God through the Son "in these last days" (1:1-2), the salvation first spoken "by the Lord" (2:3), is now styled as:

- "what would be said in the future [*tōn lalēthēsomenōn*]" (3:5; see 4:8).
- the preaching of the gospel (4:2, 4).
- the "double-edged sword" of God's word (4:12; see 4:2).

The urgency to heed God's word given through the Son in 2:1-4 is even more pronounced in chs 3—4. The preacher highlights the importance of responding to God's word "Today" (3:13; 4:7). He does this particularly through repetition of the appeal from Ps 95:7-8, "Today, if you hear his voice, do not harden your hearts" (3:7, 15; 4:7). Paying attention to the message (see 2:1) is further identified as holding fast to our confession and confidence in Christ (3:1, 6, 14; 4:14) and responding with faith (4:2) as partners of the faithful Son (3:1-2, 14). This stands in contrast with the unfaithfulness (3:12, 19; 4:2) and disobedience (3:18; 4:6, 11) of Israel's wilderness generation.

Following rhetorical convention, the preacher composed a digression that is really no digression at all. Its topics are so carefully associated with the main argument that it is integrally "part of the texture of the speech" (Quintilian, *Inst.* 4.3.15).

On the one hand, the preacher does shift his attention more pointedly to his audience, twice directly addressing them as "brothers" (3:1, 12). For the first time he issues commands (3:1, 12, 13) and prohibitions (3:8, 15; 4:7). He urges his hearers repeatedly in the first person plural ("Let us . . ." [4:1, 11, 14, 16]). A greater concentration of imperatives, prohibitives, and hortatory subjunctives will not reappear until the end of the sermon (→ introduction to 10:19—13:25; on the hortatory subjunctive, → 4:1 sidebar, "Let us . . ."). The main focus in this section is on the listeners and their response to the summons of God's word.

On the other hand, the author carefully ties this section to the thesis he will argue at length in due course—that Jesus is our Great High Priest. Hebrews 3:1-6 builds upon the preceding section (note the "Therefore" in 3:1, on the heels of 2:5-18). Hebrews 3:1 and 6 anticipate key facts that will recur in 4:14-16:

- heaven ("the heavenly calling" [3:1]; Jesus "has gone through the heavens" [4:14]).
- Jesus as "high priest" (3:1; 4:14, 15).
- Jesus as divine messenger ("apostle" [3:1]; "Son of God" [4:14]; see 1:2, 5; 3:6).
- confession (3:1; 4:14).
- boldness (3:6; 4:16).

Thus, 3:1 and 6 form links to the transitional section in 4:14-16, which itself will function as a restatement and expansion of the proposition stated in 2:17-18.

1. Commitment as Christ's Partners, God's House (3:1-6)

BEHIND THE TEXT

At first glance it may seem that the main topic of this unit is the superiority of Jesus to Moses. Indeed, Jesus' greater glory as the Son over God's house is the fact around which the preacher's comparison pivots. But the comparison of these two figures serves a greater persuasive purpose. This unit is framed by references to the listeners as holy siblings and heavenly partners with Jesus in 3:1 and members of God's household in 3:6. Their proper identity and faithfulness as God's people are crucial to the message of the larger section (3:1—4:13), which this unit introduces.

The householder over God's house, Jesus, is much more honorable than Moses, who was a servant in God's house. Then how much more accountable are present believers to the word of God delivered by the Son than were the people of Israel who heard only the testimony of Moses (see 3:16-19; 4:12-13)? The rhetorical force of both 1:1—2:4 and 3:1—4:13 is quite similar. The preacher deploys expositions of Christ's greatness to reinforce exhortations to greater commitment.

The comparison between Jesus and Moses would have been significant for Christians who had a former association with Judaism. The name "Moses" had become a cipher for the entire Jewish faith. Sufficient examples of this are Paul's reference to the children of Israel being "baptized into Moses" (1 Cor 10:2) and some Jews' accusation that Stephen had blasphemed "against Moses and against God" (Acts 6:11). Moses' stature as the renowned leader and legislator of ancient Israel was well-deserved. He was the archetypal prophet and priest who had unmediated access to God. For as Num 12:6-8 bears witness, the LORD spoke to the prophets through visions, dreams, and riddles, but with Moses "face to face" (see Exod 33:11; Deut 34:10; Sir 45:5).

The Use of Comparison (synkrisis)

Comparison (synkrisis) was a rhetorical exercise used in speeches of either praise or blame (e.g., epideictic speeches, such as eulogies; see Aristotle, *Rhet.*

1.9.38-39). *Synkrisis* could be a comparison of good with good, bad with bad, or good with bad. Its purpose was to extol virtues or to denounce unworthy behavior. It was not to denigrate the character of persons, even those with wicked actions, but to amplify or minimize (as the case may be) those behaviors that should be either emulated or avoided (see *Rhet. Her.* 1441a27-1441b28).

Young students in rhetoric were routinely required to produce biographical comparisons called *progymnasmata* (see Quintilian, *Inst.* 2.4.21). Topics used for comparison included birth, ancestry, education, health, strength, and beauty. Plutarch perfected rhetorical comparisons as an art form in his famous *Parallel Lives* (Thompson 2008, 13).

Hebrews employs *synkrisis* at many points. The author compares Christ with angels (chs 1—2), Moses (3:1-6), and the OT priesthood (5:1-10; 7:1—10:18). He compares present believers with the unfaithful wilderness generation (3:12-13; 4:2-3, 6, 10). This accords with an overall interest in amplifying the fact that Christ and the new covenant are superior to the old (→ 1:4 sidebar, "'Better' Things in Hebrews"). "Amplification," wrote Aristotle, "is with good reason ranked as one of the forms of praise, since it consists in superiority, and superiority is one of the things that are noble" (*Rhet.* 1.9.39).

By the NT period the position of Moses had risen to even greater heights. Not only was he "the noblest Hebrew of them all" (Josephus, *Ant.* 2.229), but according to Hellenistic Jewish historians, he was the father of many advances in culture. These included the invention of the alphabet (Eupolemus in Clement of Alexandria, *Strom.* 1.23.153.4; Eusebius, *Praep. ev.* 9.25.4), ships, stonework pulleys, irrigation, Egyptian weaponry, and philosophy (Artapanus in Eusebius, *Praep. ev.* 9.27.22-25); and, of course, Moses was regarded as the "first religious teacher" (Thallus in Pseudo-Justin, *Coh. ad Graec.* 9).

According to Philo, Moses was appointed by God as Israel's king, lawgiver, high priest, prophet (*Moses* 2.2-3, 6, 66, 187, 292; *Rewards* 53), and even "god and king of the whole nation" (*Moses* 1.158; see Exod 4:16; 7:1). But as God's friend, Moses partook (*metechō*) of God's self and of all God's possessions, thus taking "the whole world" for his inheritance, and gaining mastery over the elements of the cosmos (Philo, *Moses* 1.155-57; see *2 Bar.* 59:3-12).

No one ever "saw the glory of the Lord" like Moses did (Num 12:8 LXX), so that it was reflected in his face (Exod 34:29-30, 35)—until Jesus (Matt 17:1-9; Mark 9:2-10; Luke 9:28-36; 2 Cor 3:12-18). Ben Sirach states that God made Moses "equal in glory to the holy ones" (Sir 45:2), that is, to the angels. Later rabbinic tradition identified Moses as the one crowned with glory and honor in Ps 8 (*b. Rosh Hash.* 21b; *b. Ned.* 38a; *Midr. Ps.* 8:7). Some rabbis even claimed that he was accorded a rank above the ministering angels and the heavenly sanctuary (*Sipre Zuta* on Num 12:6-8; *Sipre Num* 103).

To what extent the author of Hebrews was familiar with such traditions is impossible to determine. If he were aware of a tradition that Moses surpassed the angels in power and glory, then it would not seem needless, after demonstrating Jesus' superiority to angels, to proceed to demonstrate that he is also superior to the more exalted figure of Moses (Lane 1991, 73). Yet the preacher does not offer a polemic against Moses. He offers a comparison (*synkrisis*) between Jesus and Moses. The comparison is based on a detailed look at Num 12:7 (alluded to in Heb 3:2, and loosely quoted in 3:5). The points in the comparison are based upon their order in the loose quotation in 3:5: Moses was faithful (3:1-2); in his whole house (3:3-4); as a servant (3:5-6; Koester 2001, 249).

IN THE TEXT

■ 1 **Therefore** (*hothen*) at the head of 3:1 signals that the following material builds on what the preacher has already said about Jesus' identification with humanity and perfection as high priest in 2:5-18. In terms of content, 3:1 shares several links with the preceding section. His direct address to his listeners as **holy brothers** recalls both the common bond of divine holiness shared by Jesus and believers (2:11*a*) and the sibling bond declared by Jesus in Scripture (2:11*b*, 12) and enacted through his incarnation (2:17*a*). Addressing the readers as **holy** (*hagioi*) points up the significance of holiness for authentic Christian identity. Here is the only use of the expression **holy brothers** in the entire Bible.

Holiness in Hebrews

Holiness is of principal importance in Hebrews. Words from the *hagios* ("holy") word group occur twenty-eight times in Hebrews. Their usage, not surprisingly, is indebted to the LXX and in turn based upon the *qōdeš* ("set apart," "holy") word group in the Hebrew OT. In its biblical contexts, holiness is associated not only with the trappings of worship in the temple, but also with the nature of God's self and humanity's ceremonial and moral preparation to encounter the Holy One.

In its most general sense, holiness refers to the separation of the sacred from the profane. Certain places, things, events, and people are set apart as God's very own. Thus, the "sanctuary," as in the LXX (see Num 3:28, 38), is literally "the Holy Place" or "holy things" in Hebrews (8:2; 9:1, 2, 8, 12, 24, 25; 10:19; 13:11). Once the innermost chamber of the temple is called "the Holy of Holies" (9:3 NRSV; see Exod 26:33; Heb 6:19).

God is the source of all holiness (→ 2:11). The divine character of holiness is a gift to human beings (12:10), but through the sanctifying work of Christ (2:11) and sharing in the Holy Spirit (6:4). Jesus is uniquely qualified as the high priest who brings definitive cleansing, because he is himself utterly "holy [*hosios*], blameless, pure, set apart from sinners, exalted above the heavens" (7:26).

It is particularly through the sacrifice of Jesus that people are "sanctified" or "made holy" (10:10, 14, 29; 13:12). It is more effective than the animal sacrifices under the old covenant because it is a sanctification that does more than provide an outward, ceremonial cleansing of worshipers (9:13). It effects an inward transformation of the worshiper through the purification of sins (1:3) at the deepest level: the cleansing of the conscience (9:14; 10:2, 22; see 9:9).

On this basis, the preacher calls believers "holy brothers" (3:1) or "God's people" (6:10; 13:24; lit., "holy ones" or "saints," reminiscent of Paul's address to his churches, e.g., in Rom 1:7; 1 Cor 1:2; 2 Cor 1:1; Phil 1:1; Col 1:2). The sanctification of believers is certainly a once-for-all benefit of Christ's sacrifice ("sanctified": perfect tense in Heb 10:10; aorist tense in 10:29; 13:12). But it is also an ongoing process of discipline, sovereignly administered by God the Father and endured and submitted to by God's children. Persevering in sanctification means struggling against sin (12:1, 3, 4; see 10:19-39; 11:25) and pursuing peace and holiness (12:14). This is to be done both individually (3:12) and communally (3:13). God the Father uses the hardships of life to educate us in holy living, producing a "harvest of righteousness and peace" (12:11) and allowing us to share in God's own holiness (12:10).

In the address to those **who share** [*metochoi*] **in the heavenly calling**, one is reminded of how Jesus "shared [*meteschen*]" in human nature in order to liberate people from the enslaving fear of death (2:14) and bring "many sons to glory" (2:10). Jesus shared in our lowly estate so that we might share in his heavenly one. "For we have come to share in [*metochoi*] Christ" (3:14). *Metochoi* may also connote **partners,** a sense common in ancient Greek papyri (→ 3:14 sidebar, "Partners with Christ").

The **heavenly calling** (*klēseōs epouraniou*) corresponds to Jesus' trailblazing a pathway for us into "heaven itself" (9:24; see 4:14; 7:26; 8:1). Presently believers "have tasted the heavenly [*epouraniou*] gift" of salvation (6:4) and possess a hope that is anchored in the very presence of God. There, in "the inner sanctuary behind the curtain, . . . Jesus" our forerunner "has entered" (6:19-20). The future reality to which we have been "called [*hoi keklēmenoi*]" is "the promised eternal inheritance" (9:15). It is the "better country—a heavenly [*epouraniou*] one" for which the patriarchs longed (11:16), and "the heavenly [*epourianō*] Jerusalem" (12:22). As believers, our names have already been enrolled as citizens there ("in heaven" [12:23]). It is the promised "rest" into which the preacher will urge his listeners to enter (4:1, 3, 10, 11).

The first command issued to the readers of Hebrews appears in 3:1. The imperative **fix your thoughts on** is a form of the verb *katanoeō*. It refers to the action of considering, contemplating, or observing something carefully ("consider" [ESV, HCSB, KJV, NASB, NRSV, TYNDALE]; "reflect" [NAB]; "take note" [NET]; "think carefully about" [NLT]; "turn your minds to" [NJB]). The exhortation in Col 3:1 is similar: "set your hearts on things above, where Christ is seated at the right hand of God." The immediate objects for this intense reflection are two titles for Jesus: **the apostle** and **high priest.**

Only in Hebrews do we find Jesus designated as **the apostle.** Elsewhere this title (*apostolos*, "one who is sent") is applied to Jesus' first disciples (the Twelve: Matt 10:2; Mark 3:14; Luke 6:13; Rev 21:14) or others such as Paul and Barnabas (Acts 9:27; 1 Cor 9:1-6), who were commissioned to preach the gospel. However, Jesus was the first to proclaim the gospel of God's kingdom (Mark 1:14-15). Hebrews tells us that in these last days God has spoken to us "by his Son" (1:2), and that "This salvation . . . was first announced by the Lord" (2:3). While the apostles were sent by Jesus, Jesus was sent directly from God. In the Gospel of John, Jesus is characteristically identified as the One whom the Father has sent (John 3:17, 34; 5:36, 38; 6:29, 57; 7:29; 8:42; 10:36; 11:42; 17:3, 8, 18, 21, 23, 25; 20:21).

Thus, the preacher rightly acknowledges Jesus as the **apostle** par excellence. The title is appropriate to Jesus in Heb 1—4 since he is compared to other messengers sent by God, such as prophets (1:1-2), angels (1:5-14), and Moses (3:1-6; Westfall 2005, 112). God's word or message is a prominent theme in these chapters (1:1-2; 2:2-4; 3:5; 4:12-13). Jesus is the ultimate "messenger" of God's word (3:1 NLT).

The listeners must also contemplate Jesus as **high priest.** As apostle, Jesus represents God by communicating God's word to humanity. As **high priest,** he represents his people before God and brings them into God's presence. Jesus' key high-priestly functions have already been mentioned: providing atonement for sins (1:3*c*; 2:17) and making people holy (2:11).

Given the uniqueness of these christological titles, it may come as a surprise that the preacher speaks of **the apostle and high priest** *of our confession.* By using the noun *confession* with the definite article (*tēs homologias*, **the** *confession*) he denotes not just the act of confessing (NIV's **whom we confess**), but its content. This is not to suggest that early Christians confessed Jesus as apostle and high priest in exactly those terms. If such designations had been common, the author could hardly "have much to say" later about Jesus as high priest that his listeners would find difficult to comprehend (5:11).

Nevertheless, Jesus' high-priestly functions of saving power through atonement and heavenly intercession are inherent in the earliest Christian confessions. These were confessions of Jesus as the Christ, the Son of God, who had come from God in the flesh (1 John 4:2-3, 15; 2 John 7; Gal 4:4; Phil 2:6-8), died for the forgiveness of sins (1 Cor 15:3; Col 1:20), was raised from the dead (1 Cor 15:4; Rom 10:9), and was exalted into heaven (Phil 2:9-11; 1 Tim 3:16). The concise, most primitive Christian confession of all was "Jesus is Lord" (Rom 10:9; 1 Cor 12:3; Phil 2:11).

The apostle and high priest of our confession is **Jesus.** As in 2:9, the name of Jesus is reserved for the very end of the sentence for emphasis (see the KJV of 3:1 for a reflection of the Greek word order; → 2:9 sidebar, "Use of the Name 'Jesus' in Hebrews").

■ **2** The preacher now introduces a comparison (*synkrisis*) of Jesus and Moses. It has its exegetical basis in Num 12:7, alluded to here, and quoted in 3:5. That Jesus **was faithful** has already been described in 2:6-18. The Son's identification with humanity through suffering is what perfected him (2:10). This made him a "merciful and faithful high priest" who effected atonement for sins (2:17) and deliverance from the "fear of death" (2:15-16).

Jesus was faithful **to the one who appointed him.** The form of the verb *poieō* is translated **appointed** by virtually every English translation (see the same usage in 1 Sam 12:6 LXX; Mark 3:14; Acts 2:36). The verb may legitimately be translated "made," with the sense of "created," in appropriate contexts (e.g., Gen 1:1 LXX). Recently, Luke Timothy Johnson has favored this latter rendering, since it fits with the preceding context (2:10-18) where the human Jesus is "surely a creature" (Johnson 2006, 107).

However, the initial clause in 3:2 is not independent, but connected to the command in 3:1 as follows: "Fix your thoughts on Jesus . . . ***who*** **was faithful to the one who appointed him.**" Consequently, the verb (or more accurately, participle, *poiēsanti*) is not used in an absolute or unqualified sense (as, e.g., in Isa 17:7 LXX). Chrysostom explains: "'Who was faithful,' he says, 'to Him that made Him'—made [Him] what? 'Apostle and High Priest'" (Chrysostom 1996, 390). The Son is clearly distinguished from created beings in 1:2*b*, 10-12. He is addressed as "God" in 1:8. He is aligned with God the builder, over against the house that is built (= everything), in 3:3-4. Therefore, the author is more likely speaking of Christ's appointment to the offices of apostle and high priest than the creation of his human nature (see Koester 2001, 244).

The point of comparison between Jesus and Moses is faithfulness. Jesus was faithful **just as Moses was faithful.** The lawgiver's faults have not been hidden by the biblical record. These include his murder of an Egyptian (Exod 2:11-15); his reticence and timidity to follow God's orders to lead the people of Israel (Exod 3—4); and his angry and presumptuous actions at the waters of Meribah, which disqualified him from leading the Israelites into the promised land (Num 20:9-13). However, no mention of them is made (here or in Heb 11:23-28). To have done so would have been inappropriate for this rhetorical comparison (→ 3:1-6 Behind the Text sidebar, "The Use of Comparison").

The preacher focuses instead on the virtuous quality highlighted by God himself in the text of Num 12. In that text, Miriam and Aaron, using Moses' marriage to a Cushite woman as a pretext, spoke against the primacy of Moses as God's spokesperson (Num 12:1-2). The Lord himself defended Moses, confirming him as the greatest of prophets (Num 12:6-8), and declaring that "he is faithful in all my house" (Num 12:7*b*).

Moses was faithful **in all God's** [lit., ***his***] **house.** The precise referent for **house** becomes clear only in Heb 3:6*b*. In fact, the preacher will exploit this many-sided figure as he proceeds with his comparison.

God's "House"

God's "house [*oikos*]" can mean many different things. It could simply mean the temple, as when Jesus referred to the temple as his "Father's house" (John 2:16; see Luke 2:49) in accordance with OT usage ("house of the LORD";

Heb., *bêt YHWH* = Gk. *oikos kyriou*: Exod 23:19; 34:26; Deut 23:18; 1 Kgs 3:1; 9:1; 10:5).

"House" could refer to the community of God's people ("house of Israel": Exod 16:31; Ruth 4:11; 1 Sam 7:2; Ps 115:12; Jer 31:31 [cited in Heb 8:8]; Hos 9:15; Matt 10:6; 15:24; Acts 2:36) or to the divinely favored Davidic dynasty ("house of David": 1 Sam 20:16; 2 Sam 7:11-29; 1 Kgs 12:19, 20, 26; 2 Kgs 17:21; Ps 122:5; Isa 7:2, 13; 16:5; 22:22; Jer 21:12; Zech 12:7, 8, 10, 12; 13:1; Luke 1:27, 69; 2:4). The early church also regarded the Christian community as God's dwelling place (1 Cor 3:9-17; Eph 2:22; 1 Tim 3:15; 1 Pet 2:5; 4:17).

The heavenly world, or the entire created universe, could be referred to as God's "house" (Philo, *Posterity* 5; *Planting* 50; *Sobriety* 62-64; *Dreams* 1.185; see Attridge 1989, 109 nn. 59-60).

Hebrews exploits this rich imagery in 3:1-6.

- In 3:2 one might guess that God's house refers to the people of Israel (but see the rabbinic interpretation of Num 12:7 in *Tg. Neof*.: "In the whole world I have created, [Moses] is faithful").
- In 3:3 he refers to a house as a physical building.
- In 3:4 God's house refers to the whole cosmos ("everything").
- One might even wonder if the dynastic promise to David ("I will make him faithful in my house" [1 Chr 17:14 LXX]) or the promise of a priestly house ("I will raise up . . . a faithful priest . . . and I will build a faithful house" [1 Sam 2:35 LXX]) is in the back of the preacher's thoughts.
- One must also not forget that the "household" or kinship associations of Jesus as Son and the believing community as his siblings are close at hand, and perfectly understandable within a Greco-Roman context.

In the end, the familial metaphor seems to be uppermost, as the Christian community is identified as God's house in Heb 3:6. Nevertheless, since the Son is the heir of all things (1:2b), and his siblings are promised a share in the eternal inheritance (1:14; 6:12; 9:15), God's household ultimately takes on cosmic proportions.

■ **3** The preacher explains the reason why (***For*** [*gar*]; untranslated in NIV) his listeners must turn their thoughts toward the apostle and high priest of our confession (see 3:1-2): Because **Jesus has been found worthy of greater honor** [*doxa*, **glory**] **than Moses, just as the builder of a house has greater honor** [*timē*] **than the house itself.** In ancient Mediterranean society, honor was a pivotal value. To have a good name, to be accorded high regard and esteem within one's community, was of utmost concern for men and their families. Here the author of Hebrews uses vocabulary (as noted above) associated with this social value.

That Jesus **has been found worthy** (a perfect passive verb, *exiōtai*) probably signifies a divine passive. That is, God considered him worthy. The preacher has already identified when this divine determination occurred. It is true that the Son has eternally radiated God's "glory [*doxa*]" (1:3a). But Christ's exaltation marked the point when God counted him worthy of greater honor

(1:4-5). In 2:7 and 9 Jesus' exaltation is described as his being "crowned with glory [*doxa*] and honor [*timē*]."

It is not only as Son, but as high priest, that God has considered Jesus worthy of **greater *glory*** and **greater honor**. The same honor terminology reappears in 5:4-5. There the preacher notes that no one takes the "honor [*timē*]" of the high priesthood upon himself. And neither did Christ "take upon himself the glory [*heauton edoxasen*]." God conferred it upon him in the declarations of Ps 2:7 (see Heb 1:5) and Ps 110:4.

Though the language used here is suggestive, we must not get ahead of the preacher's logic. The implications of Jesus' faithfulness as Son over God's house become explicit only in 3:6. For the present, the argument is simply that Jesus has been counted as more honorable than Moses: **the builder of a house has greater honor than the house itself.** This is a truism, a maxim that readers would have recognized, and to which they would have readily given their assent. The comic poet Menander, among others, said that "the workman is greater than the work" (Justin Martyr, *1 Apol.* 20). Philo, likewise, wrote that "he that has gained possession is better than the possession, and he that has made than that which he has made" (*Planting* 68; see *Migration* 193).

■ **4** The concrete image of a house as a building is extended to the whole of creation. The preacher's evidence is another common matter-of-fact saying: **For every house is built by someone.** Reasonable persons—both ancient and modern—would agree, as Philo states, that a carefully built house implies an architect and builder (*Alleg. Interp.* 3.98). **But God is the builder of everything** points to God as the Creator of all things. To infer from the cosmos that there is a Creator was also a common argument (see Philo, *Alleg. Interp.* 3.97-100; *Migration* 193; *Cherubim* 126-27; see Wis 13:1-9).

3:3-6a

Let us sum up the preacher's logic up to this point: Both Jesus and Moses may be compared as persons who were faithful to God (3:2). But Jesus' honor is greater than Moses' to the same extent that the builder of a house is more honorable than the house itself. Indeed, the difference in honor is as vast as that between God and creation (3:3).

But how can this be so? How can both Jesus and Moses be faithful to God, yet Jesus—like God—somehow transcend the created order? Attentive readers will anticipate the answer found in 3:5-6. As Son, Jesus shares in God's glory (1:3*a*), was instrumental in creation (1:2*c*, 10), and was made the heir of and ruler over **everything** (*panta*; see 1:2*b*; 2:8-9).

■ **5-6a** The comparison between Moses and Jesus is brought to a climactic conclusion in 3:5-6a. The contrast between them is grammatically marked, as captured in the REB: "Moses indeed was faithful [*kai Mōusēs men pistos*] . . . but Christ [*Christos de*] is faithful"—note the *men* . . . *de* (**on the one hand . . . on the other hand**) contrast, also found in 1:7-8. Hebrews loosely quotes Num 12:7, reordering the LXX in order to emphasize two key points in the biblical text:

ho therapōn mou Mōusēs en holō tō oikō mou pistos estin.
My servant Moses in all my house is faithful (Num 12:7 LXX).

kai Mōusēs men pistos en holō tō oikō autou hōs therapōn.
Moses indeed was faithful in all his [God's] **house as a servant** (Heb 3:5). First, the preacher frontloads the fact that Moses **was faithful.** He does so because that is the common virtue between Moses and Jesus around which his comparison pivots (see 3:2). Second, he defers the role of Moses as **servant** to the end of the clause, for this sets up the major point of contrast between Moses and Jesus.

The word for **servant** (*therapōn*) is not the normal word for a common "slave [*doulos*]." It differs from *doulos* in that it can refer to service rendered freely, as opposed to forced or inherited slavery (Liddell and Scott 1995, "*therapōn*," 363). *Therapōn* is often used in a religious or cultic setting (i.e., of one who renders service to a deity) and is particularly applicable to Moses in biblical, OT pseudepigraphal, and early Christian literature (BDAG, 453). Its cognate *therapeia* can refer to a "household" or "household servants" (Luke 12:42 ESV, HCSB). Such household connections are quite appropriate in Heb 3:5. Though *therapōn* takes on different shades of meaning than other words for "slave" or "servant" [*doulos, diakonos, hypēretēs*]," and in the case of Moses connotes a nobler form of service, the fact remains that *therapōn* still denotes a **servant.**

The subordinate role of Moses is expressed as **testifying to what would be said in the future.** The NIV's **testifying** translates a prepositional phrase that signifies purpose (*eis martyrion*, "for a testimony" [KJV, LEB, NASB]). Moses' faithful service to God bore testimony to God's future actions in Christ. Moses preferred "disgrace for the sake of Christ" to the treasures of Egypt, "because he was looking ahead to his reward" (11:26). So **what would be said in the future** (*tōn lalēthēsomenōn*) can be none other than the fact that God "spoke [*elalēsen*]" through the Son in these last days (1:2*a*): the salvation "first announced [*laleisthai*] by the Lord" (2:3*b*). Later this will be linked to the preaching of the gospel message (4:2, 6), and the promised rest "spoken later" by God (*elalei meta tauta* [4:8]).

The contrasting statement about Christ in 3:6*a* is more succinct in the Greek text than in the NIV. **But Christ** is followed immediately by **as a son over God's house.** The preacher uses an ellipsis, in which the phrase **is faithful** is omitted, but implied. This sharpens the two contrasts with Moses that follow the omission.

The title **Christ** appears for the first of twelve times in Hebrews. Here it probably has no explicit messianic overtones; it is simply a proper name. The floodlight, in any case, is trained on Christ **as a son.** This is in marked contrast, first, to Moses' role **as a servant.** Second, whereas Moses served faithfully **in . . . God's house,** Christ rules **as a son over God's house.** The preposition *epi* (**over**) is employed here as a marker of power, authority, or control of someone over something (BDAG, 365), as it is in 10:21. Hence, to translate the preposition so that Christ is said to be "in charge of" (GW, NLT; or "hath rule over" [TYNDALE]) God's house is right on target.

Sons vs. Slaves in Biblical Times

Ancient readers would have immediately comprehended the dramatic contrast between sons and slaves. The role and status of slaves varied in the ancient world. For example, there was a vast difference between slaves who worked in mines on the outposts of the Roman Empire and slaves serving in the imperial household. Yet in every household, freeborn sons always ranked higher than slaves, even if the latter had gained their freedom. Freed slaves could never rid themselves of the mark of slavery, being called freedmen, not free men.

The contrast was noted by Jesus: "Now a slave has no permanent place in the family, but a son belongs to it forever. So if the Son sets you free, you will be free indeed" (John 8:35-36). The contrast is also operative in Jesus' parable of the tenants in Mark 12. After sending servants to collect his share of the vine harvest without success, the owner finally sent his beloved son, saying, "They will respect my son" (Mark 12:6).

Galatians relies heavily on the distinction between the freeborn son and slaves (Gal 4:1-7, 21-31). Adoption as sons stands as one of the greatest benefits of salvation (Rom 4:5; 8:15, 23; Eph 1:5). Similarly, Jesus' sonship and believers' participation in the divine family and inheritance are strong themes in Hebrews (see Boyd 2012).

■ **6b** Here the purpose of the comparison between Moses and Jesus and the "house" imagery in vv 1-6 finally becomes clear. Once again, scriptural exposition and rhetorical argument undergird pastoral encouragement. With the words **And we are his house** (lit., ***whose house*** [*oikos*] ***we are***) the people of God are revealed as God's "household" (GW, HCSB, NJB, REB).

Continued membership in God's household is conditional: **if we hold on.** The verb translated **hold on** (*katechō*) occurs again in exhortations at 3:14 and 10:23, as does the similar verb *krateō*, "hold on firmly" (4:14; see 6:18). This kind of condition, expressed again in 3:14, prepares for the warnings against apostasy that immediately follow (see esp. 3:12; 4:1, 11). Such a warning appeared earlier in 2:1-4, and will occur repeatedly (6:1-11; 10:19-39; 12:15-16, 25-29).

The condition of holding on complements the command in 3:1 that they fix their minds on Jesus as the apostle and high priest of their confession. Jesus possesses greater honor than all of God's previous messengers (including Moses). And his brothers and sisters share in that honor. Since Jesus was not ashamed to call them siblings (2:14), delivered them from the enslaving fear of death (2:15), and atoned for their sins (which once kindled God's wrath, 2:17), it is only right for them now to stand tall in their full rights as God's children.

This requires holding on **to our courage.** The word **courage** (*parrēsia*) is better translated as "confidence" (ESV, KJV, LEB, NAB, NASB, NET, NIV[11], NRSV) or **boldness.** The Greek word conveys the inner sense of confidence and the outward boldness to speak freely. Every freeborn citizen possessed the right to speak his mind in the public assembly. In Hebrews such boldness applies to God's children in their approach to God in worship and prayer (4:16; 10:19), because their consciences have been cleansed from the defilement of sin (9:14; 10:22). Boldness is also needed within the context of being treated disgracefully by the wider community around them on account of their confession of faith, so that they will receive their promised reward (10:32-35; see Koester 2001, 247-48).

They must also hold on to their **boast** (*kauchēma*) or "pride" (NAB, NET, NRSV; "glory" [NIV[11]]). This belongs firmly within the context of honor-shame cultures. The author does not refer to empty and sinful haughtiness, but to the legitimate pride believers should have because of their membership in God's household.

The basis for this justifiable pride is **the hope of which we boast.** This is (lit.) **the boast *of hope*** (*to kauchēma tēs elpidos*) or ***the pride based on hope.*** The content of the believers' **hope** is their "heavenly calling" (→ 3:1). This involves the privilege of entering into God's presence now (6:18-19; 7:19; 10:19-23) and, in the future, realizing the end of our hope, which is final salvation, the promised eternal inheritance (6:11; see 6:9, 12; 9:15).

The faithfulness of the Son resulted in glory and salvation for God's people. This ought to be met by the listeners' own bold and faithful resolve, rather than fear and shame in the face of adversity ("shrink[ing] back" in unbelief [10:37-39]). The preacher emphasizes the importance of faithful endurance and obedience in the following warnings (3:7—4:11), but especially in the conclusion to his sermon (10:19—13:25).

FROM THE TEXT

Hebrews' comparison of Moses and Jesus supports a command in 3:1 and a condition in 3:6. The command and condition are just as applicable to Christians today as they were to the original audience. The command explains how to remain faithful to our holy and heavenly calling. The key to the Christian's sense of belonging within God's family—God's "house"—is to keep Jesus fixed in our minds.

This is not holding on to an *idea* of Jesus as apostle and high priest. It is concentrating on the *person* of Jesus, our revealer and go-between with God the Father. Jesus condescended to "share" in our human frailty (2:14), so that we might "share" his heavenly glory (3:1; see 3:14). Jesus, the Son and "heir of all things" (1:2), has deigned to call us "brothers" and sisters (2:11) and God's "children" (2:13). And he has been faithful as our Savior and champion to deliver us from the enslaving "fear of death" (2:15). Through Jesus the apostle, God has uniquely and definitively spoken to us (1:2*a*). As our "merciful and faithful high priest," Jesus died to atone for our sins and make us holy (2:10, 17).

The personal dimension of our confession is displayed not only in Jesus' quality of faithfulness and his status as God's obedient Son, but in the obligation placed upon those who are part of God's household. The condition in 3:6 is real, because the divine claim of honor applies to every member of God's household. The Reformed insistence that we do not have a true condition here, but only a description of authentic Christian life (e.g., Stedman 1992, 50), misses the point of the preacher's challenge. It fails to acknowledge the intensely personal obligation that is incumbent upon believers. If one were admitted as an adopted son into the imperial household, then to act in a way that was hopeless, fearful, and weak in the face of opposition or criticism would express disloyalty and bring dishonor to the entire family. It would be a personal affront to the emperor himself and could be legitimate grounds for being disowned from membership in the household.

So also, the preacher outlines the honorable attitude and behavior for members of the divine household. How can anyone be a member of the household of God, and claim Jesus, the universal Lord (see 2:8), as his or her brother, yet act with cowardice and despair when tested? This is all the more so in light of Jesus' own example of faithfulness. Expressed positively, how can members of God's family be anything other than hopeful, courageous, and proud of their association with Christ the Lord? Anything less would gravely insult the honor of God and God's Son.

Whereas Jesus is God's Son by nature, believers are children of God through divine grace and adoption (Augustine, *On Faith and Creed* 4.6, in Heen and Krey 2005, 44). None of us has an inherent right to be part of God's household, especially in our estranged, defiled, and unredeemed state. God purchased our inheritance by the death of his faithful Son. The preacher to the Hebrews knows no doctrine of unconditional election that insures our eternal salvation. Final salvation requires faithfulness to God's gracious calling. There is no guarantee that true Christians will naturally and inexorably respond with loyalty to God. Such a doctrine would make the condition in 3:6 and the warnings throughout Hebrews unnecessary.

Modern readers must understand what was second nature to an ancient reading of the preacher's challenge: it is unthinkable and disastrous to respond to God's grace in a way that would bring shame upon God's house. It is tantamount to apostasy, all-out rejection of our inheritance. Even if God were mercifully to withhold his judgment on apostasy, shameful and untrustworthy responses to God's grace clearly make one deserving of divine judgment (see 3:16-19; 6:7-8; 10:26-31, 35-39). Later, Esau will be presented as an example of someone whose immoral behavior was the occasion of his irrevocable loss of God's blessing and inheritance (12:16-17). But here in 3:6 the emphasis is positive: "And we are his house, if we hold on to our courage and the hope of which we boast."

2. Entering God's Rest: Warning and Promise (3:7—4:13)

a. The Peril of Defying God's Voice (3:7-19)

BEHIND THE TEXT

Hebrews 3:7—4:13 is an extended homiletical midrash on Ps 95:7-11 (LXX). It is anchored in the scriptural text (quoted in Heb 3:7-11) through the repetition of key verses (3:15; 4:3, 5, 7) and vocabulary throughout.

Hebrews 3:7-19, however, is the first of two clearly defined parts (the second is in 4:1-11, followed by a conclusion to the whole midrash in 4:12-13). It begins with the quotation from Ps 95 in Heb 3:7-11, followed by a warning against unbelief in 3:12-19. The warning is marked off by an *inclusio*—a section that begins and ends with the same point:

3:12 "See to it [*blepete*], brothers, that none of you has a sinful" **heart of unbelief** [*apistias*] . . .

3:19 "So we see [*blepomen*] that they were not able to enter, because of their unbelief [*apistian*]."

The word **unbelief** is important. It serves not only as a boundary marker for this subunit but also as an indicator of its theme. This is underscored by the use of the noun *apistia* only in these two verses in Hebrews. It also creates a striking contrast with Christ's faithfulness in 3:1-6 ("faithful [*pistos*]" [3:2, 5-6]).

Midrash

The Hebrew noun *midrash* is derived from the verb *darash*, "search [for an answer]." Accordingly, midrash means "inquiry," "examination," or "commentary." The term, then, can refer to a method of researching the Scriptures or to the resulting form of such study. Midrash has its roots in the OT itself and is well attested in the NT, at Qumran, in Philo, and abundantly in rabbinic literature (see Evans 2006, 381).

Rabbinic midrash has four main characteristics: (1) It has its point of departure in Scripture. (2) It is characteristically homiletical. (3) It is studiously attentive to the text. (4) It is an adaptation to the present. Among these, to adapt or "actualize" the Scriptures for the contemporary situation and "the attachment and constant reference to Scripture" are essential. These two traits are "the very soul of the midrashic process" (Bloch 1957, 1265-66).

Midrash is not a single, straightforward method. It involved many interpretive techniques that we find in Hebrews. These include the argument from lesser to greater (*qal wahomer*; e.g., 2:2-3*a*) and verbal analogy (→ 4:3*b*-5 sidebar, "Verbal Analogy").

Hebrews 3:7—4:13 is a midrash on Ps 95:7-11. The author compares this psalm with other OT texts, such as Num 14 and Gen 2:2. He also highlights key terms in the psalm to drive home his message: "Today," "day," "hear," "harden," "hearts," "rebellion," "declared on oath," "angry," "enter," "rest" (G. Guthrie 2002, 24).

This method of exegesis, in classic midrashic fashion, serves the preacher's exhortation to his contemporary audience. He brings relevant scriptures to their attention as the living, active, and penetrating word of God (4:12). His aim is to prevent any of them from following the pattern of disobedience on display in Israel's wilderness generation (4:6, 11).

The quotation from Ps 95:7-11 would have been familiar to Jewish listeners because of its frequent liturgical use. The psalm was employed in the preamble to synagogue services on Friday evenings and Saturday mornings (Lane 1991, 85). The first part (Ps 95:1-7c) is a moving call to worship. The second part (Ps 95:7d-11), quoted in Hebrews, is a plea not to imitate the example of the hard-hearted, wayward wilderness generation.

The Hebrew text of the psalm refers to the locations of Massah and Meribah, where the Israelites quarreled over lack of water (Exod 17:1-7; Num 20:1-13). These place names are obscured in the LXX (→ In the Text on Heb 3:8). This allows the preacher to narrow his reading of the text in line with another set of allusions in the psalm. The psalm alludes to the incident at Kadesh Barnea in Num 14 when the Israelites refused to enter the promised land. They did not heed God's voice (Num 14:22; see Ps 95:7d). They tested God, though they had seen God's miraculous works (Num 14:22; see Ps 95:9). And they suffered under God's anger for forty years (Num 14:34 LXX; see Ps 95:10), which God swore would happen to them (Num 14:21-23, 28-30, 35; see Ps 95:11). The preacher seems to have this scene in mind when interpreting Ps 95. He introduces further echoes from Num 14 in his closing series of rhetorical questions (→ Heb 3:16-18).

The purpose of the exhortations in our passage, based upon the scriptural record of Israel's disbelief, is to warn readers against following the wilderness generation's negative example. In the same vein, after relating a composite account of Israel's failings in 1 Cor 10:6-10, Paul wrote, "These things happened to them as examples and were written down as warnings for us, on whom the fulfillment of the ages has come" (1 Cor 10:11).

The warnings in Heb 3:6-19 are the flip side of the coin to 3:1-6. There the preacher encouraged readers to "hold on" to hope (3:6) as people who "share" in the heavenly calling and confess Christ as their apostle and faithful high priest (3:1). Hebrews 3:14 picks up key terms from these verses when it reminds readers that they are "partners" (NRSV) with Christ (*metochoi* [see 3:1]) as long as they "hold" to their commitment (*katechō* [see 3:6]). In 3:7-19 the obverse of holding on to one's confession is "turn[ing] away from the living God" in unbelief (3:12, 19).

IN THE TEXT

7a The preacher introduces a quotation from Ps 95:7-11 with the words, **So, as the Holy Spirit says.** The quote would seem to be an abrupt intrusion if it were not for the opening word **So** (*dio*). This inferential conjunction links the following words of warning with the preceding exhortations to concentrate on Jesus and hold on to confidence and hope (3:1, 6; see 3:14). The introductory formula **as the Holy Spirit says** conforms to the preacher's pattern of quoting Scripture as divine speech (→ 1:5-14 sidebar, "Quoting Scripture in Hebrews"). The use of the present tense verb **says** (*legei*) points to this scripture as more than a written record of God's words in the past, but the "living and active" word of God in the present (4:12-13).

7b-8 The quotation from Ps 95:7-11 opens with the plea, **Today, if you hear his voice, do not harden your hearts.** These solemn words will function as a refrain in 3:15 and 4:7. The word **Today** (*sēmeron*)—coupled with its cognate word "day [*hēmera*]"; perhaps suggested by the psalm in 3:8: **time** [lit., ***day*] of testing**—will resound like a chime throughout the preacher's exposition. It will strike either a menacing note of urgency (*sēmeron* [3:13, 15]; *hēmera* [3:13]) or a welcome signal of God's end-time promise (*sēmeron* [4:7]; *hēmera* [4:4, 7, 8]).

Hardened Hearts

3:7a-8

The expression "harden the heart" (*sklērynein tēn kardian*), repeated three times in Hebrews (3:8, 15; 4:7), originates in the OT. Of seventeen occurrences in the LXX, thirteen point to the hardening of Pharaoh's heart (Exod 4:21; 7:3, 22; 8:15; 9:12, 35; 10:1, 20, 27; 11:10; 14:4, 8, 17), two to the hardening of other kings' hearts (Deut 2:30; 2 Chr 36:13; see 1 Esd 1:46), and two to the hardening of the heart of God's people (Ps 95:8; Isa 63:17).

Cognate expressions occur a half-dozen times in the LXX: "the hard of heart [*ho sklēros tēn kardian*]" (Prov 17:20), the compound adjective "hard-hearted [*sklērokardios*]" (Prov 17:20; Ezek 3:7), and noun "hardness of heart [*sklērokardia*]" (Deut 10:16; Jer 4:4). In the last two passages, the Greek word translates the Hebrew phrase, "the foreskin of your heart" (NRSV). Akin to being hard-hearted is being "stiff-necked" (see Exod 33:3, 5; 34:9; Deut 9:6, 13; Prov 29:1; see Acts 7:51), or having a "heart of stone" (Ezek 11:19; 36:26).

Apart from Hebrews, in the NT hardness of heart is referred to chiefly in the Gospels. The term *sklērokardia* ("hardness of heart" [ESV, LEB, NASB]) occurs three times (Matt 19:8; Mark 10:5; 16:14). The same concept, involving cognates of the verb *pōroō* ("harden, petrify") instead of *sklērynō*, occurs mostly in the Gospel of Mark (3:5; 6:52; 8:17; John 12:40), as well as once in Ephesians (4:18).

The hardening of one's heart refers to a "persistent unreceptivity" to God's will (Behm 1965, 614). In some instances, perhaps, it relates to callousness or lack of compassion (Matt 19:8; Mark 3:5; 10:5). More often it is a stubborn resistance to God. It involves a refusal to listen to God's voice, and rebellion against the divine will (Exod 7:22; 8:19; 9:12; Ps 95:8; Ezek 3:7; Heb 3:8, 15; 4:7). It leads to a deadening of one's spiritual sensibilities, making it impossible to perceive or understand the truth (Mark 6:52; 8:17-18, 21; John 12:40).

According to Eph 4:18, hardness of heart accounts for ignorance about the truth of the gospel among the Gentiles. They are "darkened in their understanding and separated from the life of God" and, "having lost all sensitivity," held captive to chaotic and insatiable passions (Eph 4:19; see Philo, *Spec. Laws* 1.305). A "heart of stone" is associated with idolatry and impurities and is contrasted with a "heart of flesh" that perfectly obeys God's commands (Ezek 36:25-27; see Jer 32:39-40). The hard-hearted may also be contrasted with those who fear the Lord (Prov 28:14; see Heb 4:1 [KJV, NASB]).

The hard of heart are "always going astray" (Heb 3:10; Isa 63:17) and disbelieving God's word (Mark 16:14; see Heb 3:12, 19). Probably the best description of hard-heartedness is in Heb 3:12: to have "a sinful, unbelieving heart that turns away from the living God." To remain in this condition is a risky proposition (see Prov 28:14; Sir 3:26-27). This is illustrated by the debacle at Kadesh Barnea, recalled in Heb 3:16-18 (see also Sir 16:10; 46:8). Hence, the repeated warning in Heb 3—4, "Today, if you hear his voice, do not harden your hearts"!

With the statement, **as you did in the rebellion, during the time of testing in the desert,** Hebrews follows the LXX text, which translates rather than reproduces the descriptive place names found in the Hebrew text. After all, Meribah means "quarreling" (Exod 17:7; Num 20:13; see Deut 33:8) or **rebellion** (Ps 95:8 LXX); and Massah, **testing** (Exod 17:7; Deut 6:16; 33:8; Ps 95:8 LXX). The resulting lack of geographical precision allows the preacher to reflect more generally on the rebellion of the wilderness generation, culminating in their disobedience at Kadesh Barnea and exclusion from the promised land (Num 14).

■ **9-10** The desert is **where your fathers tested and tried me.** Hebrews 3:9-10a modifies the text of Ps 95:9-10a in two significant ways.

First, the LXX's "tested . . . tried [*epeirasan . . . edokimasan*]" is rephrased as ***tried by testing*** (*epeirasan . . . en dokimasia*; see NASB). This conveys more strongly how the children of Israel were putting God to the test in the wilderness (see Exod 17:2, 7; Num 14:22; Deut 6:16; Pss 78:18, 41; 95:9; 106:14; 1 Cor 10:9).

Second, the addition of **that is why** or ***therefore*** (*dio*) in 3:10 alters the focus of the forty-year time period. Psalm 95:10 identifies the **forty years** as a period when God **was angry with that generation**. But here Hebrews focuses more sharply on the **forty years** as a period when Israel tested the Lord, even though they **saw what I did** (lit., ***saw my works***). Thus, while Ps 95:10 speaks of forty years of God's anger, Hebrews emphasizes God's angry response to Israel's forty years of provocation: **That is why I was angry with that generation.** In 3:17, however, Hebrews reverts to the emphasis of the psalm text: "And with whom was he angry for forty years?"

God verbalized (**and I said**) the deep and abiding source of their rebellion: **Their hearts are always going astray.** That is, at the core of their being they were chronically susceptible to being misled or deceived. They were all too easily detoured from God's revealed will for them. This is because **they have not known my ways.** (The pairing of ignorance and going astray recurs in 5:2; contrast the promises of the new covenant in 8:10-11; 10:16.) Because they did not follow God's directions, they were left to wander in the desert, a fitting parable of the Israelites' inner spiritual condition, described earlier as hardness of heart (3:8).

▪ **11** The divine judgment on Israel's rebellion is pronounced. God solemnly **declared on oath** [or "swore" (CEB, ESV, HCSB, LEB, NAB, NASB, NET, NJB, NRSV)] **in my anger.** One can almost hear the exasperation: **They shall never enter my rest.** The psalmist's precise wording is *If they shall enter into my rest,* corresponding exactly with a Hebrew idiom that expresses emphatic denial. This is aposiopesis, a figure of speech in which the consequence of the stated condition is silenced due to intense emotion. The missing information would be, "May this or that happen to me, if . . ." (see Gen 14:23; Num 14:30; 1 Sam 14:45).

God's oath effectively barred that generation from **my rest,** which in the OT referred to the promised land (see Exod 33:14; Deut 12:10; 25:19; Josh 1:13, 15; 21:44; 22:4; 23:1). Hebrews' understanding of this rest as a divine, transcendent reality—the heavenly homeland—will become apparent in 4:1-11. The end of the psalm quotation (Ps 95:11 in Heb 3:11) recollects the repeated divine oaths at Kadesh Barnea, prohibiting the entrance of the disobedient into the land (Num 14:20-23, 27-30, 35; see 32:10; Deut 1:34; 2:14). That dramatic scene stands as a graphic example of God's judgment in Heb 3:16-18.

▪ **12** A homiletical midrash on the previous psalm quotation spans 3:12—4:11. Verses 12-15 consist of one finely crafted sentence that exhorts listeners to watch out for each other's spiritual welfare. They should collectively hold fast to their commitment as Christ's partners. In vv 12-15 the preacher warns about the cause of flagging commitment. In vv 16-18 he provides an example of the consequences of rebellion.

The preacher begins by catching his audience's attention: **See to it** (*blepete;* "watch out" [HCSB]; "take heed" [KJV]). As in 3:1, he addresses them as **brothers.** He urges the community to concern themselves with each and every person among them, so that there will not be ***anyone*** who copies the bad example of the wilderness generation. There is a concentration of indefinite pronouns in 3:12—4:11 (forms of *tis,* "someone, anyone, a certain one"), which refer to individual members of the community: **none** (= ***not any*** [3:12, 13; 4:1]), "some" (4:6), "one" (4:11; see also 10:25; 12:15, 16).

God's household needs to make sure **that none of you has a sinful, unbelieving heart that turns away from the living God.** This is a remarkably concise explanation and application of the warning against hardening one's heart (Ps 95:8 in Heb 3:8).

First, the hardened **heart** is **sinful** (*ponēra*). While most other English versions accurately translate this as "wicked" (GW, NJB) or "evil" (CEB, ESV, GNT, HCSB, KJV, LEB, NAB, NASB, NCV, NET, NLT, NRSV), the NIV's **sinful** nicely draws attention to the connection with "sin's deceitfulness" in 3:13 (→).

Second, it is an **unbelieving** (*apistia*) heart. This is the operative word in this passage, found in Hebrews only at 3:12 and 19. Though it does not appear in the psalm, it correctly captures God's assessment of the children of Israel at Kadesh Barnea: "How long," the Lord said, "will these people treat me with contempt? How long will they refuse to believe in me, in spite of all the miraculous signs I have performed among them?" (Num 14:11). Theirs was not merely a passive unbelief, or lack of faith. It was an actively rebellious and defiant disbelief or mistrust. It called into question God's faithfulness and providence.

Third, the outcome (**that**; "leading you to" [ESV]) of having such an evil and distrustful heart is that it **turns away from the living God**. This, too, means more than just a "fall[ing] away" (NASB; see ESV, RSV). It is the deliberate action of turning away (GNT, GW, NIV[11], NJB, NLT, NRSV), forsaking (NAB, NET), or departing from God (HCSB, KJV, TYNDALE). The expression "turn away from [*apostēnai apo*]" (usually with "Lord" [*kyriou*] or "God" [*theou*]) occurs often in the LXX to refer to apostasy, desertion, or revolt. The phrase **the living God** adds to the OT flavor of the preacher's language (see esp. Num 14:21, 28). It also forms a link with the conclusion to the midrash in Heb 4:12-13, which begins with a description of the word of God as "living" (4:12).

■ **13** The exhortation continues with clear echoes from the psalm citation in 3:7*b*-8: **daily** (*kath' hekastēn hēmeran*) ‖ "during the time [lit., **day;** *kata tēn hēmeran*]" (3:8); **Today** (*sēmeron* [also in 3:7*b*]); **hardened** (*sklērynthē*) ‖ "harden [*sklērynēte*]" (3:8). The command is for the community to **encourage** [*parakaleite*] **one another daily**. They must mutually engage in the same activity that the preacher is engaged in throughout his sermon, which he calls a "word of exhortation [*logos tēs paraklēseos*]" (13:22). In the present context the precise nuance of the imperative *parakaleite* may well be reflected in the NLT's "You must warn each other every day" (see Osborne 2007a, 99-100).

A play on words reinforces the command. They must ***admonish*** (*parakaleite*, a compound of *kaleō*, "to call") one another **daily** (*kath' hekastēn hēmeran*; lit., ***according to each day;*** that is, "every day" [NRSV]) as long as it is **called** [*kaleitai*] **Today** (*sēmeron*). The word **Today**, appropriately capitalized in the NIV, will be unpacked in 4:6-11 in terms of the final age. During "these last days" (→ 1:2) we have a final window of opportunity to enter into the divine rest.

Consistent mutual accountability is necessary to minimize the danger of apostasy for any given member of the community: **so that none of you may be hardened**. The instrument of hardening is **sin's deceitfulness**. The **deceitfulness** (*apatē*) or "deception" (HCSB, NET) of sin could also connote ***seduction*** ("the lure of sin" [NJB]). This may involve the personification of **sin** as a sinister power that lures humans to their destruction. Therefore, we must resist its enticement (see 12:4).

Particularly, this may be ***the* sin** (*hē hamartia*) of apostasy (→ 12:1, 4). It can creep into the community through any given member. Like a "bitter root," it contaminates others (12:15) and subtly makes it impossible to hear God's voice. Eventually, individuals can become so desensitized that they "drift away" (2:1), "fall away" (6:6), or find that they "have fallen short of" divine grace (4:1; see 12:15). The sin of apostasy is so perilous because, according to Hebrews, not only is its onset subtle, but its consequences are terrifying and irreversible (see 3:11, 16-19; 4:5; 6:4-8; 10:26-31; 12:15-17).

■ **14** The preacher now shifts from the second person imperatives in 3:12-13 (but see also 3:1: "fix your thoughts") to the first person plural ("we"). The second person has dominated his direct address up until now (see 2:1, 3, 5, 8, 9; 3:6). This verse harks back to 3:1 and 6. It is a reminder of his listeners' status as partners with Christ ("who share [*metochoi*] in the heavenly calling" [3:1]). And it restates the condition for maintaining this status (→ 3:6): **We have come to share** [*metochoi*] **in Christ if we hold *on*** (*eanper . . . kataschōmen*).

We have come (*gegonamen*), or rather, ***we have become*,** is in the perfect tense. This indicates that the partnership with Christ is a reality that was initiated in the past—perhaps at baptism, but in any case when they became sharers (*metochoi*) in the Holy Spirit (6:4)—and continues into the present.

The condition for remaining Christ's partners is intensified through the use of technical business terminology. The NIV's verb **to share** translates a noun that could mean ***partners*.** **To hold** (*katechein*) was used in commercial contexts of holding or retaining possession of property. **Firmly** (*bebaios*) often applied to the validity or guarantee of a legal agreement or contract (see 2:2), and **till the end** (*mechri telous*) to its date of termination (see BDAG, 1041).

Partners with Christ

>Only context can determine whether *metochoi* are ordinary "companions" (HCSB; see Heb 1:9) or associates or "partners" (CEB, GNT, GW, LEB, NAB, NET, NRSV) in the formal legal sense (as here in 3:14). In the ancient papyri the term is commonly used of business partners, such as farmers, fishermen, and especially tax collectors (see Luke 5:7). The synonym *koinōnoi* (lit., "sharers") was also used for such "partners" (see Luke 5:10; see MM, 406; Spicq 1994a).
>
>According to Hebrews, Christ's partners have a share in the spiritual realities of the age to come. We are "partakers [*metochoi*]" (KJV, NASB) of the heavenly calling (3:1) and the Holy Spirit (6:4). We "share in all that belongs to Christ" (3:14 NLT). This is because he "shared [*meteschen*]" in the flesh-and-blood mortality that we all "share [*kekoinōnēken*]" and broke the power of death through his own death (2:14). Since Christ made us his siblings (2:11, 12, 17; 3:1) and members of God's house (3:6), we are not exempt from the hardship of discipline that all children "share [*metochoi*]" (12:8 NRSV). But such discipline is necessary

if we are going to "share [*metalabein*]" in God's holiness (12:10). And we must hold fast our commitment to the partnership "till the end" (3:14) if we are finally to receive "the promised eternal inheritance" (9:15).

Commentators have struggled to understand what it is to which the listeners are to hold fast. The NIV translates *tēn archēn tēs hypostaseōs* as **the confidence we had at first** (compare "the beginning of our confidence" [KJV]). This draws a parallel with the condition in 3:6.

There is no ancient precedent for translating *hypostasis* as **confidence** (CEB, ESV, GNT, GW, KJV, NET, NJB, NRSV) or "assurance" (NASB; see Lane 1991, 82 n. q). The term *hypostasis* refers to "that which stands under," hence "basis." This could apply to anything from a commercial deposit to essential being (for the latter, → 1:3a). Thus, "reality" (HCSB, NAB; "substance" [TYNDALE]) is a possible translation. Presumably, this would be the reality of the believers' participation in the Son's inheritance.

However, *hypostasis* is also used as a technical term for a business obligation, such as the expectation of rent due or of commitment to the terms of a commercial venture (see BDAG, 1040-41). The clustering of other business terms (→ above, and sidebar, "Partners with Christ") tips the scale in favor of rendering *tēn archēn tēs hypostaseōs* as **initial commitment** (compare "original conviction" [NIV11]). This comports with the warning in 3:12 to avoid an evil and faithless disposition "that turns away" from God, as well as the exhortations to hold on to our confession (4:14; 10:23; see 3:1, 6).

The condition for continued partnership with Christ is to **hold firmly** to our **commitment** from its "beginning [*archē*]" (KJV, NAB, NASB) **till the end** (*telos*; see 6:11; for the wordplay here, → 5:9 sidebar, "Playing with Beginnings and Endings").

■ **15** This verse serves as the conclusion to the exhortations in 3:12-14 and a transition to the closing questions in 3:16-18. **As has just been said** introduces a repeated portion of the psalm (Ps 95:7d-11 in Heb 3:7b-8) that was the focus of the preacher's warnings against apostasy. The duplicated quote brings forward two terms (**hear** and **rebellion**) that will be picked up in the opening question in 3:16.

■ **16** In 3:16-18 the preacher uses a rhetorical technique (Lat. *subiectio*; Gk. *hypophora/anthypophora*; *Rhet. Her.* 4.23.33-24.34) in which a speaker poses a series of rhetorical questions. These provide vigorous movement and cumulative force to the argument. Here there are three sets of questions and responses (two pairs of rhetorical questions in 3:16-17; one two-part rhetorical question in 3:18).

The movement in the questioning follows that of the psalm quotation: from rebellion (3:8a ‖ 3:16a) to God's anger (3:10a ‖ 3:17a) to the divine oath (3:11 ‖ 3:18a). The responses to the questions are fashioned after the tragic events at Kadesh recorded in Num 14. The characters involved were those who had come out of Egypt with Moses (Heb 3:16b ǁ Num 14:2-3, 13, 19, 22; see 26:4). Their sin (see Num 14:18-19, 34, 40) incurred the divine judgment, with their corpses dropping in the desert (Heb 3:17b ǁ Num 14:29, 32). This was the result of God's oath to keep them from entering into God's rest (Ps 95:11; i.e., the land, Num 14:30), and to consign them to wilderness wandering (Num 14:33) on account of their disobedience (Num 14:43).

The first question in Heb 3:16a echoes two key terms from the repeated Ps 95 quote in Heb 3:15: **Who were they who heard** [*akousantes*] **and rebelled** [*parepikranan*]? The importance of one's response in faith to what is **heard** will be crucial to the second half of the preacher's midrash (see 4:2-3, 7). **Were they not all those Moses led out of Egypt?** (3:16b). Indeed, those rebels were "all the children of Israel" (Num 14:2) who desired to return to Egypt (Num 14:3-4).

■ **17 And with whom was he angry for forty years?** Here the preacher more straightforwardly follows Ps 95:10, which speaks of forty years of wrath on that generation, rather than his own rearrangement in Heb 3:9 (→). Numbers 14:33-34 (LXX) and 32:13 also plainly speak of forty years under God's fierce anger.

Was it not with those who sinned, whose bodies fell in the desert? God leveled his judgment on those who **sinned.** The record of the rebellion at Kadesh recounts how responsible individuals twenty years and older would suffer for their sins, one year for each of the forty days spent exploring the land (Num 14:28-35). Their children (and Caleb and Joshua) would live to see the promised land, but their **carcasses** (*kōla*, unburied corpses [BDAG, 579], a sign of great dishonor) would fall in the desert (Num 14:29, 32-33).

■ **18** The final sobering question is: **And to whom did God swear that they would never enter his rest if not to those who disobeyed?** Both Ps 95:11 and Num 14:21-23, 28-30 record God's oath to prevent that wicked generation from entering the land. Psalm 95 does not refer explicitly to **those who disobeyed** (*tois apeithēsasin*), but in Num 14:43 LXX the rebels are clearly addressed as those who "turned away from the Lord in disobedience [*apestraphēte apeithountes kyriō*]." Deuteronomy 1:26-27 and 9:23 (LXX) also characterize the incident at Kadesh Barnea as an act of disobedience.

The ancient and important manuscript 𝔓⁴⁶ has the expression "to those who disbelieved [*apistēsasin*]" instead of **to those who disobeyed** (3:18). The textual variant is probably not original. But it is interesting in light of the shift of reference to "unbelief" in the following verse. Etymologically, the transition from disobedience to faithlessness is easier in Greek than in English. As Attridge observes, "'Disobedience' (*apeitheia*) is in fact failure to be persuaded, a failure to come to 'faith' (*pistis*)" (1989, 121).

■ **19** In concluding the first part of the midrash on Ps 95:7d-11, the preacher observes (**we see**) why the wilderness generation was **not able to enter** the promised land: **because of their unbelief** (*apistia*). The beginning of the preacher's exposition warned against a "sinful, unbelieving [*apistia*] heart"

(3:12). So the dire consequences for apostasy in 3:16-18 should stand as a sober reminder for the Hebrews to maintain their commitment to hope in Christ. The promise of entering into God's rest will be emphasized in the second half of the midrash (4:1, 3, 5, 6, 10, 11). But final salvation is reserved for those who believe (4:2-3) and do not follow the pattern of disobedience left by the children of Israel (4:6, 11).

FROM THE TEXT

The first part of Hebrews (1:1—4:13) emphasizes, from beginning to end, the importance of heeding God's word. If anything, the call intensifies in chs 3 and 4. The preacher calls for his audience to listen, believe, and maintain their allegiance to Christ, or risk the consequences for not doing so.

What is striking to modern ears, and quite off-putting, is the appeal to *fear* (developed in 4:1, 11). Hebrews uses the object lesson of rebellious Israelites, whom God swore would not enter the promised land, and whose dead bodies dropped in the desert.

A professor of mine in college amplified the terror of this lesson by pointing to God's words of anger at the wilderness generation who "tested me these ten times" (Num 14:22 NRSV). He explained, "When they tested God the first time, they didn't realize they had only nine times left. When they tested him the second time, they didn't realize they only had eight times left . . ."

We live in a time when people seem to desire ever-lengthening boundaries on their bad behavior and fewer (if any) consequences for them. This has been translated into some popular forms of Christianity. The message of the Bible is often reduced to nothing more than grace and love. Little is said about the horrors of sin and death from which we need deliverance, or about God, not only as loving and forgiving, but also as holy and just.

Hebrews counters this with a view of God that C. S. Lewis echoes in *The Lion, the Witch, and the Wardrobe*. The children express fear about meeting Aslan, asking whether he is "safe." "Safe?" Mr. Beaver responds, "Who said anything about safe? 'Course he isn't safe. But he's good. He's the King, I tell you."

There are many things, including lions, that should *appropriately* fill us with fear. Who, for instance, would be so foolhardy as to claim there is no reason to fear touching "the third rail" in a subway? Likewise, in Hebrews, a healthy fear of God is important to his exhortations: "It is a dreadful thing to fall into the hands of the living God" (10:31); "God is a consuming fire" (12:29).

Ironically, fear of divine judgment on unbelief and disobedience, or of the prospect of losing out on the experience of sharing in God's rest (see 4:1, 11), should motivate us to grasp the confidence and hope we have through our partnership with Christ (3:1, 6, 14; 4:16). It is important to clarify that Hebrews does not promote a slavish fear—like the fear of death, from which believers have been delivered (2:15). Quite the contrary, he promotes courageous commitment to God. As Aristotle wisely taught, courage is not a complete absence of fear. Rather, it is the endurance of frightening dangers precisely because one fears something worse. For example, a courageous man will face death in battle, because he fears something worse: the loss of his honor (*Eth. nic.* 3.6.3, 8).

It is necessary to make two further observations. First, partnership with Christ, which includes our sharing in his holiness (2:11), is what provides us with the confidence to enter before the throne of an awesome and holy God (4:16). The preacher will have much more to say about the benefits of Christ's high-priestly ministry in subsequent chapters.

Second, the appropriate response to the potential danger of missing out on God's rest through unbelief is not one of merely wanting to "save one's own skin." Instead, we should have a fearful concern for one another (see 3:12, 13; 4:1, 11). The believer is not alone on this pilgrimage toward God's final rest. And there is no substitute for mutual encouragement, confession of sin, and accountability to other believers. Whether in the small house-church gatherings of the early church (see 10:25; Banks 1994, 26-36), Wesley's class meetings, or today's small groups and Bible studies, close and deep concern for others has always been an indispensable means of building up strong, persevering faith among Christians.

Hebrews provides a needful corrective to self-centered approaches to Christian "experience." The Hebrews approach to pastoral care is a "Let us" model of progress toward maturity, as we will continue to see in ch 4.

b. Warning Not to Fall Short of the Promised Rest (4:1-13)

BEHIND THE TEXT

Hebrews 4:1-13 completes the miniature sermon on Ps 95:7-11 in Heb 3:7—4:13. The first half accented the faithlessness of the wilderness generation, which barred them from entry into the promised land (3:7-19). The second half (4:1-11) builds upon the frightful consequences (esp. 3:16-18) in that ancient example of disobedience. The midrash closes in 4:12-13 with an ode to the word of God as a sword of divine judgment.

Hebrews 4:1-11 is a tightly organized unit, comprised of two subunits. The whole is marked by an *inclusio* of complementary admonitions. That is, the unit repeats the same point at its beginning and end:

- **Therefore, . . . let us take care** [*Phobēthōmen oun*] **that none** [*mēpote . . . tis*] **of you . . . has fallen short** (*hysterēkenai*) (4:1).
- **Let us therefore make every effort** [*Spoudasōmen oun*] **. . . so that no one** [*hina mē . . . tis*] **will fall** (*pesē*) (4:11).

Compare the similar admonition in 3:12 ("See to it . . . that none [*mēpote estai hen tini*] of you . . . turns away").

The two subunits (4:1-5, 6-11) are demarcated by references to the present opportunity for entry into God's rest. The opening to each incorporates similar expressions:
- "Therefore [*oun*] since the promise of entering [*eiselthein eis*] his rest still stands [*kataleipomenēs*], let us be careful that none [*tis*] of you be found to have fallen short of it. For we also have had the gospel preached [*euēngelismenoi*] to us . . ." (4:1-2a).
- "Therefore [*oun*] since [NIV[11]] it still remains [*apoleipetai*] that some [*tinas*] will enter [*eiselthein eis*] that rest, and those who formerly had the gospel preached [*euangelisthentes*] to them did not go in, because of their disobedience" (4:6).

We may catalogue and comment on the most important corresponding expressions:
- The promised rest "stands [*kataleipomenēs*]" (4:1) or "remains [*apoleipetai*]" (4:6); a verb that reappears strategically in the summary inference of 4:9.
- The entrance into the rest is denoted by the identical expression (*eiselthein eis*, "to enter into") in 4:1 and 4:6 and once again in the concluding admonition (4:11). (Similar references to entering the rest punctuate the midrash: 3:18, 19; 4:3 [two times], 5, 6, 10. The aorist infinitive *eiselthein* occurs also in 3:19; → 4:6-7 sidebar, "Chain-Linking.")
- The promise of rest is styled as the preached gospel in 4:2 and 6, the only occurrences of *euangelizō* ("preach the gospel") in Hebrews.

One of the preacher's goals in 4:1-11 is to hold out hope that the promise of entering God's rest remains open. However, the opportunity can only be seized by those who are faithful to God (4:1-3).

The second subunit (4:6-11) is itself marked by an *inclusio*. The only two occurrences in Hebrews of the noun for "disobedience [*apeitheia*]" may be found in 4:6 and 11. This resumes the note about disobedience in 3:18 (the verb *apeitheō*; see 11:31). The same framing technique is used in 3:12, 19 where the only two occurrences of the word "unbelief [*apistia*]" appear in Hebrews. These watchwords of the preacher's warning highlight the danger of unfaithfulness and disobedience for ruining one's prospects of entering into the rest.

Hebrews 4:12-13 forms the capstone, not only to the midrash on Ps 95 in 3:7—4:13, but to the entire sermon up to this point (Pfitzner 1997, 83; → In the Text on 4:12). It, too, is marked by an *inclusio* that plays on two different usages of the same word (*logos*: "word" [4:12a]; "account" [4:13b]). Accountability to the "message [*logos*]" (2:2) was the major thrust of the conclusion to the *exordium* in 2:1-4. Now it is again at the conclusion to this "second *exordium*."

The focus here, however, is on the power of the word of God to penetrate, discern, and expose the innermost thoughts of the heart. This ode to God's word stands as the counterpart to the quotation of Ps 95:7-11 in Heb

3:7-11 (Attridge 1989, 133). The word of God in Scripture has flashed like a sword in that soul-searching refrain, "Today, if you hear his voice, do not harden your hearts" (3:7, 15; 4:7; see 3:13).

"Rest" is the prominent theme in 4:1-11. The noun *katapausis* ("rest," "place of rest") occurs eight times (3:11, 18; 4:1, 3 [two times], 5, 10, 11), the verb *katapauō* ("stop," "rest") three times (4:4, 8, 10; BDAG, 523-24), and the rare *sabbatismos* ("Sabbath-rest") once (4:9). The theme is introduced in the first part of the midrash (3:11, 18) but is explained more fully in the second (4:1-11). The preacher has two primary messages about this rest. They relate to the rest's nature and timing.

Sabbath Rest and the World to Come

Hebrews was not the first, or last, to view the biblical image of Sabbath rest as having eschatological significance. Jewish and Christian writers in the intertestamental period spoke of "rest" in the age to come: "and the saints shall refresh themselves in Eden; the righteous shall rejoice in the New Jerusalem" (*T. Dan* 5:12); "It is for you that paradise is opened, . . . the age to come is prepared, . . . a city is built, rest is appointed" (*4 Ezra* 8:52; see *2 Bar.* 73:1; *T. Levi* 18:9). One text explains that "rest on the seventh day is a symbol of the resurrection of the age to come," for "on the seventh day the Lord rested from all his works" (*L.A.E.* 51:2; see *2 En.* 42:3).

The idea of the Sabbath as an "image of the world to come" (*Gen. Rab.* 17:12a) continued among the Jewish rabbis. The Sabbath song, Ps 92, was given the description: "This psalm is also for the Sabbath to come, for the rest of the life eternal" (*Tamid* 7:4), or "The day of the Sabbath, it is the day which is entirely rest . . .; but the righteous remain seated with their crowns on their heads and delight in the splendor of the Shekinah" (*'Abot* 1). According to another tradition, God created seven ages: six for the coming and going (of people), but only the seventh "is entirely Sabbath and rest in the life eternal" (*Pirqe R. El.* 19:9d; a similar view is reflected in the early Christian work, *Barn.* 15:4-5).

Hebrews appears to belong within this stream of interpretation that views the Sabbath rest as an eschatological reality. For more on the Jewish and Christian backgrounds concerning "rest," see Attridge 1989, 126-28; Spicq 1953, 2:95-104; → 4:3b-5 sidebar, "The Eternal Fate of the Exodus Generation."

First, with regard to timing, the preacher upholds the proposition that the promise of entry into rest is a present opportunity. The proposition that the rest "remains" is held forth in 4:1, reiterated in 4:6, then stated as a conclusion in 4:9. In 4:3a he states that believers "enter" (present tense) into the rest. The preacher employs a chronological argument, pointing to the fact that God's works were "finished since the creation of the world" (4:3c), after which he rested "on the seventh day" (4:4). God's creational rest remains open even now, since "a long time later" God designated "a certain day, . . . Today" (4:7). Joshua's conquest of Canaan could not have fulfilled the divine promise of rest; otherwise God would not have spoken "later" about another "day" (4:8). "There remains, then, a Sabbath-rest for the people of God" (4:9).

Second, the nature of the rest is more clearly defined. The promise of rest is an announcement of good news (4:2, 6), which must be heeded (4:2, 7c). It must be greeted with faith (4:3) rather than with distrust (4:2) and disobedience (4:6, 11). The rest is identified as God's own rest "on the seventh day," when "God rested from all his work" (4:4b). This is why it is called a "Sabbath-rest" (4:9). When believers enter into that rest, like God they also rest from their labor (4:10).

According to an ancient patristic reading of 3:7—4:11, there are three "rests" in Hebrews. First, the Sabbath, in which God rested from the works of creation. Second, Canaan, the promised land. Finally, there is "a third and more perfect rest," the kingdom of heaven (Photius, *Fragments on the Epistle to the Hebrews* 4.3-11). Church fathers such as Chrysostom, Theodoret, and Ephrem the Syrian also held to this view (see Heen and Krey 2005, 60-61). It was followed, e.g., by Bengel (1887, 4:378-79), Wesley (n.d., 570-71), and Whedon (1880, 66-67). William Lane succinctly expresses this line of interpretation: "The theology of rest developed in 4:1-11 takes account of the pattern of archetype (God's primal rest, v 4), type (the settlement of land under Joshua, v 8), and antitype (the Sabbath celebration of the consummation, v 9)" (1991, 104).

This interpretation is subject to a couple of major modifications. First, the author of Hebrews highlights the eschatological character of the rest. By the time of the NT, God's rest had become associated with the heavenly Jerusalem and heavenly sanctuary, or more generally with the world to come. Hebrews embraces this eschatological understanding. It is instructive that the image of rest is confined exclusively to the midrash in 3:7—4:13. Elsewhere in Hebrews, the same promise of salvation is expressed in figures that emphasize its future and transcendent dimensions.

Rest and Salvation in Hebrews

"Rest" correlates with other images of salvation described as future ("to come") or transcendent ("heavenly") in Hebrews. There are future realities such as "the world to come" (2:5), powers of the age to come (6:5), good things to come (10:1), and the city to come (13:14). Their transcendent character is expressed in references to the heavenly call (3:1), "heavenly gift" (6:4), heavenly sanctuary (8:5), "heavenly things" (9:23), heavenly homeland (11:16), and "heavenly Jerusalem" (12:22).

The rest may be compared with "the promised eternal inheritance" (9:15; see 6:12; 10:36) or salvation (1:14; see 9:28). It is an entrance into glory (2:10) or into "the inner sanctuary behind the curtain" (6:19), where Jesus has already entered as our forerunner (6:20) and champion (2:9-10; 12:2). The rest is fulfilled in the unshakable kingdom (12:28), that "enduring city" (13:14) with solid foundations, whose "architect and builder is God" (11:10). Rest, then, is one of the many images that display the multifaceted character of our eschatological hope (see Lincoln 2006, 95; deSilva 2000a, 163).

A second, related modification concerns the linkage between the promised rest of Ps 95 and God's Sabbath rest in Gen 2:2. The text from Genesis establishes God's own rest as the archetype for the promised rest spoken through David. However, it is not likely that Israel's settlement in Canaan is a type of the eschatological rest in Hebrews.

The preacher focuses on the wilderness generation's *failure* to enter God's rest (3:11, 16-19; 4:2, 3, 5, 6). Indeed, he expressly identifies them as an "example of disobedience" (4:11). Moreover, he views the conquest under Joshua as *not* providing rest (4:8). He does not point to any aspect of God's provision of rest after the conquest. He does not even mention the sanctuary on Mount Zion as God's resting place (Deut 33:12 LXX; Ps 132:8, 13-14), after God had given the people rest from all their enemies (1 Kgs 8:56). Such a reference would have had considerable typological implications, as the tabernacle does later (see Heb 8:2, 5; 9:1, 24; 10:1). But this sort of typological development would only detract from the stark contrast that stands behind the warning in this passage. The preacher wants the listeners to avoid the ancient pattern of rebellion, and instead press forward by faith to enter into God's rest.

IN THE TEXT

■ 1 Through the use of an inferential particle (*oun*, **Therefore**), this warning is linked to the previous cautionary example (3:12-19, esp. vv 16-19). In classic rhetorical fashion, the preacher employs a pathos argument: he appeals to strong human emotion in order to persuade his readers (Johnson 2006, 124). Here that emotion is fear, evoked by the very first word of this verse (*phobēthōmen*). Translations such as **let us be careful** ("let us take care" [NRSV]) or "we must be wary" (NET; "on our guard" [NAB]) are much too weak. "Let us fear" (ESV, HCSB, KJV, LEB, NASB, RSV; see NLT) and "Let us beware" (NJB) are on the mark. The consequences of the wilderness generation's apostasy should stand as a warning. As Calvin notes (1976, 45), Paul issues a similar warning about a more recent "hardening" in Israel (see Rom 11:25): "But they were broken off because of unbelief, . . . Do not be arrogant, but be afraid" (Rom 11:20).

The verb *phobēthōmen* (**let us be afraid**) is "more energetic" than *blepete* ("See to it") in Heb 3:12. The use of the first person plural (**let us**) underscores the solidarity of all the faithful in such fear (see 3:13; Spicq 1953, 2:79). All believers are liberated from the fear of death (2:15) or of human powers (11:23, 27; 13:6), but not from the fear of the Lord. Hebrews invokes a proper sense of fear before the One "to whom we must give account" (4:13), particularly in hortatory passages (e.g., 10:27, 31; 12:21; on the theme of fear, see Gray 2003; Koester 2001, 90).

The Hebrews must have a fearful concern for each member in the church. This is similar to Paul's directive to "work out your [pl.; i.e., the community's] salvation with fear and trembling" (Phil 2:12). They should work to prevent **any among you** (*tis ex hymōn*; **none**) from sharing in the fateful experience of that disobedient generation who reached no further than the edge of the promised land.

"Let us . . ."

When Greek authors wanted to urge readers to join them in their resolve to undertake a course of action, they could employ a grammatical form known as the hortatory subjunctive. It is essentially equivalent to an imperative, but in the first person plural (Wallace 1996, 464). Usually the formula "Let us . . ." is used to translate such exhortations into English. It is a favorite expression in Hebrews, occurring more often than in any other NT book (twelve times).

As a rhetorical device it is highly effective. It allows the speaker to issue a forceful command without "talking down" to the audience. Thus, the preacher expresses solidarity with his readers, as one who stands along with them under the authority of God's word.

Hortatory Subjunctives in Hebrews

Let us . . .	Hebrews
be careful (i.e., "fear")	4:1
"*make every effort* to enter that rest"	4:11
"*hold firmly* to the faith we profess"	4:14
"*approach* the throne of grace with confidence"	4:16
"*go on* to maturity"	6:1
"*draw near* to God"	10:22
"*hold unswervingly* to the hope we profess"	10:23
"*consider* how we may spur one another on toward love and good deeds"	10:24
"*run* with perseverance the race marked out for us"	12:1
"*be thankful*"	12:28
"*go* to him outside the camp, bearing the disgrace he bore"	13:13
"continually *offer* to God a sacrifice of praise"	13:15

The present opportunity **of entering his rest** is identified as a **promise**. There are more occurrences of the word **promise** (*epangelia*) in Hebrews than in any other NT book (fourteen times; compare Galatians, ten times; Morris 1981, 39). The promissory character of the entrance into rest is in line with the way the author speaks elsewhere of the nature of the Christian hope. As true descendants of Abraham (6:13, 15; see 2:16), believers are heirs of the promise (6:12, 17). The promise is an "eternal inheritance" (9:15), unrealized in the lives of ancient faithful ones (7:6; 11:9, 13, 17, 33, 39), but received by all believers at the coming of Christ (10:36-37; see 9:28; 11:40).

The promise **still stands** (*kataleipomenēs*). The verb *kataleipō* means "to leave behind, leave remaining" (Günther and Krienke 1979, 247) or "leave over" (BDAG, 521). The same verb is found, with the same sense, in Rom 11:4: *"has been left and reserved for us"* (Bengel 1877, 4:378). The cognate verb *apoleipō* ("remain") is placed strategically in 4:6 and 9 in order to underscore the point that the door of opportunity remains open. The different compound form here in 4:1 (*kataleipomenēs*) may have been chosen to produce assonance (word rhyme) with *katapausin* (**rest**), and a wordplay with *hysterēkenai* (**fallen short**): The promise *is left over* (*kataleipomenēs*), so let us be fearful lest anyone *is left behind* (*hysterēkenai*).

The last portion of this verse (**be found to have fallen short of it**) has given rise to conflicting interpretations. The debate surrounds the meaning of two Greek words (*dokeō* and *hystereō*) and boils down to two main interpretive options.

(1) It is a reassurance, meant to dispel anyone's mistaken notion that he or she has "missed the boat." The verb *dokeō* would be translated "think, suppose," and *hystereō*, "arrive too late, be left behind" (Spicq 1953, 2:80; Spicq 1994d, 428 n.18). This is reflected in the NJB: "none of you must think that he has come too late" (see GW).

It is difficult to square this view with the context, in which strong warnings are sounded about the danger of repeating the wilderness generation's fatal apostasy. Note particularly the parallel admonitions in 3:12 and 4:11 (see also 3:6). The phrasing in 4:1 itself speaks against this interpretation. One would have expected "Therefore, let us *not* fear . . . [*mē oun phobēthōmen*]," rather than the exhortation to fear that we find here (Lünemann 1890, 477; see Attridge 1989, 124). The author is not calming nerves or merely correcting misconceptions about the timing of the rest, but causing concern and urging progress toward entry into it.

(2) It is a warning against the dire consequences of failing to enter. *Hysterēkenai* is rendered in most translations as **to have fallen short,** "to have come short" (NASB, NET, NKJV; see KJV), or "to have failed to reach it" (ESV, NLT, NRSV; see NAB). Even the translations "to have come too late" (Lane 1991, 93 n. e) or "to have missed it/the opportunity/his chance" (HCSB, NEB, REB) are possible under this view, provided the idea of personal culpability is retained (Lane 1979, 954).

It remains difficult to determine how *dokeō* should be translated:

(a) As a euphemism to moderate or soften an otherwise harsh statement: "to *seem* to have fallen short," rather than the bare "have fallen short" (BDAG, 255; Oecumenius as cited in Westcott 1909, 94).

(*b*) As a suggestion concerning "the mere appearance or suspicion of failure" (Westcott 1909, 94; Bengel 1877, 4:378). Whether the rendering "seem" (ESV, KJV, NAB, NASB, NET, NRSV) indicates (*a*) or (*b*) is impossible to tell.

(*c*) As a judicial verdict: **be found** (NIV, NEB) or "be judged" (RSV) to have fallen short (see Attridge 1989, 124; Isaacs 2002, 62).

(*d*) As the equivalent to a direct statement (Clarke 1977, 3:708-9; HCSB and REB). Clarke cites the third-century A.D. Roman jurist Ulpian: "The word *dokein* is used by the ancients to express, not always what is doubtful, but oftentimes what is true and certain" (1977, 3:419).

The NIV's **be found to have fallen short of it** is a proper rendering. Yet a closer look at *hystereō* is necessary to support, not only the forensic understanding of *dokeō* (option [*c*]), but the broader, eschatological thrust of this verse.

Few commentators remark on the rare occurrence of the perfect infinitive *hysterēkenai* (**to have fallen short**). According to Westcott, the tense indicates more than a present (Rom 3:23) or past defeat (aorist; 2 Cor 12:11), "but an abiding failure" (1909, 94). It is more likely that the perfect tense has a proleptic or futuristic sense. That is, it conveys an action as a completed past action, though it is future relative to the time of speaking (see Wallace 1996, 581; for a similar use, see Heb 9:8).

This is facilitated by the identification of entry into the rest as a **promise** as well as the *"futuristic* orientation" of the sentence: **Let us be careful that none of you *will* be found** . . . (on the future time orientation of the subjunctive mood, see Hewett 1986, 163). Furthermore, the verb *hystereō* appears again in an eschatological context in 12:15 (Wilckens 1972, 8:596). Lünemann concludes, "The *infinitive perfect* characterizes that which, with the dawn of the Parousia, has become an historically completed, definite fact" (1890, 475). Likewise, Whedon detects the proleptic sense here. He states that the falling short will have occurred after "the end" (3:14; see 6:8, 11) and at the judgment day (10:25; Whedon 1880, 5:67).

■ **2** The preacher provides a warrant (**For** [*gar*]) for the warning in v 1. Both halves mirror each other in vv 1 and 2. The first half, **For we also have had the gospel preached to us,** corroborates the promise in v 1*a*. The second half of v 2 explains the biblical precedent for the potential failure forewarned in v 1*b* (Lünemann 1890, 478).

The phonetic similarity between **the gospel preached** (*euēngelismenoi*) and "promise [*epangelias*]" (4:1) is probably intentional (Attridge 1989, 124-25). There is a unity between the "good news proclaimed" (NIV[11]) to the ancient children of Israel and the gospel preached **to us** "in these last days" (see 1:2). The continuity between **the message** in the Old and New Testaments is more prominent here than in the similar comparison of 2:2-3 (see Lane 1991, 98). In Gal 3:8, Paul is more careful to note that God "*pre*-evangelized" Abraham. But here the overt Christian associations of *euēngelismenoi* are reinforced by the reference to **the message . . . heard** (*ho logos tēs akoēs*). Paul uses the same expression in 1 Thess 2:13 of the word of God that is **heard** and received **with faith** (see Rom 10:16-17; Gal 3:2, 5). Heeding God's word is crucial both in this midrash on Ps 95 (Heb 3:7, 15, 16; 4:2, 7) and at other key points in Hebrews (2:1, 3; 5:11; 12:19, 25).

The announcement of good news **was of no value to them** because the exodus generation did not respond in faith. The importance of the "beneficial" or "useful" was common in the Hellenistic world. It was one of the fundamental questions in rhetorical argumentation (Hermogenes, *Prog.* 11; see Thompson 2008, 72) and moral philosophy (Epictetus, *Diatr.* 1.4.16; 3.24.51). It was important also to Jewish wisdom writers (Wis 5:8; 6:25; Sir 5:8; 34:23, 25, 26; 38:21), Philo, *Alleg. Interp.* 3.86; *Cherubim* 121; *Migration* 55; *Posterity* 86; and scores more places), and other NT writers (Rom 2:25; 1 Cor 13:3; 14:6; 15:32; Gal 5:2; Heb 13:9; Jas 2:14, 16; see Johnson 2006, 125). Given the horrifying fate of the rebels in Heb 3:16-18, to say that they did not benefit from God's promise is surely an understatement (litotes).

The association of faith and hearing is clear, but the exact way in which they are connected is not. A jumble of variant readings appears at 4:2*d* in the Greek manuscripts. Scholars select from two principal readings. The first is reflected in the NIV's **because those who heard did not combine** [*synkekerasmenos*] **it with faith** (see also KJV, NASB, REB, RSV). The second is followed by most other English translations, such as the NRSV's "because they were not united [*synkekerasmenous*] by faith with those who listened."

In the first reading, the singular participle *synkekerasmenos* (**combine**) is grammatically linked to **the message** (*ho logos*) in the preceding clause (hence, NIV's **it**). In the second reading, the plural participle "united" (NRSV; *synkekerasmenous*) is grammatically linked to **them** (*ekeinous*) in the preceding clause. The latter is widely regarded as the most likely reading. It is represented in early and diverse textual witnesses. Since its meaning is not apprehended quite as straightforwardly as other readings, it accounts for the variety of "corrections" in the textual history (see Metzger 1994, 595).

The word for **combine** (*synkekerasmenous*) was used of the blending of paints, the tempering of metals, and figuratively of the joining of friends, moral and spiritual union, or the implication of a person in a conspiracy (Jewett 1981, 63; Ellingworth 1993, 243). If the second reading (discussed above) be accepted, it has the advantage of implying the union of the similar (persons with persons) rather than the dissimilar (God's message with persons; so Ellingworth 1993, 243).

However, it raises the difficulty of having to distinguish between **them** (*ekeinous*; note also **they**, *kakeinoi*) and **those who heard** (*tois akousasin*)—a distinction not reflected in the NIV. The preacher may be contrasting those who did not benefit from the message they heard with "those who actually listened" (Koester 2001, 270; compare ESV, NAB, NJB, NLT, NRSV; "obeyed" [NIV[11]];

or "heard it in faith" [HCSB, NET]). The true listeners have been identified as Joshua and Caleb, the only two who were willing to enter the promised land (Num 14:26-30; so Chrysostom 1996, 395; Lane 1991, 98). But Hebrews does not seem to take any interest in the positive example of Joshua and Caleb. In 3:16 "they who heard and rebelled" are "all those Moses led out of Egypt." Hebrews 4:8 negates Joshua's conquest as a provision of divine rest.

A case can be made that **those who heard** are the Christian believers who are reading Hebrews (keep in mind translations such as the NRSV: "they were not united by faith with *those who listened*" [emphasis added]). According to this interpretation, a sustained comparison is being made between the two groups who have been "evangelized." In the first half of the verse there are **we** (Christians) in the present and **they** (rebellious children of Israel) in the past. In the second half (in reverse order, forming a chiasm) we find **they** who heard without benefit (rebellious children of Israel) and "those who listened" (NRSV; i.e., **we** Christians). Then the next verse (4:3) draws the inference: "Now [*gar*] we who have believed enter that rest." Attridge suggests that such a bold comparison accounts for the many variants in the textual tradition. Additionally, 11:40 makes the similar point that God foresaw the OT faithful as not being perfected apart from "us" (Attridge 1989, 126).

■ **3a Now,** or rather **For** (*gar*), propels forward the comparison begun in v 2. The wilderness generation did not receive the promised rest because "they did not share the faith" of those who heard (4:2 NIV[11]; see 3:12, 19). But **we who have believed** are poised to realize the promise they forfeited. **We believers enter that rest** which **they shall never enter.** Faith as the operative factor—in averting destruction and attaining salvation—will once again find emphasis in 10:38-39 (see 10:22; deSilva 2000a, 164-65). The participle *hoi pisteusantes* (**we who have believed**) is in the past (aorist) tense, perhaps to signify our initial conviction or conversion (see 3:14; D. Guthrie 1983, 112).

The present tense verb *eiserchometha* (**we . . . enter**) has been critical to the debate regarding the time of entry into the rest. Some commentators take the present tense as futuristic, "we *will* enter the rest" (Ellingworth 1993, 246; Koester 2001, 270). Others think the tense must be taken as a "true present," stressing that believers are already enjoying the promised rest (Lane 1991, 99; Lincoln 1982, 215; Westcott 1909, 96). Still others are mindful, and rightly so, that a "true present" does not indicate that we have *already* entered the rest, but that we are *in the process* of entering it (deSilva 2000a, 155-56; see Johnson 2006, 123; Montefiore 1964, 83; GW).

Hebrews maintains the same tension between the "now" and "not yet," the realized and the future, that is found throughout the NT (→ 2:5 sidebar, "Eschatology in Hebrews"; 4:1-13 Behind the Text sidebar, "Rest and Salvation in Hebrews"). The present tense (**we . . . enter**) situates believers right in the middle of this tension. It is a reference to "the complex process on which 'believers' . . . are now engaged, although this process will certainly have an eschatological consummation" (Attridge 1989, 126, see also 128; Isaacs 2002, 62-63). Crucial to understanding the tension is to recognize the point of comparison between the two groups in this passage (see deSilva 2000a, 156). The children of Israel were on the cusp of entering into the rest; so also are present believers. The former did not enter because of their unbelief; the latter, as believers, are urged to enter while the "day" of opportunity—"Today" (4:7)—has not yet passed (see 3:13; 4:11).

■ **3b-5** The preacher supports the proposition that the promise of rest still stands. He argues on the basis of two passages of Scripture (Ps 95:11 and Gen 2:2). The passages are selected due to their verbal correspondence.

Verbal Analogy

The first standard set of seven rabbinic interpretive "rules" (*middot*) is attributed to Hillel the Elder (early first century A.D.). These rules were later expanded to thirteen by Ishmael ben Elisha (*fl.* ca. A.D. 110-130) and to thirty-two by Eliezer ben Jose ha-Galil (*fl.* ca. A.D. 130-160). One of the most widely used was Hillel's second rule, verbal analogy or *gezerah shawah* (lit., "similar laws," "similar verdicts"). The principle is that if the same wording occurs in two passages, the same considerations apply in both cases (on Hillel's rules, see Evans 2006, 381-82; Longenecker 1975, 33-38).

This principle is used in Acts 13:34-35 where two passages that contain the same word "holy" (Isa 55:3; Ps 16:10) are mutually interpreted as scriptural promises concerning Jesus' resurrection. In Heb 4:3b-5, Ps 95:11 and Gen 2:2 are brought together because they are the only two OT passages (in the LXX) that speak of *God's* "rest." In Ps 95:11 God refers to his "rest [*katapausin*]" (4:3b, 5). Genesis 2:2 relates that God "rested [*katepausen*]" on the seventh day (Heb 4:4). The proximity of the word **works** in both passages (Ps 95:9; Gen 2:2) strengthens the interpretive connection. Hebrews infers that the rest spoken of in Ps 95:11 is none other than the divine rest of Gen 2:2, when God "rested from all his work."

The flow of logic in the preacher's scriptural interpretation is complicated by the fact that he seems to be making two points at once. First, from the *contrast* between Ps 95:11 (exclusion from divine rest) and Gen 2:2 (establishment of divine rest), he draws the inference: the promise of rest remains in force for believers, even though the children of Israel forfeited it. The proposition that God's rest "still stands" or "remains" forms the backbone of the argument in 4:1-11 (see 4:1, 6, 9). Entry into or exclusion from the rest is governed, as it were, by the coefficients of belief or unbelief. Second, *comparison* of the two scriptural texts reveals that **my rest** in Ps 95:11 is authoritatively defined in Gen 2:2.

The first interpretive move (contrast) is launched in 4:3b. The citation formula, **just as God [lit., *he*] has said,** serves as the fulcrum between two opposites (note TYNDALE's "as contrarywyse [= contrariwise] he sayde [= said] to the other"). That believers are entering the rest (4:3*a*) is contrasted with the wilderness generation's exclusion from it in Ps 95:11: **So I declared on oath in my anger, "They shall never enter my rest"** (Heb 4:3*c*). This is an argument from the opposite, as Calvin observes (1976, 47): "It is unbelief alone that shuts us out; therefore the way in lies open to faith." (On the rhetorical topic of the "possible" as it is applied to opposites or contraries, see Aristotle, *Rhet.* 2.19.14; deSilva 2000a, 166 n. 67.)

The second interpretive move (comparison) begins in 4:3*c-d*. God's solemn oath to the desert rebels (4:3*c*) cannot be restricted to a refusal of entry into the land of Canaan. God speaks of his own rest, **my rest,** in Ps 95:11. God's rest cannot be limited to the period of the exodus, because it dates to the dawn of time: **And yet his work has been finished since the creation of the world** (Heb 4:3*d*). **And yet** (*kaitoi*) indicates a strong and notable correction (Smyth 1984, 654 §2893). God's rest was established when he completed his ***works*** (*tōn ergōn*) of creation. The phrase *from the foundation of the world* (*apo katabolēs kosmou*) connotes that the divine rest has an enduring, everlasting quality grounded in God's own nature and in the divine purpose for salvation history (Matt 13:35; 25:34; Luke 11:50; Heb 9:26; Rev 13:8; 17:8; Hauck 1965, 620). So the promise of rest was not exhausted when the wilderness generation was excluded from it.

The argument is corroborated (note the **For** [*gar*]) by two quotations from Scripture, beginning with Gen 2:2. The indefinite reference, **somewhere he has spoken** (4:4*a*), resembles the one in → 2:6*a*. Here it probably signifies a well-known passage, especially since Gen 2:2 stood toward the beginning of a scroll of Genesis in the Pentateuch (*pentateuchos* refers to the "five-scroll" work of Moses, the Torah), or on the first leaf of the later codex form of the whole Bible.

Primacy of the original instance was a common principle, used by Jesus himself (Matt 19:3-12 esp. vv 4 and 8 ‖ Mark 10:1-12). God's own, original rest at the foundation of the world stands as the archetype for the rest reserved for the faithful in the age to come (Pfitzner 1997, 81). It is "the reality itself of which the good news is given" (Attridge 1989, 130).

God has spoken **in these words** (*thus, houtōs*) in the text of Scripture (Gen 2:2) **about the seventh day.** The introduction to the quotation highlights one of two features of this scripture (namely, **the seventh day**) that will be significant later. **And on the seventh day** (4:4*b*) anticipates the identification of the divine rest as a "Sabbath-rest" in 4:9. That **God rested from all his work** will be essential to the definition of the believer's rest in 4:10.

The preacher has already quoted all of Ps 95:11 in Heb 4:3. Here he repeats (**again in the passage above**) only the words of the divine oath: **They shall never enter my rest** (4:5). In this way he brings before the eye of the reader, or ear of the hearer, the confirmation of his argument through a side-by-side comparison of the two texts of Scripture (Gen 2:2 and Ps 95:11).

The Eternal Fate of the Exodus Generation

Jewish rabbis of the first and second centuries raised a troubling question about Ps 95:11. When God swore in his wrath, "They shall never enter my rest," was he declaring that the wilderness generation would have no part in the world to come?

Rabbi Aqiba compared Ps 95:11 with Num 14:35 and concluded that they would not. Rabbi Eliezer ben Hyrcanus countered that the emphasis "I swore in my *wrath*" was crucial, because God had a change of mind later, after his wrath subsided (*b. Sanh.* 110b; *t. Sanh.* 13:10; *y. Sanh.* 10:29c). Another tradition attributed the hard-line position to Eliezer, with Rabbi Yehoshua opposing him. Yehoshua held that God's oath applied only to the spies and the truly wicked from that generation (*'Abot* 36; see Hofius 1970, 44).

How does the author of Hebrews weigh in on this issue? It depends on Hebrews' interpretation of the "rest" in Ps 95:11. Is the rest the land of Canaan, viewed as a type of the eternal, heavenly rest in the age to come? Then the punishment of those rebels was merely temporal: their corpses fell in the desert (Heb 3:17), but they will still have an inheritance in the age to come (so Gleason 2007a, 325-27). Is the rest in Ps 95:11 identical to the eternal rest spoken of in Gen 2:2? Then they have been excluded from the heavenly homeland/eternal city, which only the faithful throughout history will enter (Heb 11:1-40; 12:18-29; rightly, Cockerill 2007, 267-72).

4:3b-7   These are the only two texts in the OT in which God speaks of his own rest: **my rest** (*katapausin mou*) in Ps 95:11 (Heb 3:11; 4:3, 5) and **God rested** (*katepausen ho theos*) in Gen 2:2 (Heb 4:4; but see also Gen 2:3). They are perfect candidates for verbal analogy (*gezerah shawah*) interpretation. In comparing the two texts, it is clear that they must both be speaking of the same rest: the divine rest on the seventh day. In contrasting them, it is clear that, though some forfeited the promise through unbelief, God's rest has been established since the foundation of the world. Therefore, the promise of rest has continuing validity today.

■ **6-7** Verses 6-7 form one long sentence in Greek. Verse 6 summarizes the argument thus far and transitions to a further step in the exegesis of Ps 95 in Heb 4:7. The opening words **Therefore since** (*epei oun*; NIV[11]) mark the transitional and causal functions of v 6 (the NIV leaves *epei* [**since**] untranslated and pushes **Therefore** [*oun*] to the beginning of v 7). Two points sum up the preceding argument:

First, **it still remains** [*apoleipetai*] **that some** [*tinas*] **will enter** [*eiselthein eis*] **that rest** repeats the proposition set forth at the beginning (note the similar wording in 4:1: "still remains [*kataleipomenēs*]," "entering [*eiselthein eis*]," and "none [*mēpote . . . tis*]").

Second, **those who formerly had the gospel preached to them** [*euangelisthentes*] **did not go in** restates the point made in 4:2 (→ *euēngelismenoi*). That they did not enter **because of their disobedience** reminds one of the remark concerning that generation's lack of faith in 4:2b (see 3:12, 19). But now the preacher switches to a slightly different key in 4:6 and 11 (**disobedience,** *apeitheia*), anticipated in 3:18 (→ sidebar below, "Chain-Linking").

Chain-Linking

Hebrews uses a widespread rhetorical technique to link together the two parts of the midrash in 3:12—4:11. Lucian described the technique as chain-linking two units of text together (*History* 55). Quintilian compared it to two people holding hands (*Inst.* 9.4.129).

The chain-linking pattern may be represented as A-b/a-B. In Heb 3:12—4:11 the first chain-ring is 3:12-19 (= A). It is clearly defined by *inclusio* using the word "unbelief" (*apistia*) in 3:12 and 19. The anticipation or connection (= b) with the second chain-ring is in v 18. There it is said that the wilderness generation was unable "to enter [*eiselthein*, aorist infinitive]." This was because they "disobeyed [*apeitheō*]." The connection (= a) with the first chain-ring is found in 4:2: "they did not [*mē*] share the faith [*pistis*]" (NIV11). The second chain-ring (= B) is 4:1-11. It emphasizes the continued opportunity (*kataleipō* [4:1]; *analeipō*, "remains" [4:6, 9]) to enter (*eiselthein* [4:1, 6, 11]) into God's rest. This is contrasted with the wilderness generation's nonentry due to their "disobedience [*apeitheia*]," an *inclusio* in 4:6, 11.

Stylistically, this method of overlapping or interweaving material gives the midrash cohesion and clarity. It also helps to move smoothly from the first half to the second half of the exposition of Ps 95. This kind of fluid style is exactly what was recommended by teachers of rhetoric. Theologically, the technique interlocks the danger of unbelief and disobedience, supporting the preacher's strong warnings against being caught up in them, and their fatal consequences.

For further study of chain-link transitions, see Longenecker 2005.

Therefore since (NIV11) the entrance into God's rest remains open, and the rebellious Israelites did not avail themselves of the opportunity to enter (4:6), the preacher makes another inference from Ps 95 in Heb 4:7. He has completed a chronological argument from Gen 2:2 ("the creation of the world" [Heb 4:3]; "the seventh day" [4:4]) drawn in contrast to the *end* of the psalm (Ps 95:11). Now, in Heb 4:7, he marshals another chronological argument through a comparison of Gen 2:2 with the *beginning* of his psalm quotation (Ps 95:7-8).

God again set a certain day in the psalm (Heb 4:7). Pointing out **a day** may have been suggested by the word's appearance in Ps 95:8b (→ Heb 3:7b-8). More apropos is the connection with Gen 2:2. God's rest was established "on the seventh *day*" (Heb 4:4 [emphasis added]). Yet, **again,** God "appoints" (ESV; **set**) a certain day, **Today** (*sēmeron*). This declaration occurred **through David** in Ps 95. This, of course, was **a long time later** than the establishment of God's rest at the foundation of the world (Heb 4:3c).

A repeat quotation from Ps 95:7-8 is noted by **as was said before.** This refers to the pull quote in Heb 3:15 and the initial quote in 3:7-8. After the arguments in the second half of the midrash, and this repeat quote from the psalm, it is now clear that in Ps 95:7-8 God is renewing his offer of rest "in these last days" (Heb 1:2a). The opportunity is now but must be seized before the final "Day" approaches (10:25). This is why the preacher urged his readers in 3:13 to warn one another "daily [*kath' hekastēn hēmeran*]" ("every day" [NRSV]), "as long as it is called Today," so that no one's heart is hardened. The eschatological urgency is conveyed in the refrain from the psalm: **Today, if you hear his voice, do not harden your hearts.**

■ **8** The preacher sets forth a supporting chronological inference (**For** [*gar*]). Notice his references to **later** (*meta tauta hēmeras*; lit., ***after these days;*** compare "a long time later" in 4:7) and **another day** (*allēs*; lit., another; the word "day" is implied). He must have been aware of the OT characterization of Israel's settlement in Canaan as the fulfillment of God's oath to give the people rest (see Deut 25:19; 31:7; Josh 1:13, 15; 21:43; 22:4). However, **if Joshua had given them rest** [namely, the divine rest of Gen 2:2], **God would not have spoken later about another day** (i.e., the "Today" of Ps 95:7d). Note that Hebrews refers to **Joshua,** not "Jesus" (KJV; the two names have the same form in Greek: *Iēsous*). The rest under Joshua involved the cessation of hostilities with surrounding nations (Josh 11:23; 21:44; 22:4; 23:1). It was not the eschatological rest that remains open "Today," nor a participation in God's own creation rest.

■ **9** This verse concludes the arguments in the second half of the midrash. The statement begins with *ara* (**then;** "Consequently" [NET]). That God's rest "still stands [*kataleipomenēs*]" (4:1) or **remains** (*apoleipetai*) (4:6, 9) has now been strategically reiterated at the beginning, middle, and conclusion to the arguments in 4:1-11.

However, instead of the terms for "rest" used throughout 3:7—4:11 (*katapauō, katapausis*), here we find the rare expression **Sabbath-rest.** The word *sabbatismos* occurs in this verse for the first time in the surviving Greek literature. The notion that Hebrews coined the word is unlikely, since its only other occurrence in nonbiblical literature probably indicates independent knowledge of the term from Judaism (Plutarch, *Mor.* 166a).

The word *sabbatismos* is related to the verb *sabbatizō* ("keep the Sabbath") in the same way that *baptismos* ("baptism") is related to *baptizō* ("baptize"; Johnson 2006, 129). It denotes not just **Sabbath-rest** but "Sabbath observance" or "Sabbath celebration." Sabbath-keeping involved not only rest from work but also praise and thanks to the Lord (see 2 Macc 8:27; *Jub.* 50:8; *L.A.B.* 11:8; see Attridge 1989, 130-31; Lane 1991, 101-2; Koester 2001, 272). Use of the term was probably suggested by two things: first, the reference to "the seventh day" in Gen 2:2; and second, the well-known theological justification for Sabbath observance in God's own rest from the work of creation (Exod 20:11; 31:17), as the next verse confirms (4:10).

The preceding arguments of 4:1-8 amply demonstrate the eschatological character of this rest. The **Sabbath-rest** belongs to the age to come, which has already dawned in God's revelation in the Son (see 1:2*a*; 2:5; 9:26). But it was established at the creation of the world, with God's primordial rest (Gen 2:2). This fits in well with Jewish and Christian conceptions of Sabbath rest prior to and after Hebrews (→ Heb 4:1-13 Behind the Text sidebar, "Sabbath Rest and the World to Come").

■ **10** A clear allusion to both Gen 2:2 and Ps 95:7-8 spells out the meaning of "Sabbath-rest" in 4:9 (note the **for** [*gar*]). Two key issues are important for the interpretation of this verse: (1) The *timing* of the entrance into rest; and (2) the *nature* of the rest.

But first it should be noted that there are some who take "the one who has entered" (NASB) as Christ (Wiley 1984, 134-36; deSilva 2000a, 168; Attridge 1989, 131-32—the latter two only tentatively; see Ellingworth's critique [1993, 255-57]). The most serious objection to this interpretation is that if "Jesus" were really the subject of the first part of this verse, the author could have made this explicit.

With respect to *timing*, the past (aorist) tense "has entered" (ESV, HCSB, LEB, NASB, NKJV, NLT; *ho eiselthōn*, **anyone who enters**) is often seized upon as an indicator that Christians already experience the divine rest, at least in some sense (see D. Guthrie 1983, 115-16; Hagner 1990, 72). But, as Bengel asserts (1877, 4:381), "the people of GOD do not yet rest: therefore they have not yet entered in." This is in keeping with the eschatological thrust of the previous arguments, as well as the exhortations to be afraid of falling short (4:1) and to exert effort to enter God's rest (in the very next verse, 4:11). It is best, then, to take the aorist participle *ho eiselthōn* as proleptic or futuristic. This "involves a 'rhetorical transfer' of a future event as though it were past" (Wallace 1996, 564; see Zerwick 1983, 84-85 §257).

As for the *nature* of the rest, the preacher makes one last exegetical inference through verbal analogy. He explains entering into **God's** [lit., **his**] **rest** from Ps 95:11 through the phrase **rest[ed] from his . . . work** in Gen 2:2 (→ Heb 4:3*b*-5 sidebar, "Verbal Analogy"). He correlates **anyone** who, by entering God's rest, **rests from his own work,** with God's rest from his own works of creation (**just as God did from his**).

Questions surround what it means for the believer to rest **from his own work.** Since the text literally reads "works" (pl.), many have all too hastily concluded that "nothing could be more Pauline" (Taylor 1967, 55; see Jewett 1981, 64; and, surprisingly, Wright 2004, 37). Clarke even offers the gloss "*works of the law*" (1977, 3:711). But to interpret the rest as a ceasing from self-effort or "works righteousness" (Carter 1966, 66; Stedman 1992, 58-59; Turner 1975, 84) is entirely alien, not only to the immediate context, but to all of Hebrews. Hebrews never pits faith against works of righteousness (Hagner 1990, 72; Hagner 2002, 74-75). In fact, faith and obedience overlap in the thought of Hebrews (see 6:9-11; and in Paul, e.g., Rom 1:5; 16:26), as do unbelief and disobedience.

Several English translations render the plural "works [*ergōn*]" as **work** (sg.; GW, NIV, NJB), doubtless to arrest such a misreading. The "works" are not further defined as "dead" (6:1; 9:14) or "good" (10:24; see 6:10; 13:21; Ellingworth 1993, 257). Nor are they specifically identified with trials, temptations, or persecutions (on "work" in Hebrews, see Wray 1998, 78-79). The analogy with God's own rest is simple and complete within itself (Pfitzner 1997, 82). Rest is being contrasted with "labors" (NLT, NRSV).

The toiling and striving of this present life, the strain of running the race set before us (12:1), the pursuit of peace and holiness (12:14), will reach their goal in the heavenly city (11:10, 16; 12:22; 13:14; see Bruce 1990, 110). Only there in God's unshakable kingdom (12:28) will there be perfect rest (see Rev 7:16-17; 14:13; and Chrysostom 1996, 396, who points to Isa 35:10).

■ **11** Both parts of the exposition of Ps 95 began with an exhortation (Heb 3:12-13; 4:1). Now it ends with one. The matching admonitions in 4:1 and 4:11 form an *inclusio* around the second part of the midrash (→ Behind the Text for 4:1-13). Both 4:1 and 4:11 begin with a hortatory subjunctive, **Let us** . . . (→ 4:1 sidebar, "Let us . . .") and **therefore** (*oun*).

With his usual delight in puns, the preacher follows up his description of resting from work with an appeal to **make every effort** (KJV: "Let us labour . . . to enter into that rest"). The verb *spoudazō* conveys the idea of eager engagement (see Johnson 2006, 131; Ellingworth 1993, 258). With verbs of motion it may have the sense of "hurry" or "hasten" (2 Tim 4:9, 21; Titus 3:12; and here; so Taylor 1967, 57), but only rarely in the NT (2 Tim 4:9, as in the papyri [Spicq 1994b, 276 n. 2], but not in Titus 3:12 or elsewhere [278 n. 11]). It may be contrasted with the verb *paizō* ("play like a child, to sport") so as to indicate serious effort (see Harder 1971, 7:560). The cognate noun *spoudē* ("diligence" [Heb 6:11]) is the opposite of *anesis* ("relaxation, recreation," LSJ, 135; Spicq 1953, 2:84).

The use of *spoudazō* in Sir 11:11 is illuminating. There it is clumped together with two other terms for toiling (*kopiaō* and *poneō*) and is contrasted with two terms that are important in the present context of Hebrews: falling short (*hystereō*; see Heb 4:1) and being sluggish (*nōthros* [Sir 11:12]; see Heb 5:11; 6:12).

We must strive to enter **that rest,** the divine rest forfeited by the Israelites under Moses. The same interplay between community concern and effort (**us**) and the fate of any given individual among them (***anyone,*** *tis*; **none**) occurs here as it does in 3:12-13 and 4:1.

We should press forward together into God's rest, making sure **that no one will fall.** The consequence to avoid is equivalent to falling short of entering the rest (4:1). The word **fall** echoes the horrible and shameful fate of the wilderness generation in 3:17: their corpses "fell" in the desert (two of only three occurrences of the verb *piptō* in Hebrews: 3:17; 4:11; 11:30). This echo is amplified by the reference to the **example of disobedience**. The danger of **disobedience** is a major concern in the second part of the midrash (noun *apeitheia*; only two times in the *inclusio*: 4:6, 11). It is linked to the first half through the cognate verb "disobey [*apeitheō*]" in 3:18 (two times in Hebrews, only of the wilderness generation, see 11:31; → 4:6-7 sidebar, "Chain-Linking").

■ **12** Verses 12-13 bring the first part of Hebrews (1:1—4:13) to an eloquent conclusion. They comprise one elaborate sentence, bounded by two different uses of the word *logos* (→ Behind the Text on 4:1-13; → 4:13). They also function as the crescendo to the midrash that began in 3:7. This is borne out by significant links to the midrash:

- The **word of God** here has its counterpart in the quotation from Ps 95 in Heb 3:7-11 (Attridge 1989, 133). God clearly speaks in this scripture (3:7*a*, 9*b*, 11; see 4:3, 5, 7), and the preacher reiterates the need to listen to God's voice in both halves of the midrash (3:15; 4:7).
- The word of God as **living** has its counterpart in "the living God" of 3:12.
- The judging **word** (*logos*) in 4:12 is called the "word of hearing" (lit.) in 4:2 (*ho logos tēs akouēs*; i.e., the word that must be heeded). As Wesley notes (n.d., 571), this word is "armed with threatenings" in 4:3. The imagery of God's word as a "double-edged sword" only sharpens the fear and urgency of the exhortations in 4:1 and 4:11.
- Most importantly, the warnings against a "sinful, unbelieving heart" (3:12) and hardening one's "heart [*kardia*]" (3:8, 13, 15; 4:7) are matched by the power of the word to penetrate and judge the **heart** (4:12).

Hebrews 4:12 includes a cascade of images describing the vital, penetrating, and discerning power of God's word. The word of God is **living**. It derives this quality from "the living God" who speaks it (3:12; 9:14; 10:31; 12:22). Therefore, it is **active** (*energēs*), or rather "powerful" (KJV, NLT; Johnson 2006, 133; compare TYNDALE's "myghty in operacion") or "effective" (HCSB, NAB; Lane 1991, 103; "efficacious," Calvin 1976, 52). The word will not fail to accomplish God's purpose (Isa 55:11).

The word of God is personified as being **sharper than any double-edged sword**. Similarly, in Wis 18:14-16 the all-powerful word carries a sharp, deadly sword. A **double-edged** sword is one that is ***two-mouthed*** (*distomos*). The image of the "mouth of the sword" was very ancient, as attested by archaeological excavations in the region from northern Syria to northwestern Iran. Swords and battle-axes discovered there, dating to the second and third millennia B.C., have hilts that are carved into the shape of a lion, out of whose mouth proceeds the blade (Berman 2002, 299-300, with figures on p. 303). A sword is like a mouth in that it can lacerate flesh. The image of the double-mouthed sword referred to the power of speech (Judg 3:16; Ps 149:6; Prov 5:4; Sir 21:3; Heb 4:12; Rev 1:16; 2:12; see Berman 2002, 301-2).

There are interpreters, both ancient and modern, who think the *logos* in this passage is the Word incarnate (see Koester 2001, 273). But most commentators agree with Bengel, who counters this view with characteristic brevity (1877, 382): "For Christ, the hypostatic Word, is not said to be a *sword*, but to have a *sword* . . .; nor is He called *kritikos, judicial*, but *kritēs, Judge*" (see Rev 1:16; 2:12, 16; 19:15, 21; Acts 10:42; 2 Tim 4:8).

It is difficult to determine whether the word of God **penetrates even to dividing** "soul from spirit, joints from marrow" (NRSV), or if it divides each of these, "the division of soul and of spirit, of joints and of marrow" (ESV). It is possible that **soul and spirit, joints and marrow** reflect Platonic psychology and physiology (Johnson 2006, 134; Proulx and Schökel 1973, 336-37; → sidebar below, "Ancient Thinkers Dissect the Soul"). Division of **soul** from **spirit** would then indicate the separation of the superior, leading soul (**spirit**, the rational soul) in the head from the inferior **soul** in the chest. More likely, Hebrews is pointing simply to the division of our inner self into its most fundamental component parts.

Ancient Thinkers Dissect the Soul

The sixth-century philosopher Heraclitus, bored with the unending questions about the soul in his day, declared: "You'll never explore the furthest reaches of the soul, no matter how many roads you travel" (Tertullian, *An.* 2.6; Diog. Laert. 9.7). Speculation about the soul included questions about its origin, nature, relation to other substances or faculties (spirit, body, mind, emotions, etc.), and destiny (i.e., whether or not it is immortal). Only two questions about the soul are relevant to Heb 4:12.

First, there were many perspectives on the nature of the soul. Plato asserted that there are "three kinds of soul" (*Tim.* 89e): the rational (immortal, and lodged in the head) and the irrational (mortal), which is itself divided into two parts, the emotional (lodged in the chest) and the appetitive (in the abdomen; see *Tim.* 69d-72d, 87a). Aristotle believed that "soul" is only the body's form, and that "spirit" is the immediate vehicle through which a creature functions.

Stoics believed that both body and soul are physical (as opposed to Plato's idea of an incorporeal soul). Stoics, such as Chrysippus, believed that the soul *is* spirit that is active throughout the body. They divided the soul into eight parts: the five senses (extending to the respective sense organs), speech, the intellectual faculty (mind), and the generative faculty (seminal, extending to the testicles; see Diog. Laert. 7.110). Epicureans believed that the soul is made up of atoms that dissolve and dissipate at death.

Second, there were debates about where the ruling faculty of the soul resided. Platonists believed the rational soul rules the body through a system of "marrow" headquartered in the head (brain marrow), flowing through the backbone (spine marrow), then to the rest of the bones, as well as out of the base of the spine into the genital organs (seminal marrow; see *Tim.* 73d-75a, 90b-c). Aristotelians and Stoics generally viewed the ruling center of the soul as residing in the heart. Physicians such as Galen (second century A.D.), taking advantage of advances in neural science, located the command center of the soul in the brain. Tertullian, writing around the same time, surveyed much of the debate in his *On the Soul.* He held to the same biblical position that Hebrews did: the ruling part of the soul is the heart. For further study, see Annas 1992; Bennett 2007; de Lacy 1984.

Joints (*harmōn*) is not the usual word for bone joints but for any sort of connection or joining together. The word for **marrow,** strangely for English speakers, is plural, **marrows** (*myelōn*). For Platonists, death is brought on through the dissolution of the invisible bonds that hold together the elemental structure of the marrow. When this happens, "the root of the marrow" (i.e., the brain; Timaeus the Locrian 3.100) is no longer anchored to the body via the spinal marrow (Plato, *Tim.* 73d), and the soul flies away (*Tim.* 81d; see Timaeus the Locrian 3.102). Of course, Hebrews may instead be referring metaphorically to the way the word of God can penetrate to the center of our human frame, **joints and marrow.**

Regardless of what conception of human psychology and physiology stands behind this verse, it is clear that the sword of God's word executes judgment at the deepest, vital core of the human person. Here the dividing of components in the human person is not for philosophical analysis but for meting out the divine sentence.

The rendering of divine judgment reaches the center of human intellectual, emotional, and moral life: **the heart.** God's word **judges** or *discerns* [see ESV, KJV, NAB] **the thoughts** [*enthymēseōn*] . . . **of the heart,** which may have the emotional connotation of "desires" (NET) or "emotions" (NJB). It also judges **attitudes** (*ennoiōn*), or more accurately, "thoughts" (NAB, NET, NJB)—that is, the rational activity of formulating concepts or ideas in the mind (Spicq 1953, 2:89; Proulx and Schökel 1973, 337). No unbelief, deceitfulness of sin, or hardening of the heart (3:12-13) can escape the critical scrutiny of God's word.

■ **13** The preacher emphatically expresses the transparency of **all creation** before God through a double negative: **nothing in all creation** (*ouk . . . ktisis;* lit., "no creature" [CEB, ESV, GW, HCSB, LEB, NAB, NASB, NET, NRSV]; "no created thing" [NJB]) is **hidden** (*aphanēs;* lit., "not manifest" [KJV]; "invisible" [TYNDALE]). This is contrasted with a reference to **everything** being **uncovered** [lit., "naked," *gymna*] **and laid bare.**

The expression **laid bare** has been subject to various interpretations. The Greek participle *tetrachēlismena* is a form of the verb *trachēlizein,* which itself has a range of meanings relating to the neck (compare our word "trachea"; Johnson 2006, 135). Forms of the verb appear in the context of wrestling, in which an opponent is put into a neck hold (Philo, *Dreams* 2.34; *Rewards* 29). In the context of sacrifice it is used of bending back the neck of an animal to expose it to the sacrificial blade (Theophrastus, *Char.* 27.5). Chrysostom understands it as the image of a victim being cut open to reveal all of its inward parts (1996, 398). Sacrificial imagery best fits Hebrews' wider interest in priestly ministry, as well as the immediate reference to a sword (Attridge 1989, 136). It is also possible that we are dealing with a dead metaphor, since the ancient lexicographer Hesychius defined *tetrachēlismena* simply as *pephanerōmena* ("revealed" or "manifested"; BDAG, 1014).

In v 13 the focus has shifted from the word of God to God himself. No creature is concealed **from *his* sight** (*enōpion autou*). Everything is naked and vulnerable **before *his* eyes** (*tois ophthalmois autou*). The word *logos*, which appeared at the beginning of this concluding section (4:12), reappears here at the end, but in a different sense. God is described as the One **to whom we must give an account** (*logos*; see 13:17). This wordplay sums up the message of the conclusion: God's "word [*logos*]" (4:12) demands a human "account [*logos*]" (4:13) (Koester 2001, 275).

FROM THE TEXT

The thrust of Heb 3:7—4:13 is clearly to exhort us to enter into God's rest. A witness to this is the sheer repetition of language like "enter" (eleven times), "rest" (eight times; and "Sabbath-rest," once), and "remains" (or "still stands," three times). But what exactly does it mean to enter into God's rest, and when does it occur?

The theme of divine rest has captured the imaginations of theologians throughout the centuries. The theme forms an *inclusio* in Augustine's *Confessions* (1.1.1; 13.36.51-53), which also contains his most famous saying, "You have made us for yourself, and our heart is restless until it rests in you." A strong tradition of interpretation among the church fathers viewed the divine rest as the final rest that believers enjoy in the afterlife or after the final judgment—that is, in the kingdom of heaven (see Oden 2001b, 464; Heen and Krey 2005, 60-61).

There are also interpretations of the divine rest as a spiritual state into which believers may enter even now, if only in a way limited to our life on this side of glory. It has been described as a mystical experience of peace and divine revelation among the Eastern church fathers (see Isaac of Nineveh in Heen and Krey 2005, 60). Protestants have identified it as justification by faith, apart from works (Stedman 1992, 58-59). Calvin referred to it as that aspect of sanctification involving "mortification of the flesh" or self-renunciation (Calvin 1976, 48-49; see also Heidelberg Catechism, answer 103, in Kistemaker 1984, 111).

Possibly the richest interpretive heritage concerning this theme flows out of Methodism and the nineteenth-century holiness movement. In *A Collection of Hymns for the Use of People Called Methodists*, we find many places where the "rest" theme from Hebrews is interpreted as present entry into "The Canaan of thy perfect love" (Hymn 380, fifth stanza), "The sabbath of thy love" (Hymn 391, fourth stanza), or "The land of rest from inbred sin,/The land of perfect holiness" (Hymn 396, sixth stanza; in Hildebrandt and Beckerlegge 1989).

The most well-known reference is in Charles Wesley's "Love Divine, All Loves Excelling": "Let us all in Thee inherit, / Let us find that second rest."

Equating entrance into the divine rest with a second work of grace (entire sanctification) was so widespread in the nineteenth-century holiness movement that it scarcely requires documentation. Figures as diverse as Daniel Steele (1909, 209-42), Charles Finney (1980 and 1984), and Andrew Murray (1993, 163-78) expounded a holiness theology of rest. One holiness writer, Isaac See, wrote a treatise on entire sanctification titled *The Rest of Faith* (1871). This interpretive tradition was carried on by twentieth-century writers such as H. Orton Wiley (1984, 121-40), Richard S. Taylor (1967, 51-55), W. T. Purkiser (1974, 40-43), Milton S. Agnew (1975, 23-31), George Allen Turner (1975, 79-86, 215-17), among many others.

By the turn of the century, many holiness writers were less sure-footed in this interpretation, as illustrated by H. Ray Dunning's willingness to identify "the rest of faith" in Heb 4 with justification by faith, entire sanctification, *and* future hope (2001, 39-40). The important study by Wayne McCown (1981, 63-66) seriously undermined the holiness allegorical interpretation of Heb 3:7—4:13, while also showing the importance of sanctification within these chapters and throughout Hebrews.

Any attempt to equate the divine rest in Hebrews with a particular stage in the order of salvation (*ordo salutis*), or with a particular spiritual "experience," is doomed to failure. We will focus our attention on the holiness movement's interpretation, mainly because it is more developed than others. However, despite its faults, its emphasis on sanctification ties into a related theme that is abundantly evident in Hebrews. Four building blocks of this interpretation need to be examined.

First, it is based upon an allegorical interpretation of Israel's experiences under Moses and Joshua, which has no basis in Heb 3:7—4:13. The allegory runs like this: the exodus (= conversion, justification by faith), wilderness wanderings (= struggle with sin, carnality), and finally the conquest of Canaan (= the experience of entire sanctification, the "rest of faith," victory over sin). As we have seen, the author of Hebrews does not have the slightest interest in developing a positive typological correlation between the rest of Canaan and the divine rest. Indeed, he takes great pains to equate the rest in Ps 95 with God's Sabbath rest in Gen 2:2, *not* the settlement of Israel in Canaan. He emphasizes the *failure* of the wilderness generation to enter into the divine rest, as well as Joshua's *failure* to provide the divine rest available in these last days. The wilderness generation serves primarily as an "example of disobedience" that the readers will do well not to imitate.

Second, a faulty interpretation of Greek verb tenses is used in an attempt to demonstrate that entry into the rest occurs now (present tense *eiserchometha*, "we . . . enter" [4:3]), and that the entry is instantaneous, not gradual (aorist infinitive *eiselthein*, "enter" [4:1, 6, 11]; see Taylor 1967, 51-52).

As we have seen, the true import of the present tense in 4:3 cannot be that believers have *already* entered into the divine rest by faith, but that they are *in the process* of entering. Faithful obedience is the way to continue on the pilgrimage to our heavenly homeland; faithless disobedience is the sure way to fall short of reaching that goal. The aorist tense in 4:1, 6, and 11 cannot refer to an instantaneous work of grace in the heart, though this idea may be built upon other passages in Scripture. The complex issue of the abuse of the Greek aorist tense in holiness exegesis has already been ably discussed, most notably by Maddox (1981), and need not be rehearsed here.

Third, taking the "work" (lit., "works") in 4:10 as "works of righteousness" or "works of the law," as we have seen, is alien both to the immediate and full contexts of Hebrews. One might add that it makes for a very odd comparison to correlate resting from our own self-efforts to be righteous (works that turn out to be bad) with God's resting from the works of creation (which are repeatedly called "good" in Gen 1). The comparison becomes considerably more convoluted if "the one who enters God's rest" (NET) in 4:10 is Christ. For then Christ's finished work on the cross, the death to our "self-life," and God's rest are being correlated (see Wiley 1984, 134-38). Hebrews is distorted by reading it through the prism of Paul's theology.

Fourth, we have already shown the eschatological thrust of Hebrews' concept of rest (→ 4:1-13 Behind the Text sidebar, "Sabbath Rest and the World to Come"). There has been a tendency among some holiness expositors to downplay the eschatological character of the rest. Turner quite explicitly says that Hebrews "has risen far above the concepts of Jewish apocalypticism [e.g., *4 Ezra* 8:52] by emphasizing the spiritual nature of this relationship" (1975, 85). Taylor (1967, 55) sets forth a spiritualized interpretation of *sabbatismos* ("Sabbath rest") as a "Sabbath-state of the soul," a quiet rest in God that involves "self-crucifixion, . . . total surrender to God."

However, it is difficult to escape the eschatological urgency that stands behind the present opportunity ("Today"; see 3:13; 4:7) to enter God's rest, and the peril of failing to enter. Some hold to a present attainment of the rest of faith (i.e., ceasing from our own works of righteousness) in tension with a final fulfillment of the promised rest (e.g., Clarke 1977, 3:711). Few have been willing to hold these in tandem: a particular experience of entire sanctification (from a nineteenth-century holiness understanding) as a condition for entry into eschatological rest. W. B. Godbey followed this holiness interpretation to its logical conclusion, as stated in his provocatively titled work *Holiness or Hell?* (1893, 12-13).

If our reading is faithful to Heb 3:7—4:13, then none of the above building blocks holds up an interpretation of these chapters that points to a specific, personal experience of presently entering the rest. The divine rest cannot be equated with one particular step or experience relating to salvation or sanctification, but stands as a symbol of the terminal point in "the whole soteriological process" (Attridge 1989, 128; see McCown 1981, 66; → 4:1-13 Behind the Text sidebar, "Rest and Salvation in Hebrews"). Endeavoring to enter the rest now, while it is still "Today," is a metaphor for continued partnership with Christ and firm commitment "till the end" (3:14). The obverse is apostasy and the potential failure to enter God's rest (3:12; 4:1, 11).

We must hasten to add that holiness is an essential preparation for entering God's rest. These chapters clearly set forth the main obstacle to entering that rest: a hardened heart. This is a "sinful, unbelieving heart that turns away from the living God" (3:12; see 3:19); being "hardened by the deceitfulness of sin" (3:13 ESV, NASB, NRSV); a rebellious disobedience (3:18; 4:6, 11).

In the next chapter the preacher confronts his listeners' lackadaisical approach to faith, which has arrested their spiritual growth and clouded their moral clarity (5:11-14). But how can the preparation to enter God's rest be described more positively? How is the promise of rest in the future connected with the life of faith, obedience, and holiness now?

The eschatological reality of God's rest and the necessary sanctification of believers are brought together in Hebrews through the preacher's later teaching on Christ's entrance into the heavenly sanctuary (Pfitzner 1997, 82-83). Believers' qualification to enter into God's rest is described through images of worship and priestly ministry. It is instructive that the preacher never again uses the action of "entering [*eiserchomai*]" with regard to believers themselves, apart from the metaphor of entry into rest in chs 3—4. (Hebrews 10:19-20 does not say that we enter into the most holy place but that Christ has given us the privilege of bold access to God's presence.) Only Christ "our forerunner" has actually "entered" the heavenly sanctuary "on our behalf" (6:20 NIV[11]; see 9:12, 24 ["for us"]). What believers have that "enters the inner sanctuary" is "hope as an anchor for the soul," that is, the guarantee of our eventual entry (6:19). Otherwise the preacher consistently speaks of the Christian privilege of worship as an "approach" before God (*proserchomai*; see 4:16; 7:25; 10:22; 12:18, 22).

Our present approach and future entry into the reality of God's unshakable kingdom is made possible only through sanctification. Christ's sacrifice definitively takes away sins (9:28; 10:12), sanctifies (9:13; 10:10, 14, 29; 13:12; see 2:11), and cleanses the guilty conscience (9:14; 10:22). Christ's high-priestly ministry is based on a better covenant. The new covenant guarantees a new obedience among God's people (the antidote to a rebellious heart; see 8:10; 10:16) and a total obliteration of sins from God's memory (10:17-18). A more comprehensive sanctification cannot be imagined. Holiness is indispensable to having an audience before a holy God (12:14), or approaching God in worship "with a sincere heart in full assurance of faith" (10:22).

The necessary sanctification is accomplished through the death of Jesus. The effectiveness of Christ's high-priestly ministry will be front and center throughout the main part of the preacher's argument in 7:1—10:18. Sanctification is part of an ongoing life of faithfulness to God (see Heb 11). It is worked out in great struggle, through the divine process of discipline for God's children (12:4-13), and is crucial to receiving the promised inheritance (12:14-17).

II. JESUS' SUPERIOR HIGH PRIESTHOOD: HEBREWS 4:14—10:18

These chapters are central to the message of Hebrews.
- 4:14—5:10 introduces the subject of Christ's high-priestly ministry.
- 5:11—6:20 prepares readers to be more receptive to the in-depth teaching to follow.
- 7:1—10:18 offers a series of arguments demonstrating the superiority of Christ's high-priestly office, new covenant, heavenly sanctuary, and once-for-all sacrifice.

A. The Qualifications of the Great High Priest (4:14—5:10)

BEHIND THE TEXT

Hebrews 4:14—5:10 marks a major transition to the main argument of the homily. The opening verses (4:14-16) include, first, a restatement of the proposition for the entire homily (see 2:17-18; Bengel 1877, 4:383). Second, they repeat previous exhortations to remain committed to our **confession** (*homologias*: "the faith we profess" [4:14]; see 3:1, 14) and to hold on to our **boldness** (*parrēsias*: "confidence") before God (4:16; see 3:6). The same notes are sounded in a parallel transitional passage (10:19-23), which forms an *inclusio* with 4:14-16.

The "Bookends" of 4:14-16 and 10:19-23

The preacher frames the central part of his homily (the *probatio* or major argumentative sections in 4:14—10:18) with an impressive set of "bookends" at 4:14-16 and 10:19-23. The following table shows the many parallels between these two passages, which can hardly be accidental (Guthrie 1998, 341; deSilva 2000a, 180).

Hebrews 4:14-16	Hebrews 10:19-23
"Therefore, since we have [*Echontes oun*]" (v 14)	"Therefore, . . . since we have [*Echontes oun*]" (v 19)
"a great high priest [*archierea megan*]" (v 14)	"a great priest [*hiera megan*]" (v 21)
"Jesus" (v 14)	"Jesus" (v 19)
"the Son of God" (v 14)	"over the house of God" (v 21; see 3:6)
"let us hold firmly to the faith we profess [*kratōmen tēs homologias*]" (v 14)	"Let us hold . . . to the hope we profess [*katechōmen tēn homologian*]" (v 23)
"Let us . . . approach [*proserchōmetha*]" (v 16)	"let us draw near [*proserchōmetha*]" (v 22)
"the throne of grace with confidence [*meta parrēsias*]" (v 16)	"we have confidence [*parrēsian*] to enter the Most Holy Place" (v 19)

The first part of Hebrews focused on Jesus as the Son (1:2, 5, 8; 2:6; 3:6). The preacher explicitly named Jesus as high priest only twice (2:17; 3:1). He provided a few general descriptions of the Son's high-priestly ministry (purification or atonement for sins [1:3; 2:17]; sanctifying or making people holy [2:11; see 3:1]). Now in 4:14—5:10 he begins to delve more deeply into "Jesus the Son of God" as the "great high priest" (4:14). Jesus as the exalted high priest is "the main point" (8:1 NIV[11]) of the central arguments of the sermon (esp. 7:1—10:18). So it is no coincidence that 4:14—5:10 contains five references to "high priest [*archiereus*]" (4:14, 15; 5:1, 5, 10) in the span of thirteen verses. Of the fourteen uses of the word in the central section (and seventeen uses in all; see 2:17; 3:1; 13:11), the nine remaining occurrences are spread over four chapters (6:20; 7:26, 27, 28; 8:1, 3; 9:7, 11, 25).

Hebrews 4:14-16 reactivates the theme of high priesthood mentioned earlier, and it will be further developed in ensuing chapters. But it also prepares more immediately for 5:1-10. The unit (4:14—5:10) consists of three paragraphs: the first (4:14-16) sets up the comparison (*synkrisis*) of Levitical priests and Christ that will be expanded in the following two paragraphs (5:1-4, 5-10). Hebrews 4:14-16 is itself enclosed within two exhortations ("hold firmly" [4:14]; and "let us approach" [4:16]). As is the case throughout Hebrews, christological realities support and energize pastoral encouragement.

The preacher sets forth two aspects of Christ's priesthood in 4:14-16 that undergird his exhortations. He then amplifies these two aspects in the following two paragraphs. In fact, each of the two paragraphs (5:1-4 and 5:5-10) is carefully constructed around these two aspects:

First, in 4:14, "Therefore, since we have a great high priest who has gone through the heavens" points to God's installation of the Son as high priest (see 1:3, 5, 13; 2:9; 7:26; 8:1; 9:24). The first qualification of genuine high priesthood—namely, divine appointment—provides the frame for each of the following two paragraphs (5:1a, 4; 5:5-6, 10).

Second, 4:15-16 states the solidarity of a high priest with those for whom he ministers and his provision of access to divine benefits. This corresponds with the material forming the core of each of the following two paragraphs (vv 1b-3 in 5:1-4 and vv 7-9 in 5:5-10).

The manner of presenting these two qualifications for high priesthood reveals key differences between Christ as high priest and the Levitical high priests. With regard to the first qualification, all high priests must be appointed or called by God (5:1a, 4). But only Christ "has gone through the heavens" (4:14). That is, he alone has been glorified by God as high priest (5:5a; see 2:9). Ordinary high priests "must be called by God, just as Aaron was" (5:4), but Christ was exalted as high priest forever "in the order of Melchizedek"—a phrase that frames 5:5-10 (vv 6 and 10) and anticipates the first series of arguments in the central section (ch 7).

The second qualification is also applied to ordinary high priests and to Christ in contrasting ways. The contrast is anticipated in 4:15-16. There are three matters of importance: (1) solidarity with the human condition of those for whom the high priest ministers; (2) the relationship of the high priest to sin; and (3) the benefits of high-priestly ministry.

First, the matter of solidarity is previewed in 4:15a. The double negative, "we do not [*ou*] have a high priest who is unable [*mē dynamenon*] to sympathize with our weaknesses," suggests a contrast between Christ and the Levitical priests that is amplified in the following two paragraphs. Christ's ability to sympathize with human weakness is not diminished by his heavenly exaltation. Rather, his identification with humanity (in contrast with Levitical high priests) is at once more profound *and* altogether triumphant over human weakness. Notably, Hebrews stops short of directly ascribing weakness to Christ—facilitated by the double negative statement in 4:15, and probably in order to avoid associating Christ with the moral failure inherent in fallen humanity. Paradoxically, ordinary high priests are not able to sympathize fully with the ones they represent, precisely because they cannot transcend human weakness in order to provide real help. They are "beset with weakness" (5:2 ESV, NAB, NASB, REB; see 7:28).

This paradox unfolds through the language of ability (*dynamai*) and emotion (cognates of *pathos*, "passion") found in each of the three paragraphs. Christ is able to sympathize (*dynamenon sympathēsai*) with our weaknesses because he has been tested in every way like us (4:15). The ordinary high priest is only able to moderate his emotions (*metriopathein dynamenos*) toward others who have the same weaknesses that he himself cannot shake off (→ *sympatheō* and *metriopatheō* in 4:15 and 5:2). Christ more deeply entered into the human experience in that he went through the horror of death. His compassion was not just a fellow feeling, but a real sharing in human suffering. He "suffered" death (*epathen* [5:8]; see 2:9-10, 18; 9:26). However, he did so with the most complete devotion to God, "to the one who could save [*ton dynamenon sōzein*] him from death" (5:7). Identification with human mortality, and the divine victory over it, are what qualify him as the ultimate high priest (see 2:14-18).

The second matter regards the relationship of high priests to sin. Christ's relationship to sin is expressed succinctly: *chōris hamartias*, "without sin" (4:15). No mention is made of Christ's atoning death for sin in this passage (see 1:3; 2:17; 9:28; 10:12, 18; 13:11). Instead, a contrast is made between Levitical high priests who "offer gifts and sacrifices for sins" (5:1b) and Christ who "offered up prayers and petitions" (5:7). A critical deficiency of ordinary high priests is their obligation to offer sacrifices for sins, not only for the people, but for themselves (5:3). By contrast, Jesus offered up his whole life in devotion to God (5:7). His suffering involved obedience (5:8), which makes possible a new obedience among his people (5:9).

Finally, the benefits of high-priestly ministry are noted in 4:16. Confident approach before God by all worshipers was unthinkable under the old covenant. No such lasting benefit is mentioned in connection with ordinary high priests in 5:1-4. Only the high priest could enter into the most holy place, and then only once a year, on the Day of Atonement (9:7, 25). Later the preacher will argue that the Levitical sacrifices offered day after day, year after year (9:25; 10:2, 11) could never definitively atone for sins, unlike Christ's once-for-all sacrifice (9:12, 26, 28; 10:10). The "weakness" of ordinary high priests resulted in the ongoing ineffectiveness of their sacrifices, but Christ was "made perfect" when he offered up himself as the definitive sacrifice (5:2-3, 7-9; see 7:27-28).

This passage does not elaborate on the ineffectiveness of sacrifices under the old covenant. The fuller argument sketched in our previous paragraph (and developed later) is implied by the fact that the Levitical high priest's weakness obligated him to offer sacrifices for his own sins as well as for the people's (5:3; see 7:27; 9:7). The benefits of Christ's ministry are clearly superior. Christ's high priesthood provides worshipers with unbroken access to divine grace (note the present tense, "Let us . . . approach") for timely help (4:16) and "eternal salvation" (5:9).

IN THE TEXT

1. The Great High Priest (4:14-16)

■ **14 Therefore, since we have** (→ 10:19 and 12:1). The Greek word for **high priest** (*archiereus*) is rare in the OT (Lev 4:3; Josh 22:13; 24:33), though it is abundant in intertestamental literature (esp. the books of Maccabees) and in the historical books of the NT. The Hebrew OT uses the expression "great priest" (*kohen gadol*: "high priest"), or *hiereus megas* in the LXX, found once in Hebrews (10:21; see Lev 21:10; Num 35:25, 28; Neh 3:1, 20; Hag 1:1, 12, 14; 2:4; Zech 3:8; 6:11).

The expression **great high priest** (*archierea megan*) conveys the excellence or magnificence of Christ's office (Lane 1991, 103). This title is uncommon. It is applied to the Hasmonean high priest, Simon (1 Macc 13:42; 14:27), to the *Logos* in Philo (*Dreams* 1.214, 219; 2.183; see *Abraham* 235), and to Christ only here in Hebrews.

That Christ **has gone through the heavens** expresses his exaltation as high priest. Hebrews describes the Son's exaltation as a royal installation at God's right hand in heaven (1:3; 8:1; see 1:13; 10:12; 12:2). Later, passage through the heavens will incorporate the spatial imagery of the high priest moving through the holy place and entering "behind the curtain" into the most holy place (6:19-20; 8:1-2; 9:8, 11, 24; 10:20).

According to Hebrews' cosmology, Jesus passed through the transitory, created heavens (1:10-12; 12:26) into the permanent and true sanctuary, into "heaven itself, . . . in God's presence" (9:24; see deSilva 2000a, 181; Koester 2001, 282). The heavenly character of Christ's high-priestly ministry is essential for Hebrews. If Jesus were still on earth, he would not even be a priest (8:4). His cultic and moral perfection is heightened by the fact that he is "exalted above the heavens" (7:26; see *T. Levi* 3:4).

"The Heavens" in Ancient Cosmology and in Hebrews

Ancient Greco-Roman cosmology envisaged a geocentric universe in which the earth is surrounded by seven celestial spheres, beyond which is a realm of fixed stars (Martin 1987, 7-9). Cicero's renowned "Dream of Scipio" recounts an ascent through the spheres into "heaven" (*On the Republic* 6.15-16, 20, 24; "the heavens" [pl.] may refer only to the outermost realm [6.17] or the seven celestial spheres [6.22, 25]). The entire celestial realm surrounding the earth comprises the "temple" or "temples" of God (6.15, 17).

Jewish apocalyptic and rabbinic texts often mirror this classical scheme through references to seven heavens (*3 En.* 1-2; 17:1-3; 18:1-2; *Ques. Ezra* A 19-21; *Ascen. Isa.* 6:13; 7:8; *b. Ḥag.* 12b; *Masseket Hekalot* 4; see Alexander 1983, 239). But there are also different numberings of the heavens: two (*b. Ḥag.* 12b), three (*1 En.* 14:8-25; *T. Levi* 2:7-10; *Midr. Tehillim* 114:2), five (*3 Bar.* 11:1), eight (*b. Ḥag.* 13a), or ten (*2 En.* 20:3; 22). One tradition records that 955 heavens were created above the seventh heaven (*3 En.* A 48:1; *Masseket Hekalot* 7). In any case, the highest heaven is the location of God's throne (*2 En.* J 1a:4; 20:3; *4 Ezra* 8:20-21; *Ques. Ezra* A 21; see Rev 4:1-10), tabernacle/temple (*2 Bar.* 4:5-6; *Sib. Or.* 5:420-24; see Rev 7:15; 11:19; 15:5-8), or the holy of holies (*T. Levi* 3:4).

Hebrews has no interest in carefully describing Jesus' ascent through the heavens (see *Ascen. Isa.* 9:13-18; 11:22-33; Bruce 1990, 115; Koester 2001, 282); nor has he provided a detailed celestial schematic. Yet it is possible to discern three distinctions regarding "the heavens" in Hebrews. (The author may share Paul's idea of three heavens in 2 Cor 12:2-4; note the extrabiblical parallel in Lucian, *Icar.* 1.)

First, there are the temporary heavens that are part of the "created things" (12:27; see 1:10). They will be "shake[n]" (12:26) or "will perish," for they can wear out or be changed "like a garment" (1:11-12).

Second, there is "the city of the living God," "the heavenly Jerusalem" (12:22; see 11:10, 16). It is an "enduring city" (13:14) in God's unshakable kingdom (12:28). Here is located the true, heavenly "tabernacle [*skēnē*]" (8:2, 5; see 9:23). When Jesus passed "through the heavens [*dielēlythota tous ouranous*]" (4:14; see 8:1), he went "through [*dia*]" the "greater and more perfect tabernacle [*skēnē*] that is . . . not part of this creation [*ktisis*]" (9:11).

Third, Jesus as high priest entered "behind the curtain" (6:19-20; see 9:3; 10:20) into the most holy place (*ta hagia* [9:12; see 9:25; 10:19]). That is, "he entered [into] heaven itself [*eis auton ton ouranon*]" into the presence of God (9:24).

Thus, Jesus advanced through the heavens of this present creation (*ktisis*), through the heavenly tent (*skēnē*), and into the holy of holies (*ta hagia*). He was "exalted above the heavens" (7:26) into "heaven itself" (9:24) "at the right hand of the [divine] Majesty" (1:3; 8:1). (For further study, see deSilva 1997, 440; Traub and von Rad 1967, 527, 535.)

Hebrews has predominantly called **Jesus** "Son" up until now (1:2, 5, 8; 2:6, 10; 3:6). The fuller title **Son of God** occurs here for the first time. It will be repeated in 6:6, 7:3, and 10:29. The whole title, **Jesus the Son of God,** is placed emphatically at the end of the opening clause (→ 2:9 sidebar, "Use of the Name 'Jesus' in Hebrews").

The Son's majesty and authority over the world to come (2:5; see 1:2-3, 6-8, 13; 2:8-9) last appeared in 3:1-6. There the preacher drew attention to Jesus as "the apostle and high priest of our confession [*homologias*]" (3:1 NRSV) and "the Son over God's house" (3:6 NIV[11]; see 10:21). He addressed his audience as partners in a "heavenly calling" (3:1) and stressed the importance of their continuing commitment ("hold on [*kataschōmen*]") (3:6; see 3:14). Likewise, in 4:14 the ascendancy of the Son "who has gone through to the highest heaven" (NJB) is grounds for exhorting, **let us hold firmly to the faith we profess** (*kratōmen tēs homologias,* "let us hold fast to the confession" [HCSB]; see 10:23; 3:6, 14). The leading edge of Hebrews' "word of exhortation" (13:22) appears in repeated encouragement and warning to maintain commitment to the greater ministry and salvation in Christ.

■ **15** The word **For** introduces the negation of a false inference that might be drawn from v 14 (Zerwick and Grosvenor 1981, 662; Lane 1991, 107 n. a). It could be inferred that Jesus' heavenly exaltation makes him distant and untouched by the testing and struggles the community is experiencing. The preacher uses a double negative to counter this: **we do not** [*ou*] **have a high priest who is *not able*** [*mē dynamenon*] **to sympathize.** Note the deliberate contrast with the previous verse: "we have a great high priest" (4:14) but **we do not have a high priest.** Hebrews avoids directly associating Jesus with **our weaknesses.** "Weakness [*astheneia*]" need not imply moral deficiency (see 11:34), but it does so consistently in Hebrews with respect to Levitical high priests. Their weakness (5:2; 7:28) explains why they need regular atonement for their own sins (5:3; 7:27).

Jesus is able **to sympathize** with our weaknesses. The word **sympathize** (found in most English translations) can be misleading. The English word is often connected with the practice of expressing one's condolences for someone who has lost a loved one or has experienced some other misfortune. The Greek word *sympatheō* includes, but involves more than, relating to another's troubles emotionally or psychologically ("feeling" [NJB]; "touched with the feeling" [KJV]; "understands" [CEV, NLT]). Jesus existentially participated in human suffering, as shown in the next clause, and in 5:7-8. Since he has "been there" (as we might say), he can truly "empathize" (NIV[11]) or "have compassion" (TYNDALE, following Luther's "Mitleid haben"). The context, as well as the use of *sympatheō* elsewhere (e.g., "suffered along with" [10:34 NIV[11]]), point to an identification with the plight of others that seeks to do more than just "feel their pain," but to bring active support and assistance to them (4 Macc 4:25; 13:23; *T. Sim.* 3:6; *T. Benj.* 4:4; see Lane 1991, 108 n. c, 114).

Jesus is able to identify with the human struggle against sin because he himself was **tempted** or "tested" (NAB, NRSV; "put to the test" [NJB]). The participle *pepeirasmenon* is causal, as the NLT translates: *"for* he faced all of the same testings" (emphasis added). The participle is also in the perfect tense. This indicates that Jesus, having triumphed over temptation, is "tried and tested" (Zerwick and Grosvenor 1981, 662). The preacher describes the character of Jesus' testing in three crisp phrases, welded together by Greek prepositions beginning with hard, guttural consonants (Koester 2001, 283): **in every way** [*kata panta*], **just as we are** [*kath' homoiotēta*]—**yet was without sin** (*chōris hamartias*).

Jesus is uniquely qualified to represent us because he participated in the depths of the human experience. The preacher's statement concerning the universal applicability (**in every way**) and likeness (**just as we are**) of Jesus' testing is not intended to invite comparisons with every possible case study in temptation. The point is not that Jesus can identify with any particular, distinctive situation (compare 1 Cor 10:13). The focus is rather on the testing Jesus endured—the suffering of death—whose nature and intensity is applicable to everyone without exception. Mortality is the most basic and inescapable fact of human existence. Jesus' obedience was forged in the crucible of suffering (5:8; see 2:18). He "taste[d] death for everyone" (2:9-10).

Repeating the Proposition

Hebrews 4:14-16 clearly repeats key points made in the proposition for the whole sermon found in 2:17-18:

2:17-18	4:14-16
Jesus "had to be made like [*homoiōthēnai*]" us "in every way [*kata panta*]" (v 17)	Jesus was tempted **in every way** [*kata panta*], **just as we are** [*kath' homoiotēta*] (v 15)
He "suffered [*peponthen*] when he was tempted [*peirastheis*]," so that "he is able to help [*dynatai . . . boēthēsai*] those who are being tempted" (v 18)	He is able (*dynamenon*) **to sympathize** [*sympathēsai*] (v 15) and provide "help [*boētheian*]" (v 16) because he was "tempted [*pepeirasmenon*]" (v 15)
He became a "merciful and faithful high priest" (v 17)	A "great high priest" (vv 14-15) faithful to God (**without sin** [v 15]) and merciful toward us (we can "receive mercy and find grace" before God [v 16])

Jesus' endurance of testing is especially relevant to the readers, for they have experienced suffering in the past (10:32-34) and still identify with others who suffer (13:3). Jesus' death on the cross is the singular example of faithful endurance to fulfill God's will, for he offered his own body as a sacrifice for sins (10:9-10; see 7:27; 9:14, 25, 26). He did not waver in his faithfulness to God (2:13a, 17; 3:2, 6; 12:2), despite the cross's shame (12:2) and the fierce opposition from sinners (12:3). He was tempted to fall away and give up his mission, but he did not (Thompson 2008, 113). He ran the course set before him, all the way to the finish line—from the cross to the throne (12:2). He became our "forerunner" into the most holy place (6:20 NIV[11]). He suffered the ultimate test, **yet was without sin.**

Therefore, he is fully equipped to assist us in combating "a sinful, unbelieving heart that turns away from the living God" (3:12) or with casting off "the sin that so easily entangles" (12:1), so that we can persevere in faith (10:19-25, 36-39). His example is more than adequate to the readers' struggle against sin, for they "have not yet resisted to the point of shedding [their] blood," as he did (12:4). Our great high priest, who is completely "set apart from sinners" and "exalted above the heavens," possesses the unlimited resources of holiness to save his people completely from sin (7:25-26).

■ **16** The opening exhortation was to "hold firmly" to our confession (4:14). Verse 16 closes this paragraph (4:14-16) with a corresponding exhortation. Commitment and perseverance are impossible without the help of mercy and the strength of God's sustaining grace.

Believers avail themselves of divine enablement within the context of corporate worship. **Let us then approach** or "draw near" (ESV, NASB) refers to an action associated with the temple cult in the LXX. Priests (Lev 9:7-8; 21:17-24; 22:3; Num 16:40; 18:3-4) and people (Exod 16:9; Lev 9:5; Num 18:4) approached the sanctuary for worship (Thompson 2008, 105). In Hebrews this verb is used of approaching God in worship (4:16; 7:25; 10:1, 22; 12:18, 22; see 11:6). Here it is in the present tense, underlining the continuous access: **Let us *again and again* approach the throne of grace** (Lane 1991, 115).

Such intimate, immediate, and ongoing access to God through Jesus was never before possible, not even for high priests under the old covenant (see 9:7-8). The very first scriptural words from Jesus quoted in Hebrews (2:12) show Jesus leading his brothers and sisters in praise to God "in the assembly" (CEB, TNIV; compare "meeting together" [10:25]). Believers can make their approach—through Jesus (7:25; 13:15)—before **the throne of grace.** Christ's sacrifice of himself for our sins provides access before God in the most holy place (10:19, 22; see 9:12) and participation in heavenly worship (12:22-24, 28).

The seat of "divine majesty" (8:1 GNT, NJB; see 1:3; 12:2) and righteous rule (1:8), from which God's judgment against sin proceeds (4:12-13; 6:2; 9:27; 10:27, 30; 12:23; 13:4), is for believers **the throne of grace.** Christ's sacrificial death to remove (9:26, 28; 10:4, 11) or purge (1:3; 9:14, 22-23; 10:2, 22) sins and to sanctify his people (2:11; 10:10, 14, 29; 13:12) was initiated "by the grace of God" (2:9).

Rather than turning or shrinking away from the living God (3:12; 10:38-39), through Christ we may **approach** God **with confidence.** "Boldness [*parrēsia*]" (HCSB, NRSV) was the civic privilege of all freeborn citizens to speak their minds openly in public assembly. In Hellenistic Judaism this right was appropriated within the religious context of righteous people addressing God in prayer (Josephus, *Ant.* 2.52; 5.38; Philo, *Heir* 5, 91-92; Attridge 1989, 142; Lane 1991, 115-16; see Eph 3:12; 1 John 5:14-15).

This confidence enables believers to **receive mercy and find grace.** God's tender **mercy** (Heb 2:17) and strengthening **grace** (13:9) are extended to us **in our time of need.** The final phrase reads literally "for timely help" (NAB; see REB). Divine aid is available "whenever we need help" (NET). Hebrews 2:18 pinpoints the right time for Jesus to "help": when we are "tempted," because he also "suffered when he was tempted" (Attridge 1989, 142).

2. Qualifications of Ordinary High Priests (5:1-4)

This paragraph concerning Levitical high priests is actually one long sentence in Greek (on the periodic sentence, → In the Text for 1:1-4). It is enclosed by similar references to the high priesthood as a divine vocation:

- **Every high priest is selected** [*lambanomenos*] **from among men and is appointed . . . in matters related to God** (5:1).
- **No one takes** [*lambanei*] **this honor upon himself; he . . . [is] called by God** (5:4).

■ **1** The preacher begins with virtually a dictionary definition of **high priest** (Hagner 1990, 79). **Every high priest is selected** or **appointed** by God as a go-between God and human beings. A high priest is selected **from among men** that he might stand as a representative *for men* (to represent them; compare 5:3). He represents people **in matters related to God,** a phrase used in 2:17 of a priest's service in offering sacrifices before God.

A purpose clause defines the function of a high priest: **to offer gifts and sacrifices for sins.** The verb **offer** (*prospherō*) is frequently used in the LXX and NT in sacrificial contexts. The grammatical structure of the pairing **gifts and sacrifices** (*dōra te kai thysias,* "both gifts and sacrifices" [HCSB, KJV, LEB, NASB, NET]) may indicate two different kinds of offerings. **Gifts** may be meal or cereal offerings, while **sacrifices** are blood offerings (e.g., D. Guthrie 1983, 125; Lane 1991, 116; Wiley 1984, 155). Philo provides a better explanation when he distinguishes between Cain's "sacrifices" and Abel's "gifts" in Gen 4:4-5. A sacrifice is when someone slays an animal, pours the blood around the altar, and takes the flesh home. A gift is offered wholly to the one who receives it (QG 1.62).

The same phrase (**gifts and sacrifices**) occurs twice more (Heb 8:3; 9:9) as a comprehensive expression for the sacrificial duties of the high priest. If a distinction is intended between **gifts** and **sacrifices** in Hebrews, it may be a distinction without a difference. Hebrews 11:4 uses the two terms interchangeably. When discussing the sacrificial ministry of the Levitical priesthood, the preacher almost exclusively has in mind the sin offerings presented daily (7:27; 10:11) or on the Day of Atonement (9:25; 10:1, 3). Whatever gifts and sacrifices were, they were offered **for sins.**

■ **2** In v 2a a positive quality of ordinary high priests is presented, but is heavily counterbalanced by the consideration of their weakness in vv 2b-3. An ordinary high priest **is able to deal gently** with the people he represents. While this is a positive quality, there is a contrast between **to deal gently** here and "sympathize" in 4:15. To sympathize (*sympatheō*) involves sharing in someone's suffering. **To deal gently** (*metriopatheō*) generally denotes (e.g., in Philo, Josephus, and Plutarch) a moderation of one's emotions, especially anger. W. M. Macgregor defined it as "the mid-course between explosions of anger and lazy indulgence" (Barclay 1976, 46). The high priest must "curb his emotions" (Koester 2001, 286) so that, on the one hand, he does not vent his anger on sinners, or on the other, gush with pity over their failings.

This emotional control is directed toward **those who are ignorant and are going astray.** The two terms (**ignorant** and **going astray**) are governed by the same definite article in Greek, forming a hendiadys: "those who ignorantly go astray" (Attridge 1989, 144). The terms do not denote, respectively, sins committed in ignorance and sins committed "with a high hand" (contrary to Thompson 2008, 106). Nor is there a link with the use of these terms in 3:10 (contrary to Koester 2001, 286). There is nothing to suggest that the ignorance and waywardness of the wilderness generation were anything but willful: the hardening of their own hearts (Johnson 2006, 143). Hebrews' understanding of sin is in keeping with the OT sacrificial regulations allowing sin offerings to cover unintentional offenses (Lev 4:2, 13, 22, 27; 5:15, 18; Num 15:22-29; see Heb 9:7), but not deliberate or "high-handed" sins (Exod 21:14; Num 15:30-31; Deut 17:12; see Heb 6:4-8; 10:26-31; 12:17; Attridge 1989, 144; Bruce 1990, 120-21).

The high priest's capacity to modulate his emotions is due to his own involvement in universal human weakness: **since he himself is subject to weakness.** Weakness is an unavoidable and pervasive part of the high priest's life. The verb *perikeimai* (**is subject to**) is used of being surrounded (e.g., by a cloud [12:1]), having something hung around the neck (a millstone [Mark 9:42; Luke 17:2]), wearing clothes or jewelry (Ep Jer 1:24, 57), or being bound in chains (4 Macc 12:2; Acts 28:20). The verb can also be used in the sense of "to be fully covered with" (Herodotus, *Hist.* 1.171; Josephus, *Ant.* 3.129; Johnson 2006, 143). According to Josephus, the high priest is "clothed" with the sacred vestments, signifying his glorious and venerable position of authority (*J.W.* 4.164; see Sir 45:6-13). According to Hebrews, the high priest is "clothed with weakness" (Koester 2001, 286-87; "compassed with infirmity" [KJV]).

■ **3** The preacher accentuates, not the psychological benefit of a high priest's weakness (v 2*a*), but its limitations on his sacrificial function. **This "weakness" (v 2) is why he has to offer sacrifices for his own sins, as well as for the sins of the people.** He **has to** or "is obligated [*opheilei*]" (ESV, LEB, NASB, NET; see 2:17) to do so because of his inherent infirmity, as well as under legal necessity (7:27-28).

The Greek text tightly correlates the sins of the high priest and of the people through the repetition of the preposition **for** (*peri*), as well as through the correlative construction (lit.): *just as for the people* [*peri tou laou*], *so also for himself* [*peri autou*], **to offer** sacrifices *for sins* (*peri hamartiōn*). Thus, the preacher expresses emphatically that both high priest and people are equally susceptible to the defilement of sin. That ordinary high priests cannot transcend the deficiencies of those to whom they minister will be exploited later as a key distinction between their high priesthood and the sinless Christ's (7:26;

see 4:15). They must offer sacrifices, even for their own sins, over and over again; Christ offers himself, unblemished, once for all, to remove sins (7:27-28; 9:7, 12; 10:10-12).

■ 4 This paragraph ends where it began (5:1), with an affirmation of the Levitical high priest's divine appointment. **No one takes this honor upon himself.** The term **honor** (*timē*) was commonly used for an office or position of authority (see Attridge 1989, 144-45). Josephus frequently refers to the high-priestly office as an **honor.** Indeed, it is "the highest of all honors" (*J.W.* 4.149; see 4.164; Koester 2001, 287).

No man **takes** (*lambanei*) this esteemed position for himself, for every high priest "is selected [*lambanomenos*]" (5:1) by God. **Rather** [*alla*], **he must be called by God, just as Aaron was.** The divine ordination of **Aaron,** and the hereditary succession of his office, are unquestioned facts about the high priesthood in the OT (Exod 28:1; Lev 8:1; Num 3:10; 17:1-11; 18:1-8; see Sir 45:6-7a; Josephus, *Ant.* 3.188, 190; 20.224; Heb 7:6, 16).

3. Qualifications of the High Priest like Melchizedek (5:5-10)

Like the previous paragraph, this is one long (but even more complex) sentence. The principal verbs in Greek assist us in teasing out its main emphases: Christ did not **glorify** himself (v 5); he learned . . . from what he suffered (v 8 emphasis added); and became the source of eternal salvation (v 9 emphasis added).

This paragraph is also structured like the previous one. Statements concerning God's designation of Christ as high priest frame the discussion (5:5-6, 10). Notable is the repetition of the phrase **in the order of Melchizedek** (5:6, 10), which anticipates the first major argumentative section of the homily in ch 7. The core of the paragraph (5:7-9) presents Christ's solidarity with his people and his perfection as **the source of eternal salvation.** "Perfection" (or "maturity")—either of Christ as high priest (7:11, 19, 28; see 9:11) or of worshipers (5:14; 6:1; 10:1, 14)—is a major topic in the central section of the sermon, and beyond (11:40; 12:2, 23).

The discussion in this and the previous paragraph may be distinguished by the use of verb tenses. The first paragraph (concerning the OT high priests [5:1-4]) consistently employs present tense verbs. The second (concerning Christ [5:5-10]) uses past tense verbs—but with understandable exceptions ("to the one who could save him" [v 7]; "for all who obey him" [v 9]). The discussion about Christ is clearly presented from the vantage point of his present, exalted position (see 4:14), looking back at his "life on earth" (5:7) when his suffering perfected him as high priest.

■ **5-6** Verse 5a is hinged to v 4 through a deliberate comparison between the Levitical priests and Christ:

5:4	5:5a
"No one takes this honor [*timēn*] upon himself [*heautō*]"	He did not take upon himself the glory (*heauton edoxasen*)
"[But (*alla*)] he . . . [is] called by God"	But [*all'*] God said to him . . .
"just as [*kathōsper*] Aaron was"	So [*houtōs*] Christ also

The author has already used the language of "glory and honor" (→ 2:7, 9) in connection with Jesus' exaltation. Here he says that even as the Levitical high priests do not arrogate to themselves the "honor [*timē*]" of the high-priestly office (5:4), neither did Christ **take . . . the glory [*edoxasen*] of becoming a high priest** (5:5a).

Christ's appointment as high priest is expressed more fully and vigorously than the statements in vv 1 and 4 regarding the divine vocation of Levitical high priests. The preacher introduces the declarations of God himself from the Psalms. **But God said** is literally "the One who said [*ho lalēsas*]" (HCSB). The very first verbal form in Hebrews is the same participle (*lalēsas*) in 1:1, which (along with *elalēsen* in 1:2) focused the listeners' attention on God who "has spoken" (Attridge 1989, 145). The divine revelation in Scripture was set forth in a chain of biblical quotations in 1:5-13, beginning with Ps 2:7 (Heb 1:5a) and ending with Ps 110:1 (Heb 1:13). Now the God who has spoken is quoted again, from Ps 2:7 (Heb 5:5b) and Ps 110:4 (Heb 5:6b).

The two psalm quotations bring together the twin emphases of Hebrews' Christology: Jesus as Son of God and high priest. Though conceptually present earlier (1:2-3; 2:6, 11; 3:1, 6), the two titles are paired explicitly for the first time in the present context (4:14; 5:5-6; see 7:1-3; 7:26—8:1; 10:29). Psalm 2:7 is God's declaration of Jesus as the Son: **You are my Son; today I have become your Father** (Heb 5:5b). This is a messianic text (→ 1:5) that, in accordance with its regal function in ancient Israel, constitutes the divine coronation of Christ as the royal heir to God's throne (hence, 1:3, 13; 8:1; 10:12; 12:2).

Psalm 110:4, unlike the first verse of the same psalm quoted in Heb 1:13 (see Matt 22:44; Mark 12:36; Luke 20:42; Acts 2:34), was not in common currency in early christological formulation. But Psalm 110:1 and 4 are arguably the taproot for Hebrews' Christology (→ Heb 1:13 sidebar, "Psalm 110 in Hebrews"). The quotation from Ps 110:4 anticipates the unique comparison between Christ and Melchizedek, which the author holds in reserve until ch 7 (see 5:10-11; 6:20).

You are a priest forever establishes Christ's priesthood in perpetuity—a theme crucial to the preacher's argument (7:3, 16-17, 21-24, 28). The phrase **in the order of Melchizedek** acts as an *inclusio* for this paragraph (5:6b, 10).

The phrase **in the order of** could point to a "fixed succession or order" of priests (see Luke 1:8; *T. Naph.* 2:8; Johnson 2006, 144-45). This is unlikely for two reasons. First, Melchizedek is not the exemplar for Christ's ultimate priesthood, but vice versa. In 7:3 it is Melchizedek who was made "like the Son of God," not the other way around. Second, the perpetual nature of Christ's priesthood rules out any line of successors (a critical distinction with the Levitical priesthood [7:23-24]). Instead, **in the order of** conveys the idea of similarity or likeness: "just like Melchizedek" (BDAG, 989; compare "after the likeness of Melchizedek" [7:15 NAB]; see Ellingworth 1993, 283-84; Isaacs 2002, 75).

■ **7** This verse continues the periodic sentence that began in → 5:5. The NIV has broken up this sentence for easier reading in English. The discussion turns to how Jesus' identification with human suffering qualifies him as high priest. The preacher introduces a relative clause that stretches to the end of the passage in 5:10.

During the days of Jesus' life on earth reads (lit.) "who in the days of his flesh" (KJV). The relative pronoun "who [*hos*]" has as its antecedent "you [*sy*]" in the previous two psalm quotations (vv 5*b*, 6*b*), but ultimately "Christ" in v 5*a*. It is the subject of two main verbs, which will not appear until vv 8 and 9 ("learned" and "became"). The accompanying phrases and participial clauses in vv 7-10 describe the attendant circumstances surrounding Christ's qualification as high priest ("he learned obedience" [v 8]) and his mediation of divine favor ("he became the source of eternal salvation" [v 9]; deSilva 2000a, 191).

"In the days of his flesh" (ESV, KJV, LEB, NASB, NRSV), like the "little while" in 2:7, 9 (NIV^{mg}), denotes the period between the Son's preexistence and his exaltation (Thompson 2008, 109, 115). It is, in Johannine terms, when "the Word became flesh" (John 1:14; Hughes 1977, 182). The preacher is not making an ontological point (i.e., about Christ's being), but a historical one. He is not saying that Christ at one time shared in human bodily life but does so no longer. This would be fatal to the argument that Jesus even now has the capacity to "sympathize with our weaknesses" (4:15; see Bruce 1990, 126), and could diminish the vital significance of his sacrificial offering ("himself" [7:27; 9:14, 25-26]; "his own blood" [9:12, 25; 10:19; 12:24; 13:12]; his "flesh" or "body" [10:5, 10, 20]).

The NIV's **During the days of Jesus' life on earth** (see CEB, GW, HCSB, NCV, NET, NJB, NLT) faithfully reflects the preacher's shift in focus to the historical time of Jesus' humiliation, viewed from the present vantage point of Christ as the exalted high priest. Compare Oecumenius's comment that the phrase "in the days of his flesh" refers to "the days when the Lord was upon the earth visibly" (Heen and Krey 2005, 71; Ellingworth 1993, 287).

The Literary and Historical Background of Hebrews 5:7-10

A key issue in interpreting 5:7-10 is the question of identifying its literary or historical source. Four main proposals have been set forth: a gnostic source, an early Christian hymn, OT texts (usually from the Psalms), or the gospel tradition. The first two options have garnered little support among commentators. There is no consensus concerning the degree to which Hebrews appropriates OT or gospel material (see Attridge 1989, 147-48; Ellingworth 1993, 284-85).

Most commentators (even among the ancients; see Heen and Krey 2005, 72-74) have attempted to make sense of this passage against the backdrop of the Synoptic accounts of Christ's agony in Gethsemane (e.g., Lünemann 1890, 508; Hughes 1977, 182; Kistemaker 1984). However, it has long been recognized that the language of Hebrews is difficult to square with the Synoptic accounts. Chrysostom, for example, noted that the Gospels nowhere speak of Jesus praying with "loud cries and tears" (Heen and Krey 2005, 72). Strange interpretations have arisen from attempts to harmonize this passage with the Gethsemane narratives (e.g., Harnack's view, → 5:7). These often relate to how Jesus' prayer for deliverance (Mark 14:36 ||) was "heard" (Heb 5:7; see Bruce 1990, 127-30; Hagner 1990, 84). Therefore, many interpreters assert that this passage is a "historical reminiscence" (D. Guthrie 1983, 128) based on oral tradition about Jesus' Gethsemane prayer independent from the canonical Gospels (Hagner 1990, 81; Hagner 2002, 84; Johnson 2006, 145; Whedon 1880, 5:73; see Attridge 1989, 149 n. 147).

A number of recent commentators prefer to interpret this passage in association with the voices of the righteous sufferers found in the Psalms (see Attridge 1989, 149; Isaacs 2002, 76-77; Koester 2001, 107-8; Lane 1991, 120; Thompson 2008, 110-11). But there is no agreement on what psalm forms the backdrop. Psalms 22; 31:23; 39:13; 116, or a composite portrait from the Psalter, have been proposed as the source of Hebrews' inspiration.

Perhaps we need not choose between an origin in the Gethsemane tradition or in the Psalms. G. Guthrie suggests that this passage may best be understood as a "reflection on Jesus' experience in Gethsemane . . . in light of early Christian appropriation of righteous-sufferer psalm material" (1998, 190). It is, after all, the pattern of Hebrews to articulate the significance of Jesus through a consideration of both the Christian kerygma and the divine voice in the OT Scriptures.

5:7

Through similar vocabulary (**offered**) and an identical grammatical construction (*te kai*, "both . . . and") a comparison is drawn between Christ's offering and that of ordinary high priests (5:1 and 7). The word "offer" (forms of *prospherō*) in 5:1 (and 5:3) is used of high priests presenting "both gifts and sacrifices" for sins. This sacrificial nuance is probably retained here in 5:7. But what Christ **offered up** (*prosenenkas*, a form of *prospherō*) were **both prayers and petitions** (*deēseis te kai hiketērias*).

Prayer and sacrifice were linked together in Jewish (2 Sam 24:25; Ps 141:2; Prov 15:8; Isa 56:7) and Greco-Roman worship (Cole 1988, 889-90; Jameson 1988, 963-64; note the stock expression, "prayers and sacrifices," e.g., Pindar, *Ol.* 6.78; Newman 2009, 587). The Qumran community's prayers were seen as an alternative to the existing daily sacrifices in the temple (CD 11:21; 1QS 9:5, 26; Newman 2009, 586). Christian worship was often described in cultic language (Acts 10:4; Rom 12:1; Eph 5:2; 1 Pet 2:5; Rev 8:3), as it is in Hebrews (12:28; 13:15-16). The shift in focus from Levitical sacrifices to Jesus' prayers stresses our Great High Priest's solidarity with worshipers. More importantly, it concentrates attention on Jesus' godly and pious disposition, in contrast to the moral weakness of high priests under the old covenant (5:2-3).

The two words **prayers** and **petitions** do not occur together anywhere else in the NT, and only once in the OT (Job 41:3 LXX; see also Sir 36:16). But there are many extrabiblical instances of the two terms employed in tandem, both in cultured literature (Isocrates, *De pace* 138; Polybius, *Hist.* 2.6.1; 3.112.8; Philo, *Cherubim* 47; *Embassy* 276; see Büchsel 1965, 296; Attridge 1989, 150) and in the papyri (MM, 302). The general word for **prayers** (*deēseis*) is common (used about one hundred times throughout the Greek Bible). The word **petitions** (*hiketērias*) occurs nowhere else in the NT and only twice in the LXX (Job 41:3; 2 Macc 9:18; though its cognates appear twenty times in the LXX). It is a more colorful word, suggestive of the protocols for one's actions and demeanor as a supplicant (see Naiden 2007; Gould 2003, 22-77). Three of these are worth mentioning:

First, the massive Byzantine lexicon, the Suda, defines *hiketēria* as "a branch of olive, wound into a wreath" and "what those who beg [*deomenoi*] bring as some kind of offering or hold in their hands" (Whitehead 2011; Whitehead 2013a). This refers to the Greek custom of supplicants holding an olive branch (a classic symbol of peace) twined with wool (soft, and woven by women, symbolizing passivity). Since woolen strips were worn by priests, their use affected an air of sanctity. Supplicants thereby conveyed their non-threatening intentions and appeal for divine favor (Naiden 2007, 56).

Second, this was only one possible gesture of supplication (mentioned often by Livy; see Clarke 1977, 718), which could be combined with or replaced by others, according to one's culture. Yet the essential aspect of supplication was the expression of self-humiliation, submission, even servility. It was a surrendering of one's honor. The Suda defines a "supplicant [*hiketēs*]" as "one who beseeches and begs [*deomenos*] in a servile manner concerning anything whatever" (Whitehead 2013b). Donning mourning clothes evoked such a posture in Greek culture, matched among Hebrews by the wearing of sackcloth (Naiden 2007, 59-60, 68-69).

Loud lamentations and tears were typical in the fervent, humble entreaties of Jewish prayer (Pss 6:6-9; 22:24; 30:11; 56:8; 116:8; Lam 2:18-19;

1QH^a 5:12). Jesus' **loud cries and tears** would not have been an unexpected expression of Jewish supplication, and find eloquent parallels from the period of the Maccabees (2 Macc 11:6; 3 Macc 1:16; 5:7, 25; see deSilva 2000a, 190-91). Westcott (1909, 128) quotes a rabbinic saying concerning three types of prayer: "Prayer is made in silence: crying with a raised voice; but tears overcome all things."

Third, it goes without saying that supplication is occasioned by distress over a calamity, either expected or already in progress. Jesus' prayers **to the one who could save him from death** are in keeping with the customary requests (or praise) in the Psalms for God's rescue of the righteous from death (Pss 9:13; 33:19; 56:13; 72:13; see Isa 25:8; Hos 13:14) or from Sheol, the realm of the dead (Pss 16:10; 18:4-6; 30:3; 31:17; 49:15; 86:13; 116:3-4; see Jonah 2:2). Note especially Ps 116:8: "For you, O Lord, have delivered my soul from death, my eyes from tears, my feet from stumbling."

It is oversubtle to suggest that the phrase **to the one who could save him from death** is only a circumlocution for God (Lane 1991, 120; Thompson 2008, 110). Rather, it expresses the content of Jesus' supplication. Jesus prayed to God who could save **him** from death. Likewise, it is unnecessary to limit the phrase **from death** to a reference to the realm of death (Attridge 1989, 15), thereby concluding that Jesus' petition was really only a prayer for resurrection (see Heb 11:19; Gray 2003, 191-95).

How could Jesus truly share "in every way" in our flesh-and-blood humanity (2:17), and "taste death for everyone" (2:9), without also experiencing the recoil and dread toward death that have been the common lot of humankind (2:15)? How else could he have "suffered" (2:9-10; 5:8) when he was "tempted" (2:18)? Given the traditional character of prayers for deliverance from death, it was not an unrighteous prayer, but a human one, as the Synoptic accounts attest (Matt 26:39, 42; Mark 14:36; Luke 22:42). Nevertheless, the preacher's focus is not so much on the content of the prayers as it is on the agony involved in Jesus' offering them to God. Jesus' time on earth prepared him to relate emotionally with all those who suffer because of their chosen life of faith and obedience to God.

Jesus' prayers and petitions were not desperate demands, but cries for help offered up in complete trust in God (2:13a) and surrender to God's will (10:5-10). We find this in Jesus' Gethsemane prayer: "yet not my will, but yours be done" (Luke 22:42 ‖ Matt 26:42; Mark 14:36; see John 12:27; 14:31).

Jesus **was heard,** that is, his prayers were answered (see Pss 6:9; 18:6; 28:6; 31:22; 40:1; 66:19-20; 116:1; 1 Kgs 9:3; 2 Kgs 19:20; Luke 1:13; Acts 10:31; 1 John 5:14-15). Because Jesus clearly died, scholars have struggled with the apparent contradiction between Jesus' cry for deliverance and the assertion that **he was heard.** Adolf von Harnack offered the unwarranted conjecture that there is a textual corruption here, suggesting that the word "not" be inserted before **heard** (see Ellingworth 1993, 289; Gray 2003, 189-90).

The apparent discrepancy dissolves once we recognize the retrospective and long-range perspective of Hebrews. Of course, Jesus' offering of prayer was accepted by God, though Jesus' resolve to do God's will resulted in his own death. His death broke the power of the one "who holds the power of death" (Heb 2:14). He was raised up from the dead (13:20). Because he endured the cross, he was awarded joy and exaltation at the right hand of God (12:2; see 1:3, 13) as the Great High Priest (4:14; 5:5-6, 10; 6:20; 7:26; 8:1).

Jesus was heard **because of his reverent submission.** The word *eulabeia* denotes dealing with the transcendent or divine with extreme caution or respect—hence, "awe, fear of God" (BDAG, 407; "godly fear" [NKJV, RSV; see KJV]; "reverence" [ESV, LEB, NAB, NJB, NLT]). The added connotation of "humble submission" (NEB) or "devotion" (Balz 1991a, 79; Mundle 1979, 91; CEB, GW, NET; "piety" [NASB]) may be strengthened by the next verse's statement about Christ's obedience (5:8). The NIV rightly combines both godly fear and humble submission in its translation **reverent submission** (also NRSV). Jesus exhibited the same disposition of "reverence" that his people ought to have in their worship of God (12:28).

■ **8 Although he was a son** sets up a contrast with the following statement, **he learned obedience from what he suffered.** "Son though he was" (NAB, NIV[11], NJB) best captures the thought of the opening clause. The preacher is not talking about just any son, but "God's Son" (NLT). This is the Son who is the very image of God, through whom God made the universe, and whose powerful word holds sway over all things (1:2-3). With the exception of 2:10, 14-18 (which anticipate the present passage), Hebrews has up to this point referred to the Son in terms of his exalted status (1:2, 5, 8; 3:6; 4:14; 5:5; Johnson 2006, 147).

The author adorns the climactic points of this paragraph in 5:8-9 with several wordplays. The first is here in v 8. The expression **he learned** [*emathen*] . . . **from what he suffered** (*epathen*) is an instance of *parechesis*, "an ornament consisting of similar words with different meanings echoing the same sound" (Hermogenes, *Inv.* 4.8; Kennedy 2005, 173). This particular pun was a commonplace in the ancient world (e.g., Aeschylus, *Ag.* 177; Herodotus, *Hist.* 1.207; Aesop, *Fab.* 134.1-3; 223.2-3; Philo, *Dreams* 2.107). It was a "linguistic jingle" (Barclay 1976, 48), roughly analogous to our "no pain, no gain" in English.

What Jesus learned was **obedience.** The assertion is stunning and may at first seem theologically prickly. There is no inference that Jesus was ever disobedient. Rather, Jesus demonstrated his faithfulness to God by passing the test of suffering (2:18; 4:15). He endured the shame and disgrace of the cross (12:2; 13:12-13; see 6:6) rather than seizing the glory of the high priesthood for himself (5:5). Jesus had to experience the vulnerability of human existence in the face of death, and emerge victorious, so that his emotional equipping and moral authority as "a merciful and faithful high priest" (2:17) would be proven.

A wordplay seems to exist between "he was heard [*eisakoustheis*]" in v 7 and **obedience** (*hypakoēn*). The latter is a compound form (with *hypo* as a prefix) of the word for "hearing [*akoē*]" (see 4:2; 5:11). Obedience (*hypakoē*) is when "one listens and follows instructions" (BDAG, 1028). Jesus is the premier example of faithful obedience (3:2, 6; see 12:2). By contrast, the wilderness generation is an "example of disobedience" (4:11; see 3:18; 4:2, 6). Jesus, however, heeded God's will (10:7, 9), and therefore God heard his anguished prayers.

■ **9** Another play on words is among the preacher's favorites. Jesus, **once made perfect**, became **the source of eternal salvation**.

Playing with Beginnings and Endings

Hebrews has a fondness for wordplays involving terms related to beginnings (esp. cognates of *archē*) and endings or goals (cognates of *telos*).

Beginning	End	Hebrews
Jesus, "the author [*archēgon*] of salvation"	made "perfect [*teleiōsai*] through suffering"	2:10
"Hold firmly" to the conviction "we had at first [*tēn archēn*]"	"till the end [*mechri telous*]"	3:14
Jesus **became the source** [*aitios*] **of eternal salvation**	having been **made perfect** [*teleiōtheis*]	5:9
"Leave the elementary [lit., 'the beginning,' *tēs archēs*] teachings about Christ"	"go on to maturity [*teleiotēta*]"	6:1
Melchizedek is "without beginning [*archēn*] of days"	"or end [*telos*] of life"	7:3
"Jesus, the author [*archēgon*]"	"and perfecter [*teleiōtēn*] of our faith"	12:2

"Perfection" vocabulary is used in the LXX concerning the ordination of Levitical priests through sacrifices of consecration or "perfection" (Exod 29:22, 26, 27, 31, 34; Lev 7:37; 8:22, 26, 28, 29, 31, 33). This usage may also be reflected in Heb 7:11 (Vanhoye 1996, 330-31). The expression **once made perfect** relates back to the educative role of suffering in 5:8. Jesus' consecration to high-priestly office involved his moral excellence being proven through suffering. The ordeal of crucifixion is what fully equipped and qualified him as high priest.

First, psychologically, he possesses the superior capacity to sympathize with our weaknesses (4:15), because he suffered (2:18; 5:8). Second, morally, he is fully possessed of the virtue of holiness (7:26). Unlike ordinary high priests, "who are weak" (who had to offer sacrifices for their own sins too [see 5:2; 7:27]), the Son has been "made perfect" forever (7:28; see 7:18-19 for an additional contrast between the "weak" and the "perfect"). Third, he therefore **became the source of eternal salvation.** This is equivalent to his perfection as "the author of their salvation" (2:10). He has "the power of an indestructible life" that has vanquished death (7:16; see 2:14-15). He can "save completely those who come to God through him" because his high-priestly intercession for them is unfailing (7:25; note also the eschatological salvation in 9:28).

Jesus' consecration through the *paideia* or training of suffering also qualified him as the model for the perfection of those who believe in him. He "learned obedience in the school of suffering" (NEB), so that he could bring salvation **for all who obey [*hypakouousin*] him.** This reference to believers' obedience prepares for the following passage (5:11—6:12). That passage opens by pointing to the readers as "hard of hearing [*akoais*]" (5:11; BDAG, 683). Christ's endurance validated his expertise with "the teaching about righteousness" and his capacity for moral discernment. These are qualities lacking in infants, but possessed by the "mature" (lit., "perfect"; → 5:13-14). Thus, believers should focus their attention on Jesus as the supreme example of faithful endurance (12:2-3; see 3:1).

■ 10 This verse repeats the divine pronouncement of Jesus as high priest, already quoted from Ps 110:4 in Heb 5:6. Jesus **was designated by God to be high priest in the order of Melchizedek** (→ 5:6). The word **designated** (*prosagoreutheis*) carries the nuance of issuing a "formal and solemn ascription of an honorific title" (Lane 1991, 110 n. z). This sense is captured well in the NJB: Jesus "was acclaimed by God with the title of high priest of the order of Melchizedek." Christ's Melchizedek-like priesthood will be explored thoroughly in 7:1-28.

FROM THE TEXT

Hebrews 4:14—5:10 is a transitional passage between the introductory parts of the sermon in 1:1—4:13 and the central, argumentative sections that follow. Hebrews 4:14-16 recaps the proposition found in 2:17-18 and prepares for a preliminary amplification of its themes in 5:1-10 (→ Behind the Text above). The preacher powerfully employs both christological reflection and pastoral encouragement. He highlights Christ's qualifications (his divine calling and moral excellence) and the superior benefits of his high-priestly office (access to divine grace, timely help, and eternal salvation).

There is one constant in the midst of Christ's movement from his eternal status as Son of God, to the humiliation of his incarnation, to his exaltation at the right hand of God: his complete faithfulness to God. In the words of this passage, it is Christ's having been tested "in every way" like us, "yet . . . without sin" (4:15); it is his "reverent submission" in the crucible of suffering

(5:7). Christ's sinlessness, or what theologians have called his impeccability, is foundational to the Christian witness about Jesus.

In the Gospels, Jesus prevailed over every satanic assault, especially at his temptation (Matt 4:1-11; Mark 1:12-13; Luke 4:1-13) and during his passion (compare Luke 4:13 with Luke 22:3, 28, 31, 40, 46; John 13:2, 27). In the writings of John, Jesus is consistently characterized as being true, righteous, and free from the guilt of sin (John 7:18; 8:46; 14:30; 1 John 2:29; 3:5, 7). The apostles declare him as "the Righteous One" (Acts 3:14; 7:52; 1 John 2:1), a title of the Suffering Servant (Isa 53:11). Peter draws from the same prophetic portrait of the Servant, quoting Isa 53:9: "He committed no sin, and no deceit was found in his mouth" (1 Pet 2:22). Jesus was "our Passover lamb" (1 Cor 5:7), "a lamb without blemish or defect" (1 Pet 1:19). The effectiveness of Christ's sin offering is dependent upon his own sinlessness, as Paul wrote, "God made him who had no sin to be sin for us, so that in him we might become the righteousness of God" (2 Cor 5:21).

Hebrews does not set out to prove the impeccability of Christ. This truth was no doubt already an essential part of "such a great salvation" (Heb 2:3). It was implicit to the Christian confession (3:1; 4:14; 10:23) and explicit in the Christian witness surrounding it (as shown in the foregoing paragraph). Hebrews follows the apostolic witnesses, who speak with one voice in saying that Christ's exaltation vindicated him as "the Holy and Righteous One" (see Acts 3:14-15; 5:30-31; 10:38-42; 13:27-39; Rom 6:7-10; Phil 2:6-11). The exclamation point to Christ's holy character as our "great high priest" is his exaltation "through" and "above the heavens" (Heb 4:14; 7:26).

No other NT book, like Hebrews, develops the reality of Christ's moral purity within the matrix of the cultic, psychological, and moral requirements for his high-priestly office. Hebrews articulates the double, almost paradoxical, truth about Christ's incarnation—hundreds of years before the Definition of Chalcedon (A.D. 451). (Indeed, Chalcedon repeated Hebrews' formulation of Christ's identity with humanity: "like us in all respects, apart from sin" [Bettenson 1963, 26].) On one hand, Jesus profoundly experienced the depths of temptation shared by the whole of humanity. "He entered the gravitational field of genuine temptation," as Thomas Oden puts it (2001a, 244). Yet, on the other hand, Jesus was "without sin" (4:15). He did not falter in his faithfulness and obedience (3:2, 6; 5:8). He was undeterred in his resolve to do God's will (10:7, 9) and in his "reverent submission" before God (5:7). This double-sided reality of Christ's human- and divine-oriented qualities is expressed compactly in the phrase "merciful and faithful high priest" (2:17).

Hebrews does not loosen the tension between these two facts. In fact, it is tightened in 5:8: "Son though he was, he learned obedience from what he suffered" (NIV[11]). The eternal Son of God condescended to join the flesh-and-blood struggle of humanity with sin and death. Some scholars have suggested that Jesus must have learned obedience through a process of trial and error. He must have experienced at least some small moral failures, working up toward his ultimate act of obedience on the cross. Otherwise, they reason, how could he have fully identified with the human condition (Buchanan 1972, 130; Williamson 1974-75, 4-8)? But this reading is faithful neither to Hebrews, nor to the wider Christian witness. Three points need to be considered:

First, Hebrews is not concerned with the imagined difficulty of Christ having the "unfair advantage" of being the Son of God. God called upon the Son to be high priest (5:5) precisely because of the hopeless disadvantage in the old order of priests, who were too morally weak to bring about any real and lasting salvation (5:2-3; 7:27-28). C. S. Lewis illustrated the unreasonableness of the objection that Jesus' obedient suffering was too easy for him. It's like a child objecting to having an adult teaching him or her how to write, because "it's easy for grown-ups." It's like a drowning man protesting that the person saving him has the unfair advantage of keeping one foot on the shore (Lewis 1978, 61).

Second, we must not fall into a common misconception concerning human nature. Authentic humanity should not be gauged by our present fallen condition. True humanity is human life lived in the image of God. From this angle, Hebrews certainly understands Jesus' earthly life, not as superhuman, but truly human. Jesus' victory over sin and death, crowning with glory and honor, and inheritance of all things achieves the destiny intended for humanity. Jesus' likeness with humanity excludes sin (4:15; see Rom 8:3; Chrysostom 1996, 400), because sin is the very weakening and dehumanizing force he came to destroy. His salvation of human beings consists of his "bringing many sons to glory" (2:10), that is, restoring human beings to their divine destiny.

Third, and finally, it is important to note the proper role of temptation. It does not create moral excellence, but proves it. The church fathers (doubtless following biblical precedent, e.g., 1 Pet 1:6-7) likened temptation to the testing of metals. If it is really gold that is being tested, then there is no actual possibility that the test will reveal anything other than genuine gold (Oden 2001a, 245). Yet the test is no less arduous.

Nevertheless, in the sphere of human moral action, one may not rule out moral reinforcement as the cumulative effect of multiple tests. This was true even for Jesus, although he never sinned (see Luke 2:52). To change the metaphor to that of athletic training (see 5:14; 10:32; 12:11), temptation provides needed exercise for "the moral musculature," without which it would atrophy (Oden 2001a, 248). With every test, culminating in the suffering of the cross, Jesus' endurance was strengthened.

Jesus "learned obedience" (5:8) because obedience cannot be exercised in the abstract. It must be flexed, challenged, exerted in new situations (Koester 2001, 299). He ran the race with perseverance, reaching its glorious end. His endurance of the cross established him as a realistic (not unreachable or superhuman) example for our own struggle with sin, since we have not (like him, or at least "not yet") resisted to the death (12:1-4). We must press on toward the moral maturity he modeled. That happens to be the key exhortation in the very next passage.

B. Preparing for Advanced Teaching on Christ's High Priesthood (5:11—6:20)

BEHIND THE TEXT

Hebrews 5:11—6:20 is another digression (on digressions, → introduction to 3:1—4:13; Koester 2001, 306-7). The preacher has already taken great pains to secure his readers' attention in the *exordium* (1:1—2:4) and in the digression of 3:1—4:13. He has also just launched, in 4:14—5:10, the introduction to the major argumentative sections of the sermon, which will run from 7:1 to 10:18. So it is striking that the main arguments are "interrupted" by another digression in 5:11—6:20.

This digression is clearly demarcated. It immediately follows the first explicit reference to Jesus as "high priest in the order of Melchizedek" (5:10; see 5:6). The digression refers to this major topic in 5:11 ("We have much to say about this"), and then segues back to it in 6:20 with the repeated reference to Jesus as "high priest forever, in the order of Melchizedek." Thus, this passage is strategically placed to prepare the audience for the most crucial and difficult portion of the homily.

Cultural Imagery

The preacher draws from many facets of ancient Hellenistic and Hebrew life to amplify his reproof, warning, and encouragement with vividness and power. The highest concentration of rich cultural imagery is in Heb 5:11—6:20.

Agriculture	Land that produces good crops or thorns and thistles; harvest	6:7-8; 12:11
Athletics	Training (*gegymnasmena*); Jesus the "forerunner" (NIV[11]); "a great contest"; running a race	5:14; 6:20; 10:32; 12:1-4, 12-13
Building	Building a house; "not laying again the foundation"	3:4; 6:1
Business/Commerce	"partners" (NRSV); "property"; "rewarder [*misthapodotēs*]" (KJV; lit., "wage-payer"); "reward"; "give an account"; "unprofitable" (KJV)	3:14; 6:6; 10:34; 11:6, 26; 13:17

Education	Milk vs. solid food; infant vs. mature; "discipline [*paideia*]"	5:11-14; 12:5-11
Law	Discussion of oaths	6:13-17; → 6:13-20 sidebar, "Legal Jargon in Hebrews"
Medicine	Dislocation/healing of a joint	12:13
Seafaring	Ship missing the harbor; hope as an anchor	2:1; 6:19
Temple/priesthood	"the inner sanctuary behind the curtain"; Jesus the "high priest"; tabernacle, priesthood, and sacrifices	6:19-20; chs 7—10

The preacher "self-consciously reflects on his rhetorical enterprise" (Attridge 1989, 156). We discover why he delays a bit longer, and why he must further set his audience into the proper frame of mind to listen to his arguments. In 5:11 he reveals that his subject matter is "hard to explain." This is reminiscent of Quintilian's reference to one of the five kinds of causes in speeches, "the obscure" or "hard to follow" (*Inst.* 4.1.40). For this kind of cause, the speaker must "render [the listener] ready to receive instruction" (*Inst.* 4.1.41).

Without doubt, the preacher is about to embark on a series of arguments and scriptural exegesis marked by extraordinary creativity and sophistication. But it is not primarily the subtlety of his arguments that will make his task difficult. It is the tendency of his audience toward being "slow to learn" (lit., "sluggish in hearing" [5:11 LEB, NAB, NET]). This concern was first raised in the opening warning ("We must pay more careful attention" [2:1]), repeated in the warning drawn from the bad example of the wilderness generation (3:8, 15; 4:2, 7), and will crescendo in the sermon's final warning (12:25).

The pastoral concern for his listeners is evident in the five paragraphs that make up 5:11—6:20. The first four paragraphs (5:11—6:12) are designed to confront the danger of spiritual apathy. They are enclosed within references to the listeners' sluggishness (5:11; 6:12). The fifth paragraph (6:13-20) creates a smooth transition to the following discussion of Melchizedek (7:1-10).

(1) *Reproof* (5:11-14). The first paragraph employs biting irony to assist readers in regaining their moral and spiritual bearings. They should be mature adults who can digest the solid food of advanced truth about Christ and who possess a highly trained moral character. However, they are acting like babies who continue to drink the milk of "elementary truths" (v 12) and who are morally underdeveloped.

(2) *Exhortation* (6:1-3). This passage is an invitation for the listeners to "go on to maturity" (v 1). The author encourages them to move beyond foundational teachings. He is determined to assist them in doing so—with the help of divine providence.

(3) *Warning* (6:4-8). This is the most severe warning about apostasy up to this point. It is one of the most controversial and frightening passages in Scripture, since it asserts that final apostasy is irreversible.

(4) *Reassurance* (6:9-12). The preacher is confident that the community has a promising spiritual track record, demonstrated through their past and present acts of loving service for God's sake. He desires that each and every one of them will redouble their commitment in order to be fully assured in hope. He urges them toward an energetic imitation of those who inherited God's promises through faithful endurance.

(5) *Powerful Encouragement* (6:13-20). The digression concludes with the example of God's confirmation of his promise to Abraham with an oath, and Abraham's patience in receiving the promise. The immovable and unimpeachable character of God's promise and oath provides the strong encouragement for believers to hold onto their hope. A transition to the main arguments of the sermon is effected through the comparison of our hope to an anchor that is securely fastened in the very presence of God, where Jesus has already appeared ahead of us as our "high priest forever, in the order of Melchizedek" (6:19-20).

IN THE TEXT

I. Reproof Concerning Arrested Spiritual Development (5:11-14)

■ 11 The preacher reproves his readers for their inattentiveness. **We have much to say** is a conventional remark used by ancient writers to draw attention to the importance of what they are saying (see Lane 1991, 299; Johnson 2006, 154). In the end he will not have time to convey everything he has to say (see 11:32), for his "word of exhortation" had to be written "quite briefly" (13:22 NIV[11]).

The expression **about this** is grammatically ambiguous. If **this** is masculine, it refers back to Melchizedek mentioned in 5:10 (Peshitta; REB; Calvin 1976, 67; Whedon 1880, 5:74; Bruce 1990, 133), or to "Christ," the subject of the lengthy sentence in 5:5-10 (Johnson 2006, 154). But if the pronoun is neuter, the phrase refers to the "total-conception" of Christ as a high priest like Melchizedek (Lünemann 1890, 513-14; e.g., "on this topic" [NET]; "on this subject" [NJB]; see Attridge 1989, 156; Lane 1991, 135; Ellingworth 1993, 299; Koester 2001, 300).

The subject matter that will be pursued in 7:1—10:18 **is hard to explain;** or "it is hard to make it clear" (NIV[11]). The adjective *dysermēneutos* was used of subjects that were difficult to describe, such as dreams (Artemidorus, *Onir.* 3.66), exotic colors (Diodorus Siculus, *Library* 2.52.5), the inexpressible beauty of archetypal ideas perceptible only by the mind (Philo, *Dreams* 1.188), the world's creation, and divine rest (Origen, *Cels.* 5.59; see BDAG, 265; Koester 2001, 300). This word choice may have been calculated to brace the original hearers (and modern readers) for the lofty and complex teaching in the sermon's central section. But the major difficulty was not the subject matter but the readers' unresponsiveness: **because you are slow to learn.**

The expression (lit.) "sluggish in hearing [*nōthroi . . . tais akoais*]" (LEB, NAB, NET) was used by ancient writers of a lack of mental alertness (see Attridge 1989, n. 25). Philo writes of persons whose minds are so distracted that a speaker must address them, not as human beings, but "lifeless statues who have ears, but no hearing [*akoai*] is in those ears" (*Heir* 12; see Koester 2001, 300-301).

Given the context, and the repetition of the term *nōthroi* in 6:12, the problem ran deeper than deficient mental acuity. Being "hard of hearing" (BDAG, 683) cannot be separated from the danger of a hardened heart (see 3:7, 15; 4:7). The audience has already been cautioned to avoid repeating the example of the wilderness generation. The "message they heard" did not benefit them, because they did not share the faith of "those who heard" (4:2).

In striking contrast, in 5:7-9, Jesus "was heard because of his reverent submission." He learned "obedience [*hypakoēn*]" through suffering. Consequently, he was perfected as "the source of eternal salvation for all who obey" (*tois hypakouousin*, "those who heed").

These negative and positive illustrations involving hearing cast into relief a pastoral concern for people who are slipping into spiritual apathy. Their culpable negligence (G. Guthrie 1998, 201-2), or worse, spiritual resistance (Lane 1991, 155), is captured well in the translations, "you have become too lazy to pay attention" (GW) or "you no longer try to understand" (NIV[11]).

■ **12 In fact** introduces a description of the readers' spiritual condition. In vv 12-14 the preacher employs educational metaphors common among ancient authors, especially popular philosophers.

Education in the Hellenistic World

Hellenistic *paideia* (education, discipline) concerned the instruction, training, and maturation of individuals into cultured, civilized human beings. For centuries Greek authors repeated the judgment of Plato that education "stands first among the finest gifts that are given to the best men" (*Leg.* 1.644b).

In the Hellenistic period, formal education consisted of three stages. First, the primary education of young boys began around age seven and concluded at about age fourteen. There were no grade distinctions. Any student who had mastered the curriculum could advance to secondary education. Teaching was conducted by a *grammatistēs*, who taught reading, writing, and simple arithmetic. Music and gymnastics were also integral to education. Tedious methods of instruction were used, such as dictation, repetition, and recitation, working from simple to complex (alphabet, syllables, words, short statements, and finally brief literary passages). Ethical formation was an important goal. This included the introduction of common maxims, such as, "Letters are the beginning of wisdom."

Secondary education extended from age fourteen to eighteen. Students were taught by a *grammatikos,* who introduced them to the enduring classics of Greek literature. Readings focused on the great poets and dramatists (esp. Homer and Euripides). The approach involved careful examination of texts, as well as literary criticism aimed at drawing out moral lessons. Apart from the common focus on literary studies, the basic curriculum varied by place and era of time. Ideally, the standard subjects were grammar, rhetoric, dialectic, music, geometry, arithmetic, and astronomy. This curriculum, called *enkyklios paideia,* "general education," was the precursor to the seven liberal arts of the Middle Ages. General education was considered the foundation for higher education in "more difficult matters" (Epictetus, *Diatr.* 1.26.3).

Higher education among the Greeks included philosophy, history, and rhetoric. Philosophy encompassed a wide-ranging curriculum under the rubrics of logic, physics, and ethics (Long 1974, 118-21). Higher education was usually pursued in the great centers of learning. Athens, Pergamum, and Rhodes were renowned for philosophy and rhetoric; Cos, Pergamum, and Ephesus for medicine; and Alexandria for the entire range of advanced studies. Because the Romans regarded history as more basic and philosophy as suspect, they restricted higher studies to rhetoric. (For further study, see Marrou 1964, 137-295; Dewald 1988, 1097-1102; Wooten 1988, 1109-20; Beck and Thomas 1996; Thompson 2008, 121).

5:12

Evidently, the Christian community the preacher addressed had existed for some time (see 10:32-34). This makes them accountable for their arrested spiritual development: **Though by this time you ought to be teachers, you need someone to teach you.** The preacher's rebuke is purposely charged with irony or hyperbole (see Attridge 1989, 157-58; Lane 1991, 136; deSilva 2000a, 211). Later, he assumes his readers—God willing—are capable of pressing beyond "elementary teachings" (6:1-3), and he expresses a more hopeful prognosis concerning their salvation (6:9-12).

In the ancient world **teachers** were in the same honorable class as other authority figures, like parents, rulers, and masters (Koester 2001, 301, 308). So it would be shameful for the listeners to be in a position where they **ought to be teachers,** but **need someone to teach** them. In terms of spiritual maturity, they have not entered fully into the realities of the new covenant, wherein knowledge of God no longer requires instruction from human teachers (see 8:11, quoting Jer 31:34; 1 Thess 4:9; 1 John 2:20).

The reproof is intensified through identification of the depth of their regression. They need to be instructed once again in the most rudimentary elements of divine truth. **The elementary truths of God's word** in Greek is (lit.): *the elements of the beginning of the oracles of God.*

Ta stoicheia (**the elements**) referred to the fundamental elements or smallest constituent parts, whether of language (letters of the alphabet), music (individual tones), metaphysics (the four elements: earth, air, fire, and water), astrology (celestial bodies), or any science or art (see Delling 1971; Plümacher 1993a; BDAG, 946). Here the reference is to the "basic elements" (NAB, NRSV) or **elementary truths** of "the oracles of God" (ESV, KJV, LEB, NASB, NRSV).

Oracles were the prophetic utterances of divine beings. In Jewish and Christian contexts, "oracles" referred to God's sayings found in Scripture (Deut 33:9-10; Acts 7:38; Rom 3:2; see 1 Pet 4:11). Here the reference is to **God's word** (GW, NLT, RSV), "utterances" (NAB, NET; "sayings" [NJB]), or "revelation" (HCSB), probably as encountered in the Scriptures and understood within the context of God's speaking through the Son (1:1-2*a*).

The preacher accents how basic this curriculum was, to which they were returning: **the elementary truths** *of the beginning* of God's word. "They are at the beginning of the beginning!" (Johnson 2006, 155). They needed to rehearse "the first principles" (KJV; see TYNDALE)—"the ABC of God's oracles" (REB).

The rhetorical intensity is strengthened by the little word *palin*, **all over again.** Twice more this word will appear in the following two paragraphs: first, in the exhortation not to lay "again" the foundation of elementary Christian teachings (6:1); and, second, in the warning about the impossibility of "again" restoring an apostate to repentance (6:6). A course of spiritual regression cannot be maintained indefinitely, not without putting oneself in peril of reaching the point of no return—final apostasy.

You need milk, not solid food employs stock imagery regarding levels of Hellenistic education. **Milk** is an image of basic studies in Greek education; **solid food** relates to more advanced studies. The next two verses unpack the meaning of these images.

■ **13** It is a truism that **Anyone who lives on milk** is **still an infant.** Paul similarly rebuked the Corinthians for not being ready for solid food, but only milk, for they were "mere infants in Christ" (1 Cor 3:1-2). Paul linked spiritual immaturity with moral deficiency (being "worldly" [1 Cor 3:1, 3]). So also here, an infant **is not acquainted with the teaching about righteousness.**

Ancient Images of Educational Progress

Advancing from milk to solid food and from infancy to adulthood were common images of progress in education. Epictetus defines being a child in terms of "ignorance" and "lack of instruction" (*Diatr.* 2.1.16). Even a grown-up can appear like a child, "for it is being a child to be unmusical in things musical, to be unlettered in things literary, to be uneducated in life" (3.19.6). Using language similar to Hebrews, Epictetus chides his students: "Are you not willing, at this late date, like children, to be weaned and to partake of more solid food?" (2.16.39; see 3.24.9).

Philo contrasts milk with solid food, and childhood with adulthood (*Prelim. Studies* 19; *Agriculture* 9; *Migration* 29; see *Dreams* 2.9). Like Hebrews (5:13-14), he contrasts the infant with the full-grown person (*Sobriety* 9) and the inexperienced with the perfect (*Agriculture* 160). He correlates baby food or milk with the branches of general education (*ta enkyklia*; → 5:12 sidebar, "Education in the Hellenistic World"). This is preparatory for the perfect and solid food of real knowledge in the virtues (*Prelim. Studies* 19; *Agriculture* 9; *Sobriety* 9; *Sacrifices* 43; *Heir* 274), or, in a word, philosophy (*Drunkenness* 51; *Good Person* 160).

The expression **not acquainted** (*apeiros*) is used of youths or beginners who do not have knowledge or skill due to a lack of trial, experience, or practice (LSJ, 184; BDAG, 100; see Wis 13:18; Philo, *Agriculture* 160; Josephus, *Ant.* 7.336; 8.374). They are (lit.) "untested" (compare Jesus, who has been tested [2:18; 4:15]). In this passage it is better to translate the word as ***unskilled*** (ESV, NRSV; "unskilful" [KJV]; "inexperienced" [HCSB, NET; see GW, NAB]; "inexperte" [TYNDALE]). A usage parallel to what we find here is in Num 14:23 LXX, which refers to the "inexperienced youth" who "does not know good or evil."

Interpretation of the phrase **the teaching about righteousness** is greatly debated (see Ellingworth 1993, 306-7). It is unlikely that it indicates an infant's incapacity for correct, articulate speech (Delitzsch and Weiss, noted in Hughes 1977, 191). And it is doubtful that the phrase is a cipher for the doctrine of justification by faith—that Christ is our righteousness, as opposed to self- or works-righteousness (Clarke 1977, 3:722; Hughes 1977, 191; Wiley 1984, 176). This clearly imposes an interpretation of Paul's theology on Hebrews; and it is ill-suited to the ethical thrust of the present context (see 5:14; 6:10).

The word **teaching** (*logos*) may mean "word" (ESV, KJV, NAB, NASB, NRSV), "message" (HCSB, NET), or "doctrine" (NJB)—as elsewhere in Hebrews (2:2; 4:2; 6:1; 13:7, 17, 22). It may also have the active sense of "speaking" (Attridge 1989, 160), perhaps parallel to "oracles [*logiōn*]" ("God's word") in v 12. However, there are three factors that support the view that what is meant is ***reasoning*** about righteousness:

First, the author is concerned with proficiency, skill, or expertise, which favors taking *logos* as an activity (Koester 2001, 302).

Second, **righteousness** (*dikaiosynē*) should be taken in the sense common to Hellenistic moral discourse (Plato, *Resp.* 433a; Aristotle, *Pol.* 1291a). It is the virtue of determining what is appropriate or right action (Johnson 2006, 156).

Third, both of the previous ideas are matched in the following verse (5:14), which speaks of acquiring a sense of moral discernment through training and habit. "Righteousness" also has an ethical meaning in 12:11, 14, involving peaceful and holy behavior. There, as here, it is the product of education or training ("discipline" [12:5, 7, 8, 11]; see *gegymnasmena*, "trained" [5:14; 12:11]; so John Chrysostom 1996, 406).

■ **14** In contrast (*de*, But) to the infant's milk diet, **solid food is for the mature.** The **solid food** the preacher intends to serve his hearers is instruction about Christ's high-priestly ministry. This provides the definitive cultic, moral, and spiritual preparation of worshipers to appear before God (not least through the cleansing of their consciences [9:9, 14; 10:2, 22]).

The **mature** (*teleiōn*), viewed from the perspective of overall human development, are those who are full-grown or have reached adulthood ("adults" [NJB]; see KJV). Within the context of education, the mature are those who have completed the course of education and are prepared to excel in virtue (Philo, *Alleg. Interp.* 3.244; *Sacrifices* 7; *Agriculture* 18; *Sobriety* 9; *Prelim. Studies* 19, 154; see *Drunkenness* 33, 51; *Heir* 274). It is puzzling how certain commentators will not admit any ethical connotations for *teleiōn* in this passage (Ellingworth 1993, 308; France 2006, 80). Yet moral development is critical to the present discussion. Also, Christ's perfection in the preceding pericope definitely has an ethical component ("he learned obedience" [5:8-9]) and is set against the moral weakness of ordinary high priests (see 5:2-3; 7:28).

The mature are further described through athletic imagery. Such imagery is not out of place, since in Hellenistic culture "exercising naked" (*gegymnasmena*: **have trained**) provided necessary training for the body that complemented training of the mind (Philo, *Prelim. Studies* 27; *Dreams* 1.250; *Good Person* 111). This athletic metaphor was also used for intellectual, rhetorical, or ethical training (Philo, *Sacrifices* 85; *Giants* 60; *Sobriety* 65; *Migration* 199; *Prelim. Studies* 17, 180; *Flight* 125; *Names* 81, 84-85; *Moses* 1.48; *Spec. Laws* 4.101; *Virtues* 18; Isocrates, *Nic.* 10; *Demon.* 21; Epictetus, *Diatr.* 2.18.26-27; see 1 Tim 4:7; 2 Pet 2:14; Heb 12:11).

It is the "faculties" (NAB, NRSV) or "powers of discernment" (ESV) that must be trained. The Greek *aisthētēria* is more specific than the NIV's **themselves**. The word could refer to the physical "senses" (CEB, HCSB, KJV, NASB) or "perceptions" (NET, REB), such as sight (Philo, *Sobriety* 155) or taste (Galen, *De diagnoscendis pulsibus* 3.135). By extension, it could be used of mental or spiritual perception (hence, "minds" [GW, NJB]; Plutarch calls the mind an *aisthētērion* of the soul [*Suave viv.* 114]; see *Quaest. conv.* 4.5; 4 Macc 2:22; Delling 1964).

The moral sensibilities will have been rigorously trained **on account of habit** (see Wesley n.d., 573; Wiley 1984, 177). The phrase *dia tēn hexin* does not mean **by constant use** or "by practice" (most English translations; see Koester 2001, 303). The term *hexis* does not refer to the process of training, but to the proficiency, mastery, character, or habit resulting from practice (Attridge 1989, 161; Johnson 2006, 157; Thompson 2008, 121-22). A "state of maturity" (BDAG, 350) is possessed by those whose moral senses have been properly disciplined.

The design of such discipline is to equip persons with the ability **to distinguish good from evil**. Moral discernment is a general characteristic of maturity in the OT (Num 14:23; Deut 1:39; Isa 7:15-16). In Hellenistic philosophy the purpose of ethics was "to deal with the distinguishing of things good, bad, and indifferent" (Sextus Empiricus, *Pyr.* 3.168; see Epictetus, *Diatr.* 2.24.19).

Though Hebrews does not use the word, it is in essence describing one of the four most prized virtues in the ancient world: wisdom (*phronēsis*; see Philo, *Spec. Laws* 1.63; → 6:10 sidebar, "Virtues"). Wisdom is "intelligence capable, by a certain judicious method, of distinguishing good and evil" (*Rhet. Her.* 3.2.3; see Aristotle, *Rhet.* 1.9.13; Philo, *Creation* 154, compare 73; *Heir* 314; *Good Person* 60). Moral clarity is of particular importance for a community that is apparently wavering in its commitment to Christ (deSilva 2000a, 213). In Hebrews, discernment is more than "moral intelligence"; it extends itself in the good works and loving service that flow from a knowledge of God's will (6:10-11; 10:24, 32-36; 13:21).

2. Exhortation to Go on to Maturity (6:1-3)

■ **1a** The preacher switches from addressing his readers in the second person (5:11-12) to exhorting them in the first person plural, **let us**. Since the community should by now be mature, the preacher concludes (*Dio*, **Therefore**) that they need not rehearse the ABC's of faith, but should advance to **maturity**.

Let us leave is not an exhortation to abandon the essentials of faith, but to "progress beyond" them (NET; see CEB, NIV[11]). **The elementary teachings about Christ** (*ton tēs archēs Christou logon*) are parallel to "the elementary truths of God's word" (*ta stoicheia tēs archēs tōn logiōn tou theou* [5:12]). The following list of teachings does not appear to be distinctively Christian. Perhaps it is reflective of a retrograde form of Judaism into which some listeners have lapsed (Bruce 1990, 139; Hagner 1990, 87). Regardless of the discontinuity Hebrews envisages between divine revelation in ages past and in these last days, it does not conceive of Judaism and Christianity as two separate religions—a viewpoint only possible decades later after the "parting of the ways" (Isaacs 2002, 84).

Though devoid of any explicit Christology, the teachings are **about Christ** and form **the beginning** (*tēs archēs*) or **foundation** (*themelion*) of the Christian message. Despite items in the list that are predominantly Jewish in character, authentic Christian instruction would have related all the topics to Christ as "the rudiments of Christianity" (REB; see Pfitzner 1997, 96). The preacher may have in mind the primitive gospel "first [*archēn*] announced by the Lord" and confirmed by the apostles (2:3). Perhaps, as Bengel suggests, "the Christian Catechism of the Old Testament" is in view (1877, 4:394). These verses may provide us with a rare glimpse of catechesis within one of the earliest communities of "Messianic Judaism" (France 2006, 82; see Attridge 1989, 163; Ellingworth 1993, 313).

The encouragement to **go on to maturity** will be facilitated by the "solid food" offered in the teachings of 7:1—10:18. The concept of **maturity** (*teleiotēta*) relates back to the discussion of "the mature" in 5:14. But it also points forward to the "perfection" (KJV, NRSV; "completion" [NJB]) attainable for worshipers only through the sacrificial death of Christ (e.g., 7:19; 9:9; 10:1, 14).

The preacher is mindful that his teaching alone will not produce spiritual development. The verb **go on** is in the passive voice, and translated accordingly only in the TNIV and NIV[11]: "let us . . . be taken forward to maturity." Determination on their part (e.g., 3:6, 14; 4:11, 14; 10:23) is necessary, but insufficient. The strength of divine grace (4:16; 13:9) and providence (6:3) will bear them along toward spiritual maturity (see Turner 1975, 102).

■ **1b-2** The irony of needing someone to teach them the elementary truths of God's word **all over again** (5:12) correlates with **not laying again the foundation**. The **foundation** metaphor was commonly used for elementary instruction (deSilva 2000a, 216). For Hebrews, rehearsing the basics of the faith is out of the question. There are only two options: moving forward or falling back; apostasy or spiritual maturity. The danger of apostasy is that it makes it impossible for the apostate to be restored **again** to repentance (6:6; **again** [*palin*] is emphatic in 5:12; 6:1, 6).

The **foundation** has six stones, presented as three pairs. The six embrace the entire span of the Christian pilgrimage, from repentance at its start to eternal judgment at its end (Koester 2001, 311).

The first pair is **repentance from acts that lead to death, and of faith in God**. These are the two aspects of conversion: repenting of sin and turning to God in faith. This twofold movement is found in the earliest preaching of the apostles (Acts 3:19; 20:21; 26:20). Repentance is grounded in the OT idea of "turning" (*šûb*) from unrighteousness (Jer 18:11; Ezek 18:21; Zech 1:4) and to God (2 Chr 15:4; Isa 55:7; see Gowan 2009, 764). It was a fundamental aspect of kingdom proclamation by John the Baptist (Matt 3:2, 8, 11; Mark 1:4; Luke 3:3, 8; Acts 13:24; 19:4), Jesus (Matt 4:17; Mark 1:15; Luke 5:32), and the early church (Luke 24:47; Acts 2:38; 11:18; 17:30). Each of the references to **repentance** in Hebrews (6:1, 6; 12:17) implies a definitive, unrepeatable turning to God.

Repentance **from acts that lead to death** (lit., "dead works" [CEB, ESV, HCSB, KJV, LEB, NASB, NET, NRSV]) is viewed by some as a turning away from reliance on Jewish good works that are ineffective ("dead") for achieving righteousness before God (D. Guthrie 1983, 138). A kindred view is that dead works are "useless rituals" (NIV[mg]) of Judaism, such as the observances under the Levitical priesthood (Jewett 1981, 95-96; Lane 1991, 140; France 2006, 86). However, in Hebrews the provisions and rituals under the old covenant are "weak and useless" (7:18; see 10:3-4). They are obsolete, aging, and soon to disappear (8:13). But they should be discarded because they are not beneficial (13:9), not repented of because they are sinful or death-dealing in and of themselves.

Others see "dead works" as a reference to idolatry, since they are placed in opposition to faith and worship of God (6:1; 9:14; see deSilva 2000a, 216;

Thompson 2008, 133). But the only other occurrence of the phrase "dead works" (9:14 [CEB, ESV, HCSB, KJV, LEB, NASB, NET, NRSV]) cannot be a reference to works of the Law or cultic acts (either Jewish or pagan). Parallel to cleansing the conscience from "dead works" is cleansing the conscience from "sins" (10:2). Furthermore, the expression fits well within the Jewish and Christian "Two Ways" doctrine (see Bruce 1990, 140; Ellingworth 1993, 314). The way that leads to death involves sins or **acts that lead to death.** The way that leads to life is marked by "good works" (10:24 [CEB, ESV, HCSB, KJV, LEB, NET, RSV]; see 13:21), which give evidence to diligence and endurance in inheriting God's promises (6:9-12; 10:24-25, 32-34).

The Christian appeal for people to have **faith in God** hardly needs documentation (but see Acts 14:15; 17:24; 26:20; 1 Thess 1:9). In Hebrews, moving on to maturity calls for a deeper understanding of faith, pursued at length in ch 11. Faith in God is more than an initial confession (e.g., belief that God exists), but complete reliance on God's fidelity to keep his promises (trusting that he "rewards those who earnestly seek him" [11:6]).

The second pair is **instruction about baptisms** and **the laying on of hands.** The word **baptisms** is altogether puzzling for commentators, both ancient and modern, for two reasons. First, the word is not the usual noun for "baptism" current in NT and early Christian writings (*baptisma*), but a word that more generally designates washing or cleansing (*baptismos*; only once used indisputably of Christian baptism in Col 2:12). Second, as in its only other occurrence in Hebrews (9:10), the word is plural (*baptismōn*). In 9:10 the word surely denotes "ceremonial washings."

This unusual expression has led to much speculation (surveyed in Hughes 1977, 199-202; Ellingworth 1993, 315). Church fathers suggested that the plural refers to the baptizing of many people (Theodoret), repeat baptism (Chrysostom; for Athanasius, specifically of heretical sects), triple immersion (Tertullian), or baptisms of water, blood, and desire (Augustine). A sacramental view of "baptisms" (beginning perhaps with Grotius), distinguishes between an outward baptism with water and an inward baptism with the Spirit (deSilva [2000a, 218] holds to a variation of this, based on 10:22).

We must admit that there cannot be any certainty on this matter. It is possible that the preacher has in mind various "cleansing rites" (NIV[11]) or "ritual ways to wash with water" (CEB) known within a Jewish-Christian setting, such as proselyte baptism of Gentiles or John's baptism. These could be thought of as preparatory to the culminating rite of initiation in Christian baptism (Hughes 1977, 202; Attridge 1989, 164; Hagner 1990, 87; Ellingworth 1993, 315). Only in the primitive age of the church, during the transition of John the Baptist's disciples into full knowledge and faith in Christ, were repeated baptisms deemed acceptable. According to the Acts of the Apostles, those who had already been baptized with John's baptism needed also to be baptized into the name of the Lord Jesus in order to be initiated fully into the Christian faith (Acts 19:4-5; see 18:25).

The **laying on of hands** was a sacred act used for the purpose of blessing, healing, and commissioning or ordaining (Koester 2001, 305). If the rite of Christian baptism is included in the previous item (**baptisms**), then the **laying on of hands** here probably concerns the accompanying act of imparting the Holy Spirit on those who have been baptized (Acts 8:17-18; 19:6). The dual rites of baptism and confirmation continued on in the church (e.g., Tertullian, *Bapt.* 8; Cyprian, *Ep.* 74.5).

The final pair, **the resurrection of the dead** and **eternal judgment,** were part of the apocalyptic bedrock for Pharisaic and early Christian faith but were rejected by Sadducees (Acts 4:1-2; 23:8; Josephus, *J.W.* 2.163-65; *Ant.* 18.14-16; see Attridge 1989, 165 n. 129). For Paul, belief in the **resurrection of the dead** was foundational to belief in Jesus' resurrection, not vice versa (Acts 23:6; 26:8; 1 Cor 15:13, 15-16). Hebrews rarely mentions resurrection (11:19, 35). The preacher takes for granted that Christ was resurrected, mentioning it explicitly only once (13:20; see Lane 1998; for treatments of resurrection in the OT, intertestamental Judaism, and early Christianity, see Wright 2003; Anderson 2006).

Expectation of the final judgment was a cardinal doctrine of apocalyptic faith among Jews and Christians (Dan 7:26-27; *4 Ezra* 7:33-44; Matt 25:31-46; Acts 17:31; 2 Tim 4:1, 8; 1 Pet 4:5; 2 Pet 2:9; 3:7; Rev 20:11-15). The phrase **eternal judgment** occurs only this once in the entire Bible. The few occurrences in apocalyptic texts (*1 En.* 91:15-16; 104:5; 4Q212 4.23-26) suggest that the expression is chosen because **eternal judgment** marks the end of this age and the beginning of the eternal age (see *4 Ezra* 7:113; Rev 20:11—21:4).

This accords with other references to the judgment in Hebrews. It stands at the conclusion to mortal life (Heb 9:27) when God judges all people (10:25, 27, 30; 12:23; 13:4). Beyond the judgment lies salvation for believers (9:28) and the realization of God's unshakable kingdom (12:25-29). The **eternal** effects of divine judgment fit nicely with the many blessings of the age to come that likewise have an eternal quality (salvation [5:9]; redemption [9:12]; the Spirit [9:14]; inheritance [9:15]; covenant [13:20]).

■ **3** The preacher is determined to assist in completing his listeners' spiritual education. **We will do so** refers back to the actions encouraged in v 1. It may also allude to the difficult task mentioned in 5:11 (Lane 1991, 140), which the preacher will begin to undertake in 7:1.

The preacher is confident that his audience will take to heart his warnings and encouragement (6:9-12). But the proviso, **God permitting,** indicates that the enablement and final assessment for spiritual progress come from God. Our destiny depends decisively upon the blessing and justice of God (6:7, 10). The discipline leading us toward maturity, producing righteousness and holiness, comes ultimately from the fatherly hand of God (12:7-17). And only God can determine whether an individual has fallen short of his grace and blessing (12:15, 17; see 4:1) and entered the "impossible" situation of apostasy addressed in the next paragraph (6:4-8; see 2:1-3a; 10:26-30; 12:15-17).

3. Warning About Irreversible Apostasy (6:4-8)

This paragraph shifts from personal ("you," "we") to impersonal address (**It is . . .**). It contains two parts, each signaled by *for* (*gar*, untranslated in the NIV): a severe warning (6:4-6) followed by a supporting illustration (6:7-8; see Johnson 2006, 160). Employing a common rhetorical topic, concerning the "impossible" (Aristotle, *Rhet.* 2.19), this passage presents an argument from the contrary. The author has urged his readers to "go on to maturity" (6:1-3). Now he shows what would happen if they were to take the opposite course of action (deSilva 2000a, 215, 219-20).

■ **4a** The opening **For it is impossible** begins a thought that is not completed until the infinitive phrase in v 6, "to be brought back [*anakainizein*] to repentance." The inferential conjunction *gar* (*for,* untranslated in the NIV) links this discussion of final apostasy with the note about God's indispensable providence in the previous verse ("God permitting"). Only God can determine if an individual cannot be renewed to repentance or is doomed to be cursed (see vv 6b, 8).

Many expositors attempt to ease the severity of this warning (see Hughes 1977, 212-14; Attridge 1989, 167; Koester 2001, 312). Some offer the inadmissible translation, "difficult" (Nicholas of Lyra, Erasmus). Others posit an impossibility for humans, but not God (e.g., Ambrose, Aquinas); draw a distinction between absolute (e.g., mathematical) and relative (or moral) impossibility (Whedon 1880, 5:78-79); or apply the impossibility to second baptism (Ambrose; Chrysostom [1996, 410]; Theodoret [Heen and Krey 2005, 84]). However, this **impossible** is emphatic and unequivocal. It cannot be qualified, any more than other instances of the impossible in Hebrews, such as the impossibility "for God to lie" (6:18; see 10:4; 11:6). There is no escaping the terrifying conclusion that, for Hebrews, final apostasy is irreversible.

A description of those who have gotten into this impossible situation proceeds with a series of five participles (in the aorist tense) in vv 4-6a. The series begins with the phrase **those who . . . once** (*tous hapax*), which modifies all of the subsequent participial clauses (**those who have once been enlightened . . . have tasted . . . have shared** . . . "have tasted . . . have fallen away" [emphasis added; NIV[11] for the final clause]). This **once** stands over against the "again" in v 6 (and in 5:12 and 6:1). Thus, the preacher accents the exceptional, definitive, and privileged nature of the experience of God's grace in these last days. To turn one's back on it, or purposely regress from it, would be unspeakably contemptible (see v 6). It would place one in the untenable position of trying again to receive the very divine favor that one had rejected and disgraced (deSilva 2000a, 225).

Those who have . . . been enlightened provides the leading idea of the series. The participle *phōtisthentas* occurs again in 10:32 ("you had received the light"). There it is a clear reference to the listeners' conversion or initiation into the Christian faith. Elsewhere in the NT the same metaphor describes the dispelling of ignorance (darkness) through the knowledge (light) of God in the gospel (see John 1:9; Acts 26:18; 2 Cor 4:6; Eph 1:18; 3:9; 2 Tim 1:10; 1 Pet 2:9; 1 John 1:5). The metaphor is paralleled by the statement that the readers "have received the knowledge of the truth" (Heb 10:26).

Enlightenment and Baptism

As early as Justin Martyr, "to enlighten" meant "to baptize." Subsequent Greek fathers interpreted the enlightenment in Heb 6:4 as "baptism" or "washing" (e.g., Theodoret and Theophylact; Dods 1960, 296). The Syriac Peshitta translated the expression "enlightened" as "those who have once descended for baptism" (Lane 1991, 141). If the author of Hebrews associated enlightenment with baptism (not improbable, but unconfirmed), he may have been the first to do so among the earliest Christian writers (see Bruce 1990, 145; Johnson 2006, 162).

■ **4b-5** Two coordinated statements follow. They further describe the experience of the enlightened through the dominant metaphor of tasting (twice in vv 4-5). The first statement pairs together those **who have *both* tasted the heavenly gift *and* . . . shared in the Holy Spirit** (v 4). The word **tasted** does not denote something less than real conversion, as Calvin asserts (1976, 76). As with Jesus' tasting death in 2:9, so here the metaphor represents those who have truly "experienced" something (GW, NLT).

The **heavenly gift** is an image too general to specify the Eucharist, following the preceding (possible) metaphor for baptism (see Bruce 1990, 146). Elsewhere in the NT the word **gift** (*dōrea*) is used of God's gift of grace in Christ (Rom 5:15, 17; 2 Cor 9:15; Eph 3:7), the gift of the Holy Spirit (Acts 2:38; 8:20; 10:45; 11:17), or the gift of living water (= eternal life [John 4:10; see John 4:14; Rev 21:6; 22:17]).

Here the **gift** encompasses the divine favor and salvation available through the Son in access to the divine presence now (Heb 4:16; 10:19-22) but received in full at Christ's return (9:28). This is the "promised eternal inheritance" (9:15; see 1:14; 6:12; 10:36). Our experience of salvation is genuine, yet partial (note the genitive *tēs dōreas tes epouraniou*, "tasted *of* the heavenly gift" [KJV, NASB, emphasis added]). Both the source of our calling to salvation (3:1; see 9:15) and its full realization await us in our **heavenly** homeland (see 10:34; 11:16; 12:22, 28; 13:14).

The clause **who have shared in the Holy Spirit** contains the language of participation ("have become partakers of" [RSV; see KJV, NASB, NET]; "received a share of" [NJB]). Such terminology was used earlier of believers' "share in the heavenly calling" (3:1) and partnership with Christ (3:14). Believers share in the vital power and insight of the same **Holy Spirit** who speaks in the Scriptures (9:8; 10:15). He was the gracious means of our redemption in Christ (9:14; 10:29) and is dynamically active through spiritual gifts (2:4).

The second statement (v 5) repeats the taste metaphor. The clause, **who have tasted the goodness of the word of God,** probably relates to a favorable response to God's revelation, found in the OT Scriptures and fully disclosed in the gospel (see 4:2, 6; Hughes 1977, 210; France 2006, 83). The phrase **powers of the coming age** reminds us that our present experience of divine power is but a foretaste of "the world to come" (2:5).

■ **6** The series of images in vv 4-5 builds up a composite picture of the magnitude of salvation (see Hughes 1977, 212; Johnson 2006, 13). It is a real and personal experience of divine revelation, presence, and power. The first participle opens the description with the idea of spiritual enlightenment ("have . . . been enlightened"). The next three participles ("have tasted," "have shared," "have tasted") develop the thought with figures emphasizing experience and participation.

The final participle in the series creates an abrupt and shocking shift (v 6a): **and have fallen away.** The conditional translation, **if they fall away** (NIV, NKJV; see KJV, RSV, TYNDALE), goes as far back as Beza's version (Clarke 1977, 3:725). Reading the participle as conditional (**if**) is based on dogma rather than grammar (Wallace 1996, 633). This error has been corrected in most English translations (including the NIV[11]: "and who have fallen away").

The author is not presenting a purely hypothetical case or "straw man" (e.g., against Wuest 2004, 117-18; see Bruce 1990, 147-48). He is warning his readers to avoid a real and possible eventuality. Although they have not yet abandoned their faith, it is important to issue this warning while there is still hope. Their only option is to press forward to maturity (6:1). Their present apathy and sluggishness puts them in grave danger, because *"standing still begets apostasy"* (Whedon 1880, 5:78).

The verb *parapiptō* (**fall away**) is used only this once in the NT. In the LXX it is used of acting unfaithfully (Ezek 14:13; 15:8; 18:24; 20:27; 22:4) or breaking one's word (Esth 6:10). In the papyri it is often used of misplacing something, but it is also used of breaking the terms of a contract (MM, 488-89). A meaning associated with contractual agreements or commitments ("to fail to follow through on a commitment" [BDAG, 770]) fits well with the commercial language of partnership in Heb 6:4 ("shared in the Holy Spirit"; → 3:14 sidebar, "Partners with Christ"). The preacher is referring to those who have "committed apostasy" (NET) or "deserted [Christ]" (GW). He frequently cautions against such disloyalty (see 2:2-3; 4:1; 10:38-39; 12:15, 17), which flows from "a sinful, unbelieving heart that turns away [*apostēnai*] from the living God" (3:12).

The impossibility introduced in 6:4a is finally described in v 6b. For those who have so contemptuously repudiated the divine favor they once enjoyed, it is impossible **to be brought back to repentance.** God's blessings of salvation have a once-and-for-all character ("once [*hapax*]" [v 4*a*]). They cannot be casually repeated. The word *palin* (***again,*** not in the NIV) stands emphatically at the head of this clause. This indicator of repetition is reinforced by the infinitive *anakainizein*, which means "to renew" (KJV, LEB, NASB) or "to restore" (ESV; **to be brought back**). Apostates cannot be restored again **to repentance** (→ 6:1*b*). The impossibility of this repetition is parallel to the unacceptable options of "laying again [*palin*] the foundation of repentance" (6:1*b*) and being taught "the elementary truths of God's word all over again [*palin*]" (5:12).

Renewed repentance is not an impossibility because God is unable to restore a defector back to faith. Nor is it impossible simply because the apostate's heart has hardened beyond recovery (however true this may be; see 3:7, 12-14, 15; 4:7). The impossibility is due to God's judgment. Historical examples from the OT illustrate the results of defiant rejection of God's promises. In the case of the wilderness generation, God swore, "They shall never enter my rest" (3:11; 4:3, 5). In the case of Esau, who sold his inheritance rights, he was rejected and given no chance for "repentance" (KJV), even though he tearfully sought to be reinstated (12:17; see Koester 2001, 312-13).

No Second Repentance or No Second Baptism?

Hebrews 6:4-8 has long been a source of concern and controversy. In particular, its rigorous stance on the impossibility of apostates being renewed to repentance is one of the greatest difficulties in Scripture. The early second-century Christian, the Shepherd of Hermas, was troubled by the teaching that no repentance was available for postbaptismal sins. But a heavenly messenger revealed to him that the Lord, in his mercy toward human weakness and awareness of the devil's devices, affords one—but only one—opportunity for repentance from sins after baptism (*Herm. Mand.* 4.3.1-7). Clement of Alexandria followed this view (*Strom.* 2.13; 4.20). Many early Christians also believed that martyrdom was a means of wiping out all of one's postbaptismal sins.

In the early third century, Tertullian took a hard-line Montanist position against that "'Shepherd' of adulterers." He insisted that no second repentance was allowed for serious sins committed after baptism, such as adultery or apostasy (*Pud.* 20). After the Decian persecution of A.D. 249-250, the Novatians employed Heb 6:4-8 to claim that those who had denied their faith under persecution could not be restored to fellowship in the church. Cyprian (d. 258) opposed both Montanists and Novatians in asserting that those who had lapsed may be granted repentance, pardon, and reinstatement (*Ep.* 51). These controversies over Heb 6:4-8 contributed to the West's difficulty in accepting Hebrews as part of the NT canon.

Beginning in the fourth century a standard interpretation of 6:4-8 would endure for the next thousand years in both the East and West. Ambrose (d. 397) asserted that Hebrews does not bar the fallen from being restored to repentance. Rather, it rejects the possibility of a second baptism. Ambrose argued that baptism is a participation in Christ's death, so that rebaptism would amount to recrucifying the Son of God. He further argued that, while repentance for postbaptismal sins may appear impossible from a human standpoint, it is not impossible for God (*Paen.* 2.2). The main lines of this view were shared by John Chrysostom, Theodoret, Ephrem the Syrian, Photius, and many others. (For further details, see Heen and Krey 2005, 83-87; Hughes 1977, 213-15; Attridge 1989, 168-69; Koester 2001, 20-25.)

After the series of five past tense (aorist) participles, two vivid, present tense participles are used to convey the rationale (**because**) for the apostate's predicament. The present tense expresses the enduring indignity caused by such betrayal. Having once been partners with Christ, they have ranked themselves among the sinners who opposed him (12:3).

Their crime is so heinous that it can be described as **crucifying the Son of God all over again** (*anastarountas*). The verb *anastauroō* was widely used simply to mean "to crucify," with the prefix *ana-* suggesting the upward motion of hoisting a victim on the cross. However, ancient translators and the Greek fathers unanimously understood the prefix to mean "again" (see BDAG, 72; Kuhn 1990, 92; Ellingworth 1993, 324), hence, "recrucifying" (HCSB, NAB).

This may be an action that is **to their** own **loss** (taking *heautois* as a dative of disadvantage). But crucifying "to themselves" (KJV, NASB; see NAB, NJB) could extend the violent metaphor to mean a decisive severing of their relationship with **the Son of God**. An analogous expression is in Paul's repudiation of the world: "the world has been crucified to me, and I to the world" (Gal 6:14; see Koester 2001, 315).

The second participle, *paradeigmatizontas* (**subjecting him to public disgrace**), complements the action of crucifixion. The verb was used of public punishments designed to make an example of criminals (BDAG, 761; Koester 2001, 315). The Romans utilized the cross as an implement not simply of excruciating pain but also of horrible disgrace (see 12:2). It was meant to deter others from committing the crime being punished. The apostate, rather than identifying with Christ's shame (13:13), is "holding him up to contempt" (ESV, HCSB, NAB, NET, NRSV). He has assumed the same mocking stance as an ancient graffiti artist in Rome, who scrawled a picture of a man lifting his hand in prayer to a donkey-headed figure on a cross, with the inscription below, "Alexamenos worships god" (see Decker 2007).

■ **7-8** The inferential conjunction *gar* (***For***) introduces an example from agriculture. It illustrates the impossibility of restoration from apostasy discussed in the previous verses (4-6). Verse 7 presents the positive side of this example; v 8, the negative.

Land that drinks in the rain often falling on it is parallel to the divine favors listed in vv 4-5. Through the use of rhyme, the preacher connects God's provision of rain with the bounty the land is expected to bear. Land that soaks in **rain** [*hyeton*] . . . **produces a crop useful** [*eutheton*] **to those for whom it is**

farmed. As in Jesus' parable of the sower, seed that falls on good soil produces a bumper crop (Matt 13:8; Mark 4:8; Luke 8:8). Drinking in the rain, like tasting the goodness of God's word (v 5a), should transform God's ongoing gifts (**rain often falling on it**) into a harvest of benefits for others.

The community's service of loving and sharing is the fruitfulness lavished on others and the "sacrifice[s] of praise" to God (see 6:10; 10:32-34; 13:15-16). This pleases God (13:16, 21) and garners God's blessing. In the clause **receives the blessing of God,** we find the language of participation (*metalambanei*, **receives;** "to share or participate in someth., *have a share in*" [BDAG, 639]). The same verb in 12:10 concerns believers' "share" in God's holiness. But it is also reminiscent of the language used earlier of participation in heavenly realities (3:1, 4; 6:4; Attridge 1989, 173).

God's **blessing** will be important in 6:13-20, where Abraham is the prime example of one who received God's promised blessing (6:14-15). The noun occurs again in the reference to Esau's forfeiture of the divine blessing (12:17). God's blessing is probably "such a great salvation," which believers will inherit (2:3; see 1:14, but esp. 6:9).

But land that produces thorns and thistles (v 8) alludes to God's cursing the land after Adam and Eve's original disobedience, so that it produces "thorns and thistles" (Gen 3:18). Here the land, which has received ample showers from heaven, has surprisingly turned out to be **worthless.** The adjective *adokimos* denotes a negative judgment. Unproductive land is "rejected" (KJV, NAB). The same adjective is used by Paul in 1 Cor 9:25-27 of the rigorous discipline required to receive an eternal crown rather than being "disqualified" (1 Cor 9:27).

Land that has consumed the divine resources for fruitfulness, but is barren, does not qualify for God's blessing. Rather, **it is in danger of being cursed.** The phrasing is literally "near" (ESV, NJB; see KJV, TYNDALE) or "close" (NASB) to being cursed. The divine curse is menacingly near ("on the verge of being cursed" [NRSV]; "a curse hangs over it" [REB]). One is reminded of the image used by John the Baptist concerning those who do not produce the fruit of repentance: "The ax is already at the root of the trees, and every tree that does not produce good fruit will be cut down and thrown into the fire" (Matt 3:10).

In the end it will be burned. The image of fire in connection with eschatological judgment is common in the NT (Matt 3:10; 5:22; 7:19; 13:40, 42, 50; 18:8-9; 25:41; Mark 9:22, 43, 48; John 15:6; 1 Cor 3:13, 15; 2 Thess 1:7-8; 2 Pet 3:7; Jude 7; Rev 19:20; 20:14-15; 21:8). In Hebrews, God's fiery judgment is reserved for the enemies of God (10:27), including apostates (see 10:26-31). Refusing the One who speaks (12:25) is perilous, because "God is a consuming fire" (12:29).

4. Words of Reassurance (6:9-12)

■ **9** Having spoken forthrightly about the danger of apostasy, the preacher now reassures his listeners. The rhetorical pattern of frank speech followed by praise was useful for steering hearers clear of error without beating them down (see *Rhet. Her.* 4.37.49-50; Chrysostom 1996, 414-15; deSilva 2000a, 244-45). **Even though we speak like this,** that is, concerning the doom awaiting those who turn their backs on God's grace (vv 4-8), **we are confident** ("we are convinced" [CEB, GW, HCSB, LEB, NASB, NET, REB]) that such a "worst-case scenario" (France 2006, 82) does not yet apply to the community being addressed.

The positive shift is marked by the return of the authorial **we** (see 5:11; 6:1, 3), after speaking more impersonally in 6:4-8. The author also addresses the community as **dear friends** (*beloved*), but only here in the sermon. The rarity of this form of address may point to its selection as part of the rhetorical strategy of this paragraph (namely, to soften the blow of the foregoing severe warning). However, it is not out of keeping with the familial term "brothers" used elsewhere (3:1, 12; 10:19; 13:22) and is characteristic of homiletical style (Attridge 1989, 174). Both forms of address bespeak tender pastoral concern, not simply the clever use of rhetoric.

The preacher is persuaded that **better things** apply **in your case.** The **better things** (*ta kreissona*) pertain to the fruitfulness and blessing of v 7, as opposed to the unfruitfulness and curse of v 8. The concept of the "better" or "superior" is of key importance to the author (→ 1:4 sidebar, "'Better' Things in Hebrews"). The better things are further described as **things that accompany salvation** (*echomena sōterias*), i.e., **involve** or "have to do with salvation" (NIV[11]; on this common Greek idiom, see Attridge 1989, 174 n. 98; LSJ, 750). Salvation is final deliverance from sin and its associated effects of defilement, alienation from God, and death (see esp. 2:5-18). In Hebrews, salvation is consistently connected with the ministry of Christ (see 2:3, 10; 5:9; 7:25; 9:28).

■ **10** The declaration **God is not unjust** is an instance of understatement (Johnson 2006, 165). It is an emphatic way of saying, "God *is* just." The bond between this thought and the next is much tighter than some translations suggest (**God is not unjust; he will not forget** [NIV, HCSB, NLT; see GW, NRSV]). "For God is not unjust so as to forget" more faithfully captures the Greek turn of phrase (NASB, NET; see CEB, ESV, KJV, LEB, NAB, NJB, REB).

God is mindful of and justly disposed toward two things: **your work** and **love.** In 10:24 the preacher will urge his readers to promote "love and good works" [ESV, HCSB, LEB, NAB, NET, NJB, NKJV, RSV] within the church. These are the antithesis of "acts that lead to death" (6:1; 9:14). Thus, the author identifies his listeners with the fruitful and blessed field (6:7), rather than the barren field that will be cursed (6:8).

Virtues

In Heb 6:9-12 and 10:19-25 we find the three virtues: love (6:10; 10:24), hope (6:11; 10:23), and faith (6:12; 10:22). These are most familiar to us through their grouping in Paul (1 Cor 13:13; see Gal 5:5-6; Col 1:4-5; 1 Thess 1:3; 5:8). Theologians call them the "theological" virtues. Their role in the life of grace and their interrelations were carefully studied by the Scholastics, most notably Thomas Aquinas.

An additional set of four moral perfections were carried over into Christian theology from Plato, Aristotle, and the Stoics: wisdom (→ 5:14), moderation, justice, and courage. The giants of Christian moral theology—Ambrose, Augustine, and Aquinas—distinguished these "cardinal" or "natural" virtues from the "theological" virtues. Aquinas correlated the cardinal virtues with various human faculties (wisdom with intellect; justice with the will; and moderation and courage with two passions of the sensitive appetite, lust and fear respectively).

Together, the theological and cardinal virtues comprise the "Seven Virtues." These are set in contrast to the "Seven Deadly Sins" (pride, covetousness, lust, envy, gluttony, anger, and sloth). For further study, see Rickaby 1908; Cross and Livingstone 1997a and 1997b; Fitzgerald 1992.

Their **love** is defined as something they **have shown**. The verb *endeiknymi* ("show, demonstrate," BDAG, 331) is used in the papyri of producing legal proof (Ellingworth 1993, 331; MM, 211). Love is not simply a thought or sentiment but is proven in concrete ways (compare 1 John 3:18). It is also undertaken *for his name* (*eis to onoma autou*; **him**). This could mean that love shown to others is "done for love of his name" (REB) or "for his [i.e., God's] sake" (NRSV). Or it could mean that their love is directed toward God himself (Koester 2001, 317). We need not choose between the two, because (as 1 John 4:20-21 attests) the one implies the other.

The work and love exhibited within the community consist of service to **his people** (lit., "the saints" [e.g., ESV, HCSB, KJV, LEB, NASB, NRSV], i.e., "the holy people of God" [NJB; see GW]). The words translated **have helped** and **continue to help** are forms of *diakoneō*, which connotes humble or menial service (e.g., waiting on tables in Acts 6:1-2; see L&N, 35.19). Past acts of service included standing shoulder to shoulder with those who suffered abuse, lost property, or imprisonment (10:32-24). Present acts of service include continuing love for one another, hospitality to strangers, taking care of those in prison (13:1-3), in short, not neglecting to do good and share with others (13:16).

■ 11 Deep conviction in the previous verse is matched here by "great desire" (NLT). **We want** translates a verb that conveys very strong desire ("we passionately want" [NET]; "we earnestly desire" [NAB]). Once again the preacher expresses his concern for every individual in the community (**each of you** [see 3:12, 13; 4:1, 11; 12:15, 16]). There were at least some among them whose commitment was flagging and whose eventual apostasy could have a poisoning effect on the believers around them (12:15).

The desire is for every person **to show this same diligence.** The verb *endeiknymi* (**show**), used in the previous verse (v 10), recurs here. They should demonstrate **this same diligence** in loving God through loving service to others. The word **diligence** (*spoudēn*) is a cognate of the verb translated "make every effort" in → 4:11. In 4:11 they were exhorted to be eager to enter into God's end-time rest. Here, similarly, the desire is for them to remain diligent **to the very end.** Holding firm to their commitment to Christ "till the end" (see 3:14) will ensure that they do not meet the ultimate "end" (6:8) of those who are not "produc[ing] a harvest of righteousness and peace" (12:11).

A prepositional phrase, **in order to make your hope sure,** spells out the aim of the listeners' diligence. It is difficult to interpret because the noun *plērophoria* (lit., "fullness") could have either of two meanings in this context:

First, it could connote fullness or completeness in the sense of hope's "fulfillment" (NAB, NET; "ultimate fulfilment" [NJB]) or "final realization" (HCSB; see NRSV; "fully realized" [REB]; Lane 1991, 130; Johnson 2006, 167). But this eschatological note might create an unnecessary repetition of the phrase **to the very end**.

Second, it could connote "full assurance" (ESV, KJV, LEB, NASB, NRSV), "complete certainty" (BDAG, 827), or **to make** their **hope sure** (NRSV and NLT combine both the senses of assurance and fulfillment). The word bears the same sense of certainty in the expression "full assurance of faith" (10:22, its only other occurrence in Hebrews; see also Col 2:2; 1 Thess 1:5). This idea fits with other exhortations to hold on steadily to our hope (Heb 3:6; 10:23), confession (4:14; 10:23; see 3:1), or commitment (3:14). A closer contextual aid is the metaphor in 6:19, which illustrates the phrase "full assurance of hope." Hope is depicted there as "an anchor for the soul, firm and secure."

■ **12** In the Greek text, **We do not want you to become lazy** does not begin a new sentence. Continuing the thought of v 11, it is a purpose clause that communicates the perseverance the preacher desires to promote: "so that you may not become sluggish" (NRSV).

Lazy (*nōthroi*) contrasts with "diligence" in v 11. The word appears only here and in 5:11, forming a deliberate frame around the first four paragraphs of this section (5:11—6:18). The effect is to reemphasize the risk of slipping into spiritual apathy. There is no discrepancy between the statements in 5:11 and 6:12. As Bengel explains, they had "become sluggish in hearing [*nōthroi gegonate tais akoais*]" (5:11 NAB, NET); but "he now cautions them, not to become *slothful* [*nothroi genēsthe*] absolutely" (6:12; Bengel 1877, 4:400). A tendency not to pay careful attention (see 2:1) could lead to becoming "lax" (REB) altogether, rather than steadily engaging in the vital commitments and practices of Christian faith.

Rather than being spiritual slackers, the listeners ought to be "imitators" (*mimētai;* ESV, HCSB, LEB, NASB, NET, NRSV; **to imitate**) of those who are models of steadfast faith. The push for imitation reappears explicitly in 13:7, where the **faith** of the community's leaders is what they should "imitate [*mimeisthe*]." The OT contains examples of disobedience to avoid (4:11) and numerous examples of faithfulness to follow (3:5; 11:1-39). But Christ is the supreme example of faith (3:2; 10:5-10; 12:1-3).

Faith and patience, or rather, "faith and perseverance" (HCSB, NET, NJB) may well be a hendiadys, rendered as "faithful perseverance" or "persevering faith" (Attridge 1989, 176). The second word (*makrothymias*) means more than passive **patience**, long-suffering, or forbearance. It connotes **perseverance,** "endurance" (NLT), or "steadfastness" (BDAG, 612; in line with secular usage, Hollander 1991). Later in Hebrews, it will be replaced by the more common word for "endurance [*hypomonē*]" (10:36; 12:1]).

The idea of imitating **those who through faith and patience inherit what has been promised** prepares the way for Abraham's example in 6:13-15. Abraham's faithfulness and steadfastness are highlighted in Jewish retellings of his story (see *Jub.* 17:17-18; 19:3, 4, 8). The last three terms in Heb 6:12—**patience** (*makrothymias*), **inherit** (*klēronomountōn*), and **what has been promised** (*tas epangelias;* → 4:1)—anticipate the content of the next paragraph (6:13-20). Repeated are Abraham's patient endurance (6:15), God's promise (6:13, 15, 17), and the heirs of the promise (6:14)—but also the sure hope that warrants all of these (6:18-19; see 6:11).

5. Powerful Encouragement Based on God's Trustworthiness (6:13-20)

This fifth and final paragraph in 5:11—6:20 serves as a transition into the major arguments of the sermon, which begin in 7:1. Themes mentioned in the previous paragraph are repeated (perseverance, inheritance of the promise, and hope; → 6:11-12). The theme of God's reliability, expressed in God's oath (6:13, 17), is integral to the argument concerning the superiority of Christ's priesthood in ch 7. Jesus' appointment as the high priest, who ministers in "the inner sanctuary" (6:19-20), is guaranteed by the divine oath from Ps 110:4, alluded to in Heb 6:20*b*. In ch 7, this same oath (7:17, 21) guarantees that God has introduced "a better hope" (7:19), "better covenant" (7:22; see 8:1-13; 9:15; 10:16; 12:24; 13:20), and complete salvation through the Son who has been appointed to a permanent priesthood (7:28; see 7:24-25).

Legal Jargon in Hebrews

Since one of the principal applications of ancient rhetoric was for prosecution and defense in law courts, anyone with rhetorical training would naturally be familiar with legal argumentation. Quintilian commends the use of various kinds of legal arguments (*Inst.* 5.11.32-35). Hebrews, more than any other NT book, employs legal terms and comparisons for persuasive effect. Legal terminology is widely used throughout Hebrews, as the following table demonstrates (see Lane 1991, 149; Thompson 2008, 139).

Term	Legal Meaning	Hebrews
athetēsis	"set aside"; technical term for the annulment or abrogation of a decree or cancellation of a debt	7:18; 9:26
ametathetos	"unchangeable," "irrevocable"; used in wills or contracts of stipulations that cannot be rescinded or annulled	6:17, 18
anaireō	"do away with," "abolish" (the OT sacrificial system)	10:9
antilogia	"legal dispute"	6:16
aparabatos	Appears in legal formulae to designate provisions that are "inviolable," "unbreakable," or "unchangeable," that is, "permanent."	7:24
bebaioō, bebaios, bebaiōsis	"firm," "valid," "guaranteed"; *eis bebaiōsin* ("for confirmation" [6:16 ESV]) is a technical expression for a legal guarantee	2:2-3; 3:14; 6:16, 19; 9:17; 13:9
diathēkē	"last will and testament"	9:16, 17
engyos	"guarantee"; legal term for a security deposit, collateral, or cosigner in a commercial transaction	7:22
endeiknymi/ epideiknymi	"make . . . clear," "demonstrate," "prove"; used in the papyri of producing legal proof	6:10, 11/6:17
ischyō	Lit., "be strong"; used in the legal sense of "takes effect" or being "in force" (CEB, ESV, HCSB, LEB, NASB, NIV, NKJV, NRSV)	9:17
histēmi	"establish" God's will (vs. abolishing the OT sacrificial system)	10:9
kairou diorthōseōs epikeimena	"the time of reformation" (NKJV); referring to the force of outmoded laws, until they are repealed and replaced	9:10
kata [+ genitive noun]	Used to signify the thing or person who guarantees an oath, as in swearing "by" someone greater	6:13, 16

6:13-20

mechri telous	"till the end"; used of the termination point for a contractual agreement	3:14
mesiteuō/ *mesitēs*	"mediate"/"mediator"; *mesiteuō* has the technical sense of "to provide a guarantee" (6:17)	6:17/8:6; 9:15; 12:24
omnymi	"swear," "take an oath"	3:11, 18; 4:3; 6:13, 16; 7:21
orkos	"oath"	6:16, 17
orkōmosia	"oath," referring to the process of taking an oath: "oath-taking"	7:20, 21, 28
synepimartyreō	"testify," "provide corroborating testimony"	2:4
pheresthai	Lit., "to be brought"; used of official registration or establishment of a legally required event (such as the death of the testator for the execution of his last will and testament)	9:16
hypostasis	A business obligation, such as the expectation of rent due or commitment to the terms of a commercial venture; a guarantee of ownership, title deed	3:14; 11:1

6:13-15

The preacher returns to the mode of scriptural exposition in 6:13-20. He has not engaged in this method in a sustained way since 3:7—4:13. His text is God's oath to Abraham in Gen 22:17 (see Heb 6:14). This miniature midrash falls into three parts.

- Verses 13-15 showcase God's oath to Abraham, along with the patriarch's perseverance in receiving the promise.
- In vv 16-17, the function of oath-taking among human beings is used to illustrate God's motivation for swearing an oath: to demonstrate the unchanging nature of the divine will.
- In vv 18-20, God's trustworthiness is the basis for pastoral application. God's purpose ("so that [*hina*]" [v 18]) for confirming his promise to Abraham with an oath was to provide powerful encouragement and assurance for current believers. Indeed, our eschatological hope is fixed like an anchor in the very presence of God, where Jesus serves as our eternal high priest (vv 19-20).

■ 13-15 The inferential conjunction *gar* (**For**, untranslated in NIV) connects Abraham to those mentioned in 6:12. Abraham is the signal example of those who through faith and perseverance inherit the promises (France 2006, 87). Topically, Abraham's story of enduring faith now comes into view, with the phrase ***for* to Abraham** at the head of this paragraph. However, grammatically,

God is the subject of the opening sentence. God (*theos*) is mentioned three times (vv 13, 17, 18) as the subject of key actions in this passage (promise, oath, purpose, and inability to lie; Fanning 2007, 193-94). The theological focus on God's solid, unimpeachable fidelity serves as the basis for Abraham's perseverance (v 15; see 11:11), just as it also gives present believers strong encouragement to hold fast to hope (6:18).

The preacher appropriates a scriptural text from arguably the most important scene in Abraham's life: the test to offer up his son Isaac. Called the Akedah ("Binding" of Isaac) in rabbinic tradition, this was the supreme expression of Abraham's faith (→ 11:17-19). At the conclusion to the testing, the Lord reaffirmed **his promise** to Abraham (Gen 22:15-18; see Gen 12:2; 13:16; 15:5). That Abraham "persevered" (Heb 6:15 [NJB]; "patiently endured" [KJV]; **after waiting patiently,** *makrothymēsas;* see 6:12) may be an allusion to Abraham's costly obedience in not withholding his son (Gen 22:16, 18).

And so, because of God's confirmation of his promises after the testing, Abraham **received what was promised** (Heb 6:15). Hebrews distinguishes between the OT saints receiving God's promises (6:12, 15; 11:17, 33), and their not receiving the complete fulfillment of the promises apart from the saints of the NT era (11:13, 39-40; see Hagner 1990, 97; Koester 2001, 326). Abraham obtained the promise—Isaac—"the pledge of all the promises" (Wesley n.d., 575). "Figuratively speaking," he received Isaac back from "the dead" (11:19). Thus, he anticipated the ultimate fulfillment of God's promises at the resurrection and in the world to come.

In 6:13 there is an allusion to God's declaration, "I swear by myself" (Gen 22:16): **since there was no one greater for him to swear by, he swore by himself** (Heb 6:13). God is the one "for whom and through whom everything exists" (2:10). The divine majesty, shared by Jesus the high priest, reaches "above the heavens" (4:14; 7:26; see 1:3; 8:1). There is no higher authority by which God may take an oath. Therefore, God swears by himself (see Exod 32:13; Isa 45:23; Jer 22:5; 49:13; 51:14; Amos 6:8; Luke 1:73). This signifies that God's word of promise is bound to the steadiness of his own nature and purpose (see Heb 6:17-18; Lane 1991, 151).

Philo and Hebrews on God Swearing by Himself

Philo treats at length the subject of oath-taking throughout his writings. Hebrews does not similarly go into detail concerning the problem of God's swearing by himself, but seems to share some of the same conclusions as Philo.

From the earliest times the Greeks invoked the names of gods to swear oaths (Xenophon, *Anab.* 6.6.17). By the Classical Age, oaths had become so overused and trivialized that attempts were made among intellectuals and politicians to ban them. In the Hellenistic period the Stoics argued against oath-taking, and Philo seems to have followed this philosophical tradition. Similarly, Jesus (Matt 5:34-35, 37), James (Jas 5:12), and the covenanters at Qumran (Josephus, *J.W.* 2.135;

CD 15:1-6) advocated avoiding oath-taking. They suggested that the practice only begged the question of one's truthfulness (Link 1979, 739; Thiselton 2009, 311).

According to Philo, the best course of action is not to swear at all; the second best thing is to keep one's oath. This is because oath-taking, by its very nature, invites suspicion that the one who is swearing is not completely trustworthy (*Decalogue* 84). Oaths call upon God to bear witness in a matter that is subject to doubt (*Alleg. Interp.* 3.205; *Sacrifices* 91; *Planting* 82; *Decalogue* 86; *Spec. Laws* 2.10; *Dreams* 1.12). Oaths are entered into by those who want to be given credence because others do not believe them (*Sacrifices* 93). But "the good man's word," says Philo, "should be an oath, firm, unswerving, utterly free from falsehood, securely planted on truth" (*Spec. Laws* 2.2). "For what is better than to practice a lifelong veracity, and to have God as our witness thereto?" (*Spec. Laws* 2.10).

This raises difficulties about God swearing by himself in a text such as Gen 22:16-17, referred to by both Hebrews (6:13-14) and Philo (*Alleg. Interp.* 3.203). It may be objected that God's swearing an oath is inconsistent with his faithful character (*Alleg. Interp.* 3.204), which contains no trace of uncertainty or doubt (*Sacrifices* 91), or that it is an absurdity (*Alleg. Interp.* 3.205). Philo meets these objections in three ways.

First, God's taking an oath does not call into question his trustworthiness. God is the only faithful being, whose every word is a most sacred and holy oath (*Alleg. Interp.* 3.204; see *Sacrifices* 93). All the words of God, like oaths, are proofs of his power, because whatever he says is sure to come to pass (*Alleg. Interp.* 3.204). Hebrews agrees that God's purposes are unchangeable, and "it is impossible for God to lie" (6:17-18).

Second, like Hebrews (6:13), Philo says that God cannot be faulted for swearing by himself, for there is nothing greater for him to swear by. God is the best of all things (*Alleg. Interp.* 3.203). Nothing is better than the Cause of all things (*Sacrifices* 92). God is to God's self everything that is most honorable (*Alleg. Interp.* 3.205). So God does not become credible by stating an oath, but even the oath is confirmed by God, who is his own confirmation and unerring testimony (*Sacrifices* 93; *Alleg. Interp.* 3.208).

Third, God does not swear an oath for his own sake, but to accommodate human weakness (*Sacrifices* 94). God's oath to Abraham was designed as a pledge (*pistis*) in return for Abraham's faith (*pistis*), so that the patriarch's mind could be more firmly and immovably established (*Abraham* 273). Likewise, in Hebrews, God swears an oath in order to demonstrate his faithful purpose convincingly and to provide strong encouragement for the heirs of God's promises (6:17-18).

The oath from Gen 22:17 is quoted in Heb 6:14: **I will surely bless you and give you many descendants.** The focus is on God's promise to multiply Abraham's descendants (Gen 22:17*a*; see Heb 11:12). No mention is made of the promised land (Gen 22:17*b*). In the theology of Hebrews, the latter promise concerns our heavenly home in the age to come. This promise will not come to fulfillment for the whole people of God until the end (Heb 11:10, 13-16; 12:22; 13:14; see 3:14; 6:11; 9:28; 10:25).

■ **16-17** The explanation of the function of oath-taking in v 16 contains two parts.

First, **Men swear by someone greater than themselves** (v 16a). Both in Greek and Jewish contexts, oaths were taken in the name of God in order to call upon higher testimony to one's veracity. The oath also functioned as a self-curse that invoked divine sanctions if the oath were not kept (Schneider 1967, 458-59; Thiselton 2009, 310; see 2 Sam 3:17; 2 Kgs 6:31; *Rhet. Alex.* 17.1432a).

Second, **the oath confirms what is said and puts an end to all argument** (v 16b). Oaths are unnecessary when one's honesty and integrity will suffice (see Matt 5:33-37; Jas 5:12). An oath is designed to call upon God to testify concerning a matter that is uncertain or doubtful. "Matters that are in doubt are decided by an oath, insecure things made secure, assurance given to that which lacked it" (Philo, *Dreams* 1.12; quoted in Koester 2001, 326-27).

Hebrews does not reflect on the apparent "absurdity" of God swearing by himself, as Philo did (*Alleg. Interp.* 3.205). Nevertheless, Heb 6:17 may indicate an awareness of the difficulty, and draws a conclusion similar to Philo's regarding the divine intention for doing this (→ 6:13-15 sidebar, "Philo and Hebrews on God Swearing by Himself"). God's resolute purpose is emphasized: **Because God wanted to make the unchanging nature of his purpose very clear** (v 17a). The Son's constancy has already been set against the changeable nature of angelic beings (1:7-12). God is not like human beings, who lie or change their minds out of fickleness (Num 23:19; 1 Sam 15:29). God "does not change like shifting shadows" (Jas 1:17).

Therefore, God swore by himself, not because his truthfulness was in doubt, but because he wanted to set forth a compelling demonstration of his resolve. The expression **to make . . . very clear** includes a cognate of the verb *endeiknymi* ("show") used twice above in Heb 6:10-11. The verb is used in the papyri in legal settings where proof or verification is demanded (MM, 237; see Acts 18:28). God wanted to demonstrate his purpose "more abundantly [*perissoteron*]" (KJV) or "more convincingly" (ESV, RSV).

God's confirmation of his promise is intended for **the heirs of what was promised**. These are all the people of God throughout history (i.e., "Abraham's descendants" [2:16]), beginning with "the ancients" (11:2; see 6:12; 11:7-9), spanning to all "those who will inherit salvation" (1:14; see 9:15). In the next verse (6:18) it is clear that the preacher includes himself and his readers ("we") among those for whom God **confirmed** his promise **with an oath** (v 17b).

The verb **confirmed** is used in the legal context of mediation. A mediator "intervened" (NAB, NET) or "interposed" (NASB, RSV) in order to settle a dispute between two parties. By extension, the mediator "guaranteed" (CEB, ESV, HCSB, LEB, NRSV) the settlement. God acts as the guarantor of human oaths (Josephus, *Ant.* 4.133). In this passage, God certifies his own promise by way of **an oath**. The language of mediation is important in Hebrews, especially as it applies to Jesus as the "guarantee" (7:22) and "mediator" of the new covenant (8:6; 9:15; 12:24).

■ **18-20** The purpose (*hina*, **so that**) for God's demonstration of his fidelity is now applied by the preacher to himself and his listeners (**we**). The **two unchangeable things in which it is impossible for God to lie** are the promise and oath spoken of in vv 13 and 17. The word **impossible** is the same as that found in → 6:4. God's own nature makes it impossible for him to be untruthful or to break faith (see Num 23:19; 1 Sam 15:29; Ps 89:34; Isa 31:2). God is the "only faithful being," apart from those who are dear to God (such as Moses in Num 12:7; Philo, *Alleg. Interp.* 3.204).

Christians are described as **we who have fled**. The verb *katapheugō* connotes "fleeing to find refuge" (see Gen 19:20; Exod 21:13; Lev 26:25; Num 35:25-26 LXX), such as to one of the cities of refuge (Deut 4:42; 19:5; Josh 20:9). In the papyri it is a technical word for supplicants who are "fleeing" or "resorting" to anyone for escape from danger (MM, 334; BDAG, 529). Believers are fugitives from the perils and uncertainties of the world about them (see Heb 11:34). Like the patriarchs, they are "aliens and strangers on earth" (11:13; see 11:9); they are refugees seeking permanent residence and eternal salvation in the better, heavenly homeland (11:16; see 11:10; 12:22; 13:14).

Two attainments (indicated by the verb *echō*, "to have") are possible on the basis of the divine promise and oath:

The first (in 6:18) is that "we . . . might have strong encouragement" (ESV, HCSB, RSV; **may be greatly encouraged**). "Strong encouragement [*ischyran paraklēsin*]" is a good description for the entire sermon, which the preacher describes as a "word of exhortation" (→ 13:22). The powerful encouragement is for the listeners **to take hold of the hope offered to us**. Exhortations to hold on to hope (3:6), commitment to Christ (3:14), or to our confession (4:14; 10:23) are prominent in Hebrews. Because of God's demonstration of his unimpeachable fidelity, hope is **offered to** ("held out to" [NJB]) or "set before" us (*tēs prokeimenēs* [ESV, HCSB, KJV, LEB, NASB, NET, NIV[11], NRSV, REB]). Paradoxically, hope is something within our grasp, since it is based on God's irrevocable promise and oath. Yet it also points to a future fulfillment that "lies before us" (NAB, NLT).

The second attainment is an extension of the first. **We have this hope as an anchor for the soul** (v 19). This is the first of three different metaphors mixed together in vv 19-20:

- nautical (hope as an anchor)
- cultic (inner sanctuary of the tabernacle)
- athletic/military (forerunner)

The word **anchor** is used metaphorically only here in the entire Bible (literally only in Acts 27:29, 30, 40). The metaphor was widespread among the maritime populations around the Mediterranean Sea (see Lane 1991, 153; Koester 2001, 329). In Hellenistic philosophy it was a symbol of stability correlated with truth (Philo, *Heir* 95, 305; *Decalogue* 67), virtue (Philo, *Dreams* 1.124; 2.225; Pythagoras in Stobaeus, *Flor.* 1.29), boldness (Plutarch, *Mor.* 815d), or hope (Epictetus, *Diatr.* fragment 30; Heliodorus, *Aeth.* 7.25.4).

Hope of salvation is an anchor **for the soul**. This indicates the inner life and thoughts that form the core of one's entire being (thus, "an anchor for our lives" [GNT, GW, REB]). We need not be troubled by the turmoil, danger, and uncertainty around us. Our lives can be steadied by looking forward to the hope that lies ahead (see Heb 11:10, 14, 26; 13:14) and fixing our thoughts upward to our heavenly calling in Jesus (see 3:1; 12:2).

Christian hope, like an anchor, is **firm and secure**. This was a stock expression used to describe anything that is stable and reliable (see Attridge 1989, 183 n. 72; Koester 2001, 329). Philo uses this expression (*Heir* 314; *Prelim. Studies* 141; *Confusion* 106; *Cherubim* 103), as well as one like it ("unwavering and secure," *Virtues* 216; *Rewards* 30, 169; *Heir* 95). The adjective **secure** (*bebaian*) aptly describes this hope, given the previous discussion of the divine oath that "confirms [*bebaiōsin*]" God's promises (6:16). God's promise and oath are "two unchangeable things" grounded in God's "unchanging" purpose (6:17-18).

The anchor of hope, rather than being dropped downward into the depths of the sea, has been hoisted upward into heaven (Whedon 1880, 5:85). This image, odd yet powerful, is due to the mixture of nautical and cultic metaphors. Hope, like an anchor, **enters the inner sanctuary behind the curtain**. This is a reference to the layout of the tabernacle in the OT, in which a curtain divided the main sanctuary from the innermost chamber—the most holy place (Lev 16:2, 12, 15; see Exod 26:31-35; Lev 21:23; 24:3; Heb 9:3). In 7:19 the preacher speaks of the "better hope" made available through Christ's high-priestly ministry, "by which we draw near to God." The anchor of hope **enters** confidently where mercy flows, and grips God's throne of grace (4:16).

The verb **enters** (*eiserchomenēn*), which has already connected a nautical metaphor with a cultic one (6:19*b*), is used in v 20*a* to link these with a third metaphor (Johnson 2006, 172). The inner sanctuary is **where Jesus, who went before us, has entered**. The rendering **who went before us** obscures the athletic or military connotations of "forerunner [*prodromos*]" (most English translations, including NIV[11]). In athletics, this was a runner who took the lead and handily won the race (Pollux, *Onom.* 3.30.148; Lane 1991, 154). In a military context, forerunners could be an advance guard (often on horseback, see LSJ, 1475) or scouts (Wis 12:8; Polybius, *Hist.* 12.20.7). Metaphorically, the term could be used of anything that is a precursor, such as early ripe grapes (Num 13:20) or figs (Isa 28:4).

Prodromos ("forerunner," "precursor") is a traditional title for John the Baptist in Eastern Orthodoxy, tracing back to the ante-Nicene fathers (see *PGL*, 144). The title is shorthand for John the Baptist's role of preparing the way for Jesus. In Hebrews the title functions like *archēgos* in 2:10, which designates Jesus as the "author" of salvation who trailblazes the path leading into the divine presence (see 12:2). Our hope enters into the inner sanctuary because Jesus our "forerunner" has already **entered** there **on our behalf.**

In 6:20*b* the end of the digression that began in 5:11 is signaled by a paraphrase of Ps 110:4: **He has become a high priest forever, in the order of Melchizedek.** This completes the transition to the discussion of Jesus' Melchizedek-like priesthood in ch 7. This transition was anticipated by the allusion to Ps 110:4 in Heb 5:10 and the direct quote of it in 5:6.

Interpreting Scripture with Scripture in Hebrews

Hebrews looks to key scriptural texts (esp. from the Psalms) as an interpretive lens through which to read other scriptures. Here are some examples:

- Psalm 110:1 in Heb 1:13 is quoted as the divine declaration of the Son's exaltation. How this was possible in connection with Christ's incarnation and suffering is explained in light of Ps 8:4-6 in Heb 2:5-18.
- In 3:7—4:13, Ps 95:7-11 is the key text (Heb 3:7-11) that guides the preacher's reading of texts from Num 14 in Heb 3 (esp. 3:16-18) and Gen 2:2 in Heb 4.
- Psalm 110:4 is quoted in Heb 5:6 and paraphrased in 5:10 and 6:20 in preparation for an interpretation of Gen 14:17-20 in Heb 7. The psalm asserts the distinguishing characteristic of the Son's priesthood, which Melchizedek resembles: it lasts "forever" and is therefore superior to the entire Levitical priesthood.
- The new covenant in Jer 31:31-34 (Heb 8:8-12) is correlated with its coming to fulfillment in Christ's obedient offering of his own body according to Ps 40:6-8 (Heb 10:5-7). These two texts are mutually interpreted in 10:8-18, along with an allusion to Ps 110:1 in Heb 10:12-13. Christ's "once for all" sacrifice for sins effects the forgiveness and holiness promised in the new covenant.
- The accent on living "by . . . faith" in Hab 2:4 (Heb 10:38) suggests the operative expression for the rehearsal of the entire biblical history of God's faithful in ch 11 ("by faith" occurring eighteen times).

In the Greek text of 6:20*b* the phrase *eis ton aiōna* (**forever**) is placed in the final emphatic position (as is the word **Jesus** in v 20*a*). The perpetuity of Christ's priesthood will be of singular importance to the preacher's argument in the next chapter, employing this very phrase taken from Ps 110:4 (Heb 7:17, 21, 24, 28; see 7:3).

FROM THE TEXT

"Can Christians lose their salvation?" Many students of God's word will turn right to Heb 6 in their Bibles in search of an answer to this question. Christians in the early centuries of the church asked this question in relation to another question: Is either a second repentance or second baptism possible? (→ 6:6

sidebar, "No Second Repentance or No Second Baptism?") Especially since the Reformation, the warning in 6:4-8 has been interpreted in relation to its doctrinal coherence, both with other scriptural texts concerning apostasy, and with systems of doctrine regarding salvation (namely, Calvinism and Arminianism).

Hebrews 6:4-8 may resemble other texts that have a bearing on the scriptural teaching concerning apostasy. As early as Origen (d. 254), this passage was correlated with Jesus' warning about the unpardonable sin (Matt 12:31-32 ‖ Mark 3:28-30 ‖ Luke 16:10), his statement concerning disciples who put their hand to the plow but then turn back (Luke 9:62), and the ominous reminder concerning Lot's wife (Luke 17:32; see Koester 2001, 20-21). Others have seen a relationship with the cryptic text in 1 John 5:16-17 concerning "a sin that leads to death." It is unclear, however, whether Matt 12:31-32 (‖) or 1 John 5:16-17 are directly relevant to the danger of apostasy envisaged in Hebrews (see deSilva 2000a, 234-36).

Advocates of doctrinal systems regarding salvation, such as Calvinists and Arminians, also wrestle with this text. Calvinists point to other texts that provide assurances to believers that their salvation is secure (e.g., John 10:27-29; Rom 8:29-30). The warnings in Heb 6:4-8 and 10:26-31 seem to fly in the face of such passages. Three main approaches to 6:4-8 have therefore been proposed.

(1) The first approach views the passage as describing those who have a profession of Christian faith but are not genuine believers. They have only "tasted" (as in "sampled") the benefits of salvation without seriously embracing them. More recent interpreters call this "the phenomenological unbeliever" view. Outward "phenomena" (as in 6:4-5) give only an appearance of conversion, but without any true faith or commitment (G. Guthrie 1998, 230-31; Fanning 2007, 217-18). This view is open to several criticisms:

- No fair, straightforward reading could plausibly construe the descriptions of salvation in 6:4-5 as being primarily applicable to false professors of faith.
- This view cannot coherently explain what it is from which such false professors "fall away." Stated differently: How would one even conceive of a *renewal* of repentance for those who have never truly repented in the first place (Wiley 1984, 197)?
- If those who are reprobate can have a superficial experience of God's grace, which mimics that of true believers (as Calvin asserts [1976, 76]), it is impossible to know who would benefit from this warning. Authentic believers would have nothing to worry about anyway (for they have the assurance of salvation). False believers would not be dislodged from their state of self-deception.

(2) A second approach is to suggest that apostates will be subject to judgment or severe punishment, but with no loss of salvation. A curious version of this view proposes a specific historical setting of Jewish Christians

in Jerusalem who were lapsing into a non-Christian form of Judaism. They were exposing themselves to God's temporal judgment on the nation of Israel through Rome's destruction of Jerusalem and the temple in A.D. 70 (Gleason 2007b). However, there is nothing in 6:4-8 or 10:26-31 that would indicate anything less than a loss of eternal, heavenly blessings. In fact, the "better things" associated with "salvation" in 6:9 stand in contrast to the image of the barren field in 6:8 that has a curse hanging over it and whose end is a blazing destruction (see 10:27, 39; 12:29; Matt 13:30, 42, 50; John 15:6).

(3) A third suggestion is that the apostasy envisaged is only hypothetical. We have already called into question the translation of the participle *parapesontas* as a conditional: "if they fall away" (→ Heb 6:6). This view might be defensible if the preacher had only this once issued a warning concerning apostasy. The repetition and increasing severity of the warnings speak against identifying them as purely academic or rhetorical exercises (see 2:1-4; 3:6, 14; 4:12-13; 10:26-31, 39; 12:25-29).

Arminians (whether of the classical or Wesleyan variety) have no difficulty with the teaching that one's eternal salvation is conditional. It is based upon continued faithfulness and commitment. Thus, believers must avoid the dangers of backsliding, and ultimately apostasy (see Osborne 2007a; Cockerill 2007). But 6:4-8 presents the troublesome claim that it is "impossible" for those who have fallen away "to be brought back to repentance." Attridge (1989, 172) states the problem: "In taking this stance, our author unjustifiably limits the gracious mercy of God, and the church's later position on the possibility of repentance and reconciliation seems to be more solidly founded in the gospel message." At stake, then, in interpreting this passage, is not merely the legitimacy of a particular doctrine of soteriology, but Hebrews' faithfulness to "the gospel of God's grace" (Acts 20:24).

An interesting attempt to remove the severity of the warning is to read the present tense participles (→ Heb 6:6) as temporal rather than causal. Thus, the impossibility for renewed repentance exists only "while," "during the time," or "as long as" one is crucifying and making a mockery of the Son of God (Carter 1966, 85; Purkiser 1974, 53-54; Elliott 1977). But this goes without saying ("a truism"; Bruce 1990, 149). This text is not communicating merely a conditional set of attendant circumstances, for this would undercut other instances in Hebrews where apostates are not granted a second chance for repentance (2:1-3*a*; 3:11; 4:3; 10:26-31; and esp. 12:16-17).

In recent decades, a scholarly consensus among commentators on Hebrews has emerged that the preacher really is warning true believers about the danger of apostasy (see Osborne 2007b, 220-21). All the controversies surrounding this passage have not been resolved to everyone's satisfaction. But deeper insight has resulted from paying more careful attention to the ancient social context in which 6:4-8 functions, and understanding how the warning fits within the preacher's view of apostasy and salvation, as well as his rhetorical strategy and specific pastoral concerns.

The social context in which grace operated in the Greco-Roman world was the patronage system. Both the givers of "grace" (patrons/benefactors) and their beneficiaries (clients) were to behave according to a set of social obligations. Patrons were expected to lavish favors upon the less fortunate. Clients, who received these benefits, were expected to respond with gratitude and loyalty to their patron. Neglecting to express gratitude was a great offense, and the ingrate risked exclusion from receiving future benefits. (On patronage and reciprocity in the Greco-Roman world, see deSilva 2000b, 95-156; deSilva 2001, 5-37.)

In order to settle the problem of 6:4-8, deSilva (2000a, 240-44; 2000b, 149-56) emphasizes how the two sets of expectations (one for patrons, the other for clients) were not supposed to overlap or affect each other. Benefactors, by definition, freely bestow gifts. They are not making investments for which they anticipate a profitable return. They are not making loans, on account of which they would take legal action if they were not repaid. Neither should patrons refrain from giving again to a client who has been ungrateful.

Yet clients are subject to wider social pressure and disdain when they are ungrateful. Clients must maintain a spirit of loyalty and gratitude toward their patron and cannot presume that they will be granted further favors if they do not. DeSilva concludes that Hebrews exhibits the same tension between social scripts for patrons and client; but it focuses on the obligations pressed upon clients, not patrons. Therefore, the warnings are aimed at urging readers to avoid the dishonor and harm that result from responding ungratefully to God's blessings. But they do not make a theological statement about limitations on divine favor.

This is true so far as it goes. However, the social context of patronage is not the silver bullet for solving the problem of the warning passages in Hebrews (see Cockerill 2007, 290-91). We must take into consideration the difference between human and divine benefactors in their seeking just punishment against ingrates. The Stoic philosopher Seneca advised benefactors against suing ungrateful clients, not least because this is contradictory to the nature of favor-giving. But more to the point, it is impossible to find a human judge who could discern motives, render a just decision on what constitutes ingratitude, or determine an appropriate penalty (*Ben.* 3.7.7—3.8.4). The ungrateful should fear the gods, "the witnesses of all ingratitude" (*Ben.* 3.17.3).

In Jewish and Christian contexts, God has perfect knowledge of our hidden motives (see Heb 4:12-13), the sole right to judge (10:30-31), and can justly punish the ungrateful (Wis 16:29—17:1; Philo, *Unchangeable* 48, 74; Josephus, *Ant.* 2.312; 6.305; 4 Ezra 8:59-61).

Importantly, the offense creating the "impossible" situation of Heb 6:4-8 goes well beyond ingratitude. More than forgetting God's benefits, it is a deliberate, active, and public repudiation of them. In a word, it is apostasy.

If God's just punishment applied to those under the old covenant who broke God's laws (2:2) or challenged God's faithfulness (3:16-18), how much more severe will God's judgment be on those who decisively reject the fullest expression of divine grace? No one can legitimately claim that such judgment constitutes a limitation on divine favor. Final apostasy is scandalous precisely because it is a sin against the most far-reaching act of God's grace—in the cross of Christ (6:6; see 2:9; 10:29; 12:2; 2 Pet 2:1).

John Wesley on Restoration from Apostasy

An isolated quotation from John Wesley could give the false impression (which Gleason [2007a, 323] falls prey to) that Wesley rejected the view that the warnings in Heb 6:4-8 and 10:26-31 speak of irreversible apostasy:

> If it be asked, "Do any real apostates find mercy from God? Do any that 'have made shipwreck of faith and a good conscience,' recover what they have lost? Do you know, have you seen any instance, of persons who found redemption in the blood of Jesus, and afterwards fell away, and yet were restored? 'Renewed again to repentance'?" Yea, verily. And not one, or an hundred only; but, I am persuaded, several thousands. (Wesley 1986, 224)

A careful reading of the entire sermon "A Call to Backsliders" reveals:

First, Wesley preached with acute pastoral sensitivity to the obstacle of despair for the restoration of the backslider. He saw the need for "the full assurance of hope" (6:11 KJV) in order to persevere in the life of faith.

Second, he viewed the severe warnings in Heb 6 and 10 as needless hindrances to assurance when not interpreted in their proper light. They do indeed concern "the desperate, irrecoverable state of wilful backsliders" (1986, 220).

Wesley used the terms "backsliding" and "apostasy" almost interchangeably. But he drew a distinction between two types of apostasy. On one hand, there is apostasy in the broadest sense ("in a higher or lower degree" [1986, 224]), for which we must always hold out hope of restoration. On the other hand, there is the narrow and specific apostasy in Hebrews. In Hebrews apostasy is the public, declarative act of rejecting Jesus as an impostor. It is regarding his death as just punishment for his crimes—treating "as an unholy thing the blood of the covenant" (10:29).

Wesley believed these passages applied to many for whom "it had been better never to have known the way of righteousness" (1986, 224; see 2 Pet 2:21); but not to his audience. "Now which of you has thus 'fallen away'?" he asked. "Which of you has thus 'crucified the Son of God afresh'? Not one; nor has one of you thus 'put him to open shame.'" He was convinced that none of them had ever "formally renounced" Christ's sacrifice for sins. "Bad as you are, you shudder at the thought; therefore that *sacrifice* still remains for you. Come then, cast away your needless fears! 'Come boldly to the throne of grace.' The way is still open. You shall again 'find mercy and grace to help in time of need'" (1986, 221-22).

Another significant factor is Hebrews' eschatological conception of salvation (→ 2:5 sidebar, "Eschatology in Hebrews"; 4:1-13 Behind the Text sidebar,

"Rest and Salvation in Hebrews"). In Hebrews "salvation is more a future attainment than a present reality, though of course it is both" (Osborne 2007c, 388).

The future-orientation of salvation makes it reasonable to conclude that, in one sense, it is impossible "to lose one's salvation." This is because one cannot lose that which one has not yet fully possessed or inherited. It would be more accurate to say that it is possible to lose the presently experienced benefits of God's grace, which are but a foretaste of the future realities of salvation (e.g., "tasted . . . the powers of the coming age" [6:5]; see McKnight 1992, 58).

Nevertheless, it is clear that totally rejecting the presently experienced benefits results in a forfeiture of the future eternal realities. As Ben Witherington is fond of saying concerning Paul's doctrine of salvation, so also he says of Hebrews': "One is not eternally secure until one is securely in eternity" (Witherington 2005, 87; 2009, 434). Thus, Hebrews couples the themes of salvation as pilgrimage, promise, hope, and inheritance with exhortations to maintain a present, ongoing commitment that is crucial to the final attainment of eternal salvation (6:10-11, 18; see 3:6, 14; 10:23).

However, Hebrews is not preaching a kind of "eternal insecurity." Rather, it is promoting what the great twentieth-century preacher and scholar W. T. Purkiser called "internal security." The preacher's rhetorical strategy is aimed at fostering genuine spiritual progress and growth among his listeners. He wants them to have the intestinal fortitude to overcome every obstacle to their love, hope, and faith. The antidote for infantile spirituality heading toward apostasy is not false hope, but true spiritual and moral development toward mature faith and solid Christian commitment.

Thus, on the negative side, he shames them for their current lack of moral development (5:11-14), urges them to advance toward spiritual maturity (6:1-3), and severely warns them of the consequences of apostasy (6:4-8). On the positive side, he shares his confidence that salvation lies in their future, and he earnestly desires that each of them proves to be diligent in fortifying his or her hope (6:9-12). Finally, he points to the powerful encouragement in God's unalterable and unimpeachable purpose, accomplished climactically in Jesus' high-priestly ministry (6:13-20). Our horizontal or future hope ("the hope set before us" [6:18 ESV, HCSB, KJV, LEB, NASB, NRSV]) is inextricably linked to our vertical or present hope, which is anchored in the very presence of God in the heavenly sanctuary (6:19).

One must also consider the pastoral setting of Hebrews to put the severe warning of 6:4-8 into perspective. Today's pastors and Bible teachers must also keep in mind the spiritual condition of their audience when dealing with the topic of apostasy.

Some believers are plagued by doubts and fears and have a heart racked with needless condemnation. They need to be assured that "God is greater than [their] hearts" (1 John 3:19-20), that "underneath are the everlasting arms" (Deut 33:27), and that nothing can "separate [them] from the love of

God" (Rom 8:39; see vv 28-39) or "pluck them out of [the Father's] hand" (John 10:28; see vv 27-29).

Others, as in the case of the recipients of the Letter to the Hebrews, need to be roused from spiritual slumber. The preacher is concerned that their inattentive (5:11), lackadaisical attitude (6:12) is putting them at risk. So they need to be "pulled up sharp" (France 2006, 84-85). In such instances it is necessary to sound the alarm, to "put the fear of God in them" (see 4:1), so that they do not "drift away" (2:1), "fall away" (6:6), or "fall short" (12:15 LEB, NKJV; see HCSB) of God's grace. This is particularly true if the readers were contemplating an abandonment of their confession of Christ to revert back to a non-Christian Jewish faith (→ Introduction, F. Purpose). There seems to have been at least a minority of them who were "throwing in the towel" (see 6:11). Their detachment and indifference were apparent from their habitual absence from community gatherings (10:25). The preacher admonishes them to guard against "a sinful, unbelieving heart that turns away from the living God" (3:12).

Therefore, they all must support and encourage one another to imitate those who persevered in faith, like Abraham. Spiritual sluggishness on the part of some is sinister, for it can infect others around them. The preacher attempts to avert any of them from being "hardened by sin's deceitfulness" (3:13). This is because it could sprout up like a "bitter root," contaminating the whole community (12:15). When we look at the preacher's strong warnings from this perspective, we can see why attempts to soften them are misguided. Both severe warnings and powerful encouragement are critical, because the stakes are so high.

C. The High Priest like Melchizedek: The Son Perfected Forever (7:1-28)

BEHIND THE TEXT

After the digression in 5:11—6:20, we finally come to the principal arguments of the sermon, for which the preacher has prepared his listeners in 4:14—5:10. The first series of arguments (7:1-28) is directly concerned with what the preacher said he has "much to say about" but is difficult "to explain" (5:11).

The topic of the Son as eternal high priest was announced through the quotations from Pss 2:7 and 110:4 in Heb 5:5-6, and in the repetition of key phrases from Ps 110:4 ("according to the order of Melchizedek" in Heb 5:10; 6:20; and "forever" in 6:20). These phrases, and variations on them, are essential to the arguments in ch 7. Indeed, the likeness between Melchizedek and the Son (7:3, 15), suggested by the phrase "according to the order of Melchizedek" (7:11, 17), is to be found precisely in the fact that they possess a priesthood that remains "forever" (7:17, 21, 24, 28).

Hebrews 7 is yet another homiletical midrash (→ 3:7-19 Behind the Text sidebar, "Midrash"). It incorporates at least four different Jewish interpretive strategies: verbal analogy, typology, argument from silence, and argument from lesser to greater.

First, the foundation for the entire exposition is an analysis of the only two passages in the OT that mention "Melchizedek" (Gen 14:17-20 and Ps 110:4). The preacher has employed the rabbinic principle of "verbal analogy" before (→ 4:3b-5 sidebar, "Verbal Analogy").

Second, the preacher uses typology to draw out the comparisons between Melchizedek and the Son of God. This is apparent immediately in the use of Melchizedek, Abraham, and Levi in Heb 7:1-10. They are not only historical but also representative figures.

- Abraham, of course, is the "patriarch" of God's people (7:4).
- Levi stands at the head of the Levitical priesthood (7:5, 9; see 7:11).
- Melchizedek, having been made "like the Son of God" in his scriptural description and priestly action, is a type of Jesus' everlasting priesthood (7:3, 8).

In 7:11-28, the preacher views the oracle from Ps 110:4 as coming to its eschatological fulfillment in the historical person of Jesus through his death, resurrection, and exaltation.

Third, particularly in Heb 7:3, the preacher (like Philo and the later rabbinic tradition) employs a hermeneutic of silence: "What is not in Torah is not in the world" (see Philo, *Alleg. Interp.* 2.55; 3.79; *Abr.* 31; Str-B 3:694-95; Lane 1991, 159). This interpretive technique indicates that the preacher is not speculating about Melchizedek's nature as an angelic personage or divine power. Rather, he points simply to the silence of Scripture as significant. This silence allows Melchizedek to serve as a type of the Son of God according to the scriptural *presentation* of history.

Fourth, an argument from lesser to greater is explicit in the comparison between Abraham and Melchizedek (7:4, 7). It is also implicit in the comparison between the Levitical priesthood and Jesus (7:11, 15-16, 18-19, 20-22, 23-24, 27-28). The flow of the argument proceeds in three phases:

The first (7:1-10) focuses on Abraham's encounter with Melchizedek in Gen 14:17-20: Melchizedek "met Abraham" (Heb 7:1, 10). The preacher highlights the historical background from Genesis (Heb 7:1-2a). He then describes Melchizedek's kingship and priesthood (7:2b-3), before offering an exposition of their encounter (7:4-10). Two actions are essential to the lesser-to-greater comparison of Abraham (and the Levitical priesthood) with Melchizedek:

- Melchizedek "blessed" Abraham (7:1, 6, 7).
- Abraham gave a "tenth" to Melchizedek ("tenth" terminology occurs seven times: 7:2, 4, 5, 6, 8, 9 [twice]).

The second phase (7:11-19) switches the focus to Ps 110:4, especially the phrase "in the order of Melchizedek" (Heb 7:11, 17; see v 15). The preacher contrasts the Levitical priesthood's legal regulation of hereditary succession with the genealogical ineligibility of "our Lord" for Levitical priesthood. But he insists upon Christ's superiority as an eternal priest "in the order of Melchizedek." The old priesthood was based on a regulation regarding ancestry. But the new priest holds his office forever "on the basis of the power of an indestructible life" (7:16). The boundaries of this passage are marked by an *inclusio* that highlights the theme of the ineffectiveness of the Levitical priesthood in reaching "perfection" (7:11, 19).

The third and final phase (7:20-28) focuses on the phrase "forever" from Ps 110:4 (see Heb 7:21, 24, 28). This passage includes a fuller quotation of the psalm text in order to point out that God established Jesus' high priesthood with an oath (7:21). The importance of God's oath-taking is emphasized, again through *inclusio* ("oath" [7:20-21, 28]).

In ch 7 the preacher has begun the formal arguments of the discourse. But he cannot resist making references to how the argument about Christ's priesthood is pastorally relevant to his audience. He does this in 7:19 by shifting to the first person plural ("a better hope is introduced, by which *we* draw near to God" [emphasis added]). He declares that Jesus is the "guarantor of a better covenant" (7:22 ESV, TNIV) and is able to save completely "those who come to God through him" (7:25). He concludes the chapter with a summary of how Christ is the high priest who "meets our need" (7:26). His cultic and moral purity qualify his self-sacrifice as singularly effective (7:26-28).

The final verse sums up various contrasting themes that have been operative in this chapter (→ 7:28). One final *inclusio* identifies the focus of ch 7: "the Son," mentioned at the beginning of the chapter (7:3), is "the Son, who has been made perfect forever" (7:28). The church's confession concerning the Son (3:1; 4:14; 10:23) is the true starting point for all christological reflection (Pfitzner 1997, 106).

IN THE TEXT

1. The Greatness of Melchizedek's Priesthood (7:1-10)

■ **1-2a** The fresh topic of this chapter is introduced with another elegant periodic sentence (→ In the Text for 1:1-4). The preacher freely quotes from Gen 14:17-20 in Heb 7:1-2a, setting down only those phrases that are relevant to his exposition:

- Verse 1a-b puts a spotlight on the key points of historical background concerning **This Melchizedek.**
- Verses 1c-2a state the two principal actions associated with the king-priest's encounter with Abraham: Melchizedek's blessing and Abraham's tithing.

That Melchizedek was **king of Salem and priest of God Most High** comes from Gen 14:18. The preacher identifies him as a king-priest. The ideal quality of Melchizedek's kingship will be explored through etymological study in 7:2*b-c*. The record's silence concerning his ancestry, origins, and death will be used to point to the enduring, Son-like quality of his priesthood in 7:3.

Ancient tradition associates **Salem** with the city of Jerusalem (1QapGen 22:13; Josephus, *J.W.* 6.438; *Ant.* 1.180). Few readers would have known of other traditions that identified it with Shechem or the Salim near Aenon (John 3:23; Jerome, *Epist.* 73.7; see Koester 2001, 341). If the preacher knew such traditions, he made nothing of them.

It is even less likely that Hebrews knew **God Most High** (Heb., *El-Elyon* [Gen 14:18 MT]) was the designation for the supreme god of the ancient Canaanite pantheon. Virtually all Jews and Christians used this as one of the titles for the covenant God of Israel, Yahweh (Gen 14:18, 19, 20, 22; Num 24:16; Ps 107:11; see Pss 57:2; 78:56). The title accented his divine transcendence (Philo, *Alleg. Interp.* 3.82; Mark 5:7; Luke 1:32, 35, 76; Acts 7:48; 16:17; *1 Clem.* 59.3; see Lane 1991, 164; Koester 2001, 341).

He met Abraham returning from the defeat of the kings. This loosely quotes Gen 14:17. The encounter between Melchizedek and Abraham is central to this section, as indicated by the *inclusio*:

- He met [*ho synantēsas*] **Abraham** (Heb 7:1*b*).
- "Melchizedek met [*synēntēsen*] Abraham" (7:10).

The historical setting of the meeting is mentioned only in passing: **returning from the defeat of the kings.** The preacher assumes that his listeners recall the back-story of Genesis 14:1-16. Four Mesopotamian kings invaded Canaan to stop a rebellion of several vassal kings. Victorious in battle, the four confiscated property and food from Sodom and Gomorrah. They also seized one of the residents of Sodom: Abraham's nephew, Lot. Abraham pursued the kings and rescued Lot and his possessions in a nighttime ambush. Upon his return, Abraham met Melchizedek in the King's Valley (Gen 14:17-20).

Melchizedek's only priestly action appears in Gen 14:19. Hebrews succinctly states it in 7:1*c*: he **blessed** Abraham. Hebrews does not mention the content of Melchizedek's blessing (Gen 14:19*b*-20*b*). It also passes over Melchizedek's offering the patriarch bread and wine (Gen 14:18). Some church fathers saw these as types of Christ's body and blood, and the elements of the Eucharist (e.g., Clement, Cyprian, Eusebius, Ambrose, Epiphanius, and the Venerable Bede; see Hughes 1977, 240-41; Bruce 1990, 158 n. 11; Heen and Krey 2005, 95-98, 102, 115). But Hebrews' typological focus lies elsewhere—in the eternality of Melchizedek's priesthood, suggested by his cameo appearance in Scripture.

Abraham's response is freely quoted from Gen 14:20: **Abraham gave him a tenth of everything** (Heb 7:2*a*). Here it replaces the word **gave** in the LXX of Genesis (*edōken*; but see Heb 7:4) with a verb better translated as "apportioned [*emerisen*]" (ESV, LEB, NAB, NASB, NET, NRSV). The action and reaction (Melchizedek's blessing and Abraham's tithing) form the themes around which the exposition in 7:4-10 pivot.

■ **2b-c** Melchizedek's identification as king and as priest in 7:1*a* is the subject of 7:2*b*-3. The ideal nature of his kingship is described through an etymological analysis of his name and political title in v 2*b-c*. The ancients were fascinated by the meanings of names. They attached an air of mystery and profound meaning to foreign or esoteric terms. Since Scripture reveals so little about Melchizedek, "translation [*hermēneuomenos*]" (ESV, NASB, RSV; **means**) or "interpretation" (KJV, NJB) of his name and title offered additional insight into his person:

First, Melchizedek's name means **"king of righteousness"** or "king of justice" (NLT; see NJB). The same etymology for Melchizedek appears in both Greek (Philo, *Alleg. Interp.* 3.79; Josephus, *Ant.* 1.180; *J.W.* 6.10.1) and Hebrew sources (*Tg. Ps.-J.* Gen 14:18). The administration of justice (see Heb 11:33), foundational to ancient royal ideology (Thompson 2008, 152), was fulfilled without parallel in the Son's rule (→ 1:8-9).

Second, **"king of Salem"** means **"king of peace."** This translation, too, is not unique to Hebrews (see Philo, *Alleg. Interp.* 3.79; compare Ps 76:2 in the MT and LXX). Righteousness and peace characterize the messianic age of Jewish prophetic hopes (Isa 9:5-7; 32:17; Jer 23:5-6; Dan 9:24; Mic 5:5; Zech 9:10). *The Testament of Judah* declared that the Messiah will be a "star of Jacob in peace" and the "sun of righteousness" (*T. Jud.* 24:1; Thompson 2008, 152). We cannot tell whether the preacher has such messianic associations in mind, for he does not pursue them. He may have provided these etymologies only to fill out the biographical portrait of Melchizedek (Lane 1991, 164). Perhaps they serve simply to convey Melchizedek's moral excellence, like the Son of God's in 7:26.

■ **3** The preacher now turns to Melchizedek's priestly qualifications. They are laid out using multiple rhetorical devices: clauses of roughly equal size (isocolon), absence of conjunctions (asyndeton), alliteration, rhyme (assonance), and chiasm (see Attridge 1989, 189). At this point, the only two OT texts relating to Melchizedek converge. The preacher interprets the silence of Gen 14:17-20 regarding Melchizedek's origins and demise in light of the testimony to a perpetual priesthood "in the order of Melchizedek" in Ps 110:4.

The first clause presents a set of descriptors, in staccato fashion, that relate Melchizedek's lack of recorded lineage: **without father** [*apatōr*], **without mother** [*amētōr*], **without genealogy** (*agenealogētos*). The first two descriptions are open to interpretation. Some in antiquity viewed those **without father or mother** as illegitimate children or orphans. But they also applied such language to deities. The God of Israel, for example, is "without father, without mother, ungenerated" (*Apoc. Ab.* 17:10; see Koester 2001, 342). But Hebrews would neither cast Melchizedek in such a negative light, nor set him up as a divine figure rivaling the Son.

The key is found in the third description: **without genealogy.** The author himself may have coined this term. It refers to the lack of any recorded lineage. In the context of the following argument (esp. 7:6) it emphasizes the absence of a (Levitical) *priestly* genealogy (Lane 1991, 158 n. d). The ancient Syriac Peshitta interpretively translates the first clause in v 3: "Neither his father nor his mother is recorded in the genealogies" (compare GW, NLT).

The second clause forms a neat chiasm in Greek (*mēte archēn hēmerōn mēte zōēs telos*) and employs one of the author's signature wordplays: **without beginning of days or end of life** (→ 5:9 sidebar, "Playing with Beginnings and Endings"). The silence of the biblical narrative regarding Melchizedek's birth and death speaks loudly.

The third clause reveals that the previous descriptions show him to be **like the Son of God.** Both the nature and direction of the comparison are significant. The nature of the comparison is found, first, in the passive participle *aphōmoiōmenos,* "made to resemble" (NAB; see NASB). The implication of the divine passive is that it is *God* who, through the scriptural account, fashions Melchizedek as a kind of mirror in which we can see the reflection of the Son of God (Spicq 1953, 2:189). Second, the comparison—as is apparent from the next clause, and the arguments in 7:4-10—is limited to his priesthood mentioned in Ps 110:4.

The direction of the comparison is crucial. The Son of God does not resemble Melchizedek; Melchizedek resembles the Son of God. Therefore, Melchizedek cannot be equal to the Son of God. Nor is he a christophany—an appearance of the preincarnate Christ. Melchizedek and Jesus are similar, not identical (see Chrysostom 1996, 424; Epiphanius in Heen and Krey 2005, 100; Koester 2001, 349).

The final clause confines the portrait to Melchizedek's priestly likeness to the Son: **he remains a priest forever.** The verb **remains** (*menei*) appears again in Heb 7:24. There the preacher concludes that Christ holds a permanent priesthood, because he "lives [*menein*]" forever. The remaining wording of this clause is fashioned after Ps 110:4. The final phrase (*eis to diēnekes,* **forever**) is a deliberate stylistic variation on the psalm's phrasing. The expression occurs nowhere else in the LXX or NT, and rarely elsewhere (e.g., *T. Job* 33:7). It denotes actions that are continuous ("without interruption") or lasting ("always"; see BDAG, 245; MM, 161). Possibly, the preacher hesitated to apply the precise language of the psalm (*eis ton aiōna*) to Melchizedek to avoid suggesting that he was eternal. He repeatedly applies this language only to the Son (Heb 7:17, 21, 24, 28; see *eis to diēnekes* in 10:1, 12, 14).

■ **4** Verses 4-10 comprise an exposition of the encounter between Melchizedek and Abraham recorded in Gen 14:17-20. The opening exclamation states its argumentative thrust: **Just think how great he was.** The exposition is aimed at showing Melchizedek's greatness compared to Abraham, as well as his priesthood's superiority to that of Levi's descendants. The preacher's argument is methodical: two declarations, involving the two main actions of the encounter (Abraham's tithing [7:4]; Melchizedek's blessing [7:7]), introduce contrasts between the Levitical priests and Melchizedek (7:5-6 and 7:8). The conclusion (7:9-10) pushes the argument to its limits—indeed, as the preacher realized, nearly to the point of absurdity.

Abraham himself recognized Melchizedek's greatness. **Even the patriarch Abraham gave him a tenth of the plunder!** Two expressions adorn Hebrews' paraphrase of Gen 14:20: First, Abraham did not stand on his own, but acted as the **patriarch** who represented the entire nation of Israel. The words **patriarch** (*patriarchēs* [Heb 7:4]) and "ancestor [*patros*]" (v 10) form an *inclusio* around 7:4-10. Second, the word **plunder** (*akrothiniōn*; lit., "top of the heap") is a classical term at home in historical accounts of Greek warfare (Ellingworth 1993, 361). It denotes the most prized items taken in battle. The custom of devoting a tenth of the spoils to a deity is attested among both Greeks and Romans (Koester 2001, 343-44).

■ **5-6** Abraham's spontaneous, even reflexive, offering of a tenth of the spoils to Melchizedek is surprising in light of the legal regulations for tithing in Israel. **Now the law requires the descendants of Levi who become priests to collect a tenth from the people.** Hebrews seems to be aware of, not only the Mosaic legislation, but contemporary practice. The Mosaic law stipulated that a yearly tithe be allocated to the Levites as their inheritance (Num 18:21, 23-24; see Neh 10:37), and one-tenth of that tithe was reserved for the priests (Num 18:26; see Neh 10:38). By the first century, the priests were exclusively charged with collecting tithes (Isaacs 2002, 93-94).

Hebrews' references to **the law** (*ton nomon*) and "a commandment [*entolēn*]" (most translations; **requires**) anticipate later references to their weak and passing force (law: 7:12, 16, 19, 28; see 10:1; commandment: 7:16, 19). The **descendants of Levi** collect tithes from their fellow countrymen only through this legal warrant, not because of any better pedigree. They receive the tenth **from the people**—that is, "from their fellow Israelites" (NIV[11]). Apart from this legal authorization, the Levites are no different from their compatriots. They collect tithes **even though their brothers are descended from Abraham,** just as they are.

The Levitical legal right to collect tithes (7:5) stands in contrast to Melchizedek's innate superiority authorizing him to do so (7:6). Melchizedek's superiority is emphasized in two ways:

First, **this man . . . did not trace his descent from Levi.** The expression "this man who has not their genealogy" (RSV) corresponds to "without genealogy" in 7:3. Melchizedek stood entirely outside Israelite priestly lineage. He did not collect tithes from his equals—as the Levites did—but from those inferior to him. He did not collect under a legal command, but by divine right. He lacked priestly lineage and Mosaic authorization, **yet he collected a tenth from Abraham.** This implies that Abraham instinctively recognized Melchizedek's preeminence and divine appointment as "priest of God Most High" (7:1). Melchizedek was a shadowy anticipation of Jesus' superior priesthood, which was also established apart from Levitical descent (7:13-14).

Second, the greatness of Abraham only amplifies Melchizedek's greatness. Melchizedek **blessed him who had the promises.** The **promises** Abraham **had** included Isaac, whose birth anticipated the fulfillment of God's promise that Abraham would be the patriarch of a great nation (6:12-15). They also included the promised land (11:9), which was a token of the better country, the future city of God (11:13-16; see 12:22; 13:14). Abraham has pride of place at the genesis of God's saving history for humanity. Yet he acted in deference to Melchizedek as his superior!

■ **7-8** An initial statement concerning Melchizedek's greatness (7:4) preceded the first contrast in 7:5-6. Another statement of his greatness (7:7) links this to the second contrast between the Levitical priests and Melchizedek in 7:8.

The preacher argues: **And without doubt the lesser person is blessed by the greater.** Scholars often question the validity of this statement as a general maxim, since there are exceptions to the rule in the OT (e.g., servants blessing a king [2 Sam 14:22; 1 Kgs 1:47; 8:66]). One scholar claims it is "hardly self evident" (Attridge 1989, 186); another that it is "something of a fallacious argument" (deSilva 2000a, 267; see Koester 2001, 344-45). But such criticisms miss the point.

As a maxim, the argument makes perfect sense in the intensely hierarchical Greco-Roman world. Within the context of patronage, it is indeed "beyond all dispute" (REB; see ESV, NRSV): superior persons bestow benefits or blessings on those who are their inferiors in honor, wealth, and status. The truth has particular force within the present context, since the priest who blesses Abraham is an agent of God Most High (Whedon 1880, 5:88; Bengel 1877, 404).

The second contrast returns to the topic of tithing. **In the one case, the tenth is collected by men who die** (Heb 7:8). The Levitical priests' vulnerability to "death" is contrasted with Jesus' eternal priesthood in 7:23-24. **But in the other case,** the tithe is collected **by him who is declared to be living.** This conclusion is drawn from the preacher's reading of Gen 14:17-20, which is silent concerning Melchizedek's "end of life" (Heb 7:3).

This interpretation of Genesis is suggested by the witness of a later scripture in the Psalms, as well as its fulfillment in Jesus. The preacher employs the same verb **declared** in 7:17 to introduce the quotation of Ps 110:4. The psalm attests to Jesus' risen, immortal life. Here the scriptural picture of Melchizedek's enduring priesthood is a narrative truth, an image of its archetype in Christ's "power of an indestructible life" (Heb 7:16).

Mysterious Melchizedek

Because of the sparse record about him in the OT (only Gen 14:17-20 and Ps 110:4), mystery and speculation surrounded Melchizedek. Philo appeals to an etymological analysis similar to that found in Heb 7:1. He identifies Melchizedek as a just king, not a tyrant who commanded violent suffering and war. He had a kingly mind, piloted by right reason, the guide to peace (*Alleg. Interp.* 2.79-81). Melchizedek received a "self-instructed and self-taught priesthood," involving the proper function of his reasoning faculties (*Congr.* 99) and an exceptionally sublime comprehension of God (*Alleg. Interp.* 2.82). Josephus's historical narrative closely follows the Genesis account (*Ant.* 180-82), adding only tidbits of extrabiblical tradition or historical inference. Notably, Melchizedek was "the first priest of God," the first to designate Salem as the city of Jerusalem, and the first to build a temple there (*J.W.* 6.438).

Another early source offers a decidedly more speculative, eschatological interpretation. A fragment from the Dead Sea Scrolls, *Melchizedek* (11QMelch), presents Melchizedek as Israel's deliverer in the last days. He will proclaim a series of Jubilee periods, climaxing in a great Day of Atonement for the righteous. Then he will render final judgment on Belial (the devil) and his evil spirits and liberate those who were captives under their power. Melchizedek is a "divine being," possessing royal, priestly, and eschatological functions. Thus, he resembles, if he is not identical to, the archangel Michael depicted elsewhere in the Dead Sea Scrolls (Hughes 1977, 238).

Gnostic texts from the fourth century similarly portray Melchizedek as a conqueror of cosmic powers. But they identify him as the "image of the true High Priest of God Most High," Jesus Christ (NHC IX,1 *Melchizedek*; see *Pistis Sophia* 1.25-26).

Hebrews shows no evidence of interaction with speculations about Melchizedek as an angelic or heavenly figure. Its view is founded upon midrashic exegesis of the biblical texts (see Cockerill 2008).

Hebrews' distinctive typological reading was open to misinterpretations in the early Christian centuries. It even spawned many heretical ideas. Melchizedek was identified variously as a cosmic power, angelic being, manifestation of the Holy Spirit, God the Father, or the preincarnate Christ. By the end of the first century, Jews and Samaritans sought to neutralize the Christian interpretation of Melchizedek as a type of Christ by proposing that he was actually Noah's son, Shem. Later rabbis contended that Melchizedek's priesthood was really Levitical, and the omission of his genealogical record hid the sordid fact that his mother was a harlot and his father unknown (Hughes 1977, 245).

A surer guide to Hebrews' typological exegesis, along with refutations of erroneous interpretations, may be found among church fathers of the fourth and fifth centuries associated with the school at Antioch. Epiphanius of Salamis, in his *Panarion,* subjected a host of errors about Melchizedek to razor-sharp logic and careful attention to the scriptural texts. For example, he countered the view that Melchizedek is God the Father by pointing to the impossibility of him being both God Most High and "priest of God Most High" simultaneously. Likewise, he could not have been the Son of God, yet "resemble" himself (→ 7:3; Heen and Krey 2005, 100-101).

John Chrysostom and Theodoret of Cyr convey their grasp of Hebrews' typology with unparalleled clarity and persuasive reasoning (Heen and Krey 2005, 102, 111-13). Features such as lack of genealogy, resemblance to the Son of God, and abiding priesthood are applied to Melchizedek as a type of Christ. As a historical figure, he did not literally possess all of the qualities that properly belong to Christ—like neither beginning of days nor end of life. The properties of eternal priesthood belong by nature and in reality only to the archetype, Christ. Melchizedek shares in these qualities, not as a human being, but only insofar as the Scriptures represent his qualifications for priesthood as a type, image, or likeness of the Son of God.

■ **9-10** The conclusion to this section (7:4-10) presses the genealogical argument nearly to its breaking point. The formula **one might even say** was used for statements that were overreaching ("so to speak" [NASB]; Attridge 1989, 197) or true only "in a sense" (HCSB). The preacher acknowledges the tenuous, even amusing, drift of his final argument (Koester 2001, 345, 352).

Levi, who collects the tenth in accordance with Mosaic legislation, **paid the tenth through Abraham. How so? Because when Melchizedek met Abraham, Levi was still in the body of his ancestor.** In 7:5 all Israelites were said to have descended from Abraham—literally, they "come out of the loins of Abraham" (KJV; see NAB). Here in 7:10, Levi is said to have been "still in the loins" of Abraham (ESV, KJV, LEB, NASB, NJB, NRSV; see NAB, REB). This usage of "loins" is distinctly biblical, passing from Hebrew idiom into Greek. The idiom is used to suggest human procreation as part of the fulfillment of divine promises (Gen 35:11; 2 Chr 6:9; see Acts 2:30).

The air of scriptural authority lends credence to an inference that would otherwise seem completely far-fetched: that by virtue of heredity, Levi shared in the action of tithing performed by his great-grandfather, Abraham. But the inferiority and deficiency of the Levitical priesthood do not finally hang on this argument, but on the eschatological appearance of the reality to which Melchizedek pointed. The preacher turns to this in the next phase of his argument.

2. The Imperfection of the Levitical Priesthood (7:11-19)

Hebrews 7:11-28 shifts the focus from the narrative in Gen 14 to the divine oracle of Ps 110:4. Each half of the series of arguments is anchored by a quotation of the psalm text (v 17 in Heb 7:11-19; v 21 in Heb 7:20-28). Each also draws attention to phrasing from Ps 110:4 appropriate to the argumentative thrust in that half: **in the order of Melchizedek** (Heb 7:11, 15, 17) and **forever** (vv 21, 24, 28). All of 7:11-28 is surrounded by an *inclusio* employing the terminology of **perfection** (7:11, 28).

The first half (7:11-19) is itself marked off by a related *inclusio*. Each "literary bookend" includes a negation, as well as a reference to **the law** (7:11, 19):

the old priesthood, with its legal regulations, *cannot* attain **perfection**. Accordingly, this half incorporates legal or quasi-legal terminology (all cognates of *tithēmi*). The preacher expresses how the regulatory laws of priestly succession were set in place (*nomotheteō* [v 11]), but subject to alteration (*metatithēmi* and *metathesis* [v 12]) and repeal (*athetēsis* [v 18]; Johnson 2006, 184). The need for a new priesthood has become unmistakably "clear" (vv 14-15) through the eschatological appearance of Jesus (vv 11, 14, 15).

■ **11-12** The opening clause, **If perfection could have been attained through the Levitical priesthood,** is a contrary-to-fact condition. The Levitical priesthood could *not*, in fact, achieve **perfection** because of two deficiencies:

- The old priesthood, with its flawed legal regulations, was powerless to overcome human mortality (7:8, 16, 23).
- The Levitical priests were prone to sin. So they could not attain the moral and cultic perfection to offer sacrifices that bring comprehensive salvation and unbroken access to the divine presence (7:19, 25, 26-28).

The **Levitical priesthood** and the Mosaic **law** were integral to the religious system under the old covenant. The priesthood, however, was foundational to the entire arrangement. Thus, parenthetically, the preacher asserts, **for on the basis of it the law was given to the people.** The law is no more valid or effective than the priesthood upon which it is founded. Priests who are mortal (7:8, 16, 23) and morally weak (7:27-28) conform to priestly regulations that are equally "weak and useless" (7:18).

The eschatological appearance of **another priest** exposes the deficiencies of the Levitical priesthood. If the former priesthood had fully accomplished its divinely appointed purposes, **why was there still need for another priest to come** in accordance with the divine declaration of Ps 110:4? The adjective translated **another** (*heteron*) may suggest not just another priest, but an altogether "different kind of" priest (GNT, NJB; see GW, NLT, REB). This new priest is **one in the order of Melchizedek, not in the order of Aaron.**

The differences between the two priesthoods, already established in Hebrews' exposition of Gen 14:17-20 (see Heb 7:4-9, esp. vv 5-6, 8), are unfolded in the following discussion:

- First, the priest **in the order of Melchizedek** does not share the lineage of the priests **in the order of Aaron** (7:13-14).
- Second, the new priesthood is not predicated on a regulation concerning priestly succession, because the new priest is "a priest forever" (7:15-17).

Before explaining these differences, the preacher again highlights his corollary point about the inadequacy of the Mosaic law. **For when there is a change of the priesthood, there must also be a change of the law** (7:12). The little word **must** translates *ex anangkēs*, "of necessity" (KJV, NASB). This indicates an axiom. If the priesthood is altered (*metatithemenēs*), then the Law—legally founded (*nenomothetētai*) on the priesthood (7:11)—must by logical necessity also undergo alteration (*metathesis*). Verse 18 will strengthen this point: the legal regulation concerning priestly succession is not only altered but abolished (*athetēsis*; note the repeated use of *tithēmi* cognates).

■ **13-14** The first difference between the old and new priesthoods relates to the legal regulation concerning hereditary priestly succession. The preacher's manner of expression in v 13 has a lyrical quality: **He of whom** [*eph' hon*] **these things are said** in Ps 110:4 **belonged** [*meteschēken*] **to a different tribe, and no one from that** [*aph' hēs*] **tribe has ever served** [*proseschēken*] **at the altar.**

Jesus is a "different kind of priest" (→ Heb 7:11 GNT, NCV, NJB) because he is from **a different tribe.** The OT records both David and Solomon engaging in priestly activities (2 Sam 6:13-19; 24:25; 1 Kgs 3:4; 8:62-64), and counts David's sons among the priests (2 Sam 8:18 NIV[11]). The author of Hebrews could not have been ignorant of these instances. But he does not appeal to them to argue from precedent for Jesus' priestly prerogatives (contrast Mark 2:23-28). These "exceptions prove the rule." In terms of lifelong *vocation*, only Israelites from the tribe of Levi had the legal authorization to fulfill the priestly role. The expression **served at the altar** is a figurative way of saying (by metonymy) that the principal duty of priests is "to offer gifts and sacrifices" (Heb 5:1; see 8:3-4; 9:9).

Verse 14 states what is "evident" (ESV, HCSB, KJV, LEB, NASB, NRSV) or "obvious" (Johnson 2006, 188) to everyone familiar with the Christian tradition concerning Jesus' earthly lineage: **It is clear that our Lord descended from Judah** (see Matt 1:2-3; 2:6; Luke 3:33; Acts 2:29-36; 13:22-23; Rom 1:3; 2 Tim 2:8; Rev 5:5; 22:16). The reference to **our Lord** has a confessional ring to it (Rom 10:9; 1 Cor 12:3; Phil 2:11; see Heb 2:3; 13:20).

The exercise of lordship is appropriate to kingship; and kingship is associated with the tribe of Judah (Gen 49:10; Rev 5:5). By saying that Jesus **descended** or "sprang [*anatetalken*]" (KJV) from Judah, the preacher may be tapping into OT prophecies of a star "rising" out of Jacob (Num 24:17 LXX; see Isa 61:1; Luke 1:78; Rev 2:28) or the "rising" of a righteous Branch from David's line (Jer 23:5; Zech 3:8; 6:12 LXX; see Isa 11:1; Jer 33:15; Matt 4:16; Luke 1:78; Rev 22:16).

Since **in regard to that tribe** of Judah **Moses said nothing about priests,** Jesus is completely unqualified for service in the Levitical priesthood. But he does not need to be, for he transcends it. His appearance marks the long-awaited fulfillment of messianic prophecy "in these last days" (Heb 1:2*a*). His was not the unremarkable birth of yet another Levite in a long line of priests.

■ **15-17** The preacher connects the second difference between the old and new priesthoods to the first (Jesus' different lineage, from Judah). He uses even more emphatic reference to what is obvious: **And what we have said is even more clear.** We might translate, ***And it is even more abundantly clear*** (*kai perissoteron eti katadēlon estin*). But **what** is it that is made so obvious **if an-**

other priest like Melchizedek appears? It is likely the legal "change" (7:12) or abolition (7:18) of the former priestly regulations necessitated by the appearance of Christ's superior priesthood (Attridge 1989, 201-2; Johnson 2006, 188; see Ellingworth 1993, 377-78, for a technical treatment of this question).

The second difference goes well beyond the matter of lineage. In emphasizing the resemblance to Melchizedek (*kata tēn homoiotēta Melchisedek*, "according to the likeness of Melchizedek" [NASB; see KJV, NAB]; **like Melchizedek**; compare 4:15), Hebrews interprets the wording of Ps 110:4 (*kata tēn taxin Melchisedek*, "in the order of Melchizedek"). The expression and the ensuing argument echo the statement in Heb 7:3 that Melchizedek was made "like the Son of God" in that "he remains a priest forever."

The use of the verb *anistēmi*, both in 7:11 ("to come") and here (**appears**), suggests more than the sense of "arriving on the scene of history" (see Exod 1:8; Deut 18:15; Acts 7:18). The verb describes Jesus' resurrection elsewhere in the NT (Matt 17:9; 20:19; Luke 18:33; Acts 17:3; 1 Thess 4:14). The following declaration concerning Jesus' **indestructible life** (Heb 7:16) makes this sense attractive here (Johnson 2006, 186-87; Koester 2001, 335).

Verse 16 further contrasts Christ's priesthood with that of the Levites. The **one who has become a priest** in the likeness of Melchizedek has done so **not on the basis of a regulation as to his ancestry**. The phrase **a regulation as to his ancestry** (lit., "law of a carnal [i.e., *fleshly*] commandment" [KJV]) denotes a legal requirement concerning physical descent. The adjective *fleshly* connotes the limited, corruptible, and mortal nature of fallen human beings. The legal regulation for hereditary succession is predicated on the mortality of the priestly line.

This is in contrast to Jesus' priesthood, which has its **basis in the power of an indestructible life.** This may be one of only three references to Jesus' resurrection in Hebrews (→ 5:7 and 13:20). In the NT resurrection from the dead is associated with **power** (Rom 1:4; 1 Cor 6:14; 15:43; 2 Cor 13:4; Phil 3:10; Col 2:12; Rev 20:6; see Hagner 1990, 112) and **life** (Luke 24:5, 23; John 5:25; 11:25-26; Acts 1:3; 3:15; Rom 6:4; 8:11; Rev 20:5). Perhaps, as in Eph 1:19-20, divine **power** is seen not only in raising Jesus from the dead but also in exalting him to God's right hand (see Heb 1:3, 13; 8:1; 10:12; 12:2; 13:20).

Different Foundations, Different Priesthoods

The different foundations for the old and new priesthoods are laid out in two compact phrases in 7:16 (Koester 2001, 361):

LEVITICAL PRIESTHOOD	JESUS' PRIESTHOOD
law	power
fleshly	indestructible
commandment	life

Consequently, whereas Melchizedek lives only figuratively (7:8), Jesus "lives" eternally in reality (see 7:25). This **is declared** ("attested" [NJB, NRSV]; → 7:8) by the Scripture in Ps 110:4: **You are a priest forever, in the order of Melchizedek** (Heb 7:17).

■ **18-19** The first half of the argument in 7:11-28 closes in vv 18-19 with another contrast:

- The passing, imperfect legal regulation of the Levitical priesthood (note the *inclusio* with v 11, employing the vocabulary of "perfection") versus
- Its replacement by a **better hope**

By shifting briefly to the first person plural (**we**), the preacher draws out a significant pastoral implication from his technical, legal argumentation.

The preceding testimony to Jesus' eternal priesthood warrants a move beyond the idea of just a "change" in the OT priesthood (7:12). **The former regulation** ["commandment" (CEB, ESV, HCSB, KJV, LEB, NAB, NASB, NJB, NRSV); see 7:5, 16] **is set aside.** The word *athetēsis* (**set aside**) stands first in the sentence for emphasis. In the papyri it serves as a technical legal term for the annulment (HCSB, NAB; see KJV, TYNDALE), "abrogation" (NRSV), or repeal (REB) of a legal decree, or the cancellation of a debt (see MM, 12; Lane 1991, 185). The preacher offers two interrelated explanations for this:

First, the previous regulation was **weak and useless** (*asthenes kai anōpheles*; note the alliteration and rhyme). The commandment was **weak** because it dealt with the "fleshly" regulation of priestly succession (→ 7:16*a*). Proverbially, the flesh is inherently weak (see Matt 26:41; Mark 14:38; John 6:63; Rom 8:3; Gal 4:9; Attridge 1989, 203). The priests' weakness of mortality is complemented by their weakness or susceptibility to sin (Heb 5:2-3; 7:27-28). The commandment was **useless** because it could not effect an inward transformation of either priests or people. It could effect only an external or cultic cleansing of "flesh" (9:9-10, 13; see Lane 1991, 185).

Second, **the law made nothing perfect** (7:19*a*). Even as the old priesthood could not attain "perfection" (7:11), so also the Law was powerless to bring it about. The Law could not overcome the limitations inherent in the Levitical priesthood (death and sin). The remainder of v 19 suggests that these weaknesses affected ordinary worshipers too. The Law was powerless to sustain an arrangement in which the people would always have a close and consistent approach to God and access to the saving benefits from the divine presence.

Setting aside the earlier commandment made way for the introduction of a **better hope**. The theme of **hope** has been prominent up to this point in Hebrews, particularly in exhortations to take hold of hope (3:6; 6:11; see 10:23). The preacher addressed a community experiencing uncertainty and instability in their faith, brought on by suffering and alienation in their social environment. They needed hope as a refuge (6:18) and "an anchor" (6:19) firmly secured in God's presence, where Jesus has already entered as "our forerunner" (6:20 NIV[11]). The **better** or superior **hope**, then, cannot be detached from Jesus. He alone provides the means **by which we draw near to God** (7:19; see 7:25).

Several features of this conclusion indicate its pastoral relevance for the audience:

- By saying that this better hope **is introduced** (*epeisagōgē*), the preacher implies that it *replaces* the **former** (*proagousēs*) commandment (see Lane 1991, 185; Ellingworth 1993, 382). This was important for a community tempted to abandon their Christian confession and return to a non-Christian form of Jewish faith.
- Apart from the passing use of the pronoun "our" in 7:14, the appearance of the first-person plural **we** marks a direct address to readers, not heard since 6:20.
- To **draw near** [*engizomen*] **to God** and to "approach" God (*proserchomai*; 4:16; 7:25; 10:1, 22; 11:6; 12:18, 22) are cultic expressions for coming before God in worship with prayers for divine aid and salvation.

3. The Son's Permanent and Perfect Priesthood (7:20-28)

Hebrews 7:20-28 presents the flipside of the first half (7:11-19) of this subunit (7:11-28; → 7:11-19). Once again the theme is indicated through an *inclusio* involving the divine **oath** (7:20, 28). In contrast to the Levitical priesthood, the Son's is established by God's unchangeable oath-swearing (7:20-21) and is therefore abiding and permanent (7:23-24). Unlike the imperfection of the old priestly order (7:11, 19), the new priest **has been made perfect forever** (7:28).

■ **20-22** Hebrews 7:11-19 emphasizes the prophetic truth from Ps 110:4 concerning Jesus as the priest "like Melchizedek." But Heb 7:20-28 highlights the perpetuity of his priesthood. The preacher confirms this by appeal to the same divine oracle: **You are a priest forever** (v 21).

How can we be sure that the "better hope" in Jesus will have staying power, that it will transcend the limitations of the Levitical priesthood? The answer builds on the argument in 6:13-20 (and 3:11). The basis of our hope is in God's oath. The preacher stresses the importance of God's oath in 7:20-28 through the frequency of pertinent terminology: "oath-taking [*horkōmosia*]" (four times in vv 20, 21, 28) and "swear [*omnyō*]" (v 21).

Verses 20-22 comprise one long correlative sentence, enclosing an explanatory contrast. This complex Greek sentence requires a measure of paraphrasing in English (notable literal exceptions are KJV, NAB, NASB). The correlative frame is in vv 20*a* and 22: "And to the degree that this happened not without the taking of an oath . . . to that same degree has Jesus [also] become the guarantee of an [even] better covenant" (NAB).

The enclosed contrast explains that **others became priests without any oath** (v 20*b*), but Jesus **became a priest with an oath,** as evidenced by Ps 110:4 (Heb 7:21). The overall effect of the construction is a lesser-to-greater argument. It demonstrates the inferiority of the Levitical priesthood to Jesus (see Bruce 1990, 171 n. 68).

The words of the oath in Ps 110:4 are not the preacher's main concern. It is God's action and resolute intent in offering this solemn promise:

- The word translated **oath** (*orkōmosia*) refers to the act of oath-taking (BDAG, 723; Ellingworth 1993, 383). God's "taking of an oath" (NAB) is in view.
- The swearing of the oath occurred through God's speaking: **when God said** ("the One who said" [HCSB]).
- The preacher quotes the introduction to the oath in Ps 110:4: **The Lord has sworn and will not change his mind.** This accents "the unchanging nature of [God's] purpose" (Heb 6:17) in designating a new priest.

Therefore, God's unbreakable word and unimpeachable character guarantees the oath (see 6:18): **You are a priest forever.**

The conclusion in 7:22 is something of a surprise (Attridge 1989, 208). One would expect that God's sworn affirmation of Jesus as an eternal priest would yield the inference that he therefore holds a better priesthood. But Hebrews broadens the horizon to embrace the entire arrangement God has established to restore his relationship with human beings: **a better covenant.** This sounds a theme that will be explained at length in the succeeding chapters (8:6, 8, 9, 10; 9:4, 15, 16, 17, 20; 10:16; see also 10:29; 12:24; 13:20). This superior **covenant** replaces the weak and useless requirement of the Levitical priesthood (7:18).

Our hope (7:19; see 6:19-20) and God's oath focus on Jesus. Once again, the preacher defers the name **Jesus** to the very end of the clause in v 22 for emphasis (→ 2:9 sidebar, "Use of the Name 'Jesus' in Hebrews"). Jesus is the **guarantee** of the better covenant. The word translated **guarantee** is a commercial legal term used in contracts to designate collateral or some material guarantee for the payment of a debt or fulfillment of a promise (MM, 179; Lane 1991, 188). It sometimes refers to a cosigner who will assume responsibility if the primary signatory fails to meet the obligations of an agreement. Such a "guarantor" (NIV[11]) takes a significant risk: he offers his own life, as it were, for another (see Sir 29:15-16).

Jesus is the "mediator" who established the new covenant, particularly through his sacrificial death (Heb 8:6; 9:15; 12:24). His death is the **guarantee** that God is fulfilling his eschatological promises. It was "through the blood

7:20-22

of the eternal covenant" that God brought back Jesus from the dead (13:20) and exalted him as a priest forever.

■ **23-25** Another antithesis between the old and new priesthoods appears in vv 23-24. A conclusion concerning the comprehensive salvation achieved by Jesus follows in v 25.

Two contrasts are set forth in chiastic fashion:

A Now there have been many of those priests,
   B since death prevented them from continuing in office;
   B' but because Jesus lives forever,
A' he has a permanent priesthood.

The first contrast is between *the* **many** and *the* **one** (i.e., **Jesus**). Josephus reported that eighty-three high priests served from Aaron to the destruction of the temple in A.D. 70 (*Ant.* 20.227). The logical superiority of unity to multiplicity reflects the assumptions of Platonic philosophy and Philo (see Attridge 1989, 210). Such an argument was already implicit at the beginning of the sermon (1:1-2*a*). It will return in the opposition between the many, ineffectual sacrifices and Jesus' once-for-all sacrifice (7:27; 10:1-4, 11-14).

The second contrast explains the first. There were many Levitical priests, **since death prevented them from continuing in office** (*paramenein*). But there is only one high priest "like Melchizedek," **because Jesus lives** [*menein*, "remains" (NAB, REB; compare 7:3)] **forever**. Thus, Jesus has a **permanent** priesthood. The Greek adjective translated **permanent** appears in legal formulae to designate provisions that are "inviolable," "unbreakable," "unchangeable"— or stated positively, **permanent** or "absolute" (MM, 53; BDAG, 97; Johnson 2006, 193).

As in the conclusions to earlier contrasts (see 7:19, 22), the preacher closes with the pastoral implications of Jesus' superior priesthood (v 25). That Jesus' priesthood is permanent implies that **he is able to save completely** (*eis to panteles*). This may refer qualitatively to the all-encompassing scope of the salvation he provides—**completely** (NIV, NET, REB; see NJB). Or, it may refer temporally to its perpetual effects—"for all time" (NRSV); "forever" (NASB, NIV^{mg}); "always" (GW, HCSB, NAB; see GNT and NLT). Perhaps the ambiguity of the phrase is deliberate, so as to embrace both meanings (Hughes 1977, 269; Attridge 1989, 210). The quaint expression "to the uttermost" (KJV, ESV) aptly conveys such surplus of meaning in the Greek.

Salvation primarily has an eschatological dimension in Hebrews. It:
- is an inheritance of the world to come (1:14; see 9:15).
- involves entering into glory (2:10).
- comes to ultimate fulfillment at the second coming (9:28).

Yet salvation also has a present dimension (→ 2:5 sidebar, "Eschatology in Hebrews"). It begins in the present for **those who come to** or **approach God through** Jesus. The privilege of approaching God in worship (see 10:1) is a benefit in itself, resulting from a restored relationship with God and "full assurance of faith" in his promises (10:22; see 11:6). Worshipers also enjoy access to divine grace and mercy for help and strength on their spiritual pilgrimage (4:16; 13:9).

Jesus' saving work—"now and always" (GNT)—includes his continual intercession. The constancy of his help is possible because he **always lives** (→ 7:8; see also 7:3, 24). Jesus' "indestructible life" (7:16) and "permanent priesthood" (7:24) allow him **to intercede for** believers (7:25; "plead on their behalf" [REB]). Christ's death, resurrection, and exaltation to God's right hand made possible his ministry of intercession. His atoning death and exalted position make him the supreme advocate for God's people against every charge laid against them (see Rom 8:33-34; 1 John 2:1). His self-sacrifice and return to God as "a great priest over the house of God" provide worshipers with unparalleled access ("a new and living way") to the presence of God (Heb 10:19-22; see 4:14-16).

Priesthoods Old and New

Point of Comparison	Levitical Priesthood	Christ Our High Priest
Appointment	By God (5:1), but through birth into the order of Aaron (5:4; 7:11).	By God (5:5-6), appearing as a priest like Melchizedek (7:15-16).
Basis of Appointment	Legal regulation regarding natural ancestry (7:16), which has been set aside as "weak and useless" (7:18).	"The power of an indestructible life" (7:16) and upon God's direct oath (7:20-22, 28).
Number and Term of Office	**Many . . . priests,** for death prevents each of them **continuing in office** (7:23).	Jesus alone remains a priest forever; he holds **a permanent priesthood** (7:24).
Service	"Offer gifts and sacrifices for sins" (5:1; 8:3-4; 9:9).	Offered himself in obedience to God's will (5:7-10; 10:5-10).
Moral Fitness	"Weak," having to offer sacrifices for their own sins before making sacrifices on behalf of others (5:2-3; 7:27-28).	Able to identify with human weakness, but is completely sinless and holy (2:18; 4:15; 7:26) and was "made perfect" through his obedient suffering (2:10; 5:8; 7:28).

	Type of Offering(s)	Animal sacrifices, such as bulls and goats (9:12-13; 10:4) and food and drink offerings; also administer ceremonial washings (9:10).	Offered himself (7:27; 9:14, 25-26), that is, his body (10:5, 10, 20) and blood (9:12, 14; 10:19, 29; 12:24; 13:12, 20) when he endured the cross (12:2; see 6:6).
	Frequency	"Regularly" (9:6), "day after day" (7:27; 10:11), and "year after year" (10:1b; esp. on the annual Day of Atonement [9:25]).	"Once for all" (7:27; 9:12, 26, 28; 10:10).
	Efficacy	Temporary "external" cleansing, "applying until the . . . new order" (9:10, 13); cannot effectively remove sins or cleanse the conscience (10:4, 11), thus cannot make worshipers "perfect" (7:11, 19; 9:9; 10:1-2).	Decisively removed sins (9:26, 28) and made worshipers "perfect forever" (10:14) by completely purging their consciences from the guilt of sins (9:14; 10:22).
7:23-25	Place	"A sanctuary that is [an outline] and shadow" of the heavenly one (8:5); an earthly, man-made tabernacle (9:1, 11, 24).	"The greater and more perfect tabernacle" (9:11), "the true tabernacle set up by the Lord" (8:2); not man-made, not part of this creation, and identified with heaven itself (9:24; see 8:1, 5; 9:23).
	Covenant	A legal framework that has been annulled (7:11, 12, 18); a covenant that was faulty, obsolete, and "soon [to] disappear" (8:8, 13). In effect "until the time of the new order" (9:10).	Jesus guaranteed the "better" (7:22), "new" covenant (8:8, 13; 9:15; 12:24). Prophesied in the OT (8:8-13; 10:15-17), "it is founded on better promises" (8:6) and the superior sacrifice of Christ (9:15, 23; 12:24). It is an "eternal covenant" (13:20).

Results: Worship	Limited access to God (only by the high priest once a year) as long as the first tabernacle was standing (9:7-8).	Bold access into God's presence through the "new and living way" of Christ's sacrifice (10:19-20; see 4:16; 9:14; 13:10).
Results: Salvation	Only shadows and pointers to "the good things that are coming" (10:1; see 8:5; 9:23), providing only temporary, ceremonial cleansing (see Efficacy above).	Complete, "eternal salvation" (5:9; 7:25a), "redemption" (9:12), and "inheritance" (9:15). Christ ever "lives to intercede" for us now (7:25b) and mediates/guarantees the covenant (8:6; 9:15; 12:24). He will bring final salvation at his second coming (9:28; 10:37-39).

■ **26** Hebrews 7:26-28 is a carefully constructed paragraph that concludes the arguments of ch 7 and serves as a transition to subsequent arguments (see Ellingworth 1993, 383). It employs an *inclusio* relating law and perfection (vv 11-12, 28) and another involving oath-taking (vv 20-21, 28). Thus, vv 26-28 conclude both 7:11-28 and its second half in vv 20-28. These verses also serve as a counterpart to the introduction to Melchizedek in 7:1-3. Stylistically, both vv 1-3 and 26-27 are periodic sentences. Verses 3 and 26 employ many of the same rhetorical devices (isocolon, asyndeton, alliteration, assonance, and chiasm; → v 3; see Attridge 1989, 212).

The first word in the Greek text of v 26, **Such** (*toioutos*), points both backward and forward. It is an intensive form of the demonstrative pronoun "this [*houtos*]" used of Melchizedek in 7:1 and 4. **Such a high priest,** whose qualities have been described in 7:1-25, is further described in vv 26-28. In 8:1 the preacher identifies Jesus by the same expression, "such a high priest," thus forging a link between chs 7 and 8.

The eternal and permanent character of Jesus' priesthood dominated the preceding arguments. Here, the preacher reaffirms his moral excellence (see 4:14—5:10). Jesus is the high priest who **meets our need.** Hebrews boldly claimed in 2:10 that "it was fitting" for God to perfect the Son "through suffering." Now he declares that such a high priest was "fitting for us" (NASB, NET). That is, he is "suited to our need" (REB) for sanctification. The preacher demonstrates Jesus' moral perfection through a list of five items (v 26) and then through another contrast between Jesus and the Levitical priests (vv 27-28).

First, our high priest is **holy** (*hosios*). This term does not belong to the more common family of NT words for holiness (cognates of *hagios*, occurring twenty-eight times in Hebrews). The word *hosios* appears only here in Hebrews. Although it can convey merely cultic associations, it has a broader religious significance in the LXX. There it describes those whose relationship to God and others is characterized by faithfulness to the covenant (Pss 12:1; 18:25; 30:4; 32:6; 37:28; 50:5; 79:1-2; 132:9, 16; 149:1-2; see Lane 1991, 191; Balz 1991c). In Acts, Jesus as the "holy one" points to biblical prophecies concerning God's fulfillment of his covenant promises through the resurrection of the Messiah (Acts 2:27; 13:34-35). The term in Heb 7:26 reprises the theme of Jesus' reverent submission and obedience to God (in 5:7-8). Jesus is not merely **holy** in terms of an outward cultic consecration to the high priesthood. He is holy in his inner disposition to please God and do God's will (see 10:5-10). He is "devout," "pious," "pleasing to God" (BDAG, 728).

Second, he is **blameless** (*akakos*). This is predominantly a moral quality. It describes someone who is "innocent" (CEB, ESV, GW, HCSB, LEB, NAB, NASB, NET, NJB, REB) or who is entirely free from guile, malice, or duplicity. Chrysostom points to the messianic prophecy in Isa 53:9 to illustrate: "nor was any deceit in his mouth" (Heen and Krey 2005, 118; see 1 Pet 2:22).

Third, he is **pure** (*amiantos*) or "incorrupt" (CEB). This term can refer to cultic purity ("undefiled" [2 Macc 14:36; 15:34]). But it more often has a broader religious or moral sense (see Wis 3:13; 4:2; 8:20; Heb 13:4; Jas 1:27; 1 Clem. 29.1).

Fourth, he is **set apart from sinners**. There is division over the import of this phrase. It could be a further explication of Jesus' moral purity, belonging with the preceding three adjectives (so Chrysostom 1996, 430; Hughes 1977, 274). It could refer to Jesus' location and status in God's presence. In this case, it belongs with the following phrase (so Attridge 1989, 213; Lane 1991, 192; Ellingworth 1993, 394; Johnson 2006, 195). But perhaps this is a false dichotomy (see Koester 2001, 367). The qualitative and local senses of Jesus' holiness are inseparable.

This description of Jesus intensifies the moral thrust of the preceding adjectives, for he is "not only free from sin, but also separate from sinners" (Bengel 1877, 4:409). The linguistic resemblance to 4:15 is striking: Jesus was "tempted in every way . . . yet was without sin [*chōris hamartias*]." He is **set apart from sinners** (*kechōrismenos apo tōn hamartōlōn*). His exaltation places him permanently beyond the boundary between defilement and cultic purity. Consequently, his high priesthood is enveloped in the holiness of God, forever unthreatened by any corruption or pollution from sinful humanity.

Fifth, and finally, he is **exalted above the heavens**. This is a fundamental christological claim Hebrews makes about Jesus as Son of God and high priest: he is exalted to the right hand of God (1:3, 13; 8:1; 10:12; 12:2; see 4:14). This prepares for a key argument Hebrews will make for the superiority of Christ's priesthood. Jesus has the distinction of carrying out his high-priestly ministry in the heavenly sanctuary, not in a humanly constructed earthly tabernacle (see 8:1-2, 5-6; 9:23-24; 10:1).

■ **27** Jesus' moral excellence makes his high-priestly sacrifice unsurpassed. This is expressed through three contrasts:

First, the sacrifice he offered is superior. **Unlike the other high priests, he does not need to offer** animal **sacrifices.** Later the preacher will boldly assert: "It is impossible for the blood of bulls and goats to take away sins" (10:3). But the Son **offered himself** as an unblemished sacrifice to God (see 9:14, 25, 26). Jesus is not only the perfect priest offering the sacrifice, but also the perfect sacrificial victim. Other NT witnesses (Gal 1:4; 2:20; Eph 5:2, 25; 1 Tim 2:6; Titus 2:14; 1 Pet 2:24) similarly emphasize that Jesus gave **himself** up as a sacrifice.

Second, because of his moral purity, Jesus does not need to be one of the objects of atonement. In contrast to the other high priests, it was **not** necessary for him to sacrifice **first for his own sins, and then for the sins of the people.** Levitical high priests, due to their moral weakness (5:2-3; 7:28), had to prioritize the atonement for their own sins before they could offer sacrifices for others. Not so with Christ.

Third, therefore, Jesus' sacrifice was singular and definitive. Levitical high priests had to offer sacrifices **day after day,** but Jesus' sacrifice of himself was effective **once for all** (*ephapax*). This announces a prominent theme in chs 9 and 10: Jesus' final, unrepeatable sacrifice for sins (*hapax*: 9:7, 26, 28; 10:2; *ephapax*: 7:27; 9:12; 10:10).

■ **28** Another set of three contrasts completes the arguments of ch 7:
- The legal regulation of the Levitical high priesthood (**the law**) is set in opposition to God's reliable **oath-*taking.*** That God's oath **came after the law** indicates the divine prerogative to enact fundamental changes in the way he relates to humankind by establishing a "better covenant" (7:22; see Koester 2001, 373).
- The former priesthood was comprised of mortal **men,** while the new high priest is the exalted **Son** of God.
- As mere humans, who are mortal and always subject to moral failure, the Levitical high priests **are weak,** but the Son **has been made perfect forever.**

These three antitheses summarize the principal points of the argument in 7:11-27 (Lane 1991, 194). The first sums up vv 11-19. The second assumes the antithesis in vv 20-25 between the mortality and impermanence of the old priesthood and the permanence of the new priesthood "because Jesus lives forever" (vv 23-24). The third builds upon Jesus' moral excellence, just discussed in vv 26-27.

With the phrase **has been made perfect forever,** the theme of the Son's perfection draws to a close. From this point forward the preacher will focus on the perfection of worshipers (9:9; 10:1, 14; 11:40; 12:23) or faith (12:2). The participle **has been made perfect** (*teteleiōmenon*) is placed at the end of the sentence for emphasis. The tense of the participle in Greek (the perfect tense) conveys past action that has a continuing force or impact. This is intensified by the phrase **forever** (*eis ton aiōna*) from Ps 110:4, used for the last time in Hebrews (but see the variation of it in 13:8, 21; the equivalent phrase *eis to diēnekes* in 7:3 recurs in 10:1, 12, 14). Jesus' perfection consisted in learning obedience through suffering and dying (2:10; 5:8-9; see 10:5-10). God guaranteed this perfection for all eternity when he exalted Jesus to his right hand, designating him as "high priest forever, in the order of Melchizedek" (5:6, 10; 6:20; 7:17).

FROM THE TEXT

All too often things in life that are of tremendous importance to us (or at least we think they are) are not easy to understand completely. Many of the things that give us security, freedom of movement, convenience, or even amusement are much too complicated for most of us to explain. Just read the documentation for your computer, automobile, or the electrical system in your home. Or try to read the policies for a health insurance, life insurance, or retirement plan. Yet we can all comprehend the benefits that these bring to our lives.

Chapter 7 of Hebrews is laden with complex and imaginative interpretations of Scripture in light of Christ's death, resurrection, and exaltation. Detailed arguments involving comparisons between the Levitical priesthood and the Son require careful attention to understand them. Yet the clear impact of Christ's eternal priesthood is never far from the preacher's mind. Although extensive exhortations to the readers will not resume until 10:19-35, he cannot delay calling attention to some of the implications of Christ's eternal high priesthood.

First, Jesus is "our Lord" (7:14). Elsewhere in the NT, the confession of Jesus as Lord occurs in connection with his resurrection from the dead (e.g., Acts 2:36; 4:33; Rom 10:9; Phil 2:11). Only once more in Hebrews does such a personalized confession occur, in the benediction of 13:20-21, where "our Lord Jesus" is "that great Shepherd of the sheep" whom God brought back from the dead. Our Lord is a high priest like Melchizedek precisely because, unlike the Levitical priests, he defeated death (see 2:14). His priesthood reigns supreme because it has its basis in "the power of an indestructible life" (7:16). What other force in the world, either now or in the age to come, could possibly command our allegiance and commitment like the risen Lord?

Second, our Great High Priest has ushered in "a better hope" (7:19) and guaranteed "a better covenant" (7:22). These are eschatological blessings firmly established by God himself through an oath (7:20, 28). They are enacted through Jesus' death and exaltation and consist of unprecedented nearness and relationship to God. Christ provides us unbroken access to heaven itself.

We "draw near to God" (7:19) or "come to God through him" (7:25). No matter how far away from God we once were—or felt—we have been "brought near through the blood of Christ" (Eph 2:13). The Son of God, who is without peer among humanity in his holiness—"set apart from sinners"—has "offered himself" for our sins (Heb 7:26-27), so that we poor sinners can be cleansed for our confident "approach" to God's "throne of grace" (4:16). Again, in Paul's words, through Christ "we have gained access by faith into this grace in which we now stand" (Rom 5:2).

Third, in our eternal high priest we have a comprehensive and unending salvation. "Therefore he is able to save completely those who come to God through him" (Heb 7:25). I had a college professor who once said (alluding to the KJV's "he is able also to save them to the uttermost") that Christ is able to save us "from the gutter-most to the uttermost." No matter how far we have wandered from our Creator, no matter how low we have sunk in our rebellion, God can raise us up to "heavenly places in Christ Jesus" (Eph 2:6 ESV, KJV, NASB, NRSV). Our high priest stands before the bar of God's judgment on our behalf and advocates all-persuasively for our salvation (1 John 2:1). As "the Lamb slain from the foundation of the world" (Rev 13:8 KJV; see Rev 5:6, 9, 12), he now "ever liveth to make intercession" for us (7:25 KJV). No better commentary on Christ's intercession can be made than in the second and third stanzas of Charles Wesley's hymn, "Arise, My Soul, Arise":

> *He ever lives above*
>   *For me to intercede;*
> *His all-redeeming love,*
>   *His precious blood to plead.*
> *His blood atoned for all our race,*
> *His blood atoned for all our race,*
>   *And sprinkles now the throne of grace.*

> *Five bleeding wounds He bears,*
>   *Received on Calvary.*
> *They pour effectual prayers;*
>   *They strongly plead for me.*
> *"Forgive him, O forgive," they cry,*
> *"Forgive him, O forgive," they cry,*
>   *"Nor let that ransomed sinner die!"*

D. The Superior Ministry of the Son's High Priesthood (8:1—10:18)

BEHIND THE TEXT

Having provided scriptural demonstration and arguments in support of Christ's *office* of high priesthood (7:1-28; see also 4:14—5:10; 6:20), the preacher now turns his attention to the superior *functions* of that office (8:1—10:18). He advances beyond arguments based upon Ps 110:4, which established the Son as a high priest like Melchizedek, never again mentioning or alluding to that text.

Instead, Ps 110:1 becomes the subtext for the final series of arguments in the central section. This important text was first quoted in the *exordium* (Heb 1:13; alluded to in 1:3, and perhaps in 4:14 and 7:26; → 1:13 sidebar, "Psalm 110 in Hebrews"). The final series of arguments is flanked by clear allusions to Ps 110:1 in Heb 8:1*c* and 10:12*b*-13. These references affirm the heavenly dignity and finality of the Son's high-priestly ministry. They remind us of the preacher's exposition of the companion text, Ps 8:4-6, in Heb 2:5-18. There he described the movement of incarnation, from suffering to exalted glory, as the basis for the Son's high-priestly service.

Another text (Jer 31:31-34) plays an equal if not greater role in this long series of arguments. It also frames Heb 8:1—10:18. It is the longest, continuous quotation from the OT in the NT. As such, it occupies nearly half of ch 8 (8:8*b*-12; 131 of 274 words in Greek). Then, snatches from Jer 31:33 and 34 reappear in Heb 10:16 and 17. This text testifies to God's purpose to enact a new covenant in the final age; and it announces the "better promises" of that covenant (8:6).

Like ch 7, Heb 8:1—10:18 builds arguments for the superiority of the Son's high-priestly ministry. It does this through a series of contrasts between the Son's ministry and that of the Levitical priests under the old covenant. Chapter 8 sets the stage for the three phases of the argument in chs 9—10 by introducing three elements of the Son's superior ministry:

- sanctuary (8:1-2, 5)
- covenant (8:6-13)
- sacrifice (8:3-4)

Then, first, 9:1-14 contrasts the earthly sanctuary with Christ's "greater and more perfect tabernacle," as well as the sacrifices under each ministry, ineffective and effective respectively.

Second, 9:15-28 compares the old and new covenants, both of which required bloody sacrifice for their inauguration.

Third, 10:1-18 brings the discussion to a climax by contrasting the repeated, ineffectual animal sacrifices under the Law with the once-for-all sacrifice of Christ. The new covenant puts into effect the promised new obedience and decisive forgiveness. (For a detailed analysis of the structure of chs 8—10, see Westfall 2005, 188-230.)

IN THE TEXT

1. Introduction to Christ's Superior Ministry (8:1-13)

■ **1-2** Hebrews 8:1-2 heads the transition (8:1-13) to the final series of arguments in the central section of the homily. Verses 1-6 introduce the controlling themes for chs 9—10. An *inclusio* in 8:2 and 6 marks the overarching topic: Jesus' superior ministry (*leitourgos*, "minister" [v 2 NRSV; **who serves**]; *leitourgia*, "ministry" [v 6]). This ministry is superior with regard to its heavenly sanctuary (vv 1-2, 5), sacrifice (vv 3-4), and new covenant (v 6). Then, vv 7-10 present the oracle from Jer 31:31-34 in order to demonstrate that the faulty and obsolete old covenant necessitated the establishment of the new covenant.

The point of what we are saying is this introduces the principal contention of the homily. Orators commonly used the term *kephalaion* to refer either to the "main point" (CEB, GW, HCSB, LEB, NAB, NASB, NET, NIV[11], NKJV, NLT, NRSV, REB; "principal point" [NJB]) or a synopsis ("sum" [KJV]; "pyth" [= pith; TYNDALE]) of their main argument (BDAG, 541; Thompson 2008, 172; see Quintilian, *Inst.* 3.10.27).

The preacher expresses concisely both the hortatory and expository thrust of his sermon. **We do have such a high priest** links back to 7:26-28. There he spoke of our "need" for "such [*toioutos*]" a high priest. Here he says, "The point is, we have the kind of [*toiouton*, **such a**] high priest that I have been describing" (Westfall 2005, 195; see Ellingworth 1993, 393). That Jesus is our high priest is the essential proposition of the entire sermon (2:17-18). It is pivotal to the preacher's exhortations to deeper Christian commitment and steadfast hope, which enclose the central argumentative sections of the sermon (→ 4:14-16 and 10:19-25; see also 3:1, 6; 6:19-20).

That the Son **sat down at the right hand of the throne of the Majesty in heaven** is the fundamental Christian confession in Hebrews (3:1; 4:14; 10:23; see 12:2; 13:15). The phrasing recalls 1:3. But the origin of the claim belongs to the earliest Christian tradition (see Mark 12:36 ∥; 14:62 ∥; 16:19; Acts 2:34; Rom 8:34; 1 Cor 15:25; Eph 1:20; Col 3:1). The conviction ultimately arises from the scriptural text of Ps 110:1 (quoted in Heb 1:13; → 1:13 sidebar, "Psalm 110 in Hebrews").

The depiction of the Son's enthronement (**at the right hand of the throne**) reminds readers of God's subjection of all things to him in the world to come (2:5-9; see 10:12-13; 12:2). **Majesty** (→ 1:3) is a circumlocution for "God." The phrase **in heaven** repeats a key thought expressed earlier in 4:14 and 7:26. It will be crucial to the preacher's remaining arguments. Christ's high-priestly ministry and sanctuary are heavenly rather than earthly. Therefore, his service is superior to that of the Levitical cult (see 8:4-5; 9:11; 9:23-24).

The expansion of this thought begins immediately in 8:2. The Son **serves,** or rather, is a ***minister*** (*leitourgos;* most English translations) in a divinely constructed sanctuary. Secular usage of *leitourgos* (and its cognates) pertained to any sort of public service, but in the LXX it is restricted to the temple service of priests and Levites (Balz 1991b; Thompson 2008, 172). Hence, Lane translates, "ministering priest" (1991, 200 n. d).

The Son is a minister **in the sanctuary.** The neuter plural *tōn hagiōn* (*of holy things* [see TYNDALE]; "in holy places" [ESV]) may refer generally to the sacred precincts and objects of **the true tabernacle** (Buchanan 1972, 133). Some scholars (e.g., Hughes 1977, 281-82; Lane 1991, 200-201 n. e) construe the wording "in the sanctuary and the true tent" (NRSV) as a hendiadys: **in the sanctuary, the true tabernacle.** However, **sanctuary** may refer more specifically to the most holy place within the **tabernacle** (as in 9:3, 12, 24-25; 10:19; 13:11). The preacher's earlier reference to Jesus entering "the inner sanctuary behind the curtain" in 6:19 supports this reading (Attridge 1989, 217; Thompson 2008, 173). Other scholars are noncommittal about whether Hebrews makes a distinction between the inner sanctuary and the tent as a whole (France 2006, 106; Johnson 2006, 199).

The **true tabernacle** is not being contrasted with a false one, but one that is only an example or a mere shadow of the real one (see 8:5). That the heavenly tabernacle is exclusively of divine origin, **set up by the Lord, not man,** reinforces this point. The preacher repeats this in 9:11 and 24. His arguments are in keeping with other NT critiques of earthly temples made by human hands (Acts 7:48-50; 17:24-25; deSilva 2000a, 281 n. 36). Human sanctuaries are transitory and never fully worthy of the divine presence. The true tabernacle belongs to the same order as the promised rest (ch 4), the heavenly homeland and enduring city "whose architect and builder is God" (11:10, 16; 13:14), and the unshakable kingdom (12:28; Bruce 1990, 182).

■ **3-4** The preacher now compares and contrasts the Son's high-priestly ministry with that of ordinary high priests. **Every high priest is appointed to offer both gifts and sacrifices** repeats the definition in 5:1. The offering of **gifts and sacrifices** for sins is the primary function of a high priest (9:9), **and so it was necessary for** the Son **also to have something to offer.** If Christ is going to act as a high priest, then by logical necessity he must make a sacrificial offering (see other appeals to logical necessity in 7:12, 27; 9:16, 23).

The nondescript reference to Christ's offering **something** is puzzling, especially given how prominent sacrifice will be in chs 9—10. However, a fuller description was perhaps superfluous to the rhetorical aims here. The briefest reference to Christ's offering is sufficient in order to concentrate on introducing the themes of sanctuary and covenant. The nature and efficacy of Christ's sacrifice will be fully developed and interwoven with these themes in chs 9—10.

Verse 3 reminds readers of the definition of high-priestly function in 5:1-3, as well as the Son's reverent and obedient offerings of "prayers and petitions" in 5:7-8 (a "cohesive tie"; so Westfall 2005, 194). Plus, only moments earlier, in 7:27, the preacher had contrasted the Levitical sacrifices with Christ's once-for-all sacrifice of "himself." As part of a discernible pattern, 8:3 refers to the repeated sacrifices under the old covenant in the present tense (*prospherein*, **offer;** see 7:27; 8:4; 9:7, 9, 25; 10:1, 2, 8, 11). But he consistently refers to Christ's decisive sacrifice in the aorist tense (*prosenenkē*, "had [something] to offer" [REB]; see 7:27; 9:14, 28; 10:12; so Vanhoye 1959, followed by Lane 1991, 201 n. f; Koester 2001, 377).

The focus in 8:4 is not on Christ's sacrifice itself, but on the venue of his priestly service. It is an argument from the contrary: **If he were on earth, he would not be a priest.** Our Great High Priest is no longer on earth (see 5:7) but ministers in the true, heavenly sanctuary (8:1-2). As already noted in 7:13-14, his human lineage from the tribe of Judah would have disqualified him from being a Levitical priest, much less a high priest.

Besides, there are already men who offer the gifts prescribed by the law. The mention of gifts being offered "according to the law" (ESV, KJV, LEB, NAB, NASB, NRSV) recalls the discussion of the Law's ineffectiveness (→ 7:16, 19, 28). It also anticipates the description of the Law, with its regulations for sacrifices, as a mere shadow of Christ's new covenant sacrifice (→ 10:1-18).

■ **5** The inferior status of the earthly sanctuary is stated and supported by Scripture. Levitical priests **serve at a sanctuary that is a copy and shadow of what is in heaven.** The word *hypodeigma* does not mean **copy,** although it is translated as such in many versions (e.g., CEB, ESV, GNT, HCSB, NAB, NASB, NCV, NKJV, NLT). Contrary to Attridge (1989, 219), it is never used in this sense in the LXX, nor anywhere else in Greek literature (see Hurst 1990, 13-14). The usual sense is not a copy, but something *to be copied*, hence, "outline," "symbol" (BDAG, 1037), "sketch" (LEB, NET, NRSV), "pattern" (GW), "example" (KJV; see TYNDALE), or "model" (NJB).

The term **shadow** (*skia*) is used in Platonic philosophy. According to Platonism, earthly phenomena (perceived by the physical senses) are shadows, images, or imitations of the realities themselves (the forms or ideals, intelligible to the mind). It is debatable whether Hebrews appropriates Platonic categories of thought, and if so, to what extent (see Hurst 1990). The only other occurrence of **shadow** in Hebrews (10:1) suggests that it is more concerned with the horizontal, eschatological relationship between shadow and reality, than with the vertical, metaphysical relationship (note the eschatological perspective in 9:8, 10-11, 15, 26). The earthly tent is but a "shadowy symbol" (8:5 REB) of the heavenly sanctuary that Christ entered at "the time of the new order" (9:10).

Nevertheless, a metaphysical disparity exists between the earthly sanctuary and "the heavenly things" (ESV, HCSB, KJV, LEB, NASB). The tabernacle built by Moses was derived and secondary. The Lord's admonition to Moses in Exod 25:40 supports this: **See to it that you make everything according to the pattern [*typos*] shown you on the mountain.** The divine **pattern** or blueprint was used to construct an earthly tabernacle that was only a "copy [*antitypos*]" (9:24) or foreshadowing of the eternal, heavenly sanctuary.

■ **6** This verse is the keystone of ch 8. First, it caps off the presentation of the controlling themes in 8:1-6 for chs 9—10. The mention of Jesus' superior **ministry** (*leitourgias*) completes an *inclusio* with 8:2 (**minister**, *leitourgos*). Also, whereas v 1 contained echoes of the prologue (1:3), so also does 8:6 (1:4). Second, it formally introduces the better **covenant** (given scriptural warrant in 8:7-13). Third, the prominence of this verse is signaled by a threefold repetition of terminology, designating Christ's ministry as **superior** (*diaphorōteras*) and the new covenant with its foundational promises as **superior** or **better** (*kreittonos*, two times).

But *now* likely sounds a note of eschatological fulfillment (see 1:1-2*a*; Koester 2001, 378; compare 9:10-11, 15, 26). This is reinforced by an additional resemblance to the prologue. Just as the Son is as superior to the angels as is the superior name he inherited (1:4), so his high-priestly **ministry** is as **superior** to that under the old covenant, as is the new **covenant** that he mediates is **superior**.

In 7:22, the designation of Jesus as the "guarantor" (NIV[11]) of a "better covenant" anticipated his role as **mediator** here. In Hebrews **mediator** is a technical term always associated with **covenant** (see 9:15; 12:24). Christ's mediation involves both his earthly life and his heavenly ministry. His death was the covenant sacrifice that enacted a new divine-human relationship. By this means he decisively ransomed and cleansed worshipers from sin (→ 9:15-22). As the transcendent and eternal high priest, he is God's guarantee of his covenant promises (6:17; 7:22). Jesus secures complete, eternal salvation (7:25*a*; 9:15, 28) and effectively intercedes for God's people (7:25*b*; 12:24).

Mediator

A mediator (*mesitēs*) was an intermediary who could serve one or more functions. In legal matters, a mediator could serve as the impartial arbiter or negotiator in a dispute, or as the witness and guarantor for a contract (see 7:22). In a social context, a mediator was a broker who could bring two unequal parties together: garnering another loyal client for a patron and securing needed benefits from the patron for the client. In a religious context, a mediator was an intercessor or advocate representing worshipers before God (BDAG, 634; MM, 399; Sänger 1991).

Jesus' superior covenant **is founded on better promises**. The verb **is founded** invites a comparison with 7:11. The Mosaic law was established (*nenomothetētai*) on the basis of an imperfect Levitical priesthood (7:11); but the new covenant **is founded** (*nenomothetētai*) on **better promises.**

The **better promises** are parallel to the divine oath fulfilled in Christ's priesthood (6:18-20; 7:20-28) and the "better hope" introduced by it (7:19; see 6:18; 10:23). Surely these promises include "the promised eternal inheritance" (9:15); entry into the divine rest (4:1, 3, 6, 9, 11); the better, heavenly country (11:16); the heavenly Jerusalem (12:22); and the unshakable kingdom (12:28; Hagner 1990, 121). More immediately, the preacher may have in mind the prophetic promises of the new covenant catalogued in the scriptural quotation that follows in 8:8*b*-12. Later he will highlight the promises of new obedience and conclusive forgiveness in this text (see 10:16, 17).

■ **7-13** The second half of the introduction in ch 8 plays a supportive role. Verses 7-8*a* and 13 articulate the main purpose for quoting the prophecy from Jer 31:31-34 in Heb 8:8*b*-12: to demonstrate the need for a new covenant.

The introduction to the scriptural quotation identifies both the **first covenant** itself (8:7) and **the people** who received it (8:8*a*) as flawed. Verse 7 employs the sort of chronological and evaluative argument typical of Hebrews (1:1-2*a*; 4:8; 7:11, 17-18; 10:9; 12:26; Koester 2001, 389; Thompson 2008, 175-76): **For if there had been nothing wrong with that first covenant, no place would have been sought for another.** The first covenant had *not* been "faultless [*amemptos*]" (most English translations). This called for **another** or **second** covenant. But **God** also **found fault** (*memphomenos* [8:8*a*]) with **the people.** The preacher supports this twofold negative evaluation with a quotation from Jer 31:31-32 in Heb 8:8*b*-9.

The time is coming (lit., *the days are coming*) probably has eschatological significance for Hebrews. They are "these last days" (1:2), that is, the evangelical era dubbed "Today" (3:15), when there is still an opportunity for salvation prior to the final "Day" (10:25; Thompson 2008, 170).

The **Lord** himself **declares** that in the final age he will **make a new covenant.** This announcement implies that the first covenant was defective. But the new will **not be like the covenant I made with their forefathers** (v 9) during the exodus. Particularly, it will not fail to secure lasting commitment and obedience among the people. It was **because** Israel **did not remain faithful to** God's **covenant** with them that he **turned away from them.** The tragic drama of the wilderness generation's rebellion, and God's abandonment of them in the desert, served as a warning earlier in Hebrews (3:7—4:13).

The preacher positively sets forth the **new covenant** in 8:10-12 by quoting Jer 31:33-34. He lists four benefits ("better promises" [8:6]). Two of these will concern him later in 10:16-17. For now, he provides no commentary on the four new-covenant blessings listed in Jeremiah's prophecy, but surely he endorsed every one of them.

First, **I will put my laws in their minds and write them on their hearts** (8:10). This involves more than the internalization of God's will. It implies a transformation of the inner person toward obedience or conformity to God's will (see esp. Koester 2001, 386-87). This is facilitated by the cleansing of the conscience through Christ's self-offering (9:14; 10:22; contrast 9:9; 10:2).

Second, **I will be their God, and they will be my people.** God's action in the Son was designed to bring "many sons to glory" (2:10). Jesus came to rescue (2:15) and assemble a worshiping community of brothers and sisters (2:12-13) who "draw near to God" (7:19; 10:22; 12:22-24). He acts as the faithful Son and high priest over the divine household (3:1-2, 6; 10:21). Christ's atoning sacrifice for "the people" (13:12; see 2:17) and God's discipline of his children (12:4-17) are aimed at creating a holy people (2:11; 12:11, 14).

Third, the prophecy promises unprecedented knowledge of the Lord (**they will all know me** [8:11]). Hebrews speaks of inauguration into the Christian faith as having been "enlightened" (6:4; 10:32) or having received "the knowledge of the truth" (10:26).

Fourth, **I will forgive their wickedness and will remember their sins no more** (8:12). Christ's once-for-all sacrifice accomplishes such definitive forgiveness of sins. This will be crucial to the arguments in chs 9—10 concerning the superiority of Christ's high-priestly ministry (9:12, 26-28; 10:10).

Hebrews 8:13 takes the negative evaluation of the first covenant in vv 7-8a to its logical end. God, **by calling this covenant "new"** in Jeremiah's oracle, **has made the first one obsolete.** Literally, God "made [it] old" (KJV; see HCSB, NJB). That is, God abrogated the old covenant (see TYNDALE). This is like God's establishment of the Son's eternal priesthood, which made it necessary to "set aside" the weak and useless regulation of the old priesthood (7:18; see 10:9).

The logical conclusion is that **what is obsolete and aging will soon disappear** (lit., "close to disappearing" [NAB]; compare 6:8). It is not simply that the old will eventually "vanish" (ESV, KJV, RSV). God pronounces the inevitable dissolution or destruction of the first covenant (Johnson 2006, 109-10; Koester 2001, 388).

2. The Better and More Perfect Tabernacle (9:1-14)

■ 1 Verse 1 sets the agenda for the argument in 9:1-14. Two components of **the first covenant**'s cultic arrangements are singled out: **regulations for worship** and **an earthly sanctuary.** The preacher takes up these topics in reverse order. He discusses the arrangement of the wilderness tabernacle in 9:1-5 (note the verb *kataskeuazō* in vv 2 ["was set up"] and 6 ["had been arranged"]). Then he attends to its priestly ministry in 9:6-10. In 9:11-14 he compares the sanctuary and priestly service of the old covenant (9:1-10) to Christ's better ministry.

Regulations or "ordinances" (KJV, REB) for worship were characteristic of the old covenant (compare 7:5, 16, 18). This term (*dikaiōmata* [9:1, 10]) encloses the discussion of the tabernacle and cultic actions under the old covenant (9:1-10; i.e., another *inclusio*). **Worship** (*latreia*) involved various rites and sacrificial offerings administered by priests (8:5; 9:9). These were designed to prepare people (e.g., through ceremonial purification) to approach the sanctuary for worship (9:14; 10:2; 12:28). Worship is a key concern in the following three paragraphs: at the head of 9:1-5; toward the beginning and end of 9:6-10 (vv 6 [*latreias*, "ministry"] and 9 [*latreuonta*, "worshiper"]); and at the end of 9:11-14 (v 14 [*latreuein*, "serve"]). Worship under the new covenant is superior to that under the old because it provides a complete, rather than only external, preparation of worshipers (compare 9:9-10 with 9:14).

Under the old covenant, priests ministered in an **earthly sanctuary** (i.e., the tabernacle built by Moses [8:5]). It was only a model or shadow of the "heavenly" (8:5 CEB, ESV, HCSB, KJV, LEB, NAB, NASB, NET, NJB, NRSV) and "true" tabernacle (8:2; 9:24). The latter is "the greater and more perfect tabernacle" (9:11). It is better because it is "not made with human hands" (9:11 NIV[11]), but "set up by the Lord" (8:2).

■ **2-5** The topic of these verses is announced in 9:2a: **A tabernacle was set up.** The preacher catalogs the arrangement of the sanctuary in chiastic order (Lane 1991, 220):

    A Arrangement of the first chamber (9:2b)
      B Name of the first chamber: "Holy Place" (9:2c)
      B' Name of the second chamber: "Most Holy Place" (9:3)
    A' Arrangement of the second chamber (9:4-5)

The **first room** contained three items (9:2b):

- The **lampstand** or seven-branched menorah made of pure gold (Exod 25:31-40; 37:17-24; 40:4, 24).
- A **table** made from acacia wood, overlaid with gold (Exod 25:23-30).
- **Consecrated bread** rested on the table. It was called "the bread of the Presence" because fresh loaves were to be kept continually before the Lord (Exod 25:30; 39:36; 40:23). The twelve loaves—a sign of God's covenant with the twelve tribes of Israel—were to be replenished each Sabbath by a select group of Levites (1 Chr 9:32). Only Levitical priests could eat this bread (Lev 24:5-9), with only one historical exception—David and his men in wartime (1 Sam 21:4-6; see Mark 2:23-28 ∥).

This first chamber was called the Holy Place (9:2c). **Behind the second curtain,** the curtain dividing the two chambers of the tabernacle, **was a room called the Most Holy Place** or "the holy of holies" (9:3 CEB, HCSB, LEB, NAB, NASB, NET, NJB, NRSV). The **second curtain** was important to our author, because the high priest had to pass through it on the Day of Atonement to make atonement for the people in the sacred precincts of the most holy place (Lev 16:1-34). He spoke earlier of a metaphorical curtain through which Jesus entered the heavenly "inner sanctuary" (6:19). He will refer to this curtain again in connection with Jesus' sacrifice (10:20).

The inventory of the most holy place in vv 4-5 is not without difficulties. A perennial problem is Hebrews' locating **the golden altar of incense** in the inner sanctuary instead of the holy place. It is doubtful that the preacher is referring to a "golden censer" (KJV; "gold incense burner" [GW]). This was a relatively incidental implement in comparison to the other furnishings, and more likely made of brass, not gold. Attridge's suggestion is attractive (1989, 234), that the references in the Pentateuch to the altar's location are open to interpretation (Exod 30:6; 37:25-28; 40:5, 26). But it is finally unconvincing because the regulations for the Day of Atonement clearly place the altar of incense outside the holy of holies (Lev 16:18). Contemporaries of the author of Hebrews confirm this location (Philo, *Moses* 2.94-95, 101-4; *Heir* 226; Josephus, *J.W.* 5.216-18; *Ant.* 3.139-47; Luke 1:8-11; Lane 1991, 220). It is possible that Hebrews follows an alternate tradition concerning the placement of the altar (as in 1 Kgs 6:22 MT; 2 Macc 2:4-8; and *2 Bar.* 6:7). But even these passages do not positively locate the altar in the inner sanctum (and any mention of the altar or its location is absent from 1 Kgs 6:22 LXX; Ellingworth 1993, 426).

Perhaps Hebrews cannot be faulted for locating the altar of incense within the most holy place. Burning incense on the altar was vitally important to what took place in the holy of holies on the Day of Atonement (so that the high priest "will not die" [Lev 16:13; see Num 16:40]). After the high priest sprinkled blood on the atonement cover (Lev 16:14-15), he also sprinkled the horns of the altar (Lev 16:18-19). Although the altar of incense was not located *in* the most holy place, it was closely *associated with* it on the Day of Atonement (so Hughes 1977, 312-14; Hagner 1990, 128; France 2006, 112-13).

The central furnishing in the inner sanctuary was **the gold-covered ark of the covenant**. In the LXX it was called "the ark of the testimony" (Exod 25:10), for it contained "the testimonies" God gave Moses (Exod 25:16, 21; 40:20). In Exodus these were the **stone tablets of the covenant** God inscribed on Mount Sinai (Exod 31:18; 32:15; 34:29; see Deut 10:5).

Only Hebrews lists **the gold jar of manna** and **Aaron's staff that had budded** as additional contents inside the ark. According to the OT, these items were placed "before the LORD" (Exod 16:33) or "in front of the Testimony" (Exod 16:34; Num 17:10), not *in* the ark. When Solomon's temple was furnished, the ark contained nothing but the two stone tablets (1 Kgs 8:9; 2 Chr 5:10). Perhaps Hebrews deemed it logical that all of these tokens of God's covenant with (**stone tablets**), provision for (**gold jar of manna**), and chosen priesthood over ancient Israel (**Aaron's staff**) would have been deposited in the ark of the covenant, particularly when the tabernacle was readied for transport.

Above the ark were the cherubim of the Glory. The **cherubim** were images of winged celestial creatures, probably sphinx- or griffin-like in appearance (Harrison 1996). Two of them were fashioned out of pure gold and positioned above the ark of the covenant, facing each other with their wings **overshadowing the atonement cover** (see Exod 25:18-22; 37:7-9). The NIV's capitalization of **Glory** accurately reflects the function of the cherubim as upholders and guardians of God's throne (see 1 Sam 4:4; 2 Sam 6:2; 2 Kgs 19:15; Pss 80:1; 99:1; Isa 37:16; Ezek 9:3; 10:1-20).

The **atonement cover** was a slab of pure gold that functioned as the lid for the ark (Exod 25:17; 26:34; 31:7). Hebrews lists it emphatically at the end of the clause in 9:5*b*. It was called the **atonement cover** ("mercy seat" [ESV, HCSB, KJV, LEB, NASB, NRSV]) since it was the site where reconciliation or atonement (Heb. *kappōret*; Gk. *hilastērion*) was effected through sprinkled blood on the Day of Atonement (Lev 16:13-15). The only other NT occurrence of the term is in Paul's reference to Christ's "sacrifice of atonement [*hilastērion*]" in Rom 3:25.

The comment that closes the description of the tabernacle would strike one as a throwaway line, if it were not so tantalizing: **But we cannot discuss these things in detail now** (9:5*c*). We can only imagine what typological insights the preacher could have offered regarding these sacred objects (see France 2006, 113, for some sober speculations). We do get a glimpse of his thinking in 9:9 concerning the tabernacle as "an illustration for the present time."

■ **6-7 When everything had been arranged** [*kateskeuasmenōn*] **like this,** along with 9:2 ("A tabernacle was set up [*kateskeuasthē*]"), form a bracket around the preceding discussion of the earthly sanctuary (9:2-5). Verse 6 begins a long sentence (9:6-10) highlighting key "regulations for worship" (9:1). Verses 6-7 contrast the priestly and high-priestly ministries in each of the two chambers of the tabernacle. Then vv 8-10 detail the divine import of these contrasts, in terms of the limited access to God's presence and the ineffectiveness of the OT sacrifices for the preparation of worshipers.

The preacher presents four antitheses in vv 6-7:

9:6	9:7
outer room (= holy place)	inner room (= most holy place)
priests (pl.)	only the high priest
entered regularly	entered . . . only once a year
to carry on their ministry	never without blood to offer for sins

Ordinary **priests** had open access to the **outer room** of the tabernacle. They **entered** there **regularly** (*dia pantos*: "continually" [LEB, NASB, NET, NRSV]; "repeatedly" [HCSB]). The purpose of their frequent entry was **to carry on their ministry** (*tas latreias epitelountes*). This last expression is thoroughly cultic. The noun *latreia* denoted cultic service or worship (BDAG, 587; Lane 1991, 222), and the verb *epiteleō* was widely used in connection with the performance of religious duties such as ritual acts or sacrificial offerings (BDAG, 383; MM, 247; Johnson 2006, 222). Priestly duties included regular offerings and sacrifices (daily, Sabbath, monthly, or at annual festivals; see Lev 1—7; Num 28—29), keeping the lamps and altar fires burning (Exod 27:20-21; Lev

6:12-13; 24:1-4), and replacing the bread of the Presence each Sabbath (Lev 24:5-9). All their functions related to "the care of the sanctuary and the altar" (Num 18:5).

Access into the **inner room** was severely restricted. **Only the high priest could enter there, and that only once a year.** The occasion is clearly the annual rite of Yom Kippur/Day of Atonement. The preacher ignores the detailed prescriptions in Lev 16:1-34. But his later references to "the blood of bulls and goats" (9:13; 10:4) suggest that he was familiar with the Yom Kippur rituals.

He is interested in the essential component (**blood**) and the central purpose of the Day of Atonement (atonement for sins). The high priest entered the most holy place once annually, **never without blood** (*ou chōris haimatos*). Hebrews acknowledges blood as the indispensable medium for atonement— "not . . . without blood" (9:18) and not "without the shedding of blood" (9:22).

The high priest would sacrifice a young bull **which he offered for himself** as a sin offering. He would sprinkle the bull's blood on and in front of the atonement cover, atoning for his own sin and the sins of his household (Lev 16:6, 14). Then he would sacrifice a goat as a sin offering for the people. Hebrews specifies that this was **for the sins the people had committed in ignorance.**

The scope of the atonement according to Lev 16:16, 21 ("all their sins") seems to encompass even deliberate sins. But Hebrews rightly discerns atonement as limited to unintentional sins (see Lev 4:1—5:19; Num 15:22-29). Those who sinned defiantly were subject to the death penalty (Exod 21:14; Num 35:20-21, 30-31; Deut 17:12) or its equivalent—exclusion from the people of God (Num 15:30-31). Yom Kippur could not benefit them. Hebrews maintains the rigorist position that rebellious or high-handed sins are unpardonable (Heb 6:4-8; 10:26-31; 12:17; → 5:2). This is not simply because such sins are deliberate and with full knowledge (see 10:26), but because they defy the covenant itself and treat its promises and blessings with contempt.

■ **8-10** The arrangement of the earthly tabernacle and the regulations for priestly service in its chambers were not ends in themselves. Their inadequacy was in itself revealing, pointing to a future perfection. **The Holy Spirit was showing by this**, that is, the limited access into God's presence under the old covenant (vv 6-7), **that the way into the Most Holy Place had not yet been disclosed** (v 8). Characteristically, Hebrews attributes the scriptural revelation to **the Holy Spirit** (see 3:7; 10:15) and employs an argument from chronology (see 1:1-2*a*; 4:8; 7:11, 17-18; 8:7; 10:9).

As long as the first tabernacle was still standing, it functioned as an **illustration** or "symbol" (*parabolē*; CEB, GNT, HCSB, LEB, NAB, NASB, NET, NJB, NRSV) **for the present time** (v 9). The **present time** is the "Today" in which the readers live (3:13; 4:7), "these last days" (1:2*a*) or "the end of the ages" (9:26) inaugurated by Christ's coming. Once Christ initiated his high-priestly ministry in the real, heavenly tabernacle (8:1-2; 9:11, 23-25), he opened up "a new and living way" into the inner sanctuary (10:19-20; → 6:19-20), thus rendering defunct the old and temporary tabernacle.

The **illustration** is elaborated in v 9 with respect to the inadequacy of Levitical cultic actions. The offering of **gifts and sacrifices** comprises Hebrews' essential definition of priestly function (→ 5:1; 8:3). The value of the regulations for worship was severely limited. This is stated in the negative in 9:9 and in the affirmative in v 10.

Negatively, offerings under the old covenant **were not able to clear the conscience of the worshiper.** Surprisingly, most English versions unsuccessfully convey the Greek here. A few versions (GW, NLT, NIV) effectively obscure the reappearance of the important theme of "perfection" here. The rendering "cannot perfect the conscience of the worshiper" (ESV, NRSV; see HCSB, NET) is a slight improvement. Similarly, some commentaries insufficiently stress the exactness of the phrasing (e.g., Attridge 1989, 242).

The Greek expression clearly shows that it is not the conscience that is perfected, but the worshiper. Indeed, significantly, this verse defines how Hebrews conceives of the perfection of worshipers, noted elsewhere without qualification (7:11, 19; 10:1, 14; 11:40; 12:23). The OT cult could not "perfect the worshiper [*teleiōsai ton latreuonta*] in conscience [*kata syneidēsin*]" (NAB; see KJV, NASB, NJB, TYNDALE). The REB expresses the thought with superb clarity: it "cannot give the worshiper a clear conscience and so bring him to perfection."

The Conscience 9:8-10

Conscience is the faculty of moral consciousness in human beings. It is not only aware of the character of our thoughts and actions (good or bad, honorable or dishonorable) but also pronounces judgment on them (accusing or defending; see Rom 2:15). In Hebrews, sinful acts defile the conscience (compare 1 Cor 8:7), so that it needs to be cleansed (Heb 9:14; 10:2, 22). A defiled conscience is "evil" or "bad" (10:22 NRSV and NJB), hence, "guilty" (NIV). A cleansed conscience is "good" (13:18 KJV, NASB), that is, "clear" (NIV).

An evil conscience disqualifies and debilitates one from having free access into God's presence. The shame and timidity associated with a guilty conscience are the antitheses of the boldness and assurance needed for worshipers to approach the throne of grace (4:16; 10:19; see 3:6; 6:11; 10:22, 35; contrast 10:37-39).

Affirmatively, preparation for worship under the old covenant was **only a matter of food and drink and various ceremonial washings** (9:10). Having spoken of the role of priests in offering sacrifices for sins, the preacher shifts attention to the responsibility of worshipers to abide by the many purity laws. The reference to **food ... drink and various ceremonial washings** is a catch-all for a host of purity rules (on food and drink, see *Let. Aris.* 128, 142, 158, 162; 1 Macc 1:63; Josephus, *Ant.* 4.137; on rites of cleansing, see Lev 15; Num 19; Mark 7:4; John 11:55; see Koester 2001, 399).

These observances were doubly limited. First, with respect to their effectiveness, they were merely **external regulations** (see REB; note the *inclusio* with 9:1, "regulations for worship"). More precisely, they were "regulations for the body [*dikaiōmata sarkos*]" (ESV, NASB, NRSV; see GW, HCSB, NLT) or "the flesh" (NAB). They affected the "outward life" (NJB), not the inward life of the heart (→ 4:12). Hebrews sees no value in the consumption of ceremonially pure foods. What matters is the strengthening of the heart by grace (13:9; similarly Jesus in Mark 7:18-23).

Second, such regulations were temporary. They applied, or rather, were "imposed [*epikeimena*]" (CEB, ESV, HCSB, KJV, LEB, NAB, NASB, NET, NRSV), **until the time of the new order** (see CEB, REB). This rendering nicely captures the eschatological import of the Greek phrase, though the expression originated within the legal sphere. The term *diorthōsis* (**new order**) referred to the correction or "reformation" (ESV, KJV, NASB, RSV) of a legal code by abolishing and replacing outdated statutes (Attridge 1989, 243; Koester 2001, 400). We have already encountered this legal procedure in Hebrews (7:12, 18, 22; 8:6-7, 13; see 10:9).

The **time of the new order** was inaugurated through Christ's priestly action. Therefore, it is effective at **the present time** (9:9). But these two time stamps are not strictly identical (see Koester 2001, 398; Ellingworth 1993, 444). As elsewhere in the NT, Hebrews envisions a tension between the already and the not-yet in eschatology (→ 2:5 sidebar, "Eschatology in Hebrews"). Many benefits of the age to come are already being enjoyed (3:1, 14; 6:5; 9:11; 10:26; see Rom 13:11; 1 Cor 10:11; Gal 1:4), and the old order has been legally invalidated (see Gal 3:23-25; 4:1-7). But the old order has not entirely vanished (Heb 8:13; see 13:10). Its dissolution will not be complete until the second coming of Christ (9:28; 10:25; 12:25-27; see 1 Cor 7:31; 1 John 2:8, 17).

■ **11-12** The lengthy Greek sentence in Heb 9:11-12 begins a series of contrasts extending through v 14:
- New and old priests.
- The bloody sacrifices under the two covenants, namely, Christ's self-offering versus animal sacrifices.
- The Spirit as opposed to the flesh.
- The profound effectiveness of Christ's sacrifice (cleansing the conscience) in contrast to merely external regulations for purity.
- The realization of what was only symbolized by the old order (Ellingworth 1993, 445).

In keeping with Hebrews' understanding of legal revision in 7:12, the new order was not initiated through the establishment of a new legal code. It came with the appearance of a new high priest. **When Christ came** does not employ the usual NT verb for "coming." Instead, the author uses a verb that elsewhere denotes someone's arrival at a destination (e.g., Gen 14:13; Exod

2:17; 2 Macc 5:25; Luke 7:20; Acts 9:26; see Koester 2001, 407). The designation of Christ **as high priest,** as well as the immediate context (see 9:12), indicate his arrival in the heavenly inner sanctuary (see 4:14; 6:19-20; 7:26; 8:1; 9:25; contrast 10:5).

The use of *paraginomai* (→ 9:11) rather than *erchomai* (thirty-six times in Hebrews) conveys a suitable meaning. But it also strikes a wordplay with **the good things that are already here.** Christ **has come** (*paragenomenos*) as the **high priest of the good things that** *have come* (*genomenōn*). Hebrews' fondness for wordplay bolsters the likely originality of *genomenōn*, as opposed to the alternate reading *mellontōn* ("are to come" [NIV^mg]). The latter reading is probably an assimilation to the wording in 10:1 (see Metzger 1994, 598).

The expression **good things** evokes a broad application, perhaps encompassing all the things that are "better" as a result of Christ's priesthood (→ 1:4 sidebar, "'Better' Things in Hebrews"). They surely include all the privileges of the new order presently available to those who "share in Christ" (3:14) and "in the Holy Spirit" (6:4). These include the experience of the goodness of God's word and "the powers of the coming age" (6:5; see 2:3-4) and bold access to God's presence (4:16; 10:19-22). More apposite to this context, the **good things** involve the better ministry and covenant (8:6*a-b*). Christians enjoy unparalleled forgiveness and cleansing from sins through Christ's superior sacrifice (9:14, 23; see 10:10, 12, 14, 18). They are the beneficiaries of better promises (8:6*c*): for an eternal inheritance (6:12; 9:15; 10:36), salvation (1:14; 2:3; 5:9; 9:28), or redemption (9:12).

The location of Christ's high-priestly ministry is also superior to that of the former tabernacle (see 8:2, 5; 9:1, 24). He went through **the greater and more perfect tabernacle** (9:11) to enter **the Most Holy Place** (9:12). The same phrase **greater and more perfect** (*meizonos kai teleioteras*) is used on occasion by Philo to describe something as **much more suitable** (*Names* 128; *Spec. Laws* 2.128). This expression permits the preacher once again to utilize the language of perfection. The heavenly tabernacle more perfectly fulfills its function as the true and most sacred space where God is worshiped (see 9:23-24).

The earthly sanctuary merely foreshadowed or resembled the heavenly one (8:5; 9:9). The former tabernacle was commissioned by God. But it was set up by human hands (8:2, 5). The better and more perfect tabernacle is "the genuine article," not a **hand-made** replica (9:11; see 8:2; 9:24). Jesus, as well as other NT witnesses (Mark 14:58; John 2:19-22; Acts 7:48; 17:24), recognized the prophetic truth: God does not really dwell in a humanly constructed temple, but in the highest heaven (Isa 66:1-2; see 1 Kgs 8:27; 2 Chr 2:5-6; 6:18; Bruce 1990, 212).

Hebrews identifies (**that is to say**) the permanent and transcendent quality of the heavenly tabernacle: **not a part of this creation.** It belongs to an order different from the earthly sanctuary: the abiding and unshakable realm (deSilva 2000a, 304-5). Possibly, Hebrews traces our Great High Priest's movements with a cosmology in mind. Christ went through a heavenly counterpart to the first chamber of the old tabernacle (**the greater and more perfect tabernacle** = passing "through the heavens" [Heb 4:14]), then **entered the Most Holy Place** (= "the inner sanctuary" [6:19] or the highest "heaven itself" [7:26; 9:24]; → 4:14 sidebar, "'The Heavens' in Ancient Cosmology and in Hebrews"; Attridge 1989, 247-48; Lane 1991, 238). Or, Hebrews' language may simply be highly metaphorical (Schenck 2007).

Just as the heavenly tabernacle is superior (compare 9:11 with vv 1-5), so also is Christ's sacrificial offering (compare v 12 with vv 6-10). **He did not enter by means of the blood of goats and calves.** This was the annual means of access for the Levitical high priests on the Day of Atonement (Lev 16:3, 5-11, 15-16, 18-19; → Heb 9:6-7).

Christ **entered the Most Holy Place,** not with the blood of brute, involuntary victims of sacrifice, but **by his own blood.** The preacher did not attach any magical qualities to covenant blood that makes it effective for cleansing (→ 9:16-22). What is effective is the death of the sacrificial victim, the giving of its life, life in place of life—"for the life of a creature is in the blood" (Lev 17:11, 14).

The phrase **by his own blood** is a synecdoche (a figure of speech in which the part represents the whole). Christ's death was a voluntary and obedient offering. The hematic fluid itself was not the preacher's concern. It was not just Christ's "own blood" (see Heb 9:25; 10:19; 12:24; 13:12) that he offered. He surrendered his "flesh"/"body" (10:5, 10, 20). He gave "himself" (7:27; 9:14, 25-26), his very life, to make possible our **eternal redemption** (9:12).

Whereas ordinary high priests had to offer sin offerings once every year (see v 7), Christ offered himself **once for all** (*ephapax*; → 7:27). His sacrifice was conclusive, requiring no repetition or renewal, **having obtained eternal redemption.** The mention of **redemption** (*lytrōsin*) anticipates the reference to Christ's death as a "ransom to set [people] . . . free [*apolytrōsin*]" from sins (→ 9:15; 11:35). The language of **redemption** applies to the means of release from debt, prison, or slavery (Kertelge 1991).

Although ransom vocabulary did not occur in 2:5-18, conceptually it was already present. Christ's death frees the heirs of God's promise from the fear of death (2:9, 14-16). True, the accent here in ch 9 is on redemption from *sins;* but there, too (2:11, 17), Jesus' sanctifying and atoning work was closely allied with his act of deliverance.

So definitive is this redemption that it can be qualified as **eternal.** This corresponds with the preacher's references to "eternal salvation" (5:9; see 2:10; 9:28) or "eternal inheritance" (9:15).

■ **13-14** These verses conclude 9:1-14 with a final set of parallel antitheses. The contrast in v 12 is extended through a lesser-to-greater (*qal wahomer*) comparison of the Levitical sacrifices and Christ's self-offering (vv 13-14). Like the conclusion to 9:1-10 in vv 9-10, the preacher assesses the limited effectiveness of old covenant regulations for worship here in vv 13-14. He builds upon that conclusion to clinch the argument for the superiority and efficacy of Christ's self-offering.

The blood of goats and bulls once again alludes to the Day of Atonement (10:3-4; → 9:6-7), though a more general reference to sacrifices may be in view (Num 7:15-16, 87; 2 Chr 29:21, 33; 30:24; Ezra 6:17; 8:35; Pss 50:13; 66:15; Isa 1:11; Lane 1991, 239). Pairing an allusion to Yom Kippur with **the ashes of a heifer** is unusual. The two are never explicitly associated in the OT (see Num 19:1-22). Nevertheless, Hebrews seems to see a number of important links between them:

First, both are sin offerings (Lev 16:6, 9, 11, 15, 25; and Num 19:9).

Second, both involve sprinkling: **sprinkled** blood in both rites (Lev 16:14, 15, 19; Num 19:4); **sprinkled** water of purification prepared with the ashes of the red heifer (Num 19:13, 18, 19, 20, 21).

Third, both provide only superficial cleansing, applying only to **those who are ceremonially unclean.** This is maintained in Hebrews' references to the Day of Atonement (9:9-10; 10:1-4) and to Levitical sacrifices generally (10:11, 18). With respect to the ashes of the red heifer, the rite was intended to cleanse persons who had become **ceremonially unclean** through contact with dead bodies (Num 19:11-21). Thus, this ritual was part and parcel with all of the cleansing provisions under the old covenant. That is, they could **sanctify** people **so that they are** only **outwardly clean.** As in → 9:10, the purification could only effect "purging the flesh [*sarkos*]" (Lane 1991, 239; see ESV, HCSB, KJV, NAB, NASB, NRSV).

Fourth, both rituals were performed by the high priest. In the case of the ashes of the red heifer, this finds greater support in traditional practice (see Koester 2001, 410) than in the biblical prescriptions (Num 19:1-4).

Fifth, Hebrews seems to formulate connections between the red heifer ritual and the covenant sacrifice discussed later (→ Heb 9:18-22). Both of them are cleansing rites, involving similar components (compare Num 19:6 with Heb 9:19) and the sprinkling of blood and water (→ second item above; 9:19-21; Thompson 2008, 187).

Christ's sacrifice is superior on every level (**How much more, then**) to those of the old covenant (v 14). His sacrifice involved, not the blood of senseless beasts, but **the blood of Christ** (→ 9:12, "by his own blood"). That Christ voluntarily and obediently **offered himself** sets his sacrifice apart. His sacrifice is spiritually and morally superior both in its execution and its effects.

Christ carried out his self-offering through supreme, spiritual enablement: **through the eternal Spirit.** The interpretation of this phrase is difficult. Some scholars have interpreted it as a reference to Christ's own eternal spirit (Whedon 1880, 5:103; Hughes 1977, 358-59; Isaacs 2002, 114) or a general reference to the eternal and spiritual mode of his sacrifice (Johnson 2006, 236). But it is preferable to see this as referring to the Holy Spirit's work enabling Christ's obedient sacrifice (see Hagner 1990, 137; Ellingworth 1993, 457; Lane 1991, 240; Koester 2001, 410-11). Thus, it is analogous to Paul's view that Christ's resurrection was effected by the Spirit (Rom 1:4; 8:11; 1 Tim 3:16).

That Christ offered himself **unblemished to God** reminds us of his moral excellence. The term **unblemished** (*amōmos*) has both sacrificial and moral resonances (Num 6:14; 19:2; 1 Pet 1:19; BDAG, 56). Hebrews never describes Christ's blamelessness in terms of any lack of physical or external blemish, but spiritually and morally: his reverent and obedient disposition (5:7-8; 10:5-10) and holiness (4:15; 7:26-28; Attridge 1989, 251; Johnson 2006, 238). This is precisely what qualifies Christ's sacrifice as uniquely acceptable **to God** (→ 10:5-10).

The spiritual and moral effects of Christ's sacrifice are unsurpassed. Rather than effecting only fleshly or external cleansing (9:10, 13), Christ's sacrificial work penetrates to the moral center of human beings. What the Levitical sacrifices could not accomplish, Christ's does: it cleanses **our consciences** (→ 9:8-10 sidebar, "The Conscience"). The defilement it purges does not merely render us ceremonially clean. It cleanses us from **acts that lead to death,** namely, sins (→ 6:1). Whereas the Levitical sacrifices could not perfect worshipers (→ 9:9), Christ's sacrifice completely prepares us **so that we may serve the living God.**

The mode of discourse is argumentative in chs 7—10. But at the conclusion to this subunit the preacher once again cannot resist—either self-reflexively or by design—coloring his argument with a pastoral tone (as in ch 7; → 7:14, 15, 26). He draws his audience in as beneficiaries. Christ's self-offering cleanses **our consciences,** so that **we** are properly disposed to worship God (Thompson 2008, 187).

3. Christ's Sacrificial Death Inaugurated the New Covenant (9:15-28)

■ **15** The previous subunit (9:1-14) treated the superiority of Christ's ministry in terms of its greater tabernacle and effective sacrifice, as 8:1-5 anticipated. In 9:15-28, the preacher discusses the superiority of Christ's ministry in connection with his inauguration of **a new covenant** (→ 8:6-11). Christ is **the mediator of the new covenant** (→ 8:6; → 7:22 on "guarantor" [NIV[11]]). The preacher demonstrates at length the necessity of Christ's death for establishing the new covenant and effecting its "better promises" (8:6). The present verse orients the discussion in the following paragraphs (9:16-22 and 23-28).

First, the central point in the discussion is that Christ **has died.** More precisely, the preacher emphasizes that "a death has occurred" (ESV, NJB, NRSV; see HCSB, NAB, NASB). In 9:16-22 and 23-28 the preacher will argue that a sacrificial death was the "necessary" means (9:16, 23) for inaugurating the covenant and consecrating the heavenly sanctuary for Christ's high-priestly ministry.

Second, Hebrews describes Christ's death as **a ransom to set . . . free** (*apolytrōsis*) or "redemption" (KJV, NASB; → 9:12, "eternal redemption"). Christ's sacrifice provides decisive release **from the sins committed under the first covenant.** Christ's sacrifice achieves what sacrifices under the old covenant could not (9:13-14; 10:1-4). While provision was made for the application of blood as a cleansing agent and grounds for "forgiveness" (9:22), only Christ's final sacrifice could really "do away with" or "take away" sins (9:26, 28; see 10:4, 11).

Third, the purpose **(For this reason)** of Christ's redemptive sacrifice is **that those who are called may receive the promised eternal inheritance** (→ 8:6, "better promises"). The point will be restated at the end of this subunit with the reference to Christ's bringing "salvation" to those who are waiting for his second coming (9:28).

■ **16-17** A maxim in v 16 announces the topic of the first paragraph (9:16-22): the necessity of a death for the establishment of a covenant. However, the author suddenly shifts his reference from "covenant" to **a will.** As the NIV points out in a footnote, the same word for "covenant [*diathēkē*]" (see 7:22; 8:6, 8-10; 9:15, 20; 10:16, 29; 12:24; 13:20) is used to mean **will** in 9:16-17. The wordplay may have been suggested by the idea of "inheritance" just mentioned in v 15.

The preacher is not confusing the Jewish covenant idea (*diathēkē* in the LXX) with the Greco-Roman usage of the same word for the legal disposition of a last will and testament. Nor is he squeezing one concept into the other, as some commentators suggest (e.g., Lane [1991, 244] insists that the word must mean "covenant" throughout; see Attridge 1989, 255-56; Bruce 1990, 221-23; and Ellingworth 1993, 462-63, for the debate on this matter). He seems to be consciously playing the two uses off each other for the purpose of illustration.

The case of a will provides a suitable legal analogy. **It is necessary to prove the death of the one who made it** (i.e., the testator) in order for a will to be enacted. The verb translated **to prove** (*pheresthai*; lit., "to be brought [in/forth]") was used in a technical legal sense for submitting public record or proof of a death (Wolter 1993; L&N 70.8).

The rationale **(because)** for this principle is stated both positively and negatively in v 17. Positively, **a will is in force** ["valid" (HCSB, NASB)] **when somebody has died.** Negatively, **it never takes effect while the one who made it is living** (→ 6:13-20 sidebar, "Legal Jargon in Hebrews"). The rhetorical force of this argument exists in that it commands universal assent, even to this present day.

■ **18-22** What is true for a **will** (vv 16-17) also applies to a **covenant** (v 18). **This is why even the first covenant was not put into effect without blood. Blood** vividly symbolizes death. The shedding and sprinkling of blood in sacrifice ritually consecrated worshipers and cleansed them from sins (vv 22,

25-26). Sacrificial death was required to **put into effect,** that is, "inaugurate [*enkainizō*]" (NRSV) the **first covenant.**

The inaugural ceremony for the first covenant is recorded in Exod 24. This serves as the basis for the description in Heb 9:19-21. But Hebrews augments it with details from other OT rituals and events. The **water, scarlet wool,** and **hyssop** were used in the red heifer ritual (Num 19:6, 18) and in the cleansing of skin diseases (Lev 14:4-7, 51-52). Hyssop may have been used to apply the blood of the Passover lambs to the Hebrews' doorposts (Exod 12:22; see Lev 4:4; Num 19:18; Lane 1991, 244). Exodus makes no mention of sprinkling **the scroll** with blood (Heb 9:19). Nor could Moses have sprinkled **the tabernacle** with blood (9:21), since it had not yet been built; and once built, it was dedicated, not **with blood,** but anointing oil (Exod 40:9, 16; Lev 8:11). By telescoping rituals and events, most involving the sprinkling of blood, Hebrews offers a commentary on the entire sacrificial system under the old covenant (Thompson 2008, 191).

Hebrews (9:20) appropriately highlights the importance of sacrificial blood for inaugurating the covenant by quoting Exod 24:8: **This is the blood of the covenant, which God commanded you to keep.** The comprehensive scope of the covenant dedication is stressed throughout: **every** [*pasēs*] **commandment** (v 19*a*); **to all** [*panti*] **the people** (v 19*a*); **sprinkled the scroll and all** [*panta*] **the people** (v 19*c*); **sprinkled . . . both the tabernacle and everything** [*panta*] **used in its ceremonies** (v 21).

This emphasis leads naturally to the conclusion in v 22: **In fact, the law requires that nearly everything** [*panta*] **be cleansed with blood.** Hebrews rightly notes that **nearly** (*schedon*) or "almost" (most English versions; "practically" [NJB]) **everything** was cleansed with blood. Clearly **the law** authorized cleansing rituals with other purifying agents (e.g., water in Lev 14:4; 15:11, 13, 16-18).

Yet the general principle stands: **without the shedding of blood there is no forgiveness.** Greeks and Romans, as well as Jews, believed blood possessed a mysterious power that effected cultic purity (see Koester 2001, 420). But Hebrews' understanding of sacrificial blood's capacity to cleanse sins (9:7, 13; see 13:11) and ward off evil (11:28; see Böcher 1990) is indebted to the Jewish cultural milieu and to the OT cultic system in particular. The "pillar text" of blood sacrifice, Lev 17:11 (deSilva 2000a, 311), comes closest to explaining *how* blood atones for sins: "For the life of a creature is in the blood," so "it is the blood that makes atonement for one's life." Taking the life of a sacrificial victim releases that life for the benefit of the one making the sacrifice, somehow effecting atonement. New life arises from death.

Whether or not Hebrews coined the rare term ***bloodshed*** (*haimatekchysia*), it was probably abstracted from the violent expression "shedding of blood [*ekchysis haimatos*]" (see 1 Kgs 18:28 LXX; Sir 27:15). The image of free-flowing blood conveys the taking of life; it pictures sacrificial death. The resulting **forgiveness** may indicate cleansing from sin, since it is paired with cleansing in this very verse (9:22; see 9:14; 10:2). However, *aphesis* (**forgiveness;** also in 10:18) can indicate release or deliverance (e.g., Isa 61:1 LXX; Luke 4:18). The overlap with Christ's death as a "ransom . . . to set free [*apolytrōsis*]" (9:15) from sins can hardly be accidental.

The OT principle of atonement holds, even though the preacher asserts that the Levitical sacrifices could never actually be effective (see 9:9, 13-14; 10:4). The indispensability of sacrificial death, argued in this paragraph (9:15-22), forms the presupposition for the argument in the next paragraph (9:23-28): Christ offered himself as the definitive sacrifice.

■ **23-24** Verse 23 draws a conclusion from the preceding argument. **It was necessary, then** parallels the "it is necessary" in v 16. Sacrifices were required to inaugurate the old covenant and consecrate all of the people and objects (scroll, tabernacle, implements) associated with it (→ 9:18-21). So also with the new covenant. The argument runs from lesser to greater (*qal wahomer*). On the one hand (*men*), the **copies of the heavenly things** needed **to be purified with these sacrifices** (i.e., covenant sacrifices, such as "the blood of calves" in 9:19). On the other hand (*de*, **but**), **the heavenly things themselves** needed to be purified **with better sacrifices than these.** This raises two difficult questions:

First, Why does the preacher refer to **better sacrifices** (pl.), especially when he has already characterized Christ's sacrifice as "once for all" (7:27; 9:12)? It only begs the question to explain that the plural is generic and imprecise (Attridge 1989, 261; Hagner 1990, 146; Ellingworth 1993, 476) or simply that it grammatically matches **these sacrifices** in the preceding clause (Lane 1991, 247; see Johnson 2006, 243). Rather, the author exploits the inherent symmetry between the notion of sacrifices (pl.), necessitated for both earthly and heavenly sanctuaries, to create suspense in his argument. The singularity of the new covenant sacrifice is not immediately self-evident. It must be demonstrated. Thus, the preacher will take pains to do so in the following argument (9:25-28).

Second, the more perplexing question is: Why was it necessary for heavenly things to be purified? We consider four main proposals (for others, see Hughes 1977, 379-82; Ellingworth 1993, 477):

(1) The cleansing refers to the expulsion of Satan from heaven (Luke 10:18; John 12:31; Rev 12:7-9) or the conquest of evil spiritual forces in the heavenly realms (Eph 6:12). This view, going back to Aquinas, is alien to the present context.

(2) The purification of the heavens is purely ceremonial (Spicq 1953, 2:266-67; Lünemann 1890, 623; Ellingworth 1993, 477). It is an "inauguration" or "consecration" of the new covenant. It does not imply the removal of any previous defilement or impurity. This view simply shunts aside the notion of purification by relabeling it as "inauguration" (defining the verb "purify [*katharizō*]" here by the verb "inaugurate [*enkainizō*]" in 9:18). Such sleight

of hand will not do. The first covenant was inaugurated precisely through the blood of sacrifice, which provided *cleansing* (9:22).

(3) The heavenly things are metaphorical (Bruce 1990, 228-29; Attridge 1989, 262; Thompson 2008, 192). "The heavenly or ideal realities cleansed by Christ's sacrifice are none other than the consciences of the members of the new covenant" (Attridge 1989, 262). This view is attractive because it takes into account an important idea presented earlier in the chapter (9:9, 14; see 10:2, 22). But these references are too remote to be applicable here. Besides, the spatial references are too pronounced (**heavenly things themselves** [9:23]; **heaven itself** [9:24]; Koester 2001, 421), and the preacher's thinking too subtle, to be reduced to a spiritual or psychological concept.

(4) The heavenly sanctuary itself was defiled by human sin and required purification. This view should not be cavalierly dismissed as "fantastic" (Moffatt 1924, 132) or "nonsense" (Spicq 1953, 2:266-67). The instructions for Yom Kippur explicitly prescribe atonement for the most holy place, "because of the uncleanness and rebellion of the Israelites" (Lev 16:16; see Lev 16:18; 20:3; 21:23; Num 19:20). The sins of the people are the cause of defilement in the tabernacle. This is consonant with the description of the inaugural ceremony in Heb 9:18-22. There the blood of sacrifice was employed not only for the forgiveness of the people's sins, but to purify the tabernacle and all its implements as well (Lane 1991, 247; G. Guthrie 1998, 315).

The extent to which the defilement of sin acts as a barrier between God and his people—even to the highest heaven—to that same extent Christ's sacrifice comprehensively cleanses from sin's effects. **For Christ did not enter a man-made sanctuary** (v 24). The preeminence of Christ's high priesthood is associated with his ministry in the heavenly sanctuary. That Christ did **not** enter a **man-made sanctuary . . . only a copy of the true one** resembles the description of the heavenly sanctuary in 8:2 ("the true tabernacle set up by the Lord, not by man"). This stands in contrast to the earthly **copy** (see 8:5) and "the greater and more perfect tabernacle that is not man-made" (→ 9:11).

Christ's exaltation "through the heavens" (4:14), "above the heavens" (7:26), or (lit.) "in the heavens" (8:1) now comes to a climax with the statement that **he entered heaven itself.** This is doubtless equivalent to his entering "the inner sanctuary behind the curtain" (6:19), that is, the most holy place (9:8; 10:19-20).

The depiction of Christ's heavenly ministry is extremely compact: **now to appear for us** [*hyper hēmōn*] **in God's presence.** The verb **appear** (*emphanizō*) may hint at his appearance in an official, representative capacity (see MM, 208). The description reads like an abbreviated version of the definition of high-priestly function in 5:1: "Every high priest is selected from among men and is appointed to represent them [*hyper anthrōpōn*] in matters related to God, to offer gifts and sacrifices for sins" (→ 8:3).

Christ has entered the inner sanctuary "on our behalf [*hyper hēmōn*]" (6:20)—never "for himself [*hyper heautou*]" (9:7), like the old high priests. He always "lives to intercede for them [*hyper autōn*]" who "come to God through him" (7:25). He does not merely represent us "in matters related to God [*ta pros ton theon*]" (2:17; 5:1); he appears for us **before the face of God** (*tō prosōpō tou theou*), that is, **in God's presence.** Christ mediates directly between God and his people, as no other priest could.

■ **25-26** Christ's high-priestly ministry is different from that of other high priests, because he serves in the heavenly sanctuary. Indeed, "if he were on earth, he would not be a priest," for there are already priests who offer sacrifices in accordance with the Law (8:4). What Christ offered was **himself.** But he did not **enter heaven to offer himself again and again** (9:25). The adverb *pollakis*, **again and again,** is given emphatic priority in its clause.

This is unlike **the way the high priest** under the old covenant **enters the Most Holy Place every year** on the Day of Atonement **with blood that is not his own** (i.e., the blood of sacrificial animals [9:7, 12, 13; 10:4]). The implication is that Christ offered "his own blood" (9:12; 13:12). He offered his own life, **himself** (7:27; 9:7, 14, 25, 26). The preacher will unpack the significance of Christ's self-offering in 10:1-10.

Hebrews' argument assumes the symmetry between the sacrifices of the old covenant and the "better sacrifices" (note the pl.) of the new covenant (→ 9:23). But since Christ's "something to offer" (8:3) is **himself,** multiple sacrifices under the new covenant lead to an absurdity. **Then Christ would have had to suffer many times since the creation of the world** (9:26*a*). The verb **to suffer** (*pathein*) is used in the Christian tradition of Jesus' painful death on the cross (Matt 16:21; 17:12; Mark 8:31; 9:12; Luke 9:22; 17:25; 22:15; 24:26, 46; Acts 1:3; 3:18; 17:3; Heb 2:18 [see 2:9-10]; 5:8; 13:12; 1 Pet 2:21, 23; 3:17; 4:1).

The absurdity assumes:

- The Son of God existed before "the foundation of the world" (NRSV; **the creation of the world;** see 1:2; 4:3).
- Human beings have sinned since the dawn of time (Gen 3:1-24; Rom 5:12; see *2 Bar.* 23:4; 54:15; *4 Ezra* 3:21, 26; Koester 2001, 422).
- Sinning has continued unabated, requiring regular atonement—such as the annual Yom Kippur sacrifices (7:27; 9:7, 25; 10:1).

The simplest ground for refuting this absurdity is the empirical fact that human beings do not die repeatedly. However, this is demoted to an illustration in 9:27. The primary refutation is theological, or more specifically, eschatological: Christ **appeared once for all at the end of the ages** (v 26*b*). The verb **appeared** (*pephanerōtai*) connotes the finality and conclusiveness of eschatological revelation or manifestation ("manifested" [NASB]). It is found in christological hymns to mark the Son's appearance in the incarnation (1 Tim

3:16; 1 Pet 1:20; 1 John 1:2; see 1 Pet 5:4). Two time stamps qualify this appearance:

- First, **once for all** (*hapax*), like its antithesis **again and again** (*pollakis* [9:25, 26*a*]), is placed emphatically in the clause.
- Second, **at the end of the ages** (which contrasts with **since the creation of the world**) brings to the fore the eschatological character of Christ's appearance.

Such overt eschatological language has not occurred since the opening of the homily ("in these last days" [1:2*a*]; but see 1:6; 2:5; 4:3; 6:5). The phrase **end of the ages** (*synteleia tōn aiōnōn*) denotes the final age of the world ("the culmination of the ages" [NIV[11]]; "the consummation of the ages" [NASB, NET]; "the climax of history" [REB]). It is used in apocalyptic contexts (e.g., *T. Benj.* 11:2; *T. Levi* 10:2; *T. Job* 4:6) and is a favorite expression in Matthew (13:39, 40, 49; 24:3; 28:20; see BDAG, 974-75).

The **once for all** manifestation of Christ is supremely accomplished **by the sacrifice of himself.** The purpose of Christ's coming was **to do away with sin** (see 9:28*a*). Hebrews resorts to legal terminology to speak of the abolition ("to abolish" [REB]) or annulment of sin (*athetēsis*; MM, 12; Attridge 1989, 203; Koester 2001, 422; see 7:18; 10:28; → 6:13-20 sidebar, "Legal Jargon in Hebrews"). According to both Jewish and Christian apocalyptic traditions, the Messiah's coming would bring an end to sin (*Pss. Sol.* 17:36; *T. Levi* 18:9; *1 En.* 62:2; 69:27). First John 3:5 and 8 closely resemble these traditions, and Hebrews, in the affirmation that Christ "appeared [*ephanerōthē*]" to "take away sins" and "destroy the devil's work."

■ **27-28** A commonsense fact illustrates the definitive quality of Christ's sacrifice: **Man is destined to die once, and after that to face judgment** (v 27). It was almost universally recognized, both in the Judeo-Christian and Greco-Roman worlds, that human beings die but **once** (*hapax*). Yes, a minority of pagans held to the doctrine of reincarnation (or metempsychosis)—chiefly indebted to Pythagorean and Platonic thought. But most ancients shared Homer's verdict: "Men die once" (*hapax thnēskous' anthrōpoi*, *Od.* 12.22). The idea of a final **judgment** beyond death was also widely held, though certain intellectual elites lampooned this fearful prospect (the classic parody is Lucian's *Funerals*).

It should be kept in mind that the preacher is drawing his argument to a close in 9:15-28. The principal point of this subunit is the necessity of a death to inaugurate a covenant. The blood of calves was used to initiate the first covenant (vv 16-22). But since Christ offered his human life, and humans are appointed to die only once, **so Christ was sacrificed once** (*hapax* [v 28]) to establish the new covenant.

Echoing the thought of v 26*b*, the purpose of his death was **to take away the sins of many people.** The phrase **many people** (simply **many** [*pollōn*] in Greek) does not in any way limit the scope of the atonement. The distinctive wording is due to the Semitic idiom in the Suffering Servant formula from

Isa 53:12, which had a profound effect on the formulation of early Christian statements concerning the death of Christ (Matt 26:28; Mark 10:45; see 1 Pet 2:24; Attridge 1989, 266; Lane 1991, 250; Johnson 2006, 245).

The NT acknowledges a twofold pattern of movement in the Messiah's vocation: from suffering to glory (Luke 24:26; Heb 2:9; 1 Pet 5:1). His followers are also drawn into this pattern (Rom 8:17-18; Eph 3:13; 1 Pet 4:13; 5:10). The pattern is discernible here too. At the first coming, **Christ was sacrificed,** but **he will appear a second time.** The word **appear** (*ophthēsetai*) differs from the two previous verbs in vv 24 and 26, also translated "appear[ed]" in the NIV. Like the verb used of Christ's postresurrection appearances (*ōphthē* [Luke 24:34; Acts 13:31; 1 Cor 15:5, 6, 7, 8]), this verb is at home in apocalyptic settings (see 1 Tim 3:16; Rev 11:19; 12:1, 3). Here is the only NT use of this verb in the future passive. It denotes Christ's appearance at his second coming (the closest parallels, in the active, are Matt 24:30; 26:64; Mark 13:26; 14:62; Luke 21:27; Heb 12:14; 1 John 3:2; Rev 1:7; 22:4).

Christ's second appearance is "not to deal with sin" (ESV, GNT, GW, NRSV, REB; see NLT) or **not to bear sin** (HCSB, NET; see NAB). The Greek simply reads *chōris hamartias*: "without sin" (KJV, TYNDALE; "without *reference to* sin" [NASB]) or "apart from sin" (NKJV). His sacrificial death already effectively canceled sin (Heb 9:26*b*, 28*a*) and decisively purged its defilement (9:14, 23; 10:4, 22). So, of necessity, Christ's second coming will not require any act of atonement for sin.

The purpose of Christ's second appearance will be **to bring salvation to those who are waiting for him.** This is the last use of the term **salvation** in its full, eschatological sense in Hebrews (see 1:14; 2:3, 10; 5:9; 6:9; the reference in 11:7 is to the salvation of Noah's family from the flood). Christ "is able to save completely those who come to God through him" (7:25). He will bring salvation **to those who are waiting for him.** Hebrews is not alone in characterizing believers as those who wait expectantly for "the blessed hope—the glorious appearing of our great God and Savior, Jesus Christ" (Titus 2:13; see 1 Cor 1:7; Phil 3:20; Jude 21; see also Mark 15:43; Luke 23:51; Rom 8:19, 23, 25).

With this twofold movement involving Christ's two appearances, the end of this subunit (Heb 9:15-28) conceptually mirrors its beginning. At his first coming Christ was sacrificed **to take away the sins of many** (v 28*a*), for he "died as a ransom to set them free from the sins committed under the first covenant" (v 15*c*). At his second coming he will **bring salvation** (v 28*b*), that is, "the promised eternal inheritance" available under the new covenant (v 15*a*-*b*).

4. Christ's One Obedient Offering Perfects Worshipers Forever (10:1-18)

The subunit in 10:1-18 constitutes the conclusion, not only to the argumentative unit in 8:1—10:18, but to the entire argument (*logos*) of the central section that is "hard to explain" (5:11). In ch 7 the preacher emphasized that the Levitical system enacted through the Mosaic law could not attain "perfection" (7:11, 19). This is in contrast to the divine oath, which appointed the Son "who has been made perfect forever" (7:28). Having demonstrated the supremacy of Christ's priesthood, sanctuary, and sacrifice in chs 7—9, the preacher will now demonstrate *why* our high priest's sacrifice was decisive, whereas the sacrificial system under the Law was not. Christ's self-offering provides perfection (10:1, 14) because it was an offering in voluntary obedience to God's will.

■ **1-4** As the first of four paragraphs in this subunit (10:1-4, 5-10, 11-14, 15-18), vv 1-4 give us the point of departure. They focus on the **law**'s incapacity to provide atonement for sins. Even as the earthly tabernacle built by Moses was but "a copy and shadow" of the heavenly sanctuary (8:5; see 9:11, 23), so also **the law is only a shadow of the good things that are coming** (v 1*a*; compare Col 2:17). The preacher asserts that the Law is merely **a shadow** [*skia*] . . .—**not the realities themselves,** or rather, **not the very image/form** [*eikona*] **of the realities.** He may have in mind the figure of a statue (*eikōn*) and its shadow (Wiley 1984, 281). However, patristic commentators discerned another metaphor from the world of art. A *skia* was an outline or sketch. Only when the artist finished brushing in all the colors was it called an *eikōn* (see Chrysostom in Heen and Krey 2005, 149; Ellingworth 1993, 490-91). Therefore, "the law contains but a shadow of the good things to come, not the true picture" (v 1 REB).

The good things that are coming (*tōn mellōn agathōn*) are the same as **the realities** (*tōn pragmatōn*) but are not strictly identical to "the good things that are already here" in Heb 9:11. Indeed, the author acknowledges benefits of the age to come (2:5) already enjoyed by believers (see 3:1, 14; 6:5). Chief among them in this context is Christ's definitive removal of sin (9:26, 28*a*-*b*). But here **the good things that are coming** point to the salvation Christ will bring at his second coming (9:28*c*). This includes believers' full participation in the divine rest (4:1-10) in the unshakable kingdom (12:22-28; see Attridge 1989, 269; Koester 2001, 430).

The remainder of the paragraph unfolds the implications of the opening statement (10:1*a*). The inability of the Law is expressed through an *inclusio* in vv 1*b* and 3-4:

- **can never** (*oudepote dynata* [v 1*b*]) || **impossible** (*adynaton* [v 4]).
- **year after year** || **annual** (*kat' eniauton* [vv 1*b* and 3]).
- **the same sacrifices** (v 1*b*) || **the blood of bulls and goats** (v 4; Lane 1991, 261).

By heaping one phrase upon another in v 1*b*, the author emphasizes the futility of the sacrifices under the Law. They are **the same sacrifices,** offered **year after year,** repeated **endlessly.** The preacher once again envisions the annual sacrifices on the Day of Atonement (see 9:7, 25).

What the Law **can never** do by way of these sacrifices is **make perfect** [*teleiōsai*] **those who draw near to worship** (v 1*b*). This claim, in combination with v 2*b*, reiterates the thought of → 9:9. The perfection these sacrifices cannot achieve is *with respect to the conscience*. They cannot purge the guilty conscience from the defilement of sin. Therefore, they cannot prepare worshipers to **draw near** to a holy God.

The author presses the point with a rhetorical question in v 2: **If it could, would they not have stopped being offered?** There would be no need for repeated sacrifices, **for the worshipers would have been cleansed once for all.** One of the most significant expressions in Hebrews, **once for all** (*hapax*), along with the perfect participle **have been cleansed** (*kekatharismenous*), indicate a decisive and final purgation of sins.

If such a sacrifice had been offered under the Law, the people **would no longer have felt guilty for their sins.** Hebrews refers to the "conscience [*syneidēsis*]" (KJV; see GW), that moral faculty laden with a "consciousness" (ESV, HCSB, LEB, NAB, NASB, NET, NKJV, NRSV; BDAG, 967; "sense" [REB]; or "awareness" [NJB]) of sins. This accounts for the NIV paraphrase **felt guilty** (→ 9:8-10 sidebar, "The Conscience").

In fact, rather than effectively erasing Israel's collective sense of guilt, **those sacrifices** offered at Yom Kippur **are an annual reminder of sins** (v 3). Observant Jews agreed that the Yom Kippur sacrifices served as a remembrance of the peoples' sins, but so they might be atoned for (Lev 16:16, 19, 30, 33-34; see Philo, *Spec. Laws* 2.196).

Some commentators think Hebrews echoes a Jewish homiletical reflection on Num 5:15, 18 (see Philo, *Planting* 108; Attridge 1989, 272; deSilva 2000a, 318; Koester 2001, 432). Sacrifices are acceptable to God only in proportion to the virtue of the worshipers. The wicked cannot bribe God; when sacrifices are offered with impiety "it is not a remission but a reminder of past sins which they effect" (Philo, *Moses* 2.107; see *Spec. Laws* 1.215).

However, the reason Hebrews relegates these sacrifices to no more than a perpetual reminder of sins is closer at hand. It is suggested by its antithesis in the new covenant. Because of Christ's ultimate sacrifice, God promises, "Their sins and lawless acts I will remember no more" (Heb 10:17). Moreover, Hebrews' position is more radical and sweeping even than the critique of the temple cult leveled by the prophets (e.g., 1 Sam 15:22; Isa 1:11-13; Jer 7:21-23; Hos 6:6; Amos 5:21-25; see Pss 40:6-8; 50:7-15; 51:16-19; 69:31). The ineffectiveness of the OT sacrifices is not merely due to a deficiency of attitude or virtue on the part of the worshipers. They are ineffective, period, full stop.

The axiom in Heb 10:4 puts an exclamation point on the argument: **because it is impossible for the blood of bulls and goats to take away sins.** This is not in conflict with 9:22. There cleansing and forgiveness of sin appear as a distinct provision under the first covenant. Hebrews has already established the point that the Levitical sacrifices do not actually effect the required inward cleansing of the conscience, but only a superficial, outward cleansing (see 9:9-10, 13-14). In the next paragraph (10:5-10) the preacher will explain why the bloody sacrifices of brute beasts cannot provide profound and lasting purification of sins.

■ **5-7** The strong conjunction **Therefore** (*dio*) transitions to an exposition of Christ's all-sufficient sacrifice. Verses 5-10 are a brief midrash on Ps 40:6-8. The psalm is cited in Heb 10:5-7, followed by a succinct commentary on it in vv 8-10.

Hebrews discerns the voice of Christ in the psalm text. The preacher consistently hears God speaking in Scripture (→ 1:5-14 sidebar, "Quoting Scripture in Hebrews"). This is the second of only two passages in Hebrews in which Christ is the speaker in Scripture (→ 2:12-13). The name **Christ** does not appear in Greek but is implied; he is not explicitly named until 10:10. Perhaps, in both 2:12-13 and 10:5-7 it seemed obvious that Christ must be the speaker because of the way he addresses God (France 2006, 128). But here there are other clues to the speaker's identity:

First, the declaration **I have come** (v 7; see v 9) suggests that it was Christ who **said** these words **when** he **came into the world** (v 5*a*). In Jewish tradition the phrase **came into the world** meant being born (Str-B, 2:358; see Koester 2001, 432). Here it refers to the incarnation of the Son, when he was "made a little lower than the angels" (2:7, 9). The phrase occurs frequently of Christ's incarnation in the Gospel of John (1:9; 6:14; 9:39; 12:46; 16:28; 18:37; see 1 Tim 1:15; 2 John 1:7) and as a messianic title (John 11:27; see John 4:25; 6:14).

Second, the reference to the incarnation is yet more graphic in the statement, **a body you prepared for me** (Heb 10:5*c*). It is apparent, even in English, that the preacher is following the LXX, rather than the opaque wording of the Hebrew, "You have dug out two ears for me" (Ps 40:6 GW). Either expression seems to convey the idea of ready obedience. But the MT probably refers to "receptive ears" (Ps 40:6 REB), while the LXX refers to the availability of one's **body**—that is, one's whole self—to fulfill God's will (Bruce 1990, 241-42; see Rom 12:1-2). For Hebrews, Christ's incarnation was crucial to the completion of his saving mission (2:14, 17), for it was through the voluntary sacrifice of his **body** (*sōma*) that believers are sanctified (10:10).

Third, the speaker's statement, **Here I am, . . . I have come to do your will** (v 7)—repeated in the preacher's commentary below (v 9*a*)—is reminiscent of the earlier description of the Son in 5:7-9: "in the days of his flesh" (NRSV), the Son offered up prayers in "reverent submission," and "learned obedience" through suffering.

■ **8-10** The preacher's commentary repeats key phrases from the previously cited psalm text (10:5-7) in vv 8-9*a*. Then it draws two conclusions in vv 9*b*-10. The preacher sculpts the scriptural text to sharpen his points.

When citing once again from the first half of the psalm text (v 8), he repeats the list of four types of sacrificial offerings—**sacrifices, offerings, burnt offerings,** and **sin offerings**—making the first two items plural (compare vv 5-6). This likely emphasizes the plurality of Levitical sacrifices in contrast to

Christ's single sacrifice (7:27; 9:25-28; 10:1, 3, 11-12). He collapses together the phrases about God's disapproval: those sacrifices **you did not desire, nor were you pleased with them** (compare vv 5-6). The four types of sacrifices probably represent the entire sacrificial system under the old covenant (Bruce 1990, 240-41; Hagner 1990, 157). The parenthetical concession—**although the law required them to be made**—confirms this. It also forms a link with the earlier statements about the **law**'s inadequacy and inferiority to "the good things that are coming" (vv 1-4). The preacher omits the statement "but a body you prepared for me" (see v 5c). He reserves reference to Christ's sacrifice of his **body** for the climax of the paragraph in v 10.

The preacher's repetition of the second half of the psalm text (v 9a) retains only the essential language of obedience: **Here I am, I have come to do your will** (compare v 7). According to other NT witnesses, Jesus' life of obedience was consummated in his death (Matt 26:39, 42; Mark 14:36; Luke 22:42; John 4:34; 5:30; 6:38-40; 8:29; 12:27; 19:30; Gal 1:4).

By dividing the psalm passage in two, and taking the two parts in chronological sequence (**First he said, . . . then he said** [Heb 10:8a, 9a]), Hebrews employs an interpretive maneuver used before (2:6-9; 4:8; 7:11, 15; 8:6; 9:8-9). The method has a legal flavor, such as we find in the abrogation of the first covenant and its replacement by another (see 8:7, 13; Thompson 2008, 196).

The first interpretive conclusion in 10:9b uses legal vocabulary. **He sets aside** [*anairei*] **the first** refers to the annulment or abolition of the sacrificial system under the Mosaic law. **To establish** [*stēsē*] **the second** refers to the legal confirmation or validation of God's purpose through the death of Christ (Lane 1991, 264-65; Pfitzner 1997, 137; Koester 2001, 434; Johnson 2006, 252; → 6:13-20 sidebar, "Legal Jargon in Hebrews"). The Greek states this legal truism in a tightly constructed chiasm (abolish/first/second/establish).

The second conclusion in 10:10 unfolds the result of Christ's execution of God's will with respect to believers. The preacher appropriates key terms from Ps 40:6-8: **will** (*thelēma*), **offering** (*prosphora*), and **body** (*sōma*). The phrase **by that will** refers to God's purpose mentioned in the psalm, to which Christ's earthly life and death were conformed. The sacrifices of senseless animals could not fulfill God's **will** as did Christ's voluntary surrender of "himself" (7:27; 9:7, 14, 25, 26) through the **sacrifice** (lit., *offering*) of his **body**.

The result of Christ's self-offering is that **we have been made holy**. The author's pastoral sensibilities are evident yet again in his affirmation that **we** (7:19, 26; 8:1; 9:14) have been sanctified. The grammatical form of **we have been made holy** (perfect periphrastic participle, *hēgiasmenoi esmen*) expresses the decisiveness of the sanctification, resulting in an enduring state of holiness: "we are sanctified" (KJV). It is a final and lasting holiness that the blood of bulls and goats could never procure (9:13-14; 10:1-4).

The sanctification of believers is the object of God's **will** (1 Thess 4:3). It cannot be separated from being purged from sin (Heb 1:3; 9:14; 10:2, 22;

13:12) and having continuous access to God's presence (4:16; 9:8; 10:19). It is therefore synonymous with salvation itself (Hughes 1977, 395). God is the source of holiness (→ 2:11), and sharing in God's holiness is the condition for living in the divine presence (12:9-10, 14). Christ is the agent through whose sacrificial death atonement for sin is accomplished. He effects our holiness; he brings us to glory; he assures our final salvation (2:8b-11, 17; 5:9; 7:25; 9:28).

The full title **Jesus Christ** occurs here for the first time in Hebrews. It will appear twice more in confessional settings (13:8, 21). The name **Jesus,** associated with his necessary humanity (see 2:14, 17; 5:7), is combined with **Christ,** signifying his messianic calling. Elsewhere the title **Christ** is linked to Jesus' divine sonship (3:6, 14) and high-priestly office (5:5; 9:11, 14, 24, 28). The full title embraces the Messiah's vocation of both suffering and glory, seen in references to "the blood of Christ" (9:14), his once-for-all sacrifice (9:26, 28a), and his second coming (9:28b; Hahn 1993). As such, the **sacrifice** made by Jesus the Messiah at the culmination of the ages is finally and permanently effective. He offered himself **once for all** (*ephapax*).

■ **11-14** The third paragraph (vv 11-14) of this subunit is in many respects a counterpart to the first (vv 1-4; Lane 1991, 266; Westfall 2005, 222):

10:1-4	10:11-14
"year after year . . . [*kat' eniauton*]" (v 1)	**day after day** [*kath' hēmeran*] (v 11)
"the same sacrifices [*tais autais thysias*]" (v 1)	Levitical priest offer **the same sacrifices** [*autas . . . thysias*] (v 11)
were "repeated endlessly [*eis to diēnekes*]" (v 1)	Christ's **one sacrifice** (vv. 12, 14) offered **for all time** [*eis to diēnekes*] (v 12)
which "can never . . . make perfect [*oudepote dynatai . . . teleiōsai*]" (v 1)	**has made perfect forever** [*teteleiōken eis to diēnekes*] those who are sanctified (v 14)
"impossible" for them "to take away sins [*aphairein hamartias*]" (v 4)	offered **for sins** [*peri hamartiōn*] (v 12)

Verses 11-14 set forth antitheses between Levitical priests and Christ (compare 7:11, 20-21, 23-24, 27-28; 8:3-4). Hebrews employs an ***on the one hand*** (*men* [v 11])—***on the other hand*** (*de* [v 12]) framework to pose contrasts that are characteristically precise (Ellingworth 1993, 506).

Precise Contrasts

10:11	10:12
every priest	**this priest** (i.e., Christ)
on one hand (*men*)	on the other (*de*)

stands	sat down
offers the same sacrifices	had offered . . . one sacrifice (see v 14)
again and again	for all time (= forever [v 14])
which can never take away sins	for sins

The contrasts pivot around the postures of the respective ministers. (Observe, in passing, that the language of "ministry" [*leitourgōn*, **performs his religious duties** (v 11)] resurfaces from the beginning of the section [8:2, 6; but see 1:7, 14; 9:21].) Every Levitical priest **stands**—a posture of activity. Standing was the position priests took to carry out their cultic responsibilities (1 Kgs 8:11; 2 Chr 30:16; 35:10; Neh 12:44; Jer 28:5; Ezek 44:15 LXX; see Josephus, *Ant.* 13.372). For Hebrews this was a continuous exercise in futility. The many sacrifices they offered could **never take away** [*perielein*] **sins** (v 11), that is, they were incapable of utterly removing the defilement or guilt of sins (see 10:1-2; Lane 1991, 266).

In contrast, the finality of Christ's sacrificial act is signified by the fact that he **sat down** (v 12). In the Orient, sitting down could indicate being unoccupied (Hughes 1977, 400). But in this situation, it signaled that Christ had accomplished his task (see Rev 3:21). The allusion to Ps 110:1 conveys the posture of sitting in connection with holding an office or position of authority. This psalm—a key text for the entire homily (→ 1:13 sidebar, "Psalm 110 in Hebrews")—was first alluded to in Heb 1:3. There the Son is said to have sat down "after he had provided purification for sins." The earlier reverential paraphrase for **God**, "Majesty" (1:3; 8:1), is abandoned. The two final allusions to Ps 110:1 in Hebrews directly state that Christ sat down **at the right hand of God** (10:12; see 12:2).

The phrasing from Ps 110:1 not only helps to bring this section (Heb 8:1—10:18) to a climax, given the *inclusio* of allusions in 8:1 and 10:12-13, but also brings the principal argumentative point of the whole homily full circle. Both the *exordium* (1:1—2:4) and the statement of facts (2:5-18) affirmed that the Son presently reigns supreme over the world to come. Everything has been put "under his feet" (2:8*a*; see 1:13), even though it does not appear as though everything is subject to him (2:8*b*). It is Christ's suffering of death, through which he vanquished the ruler of death (2:9, 14), that has perfected him as the royal high priest over God's people (2:17; see 4:14-15; 5:5-8; 10:19-21). His subjugation of all things has been accomplished decisively through his sacrificial death.

All that remains is for him to wait **for his enemies to be made his footstool** (v 13). Hebrews does not specify who those **enemies** are, but simply employs the designation from Ps 110:1 (as in the citation in Heb 1:13). Surely among them are Christ's cosmic archenemy, "the devil" (2:14), the sinners who oppose him on earth (12:3), and apostates who will perish at his second coming (10:27, 37-39). Christ's **wait**ing (*ekdechomenos*) for his final victory coincides with believers' "waiting [*apekdechomenois*]" (→ 9:28) for their ultimate salvation.

The linkage between Christ's victory and that of believers is made clear in the climax to this paragraph (10:14). Christ's **one sacrifice** (lit., *offering*) seals his saving work as permanent and eternal (see 5:9; 9:12, 15). **He has made perfect forever** corresponds to the decisive cleansing and sanctification noted in 10:2 and 10. **Made perfect** (*teteleiōken*), "have been cleansed [*kekatharismenous*]" (v 2), and "have been made holy [*hēgiasmenoi*]" (v 10) are all in the perfect tense, pointing to the conclusive and lasting effects of the actions. The adverbial phrase *eis to diēnekes* (**forever**) strengthens this sense in v 14.

This is set in contrast to what the Law could not accomplish according to v 1. The same sacrifices repeated "endlessly [*eis to diēnekes*]" could never "make perfect [*teleiōsai*]" (→ 10:1). Perpetual, ineffectual sacrifices have been replaced by the one sacrifice that is effective **forever** (*eis to diēnekes*), offered by the high priest who holds his office "forever [*eis to diēnekes*]" (7:3).

The beneficiaries of this perfection are **those who are being made holy.** There is little agreement on how to take the present participle (*tous hagiazomenous*). Three options are possible:

(1) The present tense could be iterative, referring to those who are being sanctified from time to time (Wiley 1984, 290). It is difficult to see how this fits the stress on definitive cleansing/holiness in this context.

(2) It could indicate continuous action, and hence an ongoing process of sanctification (CEB, ESV, NAB, NIV, NKJV, NLT; Attridge 1989, 281; Pfitzner 1997, 139; Ellingworth 1993, 511; France 2006, 131). Hebrews 12:4-17 certainly presents sanctification as more than a gift. It is the result of divine discipline (12:10) and the communal and individual pursuit of holiness (12:14). However, these are not the points being made in 10:1-18. The emphasis, rather, is on the finality of Christ's sacrifice and the enduring effectiveness of its results (in contrast to the Law's failure to perfect anyone). Hence, a third option is more likely.

(3) The present tense participle is timeless, indicating that believers have been brought into a lasting condition or state of holiness (Bruce 1990, 247; Lane 1991, 267-68; "those who are made holy" [LEB, NET; possibly HCSB, KJV, NASB, NJB, NRSV, REB]). Such a reading is in line, not in conflict, with the perfect participle in v 10 (→). Christ, through his sacrifice, is "the one who makes . . . holy" (2:11). Believers are "those who are made holy [*hoi hagiazomenoi*]" (2:11). Therefore, they are God's "holy [ones] [*hagioi*]" (3:1; 6:10; 13:24 NAB).

The holy status of believers holds in perpetuity, but not unconditionally so. The costly purchase of sanctification by the blood of the covenant (10:29) spells great peril for those who flagrantly sin against it (10:26-31). So, having been consecrated to God and qualified to approach the inner sanctuary in worship, believers ought to yield themselves to God's ethical outworking of divine holiness in their lives (12:4-17). Indeed, in the following verses (vv 15-18), the new covenant is presented as the solution to humanity's need for definitive deliverance from sin and sustained obedience to God's will.

■ **15-18** The concluding paragraph finalizes the arguments in chs 8—10. It ends the section in a way similar to the way it began, with a quotation from Jer 31 (Heb 8:8-12; 10:16-17). Here the quote is selectively mined for its important nuggets, the "better promises" (8:6) most relevant to the present discussion. The repeated parts (Jer 31:33, 34) highlight the establishment of a new covenant, which enables a durable obedience to God (Heb 10:16) and permanent deliverance from sins (v 17).

These verses also wrap up 10:1-18 in several ways. First, the quotations from Jer 31 introduce divine testimony in support of the claim that Christ's sacrifice is absolutely effective: **The Holy Spirit also testifies to us about this** (Heb 10:15).

Second, the paragraph further defines the perfection and holiness achieved by Christ's sacrifice (see vv 1, 10, 14; France 2006, 132). These are promises of the new covenant, enacted by Christ's self-offering.

Third, and not unrelated to the second point, the promises of the new covenant are subtly contrasted with the **law**'s weakness and uselessness. On one hand, "the law [*nomos*] is only a shadow of the good things that are coming—not the realities themselves" (v 1). It is powerless to make a way out of the cycle of sinning or to offer definitive cleansing so that God can permanently banish the peoples' guilt from his mind (vv 1-4). The new covenant, on the other hand, affords God's promise: **I will put my laws [*nomos*] in their hearts, and I will write them on their minds** (v 16). In other words, God provides a deep, inward motivation for people to conform themselves fully to his will. This correlates with the preacher's references to the perfection of worshipers, consisting of the purging of the conscience from sin (9:9, 14; 10:2, 22), superior to the old covenant's provision of only external cultic purity (9:10, 13).

The once-for-all sanctification attained through Christ's death (see 10:10, 14) supports another divine promise: **Their sins and lawless acts I will remember no more** (v 17). The preacher adds the term **lawless acts** (*anomiōn*) to the quote from Jeremiah. This alludes again to the Law's inability to deal decisively with sin. The Law's sacrificial system only compounded the memory of sins year after year (v 3). But Christ "has died as a ransom to set them free from the sins committed under the first covenant" (9:15). Because the **sins and lawless acts** (10:17) themselves have been utterly removed, any remembrance of them is also removed from the eternal memory banks of God's mind!

The concluding v 18 is the antithesis to the multiple, ineffective sacrifices under the Law noted in vv 1-4 (see v 11). **And where these sins and lawless acts have been forgiven, there is no longer any sacrifice for sin.** This brief commentary on the passage from Jer 31 complements the earlier comments in Heb

8:7 and 13. The new covenant makes the old obsolete and ready to disappear. The ultimate sacrifice of Christ surpasses the ineffective Levitical sacrifices.

Christ's one sacrifice was the all-sufficient provision for "a decisive putting away [*aphesis*]" of sins (Lane 1991, 254). This is a stronger way of expressing "remission" (KJV) or "forgiveness" of sins (CEB, ESV, HCSB, NAB, NASB, NET, NRSV; **forgiven** [GW, NJB, NLT, REB]; compare 9:22). The very purpose for Christ's coming was to abolish sin (→ 9:26). Repeatedly in the preceding context we have read about sins being taken away (*anenengkein* [9:28]; *aphairein* [10:4]; *perielein* [10:11]). Since this has been accomplished conclusively, **there is no longer any sacrifice for sin.** The outmoded sacrificial system no longer has a goal to shoot for. It has been fulfilled in Christ's self-offering. Therefore, the Levitical sacrifices, like the sins they could not "take away," can themselves be "set aside [*anairei*]" (v 9).

FROM THE TEXT

The arguments of the central section of Hebrews are "hard to explain" (5:11) for ancient and modern readers alike, but for different reasons. The original audience was hampered by a spiritual condition that made them disinclined to "hear" what the preacher was saying. Modern readers, even if with open hearts, approach the text from a very foreign cultural setting. This makes it difficult for them to "hear" with full appreciation and understanding.

People living in the modern industrialized world generally know almost nothing about sacrifice. We are more likely to apply the word "sacrifice" to games of chess or baseball than to the ritual killing of an animal. Most of us would find a visit to a slaughterhouse most unpleasant. We'd rather not think that a cow had to die in order to give us the hamburger we buy in sterile, plastic packages at grocery stores. We cannot fathom how anyone imagined that a slaughtered animal could make objects or persons holy. Few appreciate that the English word "sacrifice" is derived from two Latin words meaning "to make holy." For most of us, the entire scenario of temple, priest, and bloody sacrifices evokes revulsion rather than awe. We read about such things with a strange curiosity rather than an air of sacredness.

Ironically, Hebrews has contributed to the Western sentiment that animal sacrifices are irrelevant to religious life. But it has done so, not by repudiating the idea of sacrifice, but by arguing that the sacrificial system under the first covenant has reached its *telos*—its proper end—in Christ's final sacrifice. His sacrifice, unlike those of beasts, was utterly effective because it was the unprecedented act of complete obedience to God's will (5:7-8; 10:5-10). Hebrews still emphasizes the importance of Christ's offering his own body (10:10) and blood (9:12, 14, 25; 10:19; 13:12). But his sacrifice has a profound spiritual significance because it was his willful offering up of "himself" on our behalf (7:27; 9:14, 25, 26).

People in the contemporary Western world probably recoil even more at the thought of *human sacrifice* on our behalf. The idea seems primitive and downright barbaric. Perhaps, unbeknownst to the author of Hebrews, this is for moderns his variant of Paul's scandal of the cross (1 Cor 1:23; Gal 5:11). But modern people experience a larger barrier to the message of Hebrews. Amid the discussion of Christ's better sacrifice, covenant, and greater and more perfect tabernacle, the superior benefit of Christ's atoning work encounters an even more fundamental disconnect with today's readers.

Even the object of Christ's death, as Hebrews presents it, befuddles people today. The result of Christ's sacrifice, not achievable by previous sacrifices, is a cleansed conscience. Thus, worshipers are perfected or qualified to appear before God (9:9, 14; 10:2, 22). But modern people have curious ways of dealing with conscience. In some quarters conscience is defined, not in terms of an individual sense of guilt, but in a collective fashion (i.e., "social conscience"). Others seek therapeutic methods of treating the guilty conscience, including medications—legal or otherwise. "Sin" has been repackaged under psychological euphemisms to assist people in their efforts to release themselves from responsibility for their own problems and actions—a trend noticed decades ago in Karl Menninger's aptly titled book, *Whatever Became of Sin?*

How can we recover the value of Hebrews' message for today?

First, it must be stressed that for Hebrews sin and its effects on the human conscience have not only moral implications but religious and cultic ones. Sin "defiles" the conscience, making worshipers cultically unfit. It cripples them emotionally from standing confidently before a holy God. The accusing conscience is not simply a matter of "feeling bad" about things we have done. It exposes us to the searching judgment of God (4:12-13).

Second, despite efforts to relabel or ignore the moral dimensions of our personhood, the power of the conscience remains. Of course, a person's conscience may be so "seared" that it is no longer a sensitive moral barometer (see 1 Tim 4:2). But if we have a working conscience, we can no more deny its promptings than the reality of our five senses.

I recently heard a retiring college registrar report how on numerous occasions he received letters from graduates plagued by a guilty conscience. Because they had cheated on an exam or paper—often many decades before—they were requesting that their college degrees be revoked. This, they hoped, would relieve their sense of guilt. The registrar was pleased to be an agent of redemption, granting them absolution because of their honest admission.

In a more recent example, the famous actress Keira Knightley declared her desire to be a Catholic. "It sounds much better than living with guilt," she said. "It's absolutely extraordinary. If only I wasn't an atheist, I could get away with anything. You'd just ask for forgiveness and then you'd be forgiven" (CathNewsUSA 2012). Hebrews would certainly reject her notion of forgiveness as a means of "get[ting] away with anything." That aside, both of these stories illustrate the strength of an accusing conscience. The mere passage of time cannot bring relief from its torment.

The arguments of the central section of Hebrews culminate in the new covenant promise of the decisive putting away of sins. Christ's final sacrifice provides us with subjective release from our sense of guilt (10:2). But more importantly, it is the objective grounds for God's banishment of our sins from his memory (10:17). The OT promises of forgiveness come to fruition under the new covenant. God can truly blot out our sins (Isa 43:25). He can remove them from us, "as far as the east is from the west" (Ps 103:12). He can cast them into the sea of forgetfulness (see Mic 7:19). Thus, the hymn writer Horatio Spafford could exclaim, "It Is Well with My Soul":

> *My sin—O the bliss of this glorious thought!*
> *My sin—not in part, but the whole—*
> *Is nailed to His cross, and I bear it no more!*
> *Praise the Lord, praise the Lord, O my soul!*

III. CALL TO PERSEVERING FAITH AND ACCEPTABLE WORSHIP: HEBREWS 10:19—13:25

The preacher has now concluded the main arguments of his sermon. It remains only for him to bring his "word of exhortation" to a rousing conclusion. The final section (10:19—13:25) bears the marks of a *peroratio* or conclusion (Backhaus 1996, 61-63). In ancient rhetoric, the *peroratio* had a dual function: first, to summarize the arguments of the speech; second, to move the audience emotionally toward the right decision or action (Lausberg 1998, §§431-42). The conclusion is the speaker's last opportunity to hammer home his points and make a final appeal to his listeners.

Not surprisingly, Hebrews does not devote much space to summarizing arguments. The rhetorical handbooks advise keeping the recapitulation or summary brief (*Rhet. Alex.* 1444b; *Rhet. Her.* 2.30.47; Quintilian, *Inst.* 6.1.2), and deliberative rhetoric does not ordinarily need one anyway (Cicero, *Part. or.* 17.59). On the heels of the arguments in the central section, Hebrews finds it sufficient simply to remind listeners at key points of Christ's covenant sacrifice and exalted status (10:19-20; 12:2-3, 24; 13:11-13, 20).

The opening in 10:19-25 sets the agenda for the conclusion of the sermon. Christ's high priesthood and inauguration of unprecedented access into the divine presence serve as the basis for a call to worship and enduring faithfulness. The "let us draw near [*proserchōmetha*]" of 10:22 (see 4:16) will reach a rhetorical climax in 12:18-29 with the dramatic contrast between Sinai and Zion ("you have not come [*proselēlytha*].... But you have come [*proselēlytha*]" [12:18, 22]). Worship entails commitment to Christ and solidarity with the community of the faithful (past and present; see 10:25, 32-34; 11:40—12:1; 12:23; 13:1-3, 7, 17). The fruit of faithful living under the new covenant is actively doing good deeds. These points form an *inclusio* in the conclusion: in the summary/invocation (10:19-25) and in the final benediction (13:20-21; see 13:1-6, 15-16). Persevering faith and well-doing are crucial to pleasing God and receiving the promise of salvation (10:38-39; 11:6; 12:28; 13:16, 21; see 6:9-12).

A hallmark of rhetorical conclusions is the appeal to emotions (*pathos*). Quintilian said it is in the *peroratio* where "we may give full rein to our emotions" (*Inst.* 4.1.28; see 2.5.8; 6.1.9). The goal is to coax listeners toward the right course of action. The "leading emotions" used to mobilize people are fear and hope (Lausberg 1998, §§229, 437). Appropriately, these emotions bulk large in Hebrews' *peroratio*. Here we find the most frightening warnings of the homily (10:26-31; 12:15-17, 25-29), displaying God's fiery judgment (10:27, 30-31; 12:29). Hope is also prominent, recurring in the worthwhile inheritance or reward for faithful endurance in the face of suffering (10:19-23, 32-39; 11:1—12:3; 12:18-24; 13:5-6, 13; Backhaus 1996, 62-63). A related thread woven through the conclusion is the believer's hope for a permanent (10:34; 12:27; 13:14) and heavenly home (11:10, 16): the unshakable kingdom (12:28).

The preacher's address to his readers is more direct and pointed in the conclusion. Only twice before has he addressed them as "brothers" (3:1, 12; see 2:11, 12, 17); now this form of address flanks the conclusion (10:19; 13:22). He speaks to them in the second person ("you," "your") with greater frequency than before (over fifty times in 10:19—13:25, out of eighty total occurrences; see Westfall 2005, 242). Reprised from the statement of facts (2:5-18) is the description of the readers as God's "sons" (12:5-8; see 2:10) and "children" (12:8; see 2:13-14). He demonstrates an intimate knowledge of his readers' situation (10:32-39) and—as is fitting in a *peroratio* (Aristotle, *Rhet.* 3.19.1; Quintilian, *Inst.* 6.2.8-19)—commends his own personal integrity (13:18). In line with a conclusion's function to persuade/dissuade readers regarding advantageous/disadvantageous decisions or actions, 10:19—13:25 contains the greatest concentration of imperatives (twenty-two of thirty times), prohibitives (six of ten), and hortatory subjunctives (seven of twelve; → 4:1 sidebar, "Let us . . .").

Finally, a typical feature of conclusions is the use of "commonplaces" (*loci communes*) in which certain vices are denounced and/or virtues praised (Quintilian, *Inst.* 2.4.22; 5.10.20). In Hebrews we find topics worthy of denunciation, such as sacrilege (10:29), sexual immorality (12:16; 13:4), and greed (13:5). Topics worthy of praise include mutual concern (10:24-25, 32-24; 13:1, 3), discipline (12:5-11), hospitality (13:2), marriage (13:4), acceptable worship (12:28; 13:15-16, 21), and above all faithfulness (11:1—12:13). Thus, readers are directed away from those behaviors deserving scorn and judgment, and toward those leading to honor and salvation.

The conclusion has two divisions:
A. Exhortations to Persevere in Faith (10:19—12:13)
B. Exhortations to Offer Acceptable Worship (12:14—13:25)

A. Exhortations to Persevere in Faith (10:19—12:13)

1. Confidence and Perseverance in Faith (10:19-39)

BEHIND THE TEXT

The fluid style of Hebrews is a sign of the author's remarkable rhetorical skill. The almost seamless transitions have frustrated scholars' attempts to define where one division begins and another ends. This is no more true than in 10:19-39. There is agreement that a transition between major sections occurs here. But commentators disagree as to where the central section of the homily comes to an end. Is it at verse 18, 25, 31, 34, 35, or 39? There are four reasons to recognize 10:19-39 as a cohesive unit forming a transition between the second and third major divisions of Hebrews:

First, the unit is marked by a verbal *inclusio* using the word "confidence [*parrēsia*]" (10:19, 35). This repetition creates a link to the earlier exhortations to hold on to (3:6) or approach God with "confidence" (4:16)—the only other occurrences of *parrēsia* in Hebrews. An *inclusio* involving "faith [*pistis*]" (10:22 and 10:38, 39), along with the repetition of "endurance" vocabulary (*hypomenō* [10:32]; *hypomonē* [10:36]), introduce the controlling theme of persevering faith, which extends through 12:13. Note the later recurrence of "faith" (twenty-six times in ch 11 and in 12:2) and "endurance"/"endure" (12:1/12:2, 3, 7). Additionally, one may compare the "draw[ing] near" in "full assurance of faith" at the beginning of the unit (10:22) with having "faith" (NRSV) instead of "shrink[ing] back" at its end (10:38-39).

Second, the unit is composed of four paragraphs (as in the NIV: 10:19-25, 26-31, 32-34, 35-39), arranged into two halves. The first half is dominated by appeals made in the first person plural ("we," "let us"; but see vv 25 and 29); the second, by the second person ("you"). The first person returns in v 39. The first half contains many allusions to the central section, especially its cultic language ("Most Holy Place," "blood of Jesus," "opened" [= inaugurate], "the curtain," "great priest," "draw near," "sprinkled," "cleanse," "conscience," "sacrifice for sins," "blood of the covenant"). The second half, with its references to the community's past suffering and present need for endurance, prepares for the following examples and exhortations to persevering faith (11:1—12:3).

Third, the four paragraphs are punctuated by a note of divine judgment/reward at the end of each paragraph (vv 25, 30, 34, 37-39; see also vv 35-36). The first half contains a warning about God's vengeful repayment (*antapodōsō* [10:30]) of apostates; the second half, a promise of reward (*misthapodosian* [10:35]) for those who endure. Importantly, scriptural quotations at the close of each half support the eschatological urgency of the unit (Deut 32:35, 36 in Heb 10:30; Hab 2:3-4 in Heb 10:37-38). The Hab 2:3-4 text serves as the scriptural launching pad for the following examples of faith (11:1-40).

Fourth, the integrity and transitional function of 10:19-39 is evident through comparison with earlier material. The first paragraph (10:19-25) contains close parallels to 4:14-16 (→ 4:14-16 Behind the Text sidebar, "The 'Bookends' of 4:14-16 and 10:19-23"). All of 10:19-39 resembles the content and movement found in 5:11—6:12:

- Reminder to readers of their privileged status and need to act accordingly (5:11—6:3 || 10:19-25).
- Dire warning concerning irreversible apostasy and inevitable divine judgment (6:4-8 || 10:26-31).
- Reassurance of salvation based upon a track record of exemplary conduct (6:9-12 || 10:32-34).
- Encouragement to persevere so as to receive God's sure promise (6:13-20 || 10:35-39; see Lane 1991, 279-80, 282).

Both 4:14—6:20 and 10:19-39 are transitional passages. The former provides a transition from the midrash on Ps 95 to the arguments concerning Christ's priesthood, sanctuary, and covenant sacrifice in 7:1—10:18. The latter transitions in the opposite direction, from the central arguments to the exhortations occupying the conclusion to the sermon (Attridge 1989, 283).

IN THE TEXT

a. Invocation to Worship and Faithful Living (10:19-25)

The opening paragraph to Hebrews' conclusion is another long sentence in Greek (→ 1:1-4 on the periodic sentence; see 2:2-4; 5:1-4, 5-10; 7:1-3, 26-27; 12:1-2).

Verses 19-21 of ch 10 succinctly summarize the arguments in 7:1—10:18. The upshot of the central arguments is Christ's achievement of two benefits: (1) authorization for our confident access to the divine presence; and (2) his high-priestly leadership over God's people.

Verses 22-25 present three exhortations encapsulating the ways readers ought to respond to these benefits. The preacher issues a call to true worship ("let us draw near . . ." [v 22]), firm commitment ("let us hold . . ." [v 23]), and mutual concern ("let us consider . . ." [vv 24-25]).

■ 19 **Therefore, . . . since we have** begins the conclusion. An identical expression opened the second major section of the sermon (4:14; see 12:1; for further parallels [4:14-16 || 10:19-25; 5:11—6:20 || 10:19-39] → Behind the Text above). The address to **brothers** occurs here and toward the end of the entire sermon (13:22; also in 3:1, 12). This sets a pastoral tone for the predominantly hortatory character of the conclusion. The participle **since we have** (*echontes*) has two objects, expressing the two primary benefits of Christ's death and exaltation: **confidence** in God' presence (10:19) and Christ's office as "a great priest" (v 21).

The first benefit is **confidence** (*parrēsia*; → 3:6*b* ["courage"] and 4:16). Here in 10:19, 35 it is more than a subjective feeling of "confidence" (CEB, ESV, NAB, NASB[95], NJB, NRSV; see GW) or "boldness" (HCSB, KJV; see NLT). It is an objective privilege or "authorization" (Lane 1991, 283) **to enter the Most Holy Place.** Under the old covenant, only the high priest enjoyed this privilege, and he only once each year (9:7). The accent here is not on the act of entering (**to enter**) but on the unprecedented right of *access* (*eisodos*) (see NAB; BDAG, 294; Clarke 1977, 3:755; Ellingworth 1993, 517).

All worshipers enjoy the privilege of access into God's presence **by the blood of Jesus.** Christ entered the most holy place "by his own blood," not the worthless blood of goats and calves (→ 9:12, 25). Christ's self-offering was the definitive sacrifice for:
- The inauguration of the new covenant (9:15-22).
- The purification of the heavenly sanctuary (9:23-25).
- The perfection of worshipers through the cleansing of the conscience (9:14; see 9:9; 10:2, 22).

■ 20 The "entrance into the [inner] sanctuary" (v 19 NAB) was **opened for us** by Christ. **Opened** (*enekainisen*) is the same word used of the first covenant being "put into effect" through sacrificial blood (9:18). The verb suggests newly establishing something—that is, to "ratify," "dedicate," or "inaugurate" (BDAG, 272; see HCSB, NASB, NET).

The entrance (*eisodon* [v 19]) is described as **a new and living way** (*hodon*). The way is **new** because it was not revealed under the old covenant but at "the time of the new order" (9:8, 10). The new way replaces old, ineffective ways of approaching God (Pfitzner 1997, 141; see 7:11, 18-19; 8:7, 13; 10:1-4). The way is **living,** like God (10:31; 12:22) and God's word (4:12). It is the path to complete salvation, since Christ "always lives" to plead **for us** before God (7:25; see 7:16; compare John 14:6).

The way proceeds **through the curtain.** The preacher employs the spatial imagery of the tabernacle. There a **curtain** divided the holy place from the most holy place (9:3). According to 6:19-20, Jesus has entered as our forerunner behind the **curtain** into the inner sanctuary. Elsewhere Hebrews describes Jesus as passing "through the heavens" (4:14), "above the heavens" (7:26), or entering into "heaven itself" (9:24; see 8:1). The imagery, whether cultic or celestial, indicates that Christ blazed a trail into the very presence of God.

The phrase **that is, his body** (lit., *flesh*) presents one of the most difficult interpretive problems in Hebrews. Some commentators object to the equation of Christ's **body** with the **curtain**, as though it were a veil or obstacle to the vision of God. They assert that **body** is connected, not with the **curtain**, but with the **way** (Westcott 1909, 322; Spicq 1952, 2:316; so REB: "the way of his flesh"). But this does not fit with how the author of Hebrews uses the expression **that is**. As a virtual equal sign, it joins both parts of an equation (2:14; 7:5; 9:11; 11:16; 13:15).

The parallelism in 10:19-20 helps to open up the meaning of this difficult passage (see Lane 1991, 284; Koester 2001, 443-44; Thompson 2008, 203):

10:19	10:20
"to enter" (i.e., entrance)	a new and living way
"the Most Holy Place"	through the curtain, that is,
"by the blood of Jesus"	[through] **his body** (lit., "flesh")

In vv 19 and 20 the author repeats the same basic facts concerning the access to God's presence achieved by Christ. The means of this achievement is the sacrificial death of Christ, denoted first in terms of his blood, and then in terms of his *flesh* (*sarkos*). In Hebrews the term *flesh* is applied to Jesus with respect to his mortal humanity, hence his suffering and death (2:14; 5:7). Jesus' mortality was crucial to "bringing many sons to glory" (2:10), delivering them from the "fear of death" (2:14-15), and securing "eternal salvation" (5:9). The slide from spatial movement (**through the curtain**) to means ("through his flesh" [ESV, NET, NRSV]) occurred earlier ("through the greater and more perfect tabernacle . . . by his own blood" [9:11-12]). Jesus inaugurated the way to God through the offering of his own blood (10:19) and **body** (10:20).

So the enigmatic expression **through the curtain, that is, *through his body*** is a succinct way of saying that access to God's presence has been achieved through Christ's bodily death. Christ's offering of his own "body" (10:5, 10), in obedience to God's will, is the way sin has been removed and worshipers cleansed to make their approach before God. The **way** into the most holy place, which remained undisclosed under the old covenant (9:8), has now been opened wide through the death of Christ.

Rending of the Temple Veil

Some scholars think that the equating of the curtain with Christ's flesh (Heb 10:20) suggests our author's familiarity with the tradition in the Synoptic Gospels concerning the rending of the temple veil (Mark 15:38 || Matt 27:51 || Luke 23:45; so Bruce 1990, 251; Hagner 1990, 164; France 2006, 135). Perhaps Hebrews is interpreting that dramatic scene, at the moment of Jesus' death, when the veil was torn in two. Wesley explains, "As by rending the veil in the temple, the holy of holies became visible and accessible, so by wounding the body of Christ, the God of heaven was manifested, and the way to heaven opened" (n.d., 584).

There is no way of knowing whether this scene was in the mind of the author of Hebrews. But it would be no stretch to imagine he would approve of associating the event with his typological interpretation of the tabernacle layout. The inner curtain of the tabernacle severely limited access to the most holy place (9:7). By this the Holy Spirit was demonstrating that the way into the inner sanctuary had not yet been revealed (9:8), and that animal sacrifices were incapable of preparing worshipers for full access to the divine presence (9:9-10).

So after Christ drew his last breath on the cross, and the temple veil was ripped from top to bottom, was this not a sign that "the time of the new order" had begun (9:10)? That Christ had inaugurated "a new and living way" into heaven itself—"through the curtain, that is, his body" (10:20)?

■ **21** The second benefit is Christ's installation as high priest. The reminder, **we have a great priest,** is parallel to "we have a great high priest" in 4:14 (→ 4:14—5:10 Behind the Text sidebar, "The 'Bookends' of 4:14-16 and 10:19-23"). The title **great priest** is synonymous with "high priest" (→ 4:14). Christ's exaltation as high priest has been identified as "the point of what we are saying" (8:1). The preacher has described the high-priestly work of Christ as his definitive self-offering for sins and his ongoing heavenly intercession for his people (7:1—10:18).

Christ's position as great priest **over the house of God** indicates his leadership over God's people. God used Moses to seal his covenant with Israel through the blood of beasts (9:16-22). Now God has sealed the eternal covenant with the blood of Christ, and has appointed the Son as "that great Shepherd of the sheep" (13:20). "Moses was faithful as a servant *in* . . . God's house" (3:5). Jesus, our "apostle and high priest" (3:1), is "faithful as [the Son] **over** God's house" (3:6).

The **house of God** spans the entire history of God's "people" (2:17; 4:9; 8:10; 10:30; 11:25; 13:12). It is continuous with the ancient people of God ("the house of Israel and . . . the house of Judah" [8:8; see v 10]), beginning with Abraham the patriarch (7:4; see 2:16). It includes all the "forefathers" (1:1; see 8:9) and "ancients" who were commended for their faith (11:2; see 11:1-40). The **house of God** now consists of all who maintain their commitment to Christ (3:6; see 3:14) and await his second appearance to bring them salvation (9:28).

■ **22** Three exhortations in 10:22-25 outline the appropriate responses to the divine benefits available through Christ's high-priestly ministry. The first flows naturally from the privilege of bold access into God's presence: **let us draw near** (*proserchōmetha*). The same verb occurred in the parallel exhortation in 4:16. It vividly conveys the action of priest and people approaching the sanctuary for worship (→ 4:16). Though used absolutely here, the NIV aptly adds, **let us draw near to God** (as in 7:19, 25; 11:6). In 12:18-28 the preacher displays what is at once the final destination of our Christian pilgrimage and the place we already approach in worship with our hearts: the heavenly city of the living God (→ 12:18, 22). Christ "is able to save completely those who **draw near** to God through him" (7:25 LEB).

We may approach God confidently **with a sincere** [*alēthinēs*] **heart.** This is a heart that is "true" (ESV, HCSB, KJV, LEB, NRSV), as opposed to one that is rebellious (i.e., hardened [3:8, 13; 4:7]) and "always going astray" (3:10). It is a heart that can survive the penetrating scrutiny of God (4:12)—as opposed to the "sinful, unbelieving heart that turns away from the living God" (3:12) and falls under divine judgment (3:15-19; 10:26-27). The **sincere heart** has the "knowledge of the truth [*alētheias*]" (10:26); it stays true to God by performing his will with perseverance and faithfulness (10:35-36, 39). The faithless heart "shrinks back" and is doomed to destruction (10:38-39). The true heart approaches the "true [*alēthinēs*] tabernacle" (8:2; see 9:24) and draws near to God through Christ in anticipation of complete salvation (7:25; 9:28).

It is no coincidence that the preacher mentions **heart** twice here. He has pointed to the Lord's announcement of a new covenant through the prophet Jeremiah (8:7-13; 10:15-18). The old covenant was defective because the people were never sufficiently prepared inwardly to stay true to the covenant (8:9; see 8:7-8). The new, eternal covenant is founded on better promises (8:6). The preacher has highlighted two of them: inward transformation of the **heart** and mind for a new obedience (8:10; 10:16) and decisive forgiveness of sins (8:12; 10:17).

We are to approach God **in full assurance of faith.** Similar phrasing in 6:11 accented the certainty of hope. The emphasis on the certainty of **faith** here is in keeping with the dominant note of faithfulness that follows into ch 11, climaxing in 12:2. **Full assurance** (*plērophoria*) indicates a state of complete certainty (BDAG, 827; → 6:11). The definition of **faith** in → 11:1 reinforces this. The clunky phrase **full assurance of faith** is rendered more effectively as "absolute trust" (NAB), "strong/sure faith" (GW/GNT, NCV), or "fully trusting" (NLT) God.

Two participial phrases in Greek round out the first exhortation in 10:22*b*. They indicate the comprehensive purification of worshipers for their approach to God: inwardly (**hearts**) and outwardly (**bodies**). The participles having *been* sprinkled and having *been* washed are in the perfect tense, to indicate decisive and lasting purification (compare the earlier perfect participles for cleansing and sanctification [→ 10:2, 10] and the perfect tense verb "made perfect" [→ 10:14]).

In Hebrews, sprinkling (9:13, 19, 21; 10:22; 12:24) always refers to ritual cleansing with blood. Although the preacher does not mention the blood of Christ here, he surely implies it as the means of decisive purgation (9:14; 10:29; 12:24; 13:12; → 10:4-7). Hebrews 9:14 explicitly states that "the blood of Christ . . . cleanse[s]" the **conscience** (→ 9:9, 14, and 10:2, and 9:8-10 sidebar, "The Conscience"). Thus, **having our hearts sprinkled to cleanse us from a guilty** [lit., ***evil***] **conscience** refers to the profound cleansing and forgiveness of sins afforded by Christ's final covenant sacrifice (7:27; 9:12, 15, 26, 28; 10:2, 10, 18).

Having our bodies washed with pure water employs technical language for ritual purification (Lane 1991, 287). The reference is probably to Christian baptism. A few commentators curiously resist this conclusion, insisting that both clauses in v 22*b* are metaphorical (Whedon 1880, 5:113; Taylor 1967, 125). While the cleansing of **hearts** is obviously metaphorical, the washing of **bodies** is most certainly not. Our author does not denigrate ritual washings in and of themselves. They were prescribed for worship in the tabernacle under the old covenant. Indeed, "baptisms" or "cleansing rites" (NIV[11]) are foundational to Christian faith (6:1-2). Nevertheless, ceremonial washings are of limited effectiveness, providing only external cleansing (9:10, 13), not deep, invasive purification of the heart (9:9, 14; 10:1-4, 11-12).

Outward Sign, Inward Grace

Hebrews 10:22*b* agrees with other NT texts that depict both a physical washing of the body with water and a spiritual renewal of the inner person (Eph 5:26; Titus 3:5). In the language of sacramental theology, we have the outward sign (the water of baptism) and the inward grace (cleansing of the heart or regeneration). Closely parallel to Heb 10:22 is 1 Pet 3:21, which describes baptism as "the removal of dirt from the body" (outward sign) and "the pledge of a good conscience toward God" (inward grace). The prophet Ezekiel foresaw the time when God would cleanse and transform his people comprehensively, both inside and out: "I will sprinkle clean water on you. . . . I will give you a new heart" (Ezek 36:25-26).

■ **23** The second exhortation, **Let us hold** [*katechōmen*] **unswervingly to the hope we profess** [*tēn homologian tēs elpidos*, ***the confession of hope***], is formally parallel to "let us hold fast [*kratōmen*] to the confession [*tēs homologias*]" (4:14 HCSB). **Confession** (*homologia*; most translations) is an active acknowledgment or "declaration" (GW) of one's allegiance (BDAG, 709). The objective content of the confession is Jesus as our high priest (→ 3:1 and 4:14). Attached to Christ's priesthood, established by divine oath, is the introduction of "a better hope" (7:19). Thus, confession of **hope** is inseparable from confessing Christ as Son and high priest "over God's house" (3:1, 6; 10:21). Christ our high priest is the forerunner who has anchored our "hope . . . in the inner sanctuary behind the curtain" (6:19-20).

Elsewhere Hebrews urges his readers to **hold *on*** (→ 6:18) to confidence (3:6; see 10:19, 35), **hope** (3:6; 6:18; see 6:11; 11:1), and our original commitment (3:14). These terms overlap in significance with faith (10:22, 38, 39) and perseverance (10:32, 38). Together they reinforce the principal hortatory aim of the sermon: to urge readers to maintain a solid commitment to Christ (Ellingworth 1993, 524).

They must hold their confession of hope **unswervingly.** The adjective *aklinēs* literally means "unbending," "steadfast," and "unmoved" (LSJ, 51). Importantly, **unswervingly** modifies *confession* rather than **hope** (Lünemann 1890, 649; deSilva 2000a, 340; Thompson 2008, 205). Hope is a source of strong encouragement we can hold on to (6:18), as it is grounded in the promise and oath issuing from God's unchanging purpose (6:13-18). Hope is like "an anchor . . . firm and secure," fastened inside "the inner sanctuary" (6:19). The "better hope" introduced by Christ's priesthood (7:19) is backed by God's oath (see 7:17, 20-22, 28). It is our *confession* of this hope that needs to be stabilized or kept "without wavering" (CEB, ESV, HCSB, KJV, LEB, NASB, NLT, NRSV; see NAB, NET).

10:23-25   That the God (see 6:13; 11:11) **who promised is faithful** serves as the basis **(for)** for this exhortation. Chapters 6 and 7 form part of the background for this claim. God's "promise" is "confirmed with an oath" (6:17). God's oath stands behind the "promise" of entering into divine rest (4:1-11, esp. vv 3, 5). God's oath concerning our Great High Priest makes Jesus himself "the guarantee of a better covenant" (7:22), "founded on better promises" (8:6). What is **promised**—the object of our hope—is our "eternal inheritance" (9:15; see 10:36; 11:13, 39) in God's unshakable kingdom (12:26-28).

■ **24-25** The third exhortation, **let us consider how we may spur one another on toward love and good deeds,** resembles the preacher's commendation of the readers' "work" and "love" in 6:10-11. **Let us consider** (*katanoōmen*) urges readers to direct their attention (HCSB, NJB) to one another (compare "See to it [*blepete*] . . ." [3:12]; *episkopountes* [12:15]). *Katanoeō* occurs only once more, directing our attention to Jesus (3:1; compare 12:2-3). To **consider** Jesus and other people comprises the two major foci of the Christian life (Koester 2001, 445). This third exhortation, we may note in passing, completes the theological triad of faith (10:22), hope (v 23), and love (v 24), also found in 6:9-12 (→ 6:10 sidebar, "Virtues").

The purpose of mutual concern should be to **spur one another on toward love and good deeds.** The Greek phrase employs a particularly strong word, whose flavor is hinted at in translations such as **spur . . . on** (NET) or "provoke" (KJV, NRSV; Luther has *Reizen*, "irritation"). The noun *paroxysmos*, as well as its cognate verb *paroxynō* ("to sharpen"), are typically used in a negative sense, indicating irritation, exasperation, provocation, or wrath (LSJ, 1342-43; BDAG, 780). The noun's only other occurrence in the NT refers to Paul and Barnabas's "sharp disagreement" (Acts 15:39; see also Deut 29:17 and Jer 39:37 LXX).

The verb only rarely refers to stimulation toward positive goals or actions (see Attridge 1989, 290 n. 79; Koester 2001, 445). It is sometimes paired with *parakaleō* (**encourage**) as a loose synonym (Polybius, *Hist.* 3.116.3; Appian, *Hisp.* 8.40; Plutarch, *Sol.* 30.4; compare Heb 10:24 and 25). The phrase **provocation toward love and good deeds** is arresting. It urges mutual encouragement (v 25*b*) that is challenging, even confrontational, rather than comforting (France 2006, 137).

Serious concern and motivation are required to combat the malaise that has set in among the readers. The prohibition **let us not give up meeting together** (v 25*a*) reveals the first tangible indicator of apostasy in the house church. The action is more than negligence ("neglect" [NLT; see ESV, NRSV]) or detachment ("stay away" [NAB, NCV, REB; see HCSB]; "absent yourself" [NJB]). It is a "forsaking" (KJV, NASB) or "abandoning" (NET) of the community that leaves it vulnerable ("leaving in the lurch" [Johnson 2006, 261]).

Unfortunately, the author does not tell us the reasons for the defection. Speculations have included persecution (10:32-34; 12:4; 13:3), controversial teachings and practices (13:9), disillusionment over the delay of the Parousia (9:28; 10:25*b*, 36-39), or a complex of issues. Perhaps the author himself did not know the precise causes (Attridge 1989, 290-91; → Introduction: F. Purpose). The problem is restricted to only a few members for now, but is chronic (**as some are in the habit of doing**). The preacher is concerned about the fate of the few who are slipping away (2:1; 3:12-13; 4:1, 11), as well as the corrupting effects they may have on the many (12:15).

The urgency of attending (10:24) to this problem is **all the more** critical **as you see the Day approaching** (v 25). The sudden shift to the second person (**you**) underscores the preacher's insistence. The eschatological reference to **the Day** and its imminent approach ("drawing near" [CEB, ESV, HCSB, LEB, NAB, NASB, NET, NJB, NLT, RSV]) raises the specter of looming judgment. The threat of judgment is even more emphatic in the following paragraph.

"The Day"

In Heb 10:25 "the Day" (as in 1 Cor 3:13; 2 Thess 2:3; 2 Tim 1:12, 18; 4:8) is shorthand for "the Day of the Lord." Ancient Israelites anticipated a future deliverance in which God would deliver them, judge their enemies, and establish them over the nations. However, OT prophets put the wayward people of Israel on notice. The Day of the Lord will not be a time of wholesale rejoicing. Along with all of the other nations, Israel too will be judged for its sins (Amos 5:18-20;

Joel 1:15; 2:31; Zeph 1:7-18; Zech 14:1). "That day will be darkness, not light" (Amos 5:18).

In the NT the Day of the Lord retains its double-sided character as a time of both deliverance and doom. Jesus identifies it with the coming of the Son of Man as Judge (Matt 16:27; 25:13, 31; Mark 13:26; 14:62; Luke 17:30). Paul dubs it "the day of our Lord Jesus Christ" (1 Cor 1:8), "the day of the Lord" (1 Cor 5:5; 2 Thess 2:2), "the day of the Lord Jesus" (2 Cor 1:14), or "the day of Christ [Jesus]" (Phil 1:6, 10; 2:16).

In Hebrews, clustering around "the Day" is the expectation of Christ's coming with reward (10:35-36) and judgment (4:13; 6:2; 9:27; 10:27, 30-31; 12:23; 13:4), with destruction (10:27, 39*a*) and salvation (7:25; 9:28; 10:39*b*).

b. Fearful Expectation of Judgment for Apostates (10:26-31)

The preacher now offers the sort of admonition suitable for provoking and encouraging his audience to strengthen their commitment to God and one another. As is customary in rhetorical conclusions, the author develops a powerful emotional appeal (→ 10:19—13:25). It is a textbook example of *deinōsis* (lit., "making fearful, terrible"). This is rhetorical eloquence designed to make one *feel* the strength of the case being made, the emotional impact of "things unjust, cruel, or hateful" (Quintilian, *Inst.* 6.2.24; see Thompson 2008, 124).

Fear (10:27, 31) of God's judgment (10:27, 30) explicitly frames the paragraph. The argument of the paragraph proceeds in three parts. First, the preacher articulates the dreadful consequences for defiant rejection of Christ's sacrifice (10:26-27). Second, he draws readers into the logical and emotional calculation of divine justice with a lesser-to-greater argument ("How much more severely do you think . . . ?" [10:29]). Third, he offers scriptural support for the inevitable execution of divine judgment (10:30), followed by a closing statement of how fearsome that judgment really is (10:31).

■ **26-27** *For* (*gar*; untranslated in NIV) ties the present warning to the description of apostasy in v 25. **If we deliberately keep on sinning,** then, entails abandonment of the Christian community. This includes rejection of its privilege of drawing near to God through the blood of Jesus, its confession of hope, and its mutual concern, encouragement, and participation in love and well-doing (10:19-25). The sin of apostasy is deliberate, persistent, and with full knowledge.

First, the term **deliberately** (ESV, HCSB, LEB, NAB, NET, NLT, NRSV, REB; "willfully" [KJV, NASB]) alludes to the distinction between unintentional and intentional sins in Num 15:22-31. Under the old covenant, sins committed intentionally or "defiantly" resulted in expulsion from the community and unrelieved guilt (Num 15:30-31; → 5:2).

Second, the present tense participle **keep on sinning** (*hamartanontōn*) conveys the sense of continuous or persistent sinning ("persist in sin" [NRSV, REB]).

Third, **after we have received the knowledge of the truth** implies an informed rejection of the truth. Arriving at **the knowledge of the truth** is a standard expression for conversion in the Pastoral Epistles (1 Tim 2:7; 4:3; 2 Tim 2:25; 3:7). "Knowing the truth" is also significant in the writings of John (John 8:32; 17:3; 1 John 2:21; 2 John 1). Enlightenment is a companion motif (Heb 6:4; 10:32). The intensive form for **knowledge** (*epignōsin*, "full knowledge"; Lane 1991, 292), as well as the preacher's inclusion of himself in its reception (**we have received**), preclude any suggestion that only false professors of faith are in view (France 2006, 139). Apostasy is a hazard all believers would do well to avoid.

The consequence of apostasy is stated, first, in a negation: **no sacrifice for sins is left** (v 26b). This reformulates the statement in 10:18 (Lane 1991, 292-93). The provision of conclusive forgiveness through Christ's self-offering "sets aside" (10:9) the "weak and useless" (7:18) system of Levitical sacrifices. So "there is no longer any sacrifice for sin" (10:18). Christ's definitive sacrifice, once summarily repudiated, leaves **no sacrifice** whatsoever available to atone for sins.

Christ's first coming was for the express purpose of delivering from (9:15) and "do[ing] away with sin[s]" (9:26, 28; 10:4, 11). Since Christ accomplished this with finality, his second appearance cannot and will not include any atonement for sins (9:28). The **only** thing remaining for those who sin *against* Christ's once-for-all sacrifice is **a fearful expectation of judgment and of raging fire that will consume the enemies of God** (10:27).

This second way of describing the final consequence of apostasy is diametrically opposed to the destiny of the faithful. The latter are "waiting [*apekdechomenois*]" for Christ to bring salvation (9:28). Defectors from the faith are left with nothing but a frightful **expectation** (*ekdochē*) of divine judgment. Christ himself "waits for [*ekdechomenos*]" the final judgment, when his **enemies** will be made his footstool (10:13).

The **fearful** (*phoberos* [vv 27, 31]) aspect of God's **judgment** (*kriseōs* [v 27]; "judge [*krinei*]" [v 30]) frames this paragraph. "Eternal judgment" is a basic tenet of Christian faith (6:2). It is an eschatological reality (9:27; 10:23), especially unpleasant for those whose lifestyles are in flagrant violation of God's standard of holiness (13:4; see 12:14). The reference to **raging fire that consumes the enemies of God** resembles prophetic oracles that warn of burning wrath on the Day of the Lord (Isa 26:11; 66:15; Zeph 1:18; 3:8; Ezek 38:19). Later, in an allusion to Deut 4:24, Hebrews will point out that "God is a consuming fire" (12:29).

■ **28-29** Once again the form of argument is legal, cast in a lesser-to-greater comparison (see 2:6-9; 4:8; 7:11, 15; 8:6; 9:8-9; 10:8-10). The "lesser" part of the argument (v 28) concerns the just verdict pronounced on those who repudiated the legal claims of the old covenant: **Anyone who rejected the law of Moses** refers not simply to those who violated the Law (see NRSV). It refers to actions undertaken to abrogate or nullify it (*athetēsas*, "set aside" [ESV, NASB]; Koester 2001, 452). This is treachery or breaking faith (see Polybius, *Hist.* 9.36.10; Isa 1:2; Mark 6:26; 1 Tim 5:12; Johnson 2006, 263). Only God, who established the Law through Moses, holds the prerogative to set it aside, as he has done through the sacrifice of his Son (Heb 7:18; 10:9; see 8:7-8, 13).

The death sentence (**died . . . on the testimony of two or three witnesses**) alludes to the punishment prescribed for idolaters in Deut 17:2-7. That the sentence was to be carried out **without mercy** echoes the stipulation, "Show no pity," demanded for the most egregious offenses (the OT phrase is, lit., "your eye shall not spare him/her/them" [Deut 7:16; 13:9; 19:13, 21]; Bruce 1990, 262; Ellingworth 1993, 537). The wilderness generation experienced just such an unrelenting death sentence for "turn[ing] away from the living God" (Heb 3:12, 16-19).

The "greater" part of the argument is rendered all the more potent by the preacher's interrogative formulation. He invites his readers to draw for themselves the unavoidable conclusion concerning those who turn their backs on the new covenant: **How much more severely do you think a man deserves to be punished . . . ?** (10:29; observe the shift from first ["we" (v 26)] to second person [**you**]). He presents a series of three actions so contemptible that those who perpetrate them deserve a punishment worse than death. Each action demonstrates the knowing, persistent, and deliberate character of final apostasy (→ v 26). The first graphically portrays the apostate's repudiation of the Son of God himself; the second and third articulate the blatant disregard for the gracious provisions of the new covenant.

First, the apostate is one **who has trampled the Son of God under foot**. There is no more vivid metaphor for showing contempt than "trampling underfoot" (Pss 7:5; 56:2 LXX; Isa 10:6; 26:6; Dan 8:10; Micah 7:10; Matt 5:13; 7:6; for Classical Greek uses, see Koester 2001, 452-53; Johnson 2006, 264). The treacherous betrayal of Jesus is described as Judas's "lift[ing] up his heel" against him (John 13:18, citing Ps 41:9).

This is the fourth occurrence of the full title **Son of God**. Two instances have a confessional quality (4:14; 7:3). The other two apply to apostates who flout the confession of Jesus as God's Son (6:6; 10:29). How ironic and futile for rebels to trample **the Son of God under foot**! God has already put everything "under [the Son's] feet" (2:8). The Son is "superior to the angels" (1:4-14; 2:5-7) and Moses (3:1-6). He sits enthroned at God's right hand waiting for his enemies to be made "a footstool for [his] feet" (1:13; 10:13). Rebels make themselves his enemies.

Second, the apostate is one **who has treated as an unholy thing the blood of the covenant that sanctified him**. The **blood of the covenant** originally referred to the animal blood used to seal God's first covenant with Israel (Exod 24:8, cited in Heb 9:20). Now, however, it is the blood of Christ that inaugurated the new covenant (9:15-18; 12:24; 13:20; see Matt 26:28). Christ's blood is the means of complete sanctification (**sanctified** [*hēgēsamenos*] **him**; see 13:12; compare 9:13; 10:10, 14) or cleansing from sins (9:14, 22; 10:2, 22). Yet what is all-holy, makes holy, and opens an entry into the utterly holy presence of God, apostates regard as "common" or "profane [*koinon*]" (**an unholy thing**). They declare, in effect, "that they expect no more benefit from the blood of Christ than they do from that of a cow or a sheep" (Clarke 1977, 3:758).

Third, the apostate is one **who has insulted the Spirit of grace.** The translation "outraged the Spirit of grace" misses the mark (ESV, NRSV). The verb *enybrizō* (an intensive form of *hybrizō*) denotes acting out of *hybris* ("hubris")—that is, arrogance, insolence, audacity. It is manifested in behavior that degrades, insults, or violently mistreats another. Aristotle classified "insult" as one of three kinds of slight (along with disdain and spitefulness). Insult consists of "causing injury or annoyance whereby the sufferer is disgraced." Insult is designed not to gain any legitimate advantage or redress any wrong, but only to dishonor someone out of the sheer pleasure of displaying one's superiority (*Rhet.* 2.2.5).

The act of hubris is even more egregious in this instance because its object is **the Spirit of grace.** Spicq asserts that there is no more striking contrast than that between *hybris* (**insult**) and *charis* (**grace;** 1953, 2:325). The **Spirit of grace** or "the Holy Spirit who brings God's mercy to us" (NLT) is none other than "the eternal Spirit" through whom Christ "offered himself" up for our sins (9:14). Anyone who has responded to divine benefits with such dishonor, disgrace, and ingratitude has committed a supreme act of impiety. The ancients widely recognized that such a person is headed for a downfall, and **deserves to be punished** (see deSilva 2000a, 349-51; Koester 2001, 453).

■ **30-31** The paragraph closes on the same note with which it began: the **dreadful** nature of divine judgment (→ 10:27). The preacher offers scriptural proof that God will uphold his own honor and holiness against the sacrilege and disregard of apostates described in v 29.

It is mine to avenge; I will repay is an adaptation of Deut 32:35. The near quotation does not conform either to the Hebrew text or the LXX. Paul uses exactly the same phrasing (Rom 12:19), mirrored also in the Targums (Aramaic paraphrases of the Hebrew OT). This suggests that the preacher followed the oral paraphrase in current use in Diaspora synagogues (Hagner 1990, 172; Lane 1991, 295; Koester 2001, 453).

The Lord will judge his people, like the preceding quotation, comes from the Song of Moses (Deut 32:36). The saying is repeated in Ps 135:14 LXX and the *Odes Sol.* 2:36, indicating that it, too, lived on in oral memory. Hebrews uses the identical words of the LXX, but his application is quite different from the saying's usual function. The Song of Moses celebrates God's defense of his own honor and his faithfulness in protecting and vindicating Israel. In a curious twist, Hebrews uses the oracle to remind readers that God will turn his judgment on **his people**. Judgment will be targeted on those who have turned their backs on God, purposely violated and desecrated the new covenant, and severed their ties with his people.

Possibly the most ominous statement in Scripture concludes this paragraph: **It is a dreadful thing to fall into the hands of the living God** (Heb 10:31). The idiomatic expression **fall into the hands of** means coming under the power or control of someone, often with negative repercussions (Judg 15:18; 2 Sam 21:9; Luke 10:36; see Sir 8:1; Sus 1:23). For the righteous, it is preferable to fall into the hands of God than into the hands of their adversaries (2 Sam 24:14; 1 Chr 21:13; Sir 2:18). Not so for God's sworn enemies, as the Song of Moses declares (Deut 32:39; see 2 Chr 32:14-15; Isa 43:13; 2 Macc 6:26). **The living God,** who gives life to every created thing, can also take it away (Deut 32:39; 1 Sam 2:6; 2 Kgs 5:7). This **dreadful** thought should serve as a warning to those who are "turn[ing] away from the living God" (Heb 3:12) and his people.

c. Praise for Past Endurance (10:32-34)

We find the same rhetorical pattern of frank speech (10:26-31) followed by praise (10:32-34) found in ch 6 (6:4-8, 9-12; → 6:9). John Chrysostom, an expert orator himself, recognized the technique. He likened it to a physician who, after making a deep incision, employs gentle, soothing remedies to ease the pain (1996, 461).

The aim of the opening statement of the paragraph is to call the community to remember its own past endurance of a "great contest" of sufferings (10:32). The preacher then elaborates on these sufferings in chiastic fashion (vv 33-34; Bengel 1877, 4:439):

10:33	"publicly exposed to insult and persecution"	"stood side by side with those . . . so treated"
	X	
10:34	"sympathized with those in prison"	"joyfully accepted the confiscation of your property"

The paragraph concludes with the rationale for their endurance in the face of suffering: the hope of "better and lasting possessions" (10:34*b*).

■ **32 Remember those earlier days** is an appeal to memory (Gk. *anamnēsis*). This is a rhetorical strategy aimed at motivating the audience and securing their goodwill by praising the "courage, wisdom, humanity, and nobility of past judgments they have rendered" (*Rhet. Her.* 1.5.8). Its intended effect is to favorably dispose the audience toward the speaker (expected in the *peroratio* of a speech [Aristotle, *Rhet.* 3.19.1]). Recollection of the readers' track record of honorable and courageous actions should bolster their resolve not to descend into shameful and cowardly patterns of behavior (deSilva 2000a, 355-57).

The **earlier days** being recalled occurred **after you had received the light.** The image of having "been enlightened" appeared earlier (→ 6:4*a* and sidebar, "Enlightenment and Baptism"). The time frame was perhaps at some point soon after they had "received the knowledge of the truth" (10:26) or had "come to share in Christ" (3:14). The mistreatment experienced by the community was probably due to their newfound confession of faith in Christ.

During the early life of the community **you stood your ground** [*hypemeinate*] **in a great contest in the face of suffering.** Most English versions render **you stood your ground** as *endured.* Perseverance (*makrothymia* and *makrothymeō*; → 6:12, 15) was a character trait of Abraham's that readers were urged to emulate (→ "patience" in 6:12). The reemergence of endurance vocabulary (but with *hypomenō* and *hypomonē*) occurs only here and at the beginning of ch 12. The recital of exemplary people of faith throughout history (11:1-40) is framed by calls for present endurance (10:36; 12:1, 7), based on the example of the community's own past endurance of suffering (10:32) and Jesus' endurance of the cross (12:2, 3).

Endurance was a common topic of courage, one of the four cardinal Greek virtues (→ 6:10 sidebar, "Virtues"). As Aristotle noted, "Courage endures frightful things for the sake of what is noble" (*Eth. nic.* 1115b12; deSilva 2000a, 366 n. 74). Cynic and Stoic philosophers considered endurance integral to the cultivation of all the virtues. Both Jews and Greeks frequently illustrated the endurance of hardship or suffering with athletic imagery (Croy 1998, 63-65, 174; Thompson 2008, 217-19).

Hebrews appropriates popular themes and imagery from moral philosophy to describe the community's struggles. The preacher reminds them that they endured a **great contest** (*pollēn athlēsin* [NAB, NIV]; "hard/great struggle" [ESV, HCSB, NRSV/NKJV]; "great/harsh conflict" [NASB/NET]). An *athlēsis* is an athletic contest (BDAG, 24), which could include running, boxing, wrestling, jumping, throwing, among other events. It is premature to identify the contest here as a "prize fight" (France 2006, 143; "great fight" [KJV]). When "endurance" terminology and athletic imagery resurface in ch 12, the preacher describes the struggle as a footrace (12:1) and perhaps a boxing/wrestling match (12:4). The **great contest** happened **in the face of suffering,** or rather, consisted *of sufferings* (Johnson 2006, 268).

■ **33** The preacher catalogs the prior sufferings of the community under two categories. First, there were direct, community-wide sufferings endured in full public view. Second, there were hardships that did not affect everyone in the community directly but were shouldered all the same by the community as a whole. The two categories appear twice in 10:33-34, in chiastic order (→ introduction to 10:32-34).

Sometimes this early group of Christians suffered **insult and persecution. Insult** (*oneidismois*) likely means verbal "abuse" (NAB, NET, NRSV, REB; hence, "reproach[es]" [ESV, KJV, NASB]; "ridicule" [NLT]; "taunts" [HCSB]), intended to disgrace the community (BDAG, 710; "humiliations" [NJB]; "shame" [TYNDALE]). Bearing "disgrace [*oneidismos*]" is a way in which believers identify with Christ's suffering (11:26; 13:13). **Persecution** (*thlipsesin*) is a generic term for "tribulations" (NASB, TYNDALE) or "afflictions" (ESV, HCSB, KJV, NAB, NET). Here it probably connotes physical "violence" (NJB; see Johnson 2006, 269), but it is difficult to say whether this meant being "beaten" (NLT) or "tormented" (REB).

Whatever the physical and verbal abuse, they were inflicted to maximize the impact of shame and disgrace in the public eye. The Greek expression translated **publicly exposed** (*theatrizomenoi*) is a cognate of the word for "theatre [*theatron*]" (see 1 Cor 4:9). The active verb means "to be or play on the stage"; in the passive, "to bring on the stage." It usually has the negative sense of "being made a public spectacle" (NASB; see NKJV) or "held up to shame" (LSJ, 787; BDAG, 446).

At other times, when the community was not experiencing frontal attacks from the society around them, they stood in solidarity **with those who were so treated.** The expression **stood side by side** means "partners [*koinōnoi*]" (CEB, ESV, NRSV) or "sharers" (NASB). It suggests that they shared the burden of shame with their suffering brothers and sisters, as though it were their own. The Son similarly "shared" in the humiliation of human existence through his incarnation (Heb 2:14). **Those . . . so treated** could have been certain members of the community singled out for mistreatment (perhaps leaders of the church [13:7]) or members of neighboring churches (→ 13:23-24).

■ **34** The two categories of suffering listed in → 10:33 are repeated in v 34, but in reverse order and with greater specificity. A concrete instance of standing in solidarity with others who were suffering (v 33*b*) is when the community **sympathized with those in prison.** The translation **sympathized** is at best ambiguous, at worst potentially misleading (→ 4:15). "Had compassion" (ESV, KJV, NRSV) rightly suggests more than sympathetic feelings, but rendering active help and assistance. Better yet is NIV[11]'s "suffered along with" (similarly GW, NAB, NET, NJB, NLT, REB). The imprisonment of fellow believers was still happening when Hebrews was written (13:3, 23). The exhortation in → 13:3 is a commentary on the shared suffering mentioned here. The community should care for and closely identify with prisoners, as though they were shackled alongside them.

Prison in the Ancient Roman World

The epithet, "I hope you rot in jail," was far more likely to come true in ancient prisons than in those of modern civilized countries. And that was so, despite the fact that ancient Roman custody was not even officially recognized as a form of punishment—though it could be used as such. Real punishments included fines, execution, or (a fate often thought worse than death) exile.

Conditions were dire in ancient prisons. They were usually packed beyond capacity, devoid of natural light, and poorly ventilated. Prisoners languished in noxious air and suffocating heat, and chafed in tightly fitted and heavy chains or stocks. Sleeplessness prevailed, since one had to lie in the dirt if a mat were not provided. On cold nights prisoners were lucky if they had an outer cloak to use as a blanket.

Personal hygiene and adequate diet were lacking. Prisoners could not shave or cut their hair, as barber's knives were prohibited. Only the privileged few were allowed a fresh change of clothes and visits to public baths. Most prisoners declined in health, became unrecognizable in physical appearance, and had clothing that had worn to tatters. Daily rations of food and water were barely enough for subsistence and could be withheld as a means of torture or execution. Without friends or loved ones on the outside to provide food, drink, and other permitted personal effects, existence in prison was unbearable if not impossible.

Incarceration was a devastating source of dishonor and shame. Prisoners were, by definition, social deviants; so even their closest friends and associates were pressured to abandon them. In the case of political prisoners (a category Christians fell into), visitors who provided them support and aid could fall under official suspicion. These facts about prison life shed much light on what it meant for early Christians to suffer along with those in prison. (For further study, see Rapske 1994.)

Not only did members of the community suffer attacks upon their honor, their associations, and their own persons, but the loss of their possessions. **Joyfully accepted the confiscation of your property** is an "elegant oxymoron" (Bengel 1877, 4:440), given the juxtaposition of **accepted** (or "welcomed," *prosedexasthe*; Johnson 2006, 271) with **confiscation**. Unfortunately, the Greek word *harpagē* is not specific enough to indicate whether the "seizure" (NASB, REB) of property was the result of official legal action (**confiscation** [CEB, HCSB, NAB, NET, NIV[11]]) or mob violence ("plundering" [ESV, NKJV, NRSV]; "stolen" [GW]). That these believers welcomed this injustice **joyfully** conforms to the authentic Christian pattern for accepting suffering (Matt 5:11-12; Luke 6:22-23; Acts 5:41; Rom 5:3; 2 Cor 7:4; 11:21-30; Jas 1:2; 1 Pet 1:6; 4:13). Jesus modeled this by enduring the suffering of the cross "for the joy set before him" (Heb 12:2).

The reason the community joyfully accepted the loss of their earthly belongings was their knowledge of a much greater hope. **You knew that you yourselves had better and lasting possessions.** The preacher emphasizes his point by playing on the words **property** (NAB, NASB, NIV; *ta hyparchonta*, "possessions" [CEB, GW, HCSB, NRSV, REB]) and **possessions** (CEB, NIV; *hē hyparxis*, "possession" [ESV, GW, HCSB, LEB, NAB, NASB, NKJV, REB]). These were often used interchangeably for personal possessions, belongings, or goods (LSJ, 1853-54; Ellingworth 1993, 550). However, the latter was also used in the philosophical sense of "substance" (KJV; see TYNDALE), "existence," or "reality" (LSJ, 1853; BDAG, 1029). Philo uniformly uses the word in this way, especially of God's existence (e.g., *Creation* 170; *Worse* 160, 168-69; *Unchangeable* 55, 62). Hebrews may be exploiting the philosophical overtones of the latter term. If so, the preacher contrasts temporal possessions with the **superior** (*kreittona*, **better**) and **lasting** (*menousan*, "permanent" [GW, LEB]) **reality** they have in eternity.

This anticipates the contrast between the removal of things that are shaken, with the unshakable things that will "remain [*meinē*]" (12:27). We do not now have an "enduring [*menousan*]" city, but we look for such a city to come (13:14; see 11:10, 16). This also prepares for a recurring theme in ch 11. Foundational to the life of faith is the endurance of loss and suffering now, with the guarantee (11:1) that one's true homeland, God's unseen and eternal reality, lies in the future (11:10, 13-16, 26).

d. Exhortation to Endure in Faith (10:35-39)

Praise for endurance in the past (10:32-34) turns to exhortation for enduring faith in the present (10:35-39). This new paragraph effectively completes the transition from the central arguments (7:1—10:18) to the following hortatory material (11:1—13:25). "Confidence [*parrēsia*]" occurs here for the last time in the sermon in an *inclusio* (10:19, 35) that marks off the whole transitional section (10:19-39).

Faith appears relatively infrequently earlier in the sermon (4:2, 3; 6:1, 12; 10:22). Now it becomes the major topic that will dominate 11:1—12:3. The preacher launches this topic by quoting and briefly commenting on the scriptural text from Hab 2:3*b*-4 in Heb 10:37-38.

■ **35-36** That the new paragraph opens in v 35 (NIV), rather than in v 36 (NIV[11]), is supported by two features. First, the inferential particle **So** (*oun*) signals a shift from words of praise (vv 32-34) to words of encouragement based on the audience's prior excellent performance (vv 35-36). Second, vv 35-36 form a couplet with two parallel sentences:

10:35	10:36
So do not throw away your confidence;	You need to persevere
it will be richly rewarded.	so that when you have done the will of God, you will receive what he has promised.

So do not throw away your confidence urges the readers not to abandon the **confidence** announced as a singular Christian possession in → v 19. **It will be richly rewarded** (*misthapodosian*) repeats the thought of "better and lasting possessions" awaiting believers (v 34), but accents God's justice in response to their perseverance and commitment (Koester 2001, 461; see 6:10). "Reward [*misthapodosian*]" (NRSV) in 2:2 has the negative sense of "punishment." But in 11:26 it has the positive sense of Moses' looking forward to his "reward." In

11:6 God is the "rewarder [*misthapodotēs*]" (KJV, NASB) of those who diligently seek him.

You need to persevere (v 36*a*) restates the exhortation in v 35*a* in language that brackets ch 11. The vocabulary of "perseverance [*hypomenō* and *hypomonē*]" appears only in 10:32, 36 and 12:1, 2, 3, 7. **So that when you have done [*poiēsantes*] the will [*thelēma*] of God** evokes the climax to the sermon's central arguments in 10:1-18. There the purpose of Christ's coming was "to do [*poiēsai*] God's **will** (*thelēma* [10:7, 9]); and the accomplishment of that **will** was the sanctification of God's people (10:10). According to 13:20-21, God, through Christ and his covenant sacrifice, enables believers "to do his will [*poiēsai to thelēma autou*]" (GNT). **You will receive what he has promised** is the attainment of the ultimate goal toward which all of the faithful throughout history have pressed (11:9, 11, 13, 17, 33, 39; see 4:1; 6:12; 9:15).

■ **37-39** The alternation of threat (10:25, 26-31) and encouragement (10:32-34) is concentrated in the final verses of this chapter. The preacher presents another set of reasons (**For** [*gar*]) why the community must "persevere" (v 36) in a composite biblical quotation. The quotation supplies further scriptural support for the eschatological urgency punctuating the transitional section (10:25, 27, 30-31, 34, 35, 36). "The Day" is fast approaching (10:25) because Christ is coming soon (10:37). The quote also introduces the topic of living **by faith** (v 38*a*), illustrated at length in ch 11.

The introductory line, **in just a very little while,** comes from Isa 26:20. Its original context accounts for the distinctly eschatological resonance of the phrase: the promise of resurrection (Isa 26:19), the gracious opportunity given to God's people to hide from divine wrath (26:20-21), and the broader themes of God's righteous judgment and salvation (26:1-18). The phrase fits perfectly with the following quote from Hab 2:3*b*-4 (Heb 10:37*b*-38). It reinforces the promise that the Coming One **will come and will not delay** (v 37*b*).

The author adapts the text from Habakkuk in several ways in order to drive home his points. Perhaps we can excuse his sculpting and rearranging the text. Contrary to his normal practice, he does not formally introduce it as a biblical quotation (→ 1:5-14 sidebar, "Quoting Scripture in Hebrews"). (For a technical discussion of the complicated questions regarding the form of Hab 2:3*b*-4 in the MT, the LXX, Qumran, early Christian authors, and in Hebrews, see Ellingworth 1993, 553-56.) Among the changes the preacher makes in his quotation of Hab 2:3*b*-4:

First, he cements the messianic interpretation of the passage (already present in the LXX) by adding ***the*** to the word for **coming**: *ho erchomenos*, **He who is coming** or "the Coming One" (ESV, HCSB, NLT, RSV). This leaves no doubt that the prophecy in Habakkuk concerns Christ's second coming.

Second, he transposes the two clauses in Hab 2:4 (LXX) and adds an adversative **and** (*kai*, "but" [GW, KJV, NJB, NLT]) between them. So in Hebrews the subject of the phrase **if he shrinks back** is not the coming deliverer (as in the

LXX) but is **my righteous one** (i.e., the person of faith). The inversion sets up two contrasting courses of action for believers: living by faith or shrinking back.

Third, he alters the LXX by attaching **my** to **righteous one** instead of **faith**. This (along with the inversion of clauses noted above) unambiguously identifies the **righteous one** as the believer. It switches the focus from God's faithfulness (as in the LXX) to the imperative for God's righteous people to live **by faith**. Hebrews embraces the assurance found in God's faithfulness (Heb 6:13-20; → 10:23). But here the emphasis is upon the responsibility of God's people to live in accord with divine faithfulness—**by faith**.

A bit of midrashic commentary in v 39 picks up two key terms from Hab 2:4 (Heb 10:38), in reverse order, creating a chiasm (Bengel 1877, 4:441):

10:38	But my righteous one will live by faith (*ek pisteōs*).	And if he shrinks back [*hyposteilētai*], I will not be pleased with him.
	x	
10:39	But we are not of those who shrink back [*hypostolēs*] and are destroyed,	but of those who believe [*pisteōs*] and are saved.

The author also detects alliteration in the Habakkuk text (v 38): *pisteōs* (faith), *hyposteilētai* (shrinks back), *psychē* (I). So he expands upon it in his brief commentary (v 39): *hypostolē* (shrink back), *apōleian* (**destruction**), *pisteōs* (**faith**), *peripoiēsin psychēs* (**preservation of life** [Attridge 1989, 304]). These rhetorical flourishes finalize the transition to ch 11. In an ear-catching way, v 39 presents the two paths readers may pursue, along with their respective consequences.

The preacher sets an encouraging pastoral tone in his application of the Habakkuk text (v 39). He does this by using the first person plural **we** (*hēmeis*; customary in Hebrews' hortatory sections; see 2:1-4; 3:1, 6; 4:1-3, 14-16; 6:1; 10:19-25; 12:1). Providing reassurance on the heels of a strong warning about divine judgment is an effective method of exhortation he has used before (→ 6:9 and 10:32-34).

In effect, our author invites his audience to acknowledge with him that **we are not of those who shrink back and are destroyed**. To **shrink back** (*hypostolēs*) is to be timid (BDAG, 1041). It is the opposite of having "confidence" (10:19, 35), but it also plays phonetically with another antonym, **endurance** (*hypomonēs* [10:36]). Fortitude is necessary, because slinking away from God's people (10:25) and abandoning one's confession (10:23) inevitably lead to **destruction** (*apōleian*). This is connected with the "eternal judgment" (6:2), described as the dreadful and fiery execution of divine justice (6:8; 10:27, 30-31; 12:26-29). It is falling under God's curse (6:8) and displeasure (10:38), rather than doing what is pleasing to God by aligning one's actions with his will (10:36; 13:21).

The readers must count themselves among **those who believe** (*pisteōs*) or "those who have faith" (ESV, HCSB, GW, LEB, NAB, NASB, NET, NRSV). **Faith** is directly opposed to **shrink**ing **back**. Lack of faith characterized the apostasy of the wilderness generation (3:12, 19; 4:2) and led to their destruction (3:16-18; 4:11). Readers must instead follow the example of those who through faith and perseverance inherit God's promise (6:12; 10:36).

Faith here is more than a mental assent to the truth or a mere profession of one's belief. It entails drawing near to God in "absolute trust" (10:22 NAB) and "confidence" (10:19, 35). It means holding on to the confession of hope (10:23) and committing oneself to the Christian community and its vital practices of love and well-doing (10:24-25). Such *faithfulness* involves courage and "perseverance" (10:32, 36). A long list of people who model this follows in ch 11.

The result of faithfulness is that we **are saved**. The expression is literally "preserving of the soul" (NASB). In classical literature this referred to saving one's life from death (Isocrates, *Phil.* 7; Xenophon, *Cyr.* 4.4.10). In the NT it refers to attaining eternal life (Luke 17:33; compare "receive salvation [*peripoiēsin sōterias*]" [1 Thess 5:9]; Koester 2001, 463; Thompson 2008, 223). From the beginning, the preacher has warned his audience not to ignore "such a great salvation" (2:3; see 1:14) or the Great High Priest who has procured it (2:10; 5:9; 9:28). Now, as earlier, though he must warn them about the dire consequences of apostasy, he is convinced "of better things" in their case—"things that accompany salvation" (6:9).

2. Worthy Examples of Faith (11:1-40)

BEHIND THE TEXT

Hebrews 11 has been called the faith chapter, the roll call of faith, the hall of faith, and even the Westminster Abbey of the Bible. A rhetorical jewel, it is arguably the most identifiable and accessible passage in Hebrews. Its persuasive power is as effective today as when it was first written, despite the fact that many oratorical gems lie hidden in the Greek text behind our English versions (some of which we will uncover; → In the Text below).

One rhetorical device is too prominent to be lost on anyone: the repetition of the expression "by faith" (*pistei*) to hammer home the theme of the chapter. Such repetition at the beginning of successive clauses or sentences, known as anaphora, is employed eighteen times in 11:3-31. Hebrews also uses the companion phrases "by faith [*kata pistin*]" (vv 7, 13) and "through faith [*dia (tēs) pisteōs*]" (vv 33, 39) twice each. The latter marks off the concluding paragraph (11:32-40). The noun "faith [*pistis*]" appears two more times (vv 1, 6), and the verb "believe [*pisteusai*]," once (v 6)—notably, all three in definitional statements. This brings the inventory of "faith" vocabulary in Heb 11 to twenty-five occurrences.

The author has composed an impressive list of figures from the past whose lives he considers worthy of emulation. Exempla or example lists were common among Greco-Roman orators (see Cosby 1988, esp. 93-105). Their purpose was generally not argumentative, but supportive and illustrative of the foregoing argument.

Example lists were common in Hellenistic-Jewish writings from the intertestamental period. Hebrews 11, like Sir 44—50, is a lengthy example list that begins at creation and is brought all the way up to date. It shares with Wis 10—11 and Philo (*Rewards* 10-11) the repetition of a controlling theme ("wisdom" and "hope" respectively). Hebrews 11 has in common with the lists in 4 Maccabees a focus on how the ancients endured great struggle or suffering (4 Macc 16:16-23; 18:11-19; see Thompson 2008, 227). Despite the parallels, few example lists possess the diverse and sophisticated rhetorical composition we find in Heb 11 (Cosby 1988, 17-24; see deSilva [2000a, 377-79] concerning Seneca's example list in *Ben.* 3.36.2—3.38.3).

The message of Heb 11 ought not be divorced from its surrounding context. The theme of "faith" is introduced in 10:35-39 with the quotation from Hab 2:3, 4 and finds its source and perfection in Christ (Heb 12:2). Indeed, 10:35-39 and 12:1-3 purposefully frame ch 11, particularly through the use of "endurance" vocabulary (10:32, 36; 12:1, 2, 3, 7). Hebrews 11 amply illustrates the kind of persevering faith the preacher urges his readers to emulate.

Yet Heb 11 possesses a compositional integrity of its own. This has led scholars to speculate that the author used an existing example list or synagogue sermon, which he has adapted to his purpose. Of course, it is possible that the author had previously developed a stand-alone sermonic piece, which he incorporated into the present homily (see Attridge 1989, 306-7; Lane 1991, 322-23). Such guesswork is fruitless. Signature motifs, vocabulary, and rhetorical ornamentation appear in abundance in Heb 11, as elsewhere in the sermon. The chapter is tightly integrated into the sermon as a whole (see Cosby 1988, 85-91). Thus, a prima facie case exists for the chapter as the author's own unique composition.

The chapter is enclosed within a complex *inclusio*. It includes references to "faith" (vv 1-7 || v 39), commendation of the ancients (vv 2, 4, 5 || v 39), and what is unseen (*ou/mēdepō blepomenōn* [vv 1, 7; compare vv 3, 5]) vs. what God has provided (v 40; lit., "has seen in advance [*problepsamenou*]"). The structure of individual subunits within the chapter is often difficult to discern, but the following summary captures the main lines of organization. Further patterns of organization will be noted in the In the Text comments that follow.

The example list begins with a working definition of faith (v 1), along with an explanatory note about the conferral of honor on the ancients who lived by faith (v 2). Then a large chunk is devoted to three great epochs of biblical history, dotted with anaphora ("by faith [*pistei*]"): creation to flood (vv 3-7); Abraham's sojourn in Canaan to Joseph's anticipation of the exodus out of Egypt (vv 8-22); and from Moses' upbringing to the conquest of Canaan (vv 23-31). The remainder of the recital begins with a rapid-fire naming of heroes in v 32 (four figures from the period of the Judges; Israel's greatest king, David; and Samuel and the prophets). This is followed by quick descriptions of the renowned deeds and suffering of unnamed biblical (and extrabiblical) characters (vv 33-38).

A closing comment states the import of the preceding heroes of faith (vv 39-40). The ancients were acclaimed, precisely because they persevered in faith that never attained its proper goal—at least not yet. God has planned for the whole community of faith, past and present, to experience the eschatological fulfillment of God's promises together.

IN THE TEXT

a. From Creation to Flood (11:1-7)

This paragraph opens with a definition of faith and an explanatory note about the commendation of the ancients for their faith (vv 1-2). The examples of faith proceed in vv 3-7 from creation to the salvation of Noah's family through the flood. The paragraph hangs together through repetition of the idea of commendation (in vv 2, 4, 5), which will be reprised only at the end of the example list (v 39). It is bounded by alliteration (with *p* in v 1; with *k* in v 7) and the similar phrases **we do not see** (v 1) and **things not yet seen** (v 7).

■ **I Faith** was brought into view in 10:38-39 through quotation and brief commentary on Hab 2:3*b*-4. In Heb 11:1 the preacher defines that **faith**. He continues to employ alliteration with *p* begun in 10:38-39 (→ 10:37-39). He also uses *homoioptōton* ("similar inflection") in which word endings have a similar sound (on this figure of speech, see Quintilian, *Inst.* 9.3.78-79; *Rhet. Her.* 4.20.28; see Cosby 1988, 82; → 1:3 sidebar, "Christology in Rhyme"). Observe these two figures of speech: **Now faith [*pistis*] is being sure [*hypostasis*] of what we hope for [*elpizomenōn*] and certain of what [*pragmatōn*] we do not see** (*ou blepomenōn*).

As was the custom of ancient philosophers and rhetoricians, the author presents a concise definition before elaborating on his subject (Thompson 2008, 229; see Quintilian, *Inst.* 7.3.1-35). It is not meant to be comprehensive. It is a working definition, drawing attention to those aspects of faith the preacher wishes to celebrate in the following examples. The definition was probably crystal clear to the Greek speakers who first heard it. But the supple, richly ornamented phrasing has created problems for later commentators, whose native tongue is not Koine Greek. In particular, the Greek words behind **being sure of** and **certain** have engendered considerable debate.

The noun *hypostasis* (**being sure of**) is the most difficult to translate, for it has such a broad range of possible meanings. Etymologically, the word refers to "that which stands under." This sense seems primary to its many uses: basis, foundation, support, guarantee, possession, existence, deposit, pledge (Hollander 1993; LSJ, 1895; LSJ rev. supp., 303; BDAG, 1040-41; see Hughes 1977, 439-40, and Johnson 2006, 277-78, for a review of interpretive options).

The widespread practice of translating the word in the subjective sense—**being sure of** (NCV, NET, TNIV; "assurance" [ESV, NASB, NRSV]; or "confidence" [NIV[11]; see NLT])—complicates the interpretation. Erasmus first defended this view (followed by Melanchthon and Luther in the sixteenth century). This inspired the rendering "sure confidence" in English versions (e.g., Tyndale, Coverdale, and the Great Bible; Attridge 1989, 308; Bruce 1990, 277 n. 6). A number of recent commentators hold this view (Bruce 1990, 277; Pfitzner 1997, 155; G. Guthrie 1998, 374; Koester 2001, 472; Witherington 2007, 298-300).

Strong contextual reasons support this translation. There is the proximity of "confidence" (10:19, 35) and "full assurance of faith" (10:22) in the preceding context. Their opposite, "shrinking back [*hyposteilētai, hypostolēs*]" in 10:38, 39, may also be playfully placed in contrast to *hypostasis*, "standing firm" in 11:1. But the Achilles' heel of this interpretation is that *hypostasis* is nowhere used in the subjective or psychological sense of confidence or assurance (BDAG, 1041). Nevertheless, one cannot ignore those instances in which the word could mean "steadfastness" or "perseverance" (see Koester 2001, 472; Delitzsch 1872, 2:210).

The Greek fathers universally took the word in the objective, philosophical sense of "essence" or "substance." That is, *hypostasis* is "reality" as opposed to what is merely apparent. It is "that which gives true existence" to an object (Westcott 1909, 352-53; see Chrysostom 1996, 463; Heen and Krey 2005, 176). This is reflected in the English translations "substance" (KJV; "gives substance" [REB]) or "reality" (CEB, HCSB). This view has been adopted by a number of modern commentators (see Attridge 1989, 309-10; Lane 1991, 328-29; Cosby 1988, 34). A variation sees *hypostasis* as faith's "realization" of things hoped for (NAB; Thompson 2008, 230).

The problem with this view is that it interjects a philosophical explanation that becomes entangled in confusion and contradiction. To say that the Son is the exact imprint of God's "being" or "essence [*hypostaseōs*]" (1:3) clearly utilizes the philosophical meaning of the word and makes perfect sense. But to assert, in the philosophical sense, that faith *is* the "substance" or "reality [*hypostasis*]" of our hope flatly negates the point the author is making (Johnson 2006, 277). The entire chapter reinforces the point that faith lays claim to God's promise and looks forward to its realization. But the faithful have *not* yet attained the reality of God's promised city and heavenly homeland. They only anticipate it from afar. Chrysostom's analogy of the resurrection as not now substantial (*hypostasis*), but that hope makes it substantial in our soul, fails to clarify the philosophical interpretation of 11:1 (1996, 463). It illustrates how abstract and incoherent this view is.

Other key terms in vv 1-2—"proof [*elenchos*]" (HCSB) and "were attested [*emartyrēthēsan*]" (NAB)—suggest that our author is moving in a legal, rather than philosophical, sphere. Instances in ancient Greek papyri attest to the legal usage of *hypostasis* as a "guarantee of ownership/entitlement" or "title deed" (MM, 659-60; BDAG, 1041; Spicq 1994c, 423). A number of scholars embrace this view (Spicq 1953, 2:336-38; Koester 1972, 579-80; Hughes 1977, 439-40; deSilva 2000a, 383). Others find this interpretation attractive, but reject it because of a purported lack of evidence for this meaning in the context (Bruce 1990, 277; G. Guthrie 1998, 374; Witherington 2007, 299 n. 609).

However, there is ample contextual support for understanding *hypostasis* as a "guarantee" (NJB). We should note, first, that the word was used earlier in a related, though not identical sense, within a context filled with technical legal terminology concerning business dealings (→ 3:14; deSilva 2000a, 385). Ownership, inheritance, and receiving God's promise or reward are concepts that surround and give shape to the definition in 11:1.

This is so in the preceding context. David Worley argues that we should read 11:1 in light of the community's loss of property in the past (Worley 1981, 87-92, cited in deSilva 2000a, 383). They suffered loss, knowing that they have "better and lasting possessions" (10:34). Holding on to their confidence and persevering in doing God's will eventually result in great reward and the reception of God's promise (10:35-36). Finally, "preservation" or "salvation" (*peripoiēsin*) in 10:39 refers to obtaining, acquiring, or gaining possession of something (LSJ, 1384).

The commercial legal connotation of faith as a "guarantee" or "title deed" finds further support throughout ch 11. Faith establishes one as an "heir" (vv 7, 8, 9) of God's promises (vv 11, 13, 17, 33, 39). It deems God's "reward" as more precious than earthly treasures (v 26; see v 6). It expects to enjoy fully the better, heavenly homeland (vv 15-16*a*), the city God has created for the faithful (vv 10, 16*b*).

If this interpretation is correct, faith is the certificate of ownership, the title deed that lays claim to the future realities **we hope for.** Coordinated with this is another legal expression in 11:1*b*: faith is the objective "evidence" (KJV, NAB) or "proof" (CEB, HCSB, LEB) of **what we do not see.** As with *hypostasis*, the term *elenchos* does not have a subjective meaning. Thus, translations like **certain,** "convinced" (NET; see GW, REB), "conviction" (ESV, NASB, NRSV), or "assurance" (NIV[11]) are unjustified. (On the paltry evidence for a subjective interpretation, see Koester 2001, 473.)

Forensically, *elenchos* is irrefutable evidence for the truth of something— "proof, proving" (BDAG, 315). With respect to the actual nature of things, or what is alleged to be the case, it is a necessary proof (e.g., living persons require food). With regard to one's opponent's allegations, it is a refutation based on what is impossible by nature (e.g., that a small boy stole a sum of money larger than he could carry; thus, *Rhet. Alex.* 1431a7-21; see deSilva 2000a, 384). The author of Hebrews has frequently argued on the basis either of necessity (*anankē* [7:12, 27; 8:3; 9:16, 23]; *dei* [9:26]) or impossibility (*adynaton* [6:4, 18; 10:4]). In 11:6 the author presents a proof about faith that incorporates both impossibility and necessity.

Hebrews makes a bold claim about faith—one that sounded as nonsensical in the ancient world as it does today. **Faith** (*pistis*) was a state of mind attributed to the uneducated who were not trained in rational argumentation and the rules of evidence (Lane 1991, 316). Yet Hebrews speaks of faith as guarantee and proof! It guarantees the possession **of what we hope for,** that is, future realities not yet realized (on **hope** → 6:11; 7:19; 10:23). It is evidence for unseen, transcendent realities **we do not see.**

What imbues faith with such an absolute quality of legal certainty is the nature of God himself. God's promise, confirmed by his oath, gives clear expression to his unchanging purpose (6:13-20). It "puts an end to all argument" (6:16). Faith is the necessary response to the divine promises, because the One who made them is himself utterly trustworthy (10:23; 11:11; see 2:17; 3:2, 5-6).

■ **2** The definition in 11:1 establishes the forward-looking quality of faith. Verse 2 completes the introduction to the example list by pointing backward to **the ancients** whose lives of faith received God's approval. **This,** namely, the expectant faith defined in v 1, is what they **were commended for** (*emartyrēthēsan*). Up to this point in Hebrews, the verb *martyreō* has been used to indicate the testimony of God (or the Holy Spirit) in Scripture (7:8, 17; 10:15; see also 2:4, 6). The passive form in 11:2, 4, 5, and 39 is a "theological passive," implying that God is the One who has borne testimony to the people of faith in the past.

While *martyreō* and its cognates have a distinctly legal character, they were also used to make public declarations of recognition or praise. Benefactors or city councils employed this vocabulary to confer honor on individuals deemed worthy of commendation. Their favorable testimony was officially memorialized in inscriptions (deSilva 2000a, 385). How much greater is the testimony of God to the faithful of the past, inscribed in Holy Scripture?

■ **3** The example list does not start with one of the faithful worthies, as v 2 would lead us to expect. It begins appropriately at the beginning with creation (Gen 1:1). The nature of the case allows for no direct human observation or response to God's creative acts. So the author directs his attention to the present community of faith—**we** (see Heb 10:39). He will address the Christian community again in his concluding comments (11:40), making obvious the pastoral motivation behind the historical review in this chapter.

By faith indicates the way believers know what cannot be seen with the natural eye. **We understand** (*nooumen*) expresses the cognitive function of faith. Given the choice of terminology (having to do with the "mind [*nous*]"), as well as the previous rational argument for God as Creator (3:4), it is clear that faith does not bypass the human intellect. Faith is a valid means of gaining knowledge about divine activity. Hebrews articulates the kernel of a theological truth later expanded upon by Augustine and Anselm: "faith seeking understanding" (Koester 2001, 480 n. 377).

That the universe was formed is (lit.) *the ages were arranged* ("the worlds were set in order" [NET]). *The ages* is a "grand plural" intimating that all things in heaven and earth, visible and invisible, are coursing onward in accordance with divine aims (Bengel 1877, 4:447; → 1:2c). That they are "ordered" (NAB) or "prepared" (NASB) indicates more than their creation. Their arrangement denotes God's sovereign governance and providence over every dimension of time and space. **At God's command** is (lit.) "by the word of God" (most English versions). According to 1:3b, the Son upholds all things "by his powerful word."

The affirmation **what is seen was not made out of what was visible** evokes the second half of the definition of faith in → 11:1. This is not a formulation of the doctrine of creation *ex nihilo* ("out of nothing")—true as that is. Rather, it reiterates an axiom underlying the thought-world of Hebrews: the unseen, transcendent realm is superior to the visible creation (→ 8:2; 9:11, 24). The invisible realm antedates the creation of the visible universe (11:3). The transcendent is permanent, but God will shake and remove the temporal world of "created things" (12:26-28; deSilva 2000a, 387).

The point of this verse is not metaphysical but religious. The way we relate to God and his purposes is **by faith.** This theme will be repeated throughout this chapter. But whereas faith in v 3 is the means of insight into God's grand creative action in the past, the faith of the ancients was consistently directed toward an unseen future (vv 7, 10, 16, 20, 22, 26, 27, 35).

■ **4** Notably, the first pair, Adam and Eve, do not appear in this example list—not even as examples of disbelief. Alas, they did nothing worthy of commendation, but only condemnation, so they are excluded (Clarke 1977, 3:762; contrast Wis 10:1-2). The first person of faith listed is **Abel**, the righteous son of Adam and Eve.

Verse 4 of Heb 11 alludes to the actions leading up to Abel's murder by his brother Cain recorded in Gen 4:2b-12: **By faith Abel offered God a better sacrifice than Cain did.** The preacher's midrash is developed by looking at this episode through the lenses of Hab 2:4 (Heb 10:38) and the explanatory statement in 11:2. For this reason, what made Abel's offering superior to Cain's was that Abel offered it **by faith** (*pistei*). Also **by faith** Abel was approved **as a righteous man.** The OT never describes Abel as *dikaios* (**righteous**), though it is attributed to him in later tradition (Matt 23:35; 1 John 3:12; Josephus,

Ant. 1.53; see *Jub.* 4:31). In Hebrews the oracle in Hab 2:4, "But my righteous one will live by faith," suggests that Abel's actions were guided by his **faith** and **righteous** character.

He was commended . . . when God spoke well of his offerings. This is in keeping with God's commendation of the ancients for their faith (11:2). Yet one more element from Hab 2:4 ("my righteous one *will live* by faith" [emphasis added]) is borne out in the life, or rather, the death of Abel. **And by faith he still speaks, even though he is dead** likely alludes to Abel's blood crying out to God from the ground (Gen 4:10; compare Heb 12:24). Since Abel is speaking postmortem, he must be alive in some sense (perhaps as one of "the spirits of righteous men" [12:23]; see 4 Macc 7:18-19; 16:25; Luke 20:38; Attridge 1989, 317; deSilva 2000a, 388-89; Johnson 2006, 281). Philo reads Gen 4:10 in a strikingly similar fashion (viewing Abel as an allegory of the human soul). He interprets Abel's crying out to mean that, paradoxically, he is both dead and alive. "He is dead, indeed, having been slain by the foolish mind, but he lives according to the happy life which is in God" (*Worse* 48).

■ **5** The assessment of **Enoch** depends on the biblical record (Gen 5:24 LXX). But our author surely knew other traditions about Enoch's translation into heaven. Therefore, three times he repeats: **Enoch was taken** (*metetethē*), **God had taken him away** (*metethēken*), and **before he was taken** (*metatheseōs*). The preacher also makes three interpretive additions to the biblical text:

- First, he asserts that Enoch's removal happened **by faith.**
- Second, he adds **that he did not experience death** to explain what Genesis meant by his being **taken.**
- Third, the preacher claims that God **commended** him because of his faith, like the other ancients (Heb 11:2).

The Scriptures do not explicitly state that Enoch acted in faith or that God commended him. The preacher is not content with leaving the matter implicit. He seizes upon the biblical comment that Enoch **pleased God,** the LXX's interpretation of the Hebrew text's "walked with God" (Gen 5:22, 24). In Heb 11:6 the author will argue that pleasing God is tantamount to living by faith.

■ **6** Hebrews often argues on the basis of necessity or impossibility (→ 11:1). Here the preacher presents a veritable "proof [*elenchos*]" incorporating both kinds of argument:

First, the impossibility: **without faith it is impossible to please God.** The preacher infers that, since Enoch "pleased God" (v 5), he must have been "taken away" because of his exemplary **faith.**

The second argument, from necessity (**must,** *dei*), presents two fundamental tenets of faith: belief in God's existence and justice. These apply to **anyone who comes** [*ton proserchomenon*] **to God.** This is Hebrews' standard expression for someone who "draw[s] near" (ESV, HCSB) or "approach[es]" (NAB, NET, NRSV) God in worship (4:16; 7:25; 10:1, 22; 12:18, 22). To **believe that** God exists echoes creedal formulae developed in Hellenistic-Jewish synagogues (see Lane 1991, 338). "Faith in God" (6:1) is foundational to Christian teaching. So is belief in divine justice ("eternal judgment" [6:2]), here related positively: **that he rewards [***misthpodotēs***] those who earnestly seek him** (see 2:2; 11:26; → 10:35). These comport with the nature of faith as a guarantee of "what we hope for" and proof of "what we do not see" (11:1; Thompson 2008, 233).

■ **7** The beginning of the entry on Noah clearly echoes the definition of faith in 11:1: God warned **Noah . . . about things not yet seen.** Noah heeded the prophetic warning (BDAG, 1089), just as Moses did in building the tabernacle (8:5). Noah **built an ark to save his family.** He did so **in holy fear.** This accents Noah's reverent obedience (→ 5:7).

By his faith, Noah **condemned the world.** Popular tradition styled him as "a preacher of righteousness" (2 Pet 2:5) or repentance (*1 Clem.* 7.5; *Sib. Or.* 1:125-30). Perhaps, simply by his actions, he "put the whole world in the wrong" (REB). Noah was widely regarded as a "righteous" man (Gen 6:9; 7:1; Ezek 14:14, 20; Sir 44:17; Josephus, *Ant.* 1.99; frequently in Philo, e.g., *Alleg. Interp.* 3.77; *Abraham* 27, 31). But Hebrews' claim that he **became an heir of the righteousness that comes by faith** depends on Hab 2:4 (→ Heb 10:38). Despite its "Pauline ring," the phrasing must be interpreted in light of 10:36-39 and the patriarch's bold acts noted here in 11:7. The author refers here to righteous action borne out of confident and persevering faith in God's revelation concerning the future (Attridge 1989, 319-20; deSilva 2000a, 392).

The first paragraph of the example list (vv 1-7)—spanning from the creation of the world to its destruction by the flood—ends as it began with alliteration (→ 11:1). Only here it involves the repeated *k*-sound in words: **warned** (*ch*rēmatistheis), **built** (*k*ateskeuasen), **ark** (*k*ibōton), **family** (oi*k*ou), **condemned** (*k*atekrinen), **world** (*k*osmon), **by faith** (*k*ata pistin), **righteousness** (di*k*aiosynēs), and **heir** (*k*lēronomos). The last word in the paragraph (**heir**) is a catchword linking to the next subunit. There the preacher will introduce Abraham, Isaac, and Jacob in terms of "inheritance" and as "heirs" of God's promise (11:8, 9).

b. From Abraham to Joseph (11:8-22)

Hebrews has already presented Abraham as an example of faith (6:13-18). So it is no surprise that the list in ch 11 devotes more space to Abraham than to any other OT figure. It is remarkable, however, that among the details selected to illustrate the patriarch's life "by faith" (11:8, 9, 11, 17), there is no mention of the one OT text that explicitly states that Abraham "believed" God (Gen 15:6). This text is crucial to other NT discussions of the nature of Abraham's faith (Rom 4:3, 9, 22; Gal 3:6; Jas 2:23). So it is all the more conspicuous by its absence here. This subunit has three paragraphs:

- Hebrews 11:8-12 summarizes God's two promises to Abraham: land (vv 8-10) and descendants (vv 11-12).

- Verses 13-16 take up the first of these promises, arguing that it was not Canaan but God's heavenly city that Abraham and his descendants anticipated.
- Verses 17-22 take up the promise of descendants, illustrating how faith in God's promises and blessing repeatedly looked beyond the peril of death.

■ **8-10** From the Abraham cycle in Gen 12—22, the preacher summarizes Abraham's call and subsequent sojourn in **the promised land**. Abraham undertook two sets of actions **by faith**. First, he was obedient to God's call (Heb 11:8). Second, he and his immediate descendants lived in the land of promise as nomads (v 9). Verse 10 supplies the rationale behind Abraham's implicit faith.

When called, Abraham **obeyed and went.** Obedience is rarely attributed to Abraham in explicit terms in the OT (Gen 22:18; 26:5). But it is central to Hebrews' understanding of faithfulness. The wilderness generation revealed their unbelief by their disobedience (Heb 3:18; 4:6, 11). The Son exemplified faithfulness by suffering, through which he "learned obedience" (5:8). The preacher calls upon his hearers to obey the Son (5:9). Abraham put feet to his obedience. Three times the text mentions his going:

- **when called to go** (*exelthein*)
- Abraham **obeyed and went** (*exēlthen*)
- **even though he did not know where he was going** (*erchetai*)

The future orientation of faith (→ 11:1) is obvious in Abraham's obedience to God's call to **a place he would later receive as his inheritance** (*klēronomian*). We learn in v 10, however, that this **place** is not identical with **the promised land** in which he would live out his mortal life. Abraham's descendants, **Isaac and Jacob,** were **co-heirs** [*synklēronomōn*] **with him of the same promise.** Both Jewish and Christian expectations saw the believer's **inheritance** as heavenly (*2 En.* 9:1; 10:6; 55:2; 1 Pet 1:4; Rev 21:7; see Heb 11:16).

Abraham did not put down roots in the land of Canaan. **He made his home . . . like a stranger in a foreign country.** The transient nature of Abraham's existence in Canaan is indicated by his living **in tents**, rather than building houses, planting crops or vineyards, and further leveraging his wealth and power.

On the surface it seems paradoxical that Abraham, Isaac, and Jacob would dwell in the land of promise as strangers. Why did Abraham continue to live as a "wandering Aramean" (Deut 26:5)? Why did the one who would receive the whole world as an inheritance (Rom 4:13), not even own a plot three cubits long (Theodoret of Cyr in Heen and Krey 2005, 187)? Hebrews 11:10 provides the rationale: **For he was looking forward to the city with foundations.** His **looking forward to** entailed "waiting" (GNT, GW, NCV; see NKJV). The same verb (*ekdechomai*) describes Christ's waiting for the defeat of his enemies (10:13). A cognate describes believers as waiting for Christ's second coming (9:28).

In saying that Abraham was expecting **the city,** Hebrews draws on apocalyptic expectations of the new Jerusalem. According to one Jewish apocalyptic work, God showed Abraham this transcendent heavenly city (*2 Bar.* 4:4). Another states that it has "huge foundations" (*4 Ezra* 10:27; see Rev 21:14, 19). This understanding of the heavenly Jerusalem logically extends the OT claim that God laid the foundations of the earthly city of Jerusalem (Pss 48:8; 87:1, 5; Isa 14:32 LXX). Other NT authors affirm that believers' citizenship is in heaven (Phil 3:20), in "the Jerusalem that is above" (Gal 4:26) that will come down out of heaven (Rev 21:2, 10-14, 19-20).

The stability and permanence of the city's **foundations** are in direct contrast to the patriarchs' **tents,** which signify transient, nomadic life. **The city with foundations** corresponds to the "better and lasting possessions" the readers hope for (10:34). It is the "enduring city" still to come (13:14), which the preacher describes in 12:22-24. What makes the city well-established and unshakable (see 12:28) is that its **architect and builder is God.** It belongs to that same realm, "not a part of this creation," whose greater and more perfect tabernacle was not made by human hands (9:11, 24).

■ **11-12** Students of the Bible who like to compare translations will notice that a major difference exists between the translations of 11:11 in the NIV and NIV[11]. In the NIV the subject of the sentence is **Abraham**—a word that does not even appear in the Greek text, but may be implied. In NIV[11] the subject of the sentence is **Sarah.** The issues involved are highly technical (see Greenlee 1990; Hagner 2002, 148), and commentators and translators are divided (**Abraham:** GW, NAB, NET, NRSV; Bruce 1990, 294-96; Ellingworth 1993, 586-89; Hagner 1990, 192; Lane 1991, 353-54; **Sarah:** ESV, HCSB, KJV, NASB, NJB, REB; Chrysostom 1996, 471; Hughes 1977, 471-72; France 2006, 153; Johnson 2006, 291-92).

Grammatically, **Sarah** makes the best sense as the subject of the sentence. The major impediment to this construal is the idiom *katabolē spermatos.* It is a technical expression for "sowing seed," applicable only to the male role in reproduction (BDAG, 515). This justifies the NIV's **become a father.** However, the full statement is that Sarah (lit.) *received power for the sowing of seed.* This supports the NIV[11]'s "was enabled to bear children." Sarah *received power,* although she was **barren** and **past age** for having children. Abraham, of course, deposited the seed (France 2006, 153; Johnson 2006, 292).

Regardless of who is the focus of this sentence (Sarah or Abraham), the point is unchanged. God enabled this aged couple to become parents because they trusted in his faithfulness. Hebrews passes over instances of their disbelief in God's promise (e.g., Sarah's cynical laughter in Gen 18:10-15). That a barren woman conceived a child at ninety is evidence enough that she ultimately **considered him faithful who had made the promise.** This recalls the reason why the preacher's hearers were to hold on to their confession (Heb 10:23). The statement has a creedal resonance (see 1 Cor 10:13; 2 Cor 1:18; 1 Thess 5:24; 2 Thess 3:3; 2 Tim 2:13; 1 John 1:9; Rev 1:5; Pfitzner 1997, 160).

Hebrews 11:12 concludes the summary concerning Abraham in 11:8-12: **And so from this one man . . . came descendants.** The parenthetical comment that Abraham was **as good as dead** does not express the hyperbole sharply enough. The Greek text reads ***and dead at that*** (deSilva 2000a, 398). Paul makes a similar point about the deadness of Abraham's body and Sarah's womb (Rom 4:19). That God granted progeny to one who was **dead** (reproductively speaking), introduces a theme repeated in 11:17-20. The object of true faith is the One who is able to conquer death (2:14-15; 5:7; 7:16, 25).

The vast number of Abraham's posterity, **as numerous as the stars in the sky and as countless as the sand on the seashore,** is a pastiche of descriptive language from several texts (esp. Gen 22:17; Exod 32:13; and Pr Azar 13). Note the purposeful contrast between **from this one man,** dead as he was, and his **numerous,** even **countless** descendants.

■ **13** Having summarized God's two promises to Abraham in vv 8-12 (land and descendants), the preacher now expands upon the first of them in vv 13-16. The rhythm of anaphora ("by faith [*pistei*]") is broken with these verses. Verse 13 opens with a comparable expression, *Kata pistin,* **by faith.** The author emphasizes that **all these people** who believed in God **died** without receiving what was promised. The balance of the passage (through v 22) clarifies that **all these people** were Abraham and his descendants, at least through to Joseph (note the repeated mention of death in vv 19, 21, 22).

Their actions reveal not only that **they did not receive the things promised** before they **died,** but that they did not expect to do so.

First, they **saw** and **welcomed** the promises **from a distance.** The image is of someone saluting his homeland or native city from afar (Lane 1991, 356). The idea of ***greeting*** (**welcomed**) involved embracing something or someone as dear to oneself ("embraced" [KJV]) or as a source of great satisfaction or joy ("rejoiced" [GW]). Jesus expressed a similar thought in John 8:56: "Your father Abraham rejoiced at the thought of seeing my day; he saw it and was glad" (Bengel 1877, 4:449; see also Matt 13:16-17; Luke 10:24).

Second, **they admitted that they were aliens and strangers on earth.** The content of their confession (*homologēsantes,* "they confessed" [CEB, HCSB, KJV, NASB, NRSV]; **admitted**) is reminiscent of Abraham's statement in Gen 23:4: "I am an alien and a stranger among you" (see Gen 24:37). They acknowledged that they were **aliens** (*xenoi*) or "foreigners" (HCSB, NLT). They were also **strangers** (*parepidēmoi*), "exiles" (ESV, NASB, RSV), "temporary residents" (HCSB, LEB), or "nomads" (NJB, NLT; compare "pilgrims" [KJV]). The magnitude of the patriarchs' (and the readers') alien status is in the fact that they were foreigners not simply in a particular country, but **on earth.**

Aliens and Strangers

Foreigners were disenfranchised in ancient societies. They were rootless and adrift in the land in which they temporarily dwelled. Relegated to a lower status, they had a standing only slightly higher than that of enemies. Without the privileges of citizenship or social connections, they were vulnerable to abuse, insult, loss of property, and in extreme cases even death (see deSilva 2000a, 394-95; Witherington 2007, 310-12).

The preacher's audience could identify with the plight of the patriarchs. They, too, had experienced alienation (Heb 6:18) and shame from their neighbors (10:32-34). They were treated like **aliens and strangers on earth.**

■ **14-16** Verses 14-16 draw a conclusion from the foregoing facts. Hebrews uses what Quintilian considered the most effective enthymeme: a reason joined together with a dissimilar or contrary proposition (*Inst.* 5.14.4; see *Rhet. Her.* 4.30.41). The reason is in v 14: *For* **people who say such things show that they are looking for a country of their own.** The contrary proposition (v 15) is stated in contrast to the actual state of affairs (v 16a). This is followed by a conclusion in v 16b.

It is really no paradox that the patriarchs lived as aliens and strangers in the "promised land" (11:9). Since they chose not to settle permanently in Canaan, it stands to reason that they were really **looking for a country of their own.** The author refers to their "homeland" (CEB, ESV, HCSB, LEB, NAB, NET, NJB, NKJV, NLT, NRSV; "fatherland" [BDAG, 788]). This conjured up strong feelings of belonging, attachment, and loyalty. Homer said, "Nothing is sweeter than one's native land" (*Od.* 9.34). Odysseus valued returning to his homeland above immortality (Cicero, *Leg.* 2.1 §3; Koester 2001, 490).

This reason is supported by a contrary-to-fact argument in v 15. **If they had been thinking of the country they had left, they would have had opportunity to return.** Abraham's homeland was Ur of the Chaldeans in southern Mesopotamia, then Haran in northern Mesopotamia. In obedience to God's call, the patriarchs *went out from* (→ 11:8) these places (Gen 12:4-5; 15:7). Since they never attempted to resettle in them, it is evident that these places were not their real homeland.

Instead, they were longing for a better country or *homeland* (Heb 11:16a). The object of their intense **longing** (*oregontai*; see Attridge 1989, 332) was a homeland **better** than any other. **Better** (*kreittonos*) is a favorite term in Hebrews, associated with the superior provisions and blessings of the new covenant (→ 1:4 sidebar, "'Better' Things in Hebrews"). The author explains (*that is;* a dash [—] in the NIV) that the homeland is **a heavenly one.** In so doing he echoes a sentiment popular among Greco-Roman philosophers and early Christians: their true citizenship is in the city of God or in heaven (see Attridge 1989, 330; deSilva 2000a, 401-2; → 11:10, "the city with foundations").

11:13-16

The patriarchs' expectation, desire, and loyalty for their heavenly homeland cannot be separated from their devotion to God. The city they sought is "the city with foundations, whose architect and builder is God" (11:10), in short, "the city of the living God" (12:22). **Therefore** (*dio*), the preacher concludes in v 16b, **God is not ashamed to be called their God.** This may well be an allusion to the covenant formula naming God as "the God of Abraham, Isaac, and Jacob" (see Exod 3:6, 15-16; 4:5; Matt 22:32; Mark 12:26; Luke 20:37; Acts 3:13; 7:32). **For he has prepared a city for them** illustrates how God greatly rewards those who persevere in faith (see Heb 10:35-36; 11:6, 26; Johnson 2006, 293).

■ **17-19** Verse 17 resumes the anaphoric **by faith** (*pistei*), utilized with little interruption until v 32. The topic of Abraham and his descendants, introduced in vv 11-12, is picked up again in vv 17-22. A subtheme that holds this paragraph together is the repeated mention of how faith looks beyond death for the fulfillment of God's promise and blessing (vv 19, 21, 22).

Verses 17-19 bring into view the episode in Gen 22:1-19, known in rabbinic tradition as the Akedah or "Binding" of Isaac. Hebrews, like Judaism, regards the offering of Isaac as the supreme demonstration of Abraham's faith (*Jub.* 17:15-18; 18:16; Sir 44:20; 1 Macc 2:52; *'Abot* 5:3). That **God tested** [*peirazomenos*] **him** is significant in Hebrews. It is overshadowed by the testing of Jesus through suffering, which enabled him to identify with the readers' experience of testing (2:18; 4:15).

The concise description in 11:17 captures the drama of the moment when Abraham reached for the sacrificial knife. Two forms of the verb *prospherō* tell the tale. The perfect tense (**offered . . . as a sacrifice**) indicates that, in terms of Abraham's resolve, the sacrifice was as good as done (compare Philo, *Abraham* 177). The imperfect tense (**about to sacrifice**) pictures Abraham in the process of offering up his son (Westcott 1909, 367; Hughes 1977, 482).

Abraham's faithfulness in offering up **Isaac** is sharpened by three overlapping facts, indicating how this test of obedience required the patriarch to act paradoxically in conflict with the divine promises.

- First, Abraham is **he who had received the promises** (v 17), that is, "the one who assumed the responsibility" of the promises (MM, 32; Lane 1991, 361; compare 7:6).
- Second, Abraham offered his **one and only son** (*monogenē*). Isaac was "unique" (HCSB), not only as Abraham's one true son by his wife, Sarah, but as the only son of the promise (BDAG, 658; Fitzmyer 1991).
- Third, God himself made the promise, which Hebrews quotes verbatim from Gen 21:12 LXX: **It is through Isaac that your offspring will be reckoned** (v 18).

Hebrews does not view Abraham's obedience as a sheer "leap of faith" (Kierkegaard). Verse 19 explains the rationale behind Abraham's willingness to commit such an unthinkable act: he **reasoned that God could raise the**

dead. This was a tenet of faith for Jews and Christians (Deut 32:39; 1 Sam 2:6; Rom 4:17), famously articulated in the second of the Eighteen Benedictions: "Blessed are you, O Lord, who makes the dead alive" (Koester 2001, 491). This confession was commonly integrated into retellings of the Akedah, a detail with which Hebrews may have been familiar (Lane 1991, 363).

Abraham **did receive Isaac back from death.** But he did so **figuratively speaking** (ESV, NIV, NJB, NRSV; see GNT, GW, KJV, NET, NIV[11], NLT, REB). There seems to be a typological significance in the phrase *en parabolē* ("as an illustration" [HCSB]; "as a symbol" [NAB]; "as a type" [NASB]; "in a foreshadowing" [Lane 1991, 362]). There is a typological meaning in the only other instance of the word *parabolē* in Hebrews (9:9). There it refers symbolically to the limited function of the wilderness tabernacle, which would be transcended at the end of the ages (→ 9:26). Here in 11:19, the sparing of Isaac prefigures "the resurrection of the dead" (6:2) or "better resurrection" (11:35) anticipated by the faithful.

■ **20-22** This portion of the example list, related to Abraham's descendants, touches only on the major characters of the second half of Genesis: Isaac (v 20), Jacob (v 21), and Joseph (v 22). It spotlights actions undertaken by each of them as they faced death.

Verse 20 alludes to Isaac's deathbed blessing of his two sons in Gen 27 (see Gen 27:41*b*). There is no trace of the intrigue or pathos from the scene. Esau's fatal decision will only later serve as a warning in Heb 12:16-17. The focus here is on the fact that **Isaac blessed Jacob and Esau.**

The content of the benedictions in Genesis (27:27-29, 39-40) was surely **in regard to their future.** The Greek text of Heb 11:20, however, indicates that Isaac's blessing—pronounced as it was **by faith**—was much more far-seeing (11:1). Isaac spoke "even regarding things to come" (*kai peri mellontōn,* NASB). Isaac was one of the patriarchs who saw and welcomed a better homeland from afar (vv 13-16*a*). He anticipated "the city that is to come" (13:14; see 11:10, 16*b*) and all the blessings in "the world to come" (2:5; compare "the coming age" in 6:5 and "the good things that are coming" in 10:1).

Verse 21 turns to the scene in which **Jacob . . . blessed each of Joseph's sons** (Gen 48:8-20). Nothing is made of Jacob's favoring the younger brother, Ephraim, over the firstborn, Manasseh. More important is the timing of the blessing, **when he was dying,** and the manner of its pronouncement. Though Jacob was about to expire without enjoying the fulfillment of God's promises, **by faith** he handed on God's promise of blessing to his grandsons. To the end, he **worshiped** God and exhibited complete trust in him (citing Gen 47:31; for the connection of faith and worship, see Heb 4:14, 16; 10:22; 11:6).

As with Isaac and Jacob, v 22 focuses on the dying actions of **Joseph, when his end was near.** Many incidents in Joseph's life illustrate his trust in divine providence. But the final scene in Genesis (50:22-26) accents the forward-looking aspect of his last acts. Hebrews describes them as done **by faith,** summarizing Joseph's two principal actions: First, he **spoke about the exodus of the Israelites from Egypt.** Second, his faith was such a guarantee and proof of God's promises (see 11:1) that he **gave instructions** to bury **his bones** in the "promised land" (11:9). This demonstrates his faith that God would deliver the Israelites from Egypt (Gen 50:25; Exod 13:19; Josh 24:32).

c. From Moses to Rahab (11:23-31)

Hebrews 11:8-22 devoted most of its space to celebrating the faith of Abraham and Sarah (vv 8-12, 17-19), followed by three snapshots of their immediate descendants (vv 20-22). Although lacking an explanatory interlude (like that in vv 13-16), 11:23-31 follows a similar pattern.

- Verses 23-28 present a succinct faith biography of Moses.
- Verses 29-31 recount the sequel to Moses' faith in three brief descriptions of key events related to the exodus from Egypt and the conquest of Canaan.

Structurally, the passage has two paragraphs. The first paragraph (vv 23-28) is marked by an *inclusio* that highlights a lack of fear on the basis of seeing something (vv 23, 27). The core of the paragraph (vv 24-26) emphasizes Moses' choice of solidarity with God's people and the coming Messiah. He accepted mistreatment and disgrace and renounced Egyptian privilege and wealth, preferring God's future reward. Verse 28 transitions to the next paragraph with rhetorical flair (alliteration and *homoioptōton*; → 11:1, 28). Its reference to Passover introduces the theme of the second paragraph (vv 29-31): the salvation of believers and destruction of unbelievers (see Koester 2001, 507).

■ **23** Logically, **by faith** is associated with **Moses' parents** (see CEV, GNT, GW, NCV, NET, REB). But grammatically **faith** is attached to **Moses** (see ESV, HCSB, KJV, NASB, NJB; Attridge 1989, 339). Verse 23 condenses the account in Exod 1:1—2:10 but is particularly indebted to Exod 2:2. The MT mentions only Moses' mother hiding him. But Hebrews infers from the LXX ("they hid him") that both parents **hid him for three months after he was born.** The motivation for their defiance of Pharaoh was twofold.

First, they recognized Moses' princely appearance: **because they saw he was no ordinary child.** The NIV's **no ordinary child** captures well the meaning of the only Greek word (*asteion*) Hebrews reproduces from Exod 2:2 (LXX; used once more in the NT, also of Moses [Acts 7:20]). The word can be translated "beautiful" (most English versions) or "handsome" (BDAG, 145; "fine" [NJB, REB]). It connotes the good breeding and refinement of the town, as opposed to the low-brow, rustic ways of the country (BDAG, 145; LSJ, 260). From birth, Moses had the appearance of someone marked by God with special favor and destiny, even though he was born to slaves. Philo correlates Moses' outward beauty with noble birth. He considers this the reason for his parents' defiance of Pharaoh (*Moses* 1.9, 18). Josephus credits Moses' beauty for the ease of his adoption into the royal household of Egypt (*Ant.* 2.224-25, 231-32).

Moses: Handsome and High-Class from Birth

The significance of Moses' physical attributes is a detail lost on modern readers. Our ideals of freedom and equality are far removed from those of ancient societies. They generally considered one's station in life as fixed from birth. The ancients correlated physical beauty with good breeding (see Plato, *Resp.* 10.618a-b; Aristotle, *Eth. nic.* 1.8.16; *Pol.* 3.1282b; 4.1295b; Diog. Laert. 3.1.88). This popular conception is no more forcefully expressed than by a wealthy nobleman, Dionysius, in Chariton's ancient Greek novel *Callirrhoe* (ca. A.D. 50): "It is impossible for a person not free-born to be beautiful. Have you not learned from the poets that beautiful people are children of the gods, and all the more likely children of the nobly born" (2.1.5).

The ancient audience of Hebrews would have immediately grasped the significance of Moses' natural beauty. He was destined by God for a role of tremendous privilege and responsibility. However, it also casts into bold relief the fact that Moses, who looked well-bred, was actually born to low-class nomads who were now Pharaoh's slaves. Moses would later lay aside his royal prerogatives to join his own shabby and oppressed people, whom God had called him to lead in defiance of the greatest superpower of his day, Egypt.

Second, they were motivated by courage: **they were not afraid of the king's edict.** This refers to Pharaoh's command to kill every male Hebrew child (Exod 1:15-16, 22). Exodus does not mention the fearlessness of Moses' parents. It strongly implies that the Hebrew midwives were courageous (Exod 1:17, 21). So it would be no stretch to deduce the same concerning Moses' parents (Attridge 1989, 339-40; Lane 1991, 370).

11:23-24

■ **24** The topic of Heb 11:24-26, Moses' renunciation of his royal Egyptian privileges, is introduced in v 24: **By faith Moses . . . refused to be known as the son of Pharaoh's daughter.** Verses 25-26 will elaborate on the alternatives involved in this decision and the criterion Moses utilized in making it.

The phrase **when he had grown up** is lifted directly from Exod 2:11 LXX. The preacher may have been aware of the exegetical tradition that interpreted Exod 2:11—"he went out to where his own people were and watched them at their hard labor"—as his break with the Egyptian court (Lane 1991, 370-71, following D'Angelo 1979, 36, 42-53).

That he was **known as the son of Pharaoh's daughter** may indicate that Moses was formally adopted into the royal household (see Josephus, *Ant.* 2.232; Philo, *Moses* 1.19, 32-33; *Jub.* 47:9). Hebrews does not specify the act by which Moses **refused** his association with Pharaoh. It certainly was not Josephus's fanciful tale of Moses as a toddler stomping on his crown (*Ant.* 2.233). Perhaps it alludes to Moses' murder of an abusive Egyptian taskmaster (Exod 2:11-14; an addition in a few MSS makes this explicit; see Metzger

1994, 603). In view of Heb 11:25-26, a general reference to Moses' decision to make common cause with his own enslaved people is just as likely (Whedon 1880, 5:126).

■ **25-26** The elegant Greek chiasm in vv 25-26*a* may be fairly represented through slight rearrangement of the NIV:

11:25	He chose rather to be mistreated along with the people of God	than to enjoy the pleasures of sin for a short time.
	x	
11:26	He regarded as of greater value than the treasures of Egypt,	disgrace for the sake of Christ.

Moses' options and their relative values are thus set out. Scholars attempt to trace the origin of Hebrews' thought in these verses. In particular, **disgrace for the sake of Christ** has been linked to Ps 89:51-52 LXX (Lane 1991, 373; Ellingworth 1993, 614) or Ps 68:8, 10 (deSilva 2000a, 411). However, the careful arrangement and choice of wording suggest a distinctive reading of Moses' life through a pastoral prism. Hebrews sees parallels between the choice **faith** necessitated for Moses, Jesus the Messiah, and now also for the community he addresses.

Moses' preference to be **mistreated along with the people of God** is reminiscent of the community's sharing in the suffering of fellow believers (→ Heb 10:34; see 4:15). Solidarity with God's suffering people is weighed against the enjoyment of **the pleasures of sin for a short time.** The readers have been warned about the lure of sin (→ 3:13) and will be called to slough off "the sin that so easily entangles" (12:1; see 12:4).

That Moses endured **disgrace** [*oneidismon*] **for the sake of Christ** compares with the community's past exposure to "insult [*oneidismois*] and persecution" (10:33). Christ's endurance of suffering and shame (12:2-3) is what Moses looked ahead to and shared in (thus "testifying to what would be said in the future" [3:5]). It is also what the community must look back on and emulate. Christ is the pattern of faithfulness for the past, present, and future (see 13:8)—the "pioneer and perfecter of faith" (12:2 NIV[11]). In 13:13, the preacher urges his audience to "go to him . . . bearing the disgrace [*ton oneidismon*] he bore."

Moses **regarded** his share in Christ's disgrace **as of greater value than the treasures of Egypt.** Moses' choice of mistreatment over sinful pleasures, and of Christ's disgrace over vast wealth, makes no sense apart from faith. Verse 26*b* explains the reason for his preference: **because he was looking ahead to his reward.** Moses' rationale is like that offered to the community in 10:35. His **looking ahead** (see 11:1) in expectation of God's **reward** (see 11:6) conforms to Hebrews' description of the dynamics of faith.

■ **27** Readers have long wondered where this verse fits into the chronology of Moses' life. When was it that **by faith he left Egypt**? Several views are possible:

First, it could refer to his initial flight to Midian. This is unlikely since on that occasion Moses was afraid (Exod 2:14), whereas Hebrews says he left **not fearing the king's anger** (note the *inclusio* with v 23).

Second, it could refer to the exodus itself. On that occasion, Moses urged the people not to be afraid, and they marched out triumphantly (Exod 14:8, 13). However, the exodus occurred after, not before, the celebration of Passover mentioned in the next verse (Heb 11:28).

Third, v 27 could simply be a general statement about Moses' courage, not connected to any particular event (deSilva 2000a, 412; Koester 2001, 503-4). Perhaps Hebrews refers to the whole series of bold actions Moses took prior to the exodus, such as his repeated appearances before Pharaoh to press God's command, "Let my people go!" (Exod 7:16; 8:1, 20; 9:1, 13; 10:3, 7).

Moses **persevered** for one reason: **because he saw him who is invisible.** The word **invisible** is used as one of God's titles (Col 1:15; 1 Tim 1:17) or attributes (Rom 1:20; Philo, *Moses* 1.158; 2.65). Moses did not simply keep "his reward" in sight (Heb 11:26), but the "rewarder" himself (v 6 KJV). Moses is therefore an example for Hebrews' readers. They, too, must "fix [their] eyes on Jesus" (12:2; see 3:1), "the exact imprint of God's . . . being" (1:3 NRSV).

■ **28** The preacher transitions from Moses' life to the record of God's people in subsequent events (vv 29-31). It begins with Moses (**he**) and ends with **the firstborn of Israel** (lit., ***their firstborn***). As a rhetorical flourish, the diction incorporates alliteration (with *p*) and *homoioptōton* as earlier (→ 11:1). The implicit contrast between destruction of unbelievers and salvation of God's people is the theme of vv 29-31 (compare 10:39).

By faith Moses **kept the Passover,** and so instituted the ritual Jews still perform annually to celebrate God's miraculous deliverance of the Israelites out of Egypt. Hebrews does not pause to draw any typological connections with Christ's sacrifice as our "Passover lamb" (1 Cor 5:7; see 1 Pet 1:19).

The sprinkling of blood refers to the application of blood from the paschal lamb onto the top and sides of the doorframe (Exod 12:7, 22). This act of **faith,** in connection with the first celebration of Passover, was in response to God's promise (Exod 12:13, 23). God sent **the destroyer,** or "destroying angel" (1 Cor 10:10), who caused the death of the **firstborn** of Egypt. When he saw the blood on the doorposts of the Israelites, he would "pass over" their houses, so as **not to touch the firstborn of Israel.**

■ **29-31** Three vignettes quickly summarize events from Israel's exodus from Egypt and conquest of Canaan. The contrasting salvation of God's people and destruction of their enemies provides thematic unity for these verses.

Hebrews 11:29 relates the miraculous parting of the Red Sea when the Israelites were pursued by Pharaoh's army (Exod 14:1-31). Obedient to God's command to "move on" (Exod 14:15), and confident in God's deliverance, **by faith the people passed through the Red Sea as on dry land.** Their faith is set in contrast to **the Egyptians** who, when they **tried to do** the same, **were drowned.**

Equally miraculous is how the **walls of Jericho fell** (Heb 11:30). The clause, **after the people had marched around them for seven days,** indicates how this event occurred **by faith.** Simply by marching around the city, in obedience to God's orders, the city walls came tumbling down without even a single battering ram (Josh 5:13—6:27).

Notably, Hebrews make no mention of Joshua, Moses' successor and God's chosen leader of the conquest. This may be deliberate, given the earlier negative remark that Joshua had *not* given the Israelites rest (Heb 4:8). Settlement in Canaan was not the ultimate fulfillment of God's promise. The patriarchs were looking for a heavenly homeland (11:10, 14-16).

The sparing of **Rahab** in v 31 is mentioned in the account of the fall of Jericho (Josh 6:17, 23, 25). The stated reason for her deliverance from destruction is, as in the OT record (Josh 6:17, 25), **because she welcomed the spies.** Her **faith** may have consisted of trusting the oath of protection given to her by the spies she hid (Josh 2:20; 6:23).

Rahab's mention at the conclusion to the major portion of the example list (Heb 11:3-31) delivers a persuasive punch. She was a non-Israelite, a woman (→ v 11), and a **prostitute** no less! Yet she is ranged among those who believed and were saved, rather than being **killed with those who were disobedient** (→ 10:39). Chrysostom (1996, 488) expresses a possible implication for readers: "It would then be disgraceful, if you should appear more faithless even than a harlot. Yet she [merely] heard what the men related and forthwith believed."

d. Many More Faithful: From Triumph to Suffering (11:32-40)

Since the preacher is writing to the recipients "quite briefly" (13:22 NIV[11]), he does not have space to recount in full the remaining history of the faithful. Therefore, he employs a number of rhetorical techniques to give readers a sense, in small compass (11:33-38), of the scope and magnitude of that history. These include short, punchy clauses of nearly equal length (isocolon), strung together without any conjunctions (asyndeton), with successive verbs whose opening and closing syllables match each other in sound (Cosby 1988, 57-73). Both content and form are designed to give an accurate impression of the great number of additional heroes of faith, and the extent of their triumphs and suffering.

The repetition of "by faith [*pistei*]" in vv 3-31 has come to an end. However, this subunit is framed by the similar phrase "through faith [*dia pisteōs*]" in vv 33 and 39. The passage begins with a brief list of named worthies of faith (v 32) and ends with a closing summary for the entire chapter (vv 39-40). The intervening material (vv 33-38) divides into two parts. It moves from military victories and miraculous deliverances (vv 33-35a) to tales of torture, execution, and rejection (vv 35*b*-38). The hinge between the two halves is the antithesis in v 35 between women who received back their dead through resurrection and others who endured torture in hope of "a better resurrection."

■ **32** The rhetorical question **And what more shall I say?** and the assertion **I do not have time to tell** introduce a rhetorical device known as *paraleipsis*. This occurs when a speaker mentions the very things he says he is passing over (*Rhet. Her.* 4.27.37). The preacher chooses only to list further people and experiences exemplifying faith, without elaborating on them ad nauseam. This well-known technique allowed speakers to show their command of a subject matter, without being tedious (Isocrates, *Archid.* 47; Chrysostom 1996, 488; Koester 2001, 516).

The six named individuals in v 32 are not in strict chronological order. The list mentions four heroes from Israel's period of judges: **Gideon, Barak, Samson,** and **Jephthah** (see 1 Sam 12:11 LXX). **David** is the greatest and only representative figure from the tragic history of the monarchy. **Samuel,** named last, was the head of Israel's **prophets** (see 1 Sam 19:20; Acts 3:24).

■ **33-34** The experiences recounted in Heb 11:33-38 allude to figures and events from biblical and extrabiblical history. They relate accomplishments and sufferings that came about **through faith.** Some are quite general, applicable to various times and persons; others point indubitably to particular heroes of faith. By the fourth century A.D., interpreters were attempting to identify each and every allusion with specificity (Chrysostom 1996, 488-89, 491-92; Ephrem the Syrian in Heen and Krey 2005, 204-5; Lane 1991, 385). The nine short clauses in vv 33-34 are arranged into three triplets:

The first highlights military and political achievements. **Conquered kingdoms, administered justice,** and **gained what was promised** apply to all of the figures named in v 32, and many others in the OT, but especially to Samuel and David (see 1 Sam 12:3-5, 23; 2 Sam 8:1-3, 15; 1 Chr 18:14 LXX; see Lane 1991, 385-86).

Gained what was promised (lit., ***obtained promises***) has to do with vanquishing enemies, acquiring territories, and enjoying other temporal blessings God had promised. Distinguished from it is "the promise," which the ancients did not attain (Heb 11:39).

The second triplet is devoted to those who escaped certain death. **Shut the mouths of lions** unmistakably refers to Daniel in the lions' den (Dan 6:1-28). **Quenched the fury of the flames** speaks of the deliverance of three Hebrew youths from the fiery furnace (Dan 3:1-30). **Escaped the edge of the sword** could apply to many of the prophets, such as Elijah, Elisha, and Jeremiah.

The third triplet returns to martial victory. **Whose weakness was turned to strength** seems immediately applicable to Samson. Having been weakened and humiliated by the Philistines, he was given one last opportunity to deal a strong, deadly blow to his enemies (Judg 16:20-31). The final two clauses, **became powerful in battle** and **routed foreign enemies,** have a wide application in the history of Israel (again to all of those listed in Heb 11:32), including the Maccabean revolt against "foreigners" (see 1 Macc 1:38; 2:7; 4:12, 26).

■ **35** This verse forms the hinge between the remarkable exploits of faith in vv 33-34 and the endurance of suffering by the faithful in vv 36-38. It presents an antithesis pivoting around **resurrection.**

On one hand, **women received back their dead, raised to life again.** This is true of two women in the OT: the widow of Zarephath, whose son was raised up by Elijah (1 Kgs 17:22-23); and the Shunammite woman, whose son was raised up by Elisha (2 Kgs 4:32-37).

On the other hand, others **were tortured and refused to be released, so that they might gain a better resurrection.** This is a clear allusion to the Maccabean martyrs. A certain Eleazar, as well as a mother and her seven sons, resolutely refused to recant their faith to spare their lives. Instead they endured grisly forms of torture, and death, in hopes of the resurrection (2 Macc 6:18—7:42, esp. 7:9, 14, 29, 36).

Better resurrection surpasses infinitely the resurrection miracles of Heb 11:35a. This refers to the final resurrection when believers will be raised to eternal life. It shares in "the power of an indestructible life" (7:16), which God effected in the resurrection of Jesus (13:20).

■ **36-38** The list is rounded out with references to the faithful who, rather than experiencing remarkable achievements and blessings, were tormented, imprisoned, brutally executed, and ostracized by the world.

Some faced jeers (v 36), such as the prophets (2 Chr 36:16)—Jeremiah in particular (Jer 20:2, 7-8). **Jeers and flogging** together were endured by the Maccabean martyrs (2 Macc 7:1, 7, 10; 4 Macc 6:3, 6; 9:12). **Still others,** like the prophets Jeremiah (Jer 37:15-16, 18-20), Hanani (2 Chr 16:7-10), and Micaiah (1 Kgs 22:26-27), **were chained and put in prison**. Some in the readers' community had suffered the same fate (Heb 10:34; 13:3).

They were stoned (v 37) indicates the method of choice for killing the prophets, as Jesus reminded his opponents (Matt 23:37; Luke 13:34). The only prophet whose stoning is recorded in the OT is Zechariah, son of Jehoida the priest (2 Chr 24:20-21; see Matt 23:35; Luke 11:51). The first Christian martyr, Stephen, was stoned to death (Acts 7:58-59). According to a tradition widely transmitted among Jews and Christians, Isaiah the prophet was **sawed in two.** Many prophets were also **put to death by the sword** (1 Kgs 19:10, 14; Jer 2:30; 26:20-23).

Even when the prophets were not killed, they lived on the margins of society. **They went about** in the most uncivilized clothing, **sheepskins and goatskins.** Elijah wore a hairy garment (2 Kgs 1:8), which became a trademark of the prophets (Zech 13:4; Matt 7:15; compare John the Baptist's camel-hair attire [Mark 1:6 par.]). **Destitute, persecuted and mistreated** is an accurate summary of the ministries of Elijah and Elisha (1 Kgs 17:2-16; 19:1-19; 2 Kgs 1:3-15; 2:23; 4:1-2, 8-12, 38-43; 8:1-2).

Hebrews interjects a value judgment in Heb 11:38a: **the world was not worthy of them.** However despised, abused, and impoverished they were, the faithful were far more precious than those who rejected them. "They were too good for this world" (NLT). The value system of God's kingdom is not based on that of the world. The way to greater honor and glory is not through wealth and power, but through humility and suffering in obedience to God—as supremely exemplified by Jesus (2:7, 9; 3:3; 5:4-5; 12:2).

They wandered in deserts and mountains, and in caves and holes in the ground. This is reminiscent of how many of God's faithful sought refuge and hiding places away from their persecutors (1 Kgs 19:1-3, 9; Ps 107:4; 1 Macc 5:27; 6:11; 10:6). A signal example is from the time of Elijah, when Jezebel was killing the Lord's prophets. Obadiah hid one hundred prophets in caves and supplied them with food and water (1 Kgs 18:4, 13).

■ **39-40** These verses constitute the concluding summary, not only for the last subunit, but for the entire "faith chapter." The phrase **for their faith** (lit., *through faith*) reappears from Heb 11:33 to enclose vv 32-40. Another *inclusio* ties vv 39-40 to the opening of the chapter. First, the verb **were . . . commended** appears again from vv 2, 4, and 5. Second, 11:1 defined faith, in part, as proof of "what we do not see [*ou blepomenōn*]" (see vv 3, 7). Now Hebrews asserts that God **had planned** or "foreseen [*problepsamenou*]" (NAB, RSV) something better. Bengel astutely observes: God "*provides (foresees)* what faith does not yet *see*" (1877, 4:459).

The bottom line is that **these were all** [*houtoi pantes*] **commended** by God (→ 11:2), **yet none of them received what had been promised.** This recalls the preacher's summary concerning Abraham and his immediate heirs in 11:13: "all these [*houtoi pantes*] died" without receiving God's promises. It also forms a striking contrast with the preacher's encouragement to the readers in 10:36: "You need to persevere, so that . . . you will receive what he has promised" (Ellingworth 1993, 634). Such contrast is integral to the conclusion. **These . . . all** did not receive the promise. This was because God had made better arrangements **for us** so that the ancients might finally be perfected, but not without **us.**

The **something better** that God has foreseen involves, in the immediate context, the "better and lasting possessions," better homeland, and "better resurrection" (10:34; 11:16, 35). But the accent here is upon the audience's privilege of belonging to the age of fulfillment. This he calls variously the "last days" (1:2), "end of the ages" (9:26), or "time of the new order" (9:10), when "the Day" is fast approaching (10:25). The new age commenced with Christ's offering of himself as the definitive sacrifice for sins. He thus inaugurated the "better covenant" (7:22), based on "better promises" (8:6). He also introduced a "better hope" (7:19), which will be brought to fulfillment at Christ's second coming (9:28). This explains why **only together with us** will the ancients **be made perfect.**

To **be made perfect** (*teleiōthōsin*), in its most recent instances, has meant the decisive cleansing from sin through Christ's sacrifice that "perfects" worshipers with respect to their conscience (9:9; 10:2, 14). In short, the focus has been on the profound, inward preparation of the heart to draw near to God in worship (10:19, 22). Now the perfection is viewed as the ultimate fulfillment—reaching the *telos* or goal—of the divine promises in their totality. The "perfect" comes only when the whole people of God actually enter into the promised rest (4:1, 3, 6, 9-11), heavenly homeland (11:16), "enduring city" (13:14; see 11:10, 16; 12:22), or unshakable kingdom (12:28; see Lane 1991, 393-94; deSilva 2000a, 423-24).

By this means the preacher encourages his audience to remain faithful to the very end. He will enlarge upon this in the next chapter (12:1-13). All the faithful worthies under the old covenant have accomplished and suffered so much, without being perfected. How much more, then, ought current believers—"on whom the fulfillment of the ages has come" (1 Cor 10:11; compare 9:26-28)—press on toward perfection (Heb 6:1)? The ancients are counting on us to finish the race. As Origen writes, "For they do not have perfect delight as long as they grieve for our errors and mourn for our sins. . . . You see, therefore, that Abraham is still waiting to obtain the perfect things. Isaac waits, and Jacob and all the prophets wait for us, that they may lay hold of the perfect blessedness with us" (Heen and Krey 2005, 207).

3. Training for Enduring Faith (12:1-13)

BEHIND THE TEXT

This passage concludes the exhortation for readers to persevere in faith (10:19—12:13). It completes it in five interrelated ways:

First, it is framed by two conclusive statements, using "therefore" (12:1, 12).

The conclusion in 12:1 is directly linked to the faithful witnesses listed in ch 11. The expression "since we have" (NASB) is also reminiscent of the opening to the homily's *peroratio* in 10:19 (see 4:14). As we shall see, 12:1-13 picks up a number of threads from 10:19-39.

The conclusion in 12:12-13 reinforces the primary exhortations of 12:1-13:
- "Run with perseverance" (v 1).
- Don't give in to exhaustion and fatigue (v 3).
- "Endure hardship" for the sake of discipline (v 7).

Second, the passage expands upon the exhortation to persevere in 10:36. The language of endurance from 10:32, 36 resurfaces in 12:1, 2, 3, 7.

Third, the encouragement to endure employs the imagery of an athletic contest, introduced in 10:32. A footrace is the controlling athletic metaphor in 12:1, 12-13 (Croy 1998, 58). The struggle described in → 12:4 might allude to the violent sporting event, the pancratium.

Fourth, the impediment to the readers' progress, "sin," is reiterated in 12:1 and 4. This recalls the exhortations in 10:19-39, which warn against the deliberate sin of apostasy (10:26-31). The occasion for such sin is the temptation to give up under the pressure of suffering (→ 10:35, 39 and 12:3-4, 12-13). The community had earlier endured persecution valiantly (10:31-34). They must now do so again (10:35-36; 12:4). Laying aside the entanglements of sin, they must endure training that will produce righteousness (12:11).

Fifth, the pattern for the readers' endurance is not simply their own past perseverance, or the models of faithfulness among the people of God (ch 11). Even as the source of "full assurance of faith" and confident access into God's presence is the atoning death of the Great High Priest (10:19-22), so also "the author and perfecter" of faith is Jesus. They must "fix [their] eyes on Jesus" as the supreme example of how endurance through suffering leads to ultimate glory (12:2).

Hebrews 12:1-13 begins and ends with exhortations cast in a form appropriate to runners in a race (12:1-3, 12-13). The intervening material in 12:4-11 skillfully slides into a topic closely allied with athletic imagery in Greco-Roman culture: discipline (*paideia*). This theme dominates 12:4-11, as indicated by the concentration of relevant terminology (here, and nowhere else, in Hebrews: *paideia* [12:5, 7, 8, 11]; *paideuō* ["disciplines" (12:6, 7, 10)]; *paideutēs* ["instructor, teacher" (BDAG, 749; 12:9)]).

Paideia bore wide meaning in its ancient social context. It referred to the process of training or educating youths to become responsible citizens in Hellenistic society. The term could refer, as well, to the result of such training: culture (Johnson 2006, 319; → 5:12 sidebar, "Education in the Hellenistic World"). The process included both mental and physical training, as in the gymnasium. The broader idea of *paideia* or education and the narrower metaphor of athletic training (*gegymnasmenois*) are linked in Heb 12:11.

Hebrews has already used images of education and athletic training in order to communicate the importance of reaching moral maturity (5:11—6:1). These themes now reemerge, but with a more pointed emphasis on their connection with the community's present struggle to maintain faithfulness to God.

Through the introduction of Prov 3:11 in Heb 12:5-6, the preacher reorients his readers' perspective on their suffering. Persecution is reimagined as a training ground for moral and spiritual development. Concepts from the proverb ("son [*huios*]" and "discipline[s] [*paideia*; *paideuō*]") are employed to show how hardships ought to be viewed: as the Lord's loving, fatherly education of his children (observe the repetition of "son[s]" [vv 5, 6, 7, 8] and "father[s]" [vv 7, 9]). The goal of this discipline is their participation in God's life, holiness, and righteousness (vv 9-11). The true end of *paideia* is the virtuous life (→ 5:13, 14; → 5:13 sidebar, "Ancient Images of Educational Progress").

No matter how difficult their struggle, the audience is encouraged not to become weary, dispirited, or disabled by their circumstances (vv 3, 12-13). Rather, they must endure their difficulties as performance training, so they are fit to run the race set out before them.

IN THE TEXT

■ 1 With an emphatic **Therefore** (*toigaroun*) the preacher again addresses his readers directly (**we, let us**). His exhortations are tied to the preceding example list. The worthies of ch 11 are envisioned as **a great cloud of witnesses** filling an amphitheatre or stadium. The classical figure of a **cloud** denotes a great "host" or "crowd" (BDAG, 670; NLT).

The OT faithful are **witnesses** (*martyrōn*) or spectators of the **race** the listeners are running. But they are more than spectators. They have themselves been "commended [*martyrēthentes*]" (11:39; see 11:2, 4, 5) by God. Their testimonies of triumph and tragedy in faith provide an interpretive framework for the listeners' own struggle (Westcott 1909, 393). Key to their witness is God's promise that perfection in the heavenly homeland will not be fulfilled for the ancients without "us" (11:40).

This supports the principal exhortation in 12:1-2, **let us run with perseverance the race marked out for us.** (On **perseverance** in discussions of moral virtue, using athletic imagery, → 10:32.) Enduring to the end establishes the listeners' place of honor among the past faithful. Giving up exposes them to humiliation and shame (deSilva 2000a, 428-29). The listeners stand accountable to the throng of witnesses who **surround** (*perikeimenon*) them, and to God who **marked out** (*prokeimenon*) the race for them. The preacher points out two things his audience must **throw off** for a successful race:

First, they must discard **everything that hinders,** (lit.) "every weight" (ESV, HCSB, KJV, LEB, NET, NLT, NRSV). This could refer to "excess body fat" (Croy 1998, 63). But more likely, the image is of the common practice of runners removing their clothing to reduce wind resistance. Elsewhere in the NT the verb **throw off** involves putting off immoral behaviors as if they were clothes (Rom 13:12; Eph 4:22, 25; Col 3:8; Jas 1:21; 1 Pet 2:1; Johnson 2006, 316).

Second, they must cast off **the sin that so easily entangles.** The adjective **easily entangles** means "easily surrounded," probably by difficult or distressing circumstances (MM, 264; Koester 2001, 522). A contrast is set up between a surrounding crowd who cheers us on and **the sin** that closes in on us and "trips us up" (CEB).

Some scholars insist that the reference is to **sin** in general (Croy 1998, 171-72; Lane 1991, 409: "sin itself," not apostasy). However, the sermon has focused on sin as a deceitful and hardening agent, which promotes unbelief and apostasy (3:12-13; see 11:25). Two warnings against apostasy are near at hand: earlier in this unit (10:26-31) and at the beginning of the next (12:14-17).

A major thrust of the sermon is to warn the readers against drifting away (2:1), sluggishness (5:11; 6:12), falling short of the divine rest (4:1)/grace (12:15; see 6:6), and shrinking away to destruction (10:39). Readers must revitalize their diligence (4:11; 6:11), progress toward spiritual maturity (6:1), and fortify their confidence (3:6; 4:16; 10:19, 35), faith, and endurance (see Hughes 1977, 520-21; Hagner 1990, 211-12; Johnson 2006, 316-17; Thompson 2008, 247-48). Throwing off the impediment of **sin**—the "chronic tendency to unbelief, which constantly exposes them to apostasy" (Taylor 1967, 155)—fits well within this overarching message.

■ **2** Though the faithful of old provide moral support and motivation, they should not be the "focus" (GW) of the runner's gaze. **Let us fix our eyes** [*aphorōntes*] **on Jesus.** The verb used here means "to look *away from* all others toward one" (Croy 1998, 174), to direct one's attention without distraction (BDAG, 158). We must look to Jesus, the supreme model of enduring faith, for inspiration to "run with perseverance." This is consistent with Hebrews' emphasis on Jesus as central to the readers' reflection and confession (see 2:9; 3:1; 4:14; 6:19-20; 10:19-23; 12:3, 24; 13:8).

The following descriptions of **Jesus** relate the vital elements of the Christian confession in connection with his suffering and exaltation. Jesus is **the author** [*archēgon*] **and perfecter** [*teleiōtēn*] **of . . . faith** (→ 5:9 sidebar, "Playing with Beginnings and Endings"). He is "the champion who initiates and perfects" faith (NLT; Lane 1991, 411; → 2:10 sidebar, "Jesus the Champion"). Jesus is not merely one of many exemplars of faith. His obedient suffering and subsequent exaltation make him faith's true source and culmination. Significantly, the text does not refer to **our faith** but simply **faith** (NAB, NASB, NIV[11], REB). Jesus is the progenitor of faith itself. He is the paragon of faith, who brings it to its fullest realization and expression.

The preacher applies the same metaphor of athletic contest to Jesus that he applied to the readers in v 1 (see 10:32). The correlation highlights the elements of Christ's response to suffering that readers should emulate. The motivation behind Jesus' perseverance was **for the joy set before** [*prokeimenēs*] **him.** He was looking beyond the contest itself (→ v 1) to the prize awaiting the victor.

Many texts refer to prizes **set before** those who compete in athletic contests, battle, or the quest for virtue (Koester 2001, 524). Likewise, Moses preferred mistreatment and disgrace "because he was looking ahead to his reward" (11:26). In the past, the readers "joyfully" welcomed the confiscation of their property because they knew they had "better and lasting possessions" awaiting them (10:34). For Jesus, the **joy set before him** was his exaltation, mentioned at the close of 12:2. This is similar to the "hope set before [*prokeimenēs*] us" (6:18 NRSV).

Endured the cross is a distinctive, though fitting, description of Jesus' crucifixion. This is the sole reference in Hebrews to the instrument of Jesus' death: **the cross.** Elsewhere Hebrews describes Jesus' death in terms of suffering (2:9, 10, 18; 5:8; 9:26; 13:12). The mention of crucifixion accents Jesus' death as shameful. The **cross** was "the tree of shame" (Cicero, *Rab. Perd.* 4 §13), and under Jewish law exposed one to a divine curse (Deut 21:22-23; Koester 2001, 524). Jesus **endured** the suffering of **the cross,** but more important was his attitude of **scorning its shame.** He displayed more than bravery in the face of terror and humiliation (against Lane 1991, 414). Jesus' death on the cross was his ultimate act of obedience to God's will (5:8; 10:5-10), despite the cultural estimation of it as a sign of utter disgrace (deSilva 2000a, 433-34).

The reversal of shame occurred after Jesus' death, when he **sat down at the right hand of the throne of God.** This is Hebrews' final allusion to Ps 110:1, the key text supporting the central confession of Jesus as our exalted high priest (→ Heb 4:14; 7:26; 8:1; 9:24; 10:12, 19-21). Previously the preacher simply noted that Christ "sat down [*ekathisen*]" (1:3; 8:1; 10:12). Now he emphasizes the finality and permanence of his triumph by using the perfect tense (*kekathiken*). He "has taken his seat" (NRSV) and remains seated ("is seated" [ESV, NLT]).

■ **3-4** These verses form a transition to the discussion of divine discipline in vv 5-11. They shift to addressing the listeners in the second person plural (**you**).

Verse 3 explains the preacher's aim in pointing to Christ's struggle. **Consider him who endured such opposition,** such "hostility" (ESV, HCSB, LEB, NASB, NKJV, NLT, NRSV), **from sinful men.** The note of Jesus' endurance is repeated from v 2, and expressed emphatically in the perfect tense (**endured** [*hypomemenēkota*]), to encourage the readers' perseverance (10:36; 12:1, 7). **So that you will not grow weary and lose heart** continues the athletic metaphor. The preacher does not want his readers to collapse in exhaustion before they reach the finish line (Lane 1991, 417). The expression **not . . . lose heart** anticipates the scriptural injunction, "Do not lose heart" in v 5.

Verse 4 contrasts the extent of the readers' struggle with the one in which Christ prevailed. Jesus endured **hostility** (*antilogian*) from **sinners** (*tōn hamartōlōn*); they are engaged in a **struggle** [*antagōnizomenoi*] **against sin** (*tēn hamartian*). Again, **sin** is not a variety of vices, but the temptation to commit apostasy (10:26; → 12:1; Hagner 1990, 215; Witherington 2007, 329-30; Thompson 2008, 253). Jesus endured to the death, but they **have not yet resisted** [*antikatestēte*] **to the point of shedding . . . blood.**

The antagonistic vocabulary (prefixed with *anti*-) sustains the athletic metaphor, but perhaps referring to more violent sports like boxing or the pancratium. The latter was a martial arts event in the ancient Olympiad that combined wrestling and kickboxing (Koester 2001, 525). But the mention of **shedding . . . blood** may only suggest Jesus' violent death by crucifixion (Croy 1998, 194).

The listeners must judge their past and present sufferings in proportion to Christ's suffering. They may have lost reputations, freedom, and possessions—but not their lives (10:32-34; 13:3). The example of Jesus shames them for their inclination to give up the struggle. His ultimate sacrifice should motivate them to endure proportionately less severe trials (deSilva 2000a, 446; Johnson 2006, 319). Perhaps with the little word **not yet** (*oupō*) the preacher hints that they, too, may still be called upon to give their all in devotion to Christ.

■ **5-6** The fresh but related topic of divine education (*paideia*) is introduced by quoting Prov 3:11-12. It is difficult to determine whether the introduction to the quote is cast in the form of a declarative statement (**And you have forgotten . . .**) or a question ("And have you completely forgotten . . . ? [NIV¹¹]"). The author's penchant for rhetorical styling favors the latter (Lane 1991, 420; Johnson 2006, 320). Either way, the words are a mild rebuke (contrast 10:32). The citation is characterized as **that word of encouragement** or simply *exhortation* (*tēs paraklēseōs*), which resembles the preacher's identification of his sermon ("word of exhortation" [13:22]).

That it **addresses** the listeners **as sons** is essential to the message of the entire passage (12:5-11). The proverb begins and ends with a reference to **son** (vv 5, 6). The words "father[s]" (vv 7, 9) and **sons** (vv 7-8) are repeated in the ensuing discussion. The listeners' identity as sons was important earlier in the sermon. God, through his Son, is "bringing many sons to glory" (2:10), and "Jesus is not ashamed to call them brothers" (2:11). They are members of God's household (3:6; 10:21). Now the preacher quotes a proverb to remind them that the contest they are enduring is a form of **the Lord's discipline** or *training* (*paideia*). It is a demonstration of their status as sons (on sonship in Hebrews, see Boyd 2012).

The first half of the quotation (Prov 3:11 in Heb 12:5) directs each hearer (**My son**) to respond appropriately to divine **discipline** (→ Behind the Text above). At one extreme, one must **not make light of**/*minimize* (*oligōrei*) it. At the other, one must **not lose heart when he rebukes you.** The latter admonition is particularly suitable for a community in need of encouragement: Do not give up in your struggle (see vv 3, 12-13).

The second half of the quotation (Prov 3:12 in Heb 12:6) supplies the rationale for God's instruction: **Because the Lord disciplines those he loves.** This stands in synonymous parallelism to **he punishes everyone he accepts as a son.** The preacher enlarges upon his point in the following verses: If you are among God's children, you will undergo divine moral training.

Somewhat jarring to contemporary readers is the verb **punishes** (*mastigoi*; lit., "scourges" [NAB; see KJV]; softened to "chastens" [NIV¹¹]). It would not have been in premodern times. Corporal punishment was a common, acceptable method of correction among the ancients (see Prov 10:13; 13:24; 14:3; 22:15; 23:13-14; 26:3; 29:15). Still, the following discussion (Heb 12:7-

11) does not expand upon, much less mention the sharp, punitive language in the proverb (**rebukes, punishes**). Hebrews regards the Father's instruction as decidedly educative, life-giving, and beneficial, not punitive—even if it is "painful" (v 11; see Croy 1998, 196-99; Koester 2001, 526-27). The discipline envisioned here is calculated to steer listeners away from sin, not punish them for it. Discipline is for sons; punishment is for apostates at the final judgment (6:8; 10:26-31, 39).

■ **7-8** The discussion in 12:7-11, prompted by the proverb quoted in vv 5-6, proceeds in three steps: The first (vv 7-8) establishes the inevitability or necessity of discipline for true sons. The second (vv 9-10) presents a lesser-to-greater comparison of human and divine discipline and their respective purposes. The third (v 11) assures listeners that the painful process of discipline will produce God's intended benefits.

Many translations render the opening saying in v 7 as a command: **Endure** [*hypomenete*] **hardship as discipline** (see CEB, ESV, GW, HCSB, NAB, NRSV). This makes little sense, since God's discipline makes this endurance necessary. Endurance does not invite divine *paideia*; discipline demands endurance (Johnson 2006, 320). The NJB correctly renders the statement as a maxim: "Perseverance is part of your training" (see NASB). The corollary, in v 7*b*, is that **God is treating you as sons**. The train of thought is clear in the NLT: "As you endure this divine discipline, remember that God is treating you as his own children."

The logic of these statements is unfolded and applied in vv 7*c*-8. A rhetorical question articulates an ancient truism concerning discipline: **For what son is not disciplined by his father?** The answer, of course, is "None." The notion is repeated in the parenthetical comment in v 8: **everyone undergoes discipline.**

The application to the readers is pointed. The preacher addresses them directly in the second person: **If you are not disciplined . . . then you are illegitimate children and not true sons.** In the Greco-Roman world, it was the father's responsibility to supervise the education of sons. Illegitimate sons ("bastards" [KJV]) were left outside of the father's protection, parental guidance, and line of inheritance (Koester 2001, 528; Johnson 2006, 321). Thus, the preacher boldly underscores that discipline in the community is a sure sign they are legitimate members of God's household.

■ **9-10** In these verses we encounter two lesser-to-greater (*qal wahomer*) comparisons of human and divine discipline. The first (v 9) draws a contrast between **human** ["earthly" (ESV, LEB, NAB, NASB, NET, NLT, RSV); "natural" (HCSB)] **fathers** and **the Father,** not readily apparent in contemporary translations. The KJV preserves the contrast between "fathers of our flesh [*sarkos*]" and "the Father of spirits [*pneumatōn*]." In Hebrews, whether with respect to the Son's incarnation (2:14; 5:7; 10:20) or the "fleshly" regulations under the old covenant, "flesh [*sarx*]" connotes what is weak, human, temporal, mortal (7:16;

9:10, 13; see 7:18 ["weak and useless"]). "Spirit [*pneuma*]" is associated with what is heavenly, eternal, powerful, and vital (4:12; 6:4; 9:14).

Moreover, we have all had human fathers. They **disciplined us,** acting as "instructors" or "teachers [*paideutas*]" (BDAG, 749) who provided guidance and correction (Koester 2001, 528-29). Frail and flawed as they were, and mistaken in many of their corrective measures, **we respected them,** nonetheless. **How much more,** then, **should we submit to the Father of our spirits?** Human fathers command respect; only God commands absolute submission (Croy 1998, 202-3). We may defer to our earthly fathers through mere outward conformity to their instruction. But **the Father of our spirits** enables heartfelt obedience (see 10:16).

The expression **the Father of spirits** may originate in the phrase "the Father of spirits and of all flesh" (Num 16:22 LXX). Similar titles, such as "Lord of Spirits," appear in Jewish intertestamental writings to designate God as sovereign over everything in the created order, including the exalted realm of spiritual beings (see Attridge 1989, 362-63; Lane 1991, 424). Hebrews seems to include human beings among these **spirits,** as NIV's addition "**our** spirits" implies. This finds support in the later reference to "spirits of righteous men" (12:23).

The issue is not whether or not we will ultimately **submit** (*hypotagēsometha*) to God. God has already "subjected" everything under the Son's feet (2:5, 8—the four other occurrences of the verb *hypotassō* in Hebrews; see also 10:13). The question concerns *how* we will **submit to God and live.** This gets to the heart of what the preacher has been driving at thus far in the *peroratio*. Submission to divine training requires confident, enduring faith.

Habakkuk 2:3-4 ("But my righteous one will live by faith . . ." [10:37-38]) was a key text cited in preparation for the examples of faith (ch 11) and the exhortation for readers to persevere in faith (12:1-13). From the Habakkuk text the preacher deduced two possible courses of action: shrinking back to destruction or having faith leading to the preservation of one's life (10:39). The latter is comparable to what we find here: **submit** and **live.**

The second comparison (v 10) is an extension of the first. **They** (our fathers) and *but he* (but God) have as their respective antecedents **human fathers** and **the Father of our spirits** (v 9). The discipline coming from our earthly fathers has natural limitations. It is conducted during a restricted period of time **(for a little while)** with limited, imperfect human judgment **(as they thought best).** By contrast, God's *paideia* is exercised **for our good** (*epi to sympheron*). This phrase coheres with the goal of Stoic ethical instruction: seeking what is objectively beneficial or profitable, a concept akin to "the good" (*to agathon*; Croy 1998, 204; see Koester 2001, 529).

However, Hebrews goes well beyond Hellenistic ethical ideals. The design of divine discipline is **that we may share in** God's **holiness.** This implies more than possession of moral virtue, although this cannot be excluded (see v 11). It is participation in the holy life of God, God's "eternal blessedness" (Spicq 1953, 2:396; see 2 Pet 1:4, noted by Bengel 1877, 4:464). Sharing in the divine holiness is contrasted with the temporal limitation of human instruction (**for a little while**). It transcends any attainment of moral rectitude in this life. It shares in the heavenly realities of the age to come, in good measure now (see 3:1, 4; 6:4), but in fullness at Christ's second coming (9:28). It is access to the most holy place (10:19; see 6:20), entrance into divine rest (4:1, 3, 6, 9, 11), and dwelling in "the city of the living God" (12:22; see 11:10, 16; 13:14). The goal of the Father's discipline is modeled after the perfection of the Son: "holy, blameless, pure, set apart from sinners, exalted above the heavens" (7:26).

■ **11** The final point concerning divine *paideia* echoes another ancient truism: painful discipline now brings lasting benefits later. **No discipline seems pleasant** ["enjoyable" (HCSB, NLT); "joyful" (NASB, NET, NKJV; compare 10:34; 12:2)] **at the time, but painful. However, later on, . . . it produces a harvest [*karpon*, *fruit*] of righteousness and peace.** This sort of proverbial wisdom was common among Jews (Prov 23:13-14; Wis 3:5; Philo, *Congr.* 160, 175; QG 3.25) and Greeks (Aristotle, *Pol.* 8.4.4; Seneca, *Ep.* 78.14; see Attridge 1989, 364; Croy 1998, 206 n. 182; also compare Heb 5:8-10). Aristotle reportedly said, "The roots of education [*paideias*] are bitter, but the fruit [*karpon*] is sweet" (Diog. Laert. 5.1.18).

The product of God's discipline, **a harvest of righteousness and peace**, is more exactly "the peaceful fruit of righteousness" (CEB, ESV, LEB, NAB, NASB, NRSV; "peaceful harvest of right living" [NLT]). **Righteousness** and **peace** are signs that the messianic age and the kingdom of God have come (Ps 85:10; Isa 9:6-7; 11:3-9; 32:17; Rom 14:17). In Hebrews, **righteousness** is associated with the exalted Son (1:9) and those who live lives faithful to God (10:38; 11:4, 7, 33). In 7:2, **righteousness** and **peace** are characteristics of Melchizedek's/Christ's royal priesthood. Messianic overtones, however, are absent in 12:11.

Hebrews has in mind the maturation of the ethical life through divine discipline. First, ***peaceful fruit*** designates a calm, restful frame of mind resulting from **righteousness**. This outcome stands in contrast to the unpleasantness and grief accompanying the process of education itself (v 11a; for the contrast between peace and pain or trouble, see Prov 10:10; Tob 10:12; 13:13-14; John 16:33). In Heb 12:14, **peace** will refer to harmonious dealings with others, in line with the ethical dictates of "holiness."

Second, the cultivation of **righteousness** in an educational context closely matches an earlier passage. The mature are skilled in righteousness (5:13) and possess wisdom "to distinguish good from evil" (5:14). There, as here, moral maturity results from training. **Righteousness** develops in **those who have been trained by it** (i.e., *paideia*, discipline in v 11a). The verb **trained** (*gegymnasmenois*) implies athletic exercises, a metaphor appropriate to ethical training (→ 5:14). This effectively ties the discussion of *paideia* (12:5-11) to the athletic imagery both preceding and following (vv 1-4, 12-13).

Seneca and Hebrews on Suffering and Divine Discipline

Hebrews' analysis of the community's struggle in 12:1-13 includes many concepts, images, and language resembling Stoic ethical teaching. A concentration of these exists between Hebrews and *On Providence*, written by the first-century Stoic philosopher Seneca (see Croy 1998, 205).

Divine *Paideia*	Seneca, On Providence	Hebrews
Suffering hardship is God's fatherly training of his true children.	1.6; 2.6	12:9
God's love assures that even severe suffering is meant for good.	2.6; 4.7	12:6, 11
The divine goal of enduring suffering is our progress in virtue.	2.6-10; 4.5-6	12:10-11
Endurance required in adversity is comparable to an athletic contest.	2.2-4, 7-9	12:1-3, 11
A list of great exemplars to consider.	3.4-14	11:1—12:3

Most striking in its similarity to Heb 12:6-7 is Seneca's statement, "Those, then, whom God approves, whom he loves, he hardens, reviews, and trains" (*On Providence* 4.7).

For all the resemblances, Hebrews' message about the educative aims of suffering is set apart from Stoicism in at least two primary ways:

First, Hebrews points to Jesus as the supreme example of endurance through suffering (12:2-4). Inspiration to persevere comes finally not from a cool, rational accounting of how God utilizes suffering for the ultimate good, but by looking to Jesus as the "author and perfecter of . . . faith" (12:2).

Second, the goal of divine *paideia* is not simply to produce people who are wise, unperturbed by circumstances, and self-sufficient. God's discipline goes beyond the cultivation of virtue, to prepare children who can share in the very life, holiness, and blessedness of God himself (→ 12:10).

■ **12-13** The first half of the *peroratio* (10:19—12:13) now concludes (*Dio*, **Therefore**) with a final exhortation for endurance and faithfulness. The command, **strengthen your feeble arms and weak knees,** works allusively on several levels. Generally, **feeble arms** and **weak knees** vividly portray physical exhaustion (Sir 25:23; see 2 Sam 4:1; Zeph 3:16; Sir 2:12; *Pss. Sol.* 8:5). Particularly, the phrasing echoes the supportive words spoken to languishing Jewish exiles in Isa 35:3, to enliven their hope for restoration in their homeland. This encouragement applies to the readers of Hebrews, who are on the cusp of reaching the goal of their pilgrimage, the enduring city (12:18-24; 13:14).

Thus, the preacher ingeniously reprises his earlier exhortations to endure and not grow weary (12:1, 3; see 10:36), while returning to imagery appropriate to running a race (see 12:1-2).

The injunction **Make level paths for your feet** evokes the imagery of a footrace. The quotation from Prov 4:26 also supplies a common Hebrew metaphor for the ethical life. Crooked paths represent what is perverse or evil (Prov 2:15; 5:6; 10:9). Straight or level paths represent righteous conduct (Prov 2:13; 3:6; 4:11). Philo frequently employs this metaphor (e.g., *Posterity* 102; *Giants* 64; *Unchangeable* 182; *Agriculture* 101, 177; *Spec. Laws* 3.48; 4.167). Notably, he refers to the straight or level road as the "path of virtue" (*Moses* 2.138), which leads to righteousness or holiness (*Spec. Laws* 4.62; *Virtues* 51).

Good runners prefer a straight path, rather than a crooked or uneven one, so that they will not stumble or be injured (Philo, *Agriculture* 115, 177; *Migration* 133; *Herm. Mand.* 1.2-4). Hebrews cautions readers to run on smooth, straight paths, **so that the lame may not be disabled, but rather healed.** The verb **disabled** was a medical term for the dislocation of a joint (as in a twisted or sprained ankle [BDAG, 311]; "put out of joint" [ESV, NASB, NET, NRSV]; "dislocated" [HCSB, LEB, NAB]). Runners must not run over rugged terrain, so that "the injured limb will not be maimed" (NJB) or "injured more seriously" (CEB; see GW).

The "sports medicine" metaphor suggests that failure to follow the path of virtue has debilitating effects. It can irreparably harm one's chances of endurance to the end. This thought paves the way for the climactic warning against apostasy in the following section (12:14-29).

FROM THE TEXT

Hebrews is addressed to a house church of Christ followers who were once fervent in their commitment to Christ, regardless of the cost of discipleship. The first half of the sermon's *peroratio* (10:19—12:13) directs attention to their precise situation. In the past they faced public insult and injury with courage. They accepted the plunder of their possessions with a smile. The entire community helped share the burden of suffering and rallied around those who were imprisoned on account of their faith. But a fresh wave of hardships caused many to become paralyzed by fear and immobilized by discouragement. Many of them had all but given up hope. Some had begun to cut their ties with Christian fellowship, choosing not to attend regular church worship gatherings.

Every follower of Jesus has or will at some point in life pass through a dark valley of suffering and despair. Saint John of the Cross characterized the entire journey of our spiritual life as the *Dark Night of the Soul*. Hebrews was written for people who have experienced life's shipwrecks. Some are catastrophic, like the loss of a loved one, employment, or one's health. Others may seem less severe but can pose a continual threat to our sanity. The stress of overwork or the emotional drain of handling difficult personal relationships, for example, can be sources of frustration and depression.

Big or small, life's hardships can lead us to feelings of helplessness and discouragement. We can "grow weary and lose heart" (12:3). We can feel as though our arms are dragging on the ground and our knees are wobbly (12:12). A natural impulse is simply to give up when the going gets tough. Blinded by pain, our hearts descend into a darkness of doubt and self-deception. Is God really there? Does anyone care about me? Does it really pay to go on?

The preacher was keenly aware of the psychology of trauma. He knew that people in pain often do not realize how perilous their situation really is. While giving up on oneself and others may seem like the most reasonable course of action at the time, it is in fact the counsel of moral insanity. Put in the spiritual terms of Hebrews, the deceitfulness of sin hardens our hearts, making us unreceptive to truth and unreasonable in our thinking. It bids us to turn away from the living God and from the very people who can provide us with the life-sustaining encouragement we need (see 3:12-13; 10:23-25). Chronic existence in this state can lead us to an unspeakable, life-altering rejection of the only source of wholeness (10:26-31). Sin can entangle our feet and cause us to trip (12:1). If we do not heal from the injuries we suffer, we may become irreparably damaged (12:13). Hebrews 10:19—12:13 provides a series of remedies for the fainting heart:

(1) The first comes in a *strong reaffirmation of our confidence and hope.* Confidence is not just a subjective feeling of courage or boldness, but the objective privilege all believers have through Jesus Christ. It is the right of access to come before a holy God (10:19), knowing that the sprinkled blood of Jesus has utterly cleansed our conscience from guilt (10:22). The confidence we have is not self-confidence, but a sense of absolute trust in the work of Christ on our behalf. One can hardly put it better than the hymn writer Horatio Spafford ("It Is Well with My Soul"): "Though Satan should buffet, though trials should come / Let this blest assurance control / That Christ hath regarded my helpless estate / and hath shed His own blood for my soul."

Therefore, after reminding us of the confidence we now have (10:19), the preacher encourages us to "draw near" to God (10:22), "hold unswervingly to the hope" of our confession (10:23), and engage in the Christian practices of love, well-doing, and fellowship that will empower us to go on (10:24-25). We must not miss this last step. We all need to plant ourselves within an environment of authentic Christian fellowship. There our sins and failures can be confronted (see 3:12-13). Our service of love and self-sacrificial generosity can be spurred on (10:24; see 6:10). Our commitment to Christ "till the end" (3:14), or in light of "the Day approaching," can be fortified by others who share our confession of faith (10:25). The mutual encouragement we experience will help us maintain "full assurance of hope" and "full assurance of faith" (6:11 NRSV; 10:22).

Continued confidence and hope are warranted for two reasons. First, the one "who promised"—God—"is faithful" (10:23). This is an unquestioned fact in Hebrews (see 11:11), based upon God's unchanging nature and purpose, which make it "impossible for God to lie" (6:17-18). Second, it is expedient for us not to throw away our confidence, in view of God's sure promise: a rich reward, complete with "better and lasting possessions" (10:34; see vv 34-36).

(2) Since a paralysis of fear and doubt poses a threat, the solution is *strong, enduring faith*. The preacher does not simply command us, "Believe! Persevere!"—at least not in so many words (see 10:35-36; 12:12-13). Rather, he assures us that we are among those who have faith, who will eventually reach salvation, and not "those who shrink back and are destroyed" (10:39). Then he does three things to stir our faith and resolve:

First, he defines what faith is. For Hebrews, faith is not a stab in the dark or a leap into the unknown. Quite the opposite, it is a way of seeing reality in the future (or past, → 11:3) as God does. Faith is like a title of ownership, a guarantee, securing future blessings we hope for; it is proof of things we cannot yet behold with our physical eyes (→ 11:1). Specifically, Hebrews speaks of a heavenly country, the city of God, which we will one day inhabit. Faith looks forward to this reality, shaping all of our decisions and plans, with the expectation of moving in to reside there.

What faith sees is not simply a final dwelling place. What is "better" about this place is that God is its "architect and builder" (11:10). God has prepared this city for us, because he wants to welcome us there as his people (11:16). Faith's ultimate goal is not mercenary. It is not belief and right action in the expectation of receiving from God untold riches. Faith endeavors to "please God" by living in such a way that affirms his existence as a holy and righteous God. The person of faith "earnestly seeks" God as the one who metes out just rewards and punishments (11:6; see 2:2; 10:35). Moses, to be sure, weighed the treasures of Egypt against "his reward" in the future. But he endured disgrace for Christ "because he saw him who is invisible" (11:26-27).

Second, Hebrews does more than define what faith is and urge us to live by it: he shows us how people have lived by faith in the past. A thread runs from the community's past endurance of suffering (10:32-39) back to the biblical heroes of the past who lived by faith without ever receiving God's promise (11:1-39). It extends forward to the current "race" we must run, with the faithful men and women of old as a host of witnesses (12:1), and Jesus, "the author and perfecter" of faith as the premier example of faithful endurance. The faithfulness of those who have gone before functions as a motivation for us to follow them and not disappoint them by giving up before reaching the finish line.

Third, he explains the means by which our endurance is tested and strengthened (God's discipline) and the end toward which it is directed (God's holiness). This bleeds into the final remedy for those who are disheartened and weary in the struggle to maintain their commitment to Christ.

(3) *Hebrews invites us to interpret our struggles in the light of God's big picture for our lives.* Our endurance of suffering is for the purpose of divine education/training.

Before we proceed, we must offer an important caveat. Hebrews does not and should not be taken to provide a solution to the problem of evil. This perennial question must be left to other tomes devoted to advanced philosophical and theological discourse. The scope of Hebrews' discussion pertains narrowly to the suffering and challenges people of faith face in their determination to hold on to the Christian confession.

When we experience hardships on account of our faith in Christ, we must perceive them as part of God's larger plan to form us into a holy people. Hebrews 12:5-29 recalls other NT exhortations to evaluate faith's trials and temptations in light of the ultimate glory to be revealed (Rom 8:18-39) or as opportunities for character formation (Jas 1:2-4), likened to refining gold by fire (1 Pet 1:6-7). The notion of enduring suffering as God's parental discipline is somewhat unique to Hebrews (see 1 Cor 11:32; 2 Cor 6:9), but the associated athletic imagery is not (1 Cor 9:24-27; Phil 3:12-14; see Pfitzner 1967).

Hebrews makes three main points about the work of divine discipline in our lives:

First, we ought to view the endurance of suffering as a necessary part of our spiritual training as children of God (Heb 12:7-8). What would be surprising is if we never encountered any difficulties or pain. In fact, the presence of suffering—not just any suffering, but the sort of hardship associated with our devotion to Christ—proves that we are God's dear children.

Second, God's discipline is infinitely better than that of earthly parents (12:9-10). Our natural parents discipline us for a relatively brief time. Most of them do the best they can with their limited knowledge and judgment. But our heavenly Father's discipline is lifelong and designed to prepare us to live in eternity. We can trust that God will use even the most painful chastisement for our ultimate good.

Third, while discipline is unpleasant, it results in exquisite happiness, peace, and holiness. We do not have to train for a marathon to grasp this. Even those who have dragged themselves to the gym several times a week can understand the difficulty of a training regimen. But the exhilaration and sense of well-being that follow the exhaustion of intense physical exercise are truly satisfying.

The preacher speaks of several positive outcomes from God's spiritual training. Simply put, we will live (12:9). In other words, we will experience salvation. We will have eternal life with God, enjoying the same "power of an indestructible life" that Christ has (7:16). We will gain that "better resurrection" (11:35; see Phil 3:10-11). More importantly, the end result will be participation in the very holiness of God: God's eternal blessedness, happiness, and goodness (Heb 12:10). The preacher speaks of God's arduous program of spiritual discipline reaping a "harvest of righteousness and peace" (12:11).

It is clear from a parallel discussion in 5:11-14 (and later in Hebrews: e.g., 12:14-17; 13:1-6, 15-16, 20-21), that the kind of spiritual and moral maturity God has in mind is not reserved for "the sweet bye and bye." None of us can claim to be "spirits of the righteous made perfect" until we enter into the eternal city (12:23 NIV[11]). But we can be righteous by faith now (see 11:4, 7). God provides the intensive training to give us an expertise in moral reasoning: to make us wise, discerning good from evil (see comment on 5:13-14); to make us good, so that our actions are aligned with "the will of God" (10:36) and please God (11:5-6; see 13:21).

We must emphasize that holiness is not a human achievement, even though it requires a commitment to believe, submit, and persevere under God's discipline. Neither does any garden variety of suffering or misfortune have the inherent dynamism to build our moral character. God is the ultimate source of holiness (2:11), and only God, in his infinite wisdom, can utilize life's hardships and tragedies as instruments of sanctification. For Hebrews, this means that divine providence aims at shaping men and women in accordance with their God-given nature and destiny. God designed human beings to commune with him and other people, and to do so in ways that offer up acceptable worship to him. Christ's death on the cross and God's fatherly discipline finally make this destiny a reality.

B. Exhortations to Offer Acceptable Worship (12:14—13:25)

The finale of Hebrews' *peroratio* brings into clear view the goal both of Christ's covenant sacrifice and the readers' firm commitment and enduring faith. The end point is the approach of God's people to offer acceptable worship in the divine presence.

The unity of 12:14—13:25 is indicated by an *inclusio*, using a word suggested in 12:11: "peace" (12:14; 13:20; Lane 1991, 432). The unit also features significant vocabulary and concepts:

- "grace"/"thanks [*charis*]" (12:15, 28; 13:9, 25)
- Jesus' covenant "blood" (12:24; 13:12, 20)
- the destination of believers' pilgrimage (12:22, 28; 13:14)
- acts of worship that are "pleasing" or "acceptable" to God (12:28; 13:16, 21)

Two sections clarify how the community's authentic worship links to Christ's sacrifice and true Christian commitments, rather than to the cultic sacrifices and regulations under the old covenant. The first (12:14-29) is couched within the sermon's final warnings against apostasy (12:14-17, 25-29). It contrasts the tangible and terrifying encounter with God at Mount

Sinai (12:18-21) with the joyous, heavenly scene at Mount Zion (12:22-24). The second (13:1-25) presents a variety of practical exhortations designed to enable the community to maintain its unity, holiness, and distinctive Christian identity. Each of these two sections lays stress on worship that is pleasing to God (12:28; 13:15-16, 21), in response to receiving God's eternal kingdom (12:28; 13:13-14), and based on Christ's covenant sacrifice (12:24; 13:12, 20).

I. Receive the Unshakable Kingdom with Gratitude and Worship (12:14-29)

BEHIND THE TEXT

We have reached the summit of Hebrews' rhetorical and pastoral address. This section brings to a climax principal concerns and theological motifs of the sermon:

- The preacher has frequently reminded his listeners of the hope or promise of inheritance they will receive (1:14; 4:1; 6:12, 17; 8:6; 9:15; 10:23, 36; see 11:8, 9, 11, 13, 39). Receiving the inheritance, the blessing belonging to the "firstborn" (12:16-17, 23), is now depicted as our approach to "the heavenly Jerusalem" (v 22). It is our reception of an unshakable kingdom (v 28).
- The approach itself ("you have come to" [vv 18, 22]) completes the exhortations to "approach" or "draw near" to God that precede and follow the central argumentative section of the sermon (4:16; 10:22; see 7:25; 11:6).
- The preacher urges the community to watch over anyone among them in danger of forfeiting God's grace (12:15; see 2:1-4; 3:12-15; 4:1, 11; 10:24-25). One last time he warns that apostasy is irreversible (12:16-17; see 3:12, 16—4:2; 6:4-8; 10:26-31) and will meet with God's terrible, fiery judgment (12:29; see 6:8; 10:27, 39).
- The contrast between Sinai and Zion reiterates themes from the central section of the sermon. The old and new covenants are contrasted with regard to the nature of the sanctuary (tangible, i.e., earthly [12:18] vs. heavenly [v 22]; compare 8:5; 9:1 with 8:2; 9:11; 9:23-25), their mediators (12:21 and 24; compare 3:2, 3, 5; 9:19 with 7:22; 8:6; 9:15), and the sprinkling of blood (12:24; compare 9:13, 19, 21 with 10:22). The superior sacrifice of Christ fully prepares people for worship (12:28; see 9:14; 10:2). While barriers to approaching God existed under the old covenant (12:18-21; see 9:1-10; 10:1-3, 11), members of the new covenant enjoy unfettered access to the divine presence (12:22-24; see 4:15-16; 9:11-14; 10:10, 12-14, 19-22; see Lane 1991, 448).
- A theme reverberating through the sermon rises to a crescendo. God has spoken, particularly through his Son in these last days (1:1-2a), and we must heed his voice to be saved (2:1-4; 3:7—4:14; 5:11-14;

8:8-13; 10:36-39). Now the preacher amplifies the urgency of responding appropriately to the God who speaks, for the divine voice will cause a final cosmic and celestial shaking (12:15-27).

Hebrews 12:14-29 is unified by the theme of inheritance (v 17), or what the "firstborn" rightfully receive (vv 16, 23): the city of God, the unshakable kingdom (vv 22, 28). Of primary importance, however, is *how* we should receive the inheritance. Holiness and gratitude sum up the proper disposition.

Given the relative infrequency of "grace" vocabulary in Hebrews (eight times), it is notable that the opening to the passage cautions against falling short of God's "grace [*charitos*]" (v 15), while its closing encourages us to "be thankful" (lit., "have grace [*echōmen charin*]"; v 28). The appropriate response to divine favor is gratefulness. Holiness must accompany thanksgiving, since the former is requisite to entering into God's presence (v 14), the latter to offering acceptable worship to God (v 28).

A vestige of the athletic metaphor of a footrace remains from the preceding passage (12:1-4, 12-13; note the verbs "pursue" and "falls short" [vv 14-15 HCSB]). The imagery transitions to the cultic and moral purity required for acceptable worship. These ideas are evident throughout each of the three segments of the passage:

First, in vv 14-17 the preacher warns against anyone upsetting the peace and holiness of the community. He describes the danger of a "bitter root" that can "defile many" (v 15). He points to Esau as an example of someone whose immoral and profane actions disqualified him from the inheritance of the firstborn (vv 16-17).

Second, vv 18-24 climactically depict the approach to the heavenly sanctuary. The verb *proserchomai* ("come to" [vv 18, 22]) in the LXX and Hebrews refers to priests and people drawing near to the sanctuary for worship (→ 4:16). Hebrews' vision of Mount Zion and the heavenly Jerusalem evokes Jewish apocalyptic images of heaven as God's sanctuary (Son 2005, 91-92; → 12:22*a* sidebar, "Zion and the Heavenly Jerusalem: Images of God's Temple").

The preacher contrasts the tumult and terror at Mount Sinai (vv 18-21) with the festive gathering of angels and saints at Mount Zion (vv 22-24). Under the old covenant, God's presence was altogether frightening and unapproachable. The new covenant has established bold access to the throne of God. Christ as mediator and decisive sacrifice for sins provides the necessary purity and permission to appear freely before God (v 24; see 4:14-16; 10:19-22).

Third, the preacher warns readers not to refuse the One who speaks—God. They must keep in mind the eschatological judgment that will shake not just the earth (as at Sinai), but heaven also (12:25-27). Those who heed God's voice will participate in the enduring reality of God's kingdom, which "cannot be shaken." Thus, Hebrews urges us to be thankful and "worship God acceptably with reverence and awe" (v 28). "Worship" is associated with services rendered to God in a religious or cultic setting.

Hebrews 13 will be devoted to providing instruction (parenesis) on how the recipients can maintain their character as holy worshipers.

IN THE TEXT

a. Pursue Peace and Holiness (12:14-17)

The metaphor of running in pursuit of virtue, and the danger of failing to complete the race due to injury (vv 12-13), are now explained in terms of living in peace and ethical holiness. This brief paragraph continues the running metaphor at its beginning ("pursue" [v 14 HCSB]; "falls short" [v 15 HCSB]) but shifts to imagery related to moral and cultic purity and inheritance. While the paragraph is closely bound to the preceding section, it breaks new ground in preparation for the climactic approach to the heavenly Jerusalem (vv 18-24) and warning against refusing God's voice (vv 25-29).

The structure of the paragraph reveals the author's pastoral concern for his audience. Verses 14-16 comprise one sentence in Greek.

- Verse 14 begins with a command to pursue peace and holiness.
- Verses 15-16 clarify this admonition with a call to watchfulness against three dangers.
- Verse 17 illustrates the warnings against apostasy, appealing to Esau as a cautionary example.

■ 14 The exhortation **Make every effort to live in peace with all men** was common ("Seek peace and pursue it" [Ps 34:14; 1 Pet 3:11; see Rom 12:18; 14:19; 2 Tim 2:22]). Proverbs 4:25-27 (→ 12:13) may have suggested the thought: "[God] will guide your steps in peace" (Prov 4:27 LXX; Koester 2001, 531). To "pursue" or "run after [*diōkete*]" (BDAG, 254; **Make every effort**) peace extends the running metaphor from Heb 12:1-3, 12-13.

A second object of pursuit is **holiness**. The juxtaposition of peace and holiness is natural, given the earlier reference to "righteousness and peace" as the fruit of divine discipline (v 11). God, in whose holiness true sons will share (v 10), is none other than "the God of peace" (13:20). Peace and purity are linked together elsewhere in the NT (Matt 5:8-9; 1 Thess 5:23).

Holiness here is not an essential attribute or state, such as God possesses (as is "holiness [*hagiotētos*]" in Heb 12:10; against Lane 1991, 450). The form of the noun in v 14 (*hagiasmos*) indicates the action of sanctifying or making holy, emphasizing morally pure conduct (Procksch 1964, 113-14; BDAG, 10). "Practical holiness" is intended (Bruce 1990, 348-49): "living a holy life" (NLT).

It must be borne in mind that this practical outworking of holiness in life is based upon the radical sanctification of the inner self (the conscience [9:9, 14; 10:2, 22]) through Christ's sacrificial death (see 10:10, 14, 29). The pursuit of holiness is undertaken within the context of moral training, under the providential discipline of the Father (12:5-11). The preacher defines the precise moral dimensions of holiness to some extent in vv 15-16 and more fully in 13:1-21.

We now learn why running the race with endurance is so important, and why God's ethical *paideia* is indispensable: **without holiness no one will see the Lord**. To **see the Lord** within the OT prophetic tradition was to see God enthroned in heavenly majesty (1 Kgs 22:19; 2 Chr 18:18; Isa 6:1) or standing in the sanctuary (Amos 9:1). The ultimate vision of God is an eschatological hope. It is a blessing reserved for "the pure in heart" (Matt 5:8); a long-awaited "face to face" knowledge of God (1 Cor 13:12; Rev 22:4). It is a transforming vision that will complete God's work of conforming men and women into the divine likeness (1 John 3:2). Then believers will share fully in God's very own holiness (Heb 12:10) and perfect happiness. This is what theologians call the Beatific Vision.

■ **15-16** The pastoral concern for the community's peace, holiness, and ultimate salvation unfolds in a plea for vigilance. They must assist every single member to avoid three dangers (each marked by **no one**, *mē tis*). The participle translated **See to it** (*episkopountes*) communicates the idea of pastoral oversight and care (BDAG, 379; MM, 244; "look after each other" [NLT]; compare the role of leaders who "watch over you" [13:17*b*]). The author has already repeatedly expressed concern that **no one** should fail to receive God's promised salvation rest (3:12, 13; 4:1, 11).

The first danger is comprehensive. **Look out for each other so that no one** [*mē tis*] **misses** [*hysterōn*] **the grace of God**. To "miss out on" (see CEB) or "fall short of" (LEB, NKJV; see HCSB, NIV[11]) God's grace entails personal failure to finish the race. The preacher has similarly cautioned against falling short (*hystereō*) of entering God's rest (4:1; compare 4:11). The warning is against apostasy—"falling away" from God's gracious benefits (6:4-6). It is shrinking back rather than persevering in faith (10:37-39). Apostasy is ultimate rejection of the blessings of the new covenant (10:26-31), so forfeiting God's grace (see 12:15 REB).

The second danger combines the concerns for holiness and peace: **that no one** [*mē tis*] **like a bitter root grows up to cause trouble and defile many** (see LEB, NET). The preacher loosely quotes Deut 29:18. This employs the imagery of a noxious plant to describe someone who turns from the Lord to serve idols. Apostates upset the peace and stability of the church (**to cause trouble**). They contaminate the community with their unbelief and sin (**defile many**). The notion of cultic and moral defilement (*miainō*) anticipates the final danger in Heb 12:16. It contrasts with the moral excellence of our Great High Priest (7:26, "pure/undefiled [*amiantos*]") and the purity of "the marriage bed" (13:4).

The third warning narrows down the moral and religious threat: **that no one is sexually immoral, or is godless**. *Pornos* refers to someone who is **sexually immoral** (CEB, ESV, LEB; "commits sexual sin" [GW]) or a "fornicator" (KJV; BDAG, 855). The author literally intends those who engage in extramarital sexual activity. Yet it is possible that Hebrews employs the common OT symbol of harlotry for covenant unfaithfulness or idolatry (e.g., Num 14:33; Deut 31:16; Jer 2:20; 5:7; Hos 1:2; an image vividly exploited in Rev 17, esp. v 5; see Attridge 1989, 369; Johnson 2006, 324). Lane, following this metaphorical reading, translates *pornos* as "apostate" (1991, 455). Literal and metaphorical meanings are not mutually exclusive, though the literal is more probable here in light of 13:4 (where the "sexually immoral" [*pornous*] are condemned alongside the "adulterer").

The **sexually immoral** person is paired with the **godless** (*bebēlos*; syntactically there is no warrant for the comma separating them in the NIV). The **godless** refer to those who are "profane" (KJV, NAB), "secular," or "irreligious." They are completely unconcerned with God's demands for holiness (Johnson 2006, 324). Godlessness is an antonym for "holy [*hagios*]," parallel to the antithesis of clean and unclean (Hauck 1964, 604).

Esau is the prototype of all who are so driven by their passions that they forfeit the heavenly reality in favor of transient, earthly pleasure. Readers should avoid being **like Esau, who for a single meal sold his inheritance rights as the oldest son** (*prōtotokia*, **birthright of the firstborn**). Esau's sense of proportion and value was so skewed that he traded away the double portion of inheritance due to the firstborn son **for a single meal** (Thompson 2008, 266).

This is precisely the opposite of the faithful patriarchs, who risked alienation or denied themselves the temporary pleasures of sin in order to inherit an eternal reward (11:8-10, 13, 25-26). The readers must especially identify with Christ, the Firstborn (1:6), who did not seek relief from the pain and shame of the cross in view of "the joy set before him" (12:2). Otherwise, they are in danger of forfeiting their membership among "the church of the firstborn" (12:23; Attridge 1989, 369).

Esau the Immoral in Jewish Tradition

In the OT, Esau and his descendants are objects of prophetic condemnation (Jer 49:8, 10; Obad 6, 8, 18-19, 21; Mal 1:2-3). The foundation for this ongoing reproach is the account of Esau swapping his birthright for a mess of pottage (Gen 25:27-34). Later Jewish tradition expanded upon the biblical portrait of Esau as a skilled hunter and one who "despised his birthright" in preference for satisfying his own appetite (Gen 25:34). It regarded Esau as a sexual deviant, murderer, atheist, and all-around rascally fellow.

Jewish haggadic literature interprets Esau's marriage to Hittite women (Gen 26:34-35) as an instance of sexual immorality (see *Jub.* 25:1). Esau was guilty of homosexual behavior (*Gen. Rab.* 63.9 on Gen 25:27) and the rape of a betrothed woman (*Gen. Rab.* 63.12 on Gen 25:29). As a hunter, he not only stalked game, but men. He murdered King Nimrod (*Tg. Ps.-J.* on Gen 25:27) and brought on the death of his grandfather, Abraham, by his shameful actions (*Pesiq. Rab.* 12).

Lentil stew was the traditional meal for mourners, over which words of comfort were spoken. Jacob prepared this dish for his father, Isaac, to mourn Abraham's death (*Tg. Ps.-J.* on Gen 25:29; *Pirqe R. El.* 35). Esau not only traded his birthright for it but also made blasphemous speeches (*Gen. Rab.* 43; *Pesaḥ.* 22b). He denied immortality, the resurrection, and God (*Tg. Ps.-J.* on Gen 25:29). Thus, Jewish tradition classed him among the three great atheists (*Tanḥ.,* Toledoth 24; *Sanh.* 101b; see Buhl, Hirsch, and Schechter 1925).

Philo characterized Esau's bartering away his birthright as an example of catering to one's passions rather than pursuing virtue. Esau indulged "without restraint the pleasures of the belly and the lower lying parts" (*Virtues* 208; see *Sobriety* 26) and his "craving that pursues evil" (*Sacrifices* 120; see 81). Esau "exercised himself in the basest things" (*Migration* 153). He was subservient to his bodily passions rather than to reason (*Alleg. Interp.* 3.2; 3.191) and exhibited a "savagery that knows no discipline" (QG 4.242; see Thompson 2008, 259-60).

Hebrews' description of Esau as sexually immoral and godless (12:16) comports with these Jewish traditions, although it is unclear how developed they had become or to what extent Hebrews knew them.

■ **17** The outcome of Esau's folly serves as a warning directly applicable to the readers. The verb rendered **as you know** (*iste*) could be construed as an imperative, **know this**. In either case, the appeal to the readers' knowledge implies that the story of Esau should discourage them from imitating his course of action.

Hebrews' way of describing God's response to Esau's ungrateful and contemptible act is rhetorically forceful. Esau "sold [*apedeto*]" (v 16) his birthright. **Afterward, . . . when he wanted to inherit this blessing, he was rejected** (*apedokimasthē*). Once an heir to divine blessing, he repudiated it and fell under God's "irrevocable curse" (Lane 1991, 457; see 6:7-8).

Esau's rejection was complete and permanent. In English, **he could bring about no change of mind** is as ambiguous as the literal translation "for he found no place for repentance" (NASB, NKJV). The meaning is not quite that "he could not change what he had done" (NIV[11]; see GW, NJB), true as that was. The Greek idiom "find a place" refers to a favorable circumstance for doing something, an opportunity or chance (BDAG, 1012; Attridge 1989, 370; see Acts 25:16). Hence, "he found no opportunity for repentance" (NET; see ESV, HCSB, NAB, REB).

The clause **though he sought it** [*autēn*] **with tears** underscores the irreversible nature of Esau's apostasy. Genesis 27:34-41 indicates that Esau sought and received a secondary **blessing** from his father. However, grammatically it is possible that a **change of mind** (*metanoias*, **repentance**) is what was out of reach. This word is closer in proximity to the pronoun **it** than is **blessing**, which occurs earlier in the verse. Moreover, the expressions **found** [*heuron*] **no place for repentance** and **sought** [*ekzētēsas*] **it with tears** are parallel. This reading fits Hebrews' understanding that final apostasy is irreversible (Heb

2:1-4; 6:4-8; 10:26-31)—that "it is impossible . . . to be brought back to repentance" (6:4, 6; Attridge 1989, 370).

b. Mountain of Terror and Mountain of Celebration (12:18-24)

The rhetorical climax of Hebrews contrasts the old and new covenants through vivid descriptions of two mountain scenes:

The first is at Mount Sinai. There the Israelites prepared to hear the synopsis of their covenant obligations, the Ten Commandments (Exod 19—20; Deut 4—5). By highlighting details from this scene, Hebrews demonstrates how under the old covenant the worshipers were distant from God's presence and disinclined to listen to God's voice, since they were so utterly overtaken by fear.

The second is at Mount Zion, teeming with angels and saints gathered around God the Judge and Jesus the mediator of the new covenant. The heavenly scene radiates with celebration, family belonging, and righteous perfection. The voice heard there is that of Jesus' sprinkled blood, "that speaks a better word" (Heb 12:24). The appealing eschatological vision of the city of God prepares for the final admonition not to refuse the One who is speaking from heaven (vv 25-29).

The contrast between these two sites of worship evokes emotions suited to Hebrews' rhetorical purpose. Mount Sinai is a place of terror and alienation from God. Mount Zion is a place of inclusion and jubilation in the divine presence. The preacher clearly wants to repel his listeners from going back to the temporal and tangible arrangements for worship under the old covenant. Rather, he wants them to stay committed in their pilgrimage to the heavenly Jerusalem.

■ **18-21** The preacher begins with what the readers **have not come to** ("approached" [NAB]; "drawn near to" [CEB]; on the verb *proserchomai* → 4:16; 10:22). They have not approached **what can be touched.** The word **mountain** does not appear in the earliest and best manuscripts here (including the important witness 𝔓⁴⁶). Nevertheless, that the scene in view is at a mountain is certain from v 20; and though Mount Sinai is not specified, it is indicated strongly by the textual echoes from Exod 19—20 and Deut 4—5 in these verses.

By referring more generally to **what can be touched** or "the tangible" (REB), in contrast to the heavenly scene in Heb 12:22-24, the preacher repeats a familiar distinction between the earthly and the heavenly. It is similar to the contrast between the inferior "earthly sanctuary" under the old covenant (9:1; see 8:5; 9:8) and the "true" (8:2) and "greater and more perfect tabernacle" under the new, that is "not a part of this creation" (9:11; see 10:23-25).

The preacher paints the scene with details from Exodus (19:12, 16, 19; 20:18) and Deuteronomy (4:11-12; 5:5, 22-27; 18:16). The Israelites' encounter with God at Sinai included a mountain **burning with fire** (Heb 12:18; a detail creating an *inclusio* with v 29). The mountain was shrouded menacingly with **darkness** and **gloom** and **storm**. The poetic word **gloom** has been inserted among the biblical descriptors for added rhetorical effect: **darkness** (*gnophō*) and **gloom** (*zophō*) rhyme. The people were frightened by **a trumpet blast** and **a voice speaking words** (v 19*a*).

The people recoiled from the **voice** of God: They **begged that no further word be spoken to them** (v 19*b*). The rationale for their refusal to listen anymore was **because they could not bear what was commanded** (v 20*a*) concerning the boundary of holiness around the mountain (Exod 19:12-13): **If even an animal touches the mountain, it must be stoned** (Heb 12:20*b*). Even the accidental encroachment of a senseless creature would be met with certain death! The effect was to distance the people from God, rather than draw them into his presence.

The sight or "spectacle" (v 21 NAB) of the theophany (*phantazomenon*; BDAG, 1049) **was so terrifying** that even **Moses**, the mediator of the old covenant, was afraid. Moses had been afraid when God spoke to him from the burning bush (Exod 3:6; Acts 7:32) and, according to later rabbinic tradition, at the giving of the Law (*b. Šhabb.* 88b; Koester 2001, 543-44). At this point, Hebrews may be telescoping the Ten Commandments scene with another that occurred at the foot of Mount Sinai (compare the conflation of sacrificial rituals, → Heb 9:13-14, 18-22). Moses' exact confession, **I am trembling** [*entromos*] **with fear** (*ekphobos*) (12:21), never appears in the OT. However, when God's wrath broke out against the Israelites for fashioning the golden calf, Moses said, "I am afraid [*ekphobos*] because you have provoked the wrath and anger of the Lord to destroy you" (Deut 9:19 LXX).

■ **22*a*** The earthly scene of terror in Heb 12:18-21 ("you have not come to" [v 18]) is contrasted with a majestic heavenly scene in vv 22-24 (**But you have come to** [v 22]). The important verb **come to** (*proserchomai*) occurs for the last time in Hebrews. It connotes the approach into God's presence for worship (→ 4:16; 10:22).

Eight expressions (each separated by ***and*** [*kai*]) describe the goal toward which believers are advancing (12:22-24). Two expressions in v 22*a* identify the location. Six more describe the inhabitants of the heavenly city, climaxing with Jesus and his sprinkled blood (vv 22*b*-24).

The place **you have come to** is called, first, **Mount Zion**. Since the establishment of the Davidic monarchy, Zion was God's holy mountain and earthly dwelling (Joel 2:1; 4:17, 21; Pss 9:11; 65:1; 76:2; 87:1-3, 5-6; 99:2). This was the city of the Lord (Ps 48:2; Isa 60:14), the site of God's sanctuary (Ps 20:2). By the postexilic period, Zion became the rallying point for God's salvation (2 Kgs 19:31; Isa 24:23; 35:10; 52:1, 8; 59:20; 62:1; Zech 1:14-16; 2:10; 8:3; 9:9) to which all of the nations will flow (Isa 2:2-4; 18:7; Ps 102:22-23; Balz 1993a).

By the intertestamental period, Zion became the counterpart to Sinai (and sometimes Eden, *Jub.* 8:19; *T. Dan* 5:12). The theophany at Zion "in the new creation" (*Jub.* 1:28; 4:26; 8:19) would eclipse the divine manifestation on Sinai. Sinai was an earthly place; Zion, a transcendent, heavenly place (see Gal 4:24-27; Attridge 1989, 374). Important for Hebrews is Zion's role within a complex of apocalyptic images concerning the new Jerusalem, paradise, and the heavenly temple of God.

Thus, Zion in Hebrews is not the earthly mountain in Palestine, but **the heavenly Jerusalem, the city of the living God** (NIV reverses the order of the two phrases in Greek, and in most translations, including NIV[11]). This is the "place" of the patriarchs' inheritance (11:8), the heavenly homeland (11:16), the unshakable kingdom (12:28), and the "enduring city . . . that is to come" (13:14).

Zion and the Heavenly Jerusalem: Images of God's Temple

The idea of a heavenly Jerusalem revealed at the end of time was widespread in the Second Temple period. It is prevalent in apocalyptic literature, such as Revelation in the NT and various books of the OT Pseudepigrapha. In *4 Ezra* the heavenly Jerusalem is referred to as "the city" (8:52; 10:27) or "Zion" (10:44; 13:36). In *2 Baruch* it is equated with "Paradise" (4:6; 59:4, 8).

The new Jerusalem or Zion is a transcendent reality, made manifest at the end (*4 Ezra* 13:36; *2 Bar.* 4:3; see Gal 4:26; *Apoc. El.* 1:10; *Jub.* 1:29). In *2 Enoch* it is the "highest Jerusalem" in the "highest heaven" and is Enoch's "eternal inheritance" (55:2). The picture of Mount Zion as a heavenly kingdom in *4 Ezra* 2:42-48 is akin to the description of the coming kingdom of God in Heb 12:22-24 and Rev 19:1-8 (see Rev 14:1).

A celestial temple is often associated with the new Jerusalem (Rev 21:22 is a distinct exception; but see Rev 11:19). In many cases, an entire temple appears in heaven (*1 En.* 14:10-20; *T. Levi* 3:4-10; 5:1; *2 Bar.* 4:5; Wis 9:8). In other instances, heaven itself is the inner sanctuary of God's cosmic temple, with the earth as God's footstool (1 Kgs 8:22-53; Isa 66:1; 1 Chr 28:2; Lam 2:1; Josephus, *Ant.* 3.123, 180-81; Philo, *Moses* 2.88; *Spec. Laws* 1.66). In *2 Baruch* "the likeness of the tabernacle" in paradise (4:6) is also called "the likeness of Zion," which was to be made "after the likeness of the present sanctuary" (59:6; compare Heb 8:2, 5; 9:11, 24). All of the paraphernalia of the tabernacle were shown to Adam, to Abraham, and to Moses on Mount Sinai (*2 Bar.* 4:3-6). Angels rescued these items, prior to the destruction of the earthly Jerusalem and its temple, and preserved them until the time when Zion will be restored forever (*2 Bar.* 6:7-9; 80:2).

Hebrews seems to be in touch with these traditions concerning the heavenly Jerusalem or Zion as the dwelling place of God—his holy temple and throne room. Both cultic and regal metaphors are used in Hebrews concerning the approach of the Son of God (1:3, 13; 4:14; 8:1; 9:24; 10:12; 12:2) and the people of God (4:16; 7:25; 10:1, 22) into the divine presence. Thus, coming to Zion is a powerful image of our final entrance into "the true tabernacle" of God (8:1). It is when we will ultimately receive the "promised eternal inheritance" in the kingdom of God (9:15; 12:28). (For further study of the temple symbolism related to the heavenly Jerusalem and Zion, see Son 2005, 52-56, 189-97.)

12:22a

■ **22b-23** Five expressions in vv 22-24 describe the inhabitants of Zion, with a sixth personifying Jesus' sprinkled blood.

First, **you have come to thousands upon thousands of angels in joyful assembly** (v 22b). Apocalyptic visions are never complete without the presence of *myriads* or countless angels surrounding the heavenly throne (Dan 7:10; Rev 5:11; *1 En.* 71:8-9; *2 En.* 40:3; *3 En.* B 22:4-6). This throng is **in joyful assembly.** The word *panēgyrei*, found only this once in the NT, is thoroughly classical. It denotes a gathering of the whole populace for cultic events or festivals (Seeseman 1967). Religious aspects included processions, prayers, and sacrifices (Rev 4—5 is an NT example of a festal gathering). Feasting, amusements, and wild revelry also marked such occasions in their pagan settings (see Philo's disapproving descriptions in *Cherubim* 91-92; *Embassy* 12-14). In Hebrews, the term conveys a note of delight, celebration, and worship, not unlike the Sabbath celebration (*sabbatismos*) associated with entrance into the divine rest (Heb 4:9; Lane 1991, 467).

Second, we come **to the church of the firstborn, whose names are written in heaven** (v 23a). The **church** or **assembly** (*ekklēsia*) is the entire collection of God's people. It is "the whole Church" (NJB), comprised of OT and NT saints. They are called **the firstborn** (*prōtotokōn*) to indicate their rightful share in the divine promises of inheritance and salvation (see 1:14; 6:12, 17; 9:15; 11:7-9; contrast 12:16-17).

That their **names are written in heaven** authorizes them as citizens of the heavenly Jerusalem. Ancient cities contained registries of leading citizens who were members of the **assembly,** the governing body (see Koester 2001, 545, 550-51; see Phil 3:20). Jewish apocalyptic often incorporated the analogous image of the righteous being enrolled in heavenly books, particularly within the context of God's final judgment (e.g., the Book of Life, Rev 3:5; 13:8; 17:8; 20:12, 15, 27; see Exod 32:32-33; Ps 69:28; Dan 12:1; Luke 10:20; Phil 4:3; *Jub.* 2:20; 30:22; *1 En.* 47:3-4; 104:1; 108:3; *Herm. Vis.* 1.3.2; *Sim.* 2.9).

So the third description of the city's inhabitants is fitting at this point: **and to God, the judge of all** (Heb 12:23b). God (or God's word [4:12]) is frequently described as a judge in Hebrews, especially in the sense of meting out justice on the ungodly (10:27, 30; 13:4; see 6:8). The final or eternal judgment is a major tenet of Christian faith (6:2; 9:27). Here the accent may be on God giving his just reward to the righteous (10:35; 11:6, 26; see Matt 5:12; 6:1; Luke 6:23), though the thought of the judicial rejection or destruction of the godless is not far away (Heb 12:17, 25-27, 29).

Fourth, there are **the spirits of righteous men made perfect** (v 23c). Spirits [or souls] **of *the* righteous** is a stock phrase in Jewish apocalyptic literature for righteous people who have died (*Jub.* 23:30-31; *1 En.* 22:9; 41:8; 102:4; *2 Bar.* 30:2; *3 Bar.* 10:5; *4 Ezra* 4:35; 7:99; *Herm. Mand.* 11.1.15; see Pr Azar 1:64; Philo, *Moses* 1.279; BDAG, 832; Lane 1991, 470). In saying that the spirits of the righteous are **made perfect** (*teteleiōmenōn*), the preacher refers to the faithful under both covenants who have attained the ultimate destiny and inheritance for God's people.

This final use of perfection language in Hebrews is the culmination of earlier uses regarding both the perfection of the Son of God and of those who look to him as their Great High Priest. The Son's perfection was the result of his obedience and suffering (2:10; 5:8-9). It consisted in his being qualified as the ever-living high priest who achieved eternal salvation for believers (5:9; 7:28; see 7:24-25; 9:15, 24-28). Only the Son's once-for-all sacrifice of himself achieved the needed perfection (9:9; 10:1, 14), the decisive cleansing (9:14; 10:2, 22) required for men and women to approach the holy presence of God. Christ's self-offering accomplishes what the Levitical sacrifices never could (7:11, 19, 28; 9:9; 10:1).

This is why the saints of old could not be **made perfect** without us (11:40). They needed to be perfected by the One who was himself perfected to bring "many sons to glory" (2:10). Christ was the first to enter into the inner sanctuary as our "forerunner" (6:20 NIV[11]). He is the "author and perfecter of faith" (12:2 NASB).

■ **24** The vision of Zion reaches its apex in two final descriptions. We have come to the Person—**Jesus**—who has made our access into the heavenly Jerusalem possible, and to the means—his **sprinkled blood**—by which he opened "a new and living way" (10:20, 22).

This verse recalls the central arguments of Hebrews (7:1—10:18), which sought to establish the superiority of Christ's priesthood, sacrifice, covenant, and heavenly sanctuary (Attridge 1989, 376-77). Christ is designated by the same title used in 9:15: **the mediator of a new covenant** (→ 8:6). As is his custom, the preacher reserves the name **Jesus** for the end of the clause. It is a pity no English translation preserves the rhetorical suspense of the Greek word order: ***and to the mediator of a new covenant—Jesus*** (→ 2:9 sidebar, "Use of the Name 'Jesus' in Hebrews"). The name **Jesus** hints at the necessity for the Son to share in the mortal existence of fallen humanity (2:9-10, 14-18; 5:7-10; 10:5-10). Because he did not sin (4:15; 7:26), he carries out the perfect ministry as high priest of the new covenant.

The **sprinkled blood** alludes to Christ's perfect sacrifice that inaugurated the new covenant and provided decisive purgation for both the heavenly sanctuary and worshipers (→ 9:15-28; 10:1-18). In the central section, Christ's sprinkled blood was set in contrast to the ineffective sprinkling of the blood of sacrificial animals (9:13, 19, 21; 10:22). Here the preacher contrasts the primordial shedding of Abel's blood—the first murder victim since the creation of the world—with Christ's once-for-all sacrifice of himself "at the end of the ages" (9:26).

Hebrews is aware of the biblical account of Abel's blood crying out from the ground (Gen 4:10; see Heb 11:4). As the first in a long line of martyrs (Matt 23:35; Luke 11:15; Ign. *Eph.* 12:1), righteous Abel's blood cries out for vengeance (see 2 Macc 8:3; *Sib. Or.* 3:310-13; Rev 6:10). But Christ's sprinkled blood **speaks a better word than the blood of Abel.** The expansive paraphrase of the NLT captures the thought: it "speaks of forgiveness instead of crying out for vengeance like the blood of Abel." Rather than provoking the wrath of God against sin, the blood of Christ turns away God's wrath (Heb 2:17 NIV^{mg}) by decisively removing sin and its defilement (7:27; 9:26, 28; see 10:4, 11).

Indeed, the very purpose of Christ's coming was to offer himself as the definitive sacrifice for sins at the end of the ages (9:26-28; 10:5-14). Thus, God's ancient covenant promise spoken through the prophet Jeremiah could be realized (31:34): "[I] will remember their sins no more" (Heb 8:12; 10:17). It is no coincidence that the opening to the sermon related in one breath that God "has spoken to us by his Son" (1:2*a*), and in another that "after he [the Son] had provided purification for sins, he sat down at the right hand of the Majesty in heaven" (1:3*d*). Surely, this sums up the **better word,** "the point" of the entire sermon (8:1-2). It is this message of salvation that Hebrews has repeatedly called upon his listeners to heed (2:1-4; 3:7, 15; 4:2, 7), and will again, climactically, in the next paragraph.

c. Listen to the Heavenly Voice (12:25-29)

Hebrews 12:25-29 concludes the final warning of the homily, which began in 12:14. The preacher masterfully recapitulates previous warnings (esp. 2:1-4; 3:7—4:13; 10:26-31), while also developing his final admonitions in ways that complete the rhetorical climax of 12:14-29.

■ **25** The opening formula, **See to it** (*blepete*) is similar to the formula ("See to it [*episkopountes*]") in v 15's warning against apostasy. The same formula is in the sermon's second warning (3:7—4:13), which likewise warns (*blepete* [3:14]) not to **turn away** from the living God.

See to it that you do not refuse him who speaks reprises the theme of paying attention to God's word, which dominated 1:1—4:13 (1:1-2*a*; 2:1-4; 3:7, 15; 4:7, 12-13; see also 5:11). The warning is especially reminiscent of 2:1-4 (see Bateman 2007b, 28-43). Hebrews 2:2-3 makes an analogous lesser-to-greater comparison between the punishment for neglect of the Mosaic law and of "such a great salvation." **If they did not escape** [*exephygo;* see *ekpheuxometha* in 2:3] **when they refused him who warned them** reminds us again of the deadly fate of the disobedient wilderness generation (→ 3:16-19). However, by repeating the verb *paraiteomai* (**refuse**) from 12:20 ("begged") and "voice" (v 26) from v 19, the preacher clearly builds the lesser-to-greater argument on the preceding Sinai-Zion comparison (vv 18-21, 22-24).

That God warned them **on earth** refers to the frightening scene at Sinai (compare its description as a mountain that can be "touched" [v 18]). Due to the notes of celebration and atonement for sin connected with Zion (vv 22-24), one might expect an offer of divine favor at this point. However, as in earlier warnings, at issue is the consequence for decisive *rejection* of divine grace. So once again the preacher ratchets up his warning against final apostasy. It is important to note that in the midst of the inhabitants of the heavenly Jerusalem we see "God, the judge of all" (v 23b). Thus, the lesser-to-greater (*qal wahomer*) argument: If there was no escape from divine judgment for those who rejected the voice of God on earth, **how much less** [lit., ***much more***] **will we, if we turn away from him who warns from heaven?**

■ **26-27** The vertical contrast is also interpreted chronologically between earthly Sinai (**at that time**) and heavenly Zion (**now God promises that in the future, I will shake;** Lane 1991, 478). This interpretation comes from viewing the emblems of God's two covenants (Sinai and Zion) through the prophetic lens of Hag 2:6.

The quake at Mount Sinai (Exod 19:18) was later amplified to be a shaking of the whole earth (Ps 68:8; see Judg 5:4; Pss 77:18; 114:7), as here: **At that time his voice shook the earth.** Hebrews appropriates the prophecy from Haggai as a prediction of the end-time earthquake that the prophets associated with the Day of the Lord (Isa 13:1-22; Joel 2:1-11; → Heb 10:25 and sidebar, "The Day"). In later Jewish traditions, this was seen as a truly cosmic shaking (*2 Bar.* 32:1-2; 59:3; *4 Ezra* 6:11-17; 10:25-28; *Sib. Or.* 3:675-81).

But now he has promised, "Once more I will shake not only the earth but also the heavens" (Heb 12:26b, citing Hag 2:6; see also Hag 2:21). Hebrews adds the phrases **not only** and **but also** to the LXX text and inverts the original order of "the heaven and the earth" in order to accent the cosmic scope of this shaking. The idea of shaking is crucial to Heb 12:26-28, with the appearance not only of the verb **shake** (*seisō*) from the Haggai prophecy but also four occurrences of words with the root *-saleu-*, **shake**.

Verse 27 provides a concise commentary on the oracle from Haggai. The preacher assumes that the previous shaking was at Sinai. In Haggai, the future shaking coincides with the divine conquest of all nations and the filling of God's house (i.e., temple) "with glory," so that its glory exceeds that of the former house (Hag 2:7-8). Hebrews has already associated such events with Jesus' glorification as high priest over God's house (1:3; 2:7, 9; 3:1-6; 5:5; 10:21). The subjection of all things under his feet in the world to come (1:13; 2:6-8; 10:13) occurs in "the greater and more perfect tabernacle" (9:11; see 8:1-2; 9:24-25).

The phrase **once more**, (lit.) ***yet once-for-all*** (*eti hapax*), is for Hebrews the key to interpreting Haggai's oracle (deSilva 2000a, 470-71). It is a prophecy not just of some future quake, but of the ***once-for-all*** shaking at the final judgment. The words *"yet once-for-all"* indicate [*dēloi*, an exegetical expression, see 9:8; Attridge 1989, 380] **the removing of what can be shaken.** Hebrews has used **removing** (*metathesis*), along with its related verb (*metatithēmi*), concerning "change" in the Law and Levitical priesthood (7:12) and Enoch's being "taken" from earth (11:5).

The preacher contrasts **removing** what can be shaken with what will **remain** (*meinē*) and cannot be shaken. He similarly contrasted the changeable priesthood under the old covenant with Christ's priesthood that "remains" forever (7:3, 24). **What can be shaken** is equated (**that is**) with **created things**. The eternal, heavenly sanctuary stands in contrast to the earthly sanctuary that is "part of this creation" (9:11). The earthly sanctuary, "made by human hands" (9:11, 24 CEB, GNT, GW), could be "touched" (12:18). The removal of this present, transitory sanctuary will mark the time when the new order is fully established (9:8-10).

However, Hebrews envisions a shaking and dissolution of the whole created order, with only the eternal realm remaining. He introduced this understanding in a chain of scriptural citations in ch 1. Psalms 45:6-7 (in Heb 1:8-9) and 102:25-27 (in Heb 1:10-12) point to the permanence of the Son's kingdom. His throne will last forever (1:8). He will "remain" (1:11)/"remain the same" (1:12); but the earth and the heavens will be worn out, rolled up, or changed like a garment (1:11-12).

This vision of reality supports the hortatory aims of the entire homily. The readers' faith and hope should be directed toward **what cannot be shaken** and will **remain**. They must hold on to hope, because it is an anchor "firm and secure" in the inner sanctuary of the true sanctuary (6:19). Their true hope cannot be found in the old covenant with its priesthood and sacrifices, which are passing away (8:7, 13; see 7:18). The new covenant affords "better promises" (8:6) through the establishment of Christ's priesthood that "remains" forever (7:3, 24).

Thus, readers are to look to Jesus (2:9; 3:1; 12:2) in the midst of their difficulties. They must persevere in faith, rather than "shrink back" to destruction (10:39), as they press on toward God's eternal inheritance: the "better and lasting [*menousan*] possessions" (10:34), "the enduring [*menousan*] city" (13:14).

■ **28-29** These verses function as the conclusion (**Therefore**) to this section (12:14-29). But they also prepare for the more detailed exhortations in ch 13 regarding how to lead lives of gratitude and pleasing worship to God. **Since we are receiving a kingdom that cannot be shaken** nicely sums up what has been described as our approach to the city of God (vv 22-24) or "what cannot be shaken" (v 27). The term **kingdom** is infrequent in Hebrews (1:8 and 12:28). But the motif of regal authority is prominent, not least in allusions to and quotations of Ps 110:1 (in Heb 1:3, 13; 8:1; 10:12; 12:2).

Both conceptually, and in terms of phrasing, **receiving a kingdom** [*basileian . . . paralambanontes*] **that cannot be shaken** is reminiscent of the prophecy in Dan 7 (Attridge 1989, 382). There the Son of Man receives everlasting dominion in a kingdom that will never be destroyed (Dan 7:13-14). God's holy people also "will receive the kingdom . . . and will possess it forever" (Dan 7:18 LXX; see Dan 7:27).

The participle **receiving** denotes the acceptance of a divine grant, not a human possession or achievement (Lane 1991, 484). That it is in the present tense indicates that believers are already in the process of **receiving** God's gift. The full realization of this eternal inheritance (Heb 9:15) and salvation will occur at "the end" (3:14; 6:11) when Christ returns (9:28; 10:37).

Let us be thankful, (lit.) "let us have grace [*echōmen charin*]," is a counterpart to the admonition in 12:15: "See to it that no one misses the grace [*charitos*] of God." There, "grace" is a not-to-be missed gift bestowed by the divine Patron. Godless and immoral Esau is an example of someone who thoughtlessly traded away God's gracious inheritance (v 16). Here, **grace** is the proper response of "gratitude" (CEB, NAB, NASB, NJB) to God's gifts. In Hebrews, as in the wider Greco-Roman world, ingratitude or rejection of benefactions is an unforgivable insult (see 6:4-10; 10:26-31; see deSilva 2000a, 473).

Gratitude is the appropriate attitude "by which" (NASB, NKJV, NRSV; **and so**) we may **worship** [*latreuōmen*] **God acceptably with reverence and awe.** The cultic associations of **worship** are frequent in Hebrews (8:5; 9:1, 6, 9, 14; 10:2; 13:10). Christ's sacrifice cleanses and perfects the conscience "so that we may serve [*latreuein*] the living God" (9:14; see 9:9; 10:2). It makes possible a primary summons of the sermon: "Let us draw near to God" (4:16; 10:22; see 7:25; 12:22). The exalted Christ is the object of angelic worship (1:6), as well as the leader of worship for God's people (2:12-13). The character of true worship as "pleasing" God was integrally linked to faith in → 11:5-6. The importance of worship that pleases God will resound in 13:16, 21.

Jesus' own obedience and "reverent submission" (*eulabeias*) during his earthly life (5:7) provide the pattern for our own worship **with reverence** [*eulabeias*] **and awe.** Godly fear is not incompatible with our bold approach before God (3:6; 4:16; 10:19, 35). It is, in fact, an effective emotional deterrent to ignoring God's promise (4:1) and becoming an object of divine displeasure and judgment (10:27, 31). Fear of God enables us not to fear human beings who would seek to divert our loyalties from God (11:23, 26; 13:6).

The appropriateness of fear in the divine presence is due to the awesome nature of God himself: **for our "God is a consuming fire"** (12:29). Hebrews recasts a line from Deut 4:24 (see also Deut 9:3 and Exod 24:17), which grounds a warning against forgetting the covenant and turning to idols (Deut 4:23; → Heb 10:26-31, esp. 10:27). The mention of **fire** forms an *inclusio* with the description of Mount Sinai as "burning with fire" (12:18) and amplifies the warning in 12:25. At Sinai, even the mediator of the old covenant, Moses, was paralyzed by fear. In Zion, people can stand boldly in the awesome presence of "God, the judge of all" (12:23) because of the mediator of the new covenant, Jesus, and his "sprinkled blood" (12:24).

Hebrews 12:28-29 encapsulates the preacher's rhetorical strategy throughout the sermon (deSilva 2000a, 477). He strongly urges his listeners to hold on to their commitment. The advantage of loyalty is set forth in their obligation to respond with gratitude to God's saving action and promised inheritance in Christ. The disadvantage of apostasy is revealed in the righteous judgment and destruction for those who insolently reject God's grace.

2. Instructions for Worship as a Way of Life (13:1-25)

BEHIND THE TEXT

In some ways, Heb 13 stands apart from the rest of the work. Whereas the preceding chapters read like a discourse or sermon, this final chapter reads like the closing of a letter written by Paul the apostle. Verses 1-6 contain a series of imperatives that recall the moral instructions one finds in the latter portions of Paul's letters. Verses 18-25 contain standard features of letter-closings used by early Christians:

- Request for prayer (vv 18-19).
- Benediction (vv 20-21a) ending with a doxology (v 21b).
- Comments about the composition (v 22).
- Personal news and travel plans (v 23).
- Greetings (v 24).
- Farewell wish (v 25; for a tabular comparison with other NT and early Christian letters, see Attridge 1989, 404-5).

The rhetorical climax in 12:18-29, followed by a sudden shift in genre and tone in 13:1, prompts some scholars to identify ch 13 as an editorial addition to the sermon. Some view ch 13 as a letter-like ending added by the author himself (Feine, Behm, and Kümmel 1966, 278-79) or by an early Christian who wanted to create the impression that the work was by Paul (Buchanan 1972, 242-45). The mention of Timothy in v 23 may bolster the latter view. But most scholars recognize ch 13 as an integral part of the original composition (see Filson's [1967] classic defense).

Hebrews 13 is not an appendix or afterthought, but an intentional part of the author's communication to his readers. The letter-like closing is designed to make the composition as a whole function as a long-distance sermon, delivered in written form rather than in person, and sent like a letter. This is indicated in v 22, where the preacher speaks of his work as a "word of exhortation," sent as a letter (*epesteila*).

Chapter 13 functions as the final movement in the *peroratio* or conclusion begun in 10:19. The chapter is linked structurally, stylistically, and thematically to what has gone before. The chapter completes the call to peace and holiness begun in 12:14 (Isaacs 2002, 154). Verses 1-6 of ch 13 provide concrete instructions concerning the community's obligation to show love and good deeds (see 6:10; 10:24) and maintain its purity, cohesion, and complete reliance on God. The benediction and doxology in 13:20-21 address God as "the God of peace," who will equip the community to do God's will.

Two related threads run through the last half of the *peroratio* (12:14—13:25): "grace" (*charis*) and worship that is "acceptable" (or "pleasing [*euarest-*]"). The preacher has already urged his audience not to forfeit "grace" through unholy living (12:14-17). God's kingdom must be received with "thanks [*charis*]," so that we may worship God "acceptably [*euarestōs*]" (12:28). In ch 13, the preacher stresses divine "grace" as the primary source of the community's strength, rather than ceremonial foods (v 9). He finishes his work with the blessing: "Grace be with you all" (v 25). The proper response to God's grace (as in 12:28) is holy living, expressed through love and good deeds (see vv 1-6, 15-16), and described as worship that "pleases [*euaresteitai; euareston*]" God (vv 16, 21).

Chapter 13 proceeds in three parts. First, vv 1-6 provide specific moral instructions that put flesh on earlier, more general remarks about maintaining solidarity, holiness, and commitment as members of God's family (see 2:10-18; 3:1, 6, 14; 10:24-25, 32-35; 12:14-17).

Second, 13:7-19 issues a final call to identify with Christ and his sacrifice. This recalls the central arguments in 7:1—10:18 on priesthood, sanctuary, and sacrifice. But the arguments there were framed by exhortations to "draw near" to God in worship (4:16; 10:22). Here the exhortation is to "go to him [i.e., Christ] outside the camp, bearing the disgrace he bore" (13:13). True worship is a product of genuine discipleship, that is, bold identification with Christ's shameful death. This section is marked by references to past (v 7) and present leadership ("your leaders" [v 17]) and their exemplary "way of life" (vv 7 and 18).

Third, Hebrews closes with a benediction and final remarks (vv 20-25).

IN THE TEXT

a. Exhortations to Love, Purity, and Trust (13:1-6)

■ I The opening exhortation, **Keep on loving each another as brothers,** promotes a foundational Christian virtue: love. The encouragement of ***sibling love*** is traditional in apostolic moral instruction (Rom 12:10; 1 Thess 4:9; 1 Pet 1:22; 2 Pet 1:7). Outside of Christian circles, *philadelphia* denoted simply the devotion and affection among natural brothers or sisters. Christians figuratively applied the term to the family-like relations that exist between members of God's people. In Rom 12:9-10 and 2 Pet 1:7 it is a particular expression of *agapē* (Plümacher 1993b). This is the sort of Christian "love" that Hebrews has already commended (6:10; 10:24) to those identified as "brothers" of Jesus (2:11, 12, 17; see 3:1, 12; 10:19; 13:22, 23) or God's household (3:6; 10:21).

The charge to **keep on loving each another** is more than simply a piece of traditional Christian parenesis. It suits the situation of the addressees. The preacher has already instructed them to "spur one another on toward love and good deeds" (10:24; see 6:10-11) and guard against failing to meet for mutual encouragement (10:25). He has urged them to live in peace and holiness (12:14) and warned them about any who might contaminate and disrupt their fellowship (12:15).

A characteristic play on words gives this injunction even more profound meaning within its context. "Let brotherly love continue [*menetō*]" (ESV, HCSB, KJV) expresses mutual love as a quality of the Christian life that should endure. The language echoes that about the unshakable kingdom, namely, that it will "remain [*meinē*]" (12:27). The "better and lasting [*menousan*] possessions" (10:34) and "enduring [*menousan*] city" (13:14) are hoped-for future realities. However, the eternal kingdom already manifests itself among brothers and sisters who "share in the heavenly calling" and mutually strengthen their commitment to Jesus (3:1, 6, 12-14; 4:14; 10:19-25, 34-36; Attridge 1989, 385-86).

■ **2** The plea, **Do not forget to entertain strangers,** extends Christian love beyond mutual affection among believers. Sibling love (v 1) should blossom in "hospitality to strangers [*philoxenias*]" (ESV, NASB, NLT, NRSV; **entertain strangers**). Hospitality was a sacred obligation in the ancient world. It involved welcoming strangers or travelers as guests and offering them provisions and protection. Reliance on hospitality was vital to early Christian missionary work (e.g., Luke 10:1-16; 3 John 5-8; Arterbury 2007).

The preacher offers a rationale for showing hospitality: **for by so doing some people entertained angels without knowing it.** This alludes to Abraham and Sarah's hospitality to three visitors who turned out to be divine messengers (Gen 18:1-15). Here is biblical precedent for the widespread acknowledgment of hospitality as a religious duty. Kindness to strangers is a display of devotion to God. The implications include not only the possibility of unwitting contact with divine emissaries, but also God's recognition and just reward for his peoples' love and good deeds (see 6:10-12).

Hospitality in the Ancient World

In antiquity hospitality was a sacred obligation in which God or divine persons were viewed as intimately involved. In Jewish-Christian tradition, Abraham was the father of hospitality. The patriarch's "boundless sea" of hospitality (*T. Ab.* A 17:7; see 1:1, 2, 5; 4:6) was "celebrated and all-glorious" (Philo, *Abr.* 167; see *1 Clem.* 10.7). These estimations hung on the famous account of Abraham's generosity to three strangers, who were really angels from God (Gen 18:1-15). Abraham's example of hospitality was worthy of imitation (*T. Ab.* A 20:15; *T. Jac.* 7:22-25).

Pagan readers would have easily identified with the divine sanction of hospitality. "Strangers and beggars come from Zeus" (Homer, *Od.* 6.207-8); and Hermes was the guardian and enforcer of hospitality (Antoninus Liberalis, *Metam.* 21). The requirement of hospitality was reinforced by the belief that the gods might appear in disguise as strangers (*Homeric Hymn to Demeter* 111-12; *Od.* 17.485-87). Most well-known is the charming tale of Philemon and Baucis in Phrygia. The elderly couple entertained two travelers (Zeus and Hermes in disguise) and for their piety were granted the wish of dying together (Ovid, *Metam.* 8.626; compare Acts 14:11-12, in which Barnabas and Paul were mistaken for Zeus and Hermes).

Hebrews' warrant for showing hospitality—"some have entertained angels unawares" (13:2 ESV, KJV, REB, RSV)—would not have seemed fantastical at all to people in the ancient world (Koenig 1992).

■ **3** Not only should one "not forget" to entertain strangers (13:2), but one should **remember those in prison, and those who are mistreated.** The exhortation is reminiscent of the community's past exemplary conduct, when they became "partners" with those who were being persecuted (10:33 NRSV) and "suffered along with" those in prison (10:34 NIV[11]).

As in former days, so also now the readers must possess concern for and solidarity with those who are suffering—and as directly and vividly as possible. To **remember** (*mimnēskesthe*) connotes having care and concern (BDAG, 652). They must have concern for those in prison **as if you were their fellow prisoners** (→ 10:34 and sidebar, "Prison in the Ancient Roman World"). The intensity of fellowship with prisoners is expressed in a tight wordplay: *tōn desmiōn hōs syndedemenoi*, "them that are in bonds, as bound with them" (KJV). Some early Christians voluntarily stayed in prison with other imprisoned believers (Lucian, *Peregr.* 12; *Tox.* 32).

The preacher urges his audience to identify with the mistreated **as if you yourselves were suffering.** The language is again rhetorically pointed: "as though you yourselves were in [their] body" (Attridge 1989, 386; Koester 2001, 558). Philo's nearly identical phrasing (*Spec. Laws* 3.161; Johnson 2006, 341) illuminates the usage here in 13:3: "as if you felt their pain in your own bodies" (NLT). Sharing in the suffering of other believers (2 Cor 1:6-7; 2 Tim 1:8; 1 Pet 5:9; Rev 1:9; see Heb 10:25) and participation in Christ's sufferings (Acts 5:41; Rom 8:17; 2 Cor 1:5; Phil 3:10; 1 Pet 4:13; see Heb 10:26) are common NT themes.

■ **4** A fourth exhortation returns to themes articulated at the head of the second half of the *peroratio*. In 12:14-17, the preacher urged his listeners to pursue peace and holiness. There, as here, he addresses holiness in general, and sexual ethics in particular, in terms of cultic purity, honorable status before God, and divine judgment.

The preacher emphasizes the sanctity of marriage in a pair of verbless clauses (13:4*a-b*), which could be construed as declarative statements ("Marriage is honourable in all, and the bed undefiled" [KJV]) or commands (with an implied imperative, **should** or "Let . . . be"; Bengel 1877, 4:493). In either case, the concluding justification, invoking divine justice (v 4*c*), establishes sexual purity as a moral obligation.

Marriage should be honored by all identifies marriage as "an honourable estate" (as the *Book of Common Prayer* puts it). This was not written to oppose an ascetic ideal of holiness that forbade marriage (contrary to Hagner 1990,

235; see Attridge 1989, 387). Instead, it was intended to prevent the abuse or disregard of marriage by **the sexually immoral** (v 4c). Marriage is "honourable" and to be valued as ***precious*** (*timios*; BDAG, 1005-6).

The parallel expression, **the marriage bed [*should be*] kept pure,** refers to the purity of sexual union within the context of marriage. *Koitē* (**bed**) is a common euphemism for sexual intercourse (see Rom 9:10; 13:13). **Kept pure** or "undefiled" (most English translations; *amiantos*) is a term suitable to temple purity. But it has a broader religious or moral sense (→ 7:26 of Jesus; BDAG, 54). Its cognate antonym "defile [*miainō*]" is used in 12:15 of immoral behavior that contaminates the community.

Jews and Christians viewed extramarital sex as a source of defilement (Gen 49:4; Wis 14:24; *T. Reub.* 1:6; *T. Levi* 7:3; 9:9; 14:6; *Pss. Sol.* 2:13; Josephus, *Ant.* 2.55). Even Roman poets affirmed that "our age has defiled the marriage bed" through marital infidelity (Horace, *Carm.* 3.6.17-32; see Juvenal, *Sat.* 2.29).

Jewish sources, beginning with the Holiness Code (see Lev 18), provided lengthy catalogs of sexual deviancy (Ps.-Phoc. 175-206; Josephus, *Ag. Ap.* 2.199-203; Koester 2001, 558). Hebrews, however, mentions only the illicit sexual behaviors of **the sexually immoral** and **the adulterer** (the Greek order is reversed in the NIV). **All the sexually immoral** (*pornous*; "fornicators," NASB, NKJV, NRSV) indicates persons engaged in any kind of sexual vice—not just those who frequent prostitutes ("whoremongers" [KJV]). In coordination with v 4a (**Marriage should be honored by all**), the reference is to any sexual activity outside the bonds of marriage. It is distinguished from **adulterers** (*moichous*): married persons who are unfaithful to their spouses (Plümacher 1991). This coordinates with v 4b (that **the marriage bed** should be **kept pure**).

While sexual ethics was a standard talking-point for Greco-Roman, Jewish, and Christian moralists, it is not merely a stock element here. The cautionary example of Esau as **sexually immoral** and irreligious in 12:15 indicates that 13:4 is more than a passing reference. Early Christians fought continually against popular moral laxity with regard to sexual practices (see Acts 15:20, 29; 21:25; 1 Cor 5:1-12; 6:12-20; 7:2; 2 Cor 12:21; Gal 5:19; Eph 5:3; Col 3:5). The Greek pantheon of gods, with all of their sexual intrigues, implicitly condoned immorality (Josephus, *Ag. Ap.* 2.244-46); and civil penalties for adultery were often slack (*Ag. Ap.* 2.276).

For Jews and Christians, sexual impropriety was not simply a moral or legal matter, but a religious one. Thus, Hebrews prosecutes against sexual sin at the highest court of appeal: **God will judge.** Paul likewise reminds his churches that divine punishment awaits the sexually immoral (e.g., 1 Thess 4:6; Col 3:5-6), and sexual sins exclude persons from the kingdom of God (1 Cor 6:9; Gal 5:19-21; Eph 5:5). Adulterers may attempt to conceal their affairs from other people, but cannot hide them from God (Job 24:15; *Pss. Sol.* 4:5-6; Philo, *Spec. Laws* 3.52).

■ **5-6** The last in this string of five moral exhortations (13:1-6) stands in deliberate contrast to the first two, using words with the root *phil-* ("love"). Verses 1-2 encouraged mutual love in the Christian family (*philadelphia*) and love of strangers (*philoxenia*). Verse 5 reminds readers of what they should *not* love: They should be **free from the love of money** (*aphilargyros*, lit., **not loving silver**).

Admonitions against sexual immorality (v 4) and greed (v 5*a*) were often coupled together by Jewish, Christian, and Greco-Roman moralists (see Attridge 1989, 387; Koester 2001, 559). A possible biblical precedent is the juxtaposition of commandments seven and eight, against adultery and stealing, in the Decalogue (Lane 1991, 518). Greco-Roman moral philosophers understood the vital link between sexual vice and greed, rooted in inordinate desires. They also agreed with the NT truism, "the love of money is a root of all kinds of evil" (1 Tim 6:10; see Johnson 2006, 341-43).

The preacher urges freedom from greed, not just as an action, but as a deep-seated disposition or way of life (*tropos*, **your lives;** "lifestyle" [LEB]). The alternative to the love of money is to **be content with what you have.** This was a commonplace of Hellenistic moral philosophy, especially Stoicism (Attridge 1989, 388; Koester 2001, 559). Paul also embraced the principle of contentment (Phil 4:11; 1 Tim 6:8), but not as an end in itself. He did not advocate the Stoic ideal of self-sufficiency, but radical dependence on the sufficiency of God's grace (2 Cor 12:9) and enablement through Christ (Phil 4:12).

Similar reasoning figures into the scriptural warrant given in Heb 13:5*b*-6, complementing the previous emphasis on enduring present hardship in view of future reward (10:32-39; 11:8-10, 13-16, 25-26). Hebrews quotes two passages of Scripture: the first, a divine promise; the second, a response from God's people.

The first quotation supplies the divine grounds for contentment, **because God has said** (v 5*b*). The source of the quotation is difficult to identify. It is conceptually similar to Josh 1:5 and Gen 28:15 LXX. It is most like Deut 31:6 LXX, but the statement there is in the third person (see also Deut 31:8; 1 Chr 28:20). A letter-perfect match occurs in Philo (*Confusion* 166): **Never will I leave you; never will I forsake you.** The agreement between Philo and Hebrews may point to a familiar paraphrase of Deut 31:6 originating in Hellenistic synagogue preaching or liturgy in Alexandria (Lane 1991, 519). In any case, as is customary in Hebrews, the scriptural text is cited as a direct word from God that has contemporary relevance for the readers (see Anderson 2011, 407-9). They need not be consumed with anxiety about money because of God's faithful presence among them.

The second quotation in Heb 13:6 is introduced as the community's response to the divine promise: **So** [*hōste*] **we say with confidence.** Appropriately, the quotation is from the Psalms, and in particular the last of the Hallel psalms, uniquely associated with Passover (Lane 1991, 520; see, e.g., Matt

21:9, 15, 42; 23:39). It is an exact quotation from Ps 118:6 LXX: **The Lord is my helper; I will not be afraid. What can man do to me?**

The note of **confidence** (*tharrountas*) recalls the earlier exhortations to boldness (*parrēsia;* Heb 3:6; 4:16; 10:19, 35). Confidence in divine aid (**The Lord is my helper**) serves as the basis for dispelling fear (**I will not be afraid**). The sermon has argued that God's help (2:16; 4:16) comes to us through the high-priestly ministry of Jesus. He delivers us from the fear of death (2:15). Terror awaits those who reject the new covenant (10:27, 31, 38-39; 12:18-21). But firm trust in the God who is a consuming fire (12:29) produces courage in the face of human opposition and persecution (11:23, 27; 12:1-4).

b. Final Call to Commitment and Worship (13:7-19)

This section formally completes the hortatory goals of the sermon. It is a final call for the readers to commit themselves fully to following Christ as their high priest, and to offer worship that is pleasing to God. The core of the passage (vv 10-13) is reminiscent of the central section (7:1—10:18) with its focus on the superiority of Christ's sacrificial death. The earlier summons to "approach" or "draw near" to God in worship (4:16; 10:22) takes the form of a call to follow Christ: "Let us, then, go to him outside the camp" (13:13).

This section also harks back to significant themes throughout the sermon:
- The word of God (13:7; 1:1-2*a*; 4:2, 12).
- Imitation of exemplars of faith (13:7; 6:12; 11:1—12:4).
- The eternality of Christ's ministry (13:8; 7:11-28).
- The sanctification of God's people through Jesus' suffering/blood (13:12; 2:11; 10:10, 14, 29).
- Looking for the future abiding city (13:14; 11:10, 16; 12:22).
- Offering worship that is acceptable to God (13:16; 12:28; see 13:21), especially by doing good and sharing with others (6:10-11; 10:24-25, 32-34).
- Having a clear conscience (13:18; 9:9, 14; 10:2, 22).

Therefore, it is a fitting conclusion to the sermon's *peroratio*, begun at 10:19.

The message is couched within references to heeding the community's "leaders," both past and present (vv 7 and 17); to emulating their "way of life" (vv 7 [*anastrophēs*], 18 [*anastrephesthai*]); and to the "word [*logon*]" (v 7) their leaders spoke, as well as their having to give an "account [*logon*]" (v 17) of those under their care.

■ **7 Remember your leaders** ties this section to the preceding exhortations, which included reminders not to "forget" hospitality (v 2; see also v 16) and to "remember" those in prison (v 4). In light of vv 17 and 24, **leaders** (*hēgoumenōn*) are distinguished within God's people as individuals who have authority and responsibility concerning the community's spiritual welfare (*1 Clem*. 1.3; *proēgoumenoi, 1 Clem.* 21.6; *Herm. Vis.* 2.2.6; 3.9.7).

That they **spoke the word of God to you** probably marks them as the founding pastors of the church(es) to which the readers belong. It might refer to apostolic figures, who heard the message of salvation from the Lord and confirmed it "to us" (2:3). Ancient interpreters viewed them as the earliest martyrs of the church, including the protomartyr Stephen, James the brother of John, and James the Just (see Heen and Krey 2005, 231). This is possible since **the outcome** [*ekbasin*] **of their way of life** may well be an allusion to their deaths (see Wis 2:17; BDAG, 299). However, Hebrews nowhere presents martyrdom as a reality in the community's past experience (see 10:32-34; and 12:4 may rule it out.

The preacher urges his readers to engage in three actions: First, they should **remember** their leaders, who spoke **the word of God** to them. This repeats the sermon's important theme of hearing God's word (→ 2:1-4; 3:7, 15; 4:2, 7, 12; 5:11-12; 12:25-26; Thompson 2008, 280).

Second, they should **consider** (*anatheōrountes*) the consequences of their leaders' lives. Similar language encouraged them to "consider" one another (10:24) and Jesus (12:3). The focus of consideration here is **the outcome of their** leaders' **way of life,** that is, "how they suffered, how they died, and how they found a place in the city of the living God" (Johnson 2006, 345-46). Perhaps the author has in mind their existence as "spirits of the righteous made perfect" (12:23 NIV[11]).

Third, the readers should **imitate** [*mimeisthe*] **their faith**. The past leaders of the community are part of the same trajectory of exemplary faith found in 11:1—12:4. The antidote to the readers' sluggish spiritual progress is precisely to "imitate [*mimētai*] those who through faith and patience inherit what has been promised" (→ 6:12). Paul similarly urged the imitation of others who are faithfully imitating Christ (1 Cor 4:6; 11:1; 1 Thess 1:6; 2:14; see Eph 5:1).

■ **8** The acclamation **Jesus Christ is the same yesterday and today and forever** has a liturgical ring to it. Indeed, in Hebrews the full title **Jesus Christ** is used primarily in confessional contexts (→ 10:10; 13:21). This affirmation is consonant with the confession of Jesus as apostle, high priest, and Son of God to which readers should "hold firmly" (3:1; 4:14; 10:23; see 3:14). It entails Christ's

- faithful and decisive suffering in the past, **yesterday** (2:9; 5:8; 9:26; "during the days of Jesus' life on earth" [5:7]);
- grounds for the offer of divine rest **today** (3:7, 13, 15; 4:7; see 4:1-2); and
- complete salvation **forever** (see 5:9; 7:24; 9:14-15).

It confesses again the Son's eternal constancy (1:8-12; "you remain the same" [1:12]), faithfulness (2:17; 3:2, 5), and the permanence of his priesthood—**forever** (5:6; 6:20; 7:3, 17, 21, 24, 28).

This confession of Christ's eternal dependability may have had a liturgical function outside of Hebrews. But it plays a crucial role in its present context. Looking backward, **Jesus Christ is the same** as the foundation for the past leadership's teaching and example (v 7). Christ is the source of the message they spoke (1:3; 2:3). His reverent submission and self-sacrifice was the pattern for their way of life (2:9-10; 5:7-8; 10:5-10). He is "the author and perfecter" of the leaders' "faith" (12:2), which the readers should emulate.

Looking forward, the reliability of Christ supports the following exhortations not to be drawn away by "strange teachings" (13:9) but to follow Christ, even by identifying with his suffering and shame (v 13). The following verses drive home the fundamental message of the sermon: Jesus' sacrificial death and eternal priesthood are the basis for true worship and lasting hope.

■ **9** The admonition **Do not be carried away by all kinds of strange teachings** contrasts with the familiar and true "word of God" spoken by past leaders (v 7) and the trustworthiness of Christ (v 8). The continuity and constancy of the gospel are to be preferred over variability (**all kinds of**) and unreliability (**strange;** see 1:10-12; 7:23-24; deSilva 2000a, 495-96). **Carried away** (*parapheresthe*) suggests instability, like the drifting (2:1) or falling (4:1, 11; 6:6; 12:15) warned about earlier.

Conversely, **it is good for our hearts to be strengthened by grace.** The sermon's repeated use of the cognates for "established" (HCSB, KJV) or **strengthened** (*bebaiousthai*; see 2:2, 3; 3:14; 6:16, 19; 9:17; Thompson 2008, 281) remind us of the community's need for stability and security in their hope and faith (6:11, 19; 10:22). Strength may be found in God's **grace,** the motive force behind Christ's saving death (2:9) and one of the benefits of his high-priestly ministry (4:16).

The inner core of one's life and personhood, **the heart,** needs to be **strengthened** (analogously, hope is a firm and secure "anchor for the soul" [6:19]). The **heart** is the seat of one's innermost "desires and thoughts" (4:12 NET). But it can also be the center of unbelief, waywardness, and rebellion (3:8, 10, 12, 15; 4:7). When cleansed from an evil conscience (10:22) and transformed by the Lord (8:10; 10:16), the inner life of the heart can be made true and stabilized in "full assurance of faith" (10:22).

The **grace** of Christ's ministry is the real source of spiritual strength, **not ceremonial foods.** The NIV rightly adds the word **ceremonial,** though the word is simply **foods** (*brōmasin*; compare "ritual meals" [NET]). Some commentators think this is a general reference to food, encompassing **all kinds of strange teachings,** not only Jewish practices (Koester 2001, 560-61). However, the preacher has summed up the "gifts and sacrifices" (9:9) under the old covenant as "only a matter of food and drink and various ceremonial washings" (9:10). The reference here, then, is to "rules" (GW, NLT, REB) or "regulations" (NRSV) about food, that is, Jewish "dietary laws" (Johnson 2006, 347).

This is confirmed by the expression **those who walk** in or "observe" (NRSV, TNIV; see REB) such rules. "To walk" is a common biblical metaphor for ethical conduct, and appropriated as a label for rabbinic legal rulings on how to live, known as halakah (from Heb. *halak*, "walk"; see Attridge 1989, 394; Lane 1991, 535; Johnson 2006, 347).

From a new covenant perspective, the continuation or reinstatement of such regulations is indeed foreign (**strange,** *xenais*) to genuine teaching on how to be made perfect as worshipers (France 2006, 187). Other NT writers take a similar position (see Col 2:16, 22; 1 Tim 4:1-4). In the early second century, Ignatius provided a parallel, if not an allusion, to our passage: he contrasted living according to Judaism with receiving **grace** (Ign. *Magn.* 7.2—8.1; Lane 1991, 536; Pfitzner 1997, 196).

Halakic food laws **are of no value** ("no benefit" [NIV[11]]) to those who observe them. This is because they do not affect the depths of the problem of sin in the human heart, but are only "external regulations applying until the time of the new order" (9:10). They are associated with the regulation for the Levitical priesthood, which has been set aside as "weak and useless" (7:18). Such rules belong to the old covenant, which is obsolete and disappearing (8:7, 13), and the Mosaic law, which presents only a "shadow" of the reality in Christ (8:5; 10:1; see Col 2:17).

■ **10 We have an altar** sounds like other confessions in Hebrews, not least the declaration of the central point: "We do have such a high priest" (8:1; see 4:14; 10:19-21; see also 6:19; 12:1). The **altar,** by metonymy, points to the high-priestly ministry of Christ. Specifically, in light of the following comparison between Christ's death and the Day of Atonement ritual of Lev 16:27 (Heb 13:11-13), Christ's atoning sacrifice is in view.

It is unlikely that the author is contrasting an **altar** in the heavenly sanctuary with that in the earthly **tabernacle** (against Filson 1967, 48-49; Thompson 2008, 282). No such altar is mentioned earlier in conjunction with the heavenly sanctuary (see 8:5; 9:1-10, 23-24). The sacrifices in 13:15-16, offered up "through Jesus," are spiritual and do not require a literal altar. They are responses of praise to Christ's sacrifice, which was itself a historical event on earth (v 12; see Pfitzner 1997, 198). Neither is the altar a symbol of the Eucharist. A reference to eucharistic meals might make the preacher's denunciation of "ceremonial foods" (v 9) self-defeating (so Lane 1991, 538-39; Koester 2001, 569; Isaacs 2002, 158).

The preacher argued in ch 7 that Christ's high priesthood is a radical change from the Levitical priesthood (see 7:11-17). Christ's priesthood is vastly superior in its basis ("indestructible life" [7:16]; God's oath [7:20-22, 28]), permanence (7:3, 23-24, 28), and results ("better hope" [7:19]; "better covenant" [7:22]; complete salvation [7:25]). So it comes as no surprise that **those who minister at the tabernacle have no right to eat** (13:10) at Christ's altar. They are ineligible to do so.

Cognates of *hoi latreuontes* (**those who minister**) are used of the priests who serve in the earthly tabernacle (8:4-5; 9:6; see 9:1), but also of the worshipers they represent (9:9; 10:2). **Those who minister** at the tabernacle, who have no right to share in the benefits of Christ's sacrifice (**eat at the altar**), are parallel to "those who observe" (NRSV, TNIV) the unprofitable regulations concerning ritual foods (13:9). Thus, the preacher draws a conclusion from his argument that the sacrificial system and regulations for worship under the old covenant have been set aside (7:18; 10:9). God's "grace" (2:9; 13:9), enacted through Christ's suffering (13:11-13), is the basis for true "worship [*latreuōmen*]" (12:28) and sacrifices that are pleasing to God (13:16).

■ **11-12** These verses provide the justification (*gar*, **For;** untranslated in NIV) for the claim in v 10. It consists of one last midrashic interpretation of Scripture (→ 3:7-19 Behind the Text sidebar, "Midrash"). The final action of the Day of Atonement ritual is correlated with the historical event of Christ's crucifixion.

Verse 11 is a paraphrase of Lev 16:27. The **animals** are the bull and goat that were slaughtered as a **sin offering** on Yom Kippur (see Heb 9:12; 10:4). **The high priest carries** the sacrificial **blood . . . into the Most Holy Place,** that is, into the innermost chamber of the sacred tent (see 9:3, 8, 12, 25). The last step of the ritual is crucial to the ensuing comparison with Christ's death.

The sacrificed animals' **bodies**—what Lev 16:27 enumerates as their hides, flesh, and dung—**are burned outside the camp.** Symbolically, the carcasses bear the sin of the high priest and the people, and so must be incinerated **outside the camp** in order to remove the defilement from their midst (see the kindred idea of quarantining defiled persons or things **outside the camp** [Lev 13:46; 14:3; Num 5:3-4; 12:15; 31:19; Deut 23:10, 12]). Leviticus 16:28 requires the person who burned the bodies to wash his clothes and bathe himself before returning to camp.

Hebrews 13:12 suggests that the final action of the Yom Kippur ritual is a type of Christ's death. **And so** ("That is why" [GW]) indicates that Christ's sacrifice followed the scriptural pattern of the Day of Atonement. That **Jesus also suffered outside the city gate** is a historical detail concerning Christ's crucifixion (see John 19:17). It also comports with the legal requirement for executions to take place **outside the camp** (Lev 24:14, 23; Num 15:35-36).

Rabbinic regulations verify that the walls of Jerusalem corresponded to the sacred boundaries of the ancient wilderness camp. On the Day of Atonement the carcasses of the bull and goat were, in fact, burned outside the gates of Jerusalem (*b. Yoma* 65ab; see Lane 1991, 542). Therefore, Christ's death **outside the city gate** correlates with the burning of the sacrificial animals **outside the camp** on Yom Kippur.

Jesus' suffering, however, truly fulfilled the purpose of the Day of Atonement **to make the people holy** (see Heb 2:11; 9:13-14; 10:10, 14, 29). The blood of goats and bulls was never able to cleanse people from their sins (9:13-14; 10:4). But Christ, our Great High Priest, effected decisive sanctification **through his own blood** (see 9:12, 25).

■ **13-14** The preacher applies this midrashic interpretation of the Day of Atonement ritual (vv 11-12) to the readers by issuing a bold call to discipleship (v 13): **Let us, then, go to him outside the camp, bearing the disgrace he bore.** Previous exhortations focused on urging listeners to "draw near to" or "approach" the divine presence in worship (4:16; 10:22) or to enter into divine rest (4:11). Now, in coherence with the Yom Kippur typology, the direction of motion is reversed: **go *out* [*exerchōmetha*] to him outside the camp** (Attridge 1989, 398). This summons to identify with Christ aligns with earlier exhortations for readers to fix their eyes on Jesus as high priest and consider his endurance of shame and suffering (3:1; 12:2-4; see 2:9-10). It is Hebrews' version of Christ's call to discipleship: "If anyone would come after me, he must deny himself and take up his cross and follow me" (Mark 8:34).

Bearing the disgrace [*oneidismon*] he bore is something the community has already done in the past, when they persevered in their faith despite insults (*oneidismois*) and persecution (10:33). Moses was a precursor to such Christian faith, when "he regarded disgrace [*oneidismon*] for the sake of Christ" to be greater than Egypt's treasures (11:26). Jesus himself, the author and perfecter of faith, "endured the cross, scorning its shame" (12:2).

The motivation for commitment to Christ and identifying with his reproach is given in 13:14: **For [*gar*] here we do not have an enduring [*menousan*] city, but we are looking for the city that is to come.** This is the same reason repeatedly stressed throughout the *peroratio*. The community endured in its early days because they knew they had "better and lasting [*menousan*] possessions" (10:34). Their confidence still has a great reward (10:35), and they must persevere in order to receive what God has promised (10:36). Abraham lived in faithfulness to God in a foreign land, because he looked forward to the **city** built by God (11:10), the heavenly homeland (11:16). Moses endured suffering and disgrace "because he was looking ahead to his reward" (11:26). Jesus endured the cross "for the joy set before him"—his exaltation to God's right hand (12:2).

The audience is approaching the heavenly Jerusalem, "the city of the living God" (12:22) **that is to come** (see 2:5). They are receiving an unshakable kingdom that will "remain [*meinē*]" (12:27-28). These truths should steel their resolve and commitment to Christ. This much is not controversial. But are there further implications to the preceding verses?

The traditional view is that the "altar" believers have (13:10) symbolizes the sacrificial death of Jesus (v 12) and is superior to all of the cultic trappings of the old covenant: sacrifices (v 11), priesthood and tabernacle (vv 10-11), food laws (v 9). So the readers are being called to separate themselves from the security and ostensible holiness afforded to them under the old covenant, since it has been superseded. Their commitment to Christ **outside the camp** entails abandoning any attachment to the temporal and earthly order centered in Jerusalem, even though it means embracing suffering, shame, and ostracism.

They must figuratively depart from the city of Jerusalem, the center of ancient Judaism. Earthly Jerusalem has lost its redemptive significance, because Jesus' suffering "outside the city gate" is now the true means of sanctification. Jerusalem has lost its eschatological significance, too, since real hope for salvation and holiness is in the eternal, heavenly homeland promised under the new covenant (Lane 1991, 547-48; see D. Guthrie 1983, 272-75; Bruce 1990, 381; Hagner 1990, 242-43; Pfitzner 1997, 200; Isaacs 2002, 159-60).

Alternatives to the traditional perspective have been proposed for at least two reasons. First, the notion that the author is warning readers not to fall back into a pre-Christian form of Judaism is not explicitly stated in Hebrews. Warnings against drifting away or turning from the Christian confession (e.g., 2:1; 3:12; 6:4-6; 10:35, 39), as well as the phrasing here (e.g., **outside the camp** or **city**), are highly suggestive but not definitive (see Lincoln 2006, 57).

Second, an often unstated reason involves concern for the potentially anti-Semitic overtones of Hebrews' rejection of the Mosaic cult (and therefore Jews and Judaism). This second reason, however, does not take into consideration the intra-Jewish debate presumed not only by Hebrews but NT writers generally.

Alternative interpretations do not possess the same explanatory power as the traditional view:

(1) One approach finds a parallel with Philo's allegorical interpretation. Hebrews is urging readers to abandon the Jewish cult, which is a symbol of the tangible world of sense perception and bodily passions ("objects dear to the body," Philo, *Alleg. Interp.* 2.54-55; 3.46; *Worse* 160). Instead, they must latch onto the reality and security of the ideal, heavenly world, and the true virtue it inculcates (Thompson 1982, 141-51; Thompson 2008, 283). But this view reads too much Platonic/Philonic thought into Hebrews. It emphasizes dualism, rather than the eschatology of 13:14 (**the city . . . to come**), and downplays the earthy, concrete invocation to suffering and reproach in v 13 (see Pfitzner 1997, 199).

(2) The approach of Helmut Koester (1962, 301) views our passage as a call for the readers to repudiate the sacred or cultic sphere altogether as a place of security. Believers are called to life in the secular, unclean world. But v 12 patently contradicts this reading: Jesus' sacrifice sanctifies God's people, setting them apart from what is unclean (see Koester 2001, 571).

(3) Still others want to see **the camp** as a more generalized symbol of any traditional cultic means toward establishing holiness and security (i.e., not a strictly Jewish reference; Attridge 1989, 399). Or it could indicate many facets of relinquishing the refuge and comfort of urban life (Koester 2001, 571).

All of these alternatives, however, simply do not fully account for the "thick description" in Hebrews (to borrow Clifford Geertz's famous phrase). Hebrews relentlessly employs language and imagery from Mosaic law and cult. The preacher makes specific references to food regulations, tabernacle, priesthood, and animal sacrifices. He takes great pains to demonstrate the superiority of Christ's sacrifice and high-priestly ministry to them all. It is difficult to see how his warnings and exhortations, then, add up only to a general concern for his readers not to buckle under societal pressure or to give in to earthly passions. Though the temptation to revert back to Judaism (perhaps to avoid persecution) is not explicitly spelled out in Hebrews, this traditional reading makes the best sense of its message (→ Introduction: F. Purpose).

■ **15-16** The call to commitment (v 13) is appropriately followed by an invitation to engage in true worship. The phrase **through Jesus** (lit., *through him*) recalls the preacher's contention that Jesus' past sacrifice and present high-priestly intercession are the basis for access to God (see 4:15-16; 7:19, 25; 10:19-22; Pfitzner 1997, 200). Jesus' death is the fulfillment par excellence of the Day of Atonement (vv 10-12). Thus, true worship is no longer conducted by the Levitical priesthood in the earthly sanctuary (9:1). It occurs in the "house" or family of God, led by **Jesus** (see 2:11-13; 3:6; 10:19-22). It no longer involves animal sacrifices, ceremonial washings, or the observance of food laws (9:9-10; 13:9).

Let us . . . offer and **sacrifice[s]** (vv 15, 16) reprise the language of sacrifice from the central section (→ 7:27; 8:3; 9:9, 23, 28). **Such sacrifices** with which **God is pleased** are of two types:

The first are the acts of worship we **continually offer to God.** The expression **sacrifice of praise** often denoted a category of literal sacrifice (an offering of thanksgiving, see Lev 7:12-13, 15; 2 Chr 29:31; 33:16; Jer 17:26), but was also used figuratively for a grateful heart (Ps 50:14, 23; Hagner 1990, 243). The latter usage is noted here by an explanatory addition, introduced with *that is* (a dash [—] in the NIV). **The fruit of lips** from Hos 14:2 indicates praise to God in response to forgiveness of sins. To **confess his name** in biblical parlance (esp. in Psalms) was to offer praise/thanksgiving to God (deSilva 2000a, 505). Confessing Christ in Hebrews is sacrificial in the sense that this requires the endurance of suffering (3:1, 6; 4:14; 10:23; 11:13; see 10:32-39; 12:1-4).

The second type of genuine sacrifice involves love and kindness directed toward others. **And do not forget to do good and to share with others** are detailed in more particular ways in 13:1-6 ("do not forget" [v 2]; "remember" [v 3]) and 6:10-11 (the community should remain diligent in its past demonstrations of love).

The cultic language, notes of thanksgiving, and rationale **(for with such sacrifices God is pleased** [*euaresteitai*]) mark these verses as a reformulation of the exhortation in 12:28: "Let us be thankful, and so worship God acceptably [*euarestōs*]."

■ **17** This section (vv 7-19) opened with a reminder concerning the community's past leaders (v 7). It closes with a charge to cooperate with and support their present leaders—including the author (vv 17-19).

Obey [*peithesthe*] **your leaders** may rather mean "have confidence in" (NIV[11]) or "rely on" (CEB) your leaders. Nevertheless, this imperative is paired with a clear injunction to obedience: **submit to their authority**.

The community should entrust themselves to their leaders because **they keep watch over you** (lit., *over your souls*). The leaders are guardians of the community's spiritual welfare. The verb **keep watch** (*agrypnousin*; "tireless in their care" [REB]) is never used of leaders elsewhere in the NT, but of all believers remaining alert and ready for the coming of Christ (Mark 13:33; Luke 21:36; implicit in Eph 6:18; see Thompson 2008, 284). An eschatological flavor is implicit in the reminder that leaders have to **give an account** at the final judgment. The preacher himself is practicing his charge to be watchful in the sermon we call Hebrews. He is warning and encouraging his listeners to be ready for "the Day approaching" (10:25).

Past leaders were instrumental in the genesis of the community's belief, since they "spoke the word [*logon*] of God" to them (13:7). Current leaders, **as men who must give an account** (*logon*), must attempt to keep each one of them from falling short of salvation. The identical pun in → 4:12-13 employs the word *logos* at the beginning and end of the passage with the same two different senses.

The **account** the leaders must render could concern their own actions, indicating accountability for their leadership ("as people who are going to be held responsible for you" [CEB]; "will give an account for their work" [NET; see GNT, NLT]). Or it could concern the actions of the people under their charge, indicating the community's responsibility ("because they must give an account of them [i.e., souls]" [NJB]; see Pfitzner 1997, 202). In truth, everyone must give an account before God (4:13); but the second option is more probable here in light of 13:17c-18.

The following purpose clause, **in order that they might do this . . .** , is ambiguous. The NIV creates a new sentence, adding **Obey them** as a resumption of the initial exhortation. **This** (*touto*) task that the leaders **do** (*poiōsin*; their work) could refer to their **keep**ing **watch** (Bengel 1877, 499). But could the leaders' watchfulness be conducted as **a burden** ("with groaning" [ESV, LEB]), while they claim to have a clear conscience and live honorably (v 18)?

More likely, **this** refers to the leaders' **giving an account** (rightly, Koester 2001, 572). The readers'—not the leaders'—conduct is of concern here. It is preferable that the leaders' account of it be rendered **with joy** rather than "with sighing" (NRSV). The *Shepherd of Hermas* similarly instructed his audience to live peaceably with one another, "that I also, standing joyful before your Father, may give an account of you all to your Lord" (*Herm. Vis.* 3.9.10). The participle *stenazontes* ("sigh, groan" [BDAG, 942]; **burden**) conveys, not grumbling or complaining (GW, NET; see Jas 5:9), but the leaders' "sorrow" (NAB, NLT), displeasure, or disappointment with those under their care (Balz 1993b).

The final clause in Heb 13:17 follows naturally upon this interpretation: **for that would be of no advantage to you.** This extends the accounting metaphor (**give an account**) in the expression **no advantage** (or "unprofitable" [HCSB, KJV, LEB, NASB]. *Alysitelēs* was a commercial technical term for not meeting expenses [BDAG, 48]). This is another instance of understatement (→ 4:2; 6:10). A dissatisfactory reckoning before God would not simply be of **no advantage**; it would be devastating (see 3:16-19; 6:7-8). This may be one final, though veiled, warning for those members of the community who are not heeding the admonitions of their leaders (see, e.g., 10:25; 12:15-16; deSilva 2000a, 510).

■ **18-19** As the author draws his work to a close, he solicits prayer from his readers (like Paul in Eph 6:19; Col 4:3; 1 Thess 5:25; 2 Thess 3:1). **Pray** [*proseuchesthe*, **keep praying**] **for us** is a request on behalf of the author himself and colleagues who were with him (see Heb 13:24*b*). The author seems to include himself among the community's leaders (vv 17, 24). Beginning in v 19, the author addresses his readers repeatedly in the first person (**I**; see vv 22-23; previously only in 11:32).

The reason (**For** [*gar*]—omitted in the NIV) for the request is unexpected and somewhat difficult to follow: **we are sure that we have a clear conscience and desire to live honorably in every way.** Why would the grounds for the readers' prayers be their leaders' purity of heart and sterling character?

Perhaps the author is indirectly asking for spiritual strength. In effect: "Please pray for us, because we're doing the best we can to be holy." But the manner of expression is too strong to be softened in this way. The leaders are **sure** (*peithometha*)—"confident" (NAB, NKJV) or "convinced" (HCSB, LEB; Sand 1993)—that their consciences are pure. As a result, they are "certainly determined [*thelontes*] to behave honourably in everything we do" (NJB). The NIV's **desire** is not forceful enough (see Johnson 2006, 353; O'Brien 2010, 531). The mention of a **clear conscience** reminds us of its definitive cleansing through Christ's sacrifice (→ 9:9, 14; 10:2; → 9:8-10 sidebar, "The Conscience"). But here a **good** [*kalēn*] conscience is related to the determination to **live honorably** (*kalōs . . . anastrephesthai*), thus exhibiting the same "way of life [*anastrophēs*]" (v 7) as the church's venerable leaders of the past.

Another suggestion is that that author is taking a defensive stance (Chrysostom 1996, 520; Hughes 1977, 587-88; Lane 1991, 556; Hagner 2002, 173; France 2006, 192). He may have anticipated hard feelings among some readers in response to his difficult word (5:11). Or maybe there were interpersonal problems in the background (unknown to us), causing a rift and requiring the author's relationship with the readers to be **restored** (13:19). In either case, so goes the speculation, the preacher felt the need to defend the purity of his intentions against detractors.

Comparisons may be made with Paul's appeals to his clear conscience (esp. 2 Cor 1:11-12). But Paul does so in contexts where his apostolic authority is undoubtedly under attack, as in the Corinthian correspondence. No such opposition is visible in Hebrews. Even if one infers tension between the preacher and those who promote "strange teachings" (Lane 1991, 554-55), this still does not clarify the connection with a request for prayer. Moreover, if the rhetorical situation critically demands a defense of one's integrity in order to gain a hearing, this is best tackled early on in a speech (Acts 23:1; 24:16) or letter (1 Cor 4:4; 2 Cor 1:12; also Gal 1:10—2:10), not near the end. In Hebrews there is no trace of personal apologetic anywhere, least of all in the introduction or *exordium*, where one would expect it.

A more suitable explanation coheres with the purpose of establishing one's *ethos* (moral character) in the *peroratio* of a speech: to forge an emotional bond (*pathos*) with listeners (Quintilian, *Inst.* 6.2.13-19; see Thompson 2008, 285). A speaker should commend his goodness in order to kindle the audience's affection, especially when there is an intimate connection with them, or as a follow-up to an admonition (*Inst.* 6.2.14). Both of these are applicable in Hebrews (note the preceding admonition in 13:17). The preacher is promoting the sort of bond with present leaders that existed with those past leaders so worthy of memory (v 7). The readers' prayers, then, should be motivated by admiration, affection, and identification with their leaders' nobility of character.

The content of the prayer request, given in v 19, confirms this interpretation: **I particularly urge you to pray so that I may be restored to you soon.** The switch to the first person (**I**), the fervency (*perissoterōs*, **particularly**; "the more earnestly" [ESV, RSV]), and the urgency of the request (*tachion*, **soon**; "quickly" [CEB, LEB]) exude a sense of love and longing for friends (see Quintilian, *Inst.* 6.2.17). The verb **restored** does not connote healing a broken relationship, but returning home to be reunited with friends after a time of absence (see *Let. Aris.* 318; Eup. 2.10).

c. Benediction and Postscript (13:20-25)

Hebrews concludes with a benediction (vv 20-21), final plea to be heard (v 22), then a brief travelogue (v 23), greetings (v 24), and blessing (v 25).

■ **20-21** Having asked for his listeners' prayers (vv 18-19), the author now prays for them. God's past triumph in Jesus Christ (v 20) is invoked as the pledge for divine enablement to live pleasing lives in the present (v 21). The prayer pulses with major themes from the sermon:

- Christ's exaltation as the leader over God's people.
- Christ's sacrificial death that inaugurated the new covenant.
- The resulting perfection of believers as worshipers.

May the God of peace . . . equip you is the heart of the benediction, closing with a doxology, **to whom be glory for ever and ever,** and the standard Jewish/Christian liturgical formula, **Amen.**

The invocation of God as **the God of peace** is rare in Jewish literature. But Paul used it often as a formula in benedictions (Rom 15:33; 16:20; Phil

4:9; 1 Thess 5:23; see Attridge 1989, 405). The divine title is a fitting component of the *peroratio* (Heb 10:19—13:25). An *inclusio* may be intended with 12:14, where readers were exhorted to pursue **peace** and holiness. The discipline of God the Father cultivates holiness and produces a harvest of righteousness and **peace** (12:10-11). Commitment to moral integrity and communal harmony are principal emphases in 12:14-17 and 13:1-19. But ultimately, **the God of peace** enables believers to carry out God's will (13:20-21).

Though God is the subject of the main verbs (**brought back, equip,** and **work**), the prayer is christocentric. Christ is the means (**through Jesus Christ**) by which God accomplishes his purposes. Christ is named no fewer than three times—as the **great Shepherd of the sheep, our Lord Jesus,** and **Jesus Christ.**

God is *the One* who **brought back from the dead** the Lord Jesus. This is the most explicit reference to Jesus' resurrection in Hebrews (see 5:7; 7:16). Yet the preacher varies from the usual phrasing for resurrection (see 6:2; 11:35; and possibly 7:11, 15). Rather than a form of "raise up" (*egeirō* or *anistēmi*), Hebrews has **brought back** (*anagōn*; "brought up" [HCSB, LEB, NAB, NASB, NKJV, NLT]). Thus, Hebrews maintains its emphasis on Christ's exaltation (1:3, 13; 7:26; 8:1; 10:12), not only his deliverance from death.

The expression **who . . . brought back from the dead . . . that great Shepherd of the sheep** echoes Isa 63:11-14 LXX (Lane 1991, 561). There Moses is the "shepherd of the sheep," whom the Lord brought up out of Egypt, along with the people of Israel, in the exodus. A new exodus was effected through Christ's exaltation, since it entailed "bringing many sons to glory" (Heb 2:10). The title **great Shepherd of the sheep** is reminiscent of Hebrews' earlier reference to Jesus as "a great priest over the house of God" (10:21; see 4:14).

13:20-21

The gist of the argument from the central section (7:1—10:18) is packed into the phrase **through the blood of the eternal covenant.** A comparable summary appears in 12:24: "Jesus the mediator of a new covenant" and "the sprinkled blood." Sacrificial blood was indispensable in the inauguration of the first covenant. And the once-for-all offering of Christ's **blood** established the new **covenant** (9:15-28); hence, the expression, **blood of the covenant** (9:20; 10:29; see Mark 14:24 ‖; 1 Cor 11:25). **Through** his sacrificial death (**blood**), Christ was qualified/perfected as the leader over God's people. This is the point of God bringing **back from the dead . . . that great Shepherd of the sheep** (see Heb 2:9-10, 17-18; 5:7-8; 7:27-28; 10:12-13, 19-22).

Only here does Hebrews call the new covenant the **eternal covenant,** echoing God's promise through the prophets (Isa 55:3; 61:8; Jer 32:40; 50:5; Ezek 16:60; 37:26). The designation is appropriate since this "better covenant" is guaranteed by Christ's permanent priesthood (Heb 7:22, 24; see 5:6; 6:20; 7:16-17, 21, 28). It is established on "better promises" (8:6). Chief among them is the definitive sanctification through Christ's once-for-all sacrifice (10:10-18). It provides a "better hope" (7:19): **eternal** salvation, redemption, and inheritance (5:9; 9:12, 15).

The petition in 13:21 reiterates the major thrust of the second half of the *peroratio* (12:14—13:25): authentic worship is a response to God's grace. The request, **May God equip** [*katartisai*] **you,** refers to the divine provision/preparation of the readers **with everything good** so that they will lack nothing **for doing** (*eis to poiesai*) God's **will** (*to thelēma*). Implied in this is the maturation or perfection of their moral character ("make you perfect" [KJV, REB]; "make you complete" [NKJV, NRSV]; Ellingworth [1993, 730] detects an aspect of the *teleiōsis* ["perfection"] theme). Christ's incarnation is the pattern for this perfection: God "prepared" (*katarisō*) a body for Jesus, who came "to do [God's] will" (*tou poiēsai to thelēma*; 10:5, 7, 9).

The following participial clause further describes the previous action as God's **working** [*poiōn*] **in us what is pleasing to him.** The mention of **what is pleasing** completes the theme of acceptable worship (12:28) and pleasing sacrifices ("doing good" [13:16]) that constitute the appropriate response to God's gracious gift of citizenship in the unshakable kingdom (see 12:28; 13:14).

■ **22** Ever the stylist, the preacher **exhort[s]** (*parakalō,* **I urge**) his audience to heed his **word of exhortation** (*tou logou tēs paraklēseōs*). **Bear with** or **put up with** (*anechesthe*) is a polite way of asking listeners to "pay attention" (NLT) or "listen patiently" (GNT, GW; BDAG, 78). This is in keeping with repeated warnings to pay attention (2:1, 3; 3:7, 15; 4:7; 5:11; 12:25; Thompson 2008, 286).

Word of exhortation is an apt description of Hebrews. The phrase in Acts 13:15 designates a homily/sermon that Paul delivers in a synagogue. Hebrews fits this identification well. It is filled with expositions of Scripture designed to warn readers of the consequences of disobedience and to provide "strong encouragement" (6:18 ESV, HCSB, NASB) to trust in God's promises.

For I have written you only a short letter does not identify the genre of the work, but the mode of its delivery: *I have instructed you by way of letter* (*epesteila;* BDAG, 381). The preacher delivered his **word of exhortation** by letter because he could not speak with them soon enough in person.

It was a rhetorical convention to state that one's work was not burdensome in length (see 1 Pet 5:12). In two instances, Hebrews purposely refrains from delving into details to avoid being tiresome (Heb 9:5; 11:32). Hebrews is by no means **short** compared to most ancient letters (even the shortest in the NT, 3 John, is larger than the norm; see Acts 15:23-29). At nearly 5,000 words, Hebrews is comparable to Paul's longer letters (e.g., Romans [over 7,000]; 2 Corinthians [nearly 4,500]; see Just 2005). Pseudo-Barnabas, however, claims to be sending a "brief letter" (*Barn.* 1.5), yet it is double the length of Hebrews (Lane 1991, 569).

Hebrews, however, can reasonably claim: "for in fact I have written to you quite briefly" (NIV[11]). It ranks among shorter ancient works (10,000 words or less). As a written speech, it is between a third or fourth the length of Demosthenes' longer orations (Burridge 2004, 114-15). It could easily have been heard in one sitting—forty-five to fifty minutes (Koester 2001, 175). The relative brevity or length of speeches, in any case, was judged not by the kind of speech, but by the scope of the subject under consideration (Quintilian, *Inst.* 3.8.67).

■ **23** A brief notice concerning travel plans is common in the closings of ancient letters. The author's plans are somewhat tied to the movements of **our brother Timothy.** This is probably the same Timothy who had been Paul's most trusted and beloved coworker (see 1 Cor 4:17; Phil 2:19-23); but we cannot be sure. Hebrews informs the readers (**I want you to know**) that Timothy **has been released** ("from jail" [NLT]; less likely: "departed" or been "sent off" [BDAG, 117-18; Isaacs 2002, 164]). This is the only indication in the NT of Timothy being imprisoned.

Whatever Happened to Timothy?

The book of Acts and Paul's letters provide us with a good deal of information about Paul's spiritual "son," Timothy. But what became of Timothy after Paul's death? Hebrews might be the only NT writing that gives us any information: Timothy had been set free from prison. We do not know where this imprisonment occurred, but Ephesus is a plausible guess. Paul commissioned Timothy to be a minister in Ephesus (1 Tim 1:3), and church tradition names him as the first bishop in that city, as well as "the angel of the church in Ephesus" (Rev 2:1).

Church history reports little about Timothy beyond what is in the NT. He was unmarried and remained bishop of Ephesus until he was over eighty. According to tradition, around A.D. 80 the bishop stood in opposition to a festival of the goddess Artemis in Ephesus. Pagan worshipers beat him, dragged him through the streets, and stoned him to death (Aherne 1912).

The author is eager to reunite with the community (Heb 13:19). But he hopes Timothy will be able to be his traveling companion on the journey there: **If he arrives soon, I will come with him to see you.** He implies that if Timothy does not come in time, he will regrettably have to depart without Timothy. (We can only surmise whether shipping schedules or seasonal constraints on travel were factors.)

■ **24-25** Hebrews comes to a close with greetings and a concluding blessing. There are two different kinds of greetings. The first is a request for the community to send greetings on the author's behalf (v 24*a*). The second includes greetings from the author to the community on behalf of companions who are with him (v 24*b*). The greetings, together with the final blessing (v 25), are comprehensive, as indicated by the threefold repetition of the word **all** in vv 24-25.

The request in v 24*a* to greet **all your leaders** and **all God's people** (lit., "all the saints" [KJV]; "all the holy ones" [NAB]) may suggest that the preceding sermon has been directed to a particular community or house church. This smaller group is now being asked to convey greetings to a network of churches and their respective leaders (Lane 1991, 569). Or the all-inclusive greetings may imply that the work was intended to be read at a larger gathering of house churches and that the greetings would be put into effect at this public reading (deSilva 2000a, 515).

The latter suggestion may be less probable, since Roman law prohibited large associations (Lindars 1991, 18). Nevertheless, such greetings were designed to promote goodwill and solidarity among **all God's people,** and further strengthen the position and influence of **all** the **leaders** in the churches (see vv 17-18).

The second greeting (v 24b) is susceptible to two different interpretations. First, **those from Italy** who are **sending you their greetings** may imply that the author is writing from Italy. This is an ancient interpretation, reflected in a number of manuscripts with explanatory notes following v 25. These identify Italy or Rome as the place of composition (e.g., the fifth-century Codex Alexandrinus; Brown 1997, 699 n. 42; Isaacs 2002, 9).

A second interpretation is advanced by many modern interpreters: the author is writing from somewhere outside of Italy. It would be superfluous for the author to mention **those from Italy** if he were in Italy at the time of writing. Also, it is too broad of a reference inside Italy, but appropriately narrow outside. This is by no means certain, since the statement is ambiguous, designating either residence ("God's holy people in Italy" [NJB]) or extraction ("our Italian friends" [REB]). But it makes slightly more sense that some of his companions **from Italy,** who were with him somewhere outside of Italy, wanted to send greetings to their Christian friends back home, perhaps in Rome or its environs.

The final blessing, **Grace** [*charis*] **be with you all** (v 25), is common in Paul's letters (2 Cor 13:14; Eph 6:24; 2 Thess 3:18; Titus 3:15; see Gal 6:18; Phil 4:23; Col 4:18; 1 Tim 4:22; Phlm 25). Though these words are conventional, they nevertheless bring suitable closure to the preacher's message. Christ's humiliation and death originated in God's grace (2:9), and grace is one of the benefits of Christ's high-priestly ministry (4:16). Grace should not be rejected (10:29; 12:15). It is the vital source of our spiritual strength (13:9) and our indispensable response of gratitude (*charis*) to God in worship (12:28).

FROM THE TEXT

In the second half of the *peroratio* (12:14—13:25) the preacher makes his final appeals and directives to readers. As we read this last portion of Hebrews, we may feel far removed from the situation of the little house church this sermon first addressed. Few readers in the comfort of the West sense the menacing shadow of persecution. Fewer are tempted to abandon the Christian faith through an attraction to the sacrificial cult and food laws of the Mosaic covenant. Yet there are four points (among others) from the preacher's conclusion that are just as applicable to followers of Jesus today.

(1) *Hebrews urges us to remain committed to Jesus Christ*. Though we may not be worried about an official persecution against Christians breaking out,

there are many instances and settings in our society where proclaiming one's faith in Christ can be intimidating (e.g., a secular university campus in the United States).

Insofar as we still must have courage and conviction to follow Christ, we are not *that* different from these early Roman Christians. As that great preacher Dennis Kinlaw noted in a sermon at Asbury College some years ago, even the Apostle Peter denied the Lord in response to "the curl of the lip" from a servant girl. If we are honest with ourselves, many of us might do the same in a similar situation.

Hebrews challenges us to examine our commitment to and confidence in Christ. The preacher warns us of the danger of missing out on God's grace due to other passions or preoccupations that, quite frankly, are more pressing for us (12:15-17). He bids us not to refuse the voice warning us from heaven. The voice loudly threatens to shake the temporal world that we can all too often regard as permanent (12:25-27). But if we listen more closely, we'll hear "a better word than the blood of Abel" (12:24). It is the voice of the gracious mediator of the new covenant, Jesus Christ, pleading "with loud cries and tears to the one who could save him from death" (5:7). We finally hear him say, "Here I am, I have come to do your will" (10:9; see v 7).

We see his broken body, opening up a new and living way for us into God's presence, and the sprinkled blood of his sacrifice that cleanses our conscience from the guilt of sins. In response, Hebrews calls us to the same kind of cross-bearing discipleship that Jesus commanded to his disciples (Mark 8:34 ||). "Let us, then, go to him outside the camp, bearing the disgrace he bore" (Heb 13:13). Thanks be to God, it is the same grace that brought Christ to the cross that can strengthen our hearts in devotion to him (13:9).

(2) *Hebrews calls us to live our lives in thanksgiving and worship to God.* We are directed to do this in response to God's gift of his eternal, unshakable kingdom (12:28). What is not immediately apparent in English, as it is in Greek, is that our response should be energized by "grace [*charis*]." Ancient people understood this instinctively. Grace given by someone, then received by another, automatically warranted an expression of grace (gratitude or thanks) in return from the recipient. Failure to show thanks was more than a social faux pas. It was a violation of a sacred obligation—a breach of public trust. Vestiges of this social dynamic still operate in our modern world, as reflected in an ancient expression still in currency today: "return the favor."

Modern Christians prefer to emphasize our thanksgiving and worship to God as a free response, not an obligation. But what if someone saw our dire financial need and decided to give us a lavish home to live in and a high-paying job in his company, with no strings attached? Wouldn't we feel obligated to give some token of gratitude in return, at least by striving to be his most loyal employee? Wouldn't we sing the praises of our benefactor? Wouldn't we feel responsible to maintain the home, not wanting to dishonor the gift we received, the person who gave it to us, or ourselves as the privileged beneficiaries? Of course, we *ought* to respond in such ways, if we are properly grateful.

In Hebrews, the wilderness generation (3:7-19) and Esau (12:16-17) are examples of people who cavalierly dismissed God's blessing. As a result, they found themselves locked out of God's inheritance altogether. How much more, then, does the gift of citizenship in the city of the living God compel us to respond with gratitude and worship? The preacher does not want us to make the same mistake of outrageous ingratitude.

Our expected response is described in Hebrews through worship terminology associated with the cultic sacrifices in the OT. We need to "worship God acceptably" (12:28), continually offering up "a sacrifice of praise" (13:15). We ought to exercise generosity toward others, and so present sacrifices with which "God is pleased" (13:16). Hebrews reminds us that God equips us to do his will, and works in us "what is pleasing to him" (13:21; see Phil 2:13). It has been well said that Christians ought to offer up their whole lives as a liturgy—a service of worship—to God. Come to think of it, it was the Apostle Paul who first said that (Rom 12:1).

(3) *Hebrews exhorts us to make every effort to be holy*. This command heads up the second half of the conclusion (Heb 12:14). Commitment to Christ and lives of worship and gratitude should characterize the holy life. But 13:1-6 lists a series of specific, practical applications of holiness in our everyday lives. Striking is the preponderance of terms related to love. These verses illustrate what J. Kenneth Grider meant by the saying: "Love is holiness with its overalls on."

Hebrews tells us flatly who and what we should love and what we should not love. We should love our fellow believers as our brothers and sisters (*philadelphia*, "sibling love"). The preacher has spoken repeatedly about the care and concern believers should have for one another, not always using the explicit language of love (→ 6:10; 10:24; 3:12-13; 12:15-16). We should especially provide comfort and support to the suffering and mistreated (10:33-34; 13:3).

We should love strangers (*philoxenia*; 13:2). The protocols of hospitality have become considerably weaker or nonexistent in many modern Western settings (→ 13:2 and sidebar, "Hospitality in the Ancient World"). So today's Christians have to be much more intentional in our kindness and generosity toward people whom we might be tempted to regard as "other." Justifiably, we have fears about being ripped off or taken advantage of. It is not unlikely that the hospitality Hebrews had in mind was directed toward "strangers" who were followers of Christ, often involved in the work of Christian ministry. Even if we were to narrow the scope of "love of strangers" in this way, we could still make strides toward taking risks appropriate to the love and self-sacrificial giving that flow from authentic Christian faith.

Two additional exhortations are especially applicable today. First, the preacher forcefully advocates sexual purity and the sanctity of marriage

(13:4). How can we truly love other believers or strangers if we cannot even maintain fidelity with the one to whom we have pledged lifelong love?

The ancient cultural setting in which Hebrews' original readers lived was as permissive as ours (→ 13:4). We should not imagine that sexual temptations are more difficult or prevalent today—even with the omnipresent lure of Internet pornography. Even a superficial study of ancient Greco-Roman sexual mores or the sexually explicit imagery of the statuary or frescoes in ancient cities (e.g., Pompeii) should disabuse us of the notion that nowadays seduction is so much worse (see also Prov 5). And if Hebrews' threat of God's judgment is not enough to deter us from sexually immoral activities, there are more therapeutic options than ever before for people who are struggling with sexual addiction or relational dysfunction.

Second, the preacher tells us specifically what not to love: money (*aphilargyros*; → 13:5). This admonition is particularly apropos in our world based on commercialism, materialism, and conspicuous consumption. It is so easy for us to get caught up in the prevailing values of our time, including the acquisition of more and more "stuff": the next new fashion, the newest smartphone, the latest gadget. Much of our participation in the economy is necessary, if not innocent. But we must always check the deepest motivations of our heart in relation to money.

Hebrews warns against a reliance on money that squeezes out our trust in God (13:5-6). It parallels the teaching of Jesus himself, whose parable of the sower relates how the gospel can be choked by the thorns of life's worries and wealth and desire for things (Mark 4:18-19 ||): "You cannot serve God and Money" (Matt 6:24; Luke 16:13). What matters is not what is in our bank accounts, but God who will "equip [us] with everything good for doing his will" and "work in us what is pleasing to him, through Jesus Christ" (Heb 13:21).

(4) *Hebrews insists that we honor our spiritual leaders and attend to their preaching and counsel.* It is fitting that the skilled pastoral theologian behind the "word of exhortation" we call Hebrews would have something to say about the quality of pastoral leadership. Hebrews sets a high bar for the spiritual maturity, moral character, and "shepherding" responsibility expected of pastoral leaders. They must preach the pure word of God, not strange teachings (13:7, 9). They must have a genuine faith and lifestyle worthy of imitation (13:7). Indeed, they ought to embody the moral excellence of 13:18: "We are sure that we have a clear conscience and desire to live honorably in every way."

What difference would it make in our own spiritual lives, and in our relationship to our spiritual leaders, if we took seriously Hebrews' perspective on these matters? We should have high expectations of the spiritual and moral fitness of our leaders. But we must equally recognize that they have been granted oversight over *our* spiritual welfare. If our interpretation of 13:17 is correct, the emphasis is on the responsibility of leaders to hold *our* feet to the fire. They will one day give an account, not only for their own faithfulness in ministry (e.g., 1 Cor 3:10-15; 9:24-27), but for *our* faithfulness under their care.

If we look at our pastors' responsibilities as if we were in their shoes, it is easier to see why it is so much more joyful for them, and advantageous for us, when we do our best to follow their leadership and put into practice the truths of God's word they preach. And if we are convinced of the purity of their intentions (Heb 13:18), and bound to them with great affection (13:19, 23), we should be motivated to pray for them, that their ministry will be all the more effective. A spiritual leader could have no greater joy than one day to stand before God to give an account, and be able to "present everyone perfect in Christ" (Col 1:28). But that perfect joy cannot happen without our cooperation (see Phil 2:1-2, 12).

Did the original readers of Hebrews snap out of their lethargy and stop dragging their spiritual feet? I'd like to think that they joined the ranks of that cloud of witnesses spoken of in Heb 12:1. The preacher seems to have been hopeful about their future salvation (6:9-12; 10:39).

Someday, I'm sure many of us will seek out the presently unknown author of Hebrews in glory. We'll want to know his identity, but not simply out of curiosity. We'll want to thank him for caring enough for a little struggling house church, that he devoted so much time, energy, and skill to writing this "word of exhortation." And we'll bow in worship before the throne of grace, to thank God for inspiring the serious warnings and powerful encouragement in this book that we so sorely needed, too.

www.ingramcontent.com/pod-product-compliance
Lightning Source LLC
Chambersburg PA
CBHW070232240426
43673CB00044B/1763